CW01652150

The Wiley Bicentennial–Knowledge for Generations

Each generation has its unique needs and aspirations. When Charles Wiley first opened his small printing shop in lower Manhattan in 1807, it was a generation of boundless potential searching for an identity. And we were there, helping to define a new American literary tradition. Over half a century later, in the midst of the Second Industrial Revolution, it was a generation focused on building the future. Once again, we were there, supplying the critical scientific, technical, and engineering knowledge that helped frame the world. Throughout the 20th Century, and into the new millennium, nations began to reach out beyond their own borders and a new international community was born. Wiley was there, expanding its operations around the world to enable a global exchange of ideas, opinions, and know-how.

For 200 years, Wiley has been an integral part of each generation's journey, enabling the flow of information and understanding necessary to meet their needs and fulfill their aspirations. Today, bold new technologies are changing the way we live and learn. Wiley will be there, providing you the must-have knowledge you need to imagine new worlds, new possibilities, and new opportunities.

Generations come and go, but you can always count on Wiley to provide you the knowledge you need, when and where you need it!

William J. Pesce
President and Chief Executive Officer

Peter Booth Wiley
Chairman of the Board

Microsoft Certified Application Specialist (MCAS)

Microsoft CERTIFIED Application Specialist

Approved Courseware

▪ What does this logo mean?

It means this courseware has been approved by the Microsoft® Certified Application Specialist program to be among the finest available for learning Microsoft® Office Word 2007, Microsoft® Office Excel 2007, Microsoft® Office PowerPoint 2007, Microsoft® Office Access 2007, or Microsoft® Office Outlook 2007. It also means that upon completion of this courseware, you may be prepared to take an exam for Microsoft Certified Application Specialist qualification.

▪ What is a Microsoft Certified Application Specialist?

A Microsoft Certified Application Specialist is an individual who has passed exams for certifying his or her skills in one or more of the Microsoft Office desktop applications such as Microsoft Word, Microsoft Excel, Microsoft PowerPoint, Microsoft Outlook, or Microsoft Access. The Microsoft Certified Application Specialist program is the only program approved by Microsoft for testing proficiency in Microsoft Office desktop applications. This testing program can be a valuable asset in any job search or career development.

▪ More Information

To learn more about becoming a Microsoft Certified Application Specialist and exam availability, visit www.microsoft.com/learning/msbc.

Microsoft® Official Academic Course

Microsoft® Office Word 2007

WILEY

John Wiley & Sons, Inc.

Credits

EXECUTIVE EDITOR	John Kane
SENIOR EDITOR	Gary Schwartz
DIRECTOR OF MARKETING AND SALES	Mitchell Beaton
EDITORIAL ASSISTANT	Jennifer Lartz
PRODUCTION MANAGER	Kelly Tavares
DEVELOPMENT AND PRODUCTION	Custom Editorial Productions, Inc
PRODUCTION ASSISTANT	Courtney Leshko
CREATIVE DIRECTOR	Harry Nolan
COVER DESIGNER	Harry Nolan
INTERIOR DESIGN	Brian Salisbury
COVER PHOTO	Corbis
TECHNOLOGY AND MEDIA	Phyllis Bregman

This book was set in Garamond by TechBooks and printed and bound by Bind Rite Graphics. The cover was printed by Phoenix Color.

ISBN-13 978-0-47039567-7

Printed in the United States of America

10 9 8 7 6 5 4 3 2 1

Foreword from the Publisher

Wiley's publishing vision for the Microsoft Official Academic Course series is to provide students and instructors with the skills and knowledge they need to use Microsoft technology effectively in all aspects of their personal and professional lives. Quality instruction is required to help both educators and students get the most from Microsoft's software tools and to become more productive. Thus our mission is to make our instructional programs trusted educational companions for life.

To accomplish this mission, Wiley and Microsoft have partnered to develop the highest quality educational programs for Information Workers, IT Professionals, and Developers. Materials created by this partnership carry the brand name "Microsoft Official Academic Course," assuring instructors and students alike that the content of these textbooks is fully endorsed by Microsoft, and that they provide the highest quality information and instruction on Microsoft products. The Microsoft Official Academic Course textbooks are "Official" in still one more way—they are the officially sanctioned courseware for Microsoft IT Academy members.

The Microsoft Official Academic Course series focuses on *workforce development*. These programs are aimed at those students seeking to enter the workforce, change jobs, or embark on new careers as information workers, IT professionals, and developers. Microsoft Official Academic Course programs address their needs by emphasizing authentic workplace scenarios with an abundance of projects, exercises, cases, and assessments.

The Microsoft Official Academic Courses are mapped to Microsoft's extensive research and job-task analysis, the same research and analysis used to create the Microsoft Certified Application Specialist (MCAS) and Microsoft Certified Application Professional (MCAP) exams. The textbooks focus on real skills for real jobs. As students work through the projects and exercises in the textbooks they enhance their level of knowledge and their ability to apply the latest Microsoft technology to everyday tasks. These students also gain resume-building credentials that can assist them in finding a job, keeping their current job, or in furthering their education.

The concept of life-long learning is today an utmost necessity. Job roles, and even whole job categories, are changing so quickly that none of us can stay competitive and productive without continuously updating our skills and capabilities. The Microsoft Official Academic Course offerings, and their focus on Microsoft certification exam preparation, provide a means for people to acquire and effectively update their skills and knowledge. Wiley supports students in this endeavor through the development and distribution of these courses as Microsoft's official academic publisher.

Today educational publishing requires attention to providing quality print and robust electronic content. By integrating Microsoft Official Academic Course products, *WileyPLUS*, and Microsoft certifications, we are better able to deliver efficient learning solutions for students and teachers alike.

Bonnie Lieberman
General Manager and Senior Vice President

Preface

Welcome to the Microsoft Official Academic Course (MOAC) program for the 2007 Microsoft Office system. MOAC represents the collaboration between Microsoft Learning and John Wiley & Sons, Inc. publishing company. Microsoft and Wiley teamed up to produce a series of textbooks that deliver compelling and innovative teaching solutions to instructors and superior learning experiences for students. Infused and informed by in-depth knowledge from the creators of Microsoft Office and Windows Vista™, and crafted by a publisher known worldwide for the pedagogical quality of its products, these textbooks maximize skills transfer in minimum time. With MOAC, students are hands on right away—there are no superfluous text passages to get in the way of learning and using the software. Students are challenged to reach their potential by using their new technical skills as highly productive members of the workforce.

Because this knowledge base comes directly from Microsoft, architect of the 2007 Office system and creator of the Microsoft Certified Application Specialist (MCAS) exams, you are sure to receive the topical coverage that is most relevant to students' personal and professional success. Microsoft's direct participation not only assures you that MOAC textbook content is accurate and current; it also means that students will receive the best instruction possible to enable their success on certification exams and in the workplace.

The Microsoft Official Academic Course Program

The *Microsoft Official Academic Course* series is a complete program for instructors and institutions to prepare and deliver great courses on Microsoft software technologies. With MOAC, we recognize that, because of the rapid pace of change in the technology and curriculum developed by Microsoft, there is an ongoing set of needs beyond classroom instruction tools for an instructor to be ready to teach the course. The MOAC program endeavors to provide solutions for all these needs in a systematic manner in order to ensure a successful and rewarding course experience for both instructor and student—technical and curriculum training for instructor

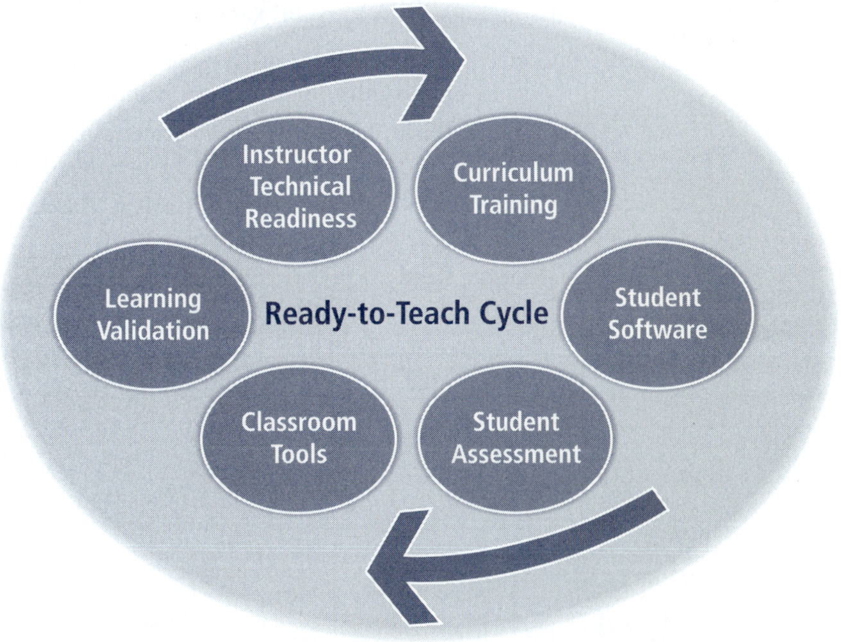

readiness with new software releases; the software itself for student use at home for building hands-on skills, assessment, and validation of skill development; and a great set of tools for delivering instruction in the classroom and lab. All are important to the smooth delivery of an interesting course on Microsoft software, and all are provided with the MOAC program. We think about the model below as a gauge for ensuring that we completely support you in your goal of teaching a great course. As you evaluate your instructional materials options, you may wish to use the model for comparison purposes with available products.

Organization

MOAC for 2007 Microsoft Office system is designed to cover all the learning objectives in the MCAS exams, referred to as "objective domains." The Microsoft Certified Application Specialist (MCAS) exam objectives are highlighted throughout the textbooks. Unique features of our task-based approach include a Lesson Skills Matrix that correlates skills taught in each lesson to the MCAS objectives; Certification, Workplace, and Internet Ready exercises; and three levels of increasingly rigorous lesson-ending activities: Competency, Proficiency, and Mastery Assessment.

Following is a list of key features in each lesson designed to prepare your students for success on these exams and in the workplace:

- Each lesson begins with a **Lesson Skill Matrix.** More than a standard list of learning objectives, the Skill Matrix correlates each software skill covered in the lesson to the specific MCAS "objective domain."
- Every lesson features a real-world **Business Case** scenario that places the software skills and knowledge to be acquired in a real-world setting.
- Every lesson opens with a **Software Orientation.** This feature provides an overview of the software features students will be working with in the lesson. The orientation includes a large, labeled screen image.
- Engaging point-of-use **Reading Aids** provide students with hints, introduce alternative methods for producing results, alert them to pitfalls, provide learning cross-references, and tell them the names of files found on the Student CD.
- **Certification Ready?** features throughout the text signal students where a specific certification objective is covered. It provides students with a chance to check their understanding of that particular MCAS objective and, if necessary, review the section of the lesson where it is covered. MOAC offers complete preparation for MCAS certification.
- Concise and frequent **Step-by-Step** instructions teach students new features and provide an opportunity for hands-on practice.
- **Circling Back.** These integrated projects provide students with an opportunity to review and practice skills learned in previous lessons.
- **Competency, Proficiency, and Mastery Assessment** provide three progressively more challenging lesson-ending activities.
- **Internet Ready.** Projects combine the knowledge students acquire in a lesson with a Web-based research task.
- **Workplace Ready.** These features preview how 2007 Microsoft Office system applications are used in real-world situations.

Illustrated Book Tour

Pedagogical Features

Many pedagogical features have been developed specifically for *Microsoft Official Academic Course* programs. Presenting the extensive procedural information and technical concepts woven throughout the textbook raises challenges for the student and instructor alike. The Illustrated Book Tour that follows provides a guide to the rich features contributing to *Microsoft Official Academic Course* program's pedagogical plan.

Each book within the *Microsoft Official Academic Course* series features:

- **Lesson Skill Matrix:** The skill matrix lists the instructional goals for the lesson so that you know what skills you will be asked to master. The Matrix previews the lesson structure, helping you grasp key concepts and prepares you for learning software skills. These skills are also linked directly to the Microsoft Certified Application Specialist (MCAS) certification skill, when appropriate.
- **Key Terms:** Important technical vocabulary is listed at the beginning of the lesson. When these terms are used later in the lesson, they appear in bold italic type and are defined. The Glossary contains all of the key terms and their definitions.
- **Software Orientation:** This feature provides an overview of the software you will be using in the lesson. The orientation will detail the general properties of the software or specific features, such as a ribbon or dialog box.
- **The Bottom Line:** Each main topic within the lesson has a summary of why this topic is relevant.
- **Hands-on practice:** Numbered steps give detailed, step-by-step instructions to help you learn software skills. The steps also show results and screen images to match what you should see on your computer screen.
- **Student CD:** The companion CD contains the data files needed for each lesson. These files are indicated by the CD icon in the margin of the textbook.
- **Informational text for each topic:** Easy-to-read, technique-focused information can be found following each exercise.
- **Illustrations:** Screen images provide visual feedback as you work through the exercises. The images reinforce key concepts, provide visual clues about the steps, and allow you to check your progress.
- **Reader aids:** Helpful hints, such as *Take Note,* and alternate ways to accomplish tasks (*Another Way*) are located throughout the lessons. Reader aids provide additional relevant or background information that adds value to the lesson. Reader aids, such as *Troubleshooting,* also point out things to watch out for or things to avoid.
- **Button images:** When the text instructs you to click a particular toolbar button, an image of the button is shown in the margin.
- **Certification Ready?:** This feature signals the point in the text where a specific certification objective is covered. It provides you with a chance to check your understanding of that particular MCAS objective and, if necessary, review the section of the lesson where it is covered.
- **New Feature:** The New Feature icon appears in the margin next to any software feature that is new to Office 2007.

- **Workplace Ready:** These special features provide a glimpse of how the software application can be put into practice in a real-world situation.
- **Circling Back:** This feature provides you with an opportunity to review and practice skills learned in previous lessons.
- **Knowledge Assessment:** True/false, multiple choice, matching, or fill-in-the-blank questions test or reinforce your understanding of key lesson topics.
- **Competency Assessment:** These projects are similar to the exercises you completed within the lesson. Specific steps for completion are provided so that you can practice what you have learned.
- **Proficiency Assessment:** These projects give you additional opportunity to practice skills that you learned in the lesson. Not all the steps for completion are provided. Completing these exercises helps you verify whether you understand the lesson and reinforces your learning.
- **Mastery Assessment:** These projects require you to work independently—as you would in the workplace. Steps needed to complete the problems are not supplied. You must apply the knowledge you have acquired in the lesson to complete the problems successfully.
- **Internet Ready:** These projects combine what you have learned with research on the Internet.
- **Glossary:** Technical vocabulary is defined in the Glossary. Terms in the Glossary also appear in boldface italic type and are defined within the lessons.
- **Index:** All Glossary terms and application features appear in the Index.

Lesson Features

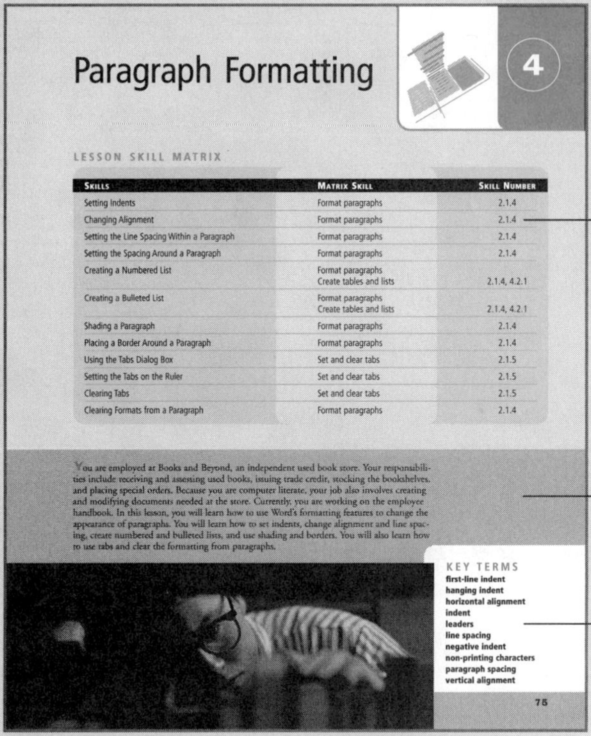

Paragraph Formatting 4

LESSON SKILL MATRIX

Skills	Matrix Skill	Skill Number
Setting Indents	Format paragraphs	2.1.4
Changing Alignment	Format paragraphs	2.1.4
Setting the Line Spacing Within a Paragraph	Format paragraphs	2.1.4
Setting the Spacing Around a Paragraph	Format paragraphs	2.1.4
Creating a Numbered List	Format paragraphs Create tables and lists	2.1.4, 4.2.1
Creating a Bulleted List	Format paragraphs Create tables and lists	2.1.4, 4.2.1
Shading a Paragraph	Format paragraphs	2.1.4
Placing a Border Around a Paragraph	Format paragraphs	2.1.4
Using the Tabs Dialog Box	Set and clear tabs	2.1.5
Setting the Tabs on the Ruler	Set and clear tabs	2.1.5
Clearing Tabs	Set and clear tabs	2.1.5
Clearing Formats from a Paragraph	Format paragraphs	2.1.4

You are employed at Books and Beyond, an independent used book store. Your responsibilities include receiving and assessing used books, issuing trade credit, stocking the bookshelves, and placing special orders. Because you are computer literate, your job also involves creating and modifying documents needed at the store. Currently, you are working on the employee handbook. In this lesson, you will learn how to use Word's formatting features to change the appearance of paragraphs. You will learn how to set indents, change alignment and line spacing, create numbered and bulleted lists, and use shading and borders. You will also learn how to use tabs and clear the formatting from paragraphs.

KEY TERMS
first-line indent
hanging indent
horizontal alignment
indent
leaders
line spacing
negative indent
non-printing characters
paragraph spacing
vertical alignment

75

Lesson Skill Matrix

Business Scenario

Key Terms

Software Orientation

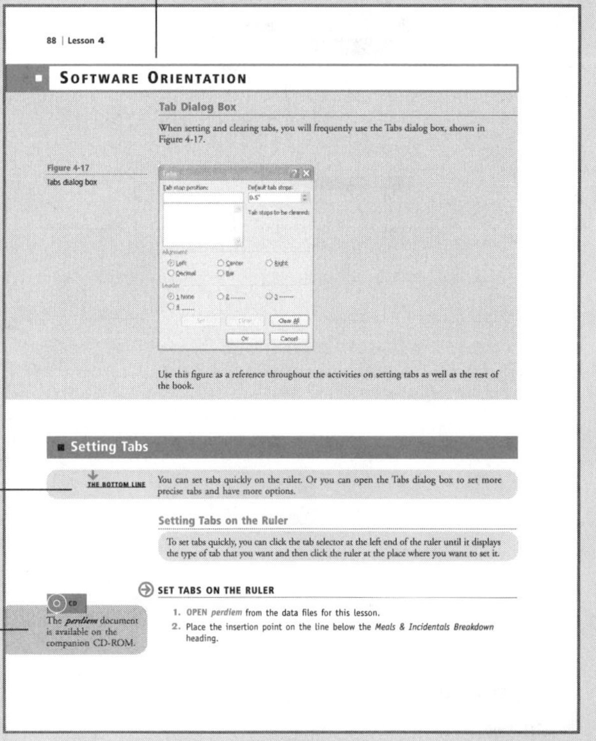

88 | Lesson 4

SOFTWARE ORIENTATION

Tab Dialog Box

When setting and clearing tabs, you will frequently use the Tabs dialog box, shown in Figure 4-17.

Figure 4-17
Tabs dialog box

Use this figure as a reference throughout the activities on setting tabs as well as the rest of the book.

Setting Tabs

THE BOTTOM LINE You can set tabs quickly on the ruler. Or you can open the Tabs dialog box to set more precise tabs and have more options.

Setting Tabs on the Ruler

To set tabs quickly, you can click the tab selector at the left end of the ruler until it displays the type of tab that you want and then click the ruler at the place where you want to set it.

CD The *perdiem* document is available on the companion CD-ROM.

SET TABS ON THE RULER

1. OPEN *perdiem* from the data files for this lesson.
2. Place the insertion point on the line below the *Meals & Incidentals Breakdown* heading.

The Bottom Line

On CD

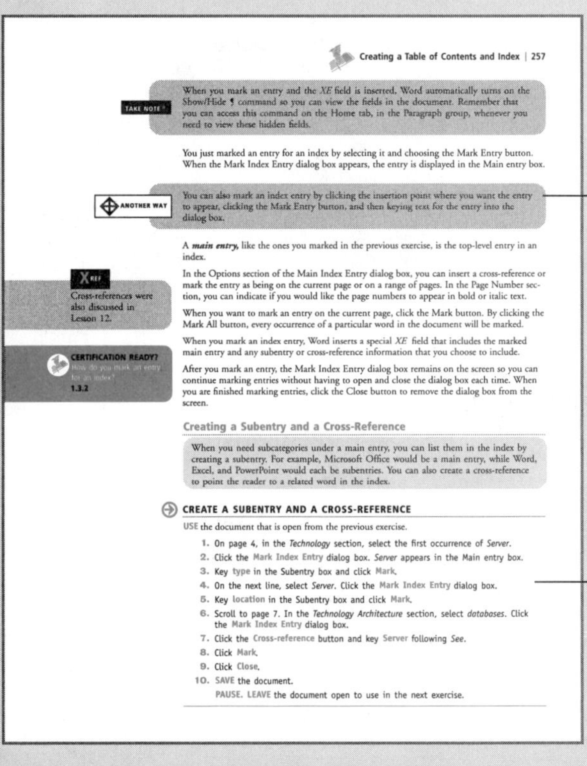

Creating a Table of Contents and Index | 257

TAKE NOTE When you mark an entry and the *XE* field is inserted, Word automatically turns on the Show/Hide ¶ command so you can view the fields in the document. Remember that you can access this command on the Home tab, in the Paragraph group, whenever you need to view these hidden fields.

You just marked an entry for an index by selecting it and choosing the Mark Entry button. When the Mark Index Entry dialog box appears, the entry is displayed in the Main entry box.

ANOTHER WAY You can also mark an index entry by clicking the insertion point where you want the entry to appear, clicking the Mark Entry button, and then keying text for the entry into the dialog box.

A ***main entry,*** like the ones you marked in the previous exercise, is the top-level entry in an index.

XREF Cross-references were also discussed in Lesson 12.

In the Options section of the Main Index Entry dialog box, you can insert a cross-reference or mark the entry as being on the current page or on a range of pages. In the Page Number section, you can indicate if you would like the page numbers to appear in bold or italic text.

When you want to mark an entry on the current page, click the Mark button. By clicking the Mark All button, every occurrence of a particular word in the document will be marked.

CERTIFICATION READY? How do you mark an entry for an index? 1.3.2

When you mark an index entry, Word inserts a special *XE* field that includes the marked main entry and any subentry or cross-reference information that you choose to include.

After you mark an entry, the Mark Index Entry dialog box remains on the screen so you can continue marking entries without having to open and close the dialog box each time. When you are finished marking entries, click the Close button to remove the dialog box from the screen.

Creating a Subentry and a Cross-Reference

When you need subcategories under a main entry, you can list them in the index by creating a subentry. For example, Microsoft Office would be a main entry, while Word, Excel, and PowerPoint would each be subentries. You can also create a cross-reference to point the reader to a related word in the index.

CREATE A SUBENTRY AND A CROSS-REFERENCE

USE the document that is open from the previous exercise.

1. On page 4, in the *Technology* section, select the first occurrence of *Server*.
2. Click the Mark Index Entry dialog box. *Server* appears in the Main entry box.
3. Key type in the Subentry box and click Mark.
4. On the next line, select *Server*. Click the Mark Index Entry dialog box.
5. Key location in the Subentry box and click Mark.
6. Scroll to page 7. In the *Technology Architecture* section, select *databases*. Click the Mark Index Entry dialog box.
7. Click the Cross-reference button and key Server following *See*.
8. Click Mark.
9. Click Close.
10. SAVE the document.
PAUSE. LEAVE the document open to use in the next exercise.

Another Way Reader Aid

Hands-On Practice

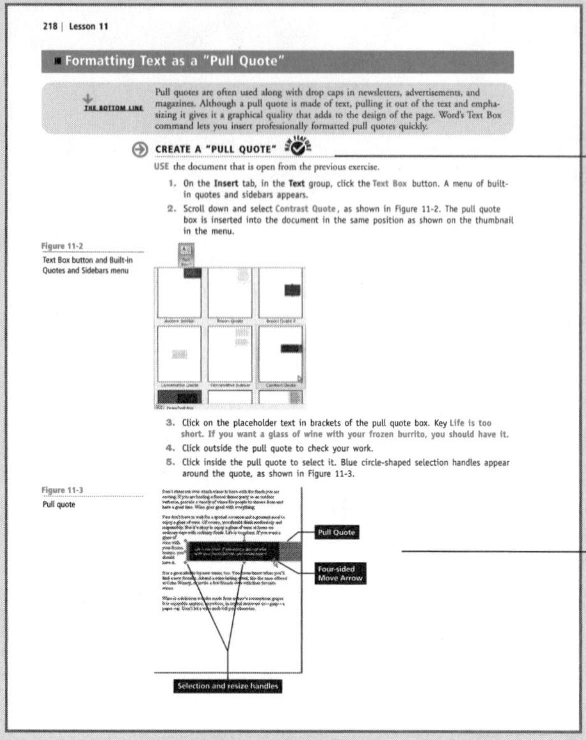

218 | Lesson 11

Formatting Text as a "Pull Quote"

THE BOTTOM LINE — Pull quotes are often used along with drop caps in newsletters, advertisements, and magazines. Although a pull quote is made of text, pulling it out of the text and emphasizing it gives it a graphical quality that adds to the design of the page. Word's Text Box command lets you insert professionally formatted pull quotes quickly.

CREATE A "PULL QUOTE"

USE the document that is open from the previous exercise.

1. On the **Insert** tab, in the **Text** group, click the Text Box button. A menu of built-in quotes and sidebars appears.
2. Scroll down and select Contrast Quote, as shown in Figure 11-2. The pull quote box is inserted into the document in the same position as shown on the thumbnail in the menu.

Figure 11-2
Text Box button and Built-in Quotes and Sidebars menu

3. Click on the placeholder text in brackets of the pull quote box. Key Life is too short. If you want a glass of wine with your frozen burrito, you should have it.
4. Click outside the pull quote to check your work.
5. Click inside the pull quote to select it. Blue circle-shaped selection handles appear around the quote, as shown in Figure 11-3.

Figure 11-3
Pull quote

New Features

Screen Images with Callouts

Cross-Reference Reader Aid

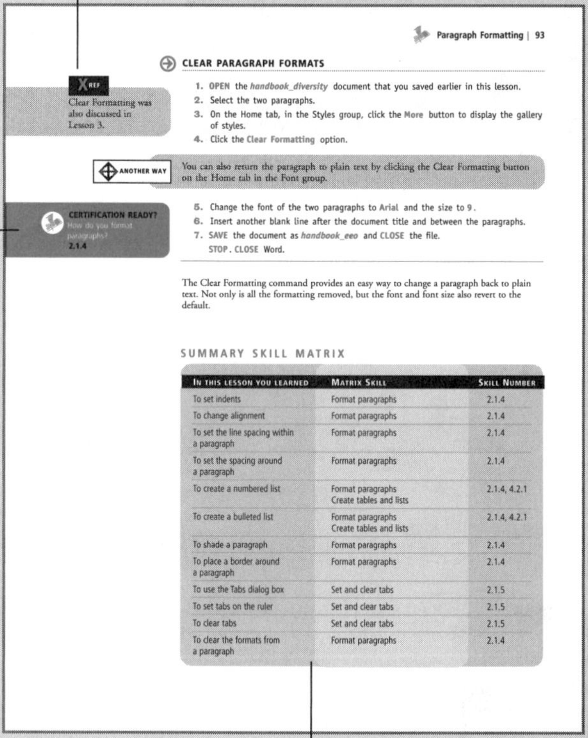

Paragraph Formatting | 93

CLEAR PARAGRAPH FORMATS

X REF — Clear Formatting was also discussed in Lesson 3.

1. OPEN the *handbook_diversity* document that you saved earlier in this lesson.
2. Select the two paragraphs.
3. On the Home tab, in the Styles group, click the More button to display the gallery of styles.
4. Click the Clear Formatting option.

ANOTHER WAY — You can also return the paragraph to plain text by clicking the Clear Formatting button on the Home tab in the Font group.

CERTIFICATION READY? How do you format paragraphs? 2.1.4

5. Change the font of the two paragraphs to Arial and the size to 9.
6. Insert another blank line after the document title and between the paragraphs.
7. SAVE the document as *handbook_eeo* and CLOSE the file.

STOP. CLOSE Word.

The Clear Formatting command provides an easy way to change a paragraph back to plain text. Not only is all the formatting removed, but the font and font size also revert to the default.

SUMMARY SKILL MATRIX

In This Lesson You Learned	Matrix Skill	Skill Number
To set indents	Format paragraphs	2.1.4
To change alignment	Format paragraphs	2.1.4
To set the line spacing within a paragraph	Format paragraphs	2.1.4
To set the spacing around a paragraph	Format paragraphs	2.1.4
To create a numbered list	Format paragraphs Create tables and lists	2.1.4, 4.2.1
To create a bulleted list	Format paragraphs Create tables and lists	2.1.4, 4.2.1
To shade a paragraph	Format paragraphs	2.1.4
To place a border around a paragraph	Format paragraphs	2.1.4
To use the Tabs dialog box	Set and clear tabs	2.1.5
To set tabs on the ruler	Set and clear tabs	2.1.5
To clear tabs	Set and clear tabs	2.1.5
To clear the formats from a paragraph	Format paragraphs	2.1.4

Microsoft Certified Application Specialist (MCAS) Certification Objective Alert

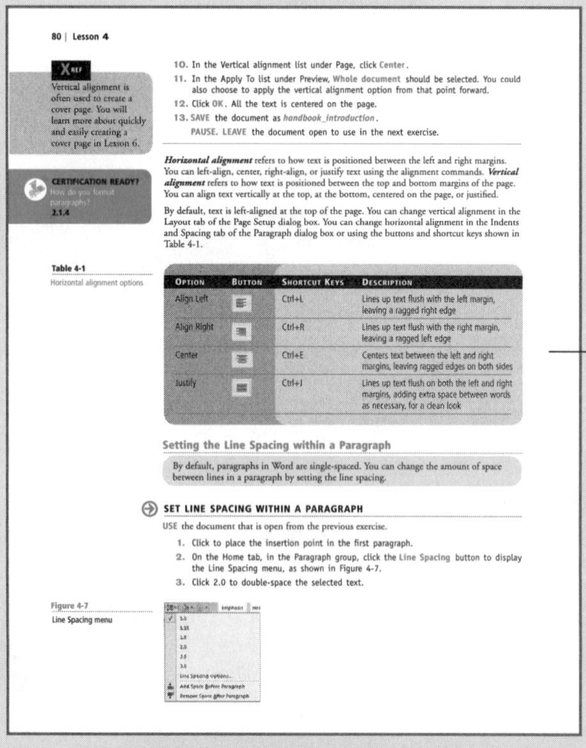

80 | Lesson 4

X REF — Vertical alignment is often used to create a cover page. You will learn more about quickly and easily creating a cover page in Lesson 6.

10. In the Vertical alignment list under Page, click Center.
11. In the Apply To list under Preview, Whole document should be selected. You could also choose to apply the vertical alignment option from that point forward.
12. Click OK. All the text is centered on the page.
13. SAVE the document as *handbook_introduction*.

PAUSE. LEAVE the document open to use in the next exercise.

CERTIFICATION READY? How do you format paragraphs? 2.1.4

Horizontal alignment refers to how text is positioned between the left and right margins. You can left-align, center, right-align, or justify text using the alignment commands. ***Vertical alignment*** refers to how text is positioned between the top and bottom margins of the page. You can align text vertically at the top, at the bottom, centered on the page, or justified.

By default, text is left-aligned at the top of the page. You can change vertical alignment in the Layout tab of the Page Setup dialog box. You can change horizontal alignment in the Indents and Spacing tab of the Paragraph dialog box or using the buttons and shortcut keys shown in Table 4-1.

Table 4-1
Horizontal alignment options

Option	Button	Shortcut Keys	Description
Align Left		Ctrl+L	Lines up text flush with the left margin, leaving a ragged right edge
Align Right		Ctrl+R	Lines up text flush with the right margin, leaving a ragged left edge
Center		Ctrl+E	Centers text between the left and right margins, leaving ragged edges on both sides
Justify		Ctrl+J	Lines up text flush on both the left and right margins, adding extra space between words as necessary, for a clean look

Setting the Line Spacing within a Paragraph

By default, paragraphs in Word are single-spaced. You can change the amount of space between lines in a paragraph by setting the line spacing.

SET LINE SPACING WITHIN A PARAGRAPH

USE the document that is open from the previous exercise.

1. Click to place the insertion point in the first paragraph.
2. On the Home tab, in the Paragraph group, click the Line Spacing button to display the Line Spacing menu, as shown in Figure 4-7.
3. Click 2.0 to double-space the selected text.

Figure 4-7
Line Spacing menu

Easy-to-Read Tables

Summary Skill Matrix

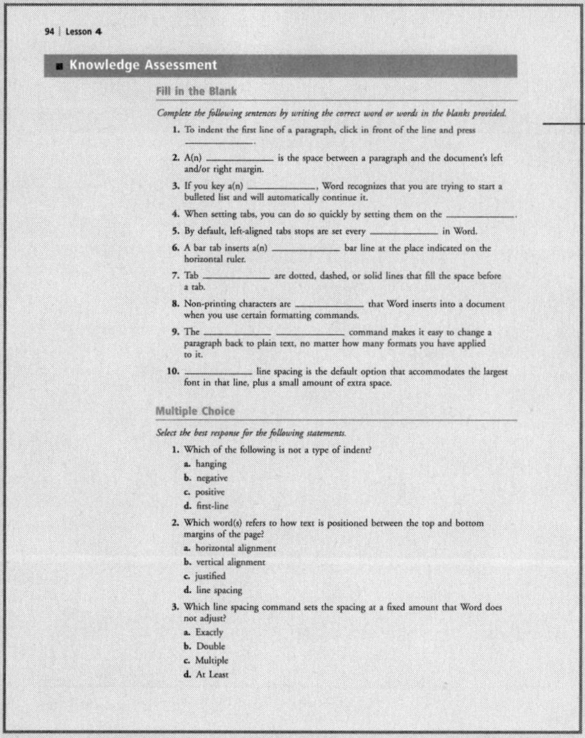

94 | Lesson 4

Knowledge Assessment

Fill in the Blank

Complete the following sentences by writing the correct word or words in the blanks provided.

1. To indent the first line of a paragraph, click in front of the line and press ________.
2. A(n) ________ is the space between a paragraph and the document's left and/or right margin.
3. If you key a(n) ________, Word recognizes that you are trying to start a bulleted list and will automatically continue it.
4. When setting tabs, you can do so quickly by setting them on the ________.
5. By default, left-aligned tabs stops are set every ________ in Word.
6. A bar tab inserts a(n) ________ bar line at the place indicated on the horizontal ruler.
7. Tab ________ are dotted, dashed, or solid lines that fill the space before a tab.
8. Non-printing characters are ________ that Word inserts into a document when you use certain formatting commands.
9. The ________ ________ command makes it easy to change a paragraph back to plain text, no matter how many formats you have applied to it.
10. ________ line spacing is the default option that accommodates the largest font in that line, plus a small amount of extra space.

Multiple Choice

Select the best response for the following statements.

1. Which of the following is not a type of indent?
   a. hanging
   b. negative
   c. positive
   d. first-line
2. Which word(s) refers to how text is positioned between the top and bottom margins of the page?
   a. horizontal alignment
   b. vertical alignment
   c. justified
   d. line spacing
3. Which line spacing command sets the spacing at a fixed amount that Word does not adjust?
   a. Exactly
   b. Double
   c. Multiple
   d. At Least

Knowledge Assessment Questions

Proficiency Assessment Projects

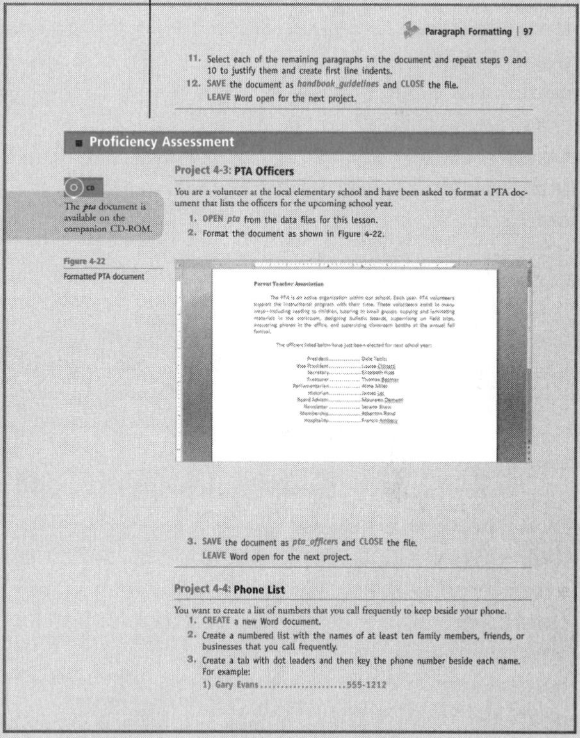

Paragraph Formatting | 97

11. Select each of the remaining paragraphs in the document and repeat steps 9 and 10 to justify them and create first line indents.
12. SAVE the document as *handbook_guidelines* and CLOSE the file.
    LEAVE Word open for the next project.

Proficiency Assessment

Project 4-3: PTA Officers

You are a volunteer at the local elementary school and have been asked to format a PTA document that lists the officers for the upcoming school year.

CD: The *pta* document is available on the companion CD-ROM.

1. OPEN *pta* from the data files for this lesson.
2. Format the document as shown in Figure 4-22.

Figure 4-22
Formatted PTA document

3. SAVE the document as *pta_officers* and CLOSE the file.
   LEAVE Word open for the next project.

Project 4-4: Phone List

You want to create a list of numbers that you call frequently to keep beside your phone.

1. CREATE a new Word document.
2. Create a numbered list with the names of at least ten family members, friends, or businesses that you call frequently.
3. Create a tab with dot leaders and then key the phone number beside each name. For example:
   1) Gary Evans....................555-1212

Competency Assessment Projects

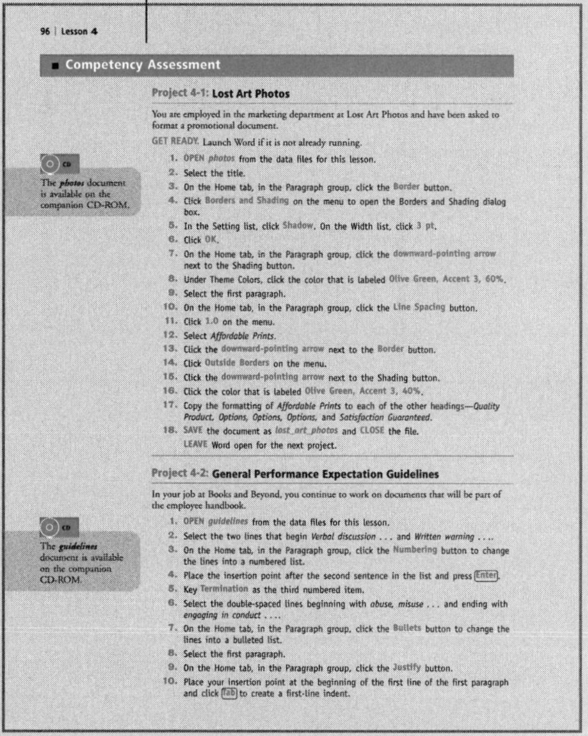

96 | Lesson 4

Competency Assessment

Project 4-1: Lost Art Photos

You are employed in the marketing department at Lost Art Photos and have been asked to format a promotional document.

GET READY. Launch Word if it is not already running.

CD: The *photos* document is available on the companion CD-ROM.

1. OPEN *photos* from the data files for this lesson.
2. Select the title.
3. On the Home tab, in the Paragraph group, click the Border button.
4. Click Borders and Shading on the menu to open the Borders and Shading dialog box.
5. In the Setting list, click Shadow. On the Width list, click 3 pt.
6. Click OK.
7. On the Home tab, in the Paragraph group, click the downward-pointing arrow next to the Shading button.
8. Under Theme Colors, click the color that is labeled Olive Green, Accent 3, 60%.
9. Select the first paragraph.
10. On the Home tab, in the Paragraph group, click the Line Spacing button.
11. Click 1.0 on the menu.
12. Select *Affordable Prints*.
13. Click the downward-pointing arrow next to the Border button.
14. Click Outside Borders on the menu.
15. Click the downward-pointing arrow next to the Shading button.
16. Click the color that is labeled Olive Green, Accent 3, 40%.
17. Copy the formatting of *Affordable Prints* to each of the other headings—*Quality Product, Options, Options, Options,* and *Satisfaction Guaranteed*.
18. SAVE the document as *lost_art_photos* and CLOSE the file.
    LEAVE Word open for the next project.

Project 4-2: General Performance Expectation Guidelines

In your job at Books and Beyond, you continue to work on documents that will be part of the employee handbook.

CD: The *guidelines* document is available on the companion CD-ROM.

1. OPEN *guidelines* from the data files for this lesson.
2. Select the two lines that begin *Verbal discussion . . .* and *Written warning . . . .*
3. On the Home tab, in the Paragraph group, click the Numbering button to change the lines into a numbered list.
4. Place the insertion point after the second sentence in the list and press Enter.
5. Key Termination as the third numbered item.
6. Select the double-spaced lines beginning with *abuse, misuse . . .* and ending with *engaging in conduct . . . .*
7. On the Home tab, in the Paragraph group, click the Bullets button to change the lines into a bulleted list.
8. Select the first paragraph.
9. On the Home tab, in the Paragraph group, click the Justify button.
10. Place your insertion point at the beginning of the first line of the first paragraph and click Tab to create a first-line indent.

Mastery Assessment Projects

Internet Ready Project

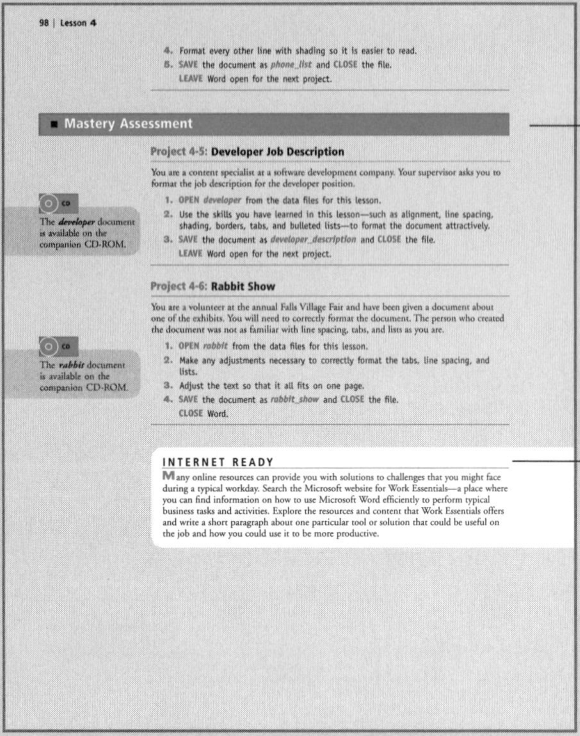

98 | Lesson 4

4. Format every other line with shading so it is easier to read.
5. SAVE the document as *phone_list* and CLOSE the file.
   LEAVE Word open for the next project.

■ Mastery Assessment

Project 4-5: Developer Job Description

You are a content specialist at a software development company. Your supervisor asks you to format the job description for the developer position.

CD — The ***developer*** document is available on the companion CD-ROM.

1. OPEN *developer* from the data files for this lesson.
2. Use the skills you have learned in this lesson—such as alignment, line spacing, shading, borders, tabs, and bulleted lists—to format the document attractively.
3. SAVE the document as *developer_description* and CLOSE the file.
   LEAVE Word open for the next project.

Project 4-6: Rabbit Show

You are a volunteer at the annual Falls Village Fair and have been given a document about one of the exhibits. You will need to correctly format the document. The person who created the document was not as familiar with line spacing, tabs, and lists as you are.

CD — The ***rabbit*** document is available on the companion CD-ROM.

1. OPEN *rabbit* from the data files for this lesson.
2. Make any adjustments necessary to correctly format the tabs, line spacing, and lists.
3. Adjust the text so that it all fits on one page.
4. SAVE the document as *rabbit_show* and CLOSE the file.
   CLOSE Word.

INTERNET READY

Many online resources can provide you with solutions to challenges that you might face during a typical workday. Search the Microsoft website for Work Essentials—a place where you can find information on how to use Microsoft Word efficiently to perform typical business tasks and activities. Explore the resources and content that Work Essentials offers and write a short paragraph about one particular tool or solution that could be useful on the job and how you could use it to be more productive.

Workplace Ready

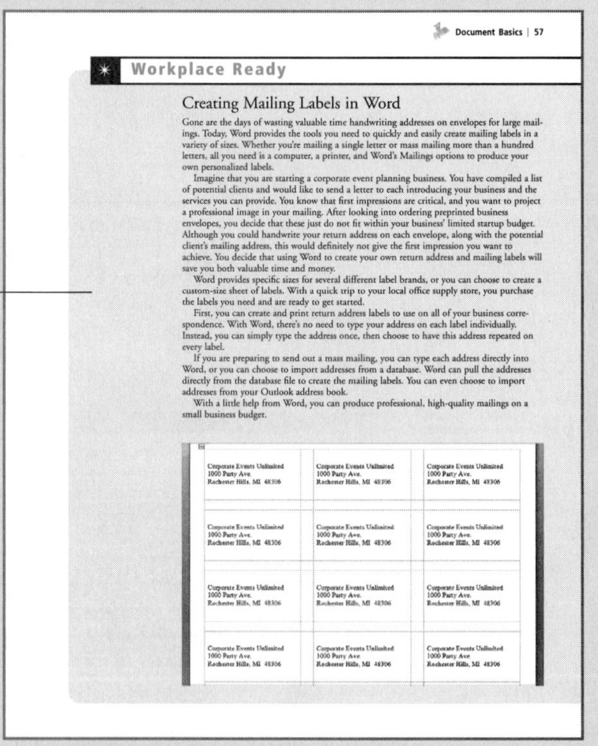

Document Basics | 57

Workplace Ready

Creating Mailing Labels in Word

Gone are the days of wasting valuable time handwriting addresses on envelopes for large mailings. Today, Word provides the tools you need to quickly and easily create mailing labels in a variety of sizes. Whether you're mailing a single letter or mass mailing more than a hundred letters, all you need is a computer, a printer, and Word's Mailings options to produce your own personalized labels.

Imagine that you are starting a corporate event planning business. You have compiled a list of potential clients and would like to send a letter to each introducing your business and the services you can provide. You know that first impressions are critical, and you want to project a professional image in your mailing. After looking into ordering preprinted business envelopes, you decide that these just do not fit within your business' limited startup budget. Although you could handwrite your return address on each envelope, along with the potential client's mailing address, this would definitely not give the first impression you want to achieve. You decide that using Word to create your own return address and mailing labels will save you both valuable time and money.

Word provides specific sizes for several different label brands, or you can choose to create a custom-size sheet of labels. With a quick trip to your local office supply store, you purchase the labels you need and are ready to get started.

First, you can create and print return address labels to use on all of your business correspondence. With Word, there's no need to type your address on each label individually. Instead, you can simply type the address once, then choose to have this address repeated on every label.

If you are preparing to send out a mass mailing, you can type each address directly into Word, or you can choose to import addresses from a database. Word can pull the addresses directly from the database file to create the mailing labels. You can even choose to import addresses from your Outlook address book.

With a little help from Word, you can produce professional, high-quality mailings on a small business budget.

Corporate Events Unlimited 1000 Party Ave. Rochester Hills, MI 48306	Corporate Events Unlimited 1000 Party Ave. Rochester Hills, MI 48306	Corporate Events Unlimited 1000 Party Ave. Rochester Hills, MI 48306
Corporate Events Unlimited 1000 Party Ave. Rochester Hills, MI 48306	Corporate Events Unlimited 1000 Party Ave. Rochester Hills, MI 48306	Corporate Events Unlimited 1000 Party Ave. Rochester Hills, MI 48306
Corporate Events Unlimited 1000 Party Ave. Rochester Hills, MI 48306	Corporate Events Unlimited 1000 Party Ave. Rochester Hills, MI 48306	Corporate Events Unlimited 1000 Party Ave. Rochester Hills, MI 48306
Corporate Events Unlimited 1000 Party Ave. Rochester Hills, MI 48306	Corporate Events Unlimited 1000 Party Ave. Rochester Hills, MI 48306	Corporate Events Unlimited 1000 Party Ave. Rochester Hills, MI 48306

Circling Back Exercises

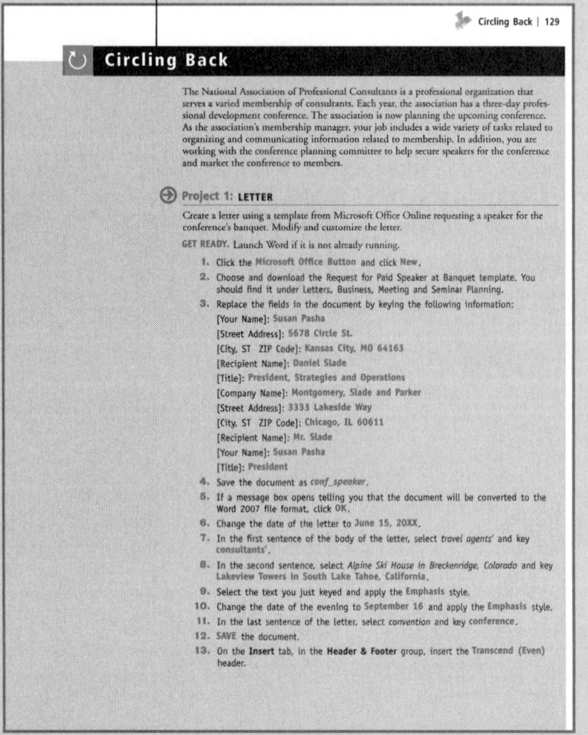

Circling Back | 129

Circling Back

The National Association of Professional Consultants is a professional organization that serves a varied membership of consultants. Each year, the association has a three-day professional development conference. The association is now planning the upcoming conference. As the association's membership manager, your job includes a wide variety of tasks related to organizing and communicating information related to membership. In addition, you are working with the conference planning committee to help secure speakers for the conference and market the conference to members.

Project 1: LETTER

Create a letter using a template from Microsoft Office Online requesting a speaker for the conference's banquet. Modify and customize the letter.

GET READY. Launch Word if it is not already running.

1. Click the Microsoft Office Button and click New.
2. Choose and download the Request for Paid Speaker at Banquet template. You should find it under Letters, Business, Meeting and Seminar Planning.
3. Replace the fields in the document by keying the following information:
   [Your Name]: Susan Pasha
   [Street Address]: 5678 Circle St.
   [City, ST ZIP Code]: Kansas City, MO 64163
   [Recipient Name]: Daniel Slade
   [Title]: President, Strategies and Operations
   [Company Name]: Montgomery, Slade and Parker
   [Street Address]: 3333 Lakeside Way
   [City, ST ZIP Code]: Chicago, IL 60611
   [Recipient Name]: Mr. Slade
   [Your Name]: Susan Pasha
   [Title]: President
4. Save the document as *conf_speaker*.
5. If a message box opens telling you that the document will be converted to the Word 2007 file format, click OK.
6. Change the date of the letter to June 15, 20XX.
7. In the first sentence of the body of the letter, select *travel agents'* and key consultants'.
8. In the second sentence, select *Alpine Ski House in Breckenridge, Colorado* and key Lakeview Towers in South Lake Tahoe, California.
9. Select the text you just keyed and apply the Emphasis style.
10. Change the date of the evening to September 16 and apply the Emphasis style.
11. In the last sentence of the letter, select *convention* and key conference.
12. SAVE the document.
13. On the **Insert** tab, in the **Header & Footer** group, insert the Transcend (Even) header.

Conventions and Features Used in This Book

This book uses particular fonts, symbols, and heading conventions to highlight important information or to call your attention to special steps. For more information about the features in each lesson, refer to the Illustrated Book Tour section.

CONVENTION	MEANING
NEW FEATURE	This icon indicates a new or greatly improved Office 2007 feature in this version of the software.
THE BOTTOM LINE	This feature provides a brief summary of the material to be covered in the section that follows.
CLOSE	Words in all capital letters and in a different font color than the rest of the text indicate instructions for opening, saving, or closing files or programs. They also point out items you should check or actions you should take.
CERTIFICATION READY?	This feature signals the point in the text where a specific certification objective is covered. It provides you with a chance to check your understanding of that particular MCAS objective and, if necessary, review the section of the lesson where it is covered.
CD	This indicates a file that is available on the student CD.
TAKE NOTE*	Reader aids appear in shaded boxes found in your text. *Take Note* provides helpful hints related to particular tasks or topics.
ANOTHER WAY	*Another Way* provides an alternative procedure for accomplishing a particular task.
TROUBLESHOOTING	*Troubleshooting* covers common problems and pitfalls.
X REF	These notes provide pointers to information discussed elsewhere in the textbook or describe interesting features of Office 2007 that are not directly addressed in the current topic or exercise.
SAVE	When a toolbar button is referenced in an exercise, the button's picture is shown in the margin.
Alt + Tab	A plus sign (+) between two key names means that you must press both keys at the same time. Keys that you are instructed to press in an exercise will appear in the font shown here.
A ***cell*** is the area where data is entered.	Key terms appear in bold italic.
Key **My Name is.**	Any text you are asked to key appears in color.
Click **OK**.	Any button on the screen you are supposed to click on or select will also appear in color.
OPEN ***FitnessClasses.***	The names of data files will appear in bold, italic, and color for easy identification.

Instructor Support Program

Instructor Support Program

The *Microsoft Official Academic Course* programs are accompanied by a rich array of resources that incorporate the extensive textbook visuals to form a pedagogically cohesive package. These resources provide all the materials instructors need to deploy and deliver their courses. Resources available online for download include:

- **6-Month Office 2007 Trial Edition (available in North America only).** Students receive 6-months' access to Microsoft Office Professional 2007 when you adopt a MOAC 2007 Microsoft Office system textbook. The textbook includes the trial CD and a product key that allows students to activate the CD for a 6-month period.
- The **Instructor's Guide** contains Solutions to all the textbook exercises, Syllabi for various term lengths, Data Files for all the documents students need to work the exercises. The Instructor's Guide also includes chapter summaries and lecture notes. The Instructor's Guide is available from the Book Companion site (http://www.wiley.com/college/microsoft) and from *WileyPLUS*.
- The **Test Bank** contains hundreds of multiple-choice, true-false, and short answer questions and is available to download from the Instructor's Book Companion site (http://www.wiley.com/college/microsoft) and from *WileyPLUS*. A complete answer key is provided. It is available as a computerized test bank and in Microsoft Word format. The easy-to-use test-generation program fully supports graphics, print tests, student answer sheets, and answer keys. The software's advanced features allow you to create an exam to meet your exact specifications. The computerized test bank provides:
    - Varied question types to test a variety of comprehension levels—multiple-choice, true-false, and short answer.
    - Allows instructors to edit, randomize, and create questions freely.
    - Allows instructors to create and print different versions of a quiz or exam.
- **PowerPoint Presentations and Images.** A complete set of PowerPoint presentations is available on the Instructor's Book Companion site (http://www.wiley.com/college/microsoft) and in *WileyPLUS* to enhance classroom presentations. Approximately 50 PowerPoint slides are provided for each lesson. Tailored to the text's topical coverage and Skills Matrix, these presentations are designed to convey key Office 2007 concepts addressed in the text.

  All figures from the text are on the Instructor's Book Companion site (http://www.wiley.com/college/microsoft) and in *WileyPLUS*. You can incorporate them into your PowerPoint presentations, or create your own overhead transparencies and handouts.

  By using these visuals in class discussions, you can help focus students' attention on key elements of Office 2007 and help them understand how to use it effectively in the workplace.
- **Microsoft Business Certification Pre-Test and Exams.** With each MOAC textbook, students receive information allowing them to access a Pre-Test, Score Report, and Learning Plan, either directly from Certiport, one of Microsoft's exam delivery partners, or through links from *WileyPLUS* Premium. They also receive a code and information for taking the certification exams.
- The **MSDN Academic Alliance** is designed to provide the easiest and most inexpensive way for university departments to make the latest Microsoft software available to faculty and students in labs, classrooms, and on student PCs. A free 1-year membership is available to qualified MOAC adopters.

MSDN ACADEMIC ALLIANCE—FREE 1-YEAR MEMBERSHIP AVAILABLE TO QUALIFIED ADOPTERS!

MSDN Academic Alliance (MSDN AA) is designed to provide the easiest and most inexpensive way for universities to make the latest Microsoft software available in labs, classrooms, and on student PCs. MSDN AA is an annual membership program for departments teaching Science, Technology, Engineering, and Mathematics (STEM) courses. The membership provides a complete solution to keep academic labs, faculty, and students on the leading edge of technology.

As a bonus to this free offer, faculty will be introduced to Microsoft's Faculty Connection and Academic Resource Center. It takes time and preparation to keep students engaged while giving them a fundamental understanding of theory, and the Microsoft Faculty Connection is designed to help STEM professors with this preparation by providing articles, curriculum, and tools that professors can use to engage and inspire today's technology students.

Software provided in the MSDN AA program carries a high retail value but is being provided here through the Wiley and Microsoft publishing partnership and is made available to your department free of charge with the adoption of any Wiley qualified textbook.*

* Contact your Wiley rep for details.

For more information about the MSDN Academic Alliance program, go to:

http://msdn.microsoft.com/academic/

- The **Wiley Faculty Network** lets you tap into a large community of your peers effortlessly. Willey Faculty Network mentors are faculty like you, from educational institutions around the country, who are passionate about enhancing instructional efficiency and effectiveness through best practices. Faculty Network activities include technology training and tutorials, virtual seminars, peer-to-peer exchanges of experiences and ideas, personal consulting, and sharing of resources. To register for a seminar, go to www.wherefacultyconnect.com or phone 1-866-4FACULTY.

WileyPLUS

Broad developments in education over the past decade have influenced the instructional approach taken in the Microsoft Official Academic Course programs. The way that students learn, especially about new technologies, has changed dramatically in the Internet era. Electronic learning materials and Internet-based instruction are now as much a part of classroom instruction as printed textbooks. *WileyPLUS* provides the technology to create an environment where students reach their full potential and experience academic success that will last them a lifetime!

WileyPLUS is a powerful and highly-integrated suite of teaching and learning resources designed to bridge the gap between what happens in the classroom and what happens at home and on the job. *WileyPLUS* provides instructors with the resources to teach their students new technologies and guide them to reach their goals of getting ahead in the job market by having the skills to become certified and advance in the workforce. For students, *WileyPLUS* provides the tools for study and practice that are available to them 24/7, wherever and whenever they want to study. *WileyPLUS* includes a complete online version of the student textbook; PowerPoint presentations; homework and practice assignments and quizzes; links to Microsoft's Pre-Test, Learning Plan, and a code for taking the certification exam (in *WileyPLUS* Premium); image galleries; test-bank questions; gradebook; and all the instructor resources in one easy-to-use website.

Organized around the everyday activities you and your students perform in the class, *WileyPLUS* helps you:

For Instructors

- **Prepare & Present** outstanding class presentations using relevant PowerPoint slides and other *WileyPLUS* materials—and you can easily upload and add your own.
- **Create Assignments** by choosing from questions organized by lesson, level of difficulty, and source—and add your own questions. Students' homework and quizzes are automatically graded, and the results are recorded in your gradebook.
- **Offer context-sensitive help to students, 24/7.** When you assign homework or quizzes, you decide if and when students get access to hints, solutions, or answers where appropriate—or they can be linked to relevant sections of their complete, online text for additional help whenever—and wherever they need it most.
- **Track Student Progress:** Analyze students' results and assess their level of understanding on an individual and class level using the *WileyPLUS* gradebook, or export data to your own personal gradebook.
- **Administer Your Course:** *WileyPLUS* can easily be integrated with another course management system, gradebook, or other resources you are using in your class, providing you with the flexibility to build your course, your way.
- **Seamlessly integrate all of the rich *WileyPLUS* content and resources with WebCT and Blackboard**—with a single sign-on.

For Students

WileyPLUS provides immediate feedback on student assignments and a wealth of support materials. This powerful study tool will help your students develop their conceptual understanding of the class material and increase their ability to answer questions.

- A **Study and Practice** area links directly to text content, allowing students to review the text while they study and answer. Access to Microsoft's Pre-Test, Learning Plan, and a code for taking the MCAS certification exam is available in Study and Practice. Additional Practice Questions tied to the MCAS certification that can be re-taken as many times as necessary, are also available.
- An **Assignment** area keeps all the work you want your students to complete in one location, making it easy for them to stay on task. Students have access to a variety of interactive self-assessment tools, as well as other resources for building their confidence and understanding. In addition, all of the assignments and quizzes contain a link to the relevant section of the multimedia book, providing students with context-sensitive help that allows them to conquer obstacles as they arise.
- A **Personal Gradebook** for each student allows students to view their results from past assignments at any time.

Please view our online demo at **www.wiley.com/college/wileyplus.** Here you will find additional information about the features and benefits of *WileyPLUS*, how to request a "test drive" of *WileyPLUS* for this title, and how to adopt it for class use.

WileyPLUS Teams with Certiport

Certiport is a leading administrator of global, performance-based certification programs and services designed to enable success and lifetime advancement through certification. As an administrator of the Microsoft Certified Application Specialist (MCAS) program, Certiport uses concurrent and simulation technologies to deliver 54,000 exams per month in 128 countries and 20 different languages around the world.

Microsoft Pre-tests, delivered by Certiport, provide a simple, low-cost way for individuals to identify their desktop computing skill level. Pre-Tests are taken online, making the first step towards certification easy and convenient. Through the Pre-Tests, individuals can receive a custom learning path with recommended training.

WileyPLUS is a powerful and highly-integrated suite of teaching and learning resources designed to bridge the gap between what happens in the classroom and what happens at home and on the job. *WileyPLUS* provides instructors with the resources to teach their students new technologies and guide them to reach their goals of getting ahead in the job market by having the skills to become certified and advance in the workforce. For students, *WileyPLUS* provides the tools for study and practice that are available to them 24/7, wherever and whenever they want to study.

WileyPLUS includes a complete online version of the student textbook, PowerPoint® presentations, homework and practice assignments and quizzes, links to Microsoft's Pre-Test, Learning Plan and a certification voucher (in *WileyPLUS* Premium), image galleries, test bank questions, gradebook, and all the instructor resources in one, easy-to-use website.

Together, with *WileyPLUS* and the MCAS Pre-Test and exams delivered through Certiport, we are creating the best of both worlds in academic learning and performance based validation in preparation for a great career and a globally recognized Microsoft certification—the higher education learning management system that accesses the industry-leading certification pre-test.

This is only available with the *Microsoft Official Academic Course* program in partnership with Certiport.

MICROSOFT BUSINESS CERTIFICATION PRE-TEST AND EXAMS AVAILABLE THROUGH *WILEYPLUS* PREMIUM

Enhance your students' knowledge and skills and increase their performance on Microsoft Business Certification exams with adoption of the Microsoft Official Academic Course program for Office 2007.

With the majority of the workforce classified as *information workers*, certification on the 2007 Microsoft Office system is a critical tool in terms of validating the desktop computing knowledge and skills required to be more productive in the workplace. Certification is the primary tool companies use to validate the proficiency of desktop computing skills among employees. It gives organizations the ability to help assess employees' actual computer skills and select job candidates based on verifiable skills applying the latest productivity tools and technology.

Microsoft Pre-tests, delivered by Certiport, provide a simple, low-cost way for individuals to identify their desktop computing skill level. Pre-Tests are taken online, making the first step towards certification easy and convenient. Through the Pre-Tests, individuals can receive a custom learning path with recommended training.

To help students to study for and pass the Microsoft Certified Application Specialist, or MCAS exam, each MOAC textbook includes information allowing students to access a Pre-Test, Score Report, and Learning Plan, either directly from Certiport or through links from the *WileyPLUS* Premium course. Students also receive a code and information for taking the certification exams. Students who do not have access to *WileyPLUS* Premium can find information on how to purchase access to the Pre-Test and a code for taking the certification exams by clicking on their textbook at:

http://www.wiley.com/college/microsoft.

The Pre-Test can only be taken once. It provides a simple, low-cost way for students to evaluate and identify their skill level. Through the Pre-Test, students receive a recommended study plan that they can print out to help them prepare for the live certification exams. The Pre-Test is comprised of a variety of selected response questions, including matching, sequencing exercises, "hot spots" where students must identify an item or function, and traditional multiple-choice questions. After students have mastered all the certification objectives, they can use their code to take the actual Microsoft Certified Application Specialist (MCAS) exams for Office 2007.

WileyPLUS Premium includes a complete online version of the student textbook, PowerPoint® presentations, homework and practice assignments and quizzes, links to Microsoft's Pre-Test, Learning Plan and a certification voucher, image galleries, test bank questions, gradebook, and all the instructor resources in one, easy-to-use website. Together, with *WileyPLUS* and the MCAS Pre-Test and exams delivered by Certiport, we are creating the best of both worlds in academic learning and performance based validation in preparation for a great career and a globally recognized Microsoft certification—the higher education learning management system that accesses the industry-leading certification pre-test.

Contact your Wiley rep today about this special offer.

Student Supplements

Book Companion Website (www.wiley.com/college/microsoft)

The book companion site for the MOAC series includes the Instructor Resources and Web links to important information for students and instructors.

Student CD

The CD-ROM included with this book contains the practice files that you will use as you perform the exercises in the book. By using the practice files, you will not waste time creating the samples used in the lessons, and you can concentrate on learning how to use Microsoft Office 2007. With the files and the step-by-step instructions in the lessons, you will learn by doing, which is an easy and effective way to acquire and remember new skills.

IMPORTANT

This course assumes that the 2007 Microsoft Office system has already been installed on the PC you are using. You can download a trial version of the 2007 Microsoft Office system by visiting Microsoft Office Online at http://office.microsoft.com. Note that Microsoft Product Support does not support these trial versions.

Copying the Practice Files

Your instructor might already have copied the practice files before you arrive in class. However, your instructor might ask you to copy the practice files on your own at the start of class. Also, if you want to work through any of the exercises in this book on your own at home or at your place of business after class, you may want to copy the practice files. Note that you can also open the files directly from the CD-ROM, but you should be cautious about carrying the CD-ROM around with you as it could become damaged.

1. Insert the CD-ROM in the CD-ROM drive of your computer.
2. Start Windows Explorer.
3. In the left pane of Explorer, locate the icon for your CD-ROM and click on this icon. The folders and files contained on the CD will appear listed on the right.

4. Locate and select the **Word Data** folder. This is the folder which contains all of the practice files, separated by Lesson folders.
5. Right-click on the **Word Data** folder and choose **Copy** from the menu.

ANOTHER WAY If you only want to copy the files for one lesson, you can open the Word Data folder and right-click the desired Lesson folder within the Word Data folder.

6. In the left pane of Windows Explorer, locate the location to which you would like to copy the practice files. This can be a drive on your local PC or an external drive.
7. Right-click on the drive/location to which you want to copy the practice files and choose **Paste**. This will copy the entire Word Data folder to your chosen location.
8. Close Windows Explorer.

Deleting the Practice Files

Use the following steps when you want to delete the practice files from your hard disk or other drive. Your instructor might ask you to perform these steps at the end of class. Also, you should perform these steps if you have worked through the exercises at home or at your place of business and want to work through the exercises again. Deleting the practice files and then reinstalling them ensures that all files and folders are in their original condition if you decide to work through the exercises again.

1. Start Windows Explorer.
2. Browse through the drives and folders to locate the practice files.
3. Select the **Word Data** folder.
4. Right-click on the **Word Data** folder and choose **Delete** from the menu.
5. Close Windows Explorer.

ANOTHER WAY If you want to delete only the files for one lesson, you can open the Word Data folder and right-click the desired Lesson folder within the Word Data folder.

Locating and Opening Practice Files

After you (or your instructor) have copied the practice files, all the files you need for this course will be stored in a folder named Word Data located on the disk you choose.

1. Click the **Office Button** in the top left corner of your application.
2. Choose **Open** from the menu.
3. In the Open dialog box, browse through the Folders panel to locate the drive and folder where you copied the files.
4. Double-click on the **Word Data** folder.
5. Double-click on the **Lesson** folder for the lesson in which you are working.
6. Select the file that you want and click **Open** or double-click on the file that you want.

ANOTHER WAY You can use the Search function in the Open dialog box to quickly find the specific file for which you are looking.

Wiley Desktop Editions

Wiley MOAC Desktop Editions are innovative, electronic versions of printed textbooks. Students buy the desktop version for 60% off the price of the printed text, and get the added value of permanence and portability. Wiley Desktop Editions provide students with numerous additional benefits that are not available with other e-text solutions:

Wiley Desktop Editions are NOT subscriptions; students download the Wiley Desktop Edition to their computer desktops. Students own the content they buy to keep for as long as they want. Once a Wiley Desktop Edition is downloaded to the computer desktop, students have instant access to all of the content without being online. Students can also print out the sections they prefer to read in hard copy. Students also have access to fully integrated resources within their Wiley Desktop Edition. From highlighting their e-text to taking and sharing notes, students can easily personalize their Wiley Desktop Edition as they are reading or following along in class.

6-Month Microsoft Office 2007 Trial Edition

MOAC textbooks provide an unparalleled value to students in today's performance-based courses. All MOAC 2007 Microsoft Office system textbooks sold in North America are packaged with a 6-month trial CD of Microsoft Office Professional 2007. The textbook includes the CD and a product key that allows students to activate Microsoft Office Professional 2007 for the 6-month trial period. After purchasing the textbook containing the Microsoft Office Professional 2007 Trial CD, students must install the CD onto their computer and, when prompted, enter the Office Trial product key that allows them to activate the software.

Installing the Microsoft Office Professional 2007 Trial CD provides students with the state-of-the-art 2007 Microsoft Office system software, allowing them to use the practice files on the Student CD and in *WileyPLUS* to learn and study by doing, which is the best and most effective way to acquire and remember new computing skills.

Important Web Addresses and Phone Numbers

To locate the Wiley Higher Education Rep in your area, go to the following Web address and click on the "*Who's My Rep?*" link at the top of the page.

http://www.wiley.com/college

Or Call the MOAC Toll Free Number: 1 + (888) 764-7001

Microsoft Office Online

Please visit Microsoft Office Online for help using Office 2007, Clip Art, Templates, and other valuable information:
http://office.microsoft.com/

Preparing to Take the Microsoft Certified Application Specialist (MCAS) Exam

The Microsoft Certified Application Specialist program is part of the new and enhanced Microsoft Certification system. It is easily attainable through a series of verifications that provide a simple and convenient framework for skills assessment and validation.

For organizations, the new certification program provides better skills verification tools that help with assessing not only in-demand skills on specific Microsoft business software programs, but also the ability to quickly complete on-the-job tasks. Individuals will find it easier to identify and work towards the certification credential that meets their personal and professional goals.

Microsoft Certified Application Specialist (MCAS) Program

The core Microsoft Office Specialist credential has been upgraded to validate skills with the 2007 Microsoft Office system as well as the new Windows Vista operating system. The Application Specialist certifications target information workers and cover the most popular business applications such as Word 2007, PowerPoint 2007, Excel 2007, Access 2007, and Outlook 2007.

By becoming certified, you demonstrate to employers that you have achieved a predictable level of skill in the use of a particular Office application. Employers often require certification either as a condition of employment or as a condition of advancement within the company or other organization. The certification examinations are sponsored by Microsoft but administered through exam delivery partners like Certiport.

http://www.certiport.com/

Preparing to Take an Exam

Unless you are a very experienced user, you will need to use a test preparation course to prepare to complete the test correctly and within the time allowed. The *Microsoft Official Academic Course* series is designed to prepare you with a strong knowledge of all exam topics, and with some additional review and practice on your own; you should feel confident in your ability to pass the appropriate exam.

After you decide which exam to take, review the list of objectives for the exam. This list can be found in the MCAS Objectives Appendix at the back of this book. You can also easily identify tasks that are included in the objective list by locating the MCAS symbol in the margin of the lessons in this book.

You can also familiarize yourself with a live MCAS certification test by downloading and installing a practice MCAS certification test from *www.certiport.com.*

To take the MCAS test, first see *www.certiport.com* to locate your nearest testing center. Then call the testing center directly to schedule your test. The amount of advance notice you should provide will vary for different testing centers, and it typically depends on the number of computers available at the testing center, the number of other testers who have already been scheduled for the day on which you want to take the test, and the number of times per week that the testing center offers MCAS testing. In general, you should call to schedule your test at least two weeks prior to the date on which you want to take the test.

When you arrive at the testing center, you might be asked for proof of identity. A driver's license or passport is an acceptable form of identification. If you do not have either of these items of documentation, call your testing center and ask what alternative forms of identification will be accepted. If you are retaking a test, bring your MCAS identification number, which will have been given to you when you previously took the test. If you have not prepaid or if your organization has not already arranged to make payment for you, you will need to pay the test-taking fee when you arrive. The current test-taking fee is $75 (U.S.). Prices are subject to change and may vary depending on the testing center.

Test Format

All MCAS certification tests are live, performance-based tests. There are no true/false or short-answer questions. Instructions are general: you are told the basic tasks to perform on the computer, but you aren't given any help in figuring out how to perform them. You are not permitted to use reference material.

As you complete the tasks stated in a particular test question, the testing software monitors your actions. An example question might be:

Open the file named *Wiley Guests* and select the word *Welcome* in the first paragraph. Change the font to 12 point, and apply bold formatting. Select the words *at your convenience* in the second paragraph, move them to the end of the first paragraph using drag and drop, and then center the first paragraph.

When the test administrator seats you at a computer, you will see an online form that you use to enter information about yourself (name, address, and other information required to process your exam results). While you complete the form, the software will generate the test from a master test bank and then prompt you to continue. The first test question will appear in a window. Read the question carefully, and then perform all the tasks stated in the test question. When you have finished completing all tasks for a question, click the Next Question button.

You have 45 to 50 minutes to complete all questions, depending on the test that you are taking. The testing software assesses your results as soon as you complete the test, and the test administrator can print the results of the test so that you will have a record of any tasks that you performed incorrectly. If you pass, you will receive a certificate in the mail within two to four weeks. If you do not pass, you can study and practice the skills that you missed and then schedule to retake the test at a later date.

Tips for Successfully Completing the Test

The following tips and suggestions are the result of feedback received from many individuals who have taken one or more MCAS tests:

- Make sure that you are thoroughly prepared. If you have extensively used the application for which you are being tested, you might feel confident that you are prepared for the test. However, the test might include questions that involve tasks that you rarely or never perform when you use the application at your place of business, at school, or at home. You must be knowledgeable in all the MCAS objectives for the test that you will take.
- Read each exam question carefully. An exam question might include several tasks that you are to perform. A partially correct response to a test question is counted as an incorrect response. In the example question on the previous page, you might apply bold formatting and move the words *at your convenience* to the correct location, but forget to center the first paragraph. This would count as an incorrect response and would result in a lower test score.
- You are not allowed to use the application's Help system. The Help function is always disabled for all exams.
- The test does display the amount of time that you have left. The test program also displays the number of items that you have completed along with the total number of test items (for example, "35 of 40 items have been completed"). Use this information to gauge your pace.
- If you skip a question, you can return to it later.

If You Do Not Pass the Test

If you do not pass, you can use the assessment printout as a guide to practice the items that you missed. There is no limit to the number of times that you can retake a test; however, you must pay the fee each time that you take the test. When you retake the test, expect to see some of the same test items on the subsequent test; the test software randomly generates the test items from a master test bank before you begin the test. Also expect to see several questions that did not appear on the previous test.

http://www.certiport.com/

Acknowledgments

MOAC Instructor Advisory Board

We would like to thank our Instructor Advisory Board, an elite group of educators who has assisted us every step of the way in building these products. Advisory Board members have acted as our sounding board on key pedagogical and design decisions leading to the development of these compelling and innovative textbooks for future Information Workers. Their dedication to technology education is truly appreciated.

Catherine Binder, Strayer University & Katharine Gibbs School–Philadelphia

Catherine currently works at both Katharine Gibbs School in Norristown, PA, and Strayer University in King of Prussia, PA. Catherine has been at Katharine Gibbs School for 4 years. Catherine is currently the Department Chair/Lead instructor for PC Networking at Gibbs and the founder/advisor of the TEK Masters Society. Since joining Strayer University a year and a half ago she has risen in the ranks from adjunct to DIT/Assistant Campus Dean.

Catherine has brought her 10+ year's industry experience as Network Administrator, Network Supervisor, Professor, Bench Tech, Manager and CTO from such places as Foster Wheeler Corp, KidsPeace Inc., Victoria Vogue, TESST College, AMC Theatres, Blue Mountain Publishing and many more to her teaching venue.

Catherine began as an adjunct in the PC Networking department and quickly became a full-time instructor. At both schools she is in charge of scheduling, curricula and departmental duties. She happily advises about 80+ students and is committed to Gibbs/Strayer life, her students, and continuing technology education every day.

Penny Gudgeon, CDI College

Penny is the Program Manager for IT curriculum at Corinthian Colleges, Inc. Until January 2006, Penny was responsible for all Canadian programming and web curriculum for five years. During that time, Corinthian Colleges, Inc. acquired CDI College of Business and Technology in 2004. Before 2000 she spent four years as IT instructor at one of the campuses. Penny joined CDI College in 1997 after her working for 10 years first in programming and later in software productivity education. Penny previously has worked in the fields of advertising, sales, engineering technology and programming. When not working from her home office or indulging her passion for life long learning, and the possibilities of what might be, Penny likes to read mysteries, garden and relax at home in Hamilton, Ontario, with her Shih-Tzu, Gracie, and husband, Al.

Jana Hambruch, School District of Lee County

Ms. Hambruch currently serves as Director for the Information Technology Magnet Programs at The School District of Lee County in Ft Myers, Florida. She is responsible for the implementation and direction of three schools that fall under this grant program. This program has been recognized as one of the top 15 most innovative technology programs in the nation. She is also co-author of the grant proposal for the IT Magnet Grant prior to taking on the role of Director.

Ms. Hambruch has over ten years experience directing the technical certification training programs at many Colleges and Universities, including Barry University, the University of South Florida, Broward Community College, and at Florida Gulf Coast University, where she served as the Director for the Center for Technology Education. She excels at developing alternative training models that focus on the tie between the education provider and the community in which it serves.

Ms. Hambruch is a past board member and treasurer of the Human Resources Management Association of SW Florida, graduate of Leadership Lee County Class of 2002, Steering Committee Member for Leadership Lee County Class of 2004 and a former board member of the Career Coalition of Southwest Florida. She has frequently lectured for organizations such as Microsoft, American Society of Training and Development, Florida Gulf Coast University, Florida State University, University of Nevada at Las Vegas, University of Wisconsin at Milwaukee, Canada's McGill University, and Florida's State Workforce Summit.

Dee Hobson, Richland College

Dee Hobson is currently a faculty member of the Business Office Systems and Support Division at Richland College. Richland is one of seven colleges in the Dallas County Community College District and has the distinction of being the first community college to receive the Malcolm Baldrige National Quality Award in 2005. Richland also received the Texas Award for Performance Excellence in 2005.

The Business Office Systems and Support Division at Richland is also a Certiport Authorized Microsoft Office testing center. All students enrolling in one of Microsoft's application software courses (Word, Excel, PowerPoint, and Access) are required to take the respective Microsoft certification exam at the end of the semester.

Dee has taught computer and business courses in K-12 public schools and at a proprietary career college in Dallas. She has also been involved with several corporate training companies and with adult education programs in the Dallas area. She began her computer career as an employee of IBM Corporation in St. Louis, Missouri. During her ten-year IBM employment, she moved to Memphis, Tennessee, to accept a managerial position and to Dallas, Texas, to work in a national sales and marketing technical support center.

Keith Hoell, Katharine Gibbs School–New York

Keith has worked in both non-profit and proprietary education for over 10 years, initially at St. John's University in New York, and then as full-time faculty, Chairperson and currently Dean of Information Systems at the Katharine Gibbs School in New York City. He also worked for General Electric in the late 80's and early 90's as the Sysop of a popular bulletin board dedicated to ASCII-Art on GE's pioneering GEnie on-line service before the advent of the World Wide Web. He has taught courses and workshops dealing with many mainstream IT issues and varied technology, especially those related to computer hardware and operating system software, networking, software applications, IT project management and ethics, and relational database technology. An avid runner and a member of The New York Road Runners, he won the Footlocker Five Borough Challenge representing Queens at the 2005 ING New York City Marathon while competing against the 4 other borough reps. He currently resides in Queens, New York.

Michael Taylor, Seattle Central Community College

Michael worked in education and training for the last 20 years in both the public and private sector. He currently teaches and coordinates the applications support program at Seattle Central Community College and also administers the Microsoft IT Academy. His experience outside the educational world is in Travel and Tourism with wholesale tour operations and cruise lines.

Interests outside of work include greyhound rescue. (He adopted 3 x-racers who bring him great joy.) He also enjoys the arts and is fortunate to live in downtown Seattle where there is much to see and do.

MOAC Office 2007 Reviewers

We also thank the many reviewers who pored over the manuscript providing invaluable feedback in the service of quality instructional materials.

Access

Susan Fry, Boise State University
Leslie Jernberg, Eastern Idaho Technical College
Dr. Deborah Jones, South Georgia Technical College
Suzanne Marks, Bellevue Community College
Kim Styles, Tri-County Technical College & Anderson School District 5

Excel

Christie Hovey, Lincoln Land Community College
Barbara Lave, Portland Community College
Donna Madsen, Kirkwood Community College
James M. Veneziano, Davenport University—Caro
Dorothy Weiner, Manchester Community College

PowerPoint

Barbara Gillespie, Cuyamaca College
Tatyana Pashnyak, Bainbridge College
Michelle Poertner, Northwestern Michigan College
Janet Sebesy, Cuyahoga Community College

Outlook

Julie Boyles, Portland Community College
Joe LaMontagne, Davenport University—Grand Rapids
Randy Nordell, American River College
Echo Rantanen, Spokane Community College

Project

Janis DeHaven, Central Community College
Dr. Susan Jennings, Stephen F. Austin State University
Diane D. Mickey, Northern Virginia Community College
Linda Nutter, Peninsula College
Marika Reinke, Bellevue Community College

Word

Diana Anderson, Big Sandy Community & Technical College
Donna Hendricks, South Arkansas Community College
Dr. Donna McGill-Cameron, Yuba Community College—Woodland Campus
Patricia McMahon, South Suburban College
Nancy Noe, Linn-Benton Community College
Teresa Roberts, Wilson Technical Community College

Focus Group and Survey Participants

Finally we thank the hundreds of instructors who participated in our focus groups and surveys to ensure that the Microsoft Official Academic Courses best met the needs of our customers.

Jean Aguilar, Mt. Hood Community College
Konrad Akens, Zane State College
Michael Albers, University of Memphis
Diana Anderson, Big Sandy Community & Technical College
Phyllis Anderson, Delaware County Community College
Judith Andrews, Feather River College
Damon Antos, American River College
Bridget Archer, Oakton Community College
Linda Arnold, Harrisburg Area Community College–Lebanon Campus

Neha Arya, Fullerton College
Mohammad Bajwa, Katharine Gibbs School–New York
Virginia Baker, University of Alaska Fairbanks
Carla Bannick, Pima Community College
Rita Barkley, Northeast Alabama Community College
Elsa Barr, Central Community College – Hastings
Ronald W. Barry, Ventura County Community College District
Elizabeth Bastedo, Central Carolina Technical College
Karen Baston, Waubonsee Community College
Karen Bean, Blinn College
Scott Beckstrand, Community College of Southern Nevada
Paulette Bell, Santa Rosa Junior College
Liz Bennett, Southeast Technical Institute
Nancy Bermea, Olympic College
Lucy Betz, Milwaukee Area Technical College
Meral Binbasioglu, Hofstra University
Catherine Binder, Strayer University & Katharine Gibbs School–Philadelphia
Terrel Blair, El Centro College
Ruth Blalock, Alamance Community College
Beverly Bohner, Reading Area Community College
Henry Bojack, Farmingdale State University
Matthew Bowie, Luna Community College
Julie Boyles, Portland Community College
Karen Brandt, College of the Albemarle
Stephen Brown, College of San Mateo
Jared Bruckner, Southern Adventist University
Pam Brune, Chattanooga State Technical Community College
Sue Buchholz, Georgia Perimeter College
Roberta Buczyna, Edison College
Angela Butler, Mississippi Gulf Coast Community College
Rebecca Byrd, Augusta Technical College
Kristen Callahan, Mercer County Community College
Judy Cameron, Spokane Community College
Dianne Campbell, Athens Technical College
Gena Casas, Florida Community College at Jacksonville
Jesus Castrejon, Latin Technologies
Gail Chambers, Southwest Tennessee Community College
Jacques Chansavang, Indiana University–Purdue University Fort Wayne
Nancy Chapko, Milwaukee Area Technical College
Rebecca Chavez, Yavapai College
Sanjiv Chopra, Thomas Nelson Community College
Greg Clements, Midland Lutheran College
Dayna Coker, Southwestern Oklahoma State University–Sayre Campus
Tamra Collins, Otero Junior College
Janet Conrey, Gavilan Community College
Carol Cornforth, West Virginia Northern Community College
Gary Cotton, American River College
Edie Cox, Chattahoochee Technical College
Rollie Cox, Madison Area Technical College
David Crawford, Northwestern Michigan College
J.K. Crowley, Victor Valley College
Rosalyn Culver, Washtenaw Community College
Sharon Custer, Huntington University
Sandra Daniels, New River Community College
Anila Das, Cedar Valley College
Brad Davis, Santa Rosa Junior College
Susan Davis, Green River Community College
Mark Dawdy, Lincoln Land Community College
Jennifer Day, Sinclair Community College
Carol Deane, Eastern Idaho Technical College
Julie DeBuhr, Lewis-Clark State College
Janis DeHaven, Central Community College
Drew Dekreon, University of Alaska–Anchorage
Joy DePover, Central Lakes College
Salli DiBartolo, Brevard Community College
Melissa Diegnau, Riverland Community College
Al Dillard, Lansdale School of Business
Marjorie Duffy, Cosumnes River College
Sarah Dunn, Southwest Tennessee Community College
Shahla Durany, Tarrant County College–South Campus
Kay Durden, University of Tennessee at Martin
Dineen Ebert, St. Louis Community College–Meramec
Donna Ehrhart, State University of New York–Brockport
Larry Elias, Montgomery County Community College
Glenda Elser, New Mexico State University at Alamogordo
Angela Evangelinos, Monroe County Community College
Angie Evans, Ivy Tech Community College of Indiana
Linda Farrington, Indian Hills Community College
Dana Fladhammer, Phoenix College
Richard Flores, Citrus College
Connie Fox, Community and Technical College at Institute of Technology West Virginia University
Wanda Freeman, Okefenokee Technical College
Brenda Freeman, Augusta Technical College
Susan Fry, Boise State University
Roger Fulk, Wright State University–Lake Campus
Sue Furnas, Collin County Community College District
Sandy Gabel, Vernon College
Laura Galvan, Fayetteville Technical Community College
Candace Garrod, Red Rocks Community College
Sherrie Geitgey, Northwest State Community College
Chris Gerig, Chattahoochee Technical College
Barb Gillespie, Cuyamaca College
Jessica Gilmore, Highline Community College
Pamela Gilmore, Reedley College
Debbie Glinert, Queensborough Community College
Steven Goldman, Polk Community College
Bettie Goodman, C.S. Mott Community College
Mike Grabill, Katharine Gibbs School–Philadelphia
Francis Green, Penn State University
Walter Griffin, Blinn College
Fillmore Guinn, Odessa College
Helen Haasch, Milwaukee Area Technical College
John Habal, Ventura College
Joy Haerens, Chaffey College
Norman Hahn, Thomas Nelson Community College

Kathy Hall, Alamance Community College
Teri Harbacheck, Boise State University
Linda Harper, Richland Community College
Maureen Harper, Indian Hills Community College
Steve Harris, Katharine Gibbs School–New York
Robyn Hart, Fresno City College
Darien Hartman, Boise State University
Gina Hatcher, Tacoma Community College
Winona T. Hatcher, Aiken Technical College
BJ Hathaway, Northeast Wisconsin Tech College
Cynthia Hauki, West Hills College – Coalinga
Mary L. Haynes, Wayne County Community College
Marcie Hawkins, Zane State College
Steve Hebrock, Ohio State University Agricultural Technical Institute
Sue Heistand, Iowa Central Community College
Heith Hennel, Valencia Community College
Donna Hendricks, South Arkansas Community College
Judy Hendrix, Dyersburg State Community College
Gloria Hensel, Matanuska-Susitna College University of Alaska Anchorage
Gwendolyn Hester, Richland College
Tammarra Holmes, Laramie County Community College
Dee Hobson, Richland College
Keith Hoell, Katharine Gibbs School–New York
Pashia Hogan, Northeast State Technical Community College
Susan Hoggard, Tulsa Community College
Kathleen Holliman, Wallace Community College Selma
Chastity Honchul, Brown Mackie College/Wright State University
Christie Hovey, Lincoln Land Community College
Peggy Hughes, Allegany College of Maryland
Sandra Hume, Chippewa Valley Technical College
John Hutson, Aims Community College
Celia Ing, Sacramento City College
Joan Ivey, Lanier Technical College
Barbara Jaffari, College of the Redwoods
Penny Jakes, University of Montana College of Technology
Eduardo Jaramillo, Peninsula College
Barbara Jauken, Southeast Community College
Susan Jennings, Stephen F. Austin State University
Leslie Jernberg, Eastern Idaho Technical College
Linda Johns, Georgia Perimeter College
Brent Johnson, Okefenokee Technical College
Mary Johnson, Mt. San Antonio College
Shirley Johnson, Trinidad State Junior College–Valley Campus
Sandra M. Jolley, Tarrant County College
Teresa Jolly, South Georgia Technical College
Dr. Deborah Jones, South Georgia Technical College
Margie Jones, Central Virginia Community College
Randall Jones, Marshall Community and Technical College
Diane Karlsbraaten, Lake Region State College
Teresa Keller, Ivy Tech Community College of Indiana
Charles Kemnitz, Pennsylvania College of Technology
Sandra Kinghorn, Ventura College
Bill Klein, Katharine Gibbs School–Philadelphia
Bea Knaapen, Fresno City College
Kit Kofoed, Western Wyoming Community College
Maria Kolatis, County College of Morris
Barry Kolb, Ocean County College
Karen Kuralt, University of Arkansas at Little Rock
Belva-Carole Lamb, Rogue Community College
Betty Lambert, Des Moines Area Community College
Anita Lande, Cabrillo College
Junnae Landry, Pratt Community College
Karen Lankisch, UC Clermont
David Lanzilla, Central Florida Community College
Nora Laredo, Cerritos Community College
Jennifer Larrabee, Chippewa Valley Technical College
Debra Larson, Idaho State University
Barb Lave, Portland Community College
Audrey Lawrence, Tidewater Community College
Deborah Layton, Eastern Oklahoma State College
Larry LeBlanc, Owen Graduate School–Vanderbilt University
Philip Lee, Nashville State Community College
Michael Lehrfeld, Brevard Community College
Vasant Limaye, Southwest Collegiate Institute for the Deaf – Howard College
Anne C. Lewis, Edgecombe Community College
Stephen Linkin, Houston Community College
Peggy Linston, Athens Technical College
Hugh Lofton, Moultrie Technical College
Donna Lohn, Lakeland Community College
Jackie Lou, Lake Tahoe Community College
Donna Love, Gaston College
Curt Lynch, Ozarks Technical Community College
Sheilah Lynn, Florida Community College–Jacksonville
Pat R. Lyon, Tomball College
Bill Madden, Bergen Community College
Heather Madden, Delaware Technical & Community College
Donna Madsen, Kirkwood Community College
Jane Maringer-Cantu, Gavilan College
Suzanne Marks, Bellevue Community College
Carol Martin, Louisiana State University–Alexandria
Cheryl Martucci, Diablo Valley College
Roberta Marvel, Eastern Wyoming College
Tom Mason, Brookdale Community College
Mindy Mass, Santa Barbara City College
Dixie Massaro, Irvine Valley College
Rebekah May, Ashland Community & Technical College
Emma Mays-Reynolds, Dyersburg State Community College
Timothy Mayes, Metropolitan State College of Denver
Reggie McCarthy, Central Lakes College
Matt McCaskill, Brevard Community College
Kevin McFarlane, Front Range Community College
Donna McGill, Yuba Community College
Terri McKeever, Ozarks Technical Community College

Patricia McMahon, South Suburban College
Sally McMillin, Katharine Gibbs School–Philadelphia
Charles McNerney, Bergen Community College
Lisa Mears, Palm Beach Community College
Imran Mehmood, ITT Technical Institute–King of Prussia Campus
Virginia Melvin, Southwest Tennessee Community College
Jeanne Mercer, Texas State Technical College
Denise Merrell, Jefferson Community & Technical College
Catherine Merrikin, Pearl River Community College
Diane D. Mickey, Northern Virginia Community College
Darrelyn Miller, Grays Harbor College
Sue Mitchell, Calhoun Community College
Jacquie Moldenhauer, Front Range Community College
Linda Motonaga, Los Angeles City College
Sam Mryyan, Allen County Community College
Cindy Murphy, Southeastern Community College
Ryan Murphy, Sinclair Community College
Sharon E. Nastav, Johnson County Community College
Christine Naylor, Kent State University Ashtabula
Haji Nazarian, Seattle Central Community College
Nancy Noe, Linn-Benton Community College
Jennie Noriega, San Joaquin Delta College
Linda Nutter, Peninsula College
Thomas Omerza, Middle Bucks Institute of Technology
Edith Orozco, St. Philip's College
Dona Orr, Boise State University
Joanne Osgood, Chaffey College
Janice Owens, Kishwaukee College
Tatyana Pashnyak, Bainbridge College
John Partacz, College of DuPage
Tim Paul, Montana State University–Great Falls
Joseph Perez, South Texas College
Mike Peterson, Chemeketa Community College
Dr. Karen R. Petitto, West Virginia Wesleyan College
Terry Pierce, Onandaga Community College
Ashlee Pieris, Raritan Valley Community College
Jamie Pinchot, Thiel College
Michelle Poertner, Northwestern Michigan College
Betty Posta, University of Toledo
Deborah Powell, West Central Technical College
Mark Pranger, Rogers State University
Carolyn Rainey, Southeast Missouri State University
Linda Raskovich, Hibbing Community College
Leslie Ratliff, Griffin Technical College
Mar-Sue Ratzke, Rio Hondo Community College
Roxy Reissen, Southeastern Community College
Silvio Reyes, Technical Career Institutes
Patricia Rishavy, Anoka Technical College
Jean Robbins, Southeast Technical Institute
Carol Roberts, Eastern Maine Community College and University of Maine
Teresa Roberts, Wilson Technical Community College
Vicki Robertson, Southwest Tennessee Community College
Betty Rogge, Ohio State Agricultural Technical Institute
Lynne Rusley, Missouri Southern State University
Claude Russo, Brevard Community College
Ginger Sabine, Northwestern Technical College
Steven Sachs, Los Angeles Valley College
Joanne Salas, Olympic College
Lloyd Sandmann, Pima Community College–Desert Vista Campus
Beverly Santillo, Georgia Perimeter College
Theresa Savarese, San Diego City College
Sharolyn Sayers, Milwaukee Area Technical College
Judith Scheeren, Westmoreland County Community College
Adolph Scheiwe, Joliet Junior College
Marilyn Schmid, Asheville-Buncombe Technical Community College
Janet Sebesy, Cuyahoga Community College
Phyllis T. Shafer, Brookdale Community College
Ralph Shafer, Truckee Meadows Community College
Anne Marie Shanley, County College of Morris
Shelia Shelton, Surry Community College
Merilyn Shepherd, Danville Area Community College
Susan Sinele, Aims Community College
Beth Sindt, Hawkeye Community College
Andrew Smith, Marian College
Brenda Smith, Southwest Tennessee Community College
Lynne Smith, State University of New York–Delhi
Rob Smith, Katharine Gibbs School–Philadelphia
Tonya Smith, Arkansas State University–Mountain Home
Del Spencer – Trinity Valley Community College
Jeri Spinner, Idaho State University
Eric Stadnik, Santa Rosa Junior College
Karen Stanton, Los Medanos College
Meg Stoner, Santa Rosa Junior College
Beverly Stowers, Ivy Tech Community College of Indiana
Marcia Stranix, Yuba College
Kim Styles, Tri-County Technical College
Sylvia Summers, Tacoma Community College
Beverly Swann, Delaware Technical & Community College
Ann Taff, Tulsa Community College
Mike Theiss, University of Wisconsin–Marathon Campus
Romy Thiele, Cañada College
Sharron Thompson, Portland Community College
Ingrid Thompson-Sellers, Georgia Perimeter College
Barbara Tietsort, University of Cincinnati–Raymond Walters College
Janine Tiffany, Reading Area Community College
Denise Tillery, University of Nevada Las Vegas
Susan Trebelhorn, Normandale Community College
Noel Trout, Santiago Canyon College
Cheryl Turgeon, Asnuntuck Community College
Steve Turner, Ventura College
Sylvia Unwin, Bellevue Community College
Lilly Vigil, Colorado Mountain College
Sabrina Vincent, College of the Mainland
Mary Vitrano, Palm Beach Community College
Brad Vogt, Northeast Community College
Cozell Wagner, Southeastern Community College

Carolyn Walker, Tri-County Technical College
Sherry Walker, Tulsa Community College
Qi Wang, Tacoma Community College
Betty Wanielista, Valencia Community College
Marge Warber, Lanier Technical College–Forsyth Campus
Marjorie Webster, Bergen Community College
Linda Wenn, Central Community College
Mark Westlund, Olympic College
Carolyn Whited, Roane State Community College
Winona Whited, Richland College
Jerry Wilkerson, Scott Community College
Joel Willenbring, Fullerton College
Barbara Williams, WITC Superior
Charlotte Williams, Jones County Junior College
Bonnie Willy, Ivy Tech Community College of Indiana
Diane Wilson, J. Sargeant Reynolds Community College
James Wolfe, Metropolitan Community College
Marjory Wooten, Lanier Technical College
Mark Yanko, Hocking College
Alexis Yusov, Pace University
Naeem Zaman, San Joaquin Delta College
Kathleen Zimmerman, Des Moines Area Community College

We would also like to thank Lutz Ziob, Sanjay Advani, Jim DiIanni, Merrick Van Dongen, and Jim LeValley at Microsoft Learning for their encourage and support in making the Microsoft Official Academic Course programs the finest instructional materials for mastering the newest Microsoft technologies for both students and instructors.

Brief Contents

Contents

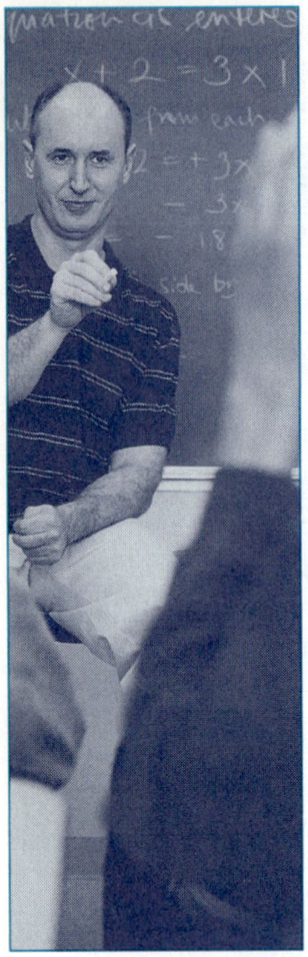

Word Essentials

1

LESSON SKILL MATRIX

Skills	Matrix Skill	Skill Number
Changing Word's View	Change window views	5.1.2
Saving an Edited Document	Save to appropriate formats	6.1.1

Star Bright Satellite Radio is the nation's leading satellite radio company. The company sells its subscription service to automobile owners, home listeners, and people on the go with portable satellite radios. The public relations department is responsible for promoting a favorable image of Star Bright Satellite Radio to the media, potential customers, and current customers. Microsoft Word 2007 is the perfect tool for creating and editing a wide variety of professional-looking documents that enhance Star Bright's image on a daily basis. In this lesson, you will learn to open, navigate, edit, save, print, and close a document.

KEY TERMS

badges
command
Connection Status menu
desktop
dialog box
dialog box launcher
gridlines
groups
I-beam
insertion point
key tips
menu
Mini toolbar
Microsoft Office Button
multi-selection
Quick Access toolbar
redo
ribbon
ruler
scrollbars
scroll box
scroll buttons
shortcut menu
tabs
thumbnails
undo

SOFTWARE ORIENTATION

Microsoft Word's Opening Screen

Before you begin working in Microsoft Word, you should be familiar with the primary user interface. When you first launch Microsoft Word, you will see a screen similar to that shown in Figure 1-1.

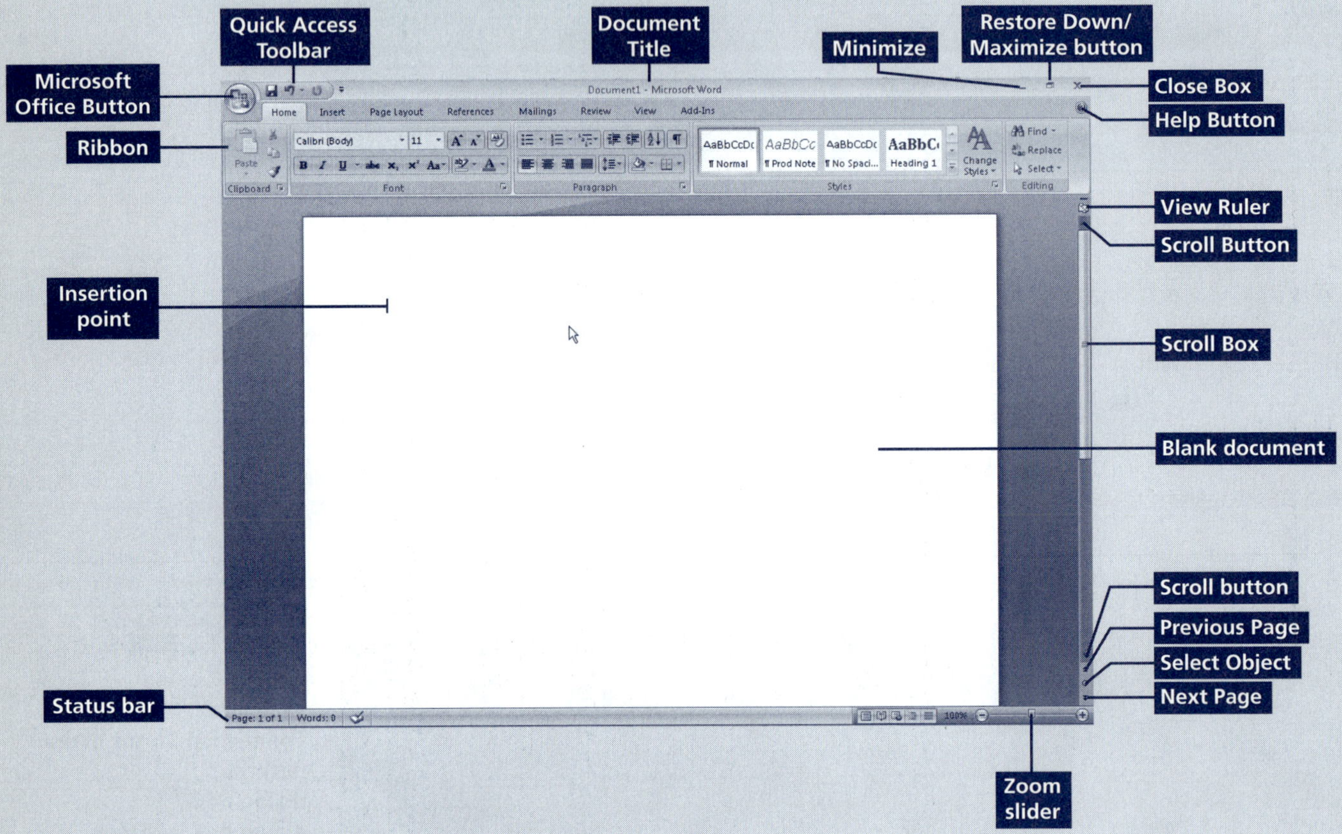

Figure 1-1

Word document window

Microsoft has designed the user interface to provide easier access to commands relevant to the document being created or edited. Your screen may vary if default settings have been changed or if other preferences have been set.

Working in Word

NEW FEATURE

THE BOTTOM LINE

To begin working in Word, first you need to start the program. When you start Word, a new, blank document will appear.

START WORD

GET READY. Before you begin these steps, be sure to turn on and/or log on to your computer.

1. On the Windows Taskbar, click the **Start** button and click **All Programs**. A menu of installed programs appears.
2. Click **Microsoft Office**. Another menu appears.

3. Click **Microsoft Office Word 2007** (see Figure 1-2). Word starts and a new, blank document appears.

Figure 1-2

Start Word

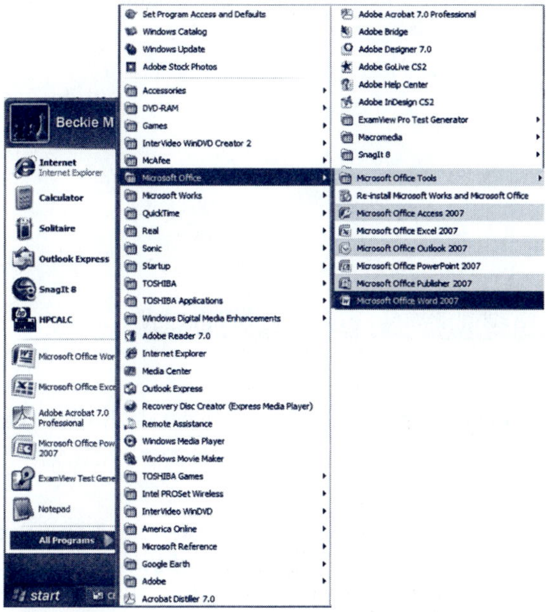

PAUSE. LEAVE the document open to use in the next exercise.

ANOTHER WAY

When Office was installed on your computer, a shortcut icon may have been added to the Start menu or to your desktop. Double-click the shortcut icon on your desktop to start Word without having to go through the Start menu.

After you have started your computer, the screen you see is called the Windows ***desktop***. Click the Start button in the lower left corner of the Taskbar to open the Start menu and then click All Programs. A pop-up menu appears where you click Microsoft Office. Another pop-up menu appears where you click Microsoft Office Word 2007.

■ Working in the Word Window

THE BOTTOM LINE

The Word 2007 window was designed to help you get your work done quickly. You will start exploring the ribbon across the top right away. Also in this lesson, you will practice using other onscreen tools and features such as the Microsoft Office Button and Word Help.

Using the Onscreen Tools

Word has many tools to help you create documents. In this section, you will explore the ribbon, which displays common commands in groups arranged by tabs. You will also learn about other onscreen tools to help you get your work done faster, such as the Mini toolbar, the Quick Access Toolbar, and key tips.

USE THE RIBBON

NEW FEATURE

USE the document that is open from the previous exercise.

1. The Home tab is the active tab. As shown in Figure 1-3, the ribbon is divided into groups of commands.

Figure 1-3

The ribbon

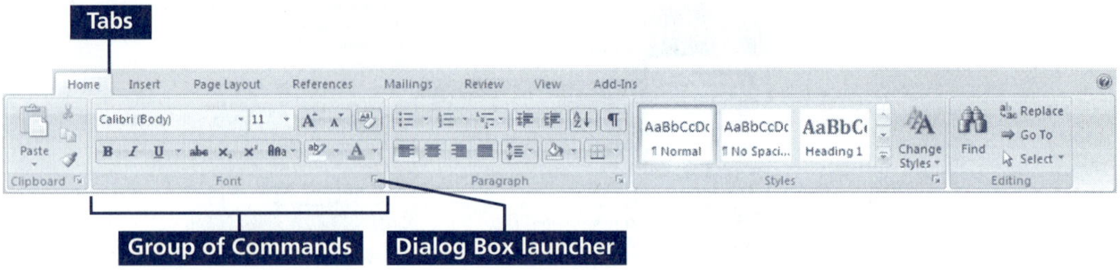

2. Click **Page Layout** to make it the active tab. Notice that the groups of commands change.
3. Click the **Home** tab.
4. Click the dialog box launcher in the lower right corner of the Font group, as shown in Figure 1-3. The Font Dialog Box, as shown in Figure 1-4, appears. Click **Cancel** to close the dialog box.

Figure 1-4

Font Dialog box

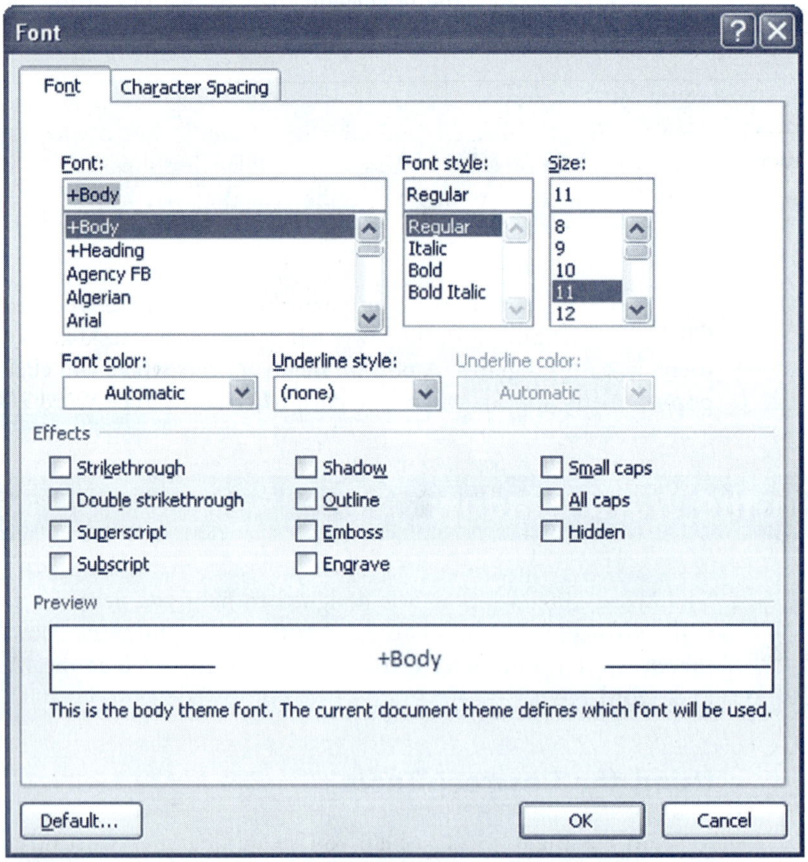

5. Click the arrow on the **Font** command in the Font group. In Figure 1-5, notice that the dropdown menu lists a variety of fonts.

Figure 1-5

Font menu

6. Click the arrow again to remove the menu.
7. Double-click the **Home** tab. Notice the groups are hidden to give you more screen space to work on your document.
8. Double-click **Home** again to redisplay the groups.
   PAUSE. LEAVE the document open to use in the next exercise.

You have just practiced using the ***ribbon***. It is divided into eight ***tabs*** or areas of activity. Each tab contains ***groups*** of related commands. The ribbon is contextual, which means it offers you commands related to the type of document or object you are working with.

Most groups have a ***dialog box launcher***—a small arrow in the lower right corner of the group—that you click to launch a dialog box. A ***dialog box*** displays additional options or information you can specify to execute a command. A ***command*** is a button you click or a box where you enter information that tells Word what you want it to do. Some commands on the ribbon have small arrows pointing down. These arrows indicate that there is a ***menu***, where you can choose from a list of options. To choose an option from a menu, just drag the mouse pointer to the command you want and click.

USE THE MINI TOOLBAR

USE the document that is open from the previous exercise.

1. Click in the left margin beside the blinking insertion point. A faint image of the Mini toolbar appears, as shown in Figure 1-6.

Figure 1-6

A faint version of the Mini toolbar appears when you point to selected text.

2. Point to the **Font** command on the Mini toolbar. Notice the toolbar brightens.
3. Click the arrow on the **Font** command. A font menu appears.
4. Move the I-beam off the Mini toolbar to a blank part of the document and click the right mouse button. In addition to the Mini toolbar, a shortcut menu with commonly used commands appears (see Figure 1-7).

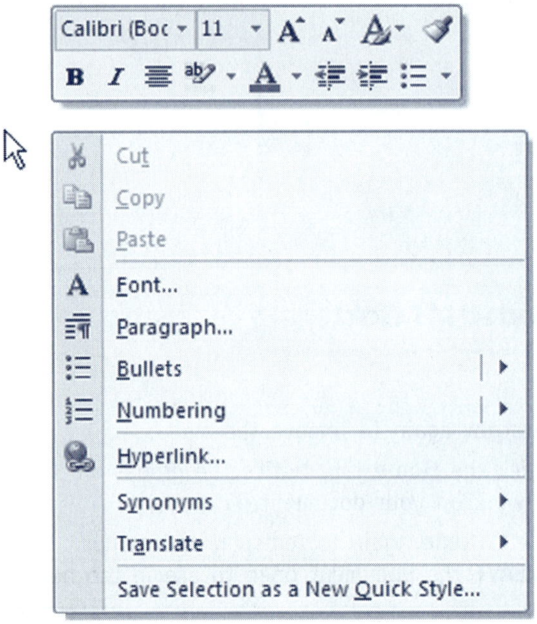

Figure 1-7

The Mini toolbar and shortcut menu

PAUSE. LEAVE the document open to use in the next exercise.

You just practiced displaying and using the ***Mini toolbar***—a small toolbar with popular commands—which appears when you point to selected text. The image is very faint until you point to a command, then it brightens and becomes active. You can also display the Mini toolbar by clicking the right mouse button, whether text is selected or not. The ***shortcut menu***, which displays a list of useful commands, also appears when you click the right mouse button.

USE THE QUICK ACCESS TOOLBAR

USE the document that is open from the previous exercise.

1. Click the **Save** button on the Quick Access Toolbar, shown in Figure 1-8.
2. The Save As dialog box appears. Click **Cancel**.
3. Click the **Customize Quick Access Toolbar** button. A menu appears, as shown in Figure 1-8.

Figure 1-8

The Quick Access toolbar

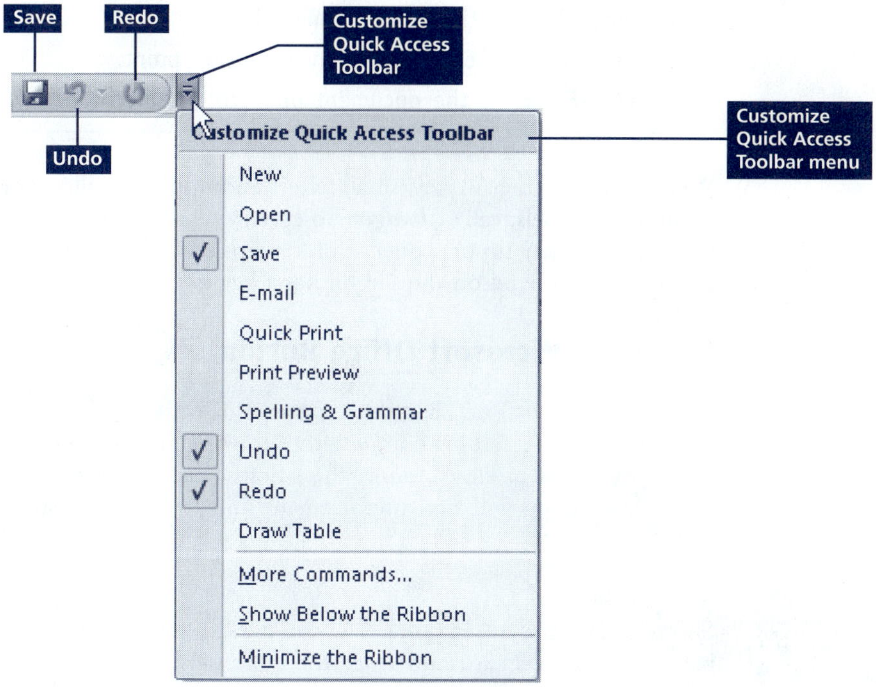

4. Click **Show Below the Ribbon.** The toolbar is moved.
5. Click the **Customize Quick Access Toolbar** button again. Click **Show Above the Ribbon.**

PAUSE. LEAVE the document open to use in the next exercise.

The ***Quick Access Toolbar*** contains the commands that you use most often, such as Save, Undo, and Redo.

Click the Save button to quickly save an existing document as you are working on it or when you have finished. If you have not yet saved a document with a filename, the Save As dialog box will launch to prompt you to do so.

The ***Undo*** command lets you cancel or undo your last command. Click it as many times as necessary to undo previous commands. Click the arrow beside the Undo command, and a menu of actions you can undo appears. In much the same way, click the ***Redo*** command to repeat your last action. A command is not available if the button is dimmed.

Later in this book, you will learn to customize the toolbar, adding buttons so you can quickly find the commands you use most often. As you practiced in the preceding exercise, you can also place the toolbar below the ribbon.

USE KEY TIPS

NEW FEATURE

USE the document that is open from the previous exercise.

1. Press Alt. Letters and numbers appear on the ribbon to let you know which key to use to access commands or tabs (see Figure 1-9).

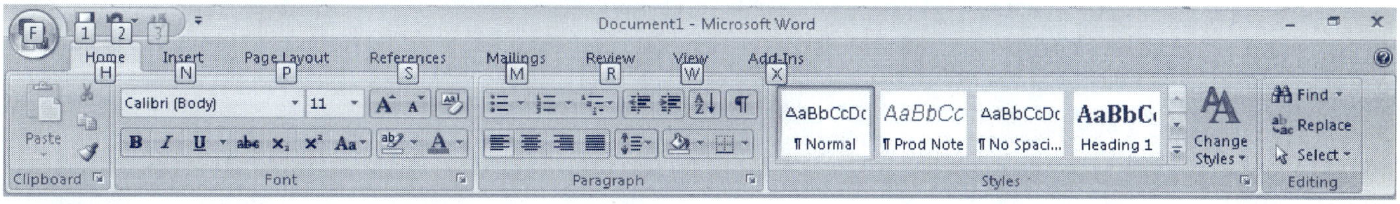

Figure 1-9

Key tips

2. Press [H] to activate the Home tab.
3. Press [A] then [C] to center the insertion point.

PAUSE. LEAVE the document open to use in the next exercise.

When you press the Alt key, small letters and numbers called ***key tips*** appear on the ribbon in small square labels, called ***badges***. To execute a command using key tips, press the Alt key then press the key tip or sequence of key tips that corresponds to the command you want to use. Every command on the ribbon has a key tip.

Using the Microsoft Office Button

NEW FEATURE

The Microsoft Office Button is a menu of commands that you will use for almost every file you create or edit, whether for opening, saving, or printing documents. As you will learn in later lessons, the Microsoft Office Button even contains some commands you will find important to know about to distribute and protect your files.

TAKE NOTE*

Shortcut keys are keys or combinations of keys pressed together to perform a command. Shortcut keys provide a quick way to give commands without having to move your hands off the keyboard and reach for a mouse. Keyboard shortcuts from previous versions of Word that began with Ctrl have remained the same. However, those that began with Alt are now different and require the use of key tips.

USE THE MICROSOFT OFFICE BUTTON

USE the document that is open from the previous exercise.

1. Click the **Microsoft Office Button**. A menu appears (see Figure 1-10).

Figure 1-10

Microsoft Office Button and menu

2. Point to the **Prepare** command to view the options available.
3. Point to other commands with the arrow to view more options.
4. Click the **Microsoft Office Button** again to remove the menu.

PAUSE. LEAVE the document open to use in the next exercise.

The ***Microsoft Office Button*** is located in the upper left corner of the screen. When clicked, it displays a menu of basic commands for opening, saving, and printing files as well as more advanced options. Some commands have arrows indicating that another menu of options is available. When you click commands that do not have an arrow, a dialog box opens.

The following is an overview of the commands on the Microsoft Office Button:

- New: Create a new document, template, or blog entry.
- Open: Open an existing document.
- Save: Save the current document using the new Word format.
- Save As: Save documents in Word 97-2003 format, as a .pdf or .xps file, or other available formats.
- Print: Open a dialog box from which to choose print options or quick-print straight to the printer. Or preview your document before printing.
- Prepare: Prepare your document for distribution by viewing and editing properties, inspecting the document for sensitive information, restricting permissions, adding a digital signature, checking compatibility, or marking a document as final so that changes cannot be made to it.
- Send: Email a document or fax it through the Internet.
- Publish: Save a document as a blog, save it to a document management server for sharing, or create a new document workspace while keeping a local copy.
- Close: Close an open document.

The Microsoft Office Button lists Recent Documents for easy access. It also displays a Word Options button at the bottom of the menu that allows you to customize Word. You can exit the Word application by clicking the Exit Word button.

Using the Microsoft Office Word Help Button

If you have questions, Microsoft Word Help has answers. In fact, you can choose to use the help topics on your computer that were installed with Office, or, if you are connected to the Internet, you can choose to use the help that is available online. Either way, you can key in search words, browse help topics, or choose a topic from the Table of Contents to get your answers.

TAKE NOTE*

When you rest the mouse pointer over a command on the ribbon, a screen tip will appear displaying the name of the command. Word 2007 also has enhanced screen tips, which give more information about the command as well as a Help button you can click to get more help.

USE THE HELP BUTTON

USE the document that is open from the previous exercise.

1. Click the **Microsoft Office Word Help** button in the upper right corner of the screen. The Word Help dialog box appears, as shown in Figure 1-11. Notice the Connection Status command in the lower right corner, indicating that Word is set to Connected to Office Online to search online for help topics. If your Connection status is set to Offline, your screen will look different.

Figure 1-11

The Word Help dialog box when you're connected to Office online.

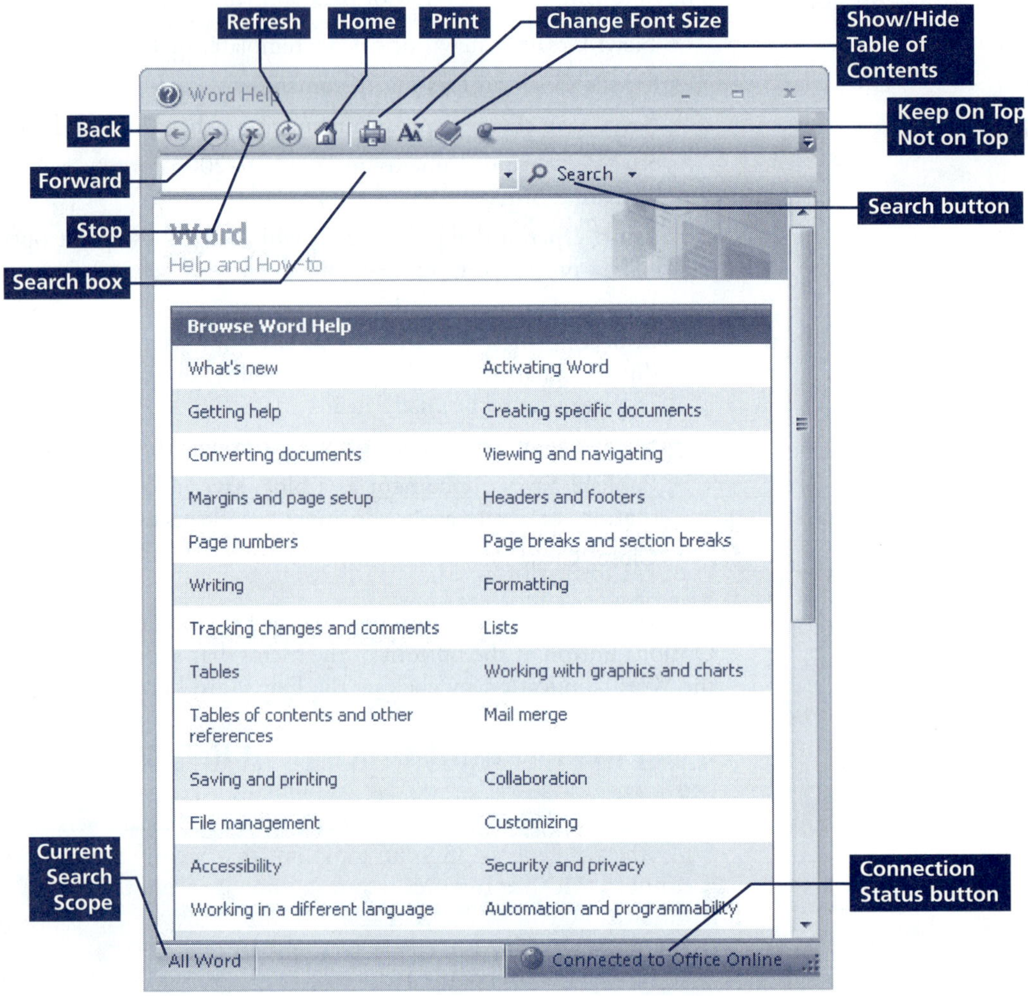

2. Click the **Connection Status** button. A menu appears, as shown in Figure 1-12.

Figure 1-12

Connection Status menu

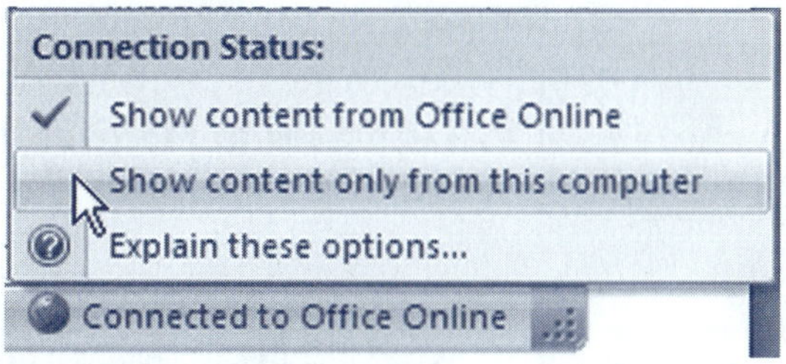

3. Click **Show content only from this computer**. Word Help appears, as shown in Figure 1-13.

Figure 1-13

Word Help dialog box when offline

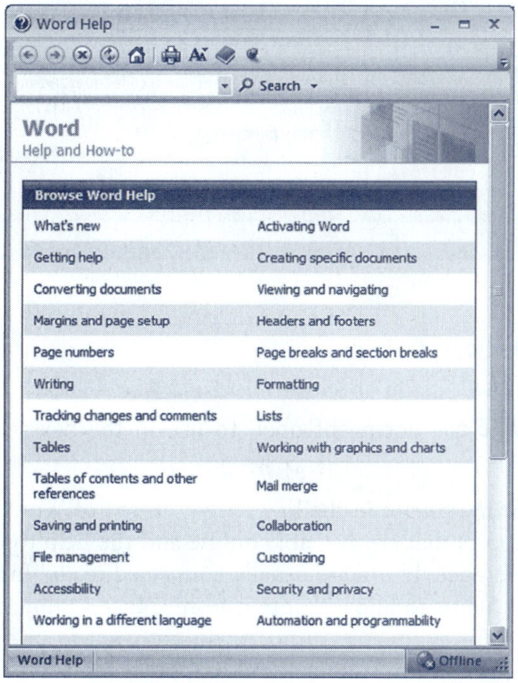

4. Key **ribbon** in the text box and click **Search**. A list of possible topics appears.
5. Click the **Use the Ribbon** link. The help topic appears.

6. Click the **Show Table of Contents** button.
7. Click the **What's new** link at the top.
8. Click **What's new in Microsoft Office Word 2007.** The text for the topic appears in the window, as shown in Figure 1-14.

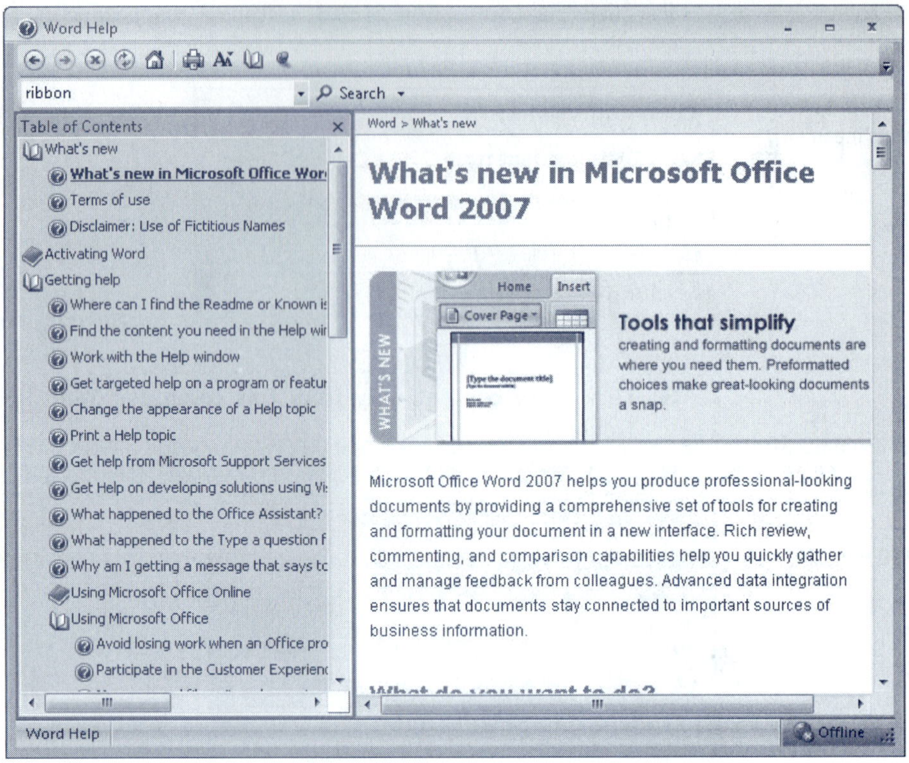

Figure 1-14

Word Help with Table of Contents and help topic displayed

9. Click the **Home** button.
10. Click the **Close** button to close Microsoft Word Help.

PAUSE. LEAVE the document open to use in the next exercise.

The ***Connection Status menu*** in the lower right corner of Word Help lets you choose between the help topics that are available online and the help topics installed on your computer for offline reference. If you are usually connected to the Internet, you might prefer to set the Connection Status to Show Content from Office Online to get the most up-to-date help available. But sometimes you cannot or do not want to be online. In those instances, you can choose Show Content Only from this Computer to get offline help topics. You can also click the Search menu to specify the scope of topics you want to search, such as All Word, Word Help, Word Templates, Word Training, or Developer References.

Microsoft Word Help works much like an Internet browser and has many of the same buttons, such as Back, Forward, Stop, Refresh, Home, and Print. A quick way to find what you need is to key a word or words into the text box and then click the Search button. Word will display a list of related topics as links.

Another way to get help is to choose one of the available topics in the Browse Word Help list. You can also click the Show Table of Contents button to list Word Help categories. Choose a category to see a list of related topics within that category.

ANOTHER WAY

The Word Help button is positioned in some dialog boxes and screen tips for quick access to context-related help. Click it wherever you see it to launch Word Help.

If you need to print a topic, just display the topic in the Word Help main window and click the Print button.

For your convenience, the Word Help window can be resized and moved to another location on the screen. The On Top button toggles between Keep On Top, which ensures that the Help window is always on top of the document you are working on, and Not On Top, which keeps the document you are editing on top. You can also use the Change Font Size button to change the font size of the text in the window.

Working with an Existing Document

THE BOTTOM LINE

The great thing about creating and editing documents using Word is the convenience with which you can later reopen documents to make changes. In this lesson, you will open an existing document and learn to navigate it. You will also enter text; select, replace, and delete text; and save, quick-print, and close a document.

Opening an Existing Document

Word has three basic options for opening existing files. You can choose to open an original document, open a copy of a document, or open a document as a read-only file that cannot be changed.

OPEN AN EXISTING DOCUMENT

1. Click the **Microsoft Office Button** to display the menu.
2. Click **Open**. The Open dialog box appears (see Figure 1-15).

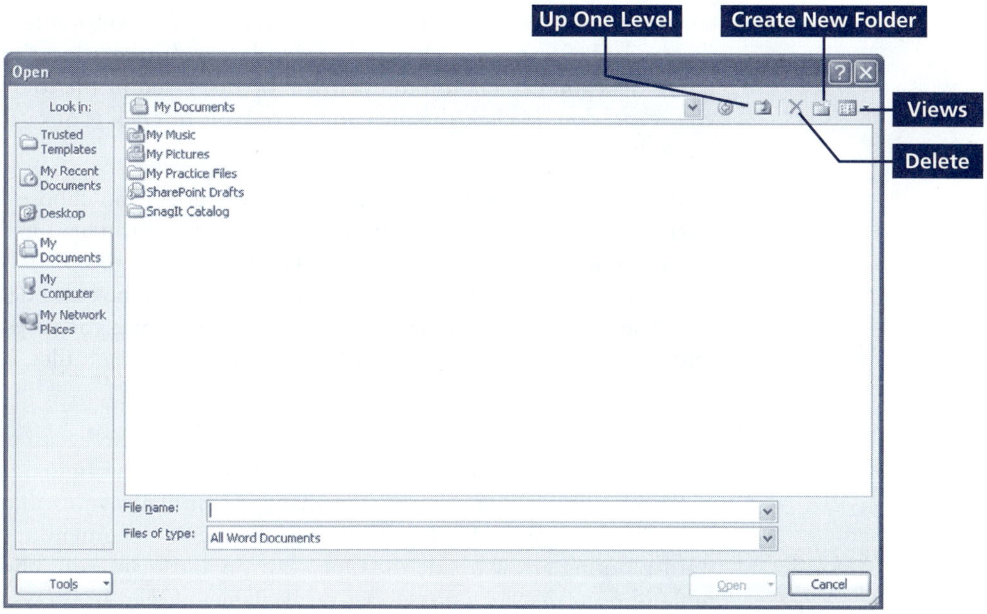

Figure 1-15

The Open dialog box

CD

The ***SBpressrelease*** document is available on the companion CD-ROM.

3. In the Look In box, click the location of the data files for this lesson. Locate and click ***SBpressrelease*** one time to select it.
4. Click the **Open** button. The document appears, as shown in Figure 1-16.

Figure 1-16

SBpressrelease document

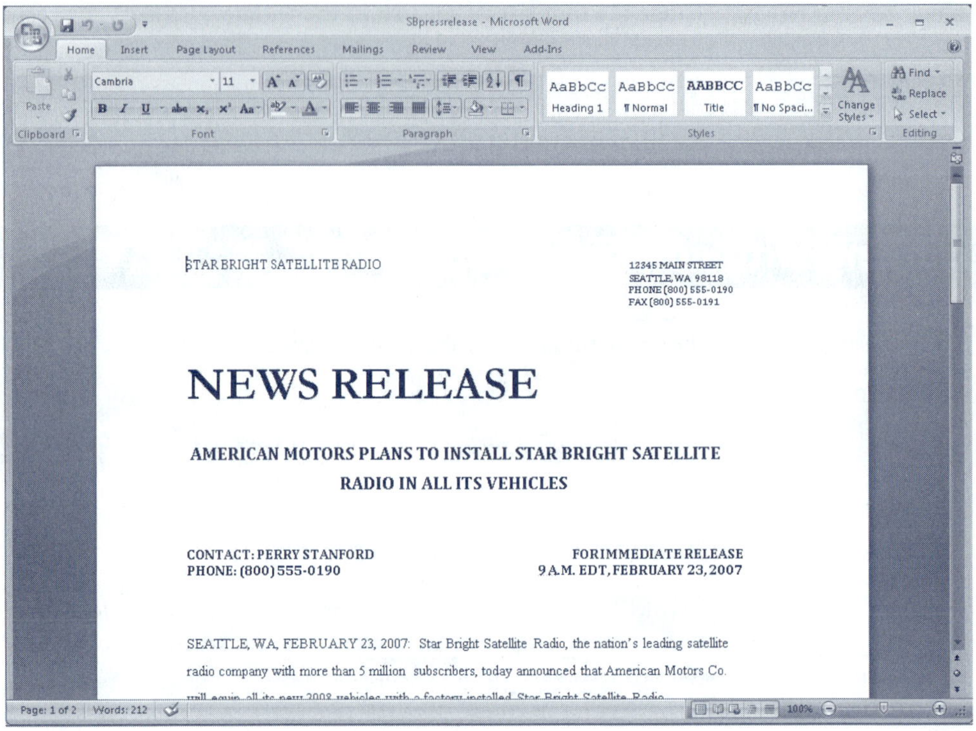

PAUSE. LEAVE the document open to use in the next exercise.

Use the Microsoft Office Button to open an existing document. The Open dialog box lets you find and open files wherever they may be located—on the desktop, in a folder on your computer, on a network drive, or on a CD or other removable media. The Look In box lists the available locations such as a folder, drive, or Internet location. Click the location, and the folders you can choose to open will be displayed in the folder list. When you find the file you want, double-click the filename to open it or click it once to select it and then click the Open button.

In the Open dialog box, the Files of Type menu lets you choose the type of file you want to open. The Tools button lets you delete, rename, print, map a network drive, or show a document's properties. The Up One Level button lets you go up a level in the folder organization to find a file. You can select a file in the Open dialog box and delete it with the Delete button. The Create New Folder button helps you organize your files with new folders. The Views button lets you display contents of a folder by thumbnail, tiles, icons, lists, details, properties, preview, or Web view.

The Open dialog box also has options for choosing whether to open a document and edit it; open a copy of the document you can edit, leaving the original intact; or open the document as a read-only file that cannot be changed. Most likely, you will open an original document and edit it, so this is the default setting. To open a document another way, click the downward-pointing arrow beside the Open button and make your choice. This menu has a few more options that may not always be available—Open in Browser, Open with Transform, or Open and Repair.

Changing Word's View

Word has different ways you can view a document. The View tab on the ribbon has groups of commands for Document Views, Show/Hide, Zoom, Window, and Macros. In this section, you will learn about various ways to view documents in Word.

CHANGE DOCUMENT VIEWS

USE the document that is open from the previous exercise.

1. Click the **View** tab to activate it, as shown in Figure 1-17. Notice the command groups that are available.

Figure 1-17

The View tab

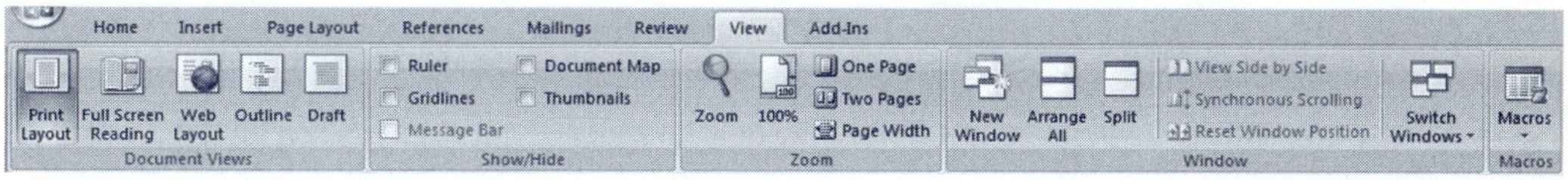

2. In the Document Views group, click the **Full Screen Reading** view button to change to Full Screen Reading view, as shown in Figure 1-18.

Figure 1-18

Full Screen Reading view

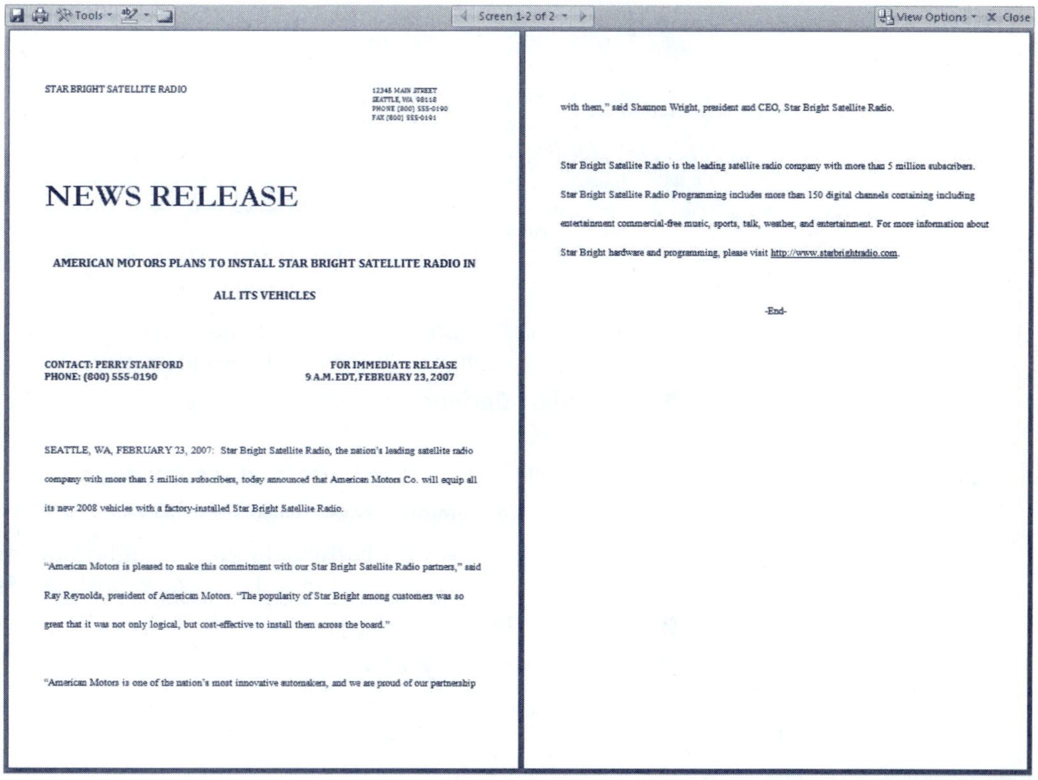

3. Click the **View Options** menu, shown in Figure 1-19.

Figure 1-19

View Options menu

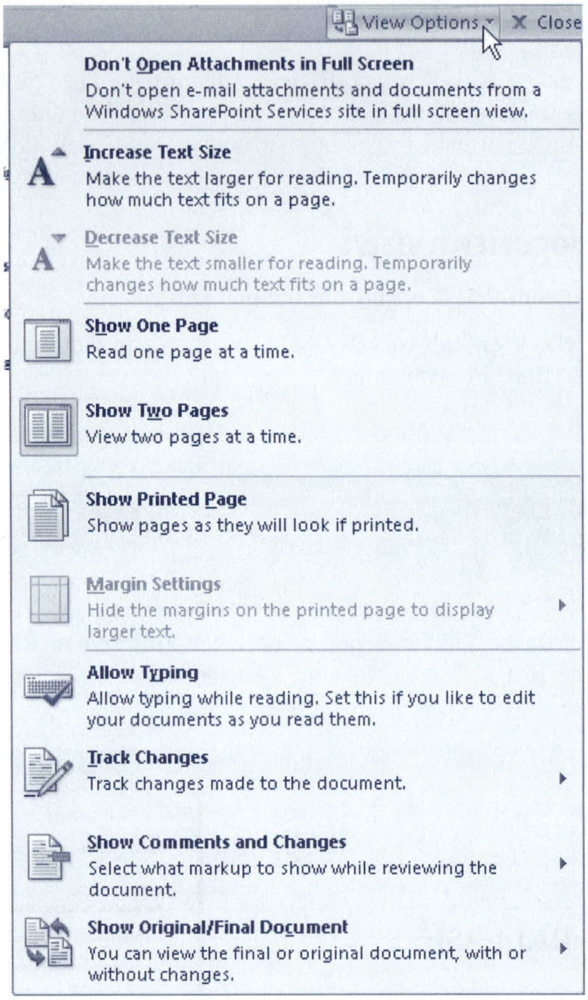

4. Notice all the options for viewing the document. Choose **Increase Text Size**. The text size is temporarily increased for better reading on the screen.
5. Click **View Options** and **Show One Page**. The document is displayed on the page one screen at a time.
6. Press Esc to turn off Full Screen Reading view.
7. Click the **Web Layout** view button.
8. Click the **Outline** view button. Notice the Outline tab and the groups of commands that appear for editing outlines. Click **Close Outline View**.
9. Click the **View** tab and click the **Draft** view button.
10. Click the **Print Layout** view button.

PAUSE. LEAVE the document open to use in the next exercise.

CERTIFICATION READY?
How do you change Word's View?
5.1.2

Word has five main views:

- Print Layout is the most common view. It displays the document as it will look when printed and enables you to use the ribbon to create and edit your document.
- Full Screen Reading view is made for reading documents on the screen. You have many options for customizing this view.
- Web Layout view shows how the document would look as a web page.

- Outline view displays the document as an outline and shows an outline tab with commands for creating and editing outlines.
- Draft view lets you view the document as a draft. Headers, footers, and other elements do not appear.

ANOTHER WAY The view commands are also accessible in the View button portion of the status bar located at the bottom of the screen.

USE SHOW/HIDE COMMANDS

USE the document that is open from the previous exercise.

1. In the Show/Hide group, click the **Ruler** box to insert a checkmark. Rulers appear, as shown in Figure 1-20.
2. Click the **Gridlines** box. A grid appears behind text on the page, as shown in Figure 1-20.
3. Click the **Thumbnails** box. Small pages appear in the left pane of the window, as shown in Figure 1-20.

Figure 1-20

Rulers, gridlines, and thumbnails

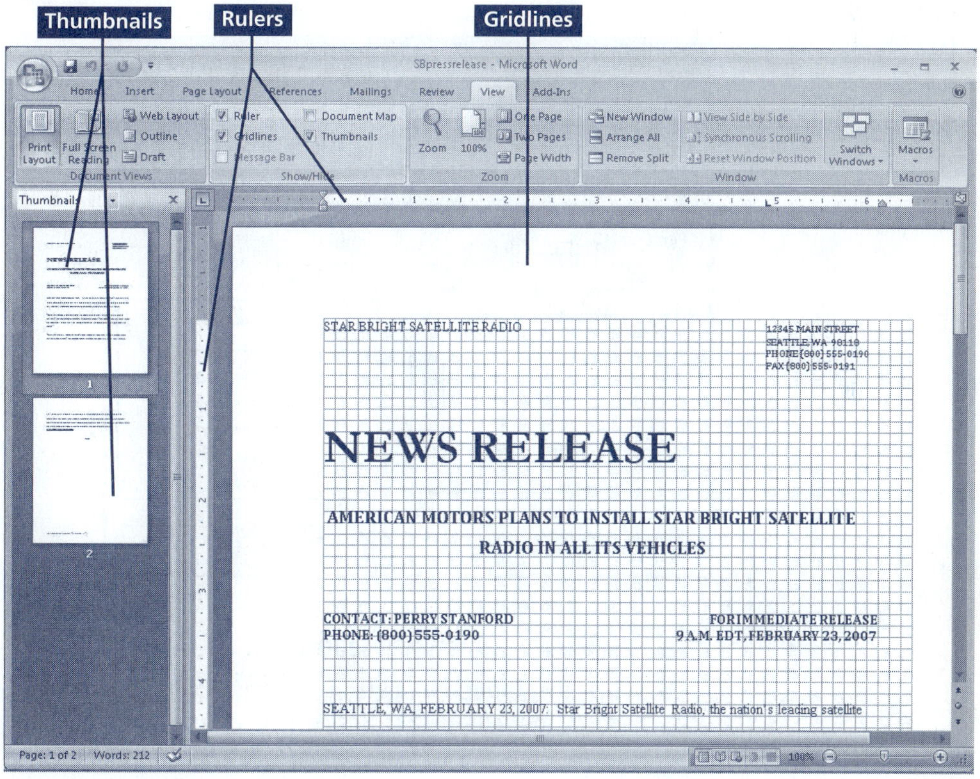

4. Click the **Document Map** box to insert a checkmark. The document map appears in the left pane, replacing the thumbnails.
5. Click the **Document Map** box to remove the checkmark. The thumbnails and window pane disappear.
6. Click the **Gridlines** box to remove the gridlines.
7. Click the **Ruler** box to remove the rulers from view.

   PAUSE. LEAVE the document open to use in the next exercise.

ANOTHER WAY

You can also use the View Ruler button on the document window to display the ruler.

The Show/Hide command group lets you show or hide various features to help with the creation, editing, and navigation of your documents. In this exercise, you displayed the ***rulers***, which are measuring tools to help you align text. Both the horizontal and vertical rulers display margins, while the horizontal ruler also displays indents and tabs.

Gridlines provide a grid of vertical and horizontal lines that help you align graphics and other objects in your documents. They can only be displayed in Print Layout view.

For long documents, it is helpful to use the document map, which appears in the left pane of the window and shows you the structure of a document. A ***thumbnail*** is a small picture of a page. Because the document map and thumbnails are both displayed in the left pane, they cannot be displayed at the same time. The message bar is a to-do list for the document, displaying tasks that need to be completed.

USE ZOOM

USE the document that is open from the previous exercise.

1. Click the **View** tab, if necessary.
2. Click the **One Page** button. The entire page is shown on the screen.
3. Click the **Two Pages** button. Two pages are shown on the screen.
4. Click the **Zoom** button. The Zoom dialog box appears, as shown in Figure 1-21.

Figure 1-21

Zoom dialog box

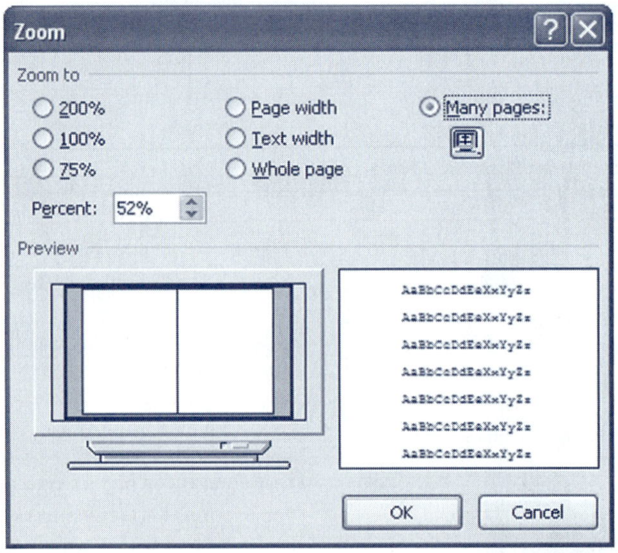

5. Click the button beside **200%** and click **OK**.
6. Click the **Zoom Out** button on the zoom slider at the bottom right of the screen, shown in Figure 1-22. Notice it decreases the zoom by 10 percent with each click.

Figure 1-22

Zoom slider

7. Drag the slider all the way to the left beside the **Zoom Out** button. Notice the document is reduced to thumbnail size.
8. In the Zoom group, click the **Page Width** button. The document expands to the width of the window.

PAUSE. LEAVE the document open to use in the next exercise.

ANOTHER WAY

You can also click the percentage displayed in the zoom slider to display the Zoom dialog box.

The Zoom group of commands lets you zoom in to get a closer view of a page or zoom out to see more of the document at a smaller size. In the previous exercise, you used the Zoom commands to view one page at a time and two pages at a time.

The Page Width button expands the document to the width of the window. The Zoom button launches the Zoom dialog box, where you have more options for zooming in and out. You can even enter a specific number in the percent box. In the Zoom To section, click to choose a specific amount of zoom, such as 200%. The preview section shows how the document will look on the screen.

You can also use the zoom slider, located on the status bar, to zoom in and out.

CHANGE WINDOW VIEWS

USE the document that is open from the previous exercise.

1. In the Window group, click the **New Window** button. A new window with the same document, titled *SBpressrelease:2* appears, as shown in Figure 1-23. It is now the active document.

Figure 1-23

New window

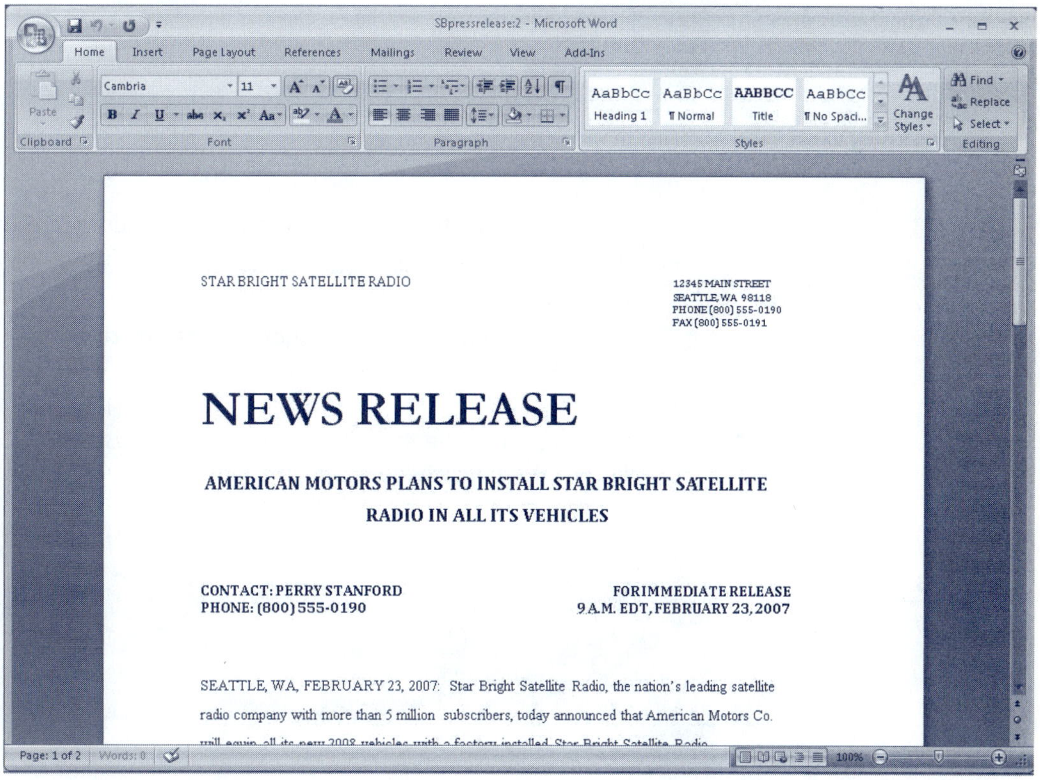

2. Click the **View** tab. In the Window group, click the **Switch Windows** button. A menu of open windows appears, as shown in Figure 1-24.

Figure 1-24

Switch Windows button and menu

3. Click **SBpressrelease:1**. The original document is now the active document.
4. Click the **Arrange All** button. The two windows are placed on the top and bottom of your screen, as shown in Figure 1-25.

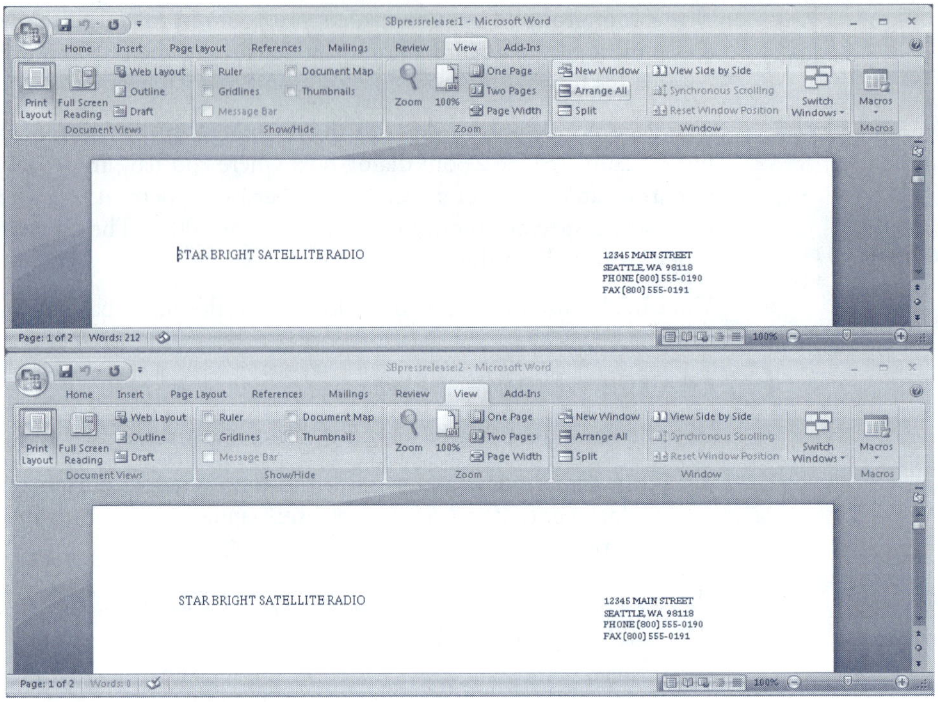

Figure 1-25

Arrange All

5. Click the **View Side by Side** button. The windows are arranged side by side.
6. Click in the window of **SBpressrelease:2** to make it the active document. Click the **Close** button to close it.
7. In the remaining document, click the **Maximize** button to make the document fill the screen again.
8. Click the **Split** button. Notice you have a vertical split bar and a double-sided arrow. Position the split bar below *News Release* and click the mouse button. The document window is now split in two (see Figure 1-26).

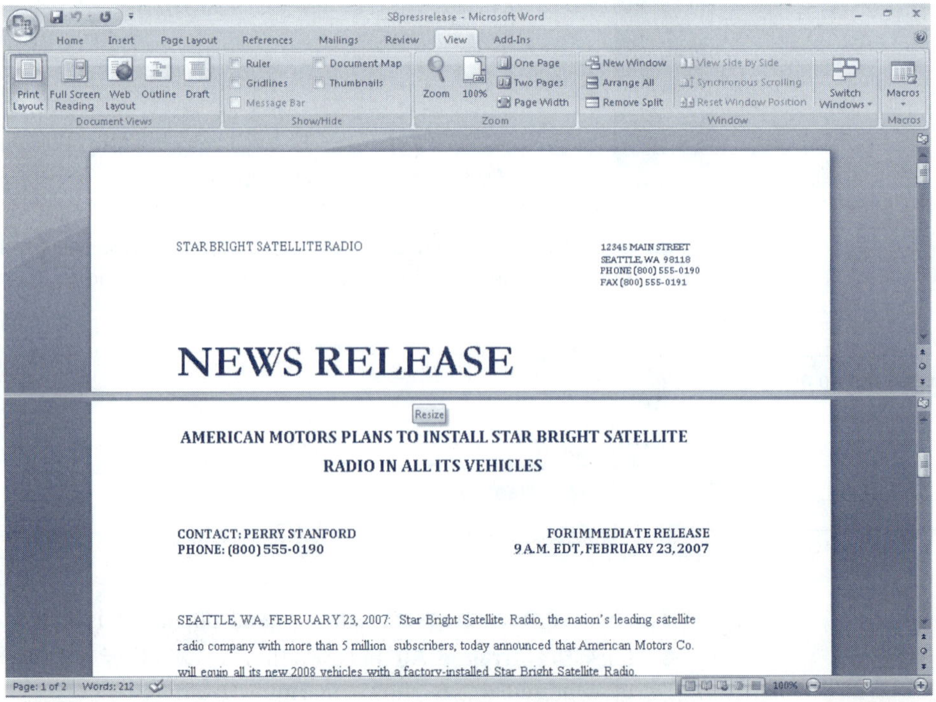

Figure 1-26

Split window

9. Click **Remove Split**.
10. Click the **Minimize** button, shown in Figure 1-27. The document is minimized to the Windows Taskbar at the bottom of the screen.

Figure 1-27

Minimize, Restore Down, and Close buttons

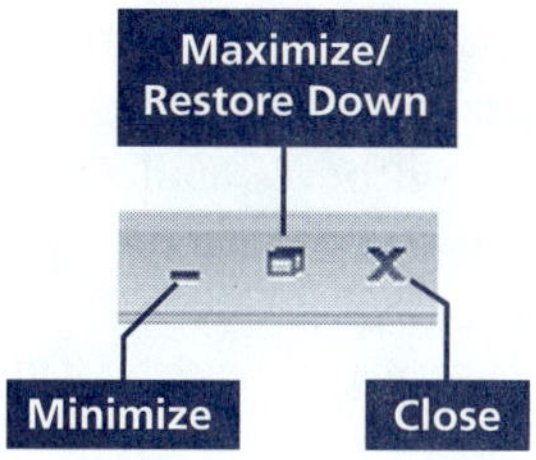

11. Click the ***SBpressrelease*** document in the Taskbar to maximize the document back on the screen.
12. Click the **Restore Down** button.
13. Position the mouse pointer on the lower right corner of the document window where you see the pattern of dots. Your mouse pointer becomes a double-sided arrow, as shown in Figure 1-28.

Figure 1-28

Size a window

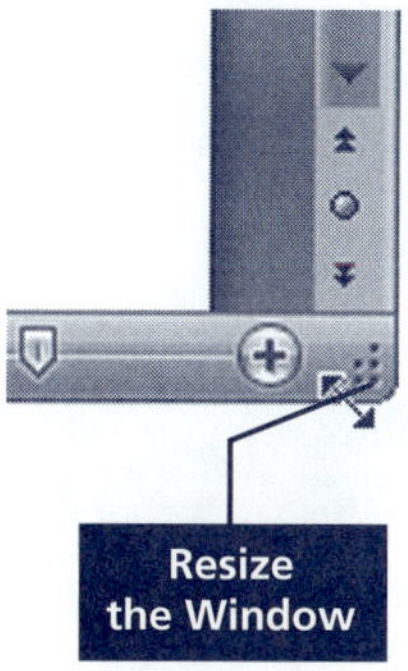

14. Click and drag toward the middle of the screen to decrease the size of the window.
15. Click the sizing corner again and drag the double-sided arrow to the lower right corner to increase the size of the window.

PAUSE. LEAVE the document open to use in the next exercise.

You can view a document in a variety of ways using the Window group of commands. In the previous exercise, you created a new window with the New Window button. The Arrange All button places two or more windows on the screen at the same time. This is useful when comparing documents or using some information from one document in another document.

The Split command divides one document window into two windows that scroll independently. This enables you to view two parts of the document at the same time.

You can view two documents next to each other using the View Side by Side button. You can use the Synchronous Scrolling command to set the scrolling of two documents to work together. And the Reset Window Position repositions two side-by-side documents equally on the screen.

You can change which window is the current active document using the Switch Windows button. When you click the button, a menu of open documents appears. Click the document you want to make active. The active document is the document that is ready to accept commands.

You may have a need to move a window on your screen out of the way without exiting the application. The three buttons in the upper right corner of Windows documents let you minimize, restore down/maximize, or close a window. Click the Minimize button to minimize the document window, removing it from the screen and sending it to the Taskbar. The Restore

Down and Maximize button toggles back and forth. Click Restore Down and you are able to size a window. Click Maximize to return the window to its maximum size on the screen. When you are finished with your document, click the Close button to remove the document from the screen.

Navigating a Document

In this section, you will use scrollbars, scroll boxes, and scroll buttons to help you navigate a document. In addition, you can use certain keystrokes to make your way through a document.

SCROLL THROUGH A DOCUMENT USING THE MOUSE

USE the document that is open from the previous exercise.

1. Click the **Scroll Down** button, shown in Figure 1-29. The document scrolls down one line at a time.

Figure 1-29

Scrollbars, scroll box, and scroll buttons

2. Click and hold the **Scroll Down** button until you scroll all the way to the end of the document.
3. Position the mouse pointer on the **scroll box**. Click and hold to see a screen tip appear, letting you know your current location in the document (see Figure 1-30).

Figure 1-30

Screen tip on scroll box

4. Drag the **scroll box** all the way to the top of the scrollbar. The page quickly scrolls to the beginning of the document.
5. Click the **Next Page** button to move to the next page, which in this case is page 2.
6. Click the **Select Browse Object** button. A menu appears with various places you can choose to browse (see Figure 1-31).

Figure 1-31

Select Browse Object menu

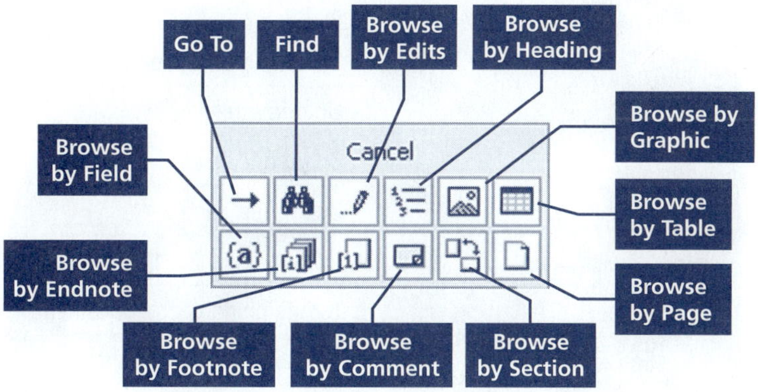

7. Move the mouse pointer over each button to see its name appear in the display box.
8. Click in a blank space in the document to remove the menu.
9. Click the **Previous Page** button to move back to page 1.

PAUSE. LEAVE the document open to use in the next exercise.

Vertical ***scrollbars*** appear on the right and/or bottom of the document window, enabling you to move up and down through the document. Click the ***scroll buttons*** to move up or down one line at a time. Click and hold a scroll button to move more quickly. Click the scroll box to see a display of your position in the document. Click and drag the ***scroll box*** to move even more quickly horizontally or vertically through a document.

You can click the Previous Page button to move back to the previous page; click the Next Page button to move to the following page. The Select Browse Object button has a pop-up menu of ways to move quickly to and browse by field, endnote, footnote, comment, edits, section, page, graphic, or table. You will learn more about these items throughout the book.

USE KEYSTROKES TO NAVIGATE A DOCUMENT

USE the document that is open from the previous exercise.

1. In the first line of the body of the document, position the insertion point before the *S* in *Seattle*.

2. On the keyboard, press the **Right arrow** key to move one character to the right.
3. Press the **Left arrow** key to move one character to the left.
4. Press the **Down arrow** key to move down one line.
5. Press the **End** key to move to the end of the line.
6. Press the **Page Down** key to move down one screen.
7. Press the **Home** key to move to the beginning of the page.

PAUSE. LEAVE the document open to use in the next exercise.

You can press certain keys on the keyboard or use a combination of keys to navigate through a document. Table 1-1 displays common keyboard shortcuts for moving through a document.

Table 1-1

Keyboard shortcuts for navigating a document

Shortcut Key	To Move
Left Arrow	One character to the left
Right Arrow	One character to the right
Up Arrow	Up one line
Down Arrow	Down one line
End	End of a line
Home	Beginning of a line
Page Up	Up one screen
Page Down	Down one screen
Ctrl+Page Down	Down one page
Ctrl+Page Up	Up one page
Ctrl+Home	To beginning of the document
Ctrl+End	To end of the document

Entering Text in a Document

In this section, you will learn how to enter text where you want it in a document.

ENTER TEXT

USE the document that is open from the previous exercise.

1. Move the pointer over the title of the document. Notice the pointer changes to an I-beam.
2. Position the I-beam on the left side of the *V* in the word *VEHICLES* and click. The I-beam becomes the blinking insertion point.
3. Key **2008** and press the **spacebar**.
4. Position the insertion point in the middle of the second paragraph, to the left of the *T* in *The popularity*.
5. Key **Their excellent programming provides our customers with an endless variety of entertainment options.** Press the **spacebar**. Your screen should look similar to Figure 1-32.

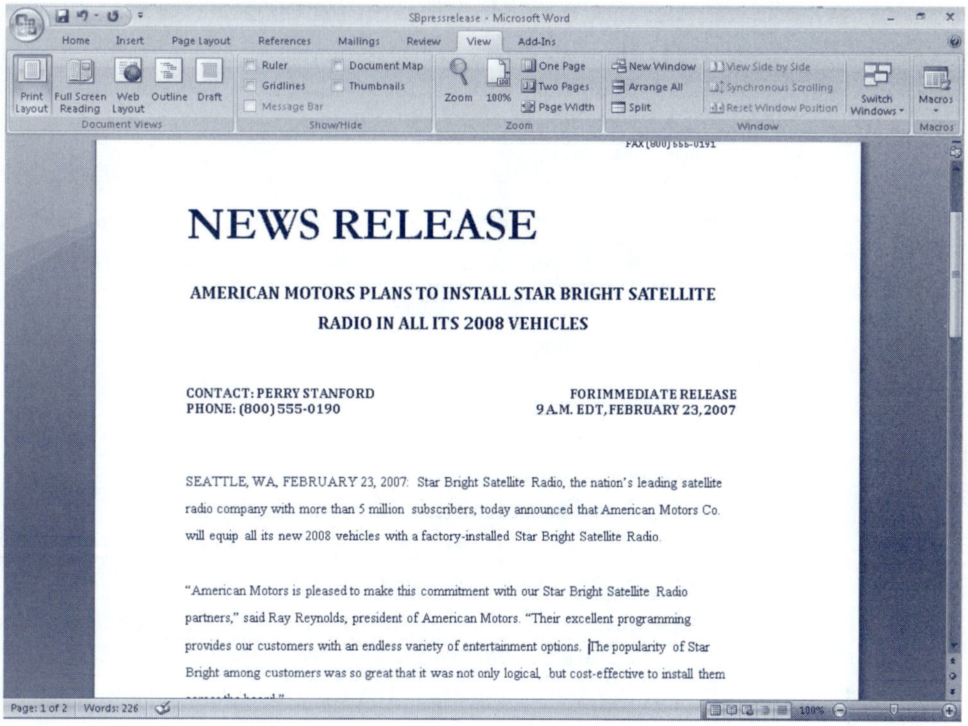

Figure 1-32

Text entered in a document

TAKE NOTE*

As you key, Word automatically checks the spelling and grammar of the words you key. If it detects a mistake, it inserts a wavy red or green line underneath. Ignore these for now. You will learn more about checking spelling and grammar in later lessons.

PAUSE. LEAVE the document open to use in the next exercise.

When you move the mouse in the text area of a document, it is shaped like an ***I-beam.*** Position the I-beam where you want to key text and click. Now it becomes a blinking ***insertion point***, ready for you to start keying. Text will be inserted to the left of the insertion point.

When you key text, Word automatically wraps text for you when you reach the end of a line. If you want to start a new paragraph, press Enter.

Selecting, Replacing, and Deleting Text

Before making any change to text, you have to select it. In this section, you will learn to use the mouse and keyboard to select text. Then you will learn to delete or replace it with new text.

SELECT, REPLACE, AND DELETE TEXT

USE the document that is open from the previous exercise.

1. At the beginning of the document, position the insertion point to the left of the *N* in *News Release*. Click and drag across the word *News* to select it.
2. Key **PRESS**. The word *NEWS* is replaced with the word *PRESS*.
3. In the first paragraph of the body of the document, position the insertion point after the *5* in *5 million*.
4. Press **Backspace** to delete the number *5*. Key **8**.
5. Scroll to the bottom of the document. Position the insertion point in any word in the last paragraph. Triple-click the mouse. The entire paragraph is selected.
6. Click in a blank part of the page, such as the margin, to deselect the paragraph.
7. Press the **Ctrl** key and click *Star*, the first word of the first sentence of the last paragraph. The sentence is selected.
8. Press **Backspace** to delete the sentence.
9. Click the **Undo** button in the Quick Access toolbar to undo the action.

10. Click the **Redo** button in the Quick Access toolbar to redo the action.
11. In what is now the first sentence, double-click the word *containing* to select it. Hold down **Ctrl** and double-click the word *entertainment*. Both words are now selected, as shown in Figure 1-33.

Figure 1-33

Multi-selection

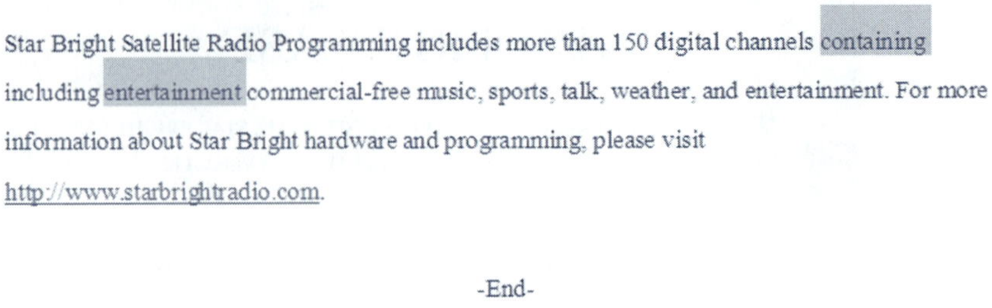
Star Bright Satellite Radio Programming includes more than 150 digital channels containing including entertainment commercial-free music, sports, talk, weather, and entertainment. For more information about Star Bright hardware and programming, please visit http://www.starbrightradio.com.

-End-

12. Press **Delete** to delete the words.
13. In the last paragraph, first sentence, position the insertion point to the left of the first *e* in *entertainment*.
14. Press and hold **Ctrl**, press and hold **Shift**, and press the **Right arrow** key. The word *entertainment* is selected.
15. Key **traffic updates**. The word *entertainment* is replaced with the words *traffic updates*.

PAUSE. LEAVE the document open to use in the next exercise.

When you select text, the text you key replaces the selected text. To cancel a selection, click on white space in the document.

When the mouse pointer is in the left margin, it changes to a selection arrow that enables you to drag to select a character, word, lines, or paragraphs of text. You can also click to position the insertion point and then drag to select text. Table 1-2 shows ways you can select text with the mouse.

Table 1-2

Selecting text with the mouse

To Select	Do This
Any amount of text	Click and drag across the text
Word	Double-click the word
Line	Click in the left margin with the mouse pointer
Multiple lines	Drag in the left margin
Sentence	Hold Ctrl and click anywhere in the sentence
Paragraph	Double-click in the left margin or triple-click in the paragraph
Entire Document	Triple-click in the left margin

ANOTHER WAY

The Select button in the Editing group of the Home tab lets you select all text in a document, select objects behind text, or select text with similar formatting.

In the previous exercise, you practiced ***multi-selection***, which is a feature of Word that enables you to select multiple pieces of text that are not next to each other. Just select the first piece of text, press the Ctrl key, and select additional items.

You can also use the keyboard to select text. Table 1-3 shows keys you can press to select text.

Table 1-3

Selecting text with the keyboard

To Select	Do This
One character to the right	Shift+Right Arrow
One character to the left	Shift+Left Arrow
To the end of a word	Ctrl+Shift+Right Arrow
To the beginning of a word	Ctrl+Shift+Left Arrow
To the end of a line	Shift+End
To the beginning of a line	Shift+Home
To the end of a document	Ctrl+Shift+End
To the beginning of a document	Ctrl+Shift+Home
The entire document	Ctrl+A
To the end of a paragraph	Ctrl+Shift+Down Arrow

You can delete text in a number of ways.

- Press the Backspace key to delete characters to the left of the insertion point.
- Press the Del key to delete characters to the right of the insertion point.
- Select text and press the Del or Backspace key.

To replace text, select the text and key new text.

Saving an Edited Document

After creating or editing a document, it is important to save your work.

SAVE A DOCUMENT

USE the document that is open from the previous exercise.

1. Click the **Microsoft Office Button**. The menu appears.
2. Click **Save As**. The Save As dialog box appears, as shown in Figure 1-34.

Figure 1-34

The Save As dialog box

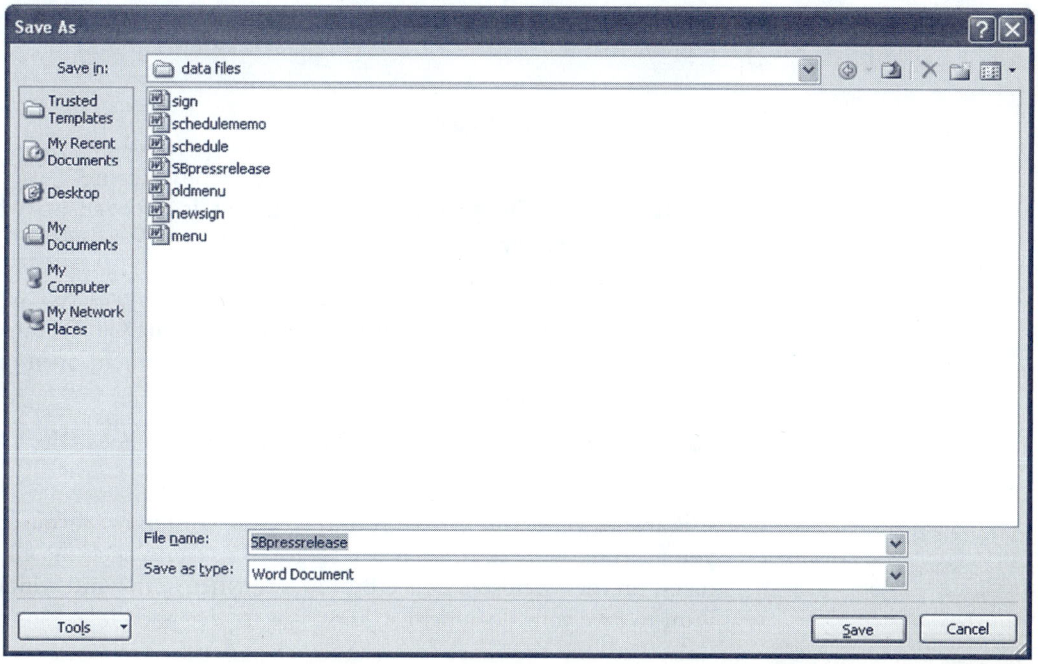

CERTIFICATION READY?
How do you save a document?
6.1.1

3. In the Save In box, click the location where you will save files.
4. If necessary, double-click a folder in the folder list where you will save your files.
5. Key **PressRelease** in the File Name box.
6. Click **Save**.

PAUSE. LEAVE the document open to use in the next exercise.

To save a document, use the Save command on the Microsoft Office Button. When saving a document for the first time or when specifying a new location or filename for a document, use the Save As command. The Save As dialog box will appear, and you can specify in the Save In window the location where you want to store the document. In the main window, you can double-click to open a folder where you are storing documents. You will then key a filename for the document and click Save. After you have the document stored with a filename in the location where you want it, just click the Save button on the Quick Access toolbar each time you make changes.

Quick-Printing a Document

Use the Quick Print command to send a document directly to the printer.

QUICK-PRINT A DOCUMENT

USE the document that is open from the previous exercise.

1. Click the **Microsoft Office Button.** The menu appears.
2. Point to **Print** and then click **Quick Print.**

PAUSE. LEAVE the document open to use in the next exercise.

When you do not need to specify a printer or set print options, simply click the Microsoft Office Button, point to Print, and click Quick Print, and the document will be sent directly to the printer. You can also access the Print command on the Microsoft Office Button menu, which opens the Print dialog box.

Closing a Document

Closing a document removes it from the screen. It is a good idea to close a document before exiting a program or turning off your computer.

CLOSE A DOCUMENT

USE the document that is open from the previous exercise.

1. Click the **Close** button. The document is removed from the screen.

STOP. CLOSE Word.

When you are ready to close the document, click the Close button on the Microsoft Word window. Clicking the Close button on the last document open in an application, such as Word, also exits the application.

You can also click the Microsoft Office Button and choose the Close command from the menu.

It is always important to save your file before closing it, so you do not lose any of the work you just finished. However, if you forget to save and click the Close button or Close command on the Microsoft Office Button, the Microsoft Word window will appear, asking if you want to save your document. Choose Yes to save and close, No to close without saving, or Cancel to stop the Close command.

SUMMARY SKILL MATRIX

In this lesson you learned	Matrix Skill	Skill Number
To change Word's view	Change window views	5.1.2
To save an edited document	Save to appropriate formats	6.1.1

Knowledge Assessment

Matching

Match the term in Column 1 to its description in Column 2.

Column 1	Column 2
1. Arrange All	**a.** helps you align text and displays indents, tabs, and margins
2. desktop	**b.** letters and numbers that appear on the ribbon when you press the Alt key
3. Ribbon	**c.** lets you choose between the help topics available online and the help topics installed on your computer offline
4. multi-selection	**d.** places all open windows on the screen at the same time
5. thumbnail	**e.** contains commands you use most often, such as Save, Undo, and Redo
6. Mini toolbar	**f.** enables you to select multiple pieces of text that are not next to each other
7. Quick Access toolbar	**g.** organized by tabs and groups of commands
8. key tips	**h.** small picture of a page
9. Connection Status menu	**i.** the first screen you see when you start Windows
10. ruler	**j.** appears when you point to selected text

True / False

Circle T if the statement is true or F if the statement is false.

T | F **1.** When you start Word, a new, blank document appears.
T | F **2.** The New Window button splits the window in two.
T | F **3.** When you select text, the first text you key replaces text.
T | F **4.** The Undo button is on the Mini toolbar.
T | F **5.** Full Screen Reading view displays the document as it will look when printed.
T | F **6.** Quick-printing a document sends the document straight to the printer.
T | F **7.** You can use the Microsoft Office Button to save and print files.
T | F **8.** The shortcut menu appears when you point to selected text.
T | F **9.** The zoom slider is located in the View menu.
T | F **10.** You can hide the ribbon by double-clicking the active tab.

Competency Assessment

Project 1-1: Coffee Shop Sign

GET READY. Launch Word if it is not already running.

The Grand Street Coffee Shop places a sign on the door and near the order counter listing the featured coffees of the day. Update today's sign.

CD

The *sign* document is available on the companion CD-ROM.

1. Click the **Microsoft Office Button** and choose **Open** from the menu.
2. In the Look In box, click the location of the data files for this lesson.
3. Locate and click **sign** one time to select it.
4. Click **Open**.
5. Position the I-beam before the *M* in *Morning Blend*. Drag over the words to select *Morning Blend*.
6. Key **Grand Street Blend**.
7. Position the I-beam before the *K* in *Kona* and click to place the insertion point.
8. Press and hold **Shift** and press the **Right arrow** key four times to select the entire word.
9. Key **Hawaiian**.
10. Position the I-beam before the *T* in *Try Me* and click to place the insertion point.
11. Key **$1** and press the **spacebar**.
12. In the last line, double-click the word *Mocha* to select it.
13. Key **White Chocolate**.
14. Click the **View** tab. In the Zoom group, click **One Page**.
15. Click **Page Width**.
16. Click the **Microsoft Office Button** and choose **Save As** from the menu.
17. In the Save In window, click the location where you will save the file. If necessary, double-click the folder in the main window where you will save files.
18. Key **newsign** in the File Name box and click **Save**.
19. Click the **Microsoft Office Button.** Point to **Print** and then click **Quick Print.**
20. Click the **Microsoft Office Button** and choose **Close** from the menu.

PAUSE. LEAVE Word open for the next project.

Project 1-2: Job Description

Star Bright Satellite Radio is hiring. Edit the job description so that it can be sent on to the human resources department for processing and posting.

CD

The *jobdescription* document is available on the companion CD-ROM.

1. Click the **Microsoft Office Button** and choose **Open** from the menu.
2. In the Look In box, click the location of the data files for this lesson. Locate and click ***jobdescription*** one time to select it.
3. Click **Open**.
4. In the second line of the document, position the I-beam before the *D* in *Date* and click to place the insertion point.
5. Beginning at the *D*, click and drag down and to the right until *Date Posted* and the line below it, *5/15/07*, is selected.
6. Press **Backspace** to delete both lines.
7. In the *Duties & Responsibilities* heading, position the insertion point before the &. Press **Shift** and then press the **Right arrow** key to select &.
8. Key **and**. The & is replaced with the word *and*.

9. Position the mouse pointer in the left margin beside the line in the first bulleted list that reads *Define the web site's look and feel.* Click to select the line.
10. Press **Del** to delete it.
11. In the *Education and/or Experience* heading, position the I-beam to the right of the letter *r* in *or.*
12. Press **Backspace** three times to delete the *r*, *o*, and */*.
13. In the first line of the bulleted list that begins *College degree required. . .*, click to position the insertion point after the last *e* in *degree.*
14. Press the **spacebar** and key **preferred**.
15. Click the **Microsoft Office Button** and choose **Save As** from the menu.
16. In the Save In window, click the location where you will save the file. If necessary, double-click the folder in the main window where you will save files.
17. Key **updatedjobdescription** in the File Name box and click **Save**.
18. Click the **Microsoft Office Button** and choose **Close** from the menu.

PAUSE: LEAVE Word open for the next project.

Proficiency Assessment

Project 1-3: Committee Meeting Schedule

You are chair of the New Neighbor Welcoming Committee in your neighborhood. The group meets monthly at a committee member's house. A different committee member is responsible for bringing refreshments to each meeting. Use Word to create a schedule to share with members.

CD

The *schedule* document is available on the companion CD-ROM.

1. **OPEN** ***schedule*** from the data files for this lesson.
2. Complete the schedule. For the May 11 meeting details, key **D. Lorenzo, 7501 Oak, 8 p.m.** Beside *refreshments*, key **S. Wilson**.
3. The June 15 meeting details are **R. Mason, 7620 Oak, 8 p.m.** and **J. Estes** is bringing the refreshments.
4. **SAVE** the document as ***updatedschedule*** and close it.

PAUSE: LEAVE Word open for the next project.

Project 1-4: Updating the Coffee Shop Sign

You already know the featured coffees for tomorrow, so go ahead and update the sign with the new coffees.

CD

The *newsign* document is available on the companion CD-ROM.

1. **OPEN** ***newsign*** from the data files for this lesson.
2. Change the light coffee to **Colombian**.
3. Change the dark coffee to **French Roast**.
4. Change the $1 Try Me Special to **French Vanilla Latte**.
5. **SAVE** the document as ***updatedsign*** and then close the file.

PAUSE: LEAVE Word open for the next project.

■ Mastery Assessment

Project 1-5: Fixing the Coffee Shop Menu

A co-worker for the Grand Coffee Shop has been working on a new menu for the coffee shop. She asks you to take a look at it before she sends it out to a graphic designer. You find the old menu file and decide to compare the two.

CD

The *menu* document is available on the companion CD-ROM.

CD

The *oldmenu* document is available on the companion CD-ROM.

1. **OPEN** ***menu*** from the data files for this lesson.
2. **OPEN** ***oldmenu*** *f*rom the data files for this lesson.
3. View the two files side by side to compare.
4. Find and insert two items that are missing from the new menu.
5. Find and change five pricing errors on the new menu.
6. **SAVE** the corrected menu as ***newmenu*** and then **CLOSE** the file.
7. **CLOSE** the ***oldmenu*** file.

PAUSE: LEAVE Word open for the next project.

Project 1-6: Meeting Schedule Memo

Create a memo to committee members to include with the schedule you created.

CD

The *schedulememo* document is available on the companion CD-ROM.

1. **OPEN** ***schedulememo*** from the data files for this lesson.
2. Leave two blank lines after the subject line and key the following:

   Thank you for volunteering to be on the New Neighbor Welcoming Committee. Enclosed please find the meeting and refreshment schedule for the next six months. See you in January!

   Committee Members:
3. **SAVE** the file as ***decschedulememo***.
4. **OPEN** the ***updatedschedule*** document you saved in Project 1-3.
5. Display both documents on your screen using the Arrange All command. Scroll through the meeting schedule document to see the names of committee members. Key the names of the eight committee members below the *Committee Members* heading in the memo.
6. **SAVE** the ***decschedulememo*** document and then **CLOSE** the file.
7. **CLOSE** the ***updatedschedule*** document without saving.

STOP: CLOSE Word.

INTERNET READY

Use Word Help to access online information about What's New in Word 2007. Up to Speed with Word 2007 provides an online short course or a demo explaining the new features. Browse these or other topics in Word Help online.

2

Document Basics

LESSON SKILL MATRIX

Skills	Matrix Skill	Skill Number
Formatting Document with Quick Styles	Apply Quick Styles to documents	1.1.2
Naming and Saving a New Document	Save to appropriate formats	6.1.1
Saving a Document Under a Different Name	Save to appropriate formats	6.1.1
Choosing a Different File Format	Save to appropriate formats	6.1.1
Formatting a Document with a Theme	Format documents using themes	1.1.3
Assigning Keywords to a Document	Add keywords to Modify document properties	1.3.3
Creating and Printing an Envelope	Create envelopes and labels	4.5.3
Creating and Printing a Label	Create envelopes and labels	4.5.3
Customizing a Theme	Customize a theme	1.1.4

Tech Terrace Real Estate is a real estate agency that works with clients to buy, sell, and rent homes in the neighborhood bordering a local university. Agents regularly create letters, sales data, and other real estate information to be mailed to current and prospective clients. Microsoft Word is the perfect tool for this task. In this lesson, you will learn how to create, save, format, and print a business letter. In addition, you will learn how to create and print the envelopes and labels you need to mail this material.

KEY TERMS

document properties
document theme
keywords
Print Preview
Quick Styles
Save
Save As

Creating a Document

THE BOTTOM LINE

When you open Word, a blank document called *Document1* is automatically displayed, as shown in Figure 2-1. Each new document you create during a Word session will be numbered consecutively. Starting a new document is like having a blank piece of paper on which you can begin keying text or entering data.

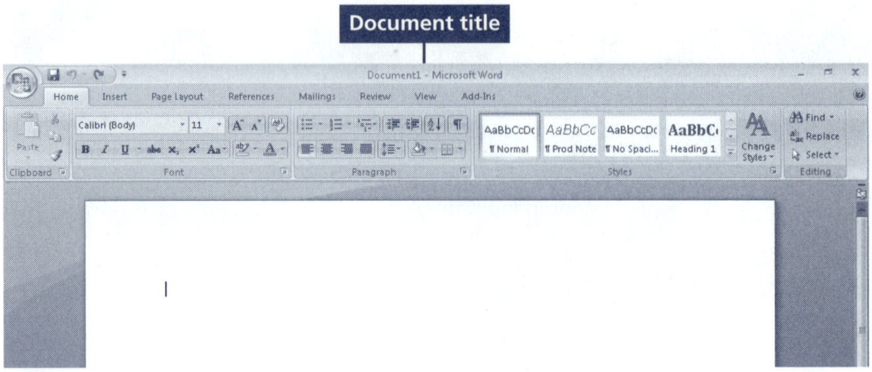

Figure 2-1

Blank document titled *Document1*

START A BUSINESS LETTER

GET READY. Before you begin these steps, be sure to launch Microsoft Office Word and open a new, blank document.

1. On the line where the blinking insertion point appears, key today's date.
2. Press **Enter** twice.
3. Key the delivery address as shown:

   Miriam Lockhart
   764 Crimson Avenue
   Boston, MA 02136
4. Press **Enter** twice.
5. Key **Dear Ms. Lockhart:**.
6. Press **Enter** twice.
7. Key the following text:

   We are pleased that you have chosen to list your home with Tech Terrace Real Estate. Our office has bought, sold, renovated, appraised, leased, and managed more homes in the Tech Terrace neighborhood than anyone—and now we will be putting that experience to work for you.

   Our goal is to sell your house quickly for the best possible price.

   The enclosed packet contains a competitive market analysis, complete listing data, a copy of the contracts, and a customized house brochure. Your home has been input into the MLS listing and an Internet ad has been posted on our website. We will be contacting you soon to determine the best time for an open house.

   We look forward to working with you to sell your home. Please don't hesitate to call if you have any questions.
8. Press **Enter** twice.
9. Key **Sincerely,**.
10. Press **Enter** twice.
11. Key **Steve Buckley**. Your document should appear as shown in Figure 2-2.

Figure 2-2

Business letter with text entered

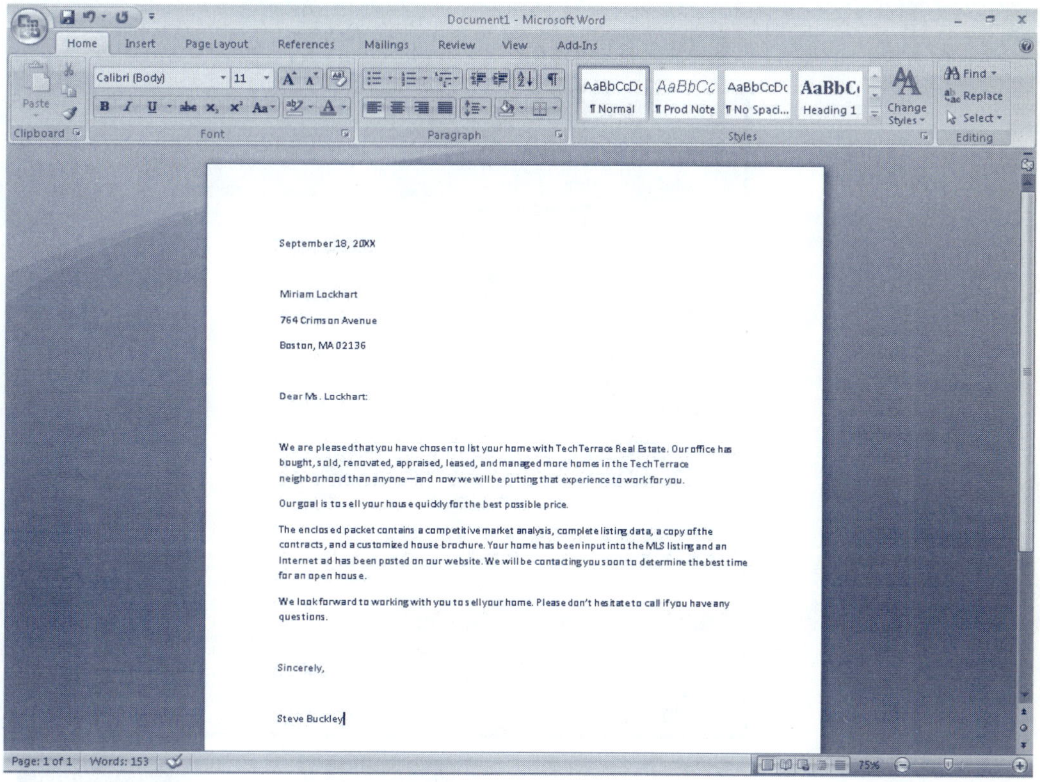

PAUSE. LEAVE the document open to use in the next exercise.

You have just created a business letter from scratch in a Word document. Later in this lesson, you will learn how to save, format, and print the document.

Saving a Document for the First Time

THE BOTTOM LINE

When saving a document for the first time, you must specify a filename and location where the document will be stored. After saving a file for the first time, the Save command will overwrite the file's previous version and save any changes.

Naming and Saving a New Document

The process for saving a document is the same every time, except the first time you save it you must name the file and choose a directory where it will be stored.

NAME AND SAVE A NEW DOCUMENT

USE the document that is open from the previous exercise.

1. Click the **Microsoft Office Button** and then click **Save**. The Save As dialog box opens, as shown in Figure 2-3.

ANOTHER WAY

You can also save a file by clicking the **Save** button on the Quick Access toolbar or by pressing **Ctrl+S**.

Figure 2-3

Save As dialog box

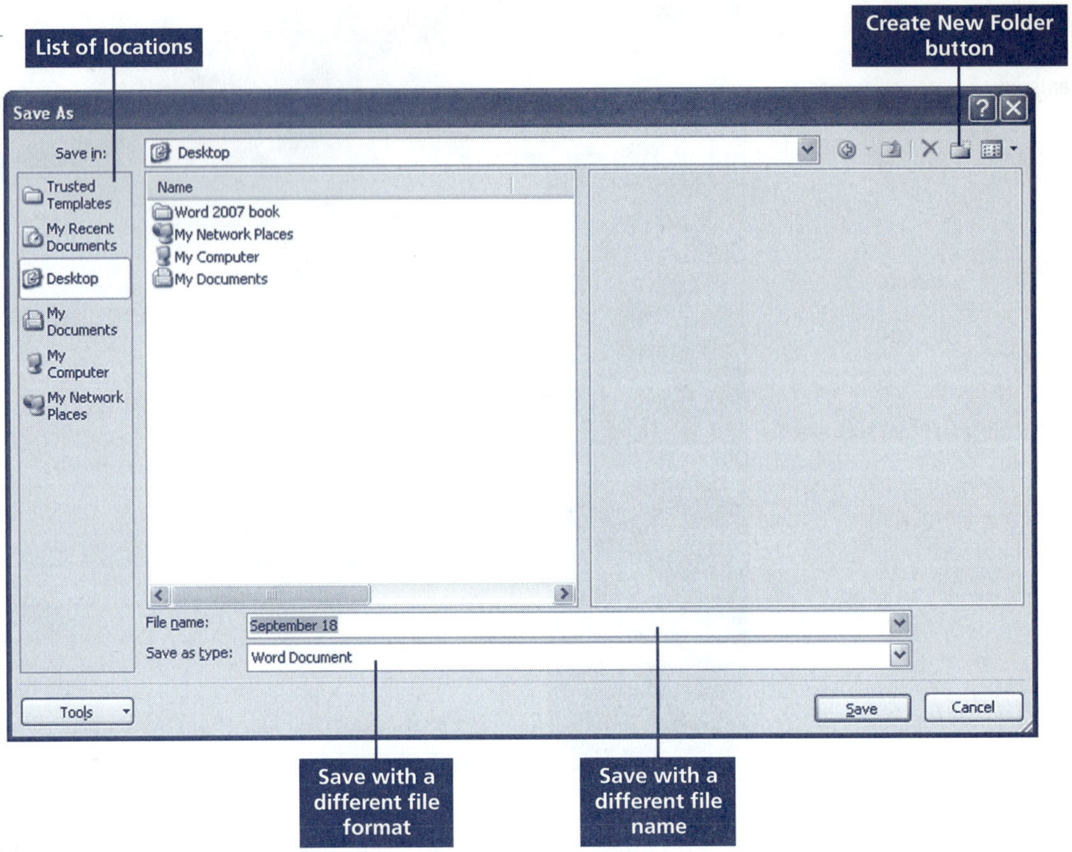

TAKE NOTE*

To create a new folder in the folder list to store your document, click the **Create New Folder** button.

2. In the Save In list, click the location where you want to store the document. You can also choose a folder in which to store the file from the folder list.
3. In the File Name box, key **TechTerrace_letter**.
4. Click **Save** to close the dialog box and save the document.

PAUSE. LEAVE the document open to use in the next exercise.

CERTIFICATION READY?
How do you save to appropriate formats?
6.1.1

You just saved the business letter that you created. When you ***save*** a document, it is stored for future use. You can save a file to a folder on your hard drive, a network location, a CD, the desktop, or another storage location.

TROUBLESHOOTING

AutoRecover is a feature that automatically saves your data at scheduled intervals. This makes it possible to recover some of your work if a problem occurs. However, this useful option is not a substitute for frequently saving your documents as you work. You should always click the Save button regularly to avoid losing work in case of a power outage or a computer crash.

Saving a Document under a Different Name

The Save As command can be used to save a copy of your document with a new filename or in a new location.

SAVE UNDER A DIFFERENT NAME

ANOTHER WAY

You can also open the Save As dialog box by pressing **F12**.

USE the document that is open from the previous exercise.

1. Click the **Microsoft Office Button** and then click **Save As** to open the Save As dialog box.
2. In the File Name box, key **TTletter_lockhart**.
3. Click **Save**.

PAUSE. LEAVE the document open to use in the next exercise.

CERTIFICATION READY?
How do you save to appropriate formats?
6.1.1

You just saved a copy of your document with a new name. You also could have chosen to save your document in a different location by choosing another directory from the Save In list or by creating a new folder. The ***Save As*** command can be used to save a document with a new name or in a different location.

Choosing a Different File Format

If you need your document available in a different format, you can choose to save it as another type of file.

CHOOSE A DIFFERENT FILE FORMAT

USE the document that is open from the previous exercise.

1. Click the **Microsoft Office Button** and then click **Save As** to open the Save As dialog box.
2. In the Save As type box, click the downward-pointing arrow and choose **Word 97-2003 Document**, as shown in Figure 2-4.

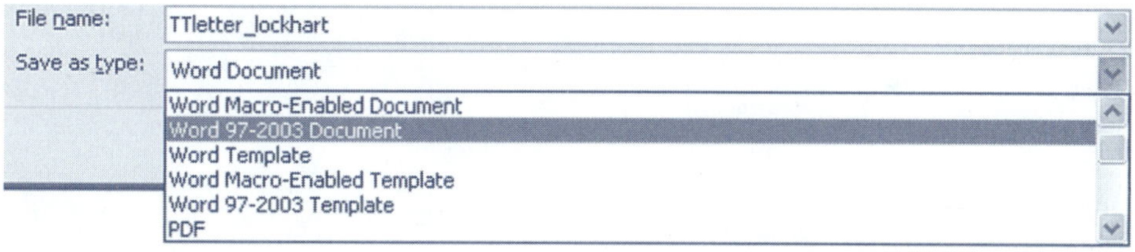

Figure 2-4
Save As type menu

3. **SAVE** the document and **CLOSE** the file.

PAUSE. LEAVE Word open for the next exercise.

CERTIFICATION READY?
How do you save to appropriate formats?
6.1.1

You just saved a copy of your document in a different file format. The format you chose enables a user who has an earlier version of Word to open your document without any difficulty. You can choose from many different file formats, depending on your needs. For example, you may choose to save the document as a web page if it will be viewed with a browser. Or, you may want to save your document as plain text if you do not want it to include any formatting. Unless you have a specific reason for saving your document in a different file format, you will usually choose to accept the default Word format when saving.

TAKE NOTE*

PDF files are a popular save-as format for documents. This preserves the formatting so that it can be viewed exactly as you intended, without allowing data to be changed or copied. In order to save in PDF format, you must download the appropriate add-in from *www.microsoft.com*.

Changing a Document's Appearance

THE BOTTOM LINE Once you have created your document, it is time to think about how you might improve its appearance. In Word, it is easy to change a document using features such as Quick Styles and themes to make it look more professional and appealing.

Formatting a Document with Quick Styles

NEW FEATURE

You can save time when formatting a document by choosing from a gallery of predefined Quick Styles available in Word.

FORMAT USING QUICK STYLES

OPEN the ***TechTerrace_letter*** file from the location where you saved it earlier.

1. Click anywhere in your document.
2. On the Home tab, in the Styles group, click the **Change Styles** button.
3. Click **Style Set** to display the menu of Quick Style options, as shown in Figure 2-5.

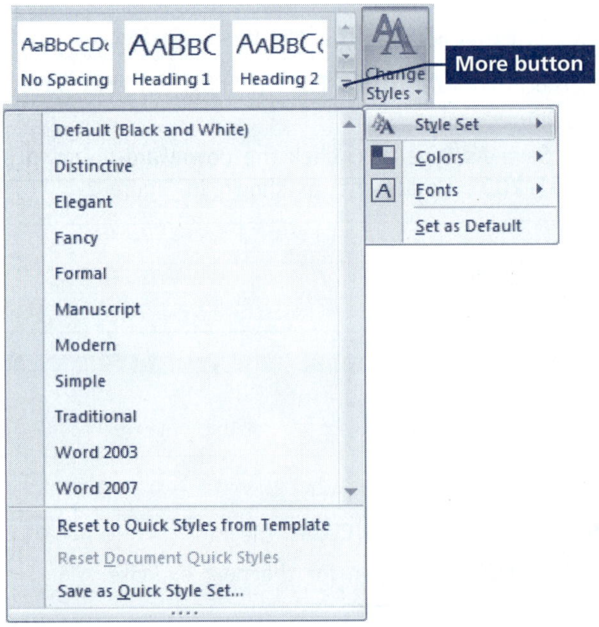

Figure 2-5
Style Set menu options

4. Place your pointer over any choice on the Style Set menu and notice that your document changes to show you a preview of that style.
5. Click **Distinctive**.
6. Select the paragraph that reads *Our goal is to sell your house quickly for the best possible price*.
7. On the Home tab, in the Styles group, click the **More** button. A Quick Style gallery appears, as shown in Figure 2-6.

Figure 2-6

Quick Style gallery

8. Place your pointer over any thumbnail in the gallery and notice that the paragraph changes to show you a preview of that style.
9. Click the **Intense Quote** thumbnail. Notice that style is applied to the paragraph you previously selected. Your document should look similar to Figure 2-7.

September 18, 2008

Miriam Lockhart

764 Crimson Avenue

Boston, MA 02136

Dear Ms. Lockhart:

We are pleased that you have chosen to list your home with Tech Terrace Real Estate. Our office has bought, sold, renovated, appraised, leased, and managed more homes in the Tech Terrace neighborhood that anyone—and now we will be putting that experience to work for you.

Our goal is to sell your house quickly for the best possible price.

The enclosed packet contains a competitive market analysis, complete listing data, a copy of the contracts, and a customized house brochure. Your home has been input into the MLS listing and an Internet ad has been posted on our web site. We will be contacting you soon to determine the best time for an open house.

We look forward to working with you to sell your home. Please don't hesitate to call if you have any questions.

Sincerely,

Steve Buckley

Figure 2-7

Document formatted with Quick Styles

CERTIFICATION READY?
How do you apply Quick Styles to a document?
1.1.2

10. SAVE your document.

PAUSE. LEAVE the document open to use in the next exercise.

You have just formatted a business letter using Quick Styles. ***Quick Styles*** are predefined formats that you can apply to your document to instantly change its look and feel. Word eliminates the guesswork by allowing you to preview the formatting changes in your document before you commit to applying the style.

Formatting a Document with a Theme

Document themes are another way to quickly change the overall design of your document using formatting choices that are predefined by Word.

FORMAT USING A DOCUMENT THEME

NEW FEATURE

USE the document that is open from the previous exercise.

1. On the Page Layout tab, in the Themes group, click **Themes**, as shown in Figure 2-8.

Figure 2-8
Document themes

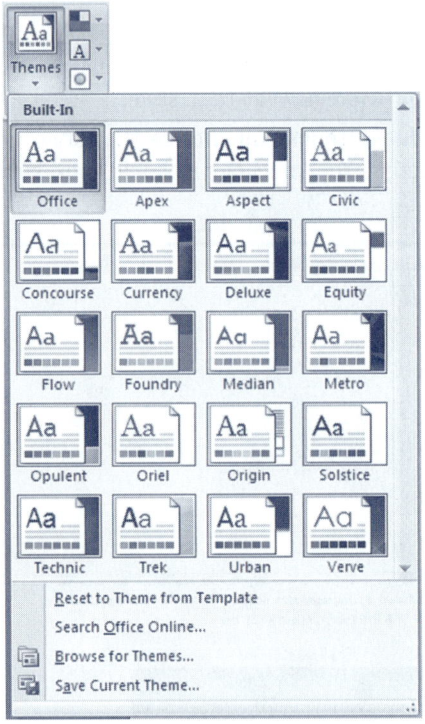

2. Place your pointer over any built-in theme and notice that the document changes to show you a preview of that theme.

TAKE NOTE*

Although you used a theme to change the overall design of the entire document, you can also change individual elements by using the Theme Colors, Theme Fonts, and Theme Effects buttons.

CERTIFICATION READY?
How do you apply a theme to a document?
1.1.3

3. Click **Concourse**. The colors, fonts, and effects for that theme are applied to your document.
4. **SAVE** your document.

PAUSE. LEAVE the document open to use in the next exercise.

You have just used a document theme to format your letter. A ***document theme*** is a set of predefined formatting options that includes theme colors, fonts, and effects. You can use the choices Word provides or you can create your own document theme. Document themes contain the following elements:

- Theme colors contain four text and background colors, six accent colors, and two hyperlink colors. Click the Theme Colors button to change the colors for the current theme, as shown in Figure 2-9.

Figure 2-9

Theme Colors menu

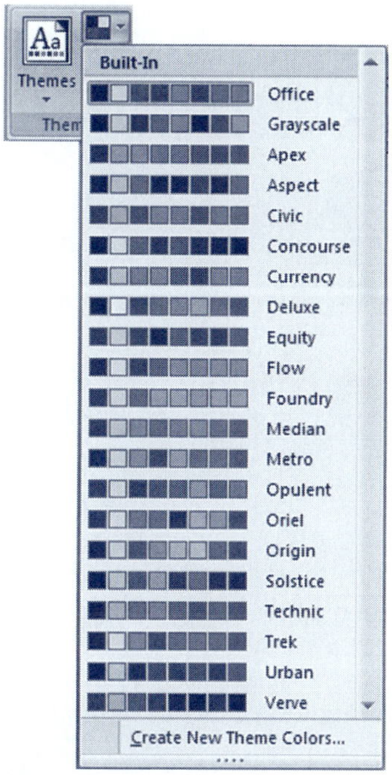

- Theme fonts contain a heading font and a body text font. Click the Theme Fonts button to change the fonts for the current theme, as shown in Figure 2-10.

Figure 2-10

Theme Fonts menu

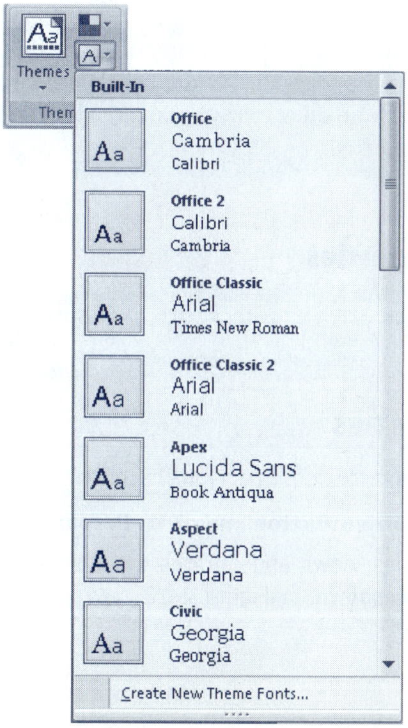

- Theme effects are sets of lines and fill effects. Click the Theme Effects button to change the effects for the current theme, as shown in Figure 2-11.

Figure 2-11

Theme Effects menu

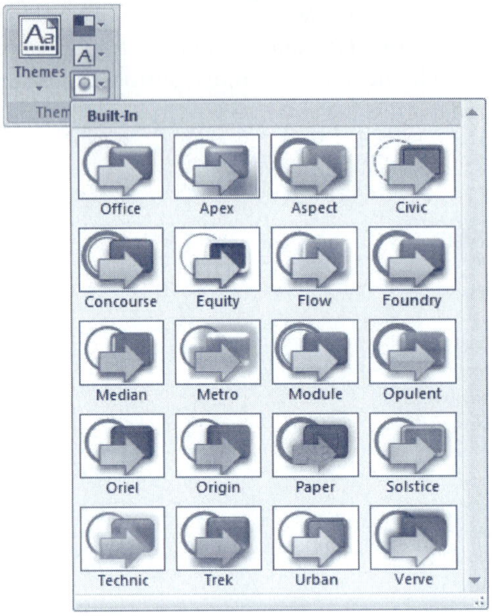

If you make any changes to the colors, fonts, or effects of the current theme, you can save it as a custom document theme and then apply it to other documents.

TAKE NOTE* Document themes are the same throughout all Office programs, so all of your Office documents can share the same look and feel.

Editing a Document's Properties

THE BOTTOM LINE Using document properties makes it easier to organize and identify them later. You can specify some document properties and Word automatically updates some document properties. You can search to find files that contain certain document properties, such as keywords, file size, or date created.

Setting Standard Properties

Standard properties are those such as author, title, and subject that are associated with a document by default.

SET STANDARD PROPERTIES

USE the document that is open from the previous exercise.

1. Click the **Microsoft Office Button**, point to **Prepare**, and then click **Properties**.
2. The standard properties views and options are displayed in the Document Information Panel, as shown in Figure 2-12.

Figure 2-12

Document Information Panel

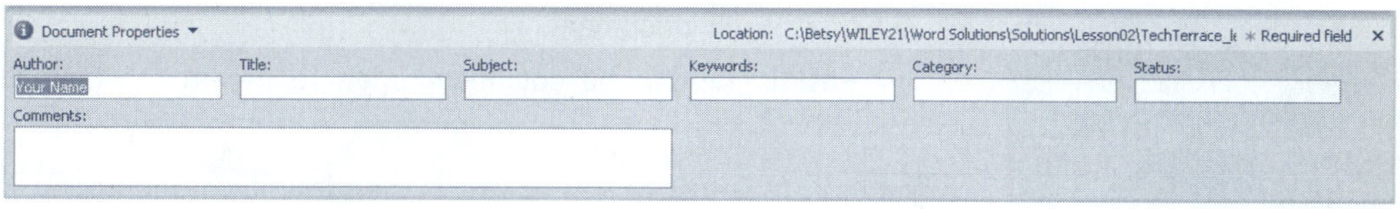

TAKE NOTE*

A document property field marked by a red asterisk indicates that the field is required and you will need to fill it in before you can save the document.

3. Key the following document properties:

   Author: **Your Name** (this may already be filled in—change if necessary)

   Title: **Miriam Lockhart letter**

   Subject: **introduction**

4. **SAVE** your document.

   PAUSE. LEAVE the document open to use in the next exercise.

You have just set some of the basic properties for a document that will help you identify and organize it later. ***Document properties*** are details that describe or identify a file. Table 2-1 describes each standard property. These properties can all be changed by the user; however, some properties—such as the file size, number of words in a document, and date the document was created or updated—are automatically updated by Word and cannot be changed.

Document properties can be useful for locating a file later. For example, you could search for all the documents created before a certain date or for all the files that were last changed yesterday. The description of each document property is listed in Table 2-1.

Table 2-1

Standard Document Properties

Property Name	Description
Author	The name of the individual who has authored the document
Title	Title of the document
Subject	Topic of the contents of the document
Keywords	A word or set of words that describes the document
Category	The category in which the document can be classified; e.g., "Documents from my manager"
Status	The status of the content e.g., "Draft," "Reviewed," or "Final"
Comments	The summary or abstract of the contents of the document

Assigning Keywords to a Document

By assigning words that describe a document, you can later organize or locate the document more easily.

ASSIGN KEYWORDS

USE the document that is open from the previous exercise.

1. The Document Information Panel should be open. If not, click the **Microsoft Office Button**, point to **Prepare**, and then click **Properties**.
2. In the Keywords box, key **Lockhart, Crimson, new listing**.
3. In the Category box, key **new listing packet**.
4. Click the **Close** button in the upper right corner of the Document Information Panel to close it.

CERTIFICATION READY?
How do you add keywords to document properties?
1.3.3

5. **SAVE** your document.

PAUSE. LEAVE the document open to use in the next exercise.

Keywords are words or sets of words that describe a document. When assigning keywords to a document, choose words that are descriptive and will help you identify it later when you are searching your files.

You can also view the keywords and other properties for any document when opening or saving a file. In the Open or Save As dialog box, clicking the downward-pointing arrow on the Views button and choosing Properties will display the document properties, as shown in Figure 2-13.

Figure 2-13

Document properties

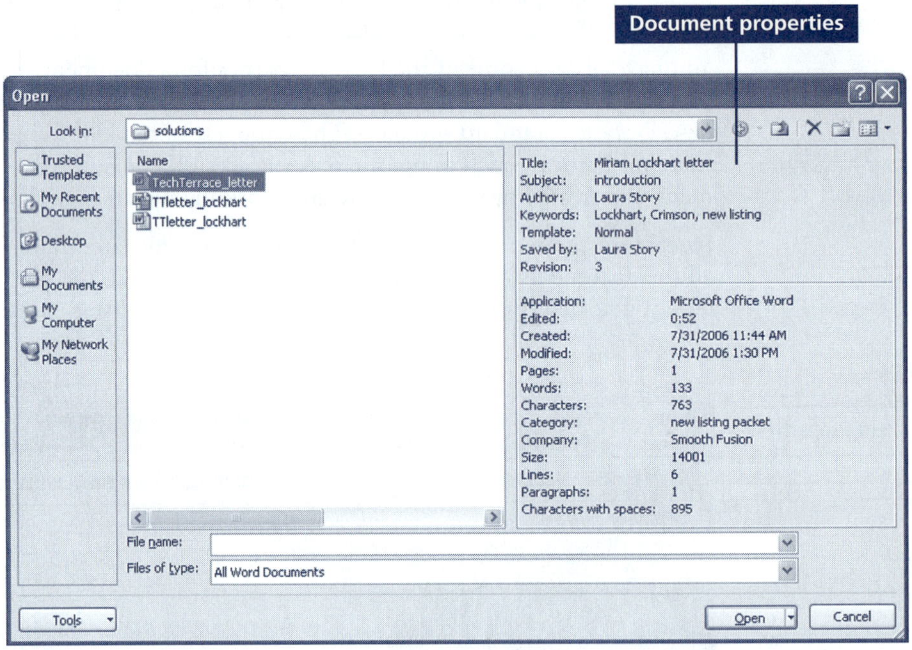

Printing a Document

THE BOTTOM LINE

After you have finished creating your document, you can preview it to see how it will look in print. This saves time and paper by enabling you to make any necessary changes before printing. When printing for the first time, you will need to choose a printer. You can choose printing options each time or simply print using the default options.

Using Print Preview

Print Preview enables you to view how the document will appear when it is printed, with options such as zoom and displaying two pages.

USE PRINT PREVIEW

USE the document that is open from the previous exercise.

1. Click the **Microsoft Office Button**, point to the arrow next to **Print**, and then click **Print Preview**. The Print Preview screen appears, as shown in Figure 2-14.

Figure 2-14

Print Preview

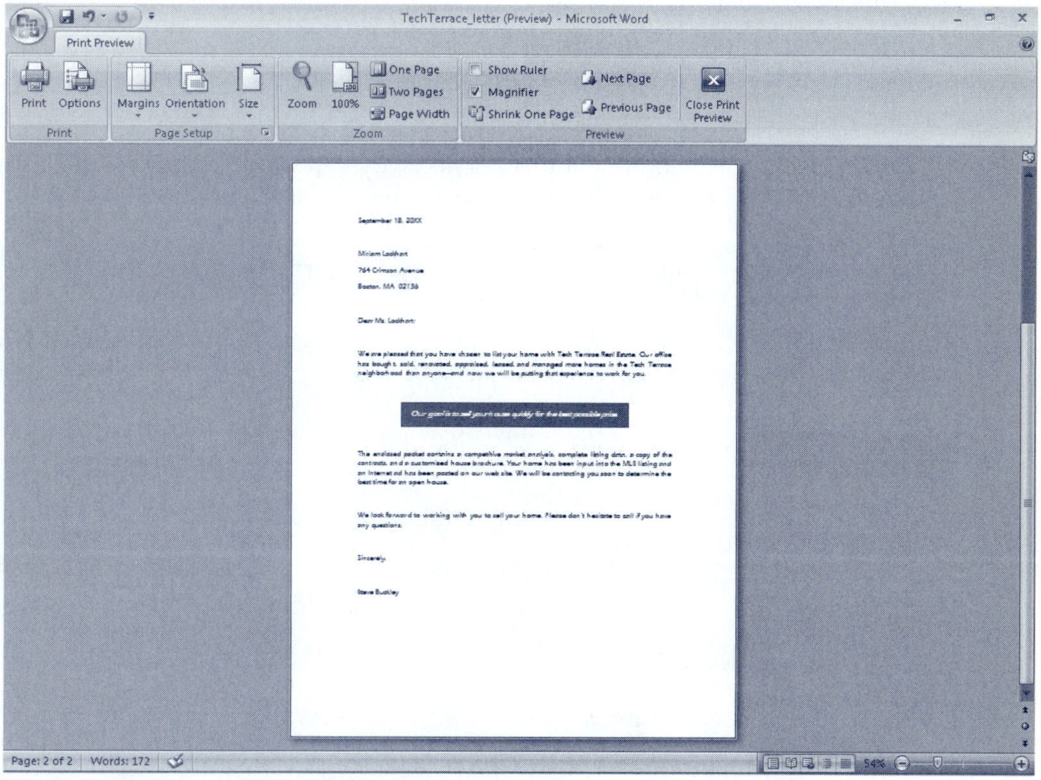

2. Use the **Zoom** controls on the bottom right of the window to zoom in to 100%.
3. In the Zoom group, click the **One Page** button so that the entire page fits in the window.
4. In the Page Setup group, click the **Margins** button and then click **Normal**. Notice the document margins change in the preview window.
5. In the Zoom group, click the **Page Width** button so that the width of the page matches the width of the window.
6. In the Preview group, click **Previous Page** to display the top of the document.
7. Click the **Close Print Preview** button.
8. **SAVE** your document.

PAUSE. LEAVE the document open to use in the next exercise.

ANOTHER WAY

Move the pointer over the document and notice that it changes to a magnifying glass. Click the document to zoom in to 100% and again to zoom out to 50%.

TAKE NOTE*

Print Preview is an example of how the standard tabs on the ribbon are replaced with program tabs relevant to the task you are performing.

Print Preview enables you to view your document as it will appear when it is printed and make any necessary changes before printing.

Choosing a Printer

Before printing your document, you will need to make sure you have selected a printer. If your computer is already set up to print, you will not need to complete this exercise.

CHOOSE A PRINTER

USE the document that is open from the previous exercise.

1. Click the **Microsoft Office Button** and click **Print** to display the Print dialog box.
2. Click **Find Printer** to display the Find Printers dialog box.
3. In the Name list, choose the printer you want to use.

ANOTHER WAY

You can also press **Ctrl+P** to display the Print dialog box.

4. Click **OK** to close the Find Printers dialog box. The Print dialog box should still be open.

PAUSE. LEAVE the document open to use in the next exercise.

Choosing a printer is a necessary step when printing for the first time. Now you are ready to set your print options and print your document.

TROUBLESHOOTING

You may need to set up a new printer before you can select it. To add a printer:

In Microsoft Windows Vista,

1. Click the **Start** button and then click **Control Panel**.
2. In Control Panel, double-click **Printers**.
3. In the Printers dialog box, click **Add a Printer**.
4. Follow the instructions in the **Add Printer Wizard**.

In Microsoft Windows XP,

1. Click the **Start** button and then click **Printers and Faxes**.
2. Under Printer Tasks, click **Add a Printer**.
3. Follow the instructions in the Add Printer Wizard.

TAKE NOTE*

To set a printer as the default, right-click the printer icon and click **Set as Default Printer** on the shortcut menu. A checkmark will appear next to the default printer.

Setting Other Printing Options

You can choose various printing options before sending your document to the printer, such as the number of copies or the range of pages to print.

SET OTHER PRINTING OPTIONS

USE the document that is open from the previous exercise.

1. The Print dialog box should still be open, as shown in Figure 2-15. If it is not, click the **Microsoft Office Button** and click **Print**.

Figure 2-15

Print dialog box

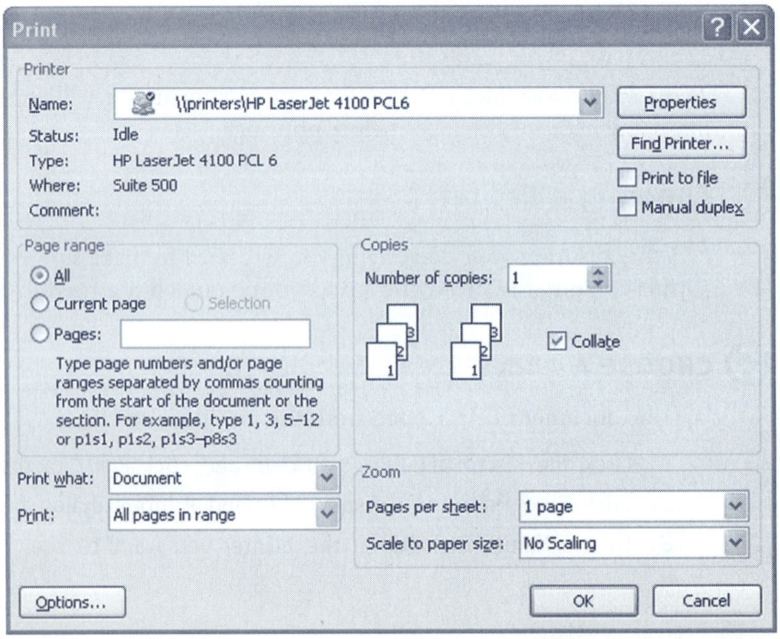

2. Click the **Options** button to display the Word Options dialog box, as shown in Figure 2-16.

Figure 2-16

Word Options dialog box

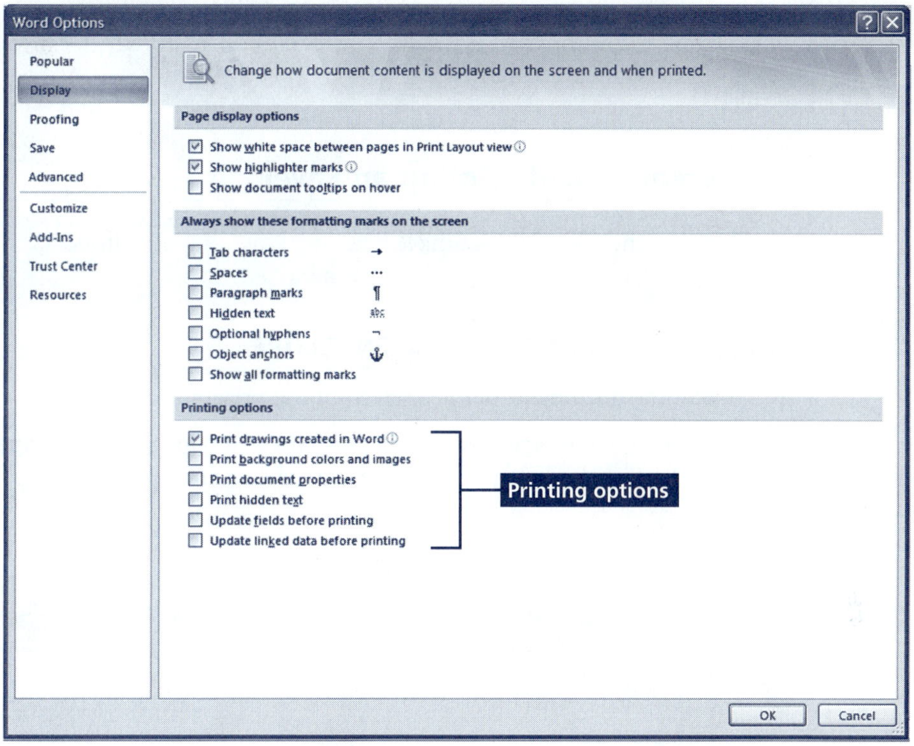

3. Notice the printing options at the bottom of the dialog box that can be selected to change the way you print your documents. Click **Cancel** to return to the Print dialog box.
4. In the Copies section, click the upward-pointing arrow next to the Number of Copies box to change it to **2**.
5. Click **OK** to print two copies of the letter.

ANOTHER WAY

To print a document quickly, you can skip the Print dialog box and use the default settings by clicking **Quick Print** from the Print option on the Microsoft Office Button menu.

PAUSE. LEAVE the document open to use in the next exercise.

In this activity, you learned about some of the options available when printing a document. When you make changes in the Word Options dialog box, they will be applied to any Word document you print. Changes that you make in the Print dialog box will only be applied to that particular document.

You chose to print two copies of the letter in this activity. If the document were longer, you could have chosen other options, such as printing a range of pages, collating the pages, or printing multiple pages per sheet.

X REF

You will learn more about printing documents with different layouts—including margins, orientations, and paper sizes—in Lesson 5.

Creating Envelopes and Labels

THE BOTTOM LINE

Creating and printing envelopes and labels in Word is a similar process that uses the same dialog box. If you have a return address stored, it can be used as the default address to save time.

Creating and Printing an Envelope

To send the letter you have been working on, you will now create and print an envelope that you can save with the document.

CREATE AND PRINT AN ENVELOPE

USE the document that is open from the previous exercise.

1. On the Mailings tab, in the Create group, click **Envelopes**. The Envelopes and Labels dialog box appears, as shown in Figure 2-17.

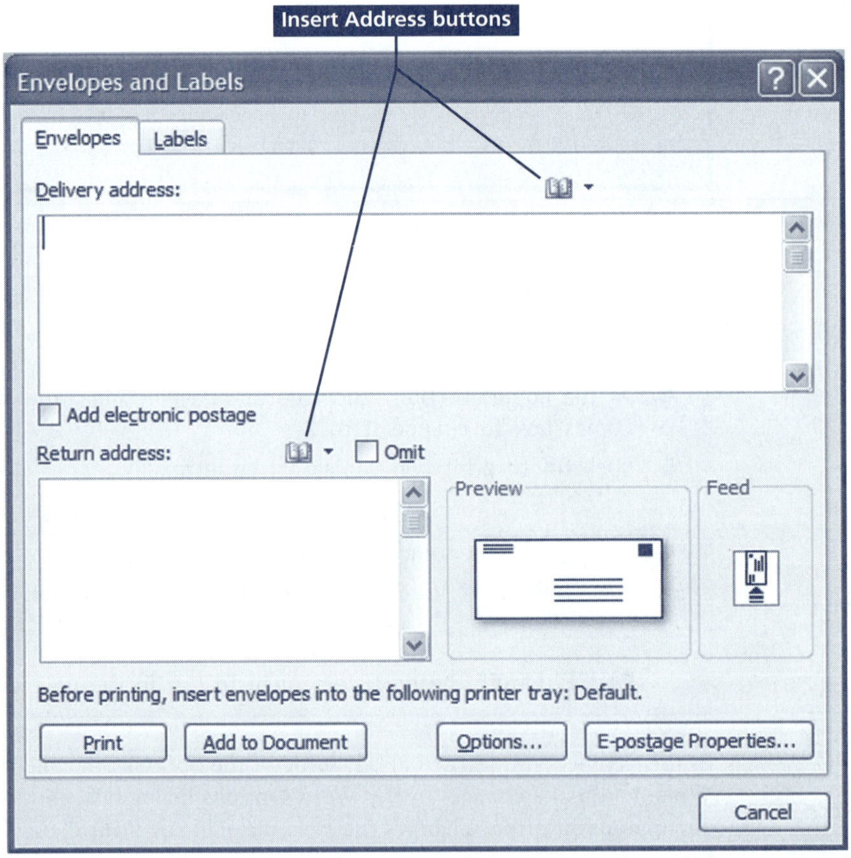

Figure 2-17

Envelopes and Labels dialog box

TAKE NOTE*

If you wanted to choose an address from the electronic address book on your computer, you could click the **Insert Address button.**

2. In the Delivery Address box, key:

   Miriam Lockhart
   764 Crimson Avenue
   Boston, MA 02136

   (Note: If the Delivery address is already pre-populated with the address above, go to the next step.)

TAKE NOTE*

The current document theme determines what font is used on the envelope. To change the font, select the address, then right-click and choose **Font** from the shortcut menu.

3. In the Return Address box, key:

   Tech Terrace Real Estate
   1218 Hutchinson Road
   Boston, MA 02136

4. Click the **Add to Document** button. (When a dialog box appears asking if you want to save the new return address as the default, click **No.**) This saves the envelope with the document you have been working on as Page 0, as shown in Figure 2-18.

Figure 2-18

Envelope added to document

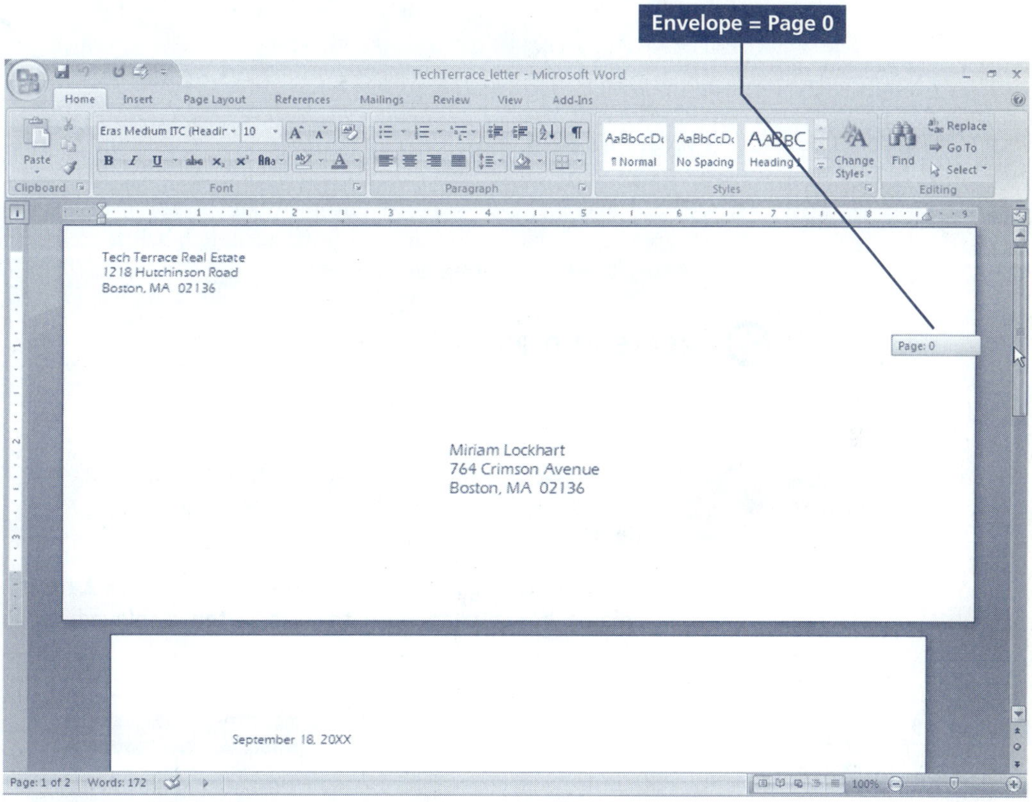

5. Click Ctrl + P to open the Print dialog box.
6. In the Print dialog box, in the Page Range section, click **Pages** and key **0**. This will print only the envelope and not the accompanying letter.
7. Insert the envelope in the printer's manual feeder and click **OK**.
8. **SAVE** the document and **CLOSE** the file.

   PAUSE. LEAVE Word open for the next exercise.

CERTIFICATION READY?
How do you create an envelope?
4.5.3

In this activity, you printed a single envelope that will enable you to mail your letter. If the return address were one that you would be using regularly, you could have chosen to save it as the default. This would save you the time of keying it again later and the address would be available for printing envelopes, labels, or inserting into a document. The Omit checkbox in the Envelopes and Labels dialog box allows you to keep the return address for future use, but not include it on the current envelope.

If you add an envelope to a document, it is stored as page 0 and saved with the document. You can print only the envelope by choosing to print page 0 of the document. If you do not add the envelope to the document, it is not stored for future use. Simply click the Print button to send it directly to the printer.

If you have electronic postage software installed, you can add electronic postage to your envelope before printing. To set postage options, click the E-postage Properties button from the Envelopes and Labels dialog box.

TROUBLESHOOTING

Before sending an envelope through your printer, you should check to make sure it is set up correctly.

1. On the Mailings tab, in the Create group, click **Envelopes**.
2. Click **Options** and then click the **Envelope Options** tab.
3. In the Envelope Size box, click the choice that matches the size of your envelope.
4. Click the **Printing Options** tab. Information about which way the envelope should be loaded into the printer is displayed here.
5. Load the envelope as indicated in the dialog box.
6. Click **OK**.

Creating and Printing a Label

Word makes it easy to create and print labels. You can select from a number of popular paper label styles and shapes to print a single label or create a full sheet of identical labels to use as return address labels.

CREATE AND PRINT A LABEL

1. **OPEN** a new, blank Word document.

TAKE NOTE*

To create labels in Word, you must first open a blank document or the label commands will not be available.

2. On the Mailings tab, in the Create group, click **Labels**. The Envelopes and Labels dialog box appears with the Labels tab displayed, as shown in Figure 2-19.

Figure 2-19

Labels tab of Envelopes and Labels dialog box

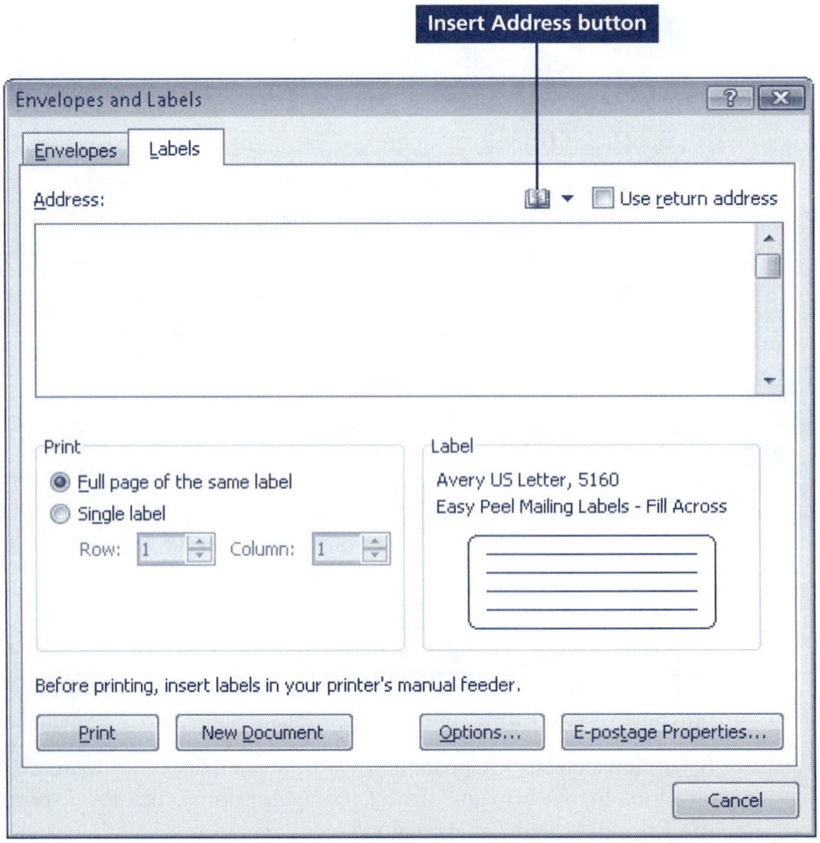

3. In the Address box, key:

   Tech Terrace Real Estate
   1218 Hutchinson Road
   Boston, MA 02136

4. Click the **Options** button. The Label Options dialog box appears, as shown in Figure 2-20.

Figure 2-20

Labels Options dialog box

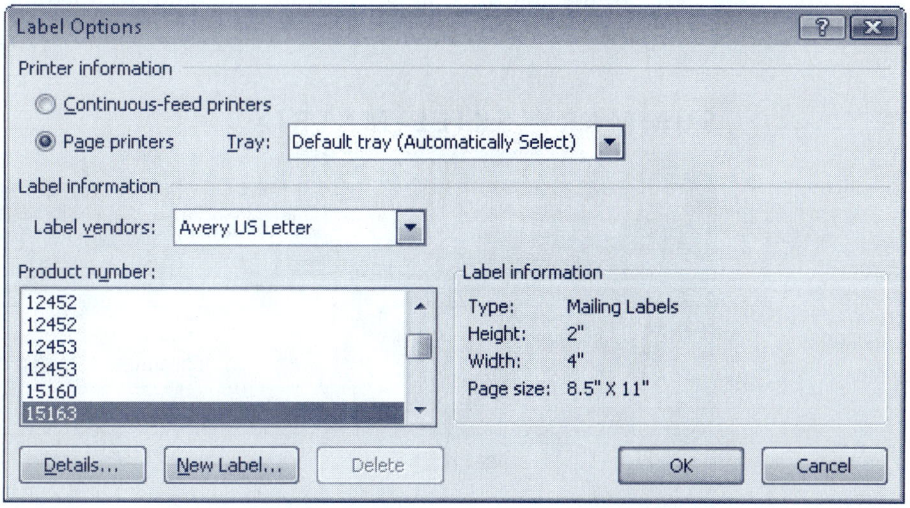

CERTIFICATION READY?
How do you create a label?
4.5.3

5. In the Label Information section, choose the type of label you are using.
6. Click **OK** to return to the Labels and Envelopes dialog box.
7. In the Print section, be sure **Full page of the same label** is selected.

TAKE NOTE* To print just one label, click the **Single Label** option and choose the numbers that correspond with the label row and column on the sheet you are using to print.

8. Click the **New Document** button. This creates a separate document with a full sheet of labels.
9. Save the document as ***TT_return_labels***.
10. Insert the labels into your printer's manual feeder.
11. Print the labels.
12. **SAVE** the document and **CLOSE** the file.

   STOP. CLOSE Word.

TAKE NOTE* When you create a full sheet of labels in a separate document, you can make formatting changes to the text on each individual label just as you would in any Word document.

In this activity, you printed a full sheet to use as return address labels. If you need only one label, it is easy to print a single label by specifying the row and column number of the label on the sheet.

Several of the options in the Label tab of the Envelopes and Labels dialog box are similar to the Envelope tab. You can use an address from the electronic address book by clicking the Insert Address button, or click the E-postage Properties button to use the electronic postage feature. To send labels directly to the printer without previewing them, click the Print button.

To change formatting, select the text, right-click and then click Font or Paragraph on the shortcut menu. To use the return address that is stored, click the Use Return Address box.

X REF You will learn about creating and printing envelopes and labels using an address list for a mail merge in Lesson 16.

TROUBLESHOOTING

If none of the choices in the Label Options dialog box match your labels, you will need to create a custom setting.

1. Click the **New Label** button to open the Label Details dialog box.
2. Key the label name.
3. Enter the dimensions and other options for your label.
4. Click **OK**.
5. To use your custom label setting, choose **Other/Custom** in the Label products list.

SUMMARY SKILL MATRIX

In This Lesson You Learned	Matrix Skill	Skill Number
To name and save a new document	Save to appropriate formats	6.1.1
To save a document under a different name	Save to appropriate formats	6.1.1
To choose a different file format	Save to appropriate formats	6.1.1
To format a document with Quick Styles	Apply Quick Styles to documents	1.1.2
To format a document with a theme	Format documents using themes	1.1.3
To assign keywords to a document	Add keywords to Modify document properties	1.3.3
To create and print an envelope	Create envelopes and labels	4.5.3
To create and print a label	Create envelopes and labels	4.5.3
To customize a theme	Customize a theme	1.1.4

■ Knowledge Assessment

Fill in the Blank

Complete the following sentences by writing the correct word or words in the blanks provided.

1. When you open Word, a ______________ document called *Document1* is automatically displayed.
2. After saving a file for the first time, the ______________ command will save any changes by overwriting the previous version.
3. If you need your document in a different ______________ you can choose to save it as another type of file.
4. Using document ______________ makes it easier to organize and identify them later.
5. When choosing the _______ _______ option, you must choose the numbers that correspond with the label row and column on the sheet you are using to print.
6. ______________ is a feature that automatically saves your data at scheduled intervals so that you can possibly recover some of your work if a problem occurs.

7. If you make any changes to the colors, fonts, or effects of the current ________ you can save it as a custom version that can be applied to other documents.
8. ______________ properties are those that are associated with a document by default.
9. To print a document quickly using the default settings, you can click the ______________ option from the Microsoft Office Button menu.
10. If you have a ______________ address stored, it can be used as the default address to save time when creating envelopes or labels.

Multiple Choice

Select the best response for the following statements and questions.

1. Which command can be used to save a copy of your document with a new filename or in a new location?
   - **a.** Save
   - **b.** Save As
   - **c.** Print Preview
   - **d.** Save New
2. Predefined formats that you can apply to your document to instantly change its look and feel are called
   - **a.** Theme Colors
   - **b.** Standard Properties
   - **c.** Pre-Formats
   - **d.** Quick Styles
3. A document theme includes sets of
   - **a.** colors
   - **b.** fonts
   - **c.** effects
   - **d.** all of the above
   - **e.** none of the above
4. A word or set of words that describes the document is called
   - **a.** Keyword
   - **b.** Abstract
   - **c.** Comment
   - **d.** Descriptor
5. When previewing a document, which command enables you to see your document close-up or see the page at a reduced size?
   - **a.** Magnify
   - **b.** Zoom
   - **c.** Percentage
   - **d.** Quick View
6. Choosing the number of copies or range of pages are options that are available when performing what process on a document?
   - **a.** Previewing
   - **b.** Assigning keywords
   - **c.** Printing
   - **d.** Saving in a different format

7. An envelope that is saved with a document is added as which page?
   a. 0
   b. 1
   c. 2
   d. the last one
8. Which is not an option when saving a document?
   a. Save in a different location
   b. Save with a different name
   c. Save with a different theme
   d. Save in a different file format
9. To preview a style or a theme,
   a. place your pointer over the choice
   b. print the document
   c. set up the document properties
   d. it is not possible to preview a style or theme
10. Document properties include
    a. file size
    b. date created
    c. author
    d. all of the above
    e. none of the above

Competency Assessment

Project 2-1: Phone Interview Selection Letter

In your position at Tech Terrace Real Estate, you have already created a letter to decline pursuing a candidate for employment any further after a phone interview. Open the document and save it in a different format and with a different name.

CD

The ***selection_letter*** document is available on the companion CD-ROM.

GET READY. Launch Word if it is not already running.

1. **OPEN** ***selection_letter*** from the data files for this lesson.
2. Click the **Microsoft Office Button** and then click **Save As** to open the Save As dialog box.
3. In the File Name box, key **decline_letter**.
4. Click **Save** to save the file with a different name.
5. Press **F12** to open the Save As dialog box again.
6. In the Save As type box, click the downward-pointing arrow and choose **Word 97-2003 Document**.
7. Click **Save** to save the document in a different format.
8. **CLOSE** the file.

LEAVE Word open for the next project.

Project 2-2: Reference Letter

A former employee at Tech Terrace Real Estate has asked for a reference letter. Open and format the document and add document properties so it will be easier to locate in the future.

CD

The ***reference_letter*** document is available on the companion CD-ROM.

1. **OPEN** ***reference_letter*** from the data files for this lesson.
2. On the Home tab, in the Styles group, click the **Change Styles** button.
3. On the Set Styles menu, click **Formal**.
4. On the Page Layout tab, in the Themes group, click **Themes**.
5. Click **Origin** on the gallery menu.
6. Click the **Microsoft Office Button**, point to **Prepare**, and then click **Properties**.
7. In the Document Information Panel, key the following:
   Author: **Your Name**
   Title: **Randall Jasmine letter**
   Subject: **reference**
   Keywords: **Jasmine, employee, reference**
   Category: **former employees**
8. **CLOSE** the Document Information Panel.
9. **SAVE** the document as ***jasmine_reference*** and then **CLOSE** the file.
   LEAVE Word open for the next project.

Proficiency Assessment

Project 2-3: Creating Return Address Labels

You are paying bills at home and decide to save time writing your return address on every envelope by creating a sheet of return address labels to use.

1. **OPEN** a new, blank Word document.
2. Create a full sheet of return address labels with your name and address. Use **Avery US Letter, 5160** as the label type.
3. **SAVE** the new document as ***personal_labels***.
4. Change the style on the labels to **Traditional**.
5. Use Print Preview to see what the labels will look like when printed.
6. **PRINT** the labels.
7. **SAVE** the document and **CLOSE** the file.
   LEAVE Word open for the next project.

Project 2-4: Welcome Back to School Letter

As a second grade teacher at the local elementary school, you have to send out letters to all your students letting them know you will be their teacher and welcoming them back to school.

CD

The ***school_letter*** document is available on the companion CD-ROM.

1. **OPEN** ***school_letter*** from the data files for this lesson.
2. Set document properties, including keywords, for the letter. Use words that apply to the document.
3. Format the document using a style that you think looks good from the Style Set menu.
4. Select the last paragraph that begins *I hope to see you...*
5. Choose an option from the Quick Style gallery to emphasize the paragraph.
6. **SAVE** the document as ***welcome_letter***.
7. Preview and then print the document.
8. **CLOSE** the file.
   LEAVE Word open for the next project.

Mastery Assessment

Project 2-5: Create a Custom Theme

CERTIFICATION READY?
How do you customize a theme?
1.1.4

Tech Terrace Real Estate has decided to give all their documents a branded look by creating a custom theme to be used for all client-facing business documents.

1. **OPEN** a new, blank Word document.
2. Use the Word Help button to get more information about creating a custom theme.
3. Choose a custom set of colors, fonts, and/or effects that you feel would be a good choice for Tech Terrace Real Estate.
4. **SAVE** the theme as ***custom_xxx*** (where xxx are your initials).
5. Key a short paragraph explaining what colors, fonts, or effects you chose. Format the paragraph with your custom theme.
6. **SAVE** the document as ***custom_theme*** and **CLOSE** the file.

   LEAVE Word open for the next project.

Project 2-6: Customizing an Envelope

Your sister needs to print an envelope for an invitation she will create and mail, but she is not as familiar with the process as you are. She has a particular size envelope and wants a certain font. She asks you to help set up the envelope, add it to a document, and be sure it prints correctly.

1. **OPEN** a new, blank Word document.
2. Create an envelope with the following information:

   Delivery address:

   Beth Patterson
   211 Spring Road
   Kearney, NE 68845

   Return address:

   Carole Bass
   14451 Cypress Lane
   Garden City, KS 67846
3. Change the format of the delivery address to **Comic Sans MS, bold, size 12.**
4. Change the format of the return address to **Comic Sans MS, regular, size 10.**
5. Set the envelope size to **Size 6¾ (3⅝ X 6½).**
6. Add the envelope to the document so that your sister can create the invitation later. Do not save the return address as the default.
7. Print just the envelope.
8. **SAVE** the document as ***invitation_envelope*** and then **CLOSE** the file.

   CLOSE Word.

INTERNET READY

You began this lesson by creating a business letter from scratch. Now you will use those skills to write a cover letter for your resume in which you request an interview for the office manager position at Tech Terrace Real Estate. Use web search tools to find out what information should be contained in a cover letter and how to format it. The OWL at Purdue is a good online source for writing help. Print the letter and an envelope or label to go with it.

Workplace Ready

Creating Mailing Labels in Word

Gone are the days of wasting valuable time handwriting addresses on envelopes for large mailings. Today, Word provides the tools you need to quickly and easily create mailing labels in a variety of sizes. Whether you're mailing a single letter or mass mailing more than a hundred letters, all you need is a computer, a printer, and Word's Mailings options to produce your own personalized labels.

Imagine that you are starting a corporate event planning business. You have compiled a list of potential clients and would like to send a letter to each introducing your business and the services you can provide. You know that first impressions are critical, and you want to project a professional image in your mailing. After looking into ordering preprinted business envelopes, you decide that these just do not fit within your business' limited startup budget. Although you could handwrite your return address on each envelope, along with the potential client's mailing address, this would definitely not give the first impression you want to achieve. You decide that using Word to create your own return address and mailing labels will save you both valuable time and money.

Word provides specific sizes for several different label brands, or you can choose to create a custom-size sheet of labels. With a quick trip to your local office supply store, you purchase the labels you need and are ready to get started.

First, you can create and print return address labels to use on all of your business correspondence. With Word, there's no need to type your address on each label individually. Instead, you can simply type the address once, then choose to have this address repeated on every label.

If you are preparing to send out a mass mailing, you can type each address directly into Word, or you can choose to import addresses from a database. Word can pull the addresses directly from the database file to create the mailing labels. You can even choose to import addresses from your Outlook address book.

With a little help from Word, you can produce professional, high-quality mailings on a small business budget.

3 Character Formatting

LESSON SKILL MATRIX

Skills	Matrix Skill	Skill Number
Choosing Fonts and Font Sizes	Format characters	2.1.3
Applying Special Character Attributes	Format characters	2.1.3
Changing Case	Format characters	2.1.3
Highlighting Text	Format characters	2.1.3
Copying Character Formatting with the Format Painter	Format characters	2.1.3
Removing Character Formatting	Format characters	2.1.3
Applying a Style	Apply styles	2.1.1
Modifying a Style	Create and modify styles	2.1.2

With more than 20 million members and 2,600 facilities, the YMCA (Y) is the nation's largest community service organization. The health and fitness programs offered at the Y include group exercise for adults and youth as well as personal fitness programs. The staff and volunteers at the Y need to create various types of documents for announcing and advertising programs throughout the year as well as organizing and registering members for participation in the programs. Microsoft Word is a great tool for creating all sorts of documents easily and quickly. In this lesson, you will learn how to format text manually and with Quick Styles to create a document that describes the group exercise classes offered at the YMCA.

KEY TERMS

character
character styles
font
paragraph styles
point size

Software Orientation

The Font Group

As you learn to format text, it is important to become familiar with the group of commands you will use. The Font group, shown in Figure 3-1, is displayed in the Home tab of the ribbon. It contains most of the commands you will need to format characters in this lesson.

Figure 3-1

The Font group

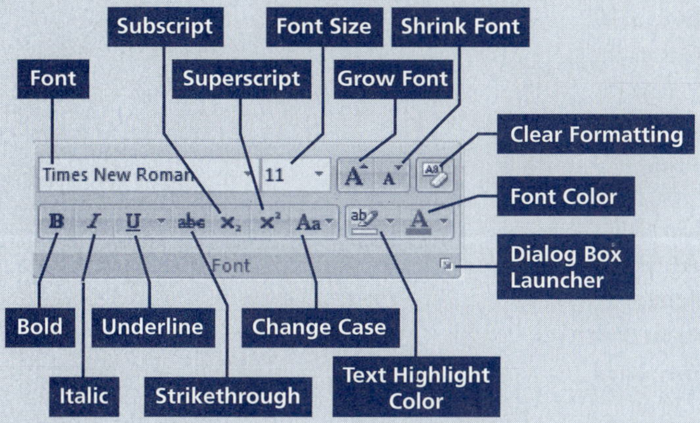

The Font group contains commands for changing the appearance of text.

Manually Formatting Characters

THE BOTTOM LINE Formatting characters makes your text more appealing and more readable.

Choosing Fonts and Font Sizes

Microsoft Word has a variety of fonts and font sizes to help you communicate your intended message in a document, whether it is casual for your personal life or formal for the workplace.

CHANGE FONTS AND FONT SIZES

OPEN the ***class_descriptions*** document from the data files for this lesson.

CD The ***class_descriptions*** document is available on the companion CD-ROM.

1. Select *Preston Creek Family YMCA*.
2. In the **Font** group of the **Home** tab, click the downward-pointing arrow on the **Font** menu. The menu appears as shown in Figure 3-2.

Figure 3-2

The Font menu

3. Scroll down the list and position the mouse pointer on **Arial**. Notice that as you point to each font in the list, the selected text changes with a live preview of what your text would look like with each different font.
4. Click **Arial**.
5. With the text still selected, click the arrow on the **Font Size** menu. The menu appears, as shown in Figure 3-3.

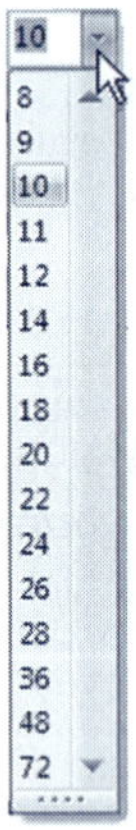

Figure 3-3

The Font Size menu

6. Click **18**.
7. Select *Group Exercise Class Descriptions*.
8. Click the **Font** menu and click **Arial**.
9. With the text still selected, click the **Font Size** menu and click **14**.
10. Select the remainder of text in the document. Point to the selected text to display the Mini toolbar. Click the **Font** menu on the Mini toolbar and choose **Calibri** (see Figure 3-4).

Figure 3-4

The Font menu on the Mini toolbar

11. With text still selected, click the **Font Size** menu on the Mini toolbar and choose **12**.

12. Click in a blank area of the document to remove the selection.

13. Select *Preston Creek Family YMCA*. In the **Font** group, click the **Grow Font** button to increase the size of the text. Notice that each time you click it, the number in the Font Size menu changes.

14. Click **Grow Font** two more times until the point size is 24.

15. Save the document as ***classes***.

PAUSE. LEAVE the document open to use in the next exercise.

A ***character*** is any single letter, number, symbol, or punctuation mark. Select a character to change its format.

A ***font*** is a set of characters that have the same design. Each font has a unique name.

Font sizes are measured in points. ***Point size*** refers to the height of characters, with one point equaling approximately 1/72 of an inch. Point sizes range from the very small 8-point size to 72 points or higher. Select text to change its font or size. Here are a few examples of fonts and sizes.

This is an example of Garamond 10 point.

This is an example of Arial 14 point.

This is an example of Juice ITC 18 point.

TAKE NOTE*

Some fonts, such as Times, have tiny lines at the ends of characters, called *serifs*. Sans serif fonts, like Calibri, don't have the lines. Serif fonts are usually more suitable for large amounts of text.

The Font group in the Home tab contains the Font menu for changing the Font, and the Font Size menu for changing its size. You can also access these commands on the Mini toolbar. The shortcut menu also has the Font command, which opens the Font dialog box.

Another way to change the size of text is to select it and click the Grow Font button to increase the size of a font, or click the Shrink Font button to decrease the size.

Applying Special Character Attributes

In addition to changing the font and font size, you can also change the appearance of characters to give them special emphasis.

APPLY SPECIAL CHARACTER ATTRIBUTES

USE the document that is open from the previous exercise.

1. Select the title of the document, *Preston Creek Family YMCA*. In the **Font** group, click the **Bold** button.

ANOTHER WAY You can also use the keyboard to apply bold. Select text and press **Ctrl+B**.

2. Select the subtitle, *Group Exercise Class Descriptions*, and click the **Italic** button.

ANOTHER WAY You can also use the keyboard to apply italics. Select text and press **Ctrl+I**.

3. Select *Active Older Adults* and click the **Bold** button.
4. With the text still selected, click the **Underline** button.

ANOTHER WAY You can also use the keyboard to apply underline. Select text and press **Ctrl+U**.

5. With text still selected, click the arrow beside the **Underline** button. A menu of underlining choices appears, as shown in Figure 3-5.

Figure 3-5

The Underline menu

6. Click **Thick Underline**, the third line down in the menu.
7. Select the title, *Preston Creek Family YMCA*. In the Font group, click the **Dialog Box Launcher**. The Font dialog box appears, as shown in Figure 3-6.

Figure 3-6

The Font dialog box

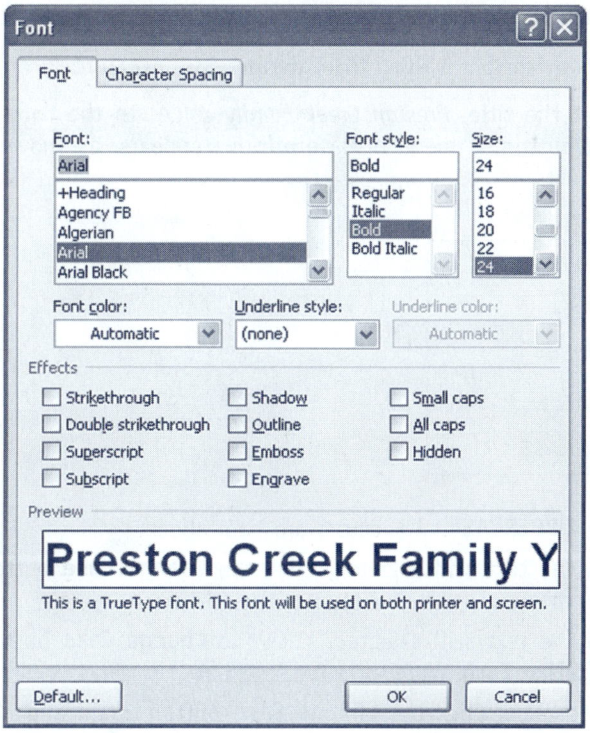

8. In the Effects section, click the **Outline** box to insert a checkmark.
9. Click the arrow on the **Font Color** menu. A menu of colors appears. Click **Red** from the Standard Colors section at the bottom.

ANOTHER WAY You can also click the Font Color button on the ribbon to launch a menu of colors you can use to change the color of text.

10. Click **OK**.
11. In the Font group, click the **Dialog Box Launcher** again. In the Font dialog box, click the **Outline** box to remove the checkmark. Click **OK**.
12. **SAVE** the document.

PAUSE. LEAVE the document open to use in the next exercise.

The Font group in the Home tab includes the commands for changing the style of text—bold, italic, and underline. You learned that applying any of these commands gives text special emphasis. You can use one at a time, such as **Bold**, or use two, such as **Bold Underline**. Just select the text you want to change and click the command in the Font group. You can also use the Bold and Italic commands on the Mini toolbar.

The Font dialog box has more options for formatting characters. You can change the Font, Font style, and Font size. In addition, you can specify a Font color, underline style, and a variety of effects, such as small caps, strikethrough, superscript, and shadow. Click the Dialog Box Launcher in the Font Group to display the Font dialog box.

Changing Case

When you need to change the case of text, Word provides several case options and an easy way to choose the one you want.

CHANGE CASE

USE the document that is open from the previous exercise.

1. Select the title, *Preston Creek Family YMCA*. In the Font group, click the **Change Case** button. A menu of case options appears, as shown in Figure 3-7.

Figure 3-7

The Change Case menu

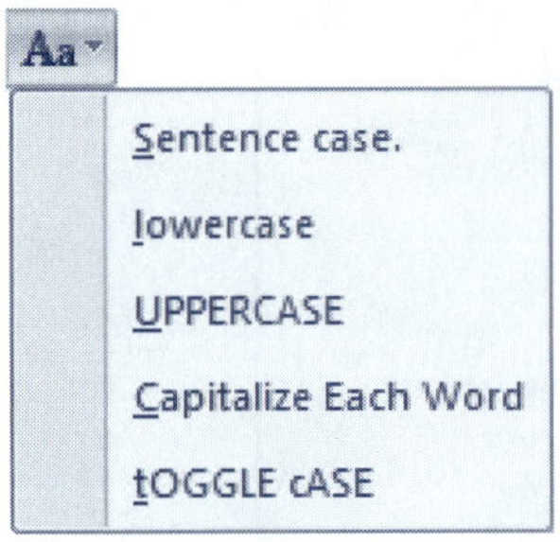

2. Click **UPPERCASE**. All letters are capitalized.
3. With the text still selected, click the **Change Case** button again and click **lowercase**.
4. With the text still selected, click the **Change Case** button again and click **Capitalize Each Word**.
5. Select *Ymca*. Click the **Change Case** button again and choose **UPPERCASE**.
6. Click in a blank area of the document to deselect the text.
7. **SAVE** the document.

PAUSE. LEAVE the document open to use in the next exercise.

The Change Case menu in the Font group has five options for changing the capitalization of text:

- Sentence case: capitalizes the first word in each sentence
- Lowercase: changes all characters to lowercase
- UPPERCASE: changes all characters to caps
- Capitalize Each Word: capitalizes the first character of each word
- tOGGLE cASE: changes each character to its opposite case

In the Effects section of the Font dialog box, you can change selected text to all caps or small caps.

Highlighting Text

Sometimes you might really want text to be noticed quickly. The Highlighting tool in the Font group lets you do just that.

HIGHLIGHT TEXT

USE the document that is open from the previous exercise.

1. In the **Font** group, click the **Text Highlight Color** button. Highlighting is turned on and the pointer changes to a highlighter pen icon.
2. Under *Core Express*, select the last sentence, *This new class is open to all fitness levels!* When you release the mouse button, the text is highlighted.
3. Click the **Text Highlight Color** button again to turn off Highlighting.
4. Select the text again. Click the arrow beside the **Text Highlight Color** button. A menu of colors appears, as shown in Figure 3-8. Click **Turquoise**. Notice the highlight color in the text and the **Text Highlight Color** button in the ribbon have changed to turquoise.

Figure 3-8

The Text Highlight Color menu

5. Select the text again. Click the **Text Highlight Color** button again to remove the highlight color.
6. **SAVE** the document.

PAUSE. LEAVE the document open to use in the next exercise.

You have just learned to use the Text Highlight Color button in the Font group to highlight text, making it look like it was marked with a highlighting pen. Click the Text Highlight Color button to turn on highlighting. Click and drag across the text you want to highlight. When you're finished, click the Text Highlight Color button again to turn off highlighting.

CERTIFICATION READY?
How do you format characters?
2.1.3

You can also select text first and click the Text Highlight Color button to apply yellow highlighting. If you'd like a different highlight color, click the arrow to display a menu of colors.

To remove highlighting, select the highlighted text and choose No Color from the Text Highlight Color menu.

Copying and Removing Formatting

THE BOTTOM LINE

Formatting text often requires copying formats or removing formats in the process of getting the look and feel you want. The Format Painter will help you copy formats to use in other areas of the document. And if you ever need to remove formatting, the Clear Formatting button will do it for you.

Using the Format Painter

When you find a tool that saves time and makes your work easier, it becomes invaluable. The Format Painter is such a tool. You can use it to copy formatting and apply it in other places, making document formatting easier and faster.

USE THE FORMAT PAINTER

USE the document that is open from the previous exercise.

1. Select the *Active Older Adults* heading.
2. On the Home tab, in the Clipboard group, click the **Format Painter** button. The pointer changes to a paintbrush icon.
3. Select the next heading, *Boot Camp*. The copied format is applied and the Format Painter is turned off.
4. With **Boot Camp** still selected, double-click the **Format Painter** button. The mouse pointer becomes a paintbrush icon.
5. Select the next heading, *Cardio Combo*. The copied format is applied.
6. Select the next heading, *Cardio Kickboxing*. The copied format is applied.

7. Select the remaining headings to apply the copied format. When you are finished with the last heading, click the **Format Painter** button to turn it off.
8. **SAVE** the document.

PAUSE. LEAVE the document open to use in the next exercise.

ANOTHER WAY

The Format Painter button is also available on the Mini toolbar.

The Format Painter command in the Clipboard group lets you copy the attributes, or format, of text and apply those attributes to different text. Select the formatted text you want to copy and click the Format Painter button. The mouse pointer becomes a paintbrush icon. Now select the text where you want to apply the format and click.

You can double-click the Format Painter button to copy the format to multiple places.

Removing Formatting

When you are formatting documents, sometimes you need to try a few different options before you get the appearance you want.

USE THE CLEAR FORMATTING BUTTON

USE the document that is open from the previous exercise.

1. Select *Active Older Adults*. In the Font group, click the **Clear Formatting** button. Formatting is removed and the plain text remains.
2. Press and hold Ctrl and select *Boot Camp*. Still holding the Ctrl key, select the remaining headings using multi-selection and click the **Clear Formatting** button. Formatting is removed on all the remaining headings at once.
3. **SAVE** the document

PAUSE. LEAVE the document open to use in the next exercise.

X REF

Refer to Lesson 1 for more information regarding multi-selection.

The Clear Formatting button in the Font group lets you clear formatting from selected text. Select the text with the formatting you want to clear and click the Clear Formatting button.

Formatting Text with Styles

THE BOTTOM LINE

Word has included predefined Quick Styles you can use to format text. When your own formatting is not producing the results you want, you might try a Quick Style. You can also modify Quick Styles to suit your needs. As you get more familiar with using the styles and exploring what is available, you'll be able to use the styles to produce results more quickly.

Applying Styles

Word's Quick Styles has two kinds of styles—paragraph styles and character styles.

APPLY A STYLE

USE the document that is open from the previous exercise.

1. Select the *Active Older Adults* heading. In the Styles group, click **Heading 1**. The style is applied to the heading.
2. Use multi-selection to select all the headings and then click **Heading 1**. The Heading 1 style is applied to all the headings.

3. In the second sentence of the *Active Older Adults* description, select *low-impact*. In the Styles group, click the **Dialog Box Launcher**. The Styles window appears, as shown in Figure 3-9.

Figure 3-9

Styles window

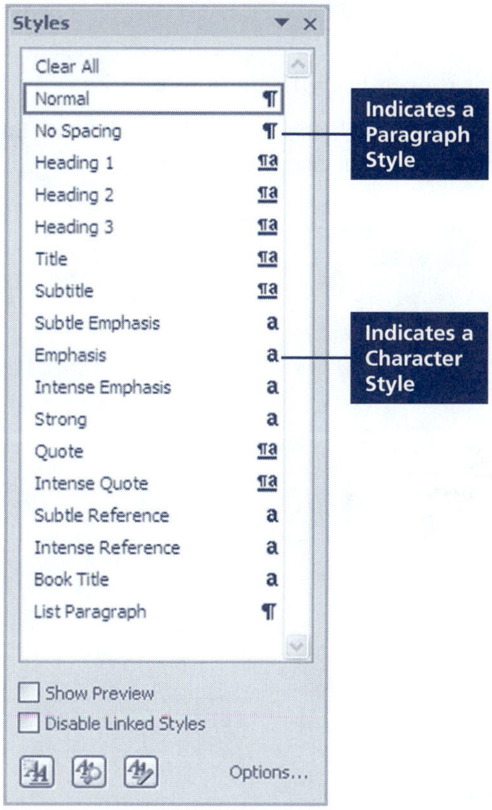

4. Point to **Subtle Emphasis**. Notice a screen tip appears and the lowercase *a* to the right of the style name becomes an arrow. Click **Subtle Emphasis**. The style is applied.
5. In the *Boot Camp* description, select *challenging* and click **Subtle Emphasis** in the Styles window.
6. In the *Core Express* description, select *strengthen* and click **Subtle Emphasis** in the Styles window.
7. In the *Indoor Cycling* description, select *high-energy* and click **Subtle Emphasis** in the Styles window.
8. In the *Yoga* description, select *breathing* and *relaxation* and click **Subtle Emphasis** in the Styles window.
9. **SAVE** the document.

PAUSE. LEAVE the document open to use in the next exercise.

The Styles window lists the same Quick Styles as are displayed in the Styles Gallery. A paragraph mark to the right of the style name denotes a style created for paragraphs. When you choose ***paragraph styles***, the formats are applied to all the text in the paragraph where your insertion point is located, whether or not you have it all selected.

Character styles have a lowercase letter *a* beside them. ***Character styles*** are applied to individual characters or words that you have selected within a paragraph rather than affecting the entire paragraph.

CERTIFICATION READY?
How do you modify a style?
2.1.1

Sometimes, a style can be used for either a paragraph or characters. These linked styles have a paragraph symbol as well as a lowercase *a* beside them. Select the text to which you want to apply a linked style.

When you point to a style in the list, a screen tip displays the style's properties.

Modifying Styles

When the style you have selected needs a little tweaking, Word lets you modify it.

MODIFY A STYLE

USE the document that is open from the previous exercise.

1. In the Styles Window, click the arrow to the right of **Subtle Emphasis** to display the Subtle Emphasis menu, shown in Figure 3-10.

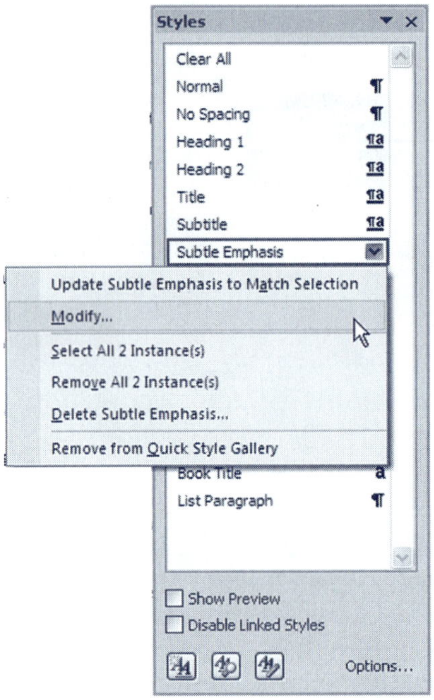

Figure 3-10
Subtle Emphasis dropdown menu

2. Click **Modify**. The Modify Style dialog box appears, as shown in Figure 3-11.

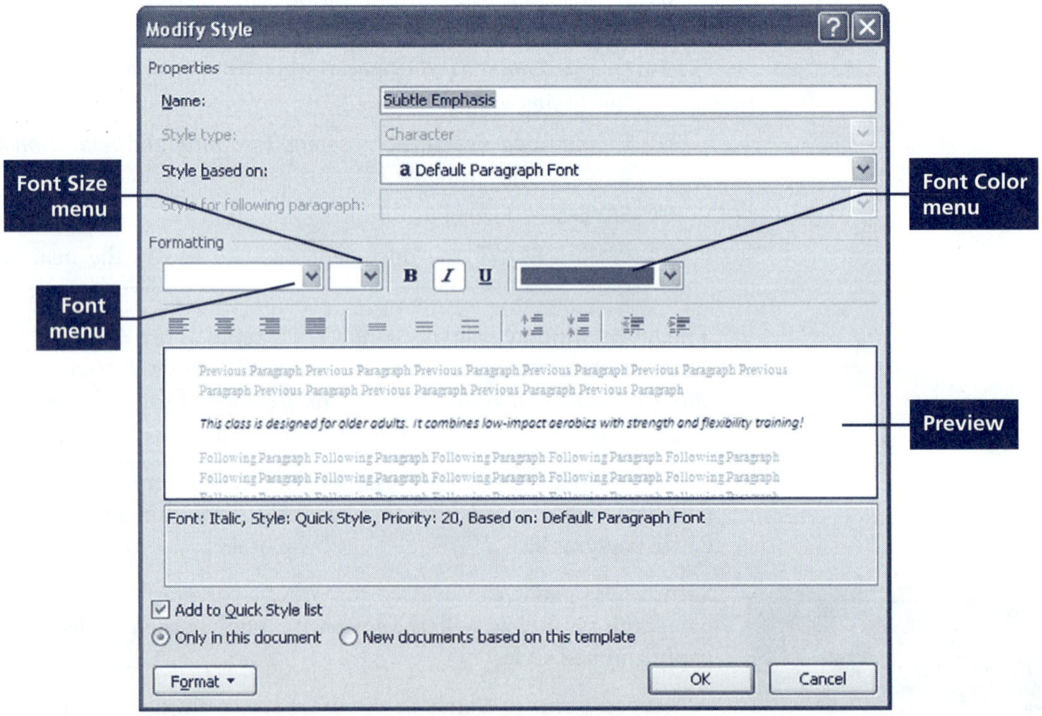

Figure 3-11
Modify Style dialog box

3. Click the **Bold** button.
4. Click the **Font Color** menu and click **Red** in the Standard Colors section. Notice the preview in the dialog box changes.
5. Click **OK**.
6. Click the arrow beside **Heading 1** and click **Modify**.
7. Click the **Font Color** menu and choose **Red**.
8. Click the **Font Size** menu and click **12**.
9. Click **OK**. All the headings with the Heading 1 style are updated to the new color and size.
10. **SAVE** the document and **CLOSE** the file.

    STOP. CLOSE Word.

CERTIFICATION READY?
How do you modify a style?
2.1.2

You just learned that the Modify Style dialog box has basic formatting commands like the Font menu; Font size menu; bold, italic, and underline buttons; and Font color menu. When you modify paragraph fonts, you can also change alignment, indents, and spacing.

When you make a change, Word automatically renames the style, or you can give it a name yourself.

You can also click the box to Add to Quick Style list or Automatically Update. Click the button to use Only in this document or New documents based on this template.

SUMMARY SKILL MATRIX

In This Lesson You Learned	Matrix Skill	Skill Number
To choose fonts and font sizes	Format characters	2.1.3
To apply special character attributes	Format characters	2.1.3
To change case	Format characters	2.1.3
To highlight text	Format characters	2.1.3
To copy character formatting with the Format Painter	Format characters	2.1.3
To remove character formatting	Format characters	2.1.3
To apply a style	Apply styles	2.1.1
To modify a style	Create and modify styles	2.1.2

Knowledge Assessment

Matching

Match the term in Column 1 to its description in Column 2.

Column 1	Column 2
1. point size	**a.** a set of characters that have the same design
2. character	**b.** makes text look like it was marked with a highlighting pen
3. font	**c.** lets you copy the format of text and apply those attributes to different text
4. change case	**d.** tiny lines at the ends of characters
5. highlighting text	**e.** removes formatting from selected text, leaving plain text
6. Format Painter	**f.** increases the size of text
7. clear formatting	**g.** refers to the height of characters, with one point equaling approximately 1/72 of an inch.
8. serifs	**h.** formats are applied to individual characters or words that you have selected within a paragraph rather than affecting the entire paragraph
9. Grow Font button	**i.** any single letter, number, symbol, or punctuation mark
10. character style	**j.** refers to changing the capitalization of text

True / False

Circle T if the statement is true or F if the statement is false.

T | F **1.** Toggle Case changes each character to its opposite case.
T | F **2.** Applying bold to text gives it special emphasis.
T | F **3.** The Format Painter is on the Mini toolbar.
T | F **4.** The Font dialog box has commands for highlighting text.
T | F **5.** The Shrink Font button increases point size.
T | F **6.** The Clear Formatting button clears text from one location and lets you apply it in another location.
T | F **7.** You can only highlight text with the colors yellow or turquoise.
T | F **8.** To apply a Quick Style, select the text and click the style you want.
T | F **9.** You cannot modify Quick Styles.
T | F **10.** The Font dialog box has options for adding effects such as strikethrough, superscript, and shadow.

Competency Assessment

Project 3-1: Sales Letter

Star Bright Satellite Radio will be sending sales letters to people who have just purchased new vehicles equipped with their radios. Add some finishing formatting touches to this letter.

GET READY. Launch Word if it is not already running.

1. **OPEN** *letter* from the data files for this lesson.

CD The ***letter*** document is available on the companion CD-ROM.

2. In the second paragraph, select the first sentence, *Star Bright Satellite....*
3. Click **Bold**.
4. In the second paragraph, select the fifth sentence, *Star Bright also broadcasts....*
5. Click the **Italic** button.
6. In the fourth paragraph, select the first sentence, *Star Bright is only $10.95 a month.*
7. Click **Bold**.
8. In the second sentence of the fourth paragraph, select *Subscribe*.
9. Click the **Change Case** button and click **UPPERCASE**.
10. With the word still selected, click **Bold**.
11. **SAVE** the document as *sales_letter* and **CLOSE** the file.

LEAVE Word open for the next project.

Project 3-2: YMCA Flyer

The YMCA's sports program needs volunteer coaches for youth sports. They ask for your help in creating a flyer.

1. **OPEN** *volunteercoaches* from the data files for this lesson.

CD The ***volunteercoaches*** document is available on the companion CD-ROM.

2. Select *We Need You!* Click the **Font** menu and click **Arial Black**.
3. Click the **Font Size** menu and click **48**.
4. Select *Volunteer Coaches Needed For Youth Sports*. Click the **Font** menu and click **Arial Black**.
5. Click the **Font Size** menu and click **18**.
6. Select *Sports include* and the four lines below it. Click the **Font** menu and click **Calibri**. Click the **Font Size** menu and click **18**.
7. Select the four sports listed and click **Italic**.
8. Select the three lines of contact information, beginning with *Contact Patrick Edelstein...* Click the **Font** menu and click **Arial Black**. Click the **Font Size** menu and click **11**.
9. Select *YMCA*. Click the **Font Color** button and click **Red** from the Standard Colors section.

10. With the text still selected, click **Bold**. Click the **Font** menu and click **Arial Black**. Click the **Font Size** menu and choose **36**.
11. **SAVE** the document as ***volunteers*** and **CLOSE** the file.

    LEAVE Word open for the next project.

Proficiency Assessment

Project 3-3: Coffee Shop Flyer

The Grand Street Coffee Shop has decided to install a wireless Internet service for customers. To announce the news, create a flyer for distribution in the coffee shop.

1. **OPEN** ***wireless*** from the data files for this lesson.

CD The ***wireless*** document is available on the companion CD-ROM.

2. Follow the directions in Figure 3-12 to format the document.

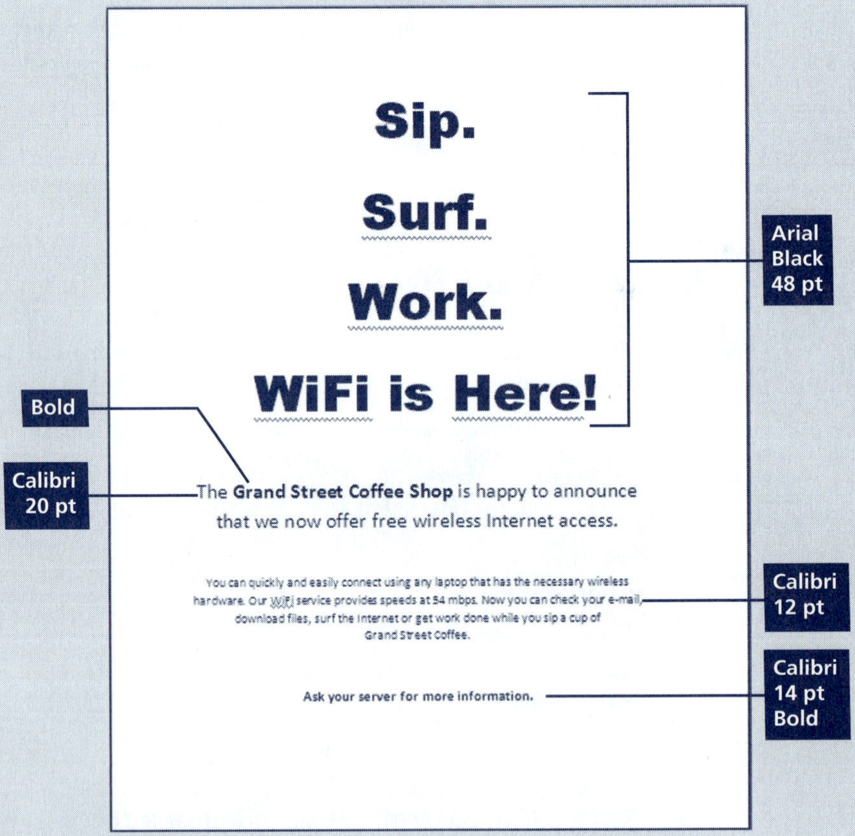

Figure 3-12

Formatting instructions for WiFi document

3. **SAVE** the document as ***WiFi*** and **CLOSE** the file.

   LEAVE Word open for the next project.

Project 3-4: Nutritional Information

Customers of the Grand Street Coffee Shop have asked about the nutritional makeup of some of the blended coffee items on the menu. Format a document you can post or make available for customers to take with them.

1. **OPEN** ***nutritioninfo*** from the data files for this lesson.

CD The ***nutritioninfo*** document is available on the companion CD-ROM.

2. Select *Grand Street Coffee Shop*. On the **Font** menu, click **Juice ITC**.
3. With the text still selected, change the font size to **28**.
4. Click the **Font Color** menu and click **Dark Blue** from the Standard Colors section.
5. Select *Nutritional Information*.
6. In the Font group, click the **Dialog Box Launcher**. Click the **Small Caps** box and change the font size to **12** and the font color to **Dark Blue**. Click **OK**.
7. Select *Brewed Coffee* and click **Title** from the Quick Styles Gallery. In the Styles group, click the **Dialog Box Launcher**.
8. In the Styles window, click the downward-pointing arrow on the **Title** style. Choose **Modify**.
9. In the Modify Style dialog box, change the font color to **Dark Blue** and the font size to **14**. Click **OK**.
10. Select the three lines of text under the *Brewed Coffee* heading. Click **Intense Emphasis** on the Styles Gallery.
11. Apply the **Title** style to the remaining headings, and apply the **Intense Emphasis** style to the remaining text.
12. **SAVE** the document as ***nutrition*** and **CLOSE** the file.

LEAVE Word open for the next project.

Mastery Assessment

Project 3-5: Resume

Your friend Mike asks you to help him with his resume. Format the resume so that it looks professional.

1. **OPEN** ***resume*** from the data files for this lesson.

CD The ***resume*** document is available on the companion CD-ROM.

2. Format the resume to the following specifications:
   - Format Mike's name with Cambria, 24 pt., bold.
   - Change his address, phone, and email information to Times New Roman 9 pt.
   - For the main headings, use the Emphasis style with Cambria font size 16 bold and italic.
   - For job titles, use Times New Roman 12 pt. small caps, bold.
   - Italicize the sentence or sentences before the bulleted lists.
   - For places and years of employment, as well as the college name, use Times New Roman 12 pt. small caps.

3. **SAVE** the document as ***mzresume*** and **CLOSE** the file.
   LEAVE Word open for the next project.

Project 3-6: References

Your friend Mike liked your work on his resume so much that he asks you to format his reference list with the same design as his resume.

1. **OPEN** ***references*** from the data files for this lesson.

CD The ***references*** document is available on the companion CD-ROM.

2. Refer to the resume you formatted in Project 3-5. Format the list of references using the same fonts, styles, sizes, and attributes as in his resume, so that they look consistent when compared side by side.
3. **SAVE** the document as ***mzreferences*** and **CLOSE** the file.
   CLOSE Word.

INTERNET READY

Search the Internet for information on the national YMCA or your local YMCA. Create a document that lists some of the programs available. The list will be mailed with a letter soliciting donations and volunteers for the Y, so make sure to choose fonts, sizes, and effects that have an appropriate look and feel. Create a heading for each program in the list with a description underneath.

Paragraph Formatting

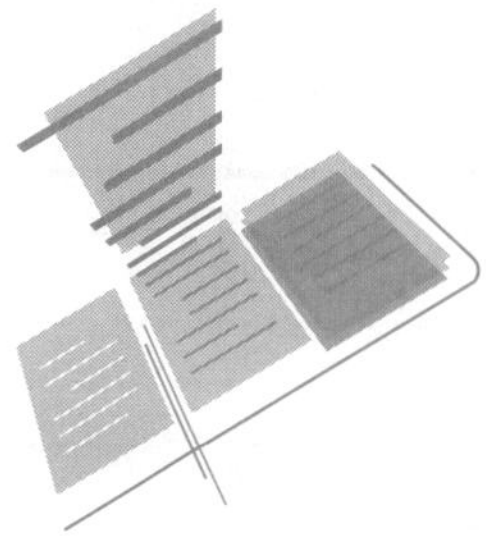

4

LESSON SKILL MATRIX

Skills	Matrix Skill	Skill Number
Setting Indents	Format paragraphs	2.1.4
Changing Alignment	Format paragraphs	2.1.4
Setting the Line Spacing Within a Paragraph	Format paragraphs	2.1.4
Setting the Spacing Around a Paragraph	Format paragraphs	2.1.4
Creating a Numbered List	Format paragraphs Create tables and lists	2.1.4, 4.2.1
Creating a Bulleted List	Format paragraphs Create tables and lists	2.1.4, 4.2.1
Shading a Paragraph	Format paragraphs	2.1.4
Placing a Border Around a Paragraph	Format paragraphs	2.1.4
Using the Tabs Dialog Box	Set and clear tabs	2.1.5
Setting the Tabs on the Ruler	Set and clear tabs	2.1.5
Clearing Tabs	Set and clear tabs	2.1.5
Clearing Formats from a Paragraph	Format paragraphs	2.1.4

You are employed at Books and Beyond, an independent used book store. Your responsibilities include receiving and assessing used books, issuing trade credit, stocking the bookshelves, and placing special orders. Because you are computer literate, your job also involves creating and modifying documents needed at the store. Currently, you are working on the employee handbook. In this lesson, you will learn how to use Word's formatting features to change the appearance of paragraphs. You will learn how to set indents, change alignment and line spacing, create numbered and bulleted lists, and use shading and borders. You will also learn how to use tabs and clear the formatting from paragraphs.

KEY TERMS

first-line indent
hanging indent
horizontal alignment
indent
leaders
line spacing
negative indent
non-printing characters
paragraph spacing
vertical alignment

Software Orientation

Indents and Spacing Tab in Paragraph Dialog Box

When formatting the alignment, indentation, and spacing of paragraphs, you will frequently utilize the Paragraph dialog box. The Indents and Spacing tab is shown in Figure 4-1.

Figure 4-1

Indents and Spacing tab of Paragraph dialog box

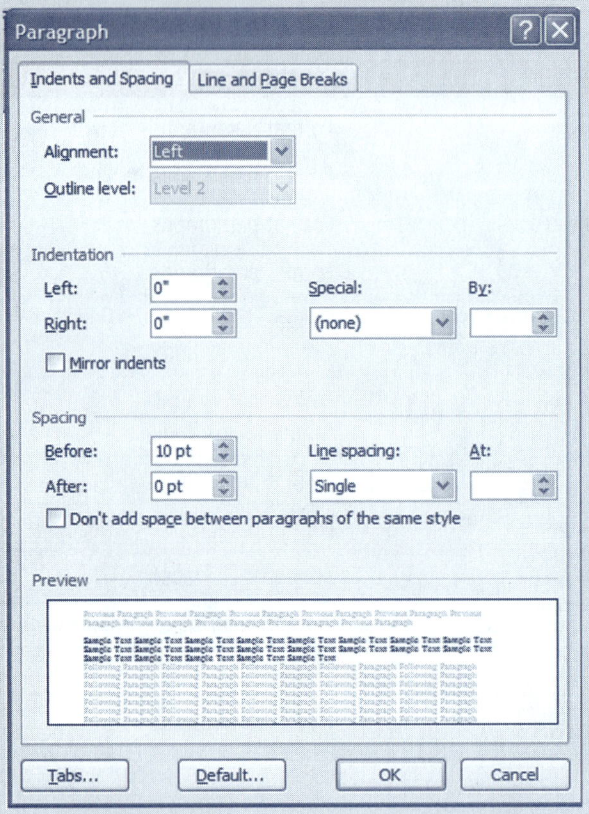

This tab of the Paragraph dialog box is used to make changes to the alignment, indentation, and spacing of paragraphs. Use this figure as a reference throughout this lesson as well as the rest of this book.

Manually Formatting Paragraphs

THE BOTTOM LINE

To apply paragraph formatting, place the insertion point anywhere in a paragraph. Word will apply any paragraph formats you chose to the entire paragraph. You cannot apply paragraph formatting to just a selection of the paragraph.

Setting Indents

Indents can be used to set paragraphs off from other text in your documents. There are various kinds of indents you can set, including first-line indents, hanging indents, and negative indents.

SET INDENTS

GET READY. Before you begin these steps, be sure to launch Microsoft Word.

CD

The *acknowledgement* document is available on the companion CD-ROM.

1. **OPEN** ***acknowledgement*** from the data files for this lesson.
2. Click to place the insertion point in the first paragraph.
3. On the Home tab, in the Paragraph group, click the **Dialog Box Launcher** to display the Paragraph dialog box. The **Indents and Spacing** tab should be selected.
4. In the Special list under Indentation, click **First line**. In the By box, the amount of space that you want the first line to be indented should be set to 0.5 inches.
5. Click **OK**.

ANOTHER WAY

Click to place the insertion point before the first line in the paragraph and drag the First Line Indent marker on the ruler (see Figure 4-2) to the place where you want the text to be indented.

6. Place the insertion point in the second paragraph.
7. On the horizontal ruler, drag the **Hanging Indent** marker to 0.5 inches, as shown in Figure 4-2.

Figure 4-2

Ruler with hanging indent marker

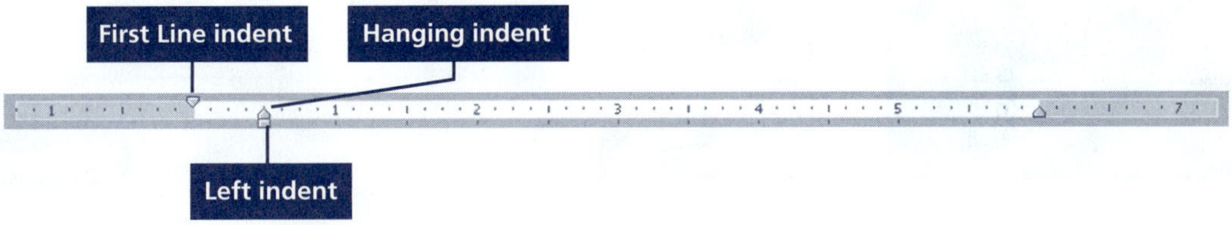

TROUBLESHOOTING

If the horizontal ruler is not visible along the top of the document, click the View Ruler button at the top of the vertical scrollbar to display it.

8. Place the insertion point in the third paragraph.
9. On the Page Layout tab, in the Paragraph group, click the upward-pointing arrow next to Indent Left five times to indent the left side of the paragraph by **0.5 inches**.
10. Click the **upward-pointing arrow** next to Indent Right five times to indent the right side of the paragraph by **0.5 inches**.

ANOTHER WAY

To indent the first line of a paragraph, click in front of the line and press Tab. To indent an entire paragraph, click in front of any line but the first line and click Tab.

11. Place the insertion point in the last paragraph.
12. On the ruler, drag the **Left Indent** marker into the left margin at –0.5 inches, as shown in Figure 4-3.

Figure 4-3

Ruler with negative indent

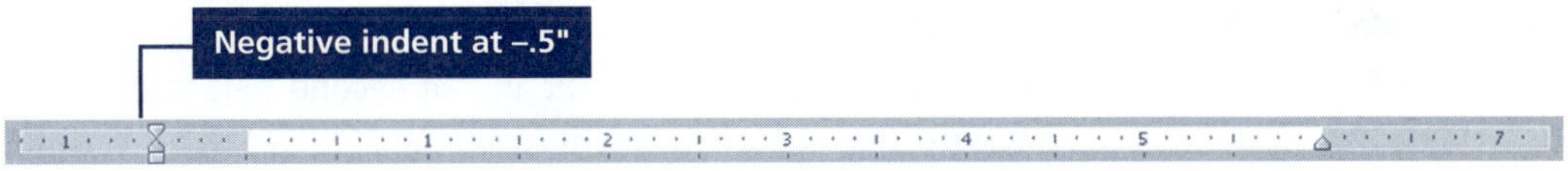

13. Your document should look similar to Figure 4-4.

Figure 4-4
Document with indents

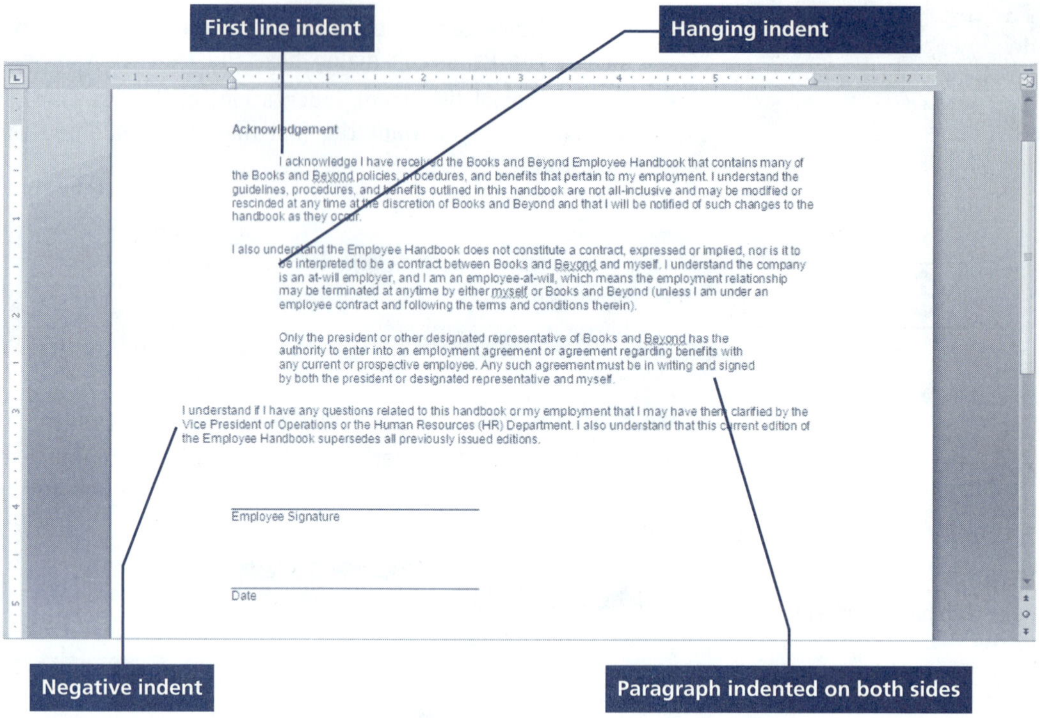

CERTIFICATION READY?
How do you format paragraphs?
2.1.4

14. SAVE the document as ***handbook_acknowledgement*** and close the file.

PAUSE. LEAVE Word open for the next exercise.

An ***indent*** is the space between a paragraph and the document's left and/or right margin. In this activity, you learned about various types of indents. A ***first-line indent*** is where the first line of a paragraph indents more than the following lines. A ***hanging indent*** is created when the first full line of text in a paragraph is not indented, but the following lines are. Hanging indents are common in legal documents or reference lists. A ***negative indent*** is when the paragraph extends into the left margin. You can also increase or decrease the indentation of a whole paragraph from the left or right margin, or both. This is often done to set off a long quotation.

Changing Alignment

Depending on the document you are creating, you may need to change the horizontal or vertical alignment of text. Alignment refers to how text is positioned between the margins.

CHANGE ALIGNMENT

CD
The ***introduction*** document is available on the companion CD-ROM.

1. **OPEN** ***introduction*** from the data files for this lesson.
2. Click to place the insertion point in the first paragraph.
3. On the Home tab, in the Paragraph group, click the **Justify** button (shown in Table 4-1).
4. Place the insertion point in the second paragraph.
5. On the Home tab, in the Paragraph group, click the **Dialog Box Launcher** to display the Paragraph dialog box. The **Indents and Spacing** tab should be selected.
6. In the Alignment list under General, click **Centered** and then click **OK**.

7. Place the insertion point in the third paragraph.
8. Press Ctrl+R to align the text on the right. Your document should appear similar to Figure 4-5.

Figure 4-5

Document with various horizontal alignments

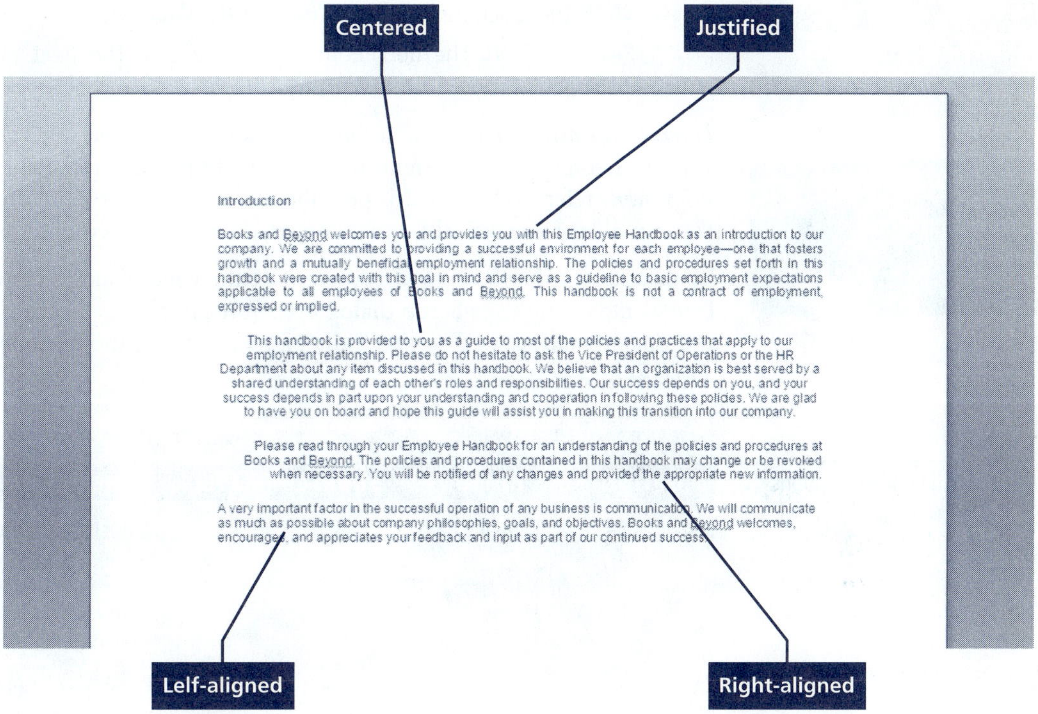

9. On the Page Layout tab, in the Page Setup group, click the **Dialog Box Launcher** and then click the Layout tab, shown in Figure 4-6.

Figure 4-6

Layout tab of Page Setup dialog box

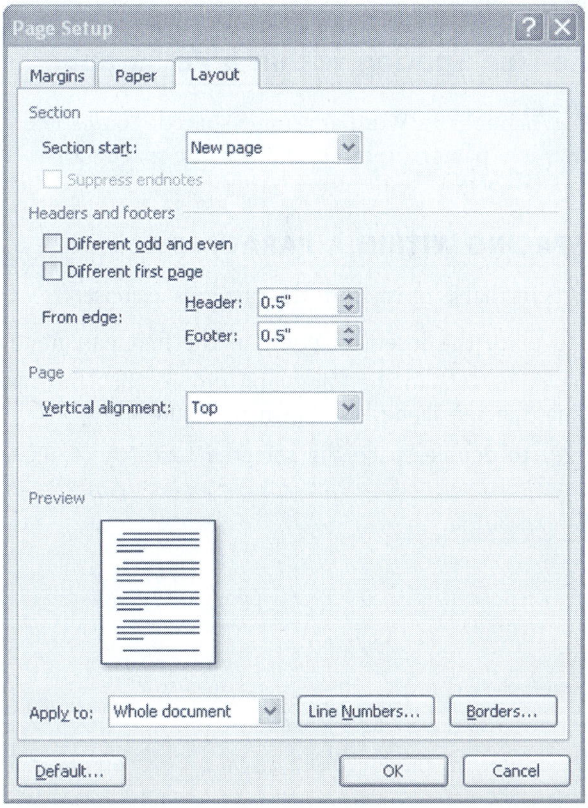

X REF

Vertical alignment is often used to create a cover page. You will learn more about quickly and easily creating a cover page in Lesson 6.

CERTIFICATION READY?
How do you format paragraphs?
2.1.4

10. In the Vertical alignment list under Page, click **Center**.
11. In the Apply To list under Preview, **Whole document** should be selected. You could also choose to apply the vertical alignment option from that point forward.
12. Click **OK**. All the text is centered on the page.
13. **SAVE** the document as ***handbook_introduction***.

    PAUSE. LEAVE the document open to use in the next exercise.

Horizontal alignment refers to how text is positioned between the left and right margins. You can left-align, center, right-align, or justify text using the alignment commands. ***Vertical alignment*** refers to how text is positioned between the top and bottom margins of the page. You can align text vertically at the top, at the bottom, centered on the page, or justified.

By default, text is left-aligned at the top of the page. You can change vertical alignment in the Layout tab of the Page Setup dialog box. You can change horizontal alignment in the Indents and Spacing tab of the Paragraph dialog box or using the buttons and shortcut keys shown in Table 4-1.

Table 4-1
Horizontal alignment options

Option	Button	Shortcut Keys	Description
Align Left		Ctrl+L	Lines up text flush with the left margin, leaving a ragged right edge
Align Right		Ctrl+R	Lines up text flush with the right margin, leaving a ragged left edge
Center		Ctrl+E	Centers text between the left and right margins, leaving ragged edges on both sides
Justify		Ctrl+J	Lines up text flush on both the left and right margins, adding extra space between words as necessary, for a clean look

Setting the Line Spacing within a Paragraph

By default, paragraphs in Word are single-spaced. You can change the amount of space between lines in a paragraph by setting the line spacing.

SET LINE SPACING WITHIN A PARAGRAPH

USE the document that is open from the previous exercise.

1. Click to place the insertion point in the first paragraph.
2. On the Home tab, in the Paragraph group, click the **Line Spacing** button to display the Line Spacing menu, as shown in Figure 4-7.
3. Click 2.0 to double-space the selected text.

Figure 4-7
Line Spacing menu

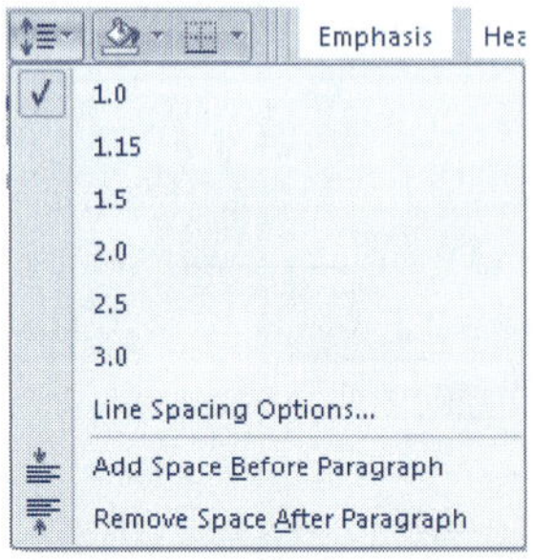

4. Place the insertion point in the second paragraph.
5. On the Home tab, in the Paragraph group, click the **Line Spacing** button to display the menu.
6. To set more precise spacing measurements, click Line Spacing Options to display the Indents and Spacing tab of the Paragraph dialog box.
7. In the Line Spacing list under Spacing, click **Exactly**. In the At list, click the **upward-pointing arrow** until it reads 14 pt.
8. Click **OK**.
9. **SAVE** the document.

PAUSE. LEAVE the document open to use in the next exercise.

CERTIFICATION READY?
How do you format paragraphs?
2.1.4

Line spacing is the amount of space between lines of text in a paragraph. The lines in a paragraph are single-spaced by default. Line spacing options available in the Indents and Spacing tab of the Paragraph dialog box are explained in Table 4-2.

Table 4-2
Line spacing options

Option	Description
Single	Default option that accommodates the largest font in that line, plus a small amount of extra space
1.5	One-and-one-half times the amount of space as single
Double	Twice as much space as single
At least	Sets the spacing at the minimum amount needed to fit the largest font on the line
Exactly	Sets the spacing at a fixed amount that Word does not adjust
Multiple	Sets the spacing at an amount that is increased or decreased from single spacing by a percentage that you specify e.g., Setting the line spacing to 1.3 will increase the space by 30%

Setting the Spacing around a Paragraph

By default, the space after a paragraph is slightly more than single-spaced lines. You can change the amount of space before or after a paragraph by setting the paragraph spacing.

SET SPACING AROUND A PARAGRAPH

USE the document that is open from the previous exercise.

1. Click to place the insertion point in the third paragraph.
2. On the Home tab, in the Paragraph group, click the **Dialog Box Launcher** to display the Paragraph dialog box. The **Indents and Spacing** tab should be selected.
3. In the Spacing section, click the **upward-pointing arrow** next to Before until it reads **24 pt**.
4. Click the **upward-pointing arrow** next to After until it reads **24 pt**.
5. Click **OK**.
6. With the insertion point still in the third paragraph, click the **Line Spacing** button in the Paragraph group to display the Line Spacing menu.
7. Click **Remove Space Before Paragraph**.
8. **SAVE** the document and **CLOSE** the file.

PAUSE. LEAVE Word open for the next exercise.

CERTIFICATION READY?
How do you format paragraphs?
2.1.4

Paragraph spacing is the amount of space above or below a paragraph. To increase or decrease paragraph spacing, click the Before and After upward-pointing or downward-pointing arrows in the Indents and Spacing tab of the Paragraph dialog box. You can also click the Line Spacing button in the Paragraph group and use the Remove Space Before Paragraph and Remove Space After Paragraph commands. If no space is currently before or after the selected paragraph, the commands will be Add Space Before Paragraph and Add Space After Paragraph.

Creating a Numbered List

You can quickly add numbers to existing lines of text to create a list, or Word can automatically create a numbered list as you key.

CREATE A NUMBERED LIST

CD

The ***alarm*** document is available on the companion CD-ROM.

1. **OPEN *alarm*** from the data files for this lesson.
2. Select the four sentences under the *Set Alarm* heading.
3. On the Home tab, in the Paragraph group, click the **Numbering** button (see Figure 4-8).
4. Click to place the insertion point at the end of the fourth numbered sentence.
5. Press **Enter**. Notice that Word automatically numbers the next line sequentially.
6. Key **Leave the premises immediately**.
7. Select the four sentences under the *Deactivate Alarm* heading.
8. On the Home tab, in the Paragraph group, click the **Numbering** button.
9. Select the numbered list under the *Set Alarm* heading.
10. To change the format of the numbered list, click the **downward-pointing arrow** next to the Numbering button to display the menu shown in Figure 4-8.

Figure 4-8

Number formatting options

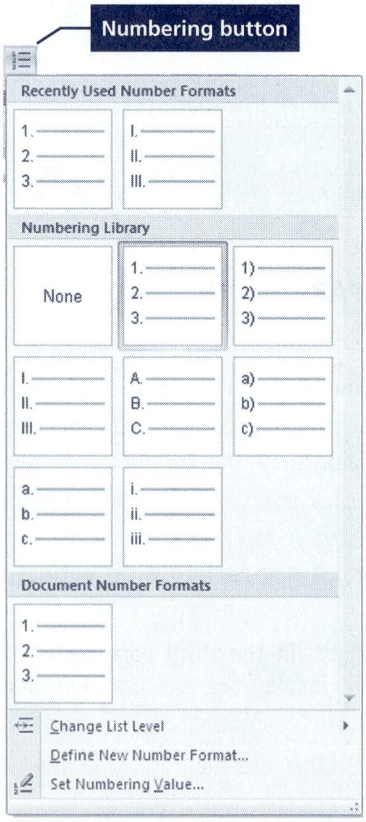

11. Notice that when you point your mouse to an option on the menu, the changes are previewed in your document. Click the last option on the first row in the Numbering Library.

TAKE NOTE*

To change the formatting of the numbers, click any number to select the entire list. If you select the text, the formatting of both the text and the numbering changes.

CERTIFICATION READY?
How do you format paragraphs?
2.1.4
How do you create tables and lists?
4.2.1

12. Select the numbered list under the *Deactivate Alarm* heading.
13. Click the **downward-pointing arrow** next to the Numbering button.
14. On the menu under Recently Used Number Formats, choose the same number format that you just applied.
15. **SAVE** the document as ***handbook_alarm***.

PAUSE. LEAVE the document open to use in the next exercise.

Numbers can be added to an already existing list or you can create a numbered list from scratch. To remove the numbers, select the list and then click the Numbers button. To change the format of a numbered list, select it and click the downward-pointing arrow next to the Numbering button.

TROUBLESHOOTING

If you key an asterisk (*) or a number one (1.), Word recognizes that you are trying to start a bulleted or numbered list and will automatically continue it. If you occasionally don't want the text you are keying to be turned into a list, you can undo a list by clicking the AutoCorrect Options button that appears.

To turn the feature off completely, click the Microsoft Office button, then choose Word Options, Proofing, AutoCorrect Options, and then the AutoFormat As You Type tab. Under Apply as You Type, select or clear the Automatic Bulleted Lists checkbox or the Automatic Numbered Lists checkbox.

Creating a Bulleted List

Bulleted lists are very similar to numbered lists. You can change existing lines of text to a bulleted list or Word can automatically create one as you key.

CREATE A BULLETED LIST

USE the document that is open from the previous exercise.

1. Select the two sentences below the phrase *Please keep in mind:*.
2. On the Home tab, in the Paragraph group, click the **Bullets** button.
3. Click to place the insertion point at the end of the second bulleted sentence.
4. Press **Enter**. Notice that Word automatically continues the bulleted list.
5. Key **If you do not know your four-digit code and password, please get it from the HR department**.
6. Select the entire bulleted list.
7. To change the format of the bulleted list, click the **downward-pointing arrow** next to the Bullets button to display the menu shown in Figure 4-9.

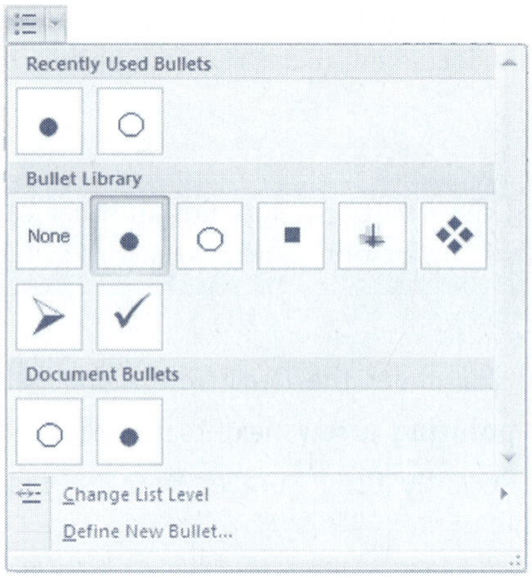

Figure 4-9

Bullet formatting options

TAKE NOTE* To change a bulleted list to a numbered list (or vice versa), select the list and then click either the Numbering or Bullets button.

8. Click the last option on the first row of the Bullets Library.
9. Your document should look similar to the one shown in Figure 4-10.

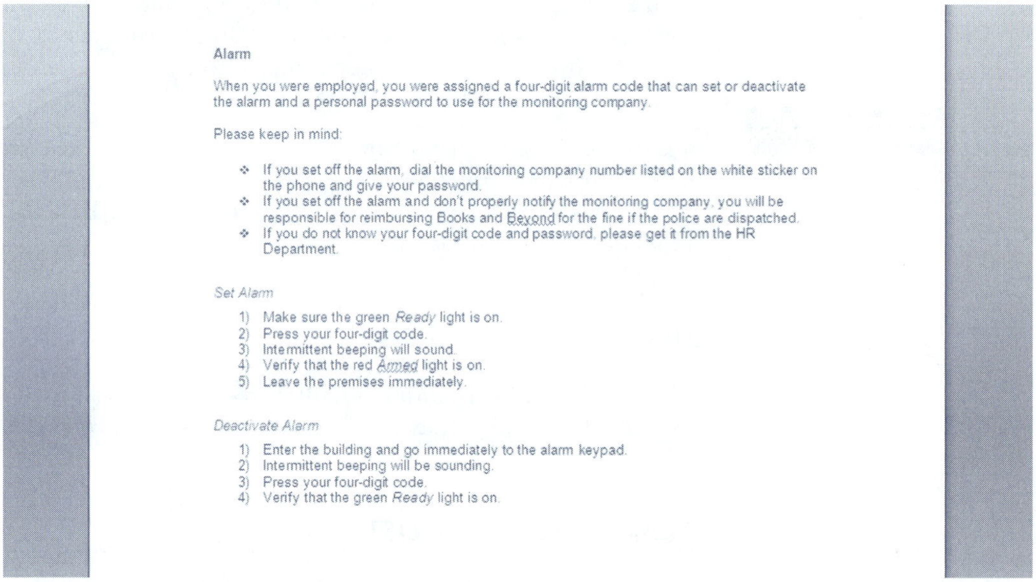
Alarm

When you were employed, you were assigned a four-digit alarm code that can set or deactivate the alarm and a personal password to use for the monitoring company.

Please keep in mind:

- If you set off the alarm, dial the monitoring company number listed on the white sticker on the phone and give your password.
- If you set off the alarm and don't properly notify the monitoring company, you will be responsible for reimbursing Books and Beyond for the fine if the police are dispatched.
- If you do not know your four-digit code and password, please get it from the HR Department.

Set Alarm

1) Make sure the green *Ready* light is on.
2) Press your four-digit code.
3) Intermittent beeping will sound.
4) Verify that the red *Armed* light is on.
5) Leave the premises immediately.

Deactivate Alarm

1) Enter the building and go immediately to the alarm keypad.
2) Intermittent beeping will be sounding.
3) Press your four-digit code.
4) Verify that the green *Ready* light is on.

Figure 4-10

Document with bulleted and numbered lists

CERTIFICATION READY?
How do you format paragraphs?
2.1.4
How do you create tables and lists?
4.2.1

10. **SAVE** the document and **CLOSE** the file.

PAUSE. LEAVE Word open for the next exercise.

Bullets can be added to an already existing list or you can create a bulleted list from scratch. To remove the bullets, select the list and then click the Bullets button. To change the format of a bulleted list, select it and click the downward-pointing arrow next to the Bullets button.

X REF You will learn more about working with lists and multilevel lists in Lesson 9.

Shading a Paragraph

You can use the Shading feature to color the background behind the selected text or paragraph.

SHADE A PARAGRAPH

CD The ***diversity*** document is available on the companion CD-ROM.

1. **OPEN** ***diversity*** from the data files for this lesson.
2. Click to place the insertion point in the first paragraph.
3. On the Home tab, in the Paragraph group, click the **downward-pointing arrow** next to the **Shading** button to display the menu shown in Figure 4-11.

Figure 4-11

Shading menu

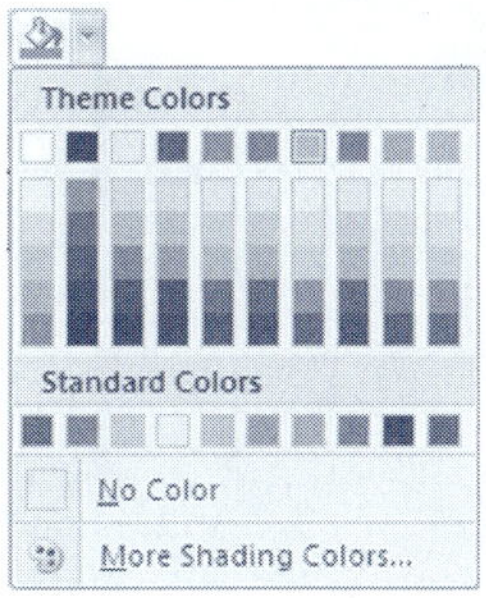

CERTIFICATION READY?
How do you format paragraphs?
2.1.4

4. In the Theme Colors palette, click the color on the third row down on the last column (Orange, Accent 6, Lighter 40%).
5. **SAVE** the document as ***handbook_diversity***.

PAUSE. LEAVE the document open to use in the next exercise.

If you want to apply the previously chosen shading to a paragraph, click the Shading button. To choose another color, click the downward-pointing arrow next to the Shading button, and you will be able to choose a color in the current theme or a standard color from the Shading menu. To remove shading, click No Color.

If you want more color choices, click More Colors to open the Colors dialog box, where you can choose standard colors in the Standard tab, shown in Figure 4-12. In the Custom tab, shown in Figure 4-13, you can create a custom color and even enter the exact RGB numbers if you know them.

Figure 4-12

Standard tab of Colors dialog box

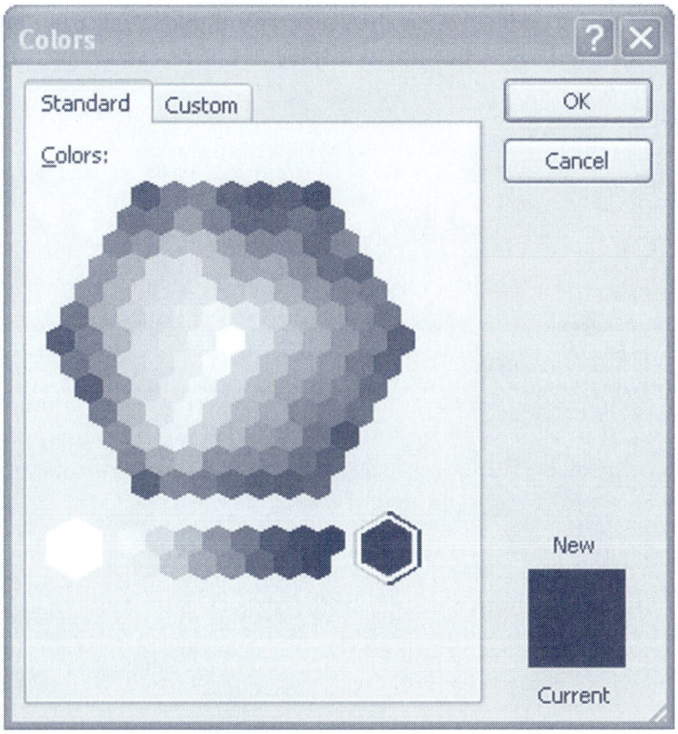

Figure 4-13

Custom tab of Colors dialog box

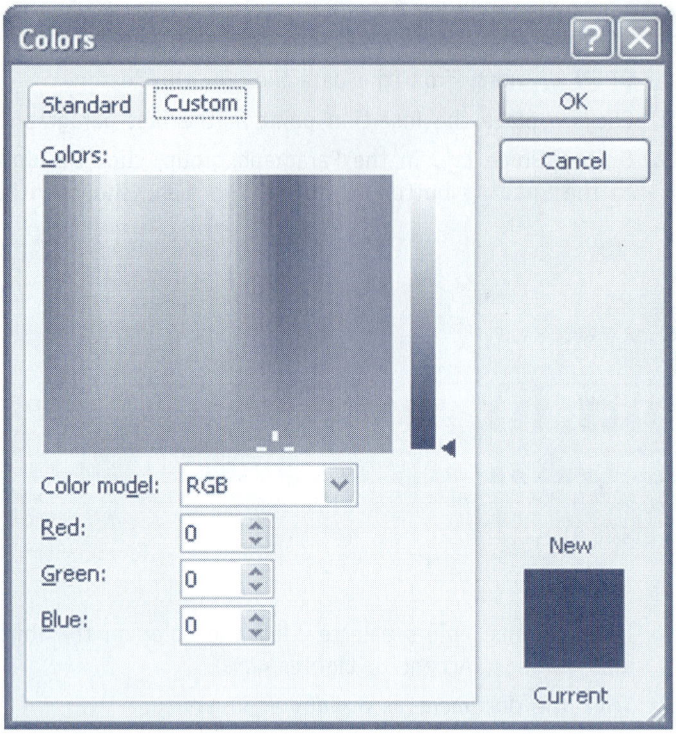

Placing a Border around a Paragraph

Like shading, borders can add interest and emphasis to paragraphs. Borders can be formatted with a variety of styles, colors, and widths.

PLACE A BORDER AROUND A PARAGRAPH

USE the document that is open from the previous exercise.

1. Click to place the insertion point in the second paragraph.
2. On the Home tab, in the Paragraph group, click the **downward-pointing arrow** next to the **Border** button to display the menu shown in Figure 4-14.

Figure 4-14

Border menu

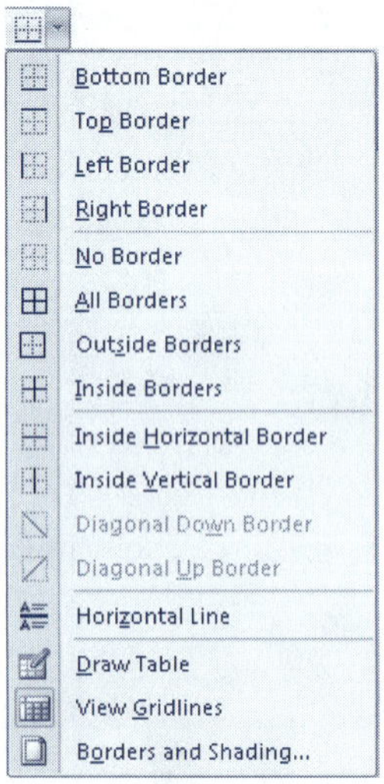

3. Click **Outside Borders** on the menu.
4. Your document should look similar to Figure 4-15.

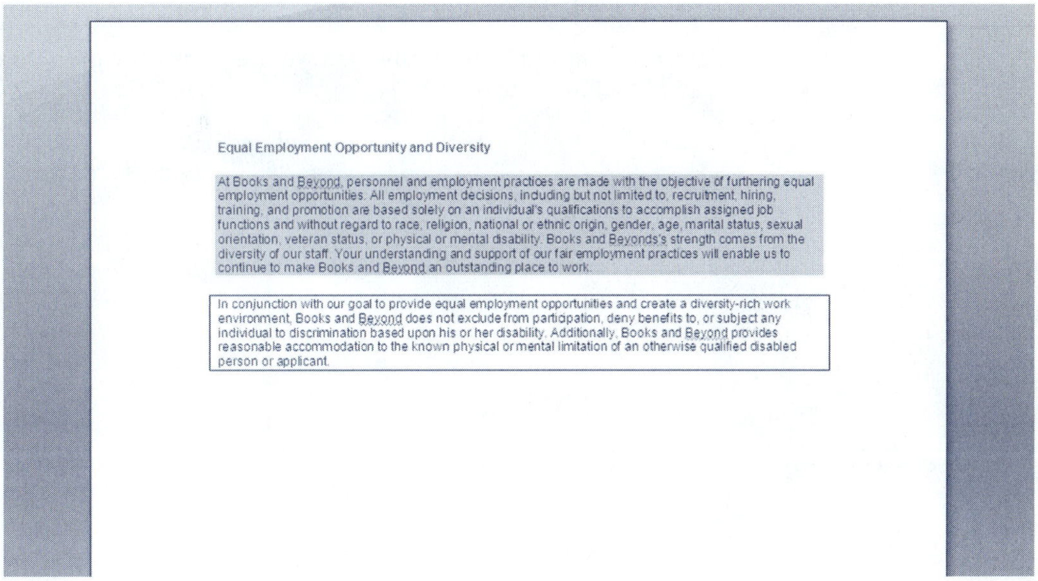

Figure 4-15

Document with shading and border

CERTIFICATION READY?
How do you format paragraphs?
2.1.4

5. **SAVE** the document and **CLOSE** the file.

   PAUSE. LEAVE Word open for the next exercise.

If you want to apply the previously chosen border to a paragraph, click the Border button. To place a different border around selected text, click the downward-pointing arrow next to the Border button.

For more options, click the Borders and Shading option on the Border menu to display the Borders tab of the Borders and Shading dialog box, shown in Figure 4-16. Here you can change the style, color, and width of the borders and preview the changes. To remove a border, click None in the Setting section. This dialog box also contains tabs for page border options and shading.

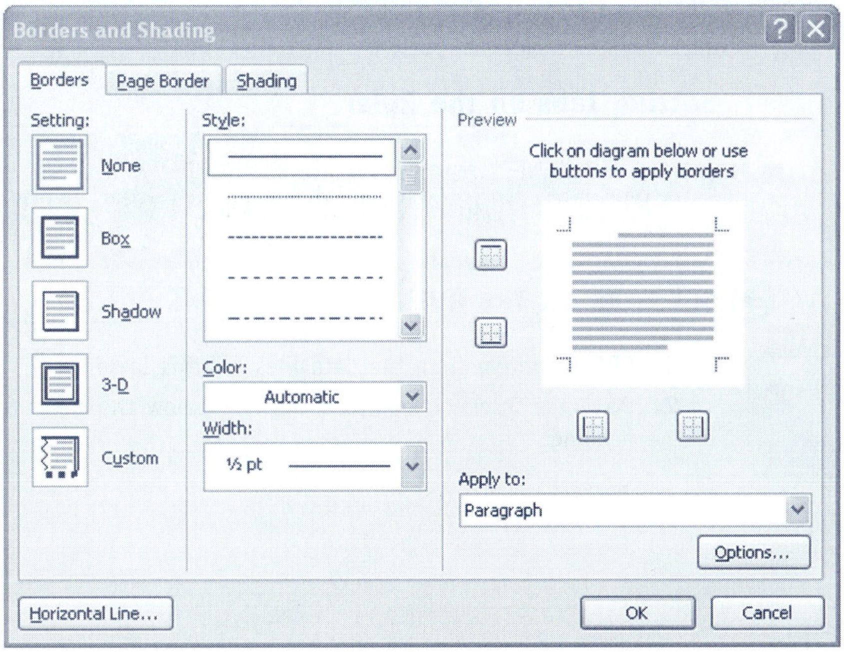

Figure 4-16

Borders tab of the Borders and Shading dialog box

TAKE NOTE*

Borders can also be added to pages, sections, tables, cells, graphic objects, and pictures.

Software Orientation

Tab Dialog Box

When setting and clearing tabs, you will frequently use the Tabs dialog box, shown in Figure 4-17.

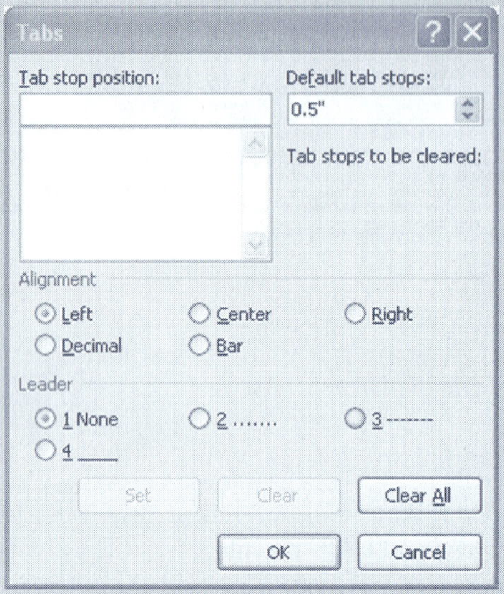

Figure 4-17
Tabs dialog box

Use this figure as a reference throughout the activities on setting tabs as well as the rest of the book.

Setting Tabs

THE BOTTOM LINE You can set tabs quickly on the ruler. Or you can open the Tabs dialog box to set more precise tabs and have more options.

Setting Tabs on the Ruler

To set tabs quickly, you can click the tab selector at the left end of the ruler until it displays the type of tab that you want and then click the ruler at the place where you want to set it.

SET TABS ON THE RULER

CD: The *perdiem* document is available on the companion CD-ROM.

1. **OPEN** ***perdiem*** from the data files for this lesson.
2. Place the insertion point on the line below the *Meals & Incidentals Breakdown* heading.

3. Click the tab selector at the left of the ruler until the Center tab appears. The tab selector and horizontal ruler are shown in Figure 4-18.

Figure 4-18

Tab selector and horizontal ruler with tabs set

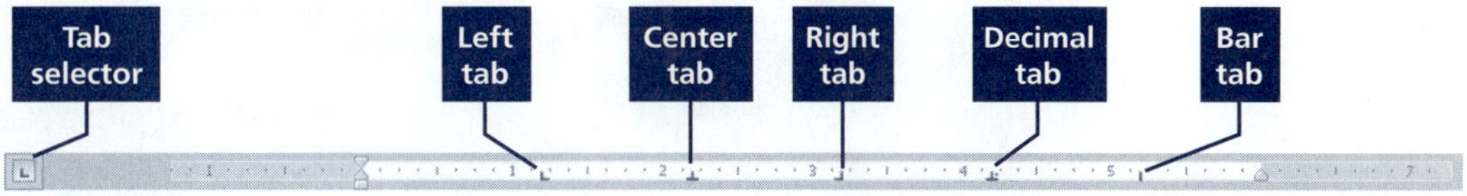

TROUBLESHOOTING If the horizontal ruler is not visible along the top of the document, click the View Ruler button at the top of the vertical scrollbar to display it.

4. Click the ruler at the 2.5-inch mark to set a center tab.
5. Click the ruler at the 4-inch mark to set a center tab.
6. Press Tab and key **Chicago**.
7. Press Tab and key **New York**.
8. Select the list of words at the end of the document, starting with *Breakfast*.
9. Click the tab selector until the right tab appears.
10. Click the ruler at the 1-inch mark to set a right tab.
11. Place the insertion point in front of each word and press Tab to align it at the right tab. Your document should look similar to Figure 4-19.

Figure 4-19

Document formatted with tabs

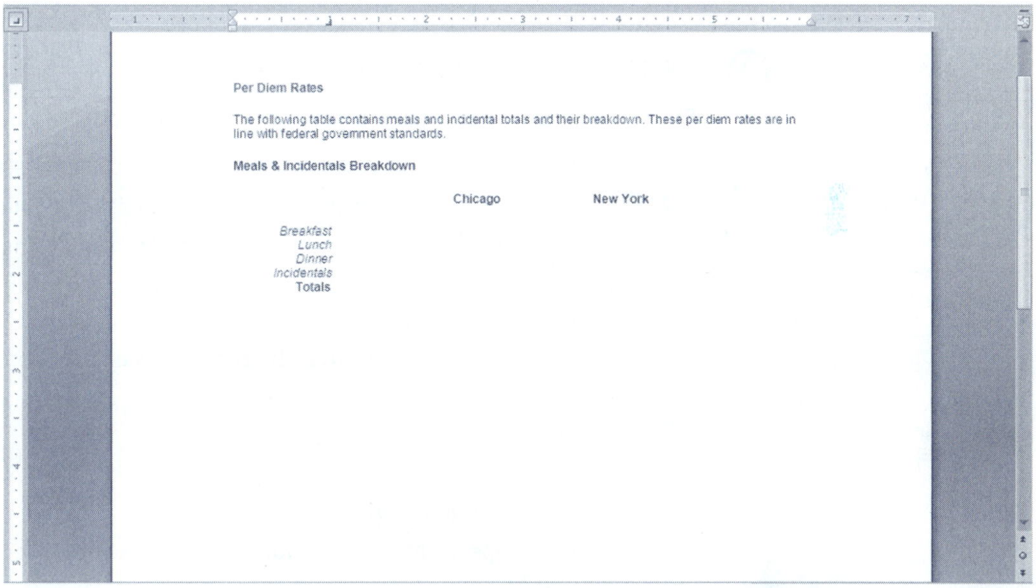

12. **SAVE** the document as ***handbook_perdiem***.

PAUSE. LEAVE the document open to use in the next exercise.

CERTIFICATION READY?
How do you set and clear tabs?
2.1.5

By default, left-aligned tab stops are set every half inch in Word. To set a tab at a different place on the ruler, click the tab selector at the left end of the ruler and then click on the ruler where you want to place the tab. The various types of tabs and their descriptions are shown in Table 4-3.

Table 4-3
Tab stops on the ruler

Name	Button	Description
Left Tab		Left aligns text at the tab place indicated on the horizontal ruler
Center Tab		Centers text at the place indicated on the horizontal ruler
Right Tab		Right-aligns text at the place indicated on the horizontal ruler
Decimal Tab		Aligns numbers around a decimal point at the place indicated on the horizontal ruler
Bar Tab		Inserts a vertical bar line at the place indicated on the horizontal ruler

After tabs are set, when you press the Tab key, the insertion point will stop at the place you specified with a tab stop. To move a tab stop to a different position on the ruler, click and drag it left or right to a new position.

Using the Tabs Dialog Box

The Tabs dialog box is useful for setting tabs at precise locations on the ruler, clearing all tabs, and setting tab leaders.

USE THE TABS DIALOG BOX

USE the document that is open from the previous exercise.

1. Select the list of words at the end of the document, starting with *Breakfast*.
2. On the Home tab, in the Paragraph group, click the **Dialog Box Launcher**.
3. Click the **Tabs** button on the bottom left to display the Tabs dialog box.
4. In the Tab stop box, key **2.6** In the Alignment section, select **Right**. In the Leader section, select **2** Then click **Set**.
5. In the Tab stop box, key **4.1** In the Alignment section, select **Right**. In the Leader section, select **2**. Then click **Set**.
6. Click **OK**.
7. Place the insertion point after the word *Breakfast* and press **Tab**.
8. Key **$10** and press **Tab**.
9. Key **$12**. Repeat this process for each line, keying the numbers shown in Figure 4-20.

ANOTHER WAY

To open the Tabs dialog box, double-click any tab stop on the ruler.

CERTIFICATION READY?
How do you set and clear tabs?
2.1.5

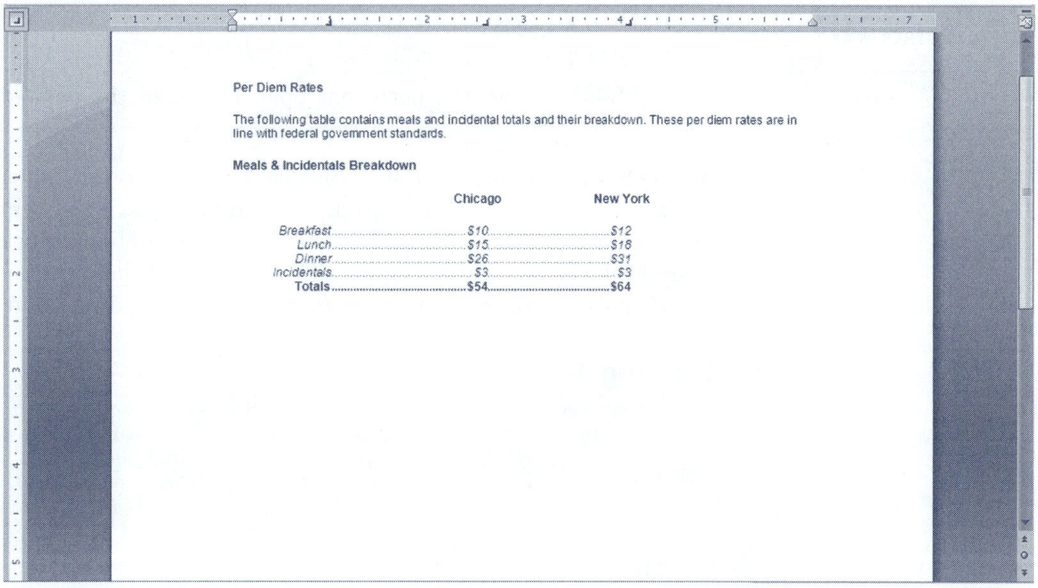

Figure 4-20

Document formatted with tabs

10. **SAVE** the document.

PAUSE. LEAVE the document open to use in the next exercise.

In this activity, you learned how to use the Tabs dialog box to set tabs and specify leaders. Tab ***leaders*** are dotted, dashed, or solid lines that fill the space before a tab.

Displaying Non-Printing Characters

> When you format documents, Word inserts symbols in the document that are usually hidden from view. However, these non-printing characters—such as paragraph marks or tab indents—can be displayed.

DISPLAY NON-PRINTING CHARACTERS

USE the document that is open from the previous exercise.

1. On the Home tab, in the Paragraph group, click the **Show/Hide Paragraph**  button to display the non-printing characters in the document. Your screen should look similar to Figure 4-21.

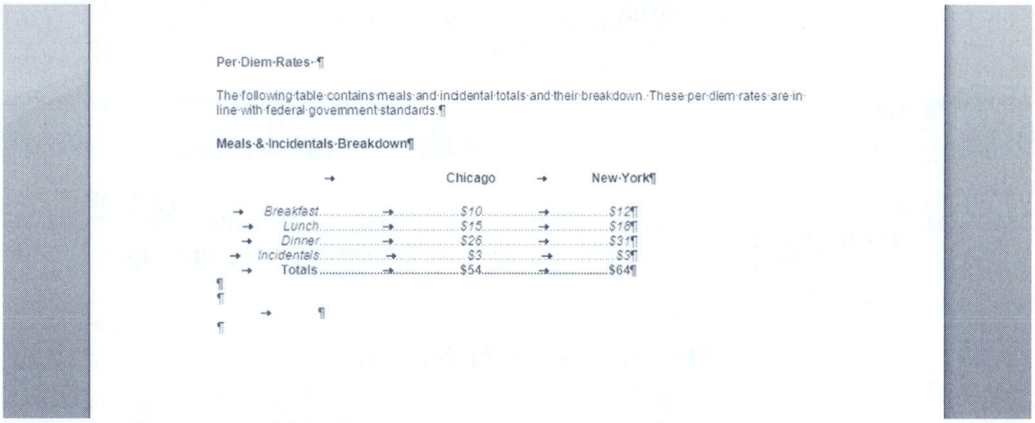

Figure 4-21

Document with non-printing characters displayed

ANOTHER WAY

To display non-printing characters, press **Ctrl+Shift+***.

2. Click the Show/Hide Paragraph button again to hide the non-printing characters.
3. **SAVE** the document.

PAUSE. LEAVE the document open to use in the next exercise.

Non-printing characters are symbols that Word inserts into a document when you use certain formatting commands, such as paragraphs and indents. These symbols are usually hidden from view, but you can display them by clicking the Show/Hide Paragraph button in the Paragraph group of the Home tab. Seeing the exact locations of these symbols can help you edit text. When you are done, click the Show/Hide Paragraph button again to hide the symbols.

Clearing Tabs

You can quickly remove a single tab by dragging it off the ruler, or you can use the Tabs dialog box to clear one or all tabs.

CLEAR TABS

USE the document that is open from the previous exercise.

1. Click to place the insertion point on the last line (*Total*).
2. Click the tab stop at **4.1″**.
3. Drag it down off the ruler and release the mouse button to remove it.
4. On the Home tab, in the Paragraph group, click the **Dialog Box Launcher**.
5. Click the **Tabs** button on the bottom left to display the Tabs dialog box.
6. In the Tab stop position list, click **2.6″** and then click **Clear** to clear that tab.
7. Click the **Clear All** button to clear all tabs on that line.
8. Click **OK**.
9. Select all the text on the *Totals* line and click the **Delete** button to delete it.
10. **SAVE** the document and **CLOSE** the file.

PAUSE. LEAVE Word open for the next exercise.

CERTIFICATION READY?
How do you set and clear tabs?
2.1.5

To remove a tab stop from the ruler, click and drag it off the ruler. When you release the mouse button, the tab stop disappears. Or open the Tabs dialog box, where you can choose to clear one tab or all of them.

TAKE NOTE*

Many of the predesigned document layout options in Word 2007 make it possible to create documents such as an index or table of contents without having to set any tabs manually.

Clearing the Formats from a Paragraph

THE BOTTOM LINE

Just as you learned how to clear the formatting from characters in the previous lesson, you can similarly clear the formatting from an entire paragraph.

Clearing Formats from a Paragraph

You may decide after making changes that you no longer want any formatting in a paragraph or that you want to start over. The Clear Formatting command makes it easy to change a paragraph back to plain text, no matter how many formats you have applied to it.

CLEAR PARAGRAPH FORMATS

X REF
Clear Formatting was also discussed in Lesson 3.

1. **OPEN** the *handbook_diversity* document that you saved earlier in this lesson.
2. Select the two paragraphs.
3. On the Home tab, in the Styles group, click the **More** button to display the gallery of styles.
4. Click the **Clear Formatting** option.

ANOTHER WAY
You can also return the paragraph to plain text by clicking the Clear Formatting button on the Home tab in the Font group.

CERTIFICATION READY?
How do you format paragraphs?
2.1.4

5. Change the font of the two paragraphs to **Arial** and the size to **9**.
6. Insert another blank line after the document title and between the paragraphs.
7. **SAVE** the document as *handbook_eeo* and **CLOSE** the file.

STOP. **CLOSE** Word.

The Clear Formatting command provides an easy way to change a paragraph back to plain text. Not only is all the formatting removed, but the font and font size also revert to the default.

SUMMARY SKILL MATRIX

In this lesson you learned	Matrix Skill	Skill Number
To set indents	Format paragraphs	2.1.4
To change alignment	Format paragraphs	2.1.4
To set the line spacing within a paragraph	Format paragraphs	2.1.4
To set the spacing around a paragraph	Format paragraphs	2.1.4
To create a numbered list	Format paragraphs Create tables and lists	2.1.4, 4.2.1
To create a bulleted list	Format paragraphs Create tables and lists	2.1.4, 4.2.1
To shade a paragraph	Format paragraphs	2.1.4
To place a border around a paragraph	Format paragraphs	2.1.4
To use the Tabs dialog box	Set and clear tabs	2.1.5
To set tabs on the ruler	Set and clear tabs	2.1.5
To clear tabs	Set and clear tabs	2.1.5
To clear the formats from a paragraph	Format paragraphs	2.1.4

Knowledge Assessment

Fill in the Blank

Complete the following sentences by writing the correct word or words in the blanks provided.

1. To indent the first line of a paragraph, click in front of the line and press ________________.
2. A(n) ________________ is the space between a paragraph and the document's left and/or right margin.
3. If you key a(n) ________________, Word recognizes that you are trying to start a bulleted list and will automatically continue it.
4. When setting tabs, you can do so quickly by setting them on the ________________.
5. By default, left-aligned tabs stops are set every ________________ in Word.
6. A bar tab inserts a(n) ________________ bar line at the place indicated on the horizontal ruler.
7. Tab ________________ are dotted, dashed, or solid lines that fill the space before a tab.
8. Non-printing characters are ________________ that Word inserts into a document when you use certain formatting commands.
9. The ________________ ________________ command makes it easy to change a paragraph back to plain text, no matter how many formats you have applied to it.
10. ________________ line spacing is the default option that accommodates the largest font in that line, plus a small amount of extra space.

Multiple Choice

Select the best response for the following statements.

1. Which of the following is not a type of indent?
   a. hanging
   b. negative
   c. positive
   d. first-line
2. Which word(s) refers to how text is positioned between the top and bottom margins of the page?
   a. horizontal alignment
   b. vertical alignment
   c. justified
   d. line spacing
3. Which line spacing command sets the spacing at a fixed amount that Word does not adjust?
   a. Exactly
   b. Double
   c. Multiple
   d. At Least

4. Which command do you use to remove shading from a paragraph?
   a. Remove Shading
   b. Delete Color
   c. Undo Shading
   d. No Color
5. Which property of borders can be changed in the Borders tab of the Borders and Shading dialog box?
   a. color
   b. width
   c. style
   d. all of the above
   e. none of the above
6. Where is the View Ruler button located?
   a. in the Tabs dialog box
   b. at the top of the vertical scrollbar
   c. in the Paragraph group
   d. all of the above
   e. none of the above
7. What does dragging a tab off the ruler do?
   a. moves it to another position
   b. turns it into a left-aligned tab
   c. clears it
   d. hides it from view
8. When applying shading to text or a paragraph, you can choose which of the following?
   a. a color in the current theme
   b. a standard color
   c. a custom color
   d. all of the above
9. Which Word feature would you use to extend a paragraph into the left margin?
   a. indent
   b. line spacing
   c. horizontal alignment
   d. shading
10. Which button do you click to display non-printing characters?
    a. Display Non-Printing Characters
    b. Show/Hide Paragraph
    c. View Formatting Commands
    d. none of the above

Competency Assessment

Project 4-1: Lost Art Photos

You are employed in the marketing department at Lost Art Photos and have been asked to format a promotional document.

GET READY. Launch Word if it is not already running.

CD

The ***photos*** document is available on the companion CD-ROM.

1. **OPEN** ***photos*** from the data files for this lesson.
2. Select the title.
3. On the Home tab, in the Paragraph group, click the **Border** button.
4. Click **Borders and Shading** on the menu to open the Borders and Shading dialog box.
5. In the Setting list, click **Shadow**. On the Width list, click **3 pt**.
6. Click **OK**.
7. On the Home tab, in the Paragraph group, click the **downward-pointing arrow** next to the Shading button.
8. Under Theme Colors, click the color that is labeled **Olive Green, Accent 3, 60%**.
9. Select the first paragraph.
10. On the Home tab, in the Paragraph group, click the **Line Spacing** button.
11. Click **1.0** on the menu.
12. Select *Affordable Prints*.
13. Click the **downward-pointing arrow** next to the **Border** button.
14. Click **Outside Borders** on the menu.
15. Click the **downward-pointing arrow** next to the Shading button.
16. Click the color that is labeled **Olive Green, Accent 3, 40%**.
17. Copy the formatting of *Affordable Prints* to each of the other headings—*Quality Product, Options, Options, Options,* and *Satisfaction Guaranteed*.
18. **SAVE** the document as ***lost_art_photos*** and **CLOSE** the file.

    LEAVE Word open for the next project.

Project 4-2: General Performance Expectation Guidelines

In your job at Books and Beyond, you continue to work on documents that will be part of the employee handbook.

CD

The ***guidelines*** document is available on the companion CD-ROM.

1. **OPEN** ***guidelines*** from the data files for this lesson.
2. Select the two lines that begin *Verbal discussion . . .* and *Written warning . . . .*
3. On the Home tab, in the Paragraph group, click the **Numbering** button to change the lines into a numbered list.
4. Place the insertion point after the second sentence in the list and press **Enter**.
5. Key **Termination** as the third numbered item.
6. Select the double-spaced lines beginning with *abuse, misuse . . .* and ending with *engaging in conduct . . . .*
7. On the Home tab, in the Paragraph group, click the **Bullets** button to change the lines into a bulleted list.
8. Select the first paragraph.
9. On the Home tab, in the Paragraph group, click the **Justify** button.
10. Place your insertion point at the beginning of the first line of the first paragraph and click **Tab** to create a first-line indent.

11. Select each of the remaining paragraphs in the document and repeat steps 9 and 10 to justify them and create first line indents.
12. **SAVE** the document as ***handbook_guidelines*** and **CLOSE** the file.

    LEAVE Word open for the next project.

Proficiency Assessment

Project 4-3: PTA Officers

CD

The *pta* document is available on the companion CD-ROM.

You are a volunteer at the local elementary school and have been asked to format a PTA document that lists the officers for the upcoming school year.

1. **OPEN** ***pta*** from the data files for this lesson.
2. Format the document as shown in Figure 4-22.

Figure 4-22

Formatted PTA document

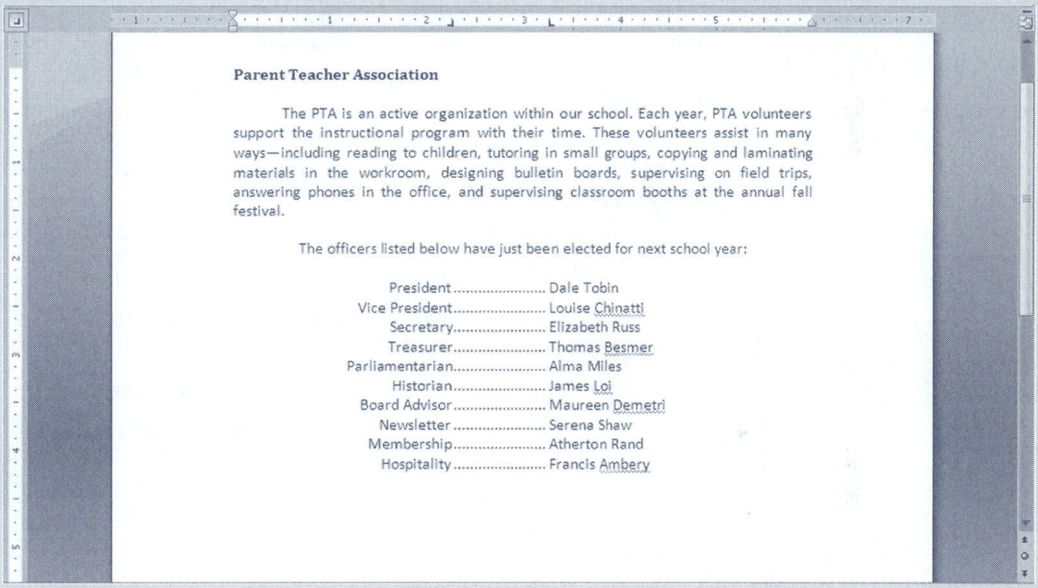

Parent Teacher Association

The PTA is an active organization within our school. Each year, PTA volunteers support the instructional program with their time. These volunteers assist in many ways—including reading to children, tutoring in small groups, copying and laminating materials in the workroom, designing bulletin boards, supervising on field trips, answering phones in the office, and supervising classroom booths at the annual fall festival.

The officers listed below have just been elected for next school year:

President....................... Dale Tobin
Vice President....................... Louise Chinatti
Secretary....................... Elizabeth Russ
Treasurer....................... Thomas Besmer
Parliamentarian....................... Alma Miles
Historian....................... James Loi
Board Advisor....................... Maureen Demetri
Newsletter....................... Serena Shaw
Membership....................... Atherton Rand
Hospitality....................... Francis Ambery

3. **SAVE** the document as ***pta_officers*** and **CLOSE** the file.

   LEAVE Word open for the next project.

Project 4-4: Phone List

You want to create a list of numbers that you call frequently to keep beside your phone.

1. **CREATE** a new Word document.
2. Create a numbered list with the names of at least ten family members, friends, or businesses that you call frequently.
3. Create a tab with dot leaders and then key the phone number beside each name. For example:

   1) Gary Evans.....................555-1212

4. Format every other line with shading so it is easier to read.
5. **SAVE** the document as ***phone_list*** and **CLOSE** the file.

   LEAVE Word open for the next project.

Mastery Assessment

Project 4-5: Developer Job Description

You are a content specialist at a software development company. Your supervisor asks you to format the job description for the developer position.

CD

The ***developer*** document is available on the companion CD-ROM.

1. **OPEN** ***developer*** from the data files for this lesson.
2. Use the skills you have learned in this lesson—such as alignment, line spacing, shading, borders, tabs, and bulleted lists—to format the document attractively.
3. **SAVE** the document as ***developer_description*** and **CLOSE** the file.

   LEAVE Word open for the next project.

Project 4-6: Rabbit Show

You are a volunteer at the annual Falls Village Fair and have been given a document about one of the exhibits. You will need to correctly format the document. The person who created the document was not as familiar with line spacing, tabs, and lists as you are.

CD

The ***rabbit*** document is available on the companion CD-ROM.

1. **OPEN** ***rabbit*** from the data files for this lesson.
2. Make any adjustments necessary to correctly format the tabs, line spacing, and lists.
3. Adjust the text so that it all fits on one page.
4. **SAVE** the document as ***rabbit_show*** and **CLOSE** the file.

   CLOSE Word.

INTERNET READY

Many online resources can provide you with solutions to challenges that you might face during a typical workday. Search the Microsoft website for Work Essentials—a place where you can find information on how to use Microsoft Word efficiently to perform typical business tasks and activities. Explore the resources and content that Work Essentials offers and write a short paragraph about one particular tool or solution that could be useful on the job and how you could use it to be more productive.

Document Formatting

5

LESSON SKILL MATRIX

Skills	Matrix Skill	Skill Number
Setting a Colored Background	Format document backgrounds	1.1.5
Adding a Watermark	Format document backgrounds	1.1.5
Placing a Border Around a Document's Pages	Format document backgrounds	1.1.5
Adding Page Numbers to a Document	Create and modify headers and footers	1.2.2
Inserting a Built-In Header or Footer	Create and modify headers and footers	1.2.2
Inserting a Formatted Header or Footer from Quick Parts	Insert formatted headers and footers from Quick Parts	4.1.3
Adding Content to a Header or Footer	Create and modify headers and footers	1.2.2
Setting Margins	Format pages	1.2.1
Selecting a Page Orientation	Format pages	1.2.1
Choosing a Paper Size	Format pages	1.2.1

You are employed at Montgomery, Slade & Parker, a global strategic management consulting firm offering consulting services to senior management in a wide variety of industries. A large healthcare corporation that owns hospitals in many major cities in the United States has hired your company to research and recommend the best place to relocate their corporate headquarters. As part of the strategy and operations team, you will be involved in this process. In this lesson, you will format the first draft of a short proposal to submit to the client.

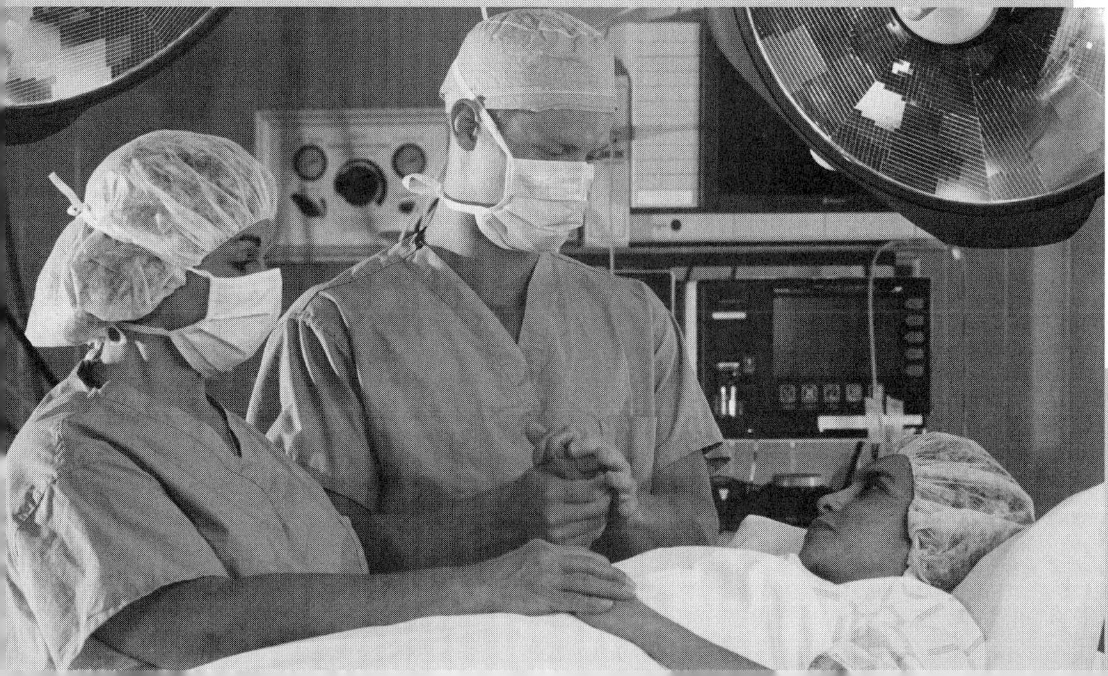

KEY TERMS

content controls
footer
header
landscape orientation
margins
portrait orientation
watermark

■ Formatting a Document's Background

THE BOTTOM LINE Word has three commands for formatting a document's background. You can insert a watermark, change the page color, or add a border. Adding these elements to a page can give a document visual importance and help set it apart from other printed materials.

Setting a Colored Background

You are probably familiar with the use of colored backgrounds for text on Web pages. Colored backgrounds can also be used when creating print documents. Adding a colored background to the title page of a report, for example, can help to establish a certain feel for the content of the report and make it easily recognizable. However, it is important to use colored backgrounds in moderation and to use light colors that will not interfere with the text on a page.

INSERT A PAGE COLOR

CD: The ***proposal*** document is available on the companion CD-ROM.

GET READY. Before you begin these steps, be sure to launch Microsoft Word.

1. **OPEN** ***proposal*** from the data files for this lesson.
2. Click the **Page Layout** tab.
3. In the Page Background group, click the **Page Color** menu and click **Aqua, Accent 5, Lighter 80%**, as shown in Figure 5-1. The page color is applied.

Figure 5-1

The Page Color menu

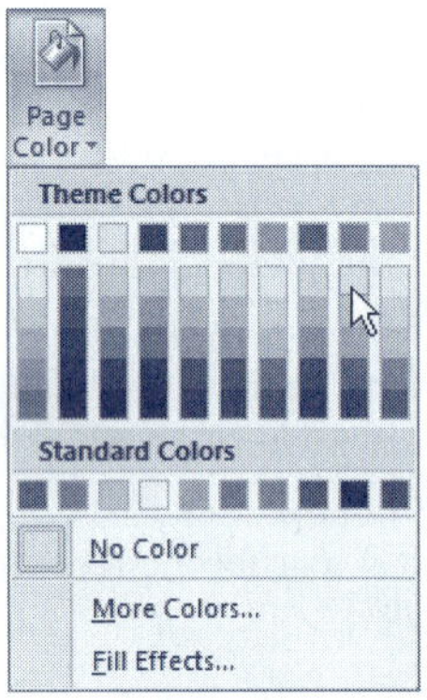

4. Save the document as ***USA_proposal.***

PAUSE. LEAVE the document open to use in the next exercise.

CERTIFICATION READY? How do you insert a page color? **1.1.5**

You can change a page's background color using the Page Color menu from the Page Background group. The Page Color menu lists Theme colors and Standard colors as well as a No Color option. The More Colors command lets you choose a custom color and the Fill Effects command displays the Fill Effects dialog box, where you can insert a page background with a gradient, texture, pattern, or picture.

Adding a Watermark

Words such as *confidential*, *draft*, or *urgent* are often used as watermarks to identify a document as needing special treatment. Graphic images are sometimes used as watermarks for added interest.

ADD A WATERMARK

USE the document that is open from the previous exercise.

1. In the Page Background group of the Page Layout tab, click the **Watermark** menu and scroll down to select **DRAFT 1: "DRAFT" Watermark with Gray Diagonal Text**, as shown in Figure 5-2. The watermark is inserted on all pages (see Figure 5-3).

Figure 5-2

The Watermark menu

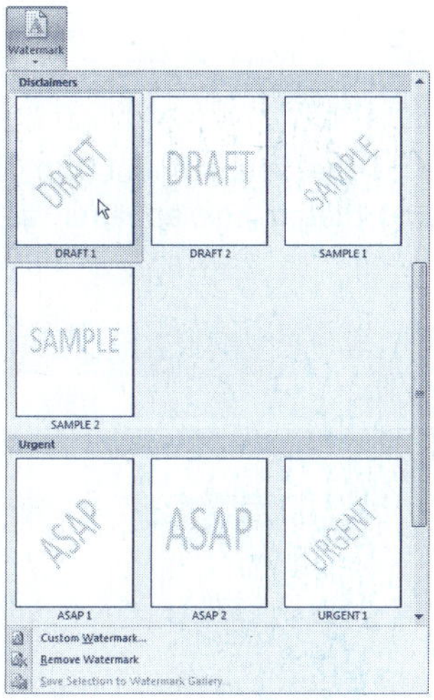

Figure 5-3

Watermark

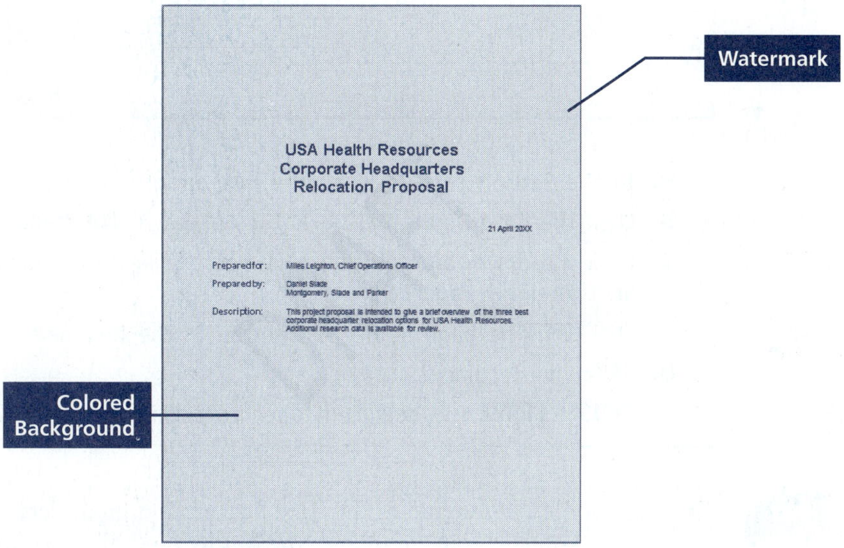

2. **SAVE** the document.

PAUSE. LEAVE the document open to use in the next exercise.

CERTIFICATION READY?
How do you add a watermark?
1.1.5

A ***watermark*** is text or a graphic that is printed lightly behind the text of a document. To insert a watermark, click the Watermark menu in the Page Background group. The menu displays a list of watermark choices as well as the Custom Watermark and Remove Watermark commands.

Choose the Custom Watermark command to create a custom watermark with a picture or custom text in the Printed Watermark dialog box. When you want to delete a watermark from the page, click the Remove Watermark command.

Placing a Border around a Document's Pages

Adding a line or border around a document's pages can help add a graphic element to the page or frame a page. Because you can change the color, width, and style of the border to zigzag, dotted, thick, thin, or double lines, page borders can also serve the purpose of surrounding text that you want to emphasize.

INSERT A PAGE BORDER

USE the document that is open from the previous exercise.

1. In the Page Background group of the Page Layout tab, click the **Page Borders** button. The Borders and Shading dialog box appears, as shown in Figure 5-4.

Figure 5-4

The Borders and Shading dialog box

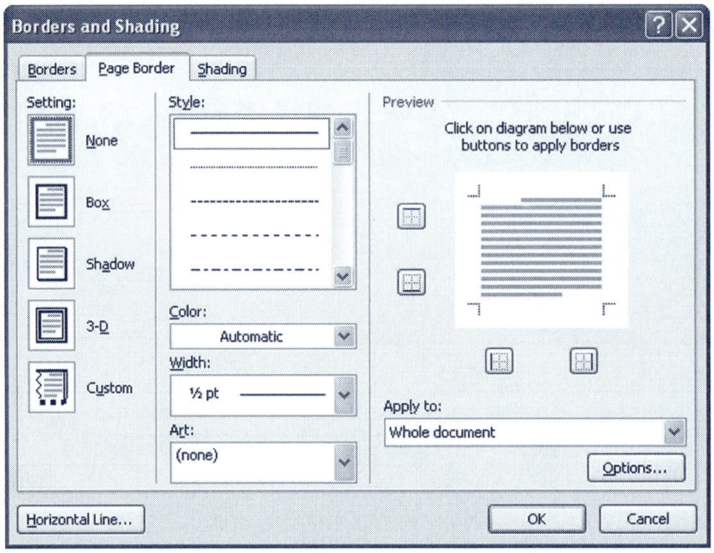

2. In the Setting section, click the **Box** option.
3. Click the downward-pointing arrow on the **Width** menu and choose **1/4** pt.
4. Click the downward-pointing arrow on the **Apply To** menu and click **This Section–First Page Only.**
5. Click **OK**. The page border is inserted in the first page only.
6. **SAVE** the document.

PAUSE. LEAVE the document open to use in the next exercise.

CERTIFICATION READY?
How do you insert a page border?
1.1.5

The Page Borders command in the Page Background group lets you insert a border around a page. When you click the command, the Borders and Shading dialog box appears. The Page Border tab has options for the setting, style, color, width, and art, if any, you want to use in the border you are inserting.

Inserting Headers and Footers

THE BOTTOM LINE

When you need to repeat information in the same place on every page of a document, use headers and footers to arrange and display that information.

Adding Page Numbers to a Document

It is often necessary to number the pages of documents that contain multiple pages, especially if the document will be printed. Not only does this help the reader keep loose pages in order, but it also enables the recipient to refer to information on a specific page when discussing a document.

ADD PAGE NUMBERS

USE the document that is open from the previous exercise.

1. Make sure the insertion point is located at the top of the first page.
2. Click the **Insert** tab.
3. In the Header and Footer group, click the **Page Number** menu, click **Bottom of Page**, and scroll down to select **Plain Number 2**, as shown in Figure 5-5. Page numbers are inserted on all pages.

Figure 5-5

Page Number menu and submenus

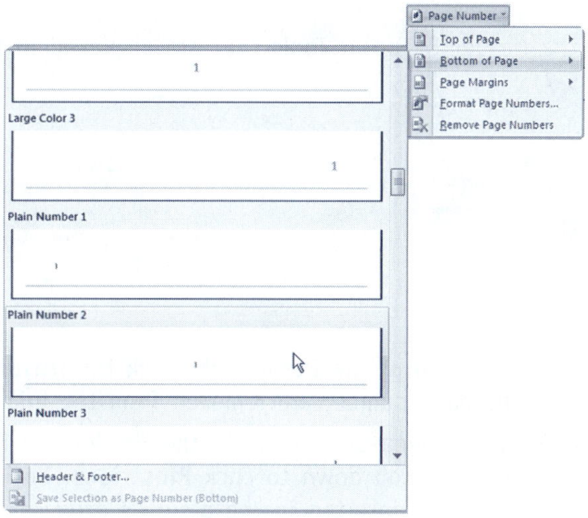

4. **SAVE** the document.

   PAUSE. LEAVE the document open to use in the next exercise.

CERTIFICATION READY?
How do you add page numbers?
1.2.2

The Page Number menu in the Header and Footer group has commands for inserting page numbers at the top, bottom, or in the margin of a page. You can also use the Format Page Numbers command to choose the type of numbering you want, such as 1, 2, 3. . . or i, ii, iii. . . and the number you want to start with. To delete page numbers, click the Remove Page Numbers command.

Inserting a Built-In Header or Footer

Word's built-in headers and footers offer you instant design for page numbers and other text that you want to appear on each page of a document.

INSERT A HEADER OR FOOTER

USE the document that is open from the previous exercise.

1. In the Header and Footer group of the Insert tab, click the **Header** menu and scroll down to select **Pinstripes**, as shown in Figure 5-6. The header is inserted.

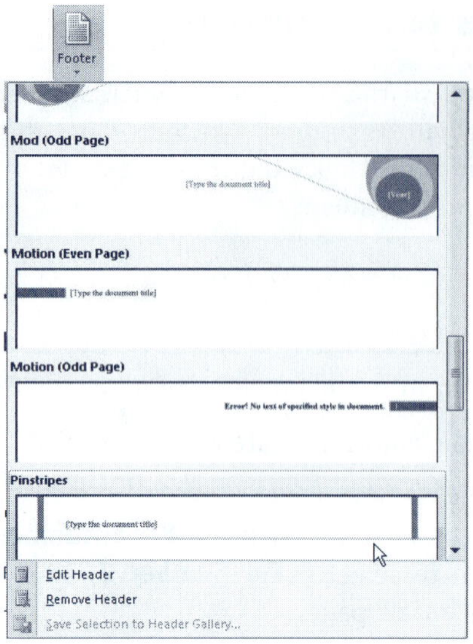

Figure 5-6
Header menu

2. Notice the Header & Footer Tools that are displayed in the Design tab's ribbon (see Figure 5-7).

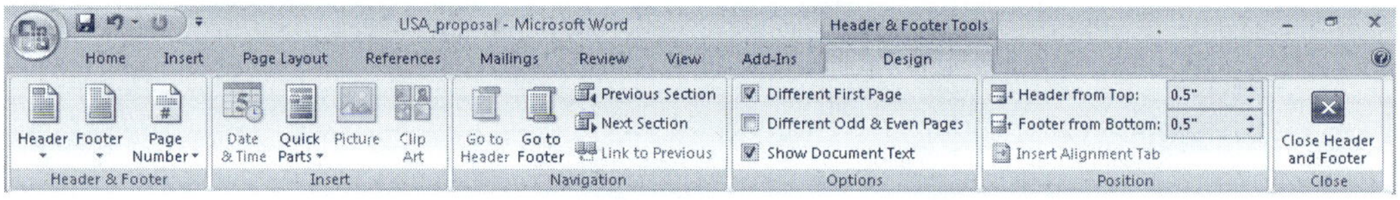

Figure 5-7
Header & Footer Tools

3. In the Options group of the Design tab, click the **Different First Page** box. The header and the page number are removed from the first page.
4. Click in the header area of page 2. In the Header and Footer group, click the **Footer** button and scroll down to click **Pinstripes**. Notice the new footer replaces the page number you inserted in the previous exercise (see Figure 5-8).

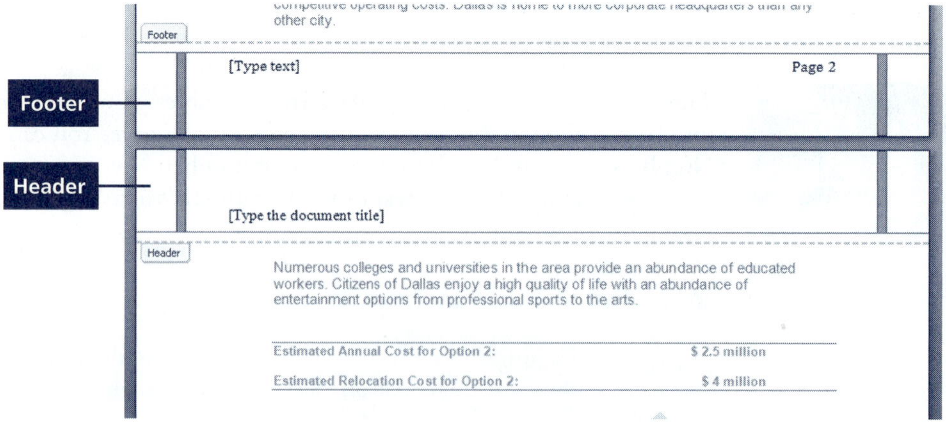

Figure 5-8
Header and Footer

5. **SAVE** the document.

PAUSE. LEAVE the document open to use in the next exercise.

CERTIFICATION READY?
How do you insert a built-in header or footer?
1.2.2

CERTIFICATION READY?
How do you insert a formatted header or footer from Quick Parts?
4.1.3

X REF
You will learn more about Quick Parts in Lesson 8.

A ***header*** is text such as the title of a document that is located at the top of the page. A ***footer*** includes the text, such as a page number, at the bottom of the page. Headers and footers are usually printed on all or most of the pages of a document. To insert a header or footer, click the Insert tab. The Header and Footer group has commands for inserting headers, footers, and page numbers. Word provides a variety of built-in header and footer designs. Just click the one you want.

When you insert a header, Word displays Header & Footer Tools in the ribbon. The Header and Footer group displays the Header, Footer, and Page Number commands. The Insert group lets you insert the Date & Time, Quick Parts (reusable pieces of content), Picture, or Clip Art you want in a header or footer. In the Navigation group, you can switch between Go To Header and Go To Footer. You can also navigate the document by Previous Section, Next Section, or Link To Previous. In the Options group, click Different First Page to remove the header or footer from the first page. Click Different Odd & Even pages if you want one header or footer on the odd pages and a different one on the even pages. The Show Document Text command toggles to show the text of the document or hide it when you are working with a header or footer.

The Position group lets you specify the location of the header from the top of the document or the location of the footer from the bottom of the document. You can also click the Insert Alignment tab to align text within a header.

Adding Content to a Header or Footer

Headers and footers can provide a convenient and functional place to insert a company logo, the title of a document, or other content that you want to display on each page of a document.

ADD CONTENT TO A HEADER OR FOOTER

USE the document that is open from the previous exercise.

1. Move the mouse pointer to the header on the second page of the document and click to activate the header.
2. Click **[Type the Document Title]** to select it.
3. Key **Relocation Proposal** (see Figure 5-9).

Figure 5-9

Title in header

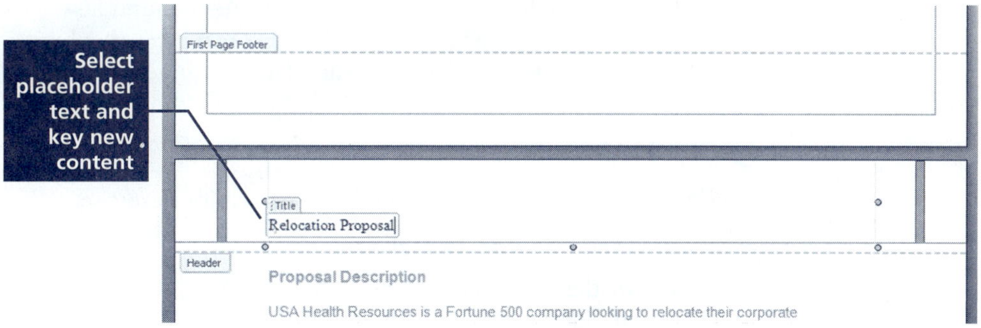

4. Scroll down to the footer of page 2. Click **[Type Text]** to select it. Key **Montgomery, Slade & Parker**.
5. Select all the text in the footer. Point to selected text to display the Mini toolbar. Click the **Font** menu and select **Arial**.
6. Click the **Font Size** menu and select **11**.
7. Click the **Italic** button.
8. Click outside the footer to deselect it.
9. Select the text in the header and display the Mini toolbar.

10. Click the **Font** menu and select **Arial**.
11. Click the **Font Size** menu and select **12**.
12. Click the **Italic** button and then click the **Bold** button.
13. **SAVE** the document

PAUSE. LEAVE the document open to use in the next exercise.

CERTIFICATION READY?
How do you add content to a header or footer?
1.2.2

After you insert a header or footer, you will want to add your own content. Just double-click the header or footer, which is grayed out, to make it active. When you activate a header or footer, the Header & Footer Tools appear with options for inserting content, such as Date & Time, Quick Parts, a Picture, or Clip Art.

Some built-in headers and footers contain ***content controls***, which are tiny programs that include a label for instructing you on the type of text to include and a placeholder that reserves a place for your new text. Click the placeholder text in the header or footer to select it, and then key your content. After you key your own content, the content control will disappear. You can remove a content control by right-clicking it and choosing Remove Content Control from the shortcut menu.

After inserting your content, you can format it with the Mini toolbar or commands in the ribbon.

Page Layout

THE BOTTOM LINE

The layout of a page helps to communicate your message. Obviously, the content of your document is very important, but having appropriate margins, page orientation, and paper size all contribute to the success of your document.

Setting Margins

Changing the size of the margins in a document can change not only the look of the document, but also the number of pages it includes. Sometimes you might want to adjust margin sizes slightly to decrease or increase the number of pages in a document. When choosing margin sizes, it is important to keep in mind how the document will be used. For example, a document that will be inserted in a three-ring binder should have plenty of space in the left margin to accommodate the binder.

SET MARGINS

USE the document that is open from the previous exercise.

1. Click the **Page Layout** tab.
2. In the Page Setup group, click the **Margins** menu and choose **Moderate**, as shown in Figure 5-10.

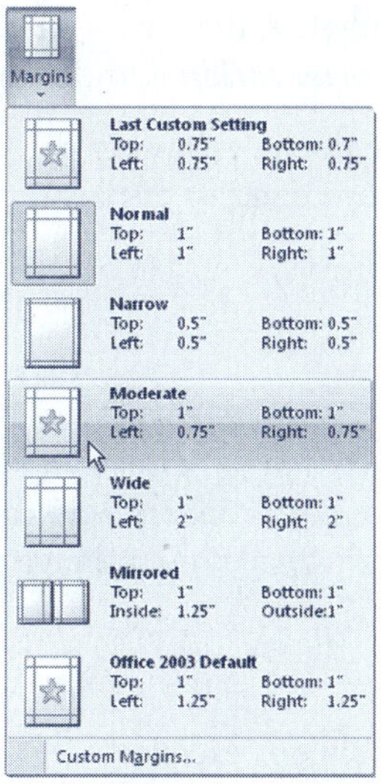

Figure 5-10

Margins menu

3. **SAVE** the document.

PAUSE. LEAVE the document open to use in the next exercise.

Margins are the blank spaces at the top, bottom, and sides of the page. To change the margins of a document, click the Page Layout tab. In the Page Setup group, click the Margins menu. Predefined margin settings are available for you to choose from. A good margin size to use for most documents is the default margin size of 1 inch for the top, bottom, left, and right margins. Click the setting of your choice and all the pages in the document will change to the setting. Click the Custom Margins command to display the Page Setup dialog box, where you can specify custom margin sizes.

CERTIFICATION READY?
How do you set margins?
1.2.1

Selecting a Page Orientation

As you plan and format your document, you also need to decide on the page orientation that best displays the content of your document. Word lets you change the orientation easily from portrait to landscape and back again if you need to, so you can choose the layout that is best for your document.

SELECT A PAGE ORIENTATION

USE the document that is open from the previous exercise.

1. In the Page Setup group of the Page Layout tab, click the **Orientation** menu and select **Landscape**, as shown in Figure 5-11. The page orientation changes to Landscape.

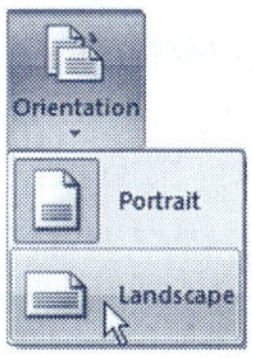

Figure 5-11

Orientation menu

2. Click the Orientation menu and select **Portrait**. The orientation is changed back to portrait.
3. **SAVE** the document.

PAUSE. LEAVE the document open to use in the next exercise.

> **CERTIFICATION READY?**
> How do you select a page orientation?
> **1.2.1**

Orientation refers to the layout of a document. A document in ***portrait orientation*** is taller than it is wide. A document in ***landscape orientation*** is wider than it is tall.

Change the orientation for a page or entire document using the Orientation command in the Page Setup group. Click the Orientation command to display a menu with the choices of Portrait or Landscape orientation.

Choosing a Paper Size

Microsoft Word helps you create documents of all kinds and sizes. When you need to print an invitation, postcard, legal document, or report, you can choose the paper size you need so that your document will print correctly on the paper.

CHOOSE A PAPER SIZE

USE the document that is open from the previous exercise.

1. From the Page Setup group of the Page Layout tab, click the **Size** menu and select **Legal**, as shown in Figure 5-12.

Figure 5-12

Size menu

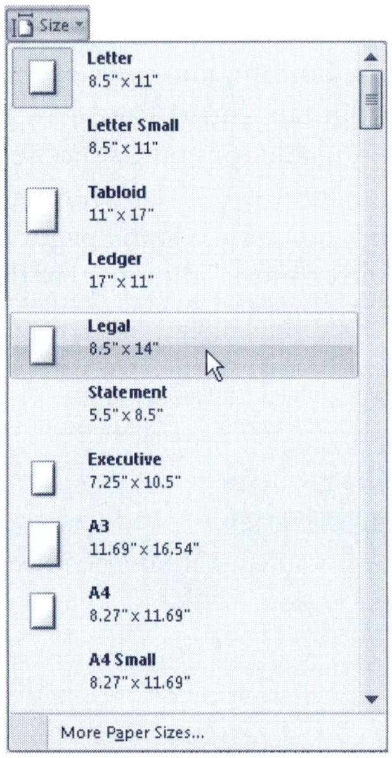

2. Click the **Size** menu and click **Letter**.
3. **SAVE** and **CLOSE** the document.

   STOP. CLOSE Word.

> **CERTIFICATION READY?**
> How do you choose a paper size?
> **1.2.1**

Many printers provide options for printing on various sizes of paper. In the Page Setup group, click the Size menu to choose a paper size. A menu appears with common paper sizes. If you need a custom paper size, click More Paper Sizes to display the Page Setup dialog box. In the Paper tab, you can enter a custom paper size and select the paper source. A preview shows what your printed page will look like. Click the Print Options button for more printing specifications.

SUMMARY SKILL MATRIX

In This Lesson You Learned	Matrix Skill	Skill Number
To set a colored background	Format document backgrounds	1.1.5
To add a watermark	Format document backgrounds	1.1.5
To place a border around a document's pages	Format document backgrounds	1.1.5
To add page numbers to a document	Create and modify headers and footers	1.2.2
To insert a built-in header or footer	Create and modify headers and footers	1.2.2
To insert a formatted header or footer from Quick Parts	Insert formatted headers and footers from Quick Parts	4.1.3
To add content to a header or footer	Create and modify headers and footers	1.2.2
To set margins	Format pages	1.2.1
To select a page orientation	Format pages	1.2.1
To choose a paper size	Format pages	1.2.1

Knowledge Assessment

Matching

Match the term in Column 1 to its description in Column 2.

Column 1	Column 2
1. watermark	**a.** a line inserted around the page
2. Header & Footer Tools	**b.** text or graphics located at the top of the document
3. content controls	**c.** a page that is taller than it is wide
4. page border	**d.** the blank spaces at the sides, top, and bottom of a document
5. page color	**e.** tiny programs that include a label for instructing you on the type of text to include and a placeholder that reserves a place for your new text
6. footer	**f.** are displayed in the ribbon after you insert a header or footer
7. portrait orientation	**g.** text or a graphic that is printed lightly behind the text of a document
8. landscape orientation	**h.** refers to the background color of a page
9. margins	**i.** text or graphics located at the bottom of a document
10. header	**j.** a page that is wider than it is tall

True / False

Circle T if the statement is true or F if the statement is false.

T | F **1.** You can only insert page numbers at the top or bottom of a document.

T | F **2.** Watermarks can be text or graphics.

T | F **3.** Triple-click to activate a header or footer.

T | F **4.** The default margin size is 1.5 inches for the top, bottom, left, and right margins.

T | F **5.** Built-in headers and footers provide instant design.

T | F **6.** In the Borders and Shading dialog box, you can specify to insert a page border on only the first page of a document.

T | F **7.** Paper size refers to landscape or portrait orientation.

T | F **8.** You can insert a picture as a page background.

T | F **9.** You cannot use a header in a document without also inserting a footer.

T | F **10.** You can specify a different header for odd and even pages.

Competency Assessment

Project 5-1: Certificate of Appreciation

Create a Certificate of Appreciation for a volunteer who has helped with the health and fitness programs at the YMCA this year.

GET READY. Launch Word if it is not already running.

1. **OPEN** ***Certificate of Appreciation*** from the data files for this lesson.

CD The ***Certificate of Appreciation*** document is available on the companion CD-ROM.

2. In the Page Layout tab, click the **Orientation** menu and select **Landscape**.
3. Click the **Margins** menu and select **Narrow**.
4. Click the **Page Borders** button and choose a box border with a rope style.
5. **SAVE** the document as ***certificate*** and **CLOSE** the file.

LEAVE Word open for the next project.

Project 5-2: Elevator Communications

Montgomery, Slade & Parker uses elevator communications for in-house announcements, invitations, and other employee relations documents. In each elevator, a durable 8 1/2 × 14-inch clear plastic frame has been installed in which announcements can be inserted and changed on a regular basis. Create a document that recognizes employee award winners and also invites employees to a reception to honor these award winners.

1. **OPEN** ***congratulations*** from the data files for this lesson.

CD The ***congratulations*** document is available on the companion CD-ROM.

2. Click the **Page Layout** tab. In the **Page Background** group, click the **Page Color** menu. In the Theme Colors section, choose a green for the background color. Choose **Olive Green, Accent 3, Lighter 60%**.

3. Click the **Page Borders** button. In the Borders and Shading dialog box, click **Shadow** in the Setting section. Click the **Width** menu and choose 3/4 pt.
4. In the Page Setup group, click the **Orientation** menu and select **Portrait**.
5. Click the **Size** menu and click **Legal**.
6. **SAVE** the document as ***elevatorcom*** and **CLOSE** the file.

LEAVE Word open for the next project.

Proficiency Assessment

Project 5-3: Two-Page Resume

Your friend Mike has revised and added some information to his resume, and it is now two pages. Update the formatting to include a header.

1. **OPEN** ***mzresume2*** from the data files for this lesson.

CD The ***mzresume2*** document is available on the companion CD-ROM.

2. Click the **Page Layout** tab. Click the **Margins** menu and select **Custom Margins**. In the Page Setup dialog box, key **1.25** in the Top box. Press the Tab key and key **1.25** in the Bottom box.
3. Press Tab and key **1.25** in the Left box. Press Tab and key **1.25** in the Right box.
4. Click **OK**.
5. Click the **Insert** tab. In the Header and Footer group, click the **Header** menu and select **Stacks**.
6. In the header, click **[Type the document title]** and key **Resume of Michael J. Zuberi.**
7. In the Options group, click the **Different First Page** box.
8. Click on page 2 to insert the insertion point anywhere on the page.
9. Click the **Footer** button and click **Stacks**.
10. Right-click **[Type the Company Name]**. In the shortcut menu, click **Remove Content Control**.
11. **SAVE** the document as ***mzresume2updated*** and **CLOSE** it.

LEAVE Word open for the next project.

Project 5-4: Letterhead

The Grand Street Coffee Shop needs new letterhead. Create one using Word.

1. **OPEN** a new blank document.
2. Insert the **Tiles** built-in header and key the document title as **Grand Street Coffee Shop**. Change the text to bold, size 18 point.
3. Click the **Year** content control and then click the downward-pointing arrow. In the calendar that appears, click **Today**.
4. Insert the Tiles built-in footer and key the company address as **1234 Grand Street, Forest Grove, OR 97116**.
5. **SAVE** the document as ***gsletterhead*** and **CLOSE** the file.

LEAVE Word open for the next project.

Mastery Assessment

Project 5-5: Postcard

It's soccer season again, and the YMCA is sending out postcards to all participants who played last season. Use Word to create the postcard.

1. **OPEN** ***soccer*** from the data files for this lesson.

CD The ***soccer*** document is available on the companion CD-ROM.

2. In the Page Setup group, change the Page Size to **4 X 6 in**, the page orientation to **Landscape**, and the margins to **Narrow**.
3. In the Page Background group, click the **Page Borders** button and insert a red double-line page border (Box setting) that is 3/4 pt. wide.
4. Click the **Page Color** menu and click **Fill Effects**. In the Fill Effects dialog box in the Colors section, click **One Color**. In the Shading styles section, click **Horizontal**. Click the sample **horizontal** pattern in the lower right corner.
5. Click the **Watermark** menu and click **Custom Watermark**. In the Printed Watermark dialog box, click **Text Watermark** and select **ASAP**. Key **YMCA SOCCER**. Click the **Horizontal** button and click **OK**.
6. **SAVE** the document as ***postcard*** and **CLOSE** the file.

   LEAVE Word open for the next project.

Project 5-6: Thank You Notes

Create thank you notes that match the style of Mike's new two-page resume.

1. Create a new blank document.
2. Choose the **Statement** (5.5 × 8.5) paper size, portrait orientation, and narrow margins. Keep in mind that the note will be folded in the middle and the words *Thank You* will be on the front of the note.
3. Referring to the ***mzresume2updated*** document, insert the same footer. Key **Thank You** where the company name would go. Be sure to use the same font, size, and style as Mike's name on the resume.
4. **SAVE** the document as ***thankyou*** and **CLOSE** the file.

   CLOSE Word.

INTERNET READY

Research the cities that have been rated the "Best Places to Live." Choose one of the top ten and find out why it ranked so high. Create a promotional document touting the positive ranking and listing reasons for the ranking. The document could be a flyer, postcard, or letter that city officials could mail to prospective businesses and families who request information about the city.

Working with Templates

6

LESSON SKILL MATRIX

Skills	Matrix Skill	Skill Number
Locating a Template Installed on Your Computer	Work with templates	1.1.1
Finding Templates on the Internet	Work with templates	1.1.1
Creating a Business Letter from a Template	Work with templates	1.1.1
Creating a Memo from a Template	Work with templates	1.1.1
Adding a Cover Sheet	Insert blank pages or cover pages	1.1.6
Modifying an Existing Template	Work with templates	1.1.1
Creating a New Template	Work with templates	1.1.1

You are the president of the Lakeville .NET User's Group, a group of students, faculty, and professionals in the community whose purpose is to educate, help build development skills, and provide a forum for networking. This group meets monthly and regularly schedules workshops and speakers on relevant topics. In this role, you are discovering that you use many of the same types of documents on a regular basis, and it would be helpful to streamline the process of creating similar documents. In this lesson, you will learn how to locate a template, create different kinds of documents using templates, modify an existing template, and create your own template.

KEY TERMS

cover sheet
template

SOFTWARE ORIENTATION

Template Options in the New Document Dialog Box

You can work more efficiently by basing many of your new documents on templates that Word provides. When you create a new document in Word, you have many choices for working with templates, as shown in Figure 6-1.

Figure 6-1

New Document dialog box

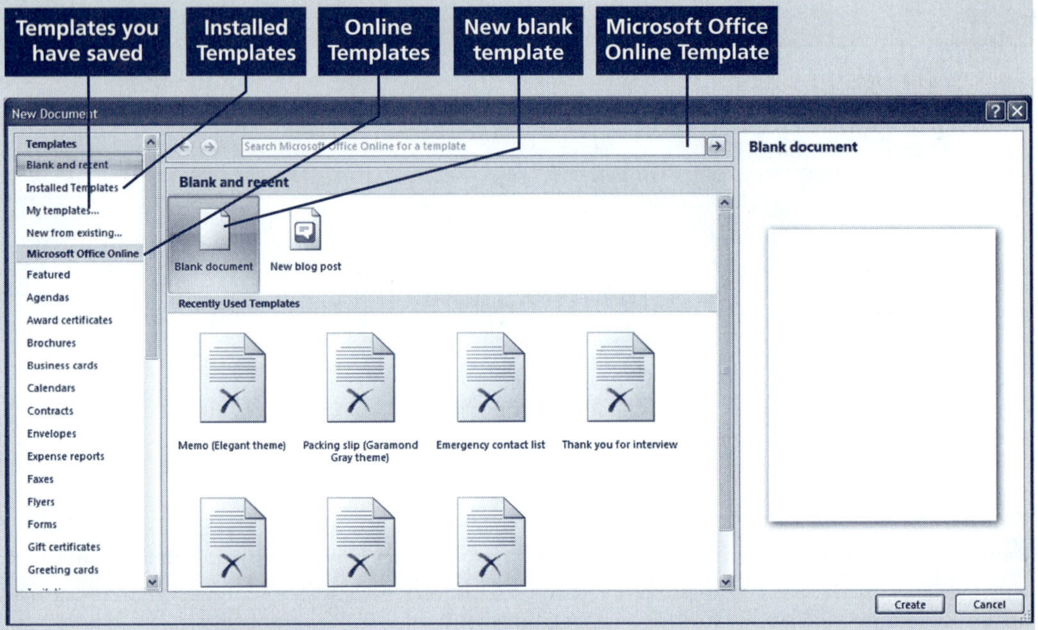

Templates save you the work of recreating documents each time you need one that is similar. In the New Document dialog box, you can choose to work with a template that is already installed, search for a template online, open a blank template, or create your own template.

Finding Templates

THE BOTTOM LINE

The first step in working with templates is finding the one you need. You can choose from many different categories of templates, including letters, memos, resumes, flyers, and forms. Some templates come installed with Word, and many more options are available online.

Locating a Template Installed on Your Computer

Although you can always search online for specific templates to create just about any type of document, Word does come with some of the more basic templates already installed.

LOCATE A TEMPLATE INSTALLED ON YOUR COMPUTER

GET READY. Before you begin these steps, be sure to launch Microsoft Word.

1. Click the **Microsoft Office Button** and then click **New** to open the New Document dialog box.
2. In the Template Categories list on the left, click **Installed Templates**.
3. In the Installed Templates list that appears, scroll down and click **Origin Fax**. A preview of the template appears in the right pane, as shown in Figure 6-2.

TROUBLESHOOTING Your computer may not have all the same pre-installed templates. If the ones used in these activities do not appear in your Installed Templates list, simply choose another.

Figure 6-2

Installed Templates

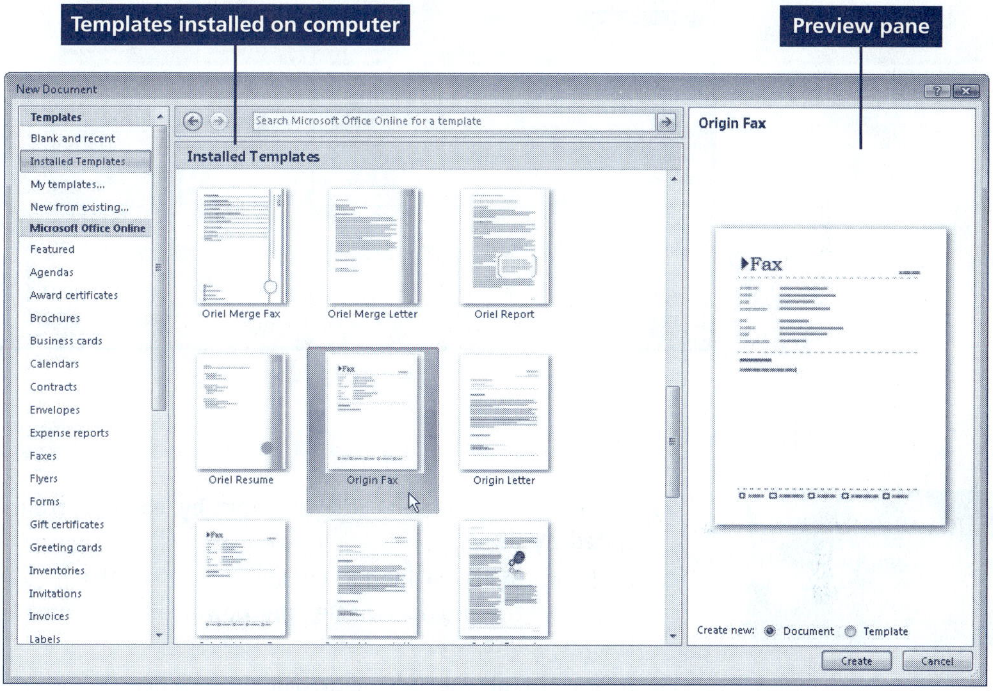

4. To see the other templates that are available, scroll through the list and click one to show a preview.

PAUSE. LEAVE the New Document dialog box open for the next exercise.

CERTIFICATION READY? How do you work with templates? **1.1.1**

A ***template*** is a master document that has predefined page layout, fonts, margins, and styles and is used to create new documents that will share the same basic formatting. To see a list of templates that come installed with Word, click Installed Templates in the New Document box. As you scroll through the list, you can click a template to preview it.

Finding Templates on the Internet

If you cannot find an already-installed template that you want, many more options are available on the Internet. Microsoft offers numerous templates online, and templates are also available from third-party providers, as well as other users in the community.

FIND TEMPLATES ON THE INTERNET

1. In the New Document dialog box, on the left below Microsoft Office Online, click **Agendas**.
2. A list of agenda templates available online is displayed, as shown in Figure 6-3.

Figure 6-3

Online Templates in the New Document dialog box

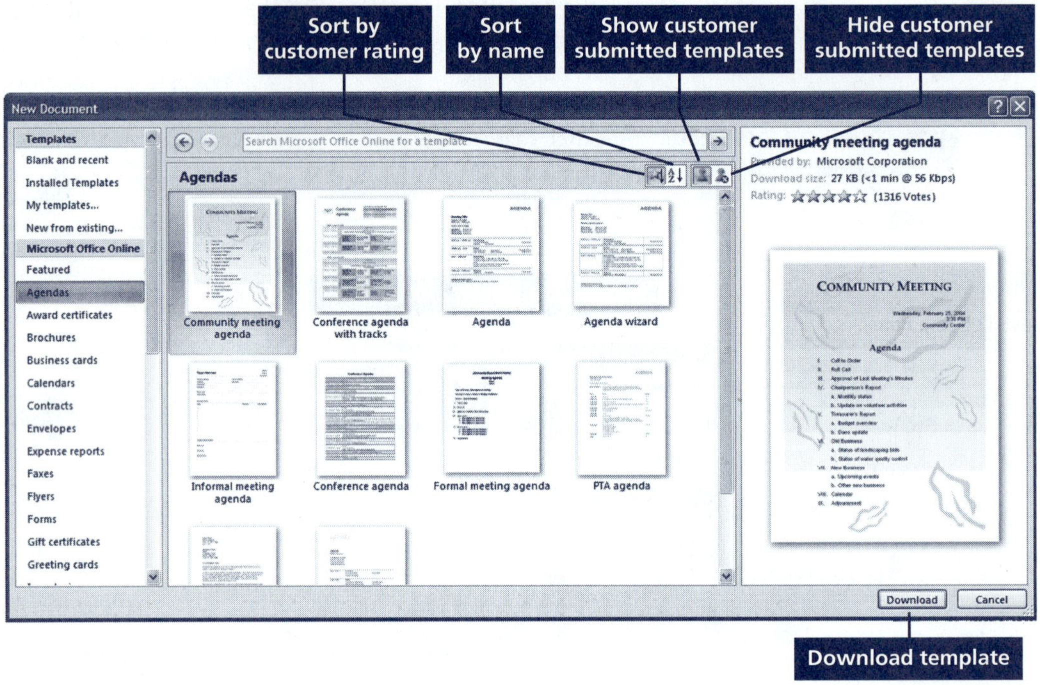

TAKE NOTE*

You must be connected to the Internet to view online templates.

CERTIFICATION READY?
How do you work with templates?
1.1.1

3. In the *Sort by* section, click the **Sort by name** button. The list of templates is sorted by name.
4. Click any template in the window. Notice in the preview pane that details, including the provider name, the download size, and the rating, are shown for that template.
5. In the list on the left below Microsoft Office Online, click **Flyers**. Notice that categories like this one have numerous options, which are divided into subcategories.
6. Click **Event** to see the templates in that subcategory.

PAUSE. LEAVE the New Document dialog box open for the next exercise.

You can use the Microsoft Office Online list on the left of the New Document box to browse for templates by category. You can also use the Search bar at the top to search by keywords.

Users can vote to rate online templates. Each template's rating information appears above its preview, in the right portion of the New Document window. This rating system is helpful in determining which template you want to use. After searching for templates on the Internet, you can sort them by rating or name. Community templates are those submitted by other users. You can choose to show or hide these community templates from your list of search results.

When you locate the template you want to use, click the Download button. The document will automatically be downloaded to your computer and opened in Word.

Using Templates to Create Documents

THE BOTTOM LINE

Now that you are familiar with locating templates, you can use them to create new documents by choosing ones that suit your tasks. When you use a template, you make changes and then save it as a different file while the original template remains unchanged. You can use a template as many times as needed.

Creating a Business Letter from a Template

Letters are among the most common type of document produced on the job. Word provides many templates for business letters so that you can pick one that is just right for your needs.

CREATE A BUSINESS LETTER FROM A TEMPLATE

1. In the list of template categories on the left of the New Document dialog box, click **Letters**.
2. In the Letters Subcategories list that appears, click **Business**.
3. In the Business Letters Subcategories list, click **Meeting and Seminar Planning.**
4. Scroll down and select the **Thank You Letter to Speaker** template.
5. Click the **Download** button.
6. Replace the fields in the document by keying the following information:

   [Your Name]: **Kwame Alford**

   [Street Address]: **89 Skipper Road**
   [City, ST ZIP Code]: **Lakeville, CT 06039**
   [the date will automatically be added here]
   [Recipient Name]: **Dalia Weaver**
   [Title]: **Regional Director**
   [Company Name]: **ConnectIT Consulting**
   [Street Address]: **764 Housatonic Boulevard**
   [City, ST ZIP Code]: **Millerton, NY 12546**
   [Recipient Name]: **Dalia**
   [Organization Name]: **Lakeville .NET User's Group**
   [Date]: **October 17**
   [topic]: **reporting**
   [topic]: **related technology**
   [Organization Name]: **Lakeville .NET User's Group**
   [Your Name]: **Kwame Alford**
   [Title]: **President**
7. To save the document as ***speaker_thanks,*** click **OK** in the message box that says the document will be saved in Word 2007 format. Then **CLOSE** the file.

   PAUSE. LEAVE Word open for the next exercise.

In this activity, you saw how easy it is to create a business letter based on a template. The layout and formatting is already part of the document, and all you have to do is key your specific information. You can even use the same text—or simply customize it to fit your needs.

CERTIFICATION READY?
How do you work with templates?
1.1.1

Creating a Memo from a Template

Memos are also often needed at any company or organization. You can quickly create an attractive memo by choosing one of the available templates.

CREATE A MEMO FROM A TEMPLATE

CERTIFICATION READY?
How do you work with templates?
1.1.1

1. Click the **Microsoft Office Button** and then click **New** to open the New Document dialog box.
2. On the left below Microsoft Office Online, click **Memos**.
3. In the list of memos, click **Memo (Professional Design)** if it is not already selected.
4. Click the **Download** button.
5. Delete the *CC:* line and key text so that your memo looks similar to Figure 6-4.

Figure 6-4
Memo

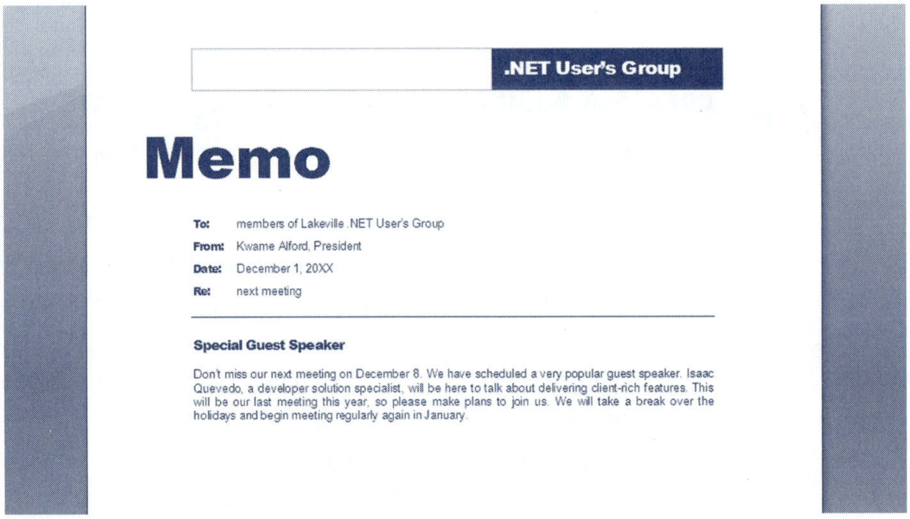

6. **SAVE** the document as ***meeting_memo*** and **CLOSE** the file.

PAUSE. LEAVE Word open for the next exercise.

When creating a memo from scratch, you would typically need to set up tabs along with other formatting. By using a memo template, you can save a lot of time and effort by just keying your text in the fields provided.

Adding a Cover Sheet

NEW FEATURE

Even if you do not have design skills, you can still add a professional-looking cover page to your documents by using the gallery of choices Word offers.

ADD A COVER SHEET

CD

The *group_info* document is available on the companion CD-ROM.

1. **OPEN** ***group_info*** from the data files for this lesson.
2. On the Insert tab, in the Pages group, click **Cover Page**. The cover page gallery options are displayed, as shown in Figure 6-5.

Figure 6-5

Cover Page options

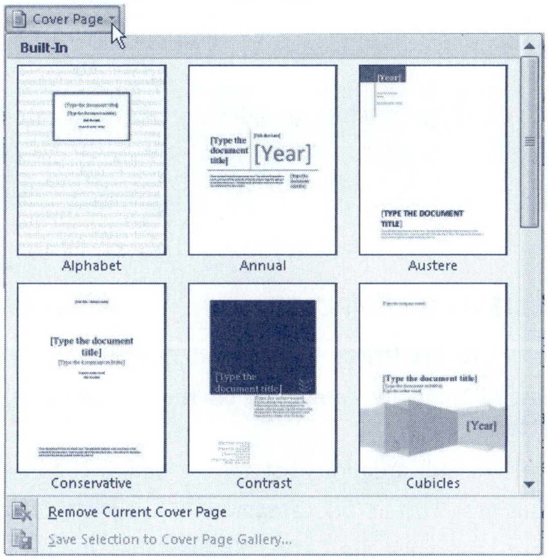

3. Scroll down and select **Stacks**. A cover page with that format is inserted at the beginning of the document.
4. Key **Lakeville .NET User's Group** as the document title.
5. Key **Information** as the document subtitle.
6. Key your name as the author name. Your cover page should look similar to Figure 6-6.

Figure 6-6

Cover page

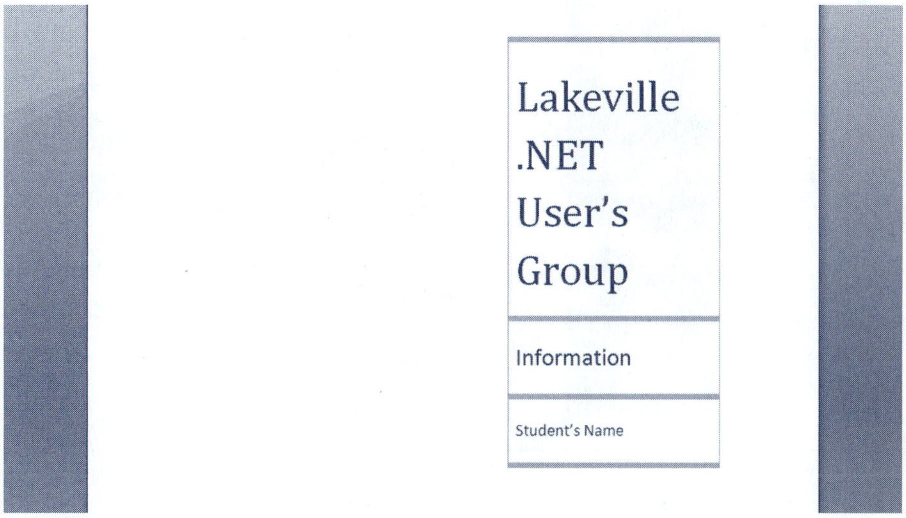

7. **SAVE** the document as ***group_cover*** and **CLOSE** the file.

PAUSE. LEAVE Word open for the next exercise.

CERTIFICATION READY?
How do you insert blank pages or cover pages?
1.1.6

A ***cover sheet*** is the first page of a document that typically includes an author, title, and date. If you cannot find a cover sheet style that fits your exact needs, you can modify an existing design. Or if your company has cover page designs with a corporate logo, you can easily incorporate them.

■ Managing Templates

THE BOTTOM LINE

If you use a certain document frequently, you can work more efficiently by turning it into a template so that it is available each time you need it. You can either modify an existing template or create a new one.

Modifying an Existing Template

To create a new template based on an existing one, choose the template that is similar to the one you need and make the changes you want to the format and/or text. Then you can save it as a new template for future use.

MODIFY AN EXISTING TEMPLATE

1. Click the **Microsoft Office Button** and then click **New**.
2. In the list of template categories on the left of the New Document dialog box, click **Letters**.
3. In the Letters Subcategories list that appears, click **Business**.
4. In the Business Letters Subcategories list, click **Meeting and Seminar Planning**.
5. Scroll down and click the **Letter Requesting Unpaid Speaker for Meeting** template.
6. Click the **Download** button.
7. Replace the fields with the text shown shaded on Figure 6-7.

TAKE NOTE*

You can also modify an existing document to create a new template.

Figure 6-7

Modify an existing template

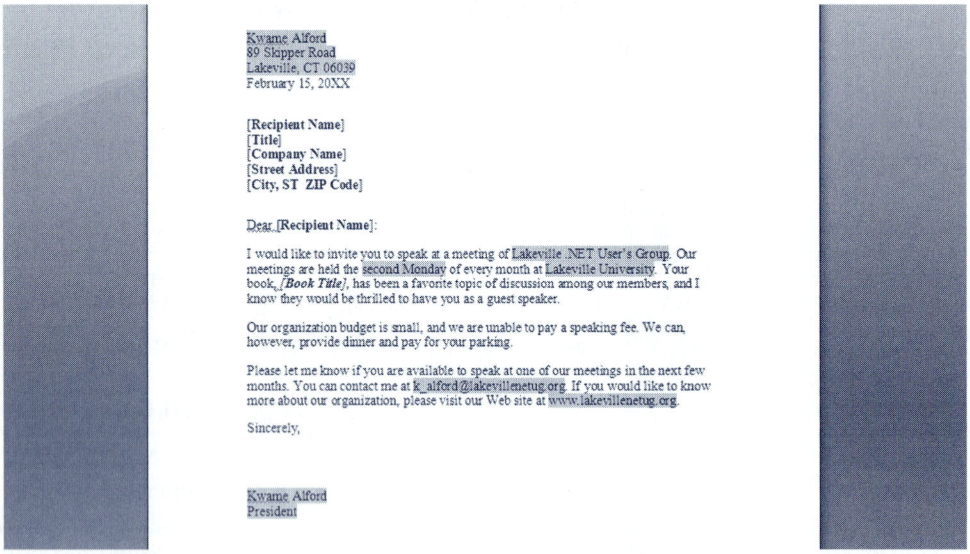

Kwame Alford
89 Skipper Road
Lakeville, CT 06039
February 15, 20XX

[Recipient Name]
[Title]
[Company Name]
[Street Address]
[City, ST ZIP Code]

Dear [Recipient Name]:

I would like to invite you to speak at a meeting of Lakeville .NET User's Group. Our meetings are held the second Monday of every month at Lakeville University. Your book, *[Book Title]*, has been a favorite topic of discussion among our members, and I know they would be thrilled to have you as a guest speaker.

Our organization budget is small, and we are unable to pay a speaking fee. We can, however, provide dinner and pay for your parking.

Please let me know if you are available to speak at one of our meetings in the next few months. You can contact me at k_alford@lakevillenetug.org. If you would like to know more about our organization, please visit our Web site at www.lakevillenetug.org.

Sincerely,

Kwame Alford
President

8. Click the **Microsoft Office Button**, and then click **Save As**.
9. In the Save As dialog box, click **Trusted Templates**, as shown in Figure 6-8.

Figure 6-8

Save a modified template

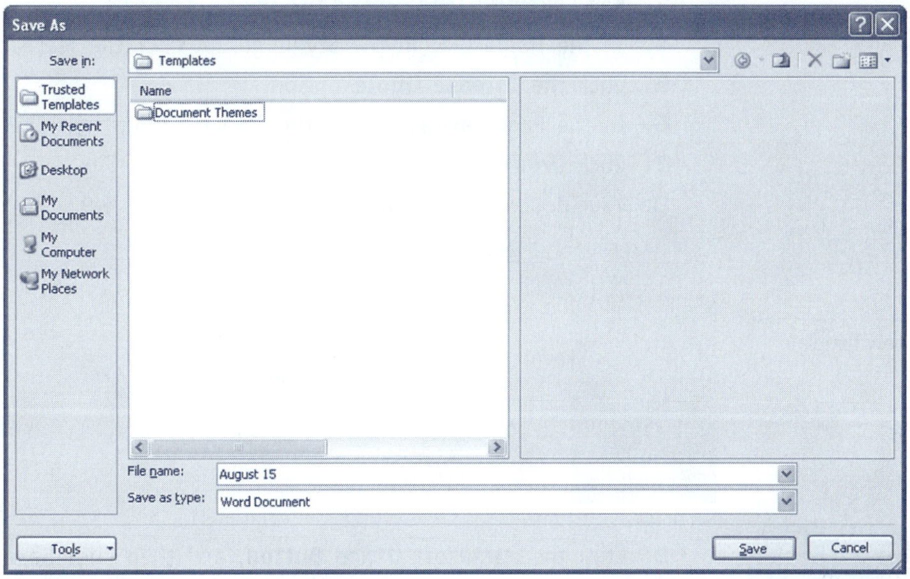

10. In the File Name box, key **speaker_request_XXX (where XXX is your initials)**.
11. In the Save As Type list, choose **Word Macro-Enabled Template**.

TAKE NOTE*

Template file types can be either Word Template (.dotx files), Word Macro-Enabled Template (.dotm files), or Word 97-2003 Template (.dot files).

12. Click the **SAVE** button and **CLOSE** the file.

PAUSE. LEAVE Word open for the next exercise.

CERTIFICATION READY?
How do you work with templates?
1.1.1

In this activity, you opened an existing template, modified it with the information you want to be a permanent part of the document, and then saved it as a new template. It is now ready to be opened and used just as other templates are.

TROUBLESHOOTING

Do not modify the ***Normal.dotm*** template. This is the template that is used whenever you start Microsoft Office Word 2007 and open a blank document, and it includes default styles and customizations that determine the basic look of a document. If you make any changes to the ***Normal.dotm*** template, they will be applied to any documents that you create in the future.

Creating a New Template

You can create a new template with formatting or text that you want to use frequently. For example, you could create a company letterhead and then save it as a template to use for all of your correspondence.

CREATE A NEW TEMPLATE

1. Click the **Microsoft Office Button** and then click **New**.
2. Click **Blank document** and then click **Create**.
3. Key **Lakeville .NET User's Group**.
4. In the Home tab, in the Styles group, click the **More** button.
5. Click the **Intense Quote** option.
6. In the Page Layout tab, in the Themes group, click the **Themes** button.
7. Click **Urban** on the Themes menu.
8. Your document should look similar to Figure 6-9.

Figure 6-9

Document for new template

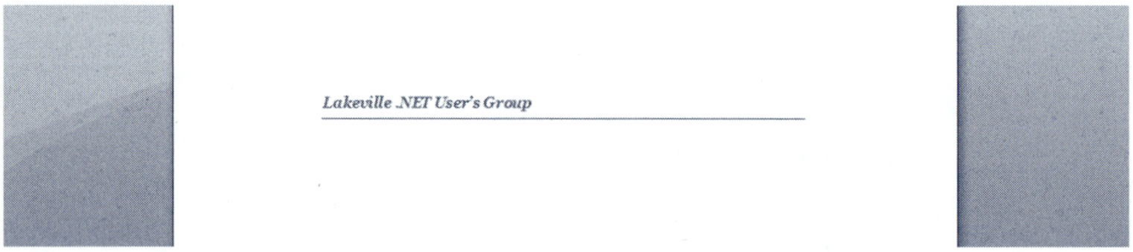

CERTIFICATION READY?
How do you work with templates?
1.1.1

9. Click the **Microsoft Office Button**, and then click **Save As**.
10. In the Save As dialog box, click **Trusted Templates**.
11. In the File Name box, key **letterhead_XXX (where XXX is your initials)**.
12. In the Save As Type list, choose **Word Template**.
13. Click the **Save** button and **CLOSE** the file.

    STOP. CLOSE Word.

In this activity, you created a new template from scratch. By saving a template in Trusted Templates, it will be available in your template folder when you are ready to use it.

X REF

You can also save and distribute building blocks with a template. You will learn about building blocks in Lesson 8.

SUMMARY SKILL MATRIX

In This Lesson You Learned	Matrix Skill	Skill Number
To locate a template installed on your computer	Work with templates	1.1.1
To find templates on the Internet	Work with templates	1.1.1
To create a business letter from a template	Work with templates	1.1.1
To create a memo from a template	Work with templates	1.1.1
To add a cover sheet	Insert blank pages or cover sheets	1.1.6
To modify an existing template	Work with templates	1.1.1
To create a new template	Work with templates	1.1.1

■ Knowledge Assessment

Fill in the Blank

Complete the following sentences by writing the correct word or words in the blanks provided.

1. A ____________ is a master document that has predefined page layout, fonts, margins, and styles.
2. There are many different ____________ of templates to choose from, including letters, memos, resumes, flyers, and forms.
3. Some templates come ____________ with Word, many more options are available online.
4. As you scroll through the list of available templates, you can click a template to ____________ it in the pane on the right.
5. You can use the Search bar to search for templates by ____________.
6. You can choose to show or hide ____________ templates, which are those submitted by other users.
7. When you have found the template you want online, click the ____________ button.
8. By saving a template you create in ____________ Templates, it will be available in your template folder when you are ready to use it.
9. You must be connected to the Internet to view ____________ templates.
10. Categories of templates that have numerous options are divided into ____________.

Multiple Choice

Select the best response for the following statements.

1. Template options are displayed in which dialog box?
   - **a.** New Template
   - **b.** New Document
   - **c.** Template Options
   - **d.** Locate Template
2. Which is NOT an option for working with templates?
   - **a.** Delete the ***Normal.dotm*** template
   - **b.** Search for a template online
   - **c.** Open a blank template
   - **d.** Create your own template
3. Templates are available from what source?
   - **a.** Installed with Word
   - **b.** Third-party providers
   - **c.** Users in the community
   - **d.** All of the above
   - **e.** None of the above

4. What determines the rating of a template?
   a. The level of detail it has
   b. The number of stars assigned by Microsoft
   c. How often it is downloaded
   d. Community user votes
5. In the preview pane of the New Document dialog box, what details about a template are listed?
   a. Number of times it has been downloaded
   b. Date of last download
   c. Author comments
   d. All of the above
   e. None of the above
6. How many times can you use a template?
   a. Once
   b. Ten
   c. 100
   d. As many as needed
7. When you use a template, make changes, and then save it as a different file, what happens to the original template?
   a. Remains unchanged
   b. Goes to the Recycle Bin
   c. Saved at the end of the new file
   d. Moved to the Installed Templates folder
8. What is the first page of a document that typically includes an author, title, and date called?
   a. Information sheet
   b. Cover sheet
   c. Document cover
   d. Template cover
9. Which is NOT an option for creating a new template?
   a. Insert the ***Normal.dotm*** template into a blank document
   b. Modify an existing document
   c. Modify an existing template
   d. Create a new template from scratch
10. To find a template on the Internet, you can browse through categories in what dialog box list?
    a. Community Templates
    b. Internet Documents
    c. Web Templates
    d. Microsoft Office Online

Competency Assessment

Project 6-1: Using a Template You Created

You want to invite a guest speaker to a future meeting of Lakeville .NET User's Group. Because you have already created a customized letter template, all you have to do is open it and insert the new information.

GET READY. Launch Word if it is not already running.

1. Click the **Microsoft Office Button** and then click **New** to open the New Document dialog box.
2. In the New Blank section, click **My Templates...**.
3. In the New dialog box, shown in Figure 6-10, click the ***speaker_request_XXX*** file (**where XXX is your initials**) that you saved earlier in this lesson.

Figure 6-10
New dialog box

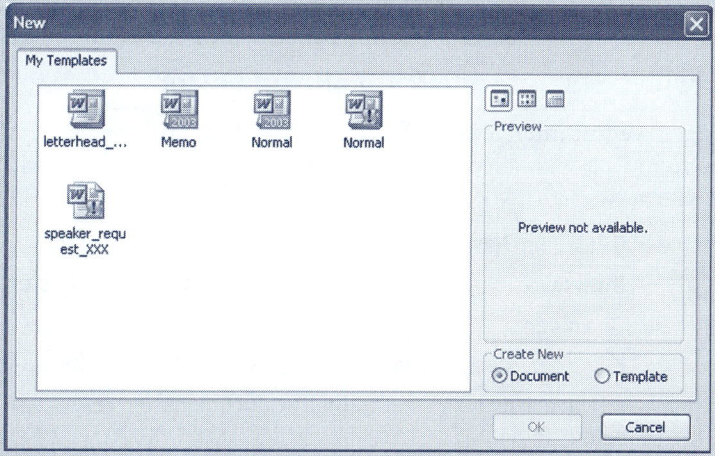

4. In the Create New section, **Document** should be selected.
5. Click **OK**.
6. Replace the fields in the document by keying the following information:
   [Recipient Name]: Luke Ibarra
   [Title]: Development Architect
   [Company Name]: Ibarra Solutions Company
   [Street Address]: 3435 Olton Road
   [City, ST ZIP Code]: Great Barrington, MA 01230
   [Recipient Name]: Mr. Ibarra
   [*Book Title*]: *Changing the Way You Interact with Databases*
7. **SAVE** the document as ***speaker_request*** and **CLOSE** the file.
   LEAVE Word open for the next project.

Project 6-2: Add a Cover Page

In your job at Books and Beyond, you continue to work on documents that will be part of the employee handbook. Now that you know how to add a cover page, you will add one to the acknowledgment document.

1. **OPEN** ***handbook_acknowledge*** from the data files for this lesson.

CD The ***handbook_acknowledge*** document is available on the companion CD-ROM.

2. On the Insert tab, in the Pages group, click **Cover Page**.
3. Scroll down and select **Cubicles**. A cover page with that format is inserted at the beginning of the document.
4. Key **Books and Beyond** as the company name.
5. Key **Employee Handbook** as the document title.
6. Key **First Edition** as the document subtitle.
7. The author's name should have been inserted automatically. If it is not your name, replace it with yours.
8. Key the current year in the Year field.
9. **SAVE** the document as ***handbook_cover*** and **CLOSE** the file.

   LEAVE Word open for the next project.

Proficiency Assessment

Project 6-3: Interview Thank You Letter

You have just interviewed for a project manager position at Whitbeck Technologies. You want to follow up with a letter to the person who interviewed you and decide to find a template to help you with the wording and format.

1. **OPEN** the New dialog box.
2. Browse to the **Letters: Employment: Interview Letters** category.
3. Download the **Thank You for Interview** letter.
4. Key your name, address, phone, and a date in the appropriate fields.
5. Replace the other fields in the document by keying the following information where indicated:

   [Recipient Name]: **Kim Preston**
   [Title]: **Vice President of Production**
   [Company Name]: **Whitbeck Technologies**
   [Street Address]: **1218 Joliet Avenue**
   [City, ST ZIP Code]: **Wilmore, KY 40390**
   [Recipient Name]: **Ms. Preston**
   [Job Title]: **project manager**
6. **SAVE** the document as ***interview_thanks*** and **CLOSE** the file.

   LEAVE Word open for the next project.

Project 6-4: Emergency Contact List

Templates provide an easy way to create documents that you might use around your home, as well as at work. In an earlier lesson, you created a list of numbers that you call frequently to keep beside your phone. Now you decide to look for a template that would simplify that process.

1. **OPEN** the New dialog box.
2. Browse the online **Lists** category.
3. Download **Emergency Contact List**.
4. Fill in the emergency contact names and numbers.
5. **SAVE** the document as ***emergency_contacts*** and **CLOSE** the file.

   LEAVE Word open for the next project.

Mastery Assessment

Project 6-5: Fax Cover Sheet

In your position at Tech Terrace Real Estate, you frequently have to fax documents and need an attractive cover sheet. You decide to see what templates are available, choose one, modify it, and save it as a new template for future use.

1. Search the templates for a fax cover sheet that you like.
2. Fill out any of the information that would likely stay the same for each fax.
3. **SAVE** the document as ***fax_cover*** and **CLOSE** the file.

   LEAVE Word open for the next project.

Project 6-6: Create a Resume

Templates are a great way to help you create a resume. Resume templates provide all the structure and formatting needed—you can just fill in your own information.

1. Search or browse the template options available to find resume templates.
2. Download a resume template that you like.
3. Fill in the document with as much information as you have.
4. **SAVE** the document as ***my_resume*** and **CLOSE** the file.

   CLOSE Word.

INTERNET READY

For more information and template options, visit the Microsoft Office Online Templates site by clicking Featured in the list on the left under Microsoft Office Online of the New Document dialog box. In the section at the bottom, click Templates below More on Office Online. A Web browser opens with a whole site about Microsoft templates, as on shown in Figure 6-11.

Figure 6-11

Microsoft Office Online Templates site

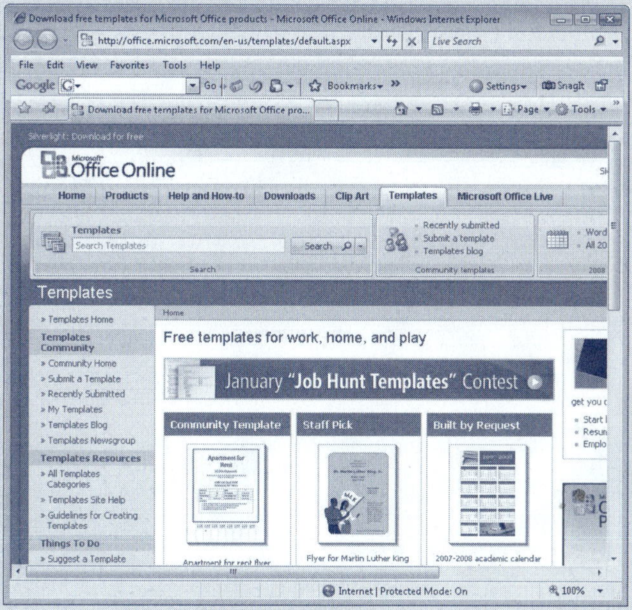

Explore the resources available on this site and then close the browser.

Workplace Ready

Working with Templates in Word

In today's business world, coming up with new ideas for various business documents can be easy. Actually trying to produce those documents may prove slightly more challenging. Time equals money in the workplace. Using any one of the many templates available in Word is the best way to quickly create a new document. The use of templates can also help to avoid the frustrations often associated with creating documents from scratch.

Your family owns and operates Tailspin Toys, a company that sells vintage and collectible toys. You decide to take on the task of streamlining the company's packing and shipping process. When doing this, you find that the packing slips currently accompanying your company's shipments do not contain all of the necessary information for each shipment.

With Word, you can choose from a wide variety of templates, from business letters and calendars to packing slips. Although two or more templates may contain the same information, each has a unique style of formatting. You can choose not only the appropriate type of template, but also the style that best fits your needs. You can also create your own template to include customized information and formatting.

Once you have chosen an appropriate packing slip template, you can add standard information, such as your company logo, company name, address, phone number, and email address. You can then save this template with a unique name, such as Tailspin Toys Packing Slip, so it will be easily recognizable when you later need to locate the file. Then, for each individual shipment, you can enter the appropriate information into preset fields, such as the ship to and bill to addresses, order date, order number, job, item number, description, and quantity.

By starting with a Word template, you can easily produce documents to fit all of your needs in a relatively short amount of time.

Circling Back

The National Association of Professional Consultants is a professional organization that serves a varied membership of consultants. Each year, the association has a three-day professional development conference. The association is now planning the upcoming conference. As the association's membership manager, your job includes a wide variety of tasks related to organizing and communicating information related to membership. In addition, you are working with the conference planning committee to help secure speakers for the conference and market the conference to members.

Project 1: LETTER

Create a letter using a template from Microsoft Office Online requesting a speaker for the conference's banquet. Modify and customize the letter.

GET READY. Launch Word if it is not already running.

1. Click the **Microsoft Office Button** and click **New**.
2. Choose and download the Request for Paid Speaker at Banquet template. You should find it under Letters, Business, Meeting and Seminar Planning.
3. Replace the fields in the document by keying the following information:
   [Your Name]: **Susan Pasha**
   [Street Address]: **5678 Circle St.**
   [City, ST ZIP Code]: **Kansas City, MO 64163**
   [Recipient Name]: **Daniel Slade**
   [Title]: **President, Strategies and Operations**
   [Company Name]: **Montgomery, Slade and Parker**
   [Street Address]: **3333 Lakeside Way**
   [City, ST ZIP Code]: **Chicago, IL 60611**
   [Recipient Name]: **Mr. Slade**
   [Your Name]: **Susan Pasha**
   [Title]: **President**
4. Save the document as ***conf_speaker***.
5. If a message box opens telling you that the document will be converted to the Word 2007 file format, click **OK**.
6. Change the date of the letter to **June 15, 20XX**.
7. In the first sentence of the body of the letter, select *travel agents'* and key **consultants'**.
8. In the second sentence, select *Alpine Ski House in Breckenridge, Colorado* and key **Lakeview Towers in South Lake Tahoe, California**.
9. Select the text you just keyed and apply the **Emphasis** style.
10. Change the date of the evening to **September 16** and apply the **Emphasis** style.
11. In the last sentence of the letter, select *convention* and key **conference**.
12. **SAVE** the document.
13. On the **Insert** tab, in the **Header & Footer** group, insert the **Transcend (Even)** header.

14. Select the **Title** placeholder text and key **National Association of Professional Consultants**.
15. Change the font to **Arial Unicode MS 12 pt. bold**.
16. Click the **arrow** on the Pick the Date content control and click **Today**.
17. Click the **Date** content control to select it. In the **Header and Footer Tools** tab, **Insert** group, click **Date & Time**. Change the format to **00-Month-00**.
18. Change the font to **Arial Unicode MS 10 pt**.
19. Insert the **Transcend (Odd Page)** footer.
20. At the blinking insertion point, key **5678 Circle Street, Kansas City, MO 64163**. (The address should be right aligned.)
21. Change the font to **Arial Unicode MS 12 pt**.
22. Select the page number and change its font to **Arial Unicode MS 12 pt**.
23. Change the margins of the page to **Moderate**.
24. Double-click in the body of the document to de-activate the headers.
25. On the **View** tab, in the **Zoom** group, click the **One Page** button to view the document on the screen.
26. Click **Page Width**.
27. Insert three blank lines before the return address to center the letter on the page.
28. On the **Page Layout** tab, in the **Themes** group, click the **Theme Colors** menu and choose **Opulent**.
29. **SAVE** the changes.

    PAUSE. LEAVE Word and the document open for the next project.

Project 2: Envelope

Create an envelope in which you can mail the letter.

USE the document that is open from the previous project.

1. Select the recipient's name, title, company name, and address.
2. On the **Mailings** tab, in the **Create** group, click **Envelopes**. The selected address should appear in the Delivery Address box.
3. In the Return Address box, key:

   Susan Pasha

   5678 Circle St.

   Kansas City, MO 64163
4. Click the **Add to Document** button. (When a dialog box appears asking if you want to save the new return address as the default, click **No**.)
5. Click **Ctrl** + **P** to open the Print dialog box.
6. In the Print dialog box, in the Page Range section, click **Pages** and key **0**. This will print only the envelope and not the accompanying letter.
7. Insert the envelope in the printer's manual feeder and click **OK**.
8. **SAVE** the changes and **CLOSE** the file.

   PAUSE. LEAVE Word open for the next project.

Project 3: Postcard

Create a postcard to announce the date of the conference to members and to solicit early registrations.

1. Create a new blank document.
2. On the **Page Layout** tab, in the **Page Setup** group, use the **Size** command to create a custom paper size of **4.25″** wide and **5.5″** high.
3. Change the document to landscape orientation with narrow margins.
4. On the **Insert** tab, in the **Header & Footer** group, insert the **Transcend (Even)** header.
5. Select the **Date** placeholder text and key **20XX**. Change the font to **Calibri 18 pt. bold**.
6. Select the **Title** placeholder and key **NAPC PROFESSIONAL CONFERENCE**. Change the font to 18 pt. bold.
7. Double-click in the body of the postcard and key the following text:

   September 14–16

   Lakeview Towers in South Lake Tahoe, California

   Early Bird Registration $329; Regular Rate $389

   Admission to all keynotes, seminars, and breakout sessions

   Ticket to Saturday night banquet

   All meals included

   Early Bird Deadline is August 1, 20XX

   Register online at www.napc20XX.com or call 800-555-5678
8. Make sure you do not press Enter after the last line of keyed text.
9. Select *September 14–16,* change the font to Calibri 20 pt. Bold, and center it.
10. Select the *Lakeview Towers . . .* line of text, change it to 14 pt., and center it.
11. Click the **View Ruler** button to display the ruler if it isn't displayed already.
12. Place the insertion point before the *E* in *Early Bird Registration. . . .* Click on the .5″ position to insert a left tab.
13. Press the Tab key to indent the paragraph.
14. Select the three lines of text under the registration costs information and format them as a bulleted list.
15. Select *$329*. Change the font color to **Purple, Accent 4, Lighter 40%** and bold it.
16. On the **Home** tab, in the **Clipboard** group, use the Format Painter to copy the format of $329 and apply it to **$389, August 1, 20XX, www.napc20XX.com**, and **800-555-5678**.
17. Beginning with *Lakeview Towers,* select all the remaining text. On the Page Layout tab, in the Paragraph group, adjust the spacing after the paragraph to **6 pt**.
18. Select the last two lines of text and center them.
19. In the **Page Background** group, use the Page Borders command to insert a **½ pt.** wide box page border, using the color **Purple, Accent 4, Lighter 60%**.
20. Use the **Watermark** command to create a custom horizontal watermark with the text **SAVE THE DATE** using **Calibri font**.
21. Select the last paragraph, which begins *Register online . . . .*
22. On the **Home** tab, in the **Paragraph** group, use the Shading command to insert shading using the color **Purple, Accent 4, Lighter 40%**.

23. In the **Page Layout** tab, in the **Themes** group, use the Theme Colors menu to change the color to **Opulent**.
24. Your document should look similar to Figure 1. Make any necessary adjustments.

Figure 1
NAPC Postcard

25. **SAVE** the document as *napc_postcard* and **CLOSE** the file.
    CLOSE Word.

Managing Text Flow

7

LESSON SKILL MATRIX

Skills	Matrix Skill	Skill Number
Controlling Widows and Orphans	Control pagination	2.3
Keeping a Paragraph's Lines on the Same Page	Control pagination	2.3
Keeping Two Paragraphs on the Same Page	Control pagination	2.3
Forcing a Paragraph to the Top of a Page	Control pagination	2.3
Forcing a Page Break	Control pagination	2.3
Inserting Section Breaks	Control pagination, Insert sections, Create and modify sections	2.3, 2.5, 2.3.2
Creating Columns	Create and format columns	1.2.3
Formatting Columns	Create and format columns	1.2.3
Changing Column Widths	Create and format columns	1.2.3
Inserting a Blank Page into a Document	Insert blank pages or cover pages	1.1.6

As a marketing associate for First Bank, you are involved in a wide variety of marketing and communications projects. You are responsible for creating and maintaining marketing collateral—brochures, posters, and other printed product information—that supports the sale of a product. It is time to update the Personal Checking Choices document that your bank provides to people interested in opening new accounts. Microsoft Word is a great tool for producing documents such as this that can be easily updated. In this lesson, you will learn to control paragraph behavior, work with section and page breaks, create and format columns, and insert a blank page.

KEY TERMS

columns
orphan
page break
section break
widow

■ Controlling Paragraph Behavior

THE BOTTOM LINE

Word works behind the scenes to control how text flows in your document. Automatic page breaks are inserted within multi-page documents, helping you create professional-looking documents. However, you may need to adjust or override automatic page breaks from time to time so that you can control where a paragraph ends or begins.

Controlling Widows and Orphans

For professional-looking documents, it is best to avoid leaving a single line of text at the bottom or top of a page. Word can help you avoid this situation by keeping at least two lines together at the bottom of the page or at the top of a new page.

TURN ON WIDOW/ORPHAN CONTROL

OPEN the ***checking*** document from the data files for this lesson.

CD

The ***checking*** document is available on the companion CD-ROM.

1. Scroll to the top of page 2 and notice the widow *experience...* at the top of the page.
2. Select the four-line paragraph under *Preferred Checking,* including the widow.
3. On the **Home** tab, in the **Paragraph** group, click the **dialog box launcher.** The Paragraph dialog box appears.
4. Click the **Line and Page Breaks** tab, as shown in Figure 7-1.

Figure 7-1

Paragraph dialog box

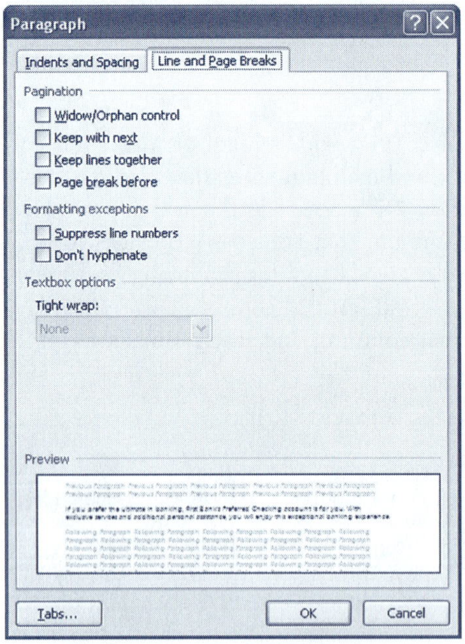

CERTIFICATION READY?
How do you control widows and orphans?
2.3

5. Click to select the **Widow/Orphan Control** box and then click **OK**. Notice that another line of the paragraph is moved to the second page.
6. Save the document as ***checkingchoices***.

PAUSE. LEAVE the document open to use in the next exercise.

A ***widow*** is the last line of a paragraph that is left alone at the top of a page. See Figure 7-2.

Figure 7-2

Widow

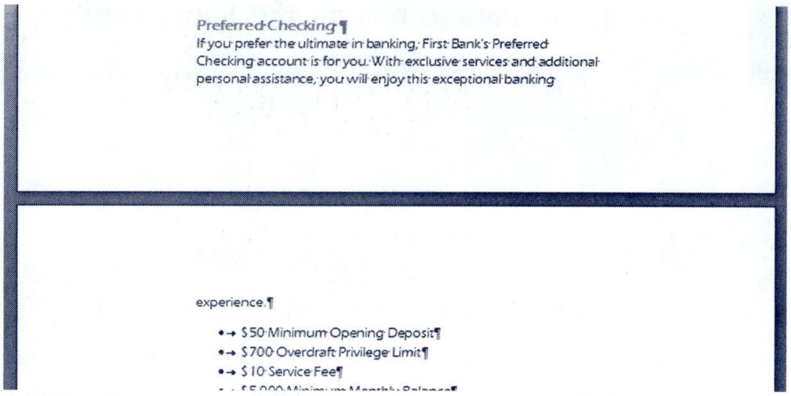

An ***orphan*** is the first line of a paragraph that is left alone at the bottom of a page. See Figure 7-3.

Figure 7-3

Orphan

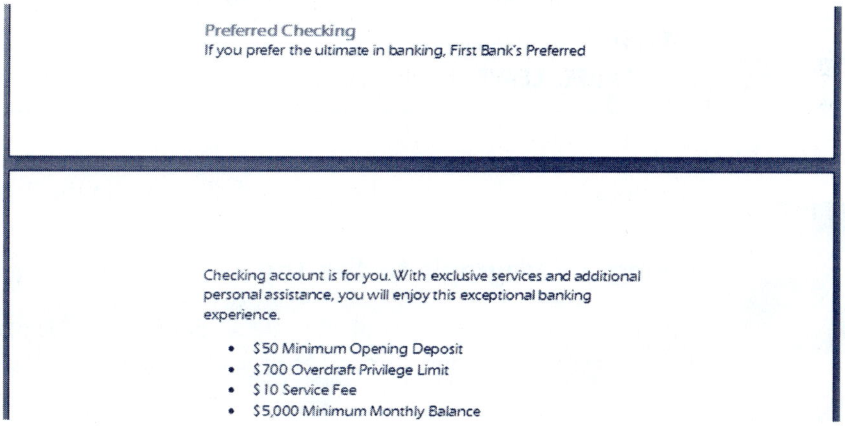

You can avoid having widows and orphans in your document by turning on Widow/Orphan Control in the Paragraph dialog box. When creating a new document, this option is turned on by default. Click to select or deselect the Widow/Orphan Control box to turn the option on or off.

Keeping a Paragraph's Lines on the Same Page

Sometimes you may not want a paragraph to split across two pages. Word's Keep Lines Together command can solve this problem.

KEEP LINES TOGETHER

USE the document that is open from the previous exercise.

1. Select the four-line paragraph under *Preferred Checking*, if necessary.
2. On the **Home** tab, in the **Paragraph** group, click the **dialog box launcher**. The Paragraph dialog box appears.
3. On the **Line and Page Breaks** tab, click to select the **Keep Lines Together** box and then click **OK**. Notice that the two lines that were at the bottom of page 1 moved to page 2.
4. **SAVE** the document.

   PAUSE. LEAVE the document open to use in the next exercise.

CERTIFICATION READY?
How do you keep a paragraph's lines on the same page?
2.3

When you need to keep all the lines of a paragraph together on the same page, select the entire paragraph and click to select the Keep Lines Together box in the Paragraph dialog box.

Keeping Two Paragraphs on the Same Page

Word considers any line of text that is followed by a return to be a paragraph. So, a heading, even if it is only one or two words, is considered a paragraph. When you need to keep two paragraphs together on the same page, such as a heading and the text below it, use Word's Keep with Next command.

KEEP TWO PARAGRAPHS ON THE SAME PAGE

USE the document that is open from the previous exercise.

1. Select the *Preferred Checking* heading and the four-line paragraph below it.
2. On the **Home** tab, in the **Paragraph** group, click the **dialog box launcher**. The Paragraph dialog box appears.
3. On the **Line and Page Breaks** tab, click to select the **Keep with Next** box and then click **OK**. Notice that the two paragraphs (the heading and paragraph that follows) stayed together and moved to page 2.
4. **SAVE** the document.

   PAUSE. LEAVE the document open to use in the next exercise.

Keeping two paragraphs together on the same page is easy in Word. To do so, select both paragraphs and click to select the Keep with Next box in the Paragraph dialog box.

CERTIFICATION READY?
How do you keep two paragraphs on the same page?
2.3

Forcing a Paragraph to the Top of a Page

Although automatic page breaks usually occur at acceptable places in a Word document, there may be times when you need to force a paragraph to the top of a page.

FORCE A PARAGRAPH TO THE TOP OF A PAGE

USE the document that is open from the previous exercise.

1. Position the insertion point before the *S* in the *Senior Preferred Checking* heading.
2. On the **Home** tab, in the **Paragraph** group, click the **dialog box launcher**. The Paragraph dialog box appears.
3. On the **Line and Page Breaks** tab, click to select the **Page Break Before** box and then click **OK**. Notice that the paragraph is forced to the top of a new page.
4. **SAVE** the document.

   PAUSE. LEAVE the document open to use in the next exercise.

CERTIFICATION READY?
How do you force a paragraph to the top of a page?
2.3

You just read about how you can force a paragraph to begin at the top of a page by clicking to select the Page Break Before box in the Paragraph dialog box.

Working with Breaks

THE BOTTOM LINE

There may be times when you will be working with documents that contain various objects or special layouts that require you to step in and control where a page or section breaks. When you need to be in control, you can do so with Word's page breaks and section breaks commands.

Forcing a Page Break

You just learned about how Word not only inserts automatic page breaks into a document, but also about how you can set specific options for those page breaks. There may also be times when you need to insert a manual page break.

INSERT AND DELETE A MANUAL PAGE BREAK

USE the document that is open from the previous exercise.

1. Position the insertion point before the *V* in the *Value Checking* heading.

2. On the **Insert** tab, in the **Pages** group, click the **Page Break** button. A manual page break is inserted and the *Value Checking* paragraphs start a new page, as shown in Figure 7-4.

Figure 7-4

Page Break in Print Layout view

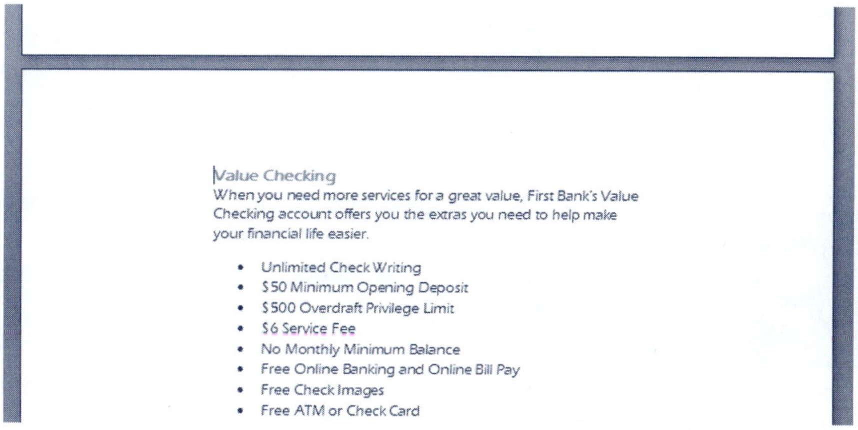

3. Position the insertion point before the *P* in the *Preferred Checking* heading.
4. On the **Page Layout** tab, in the **Page Setup** group, click the **Breaks** menu. The Breaks menu appears, as shown in Figure 7-5.

Figure 7-5

Breaks menu

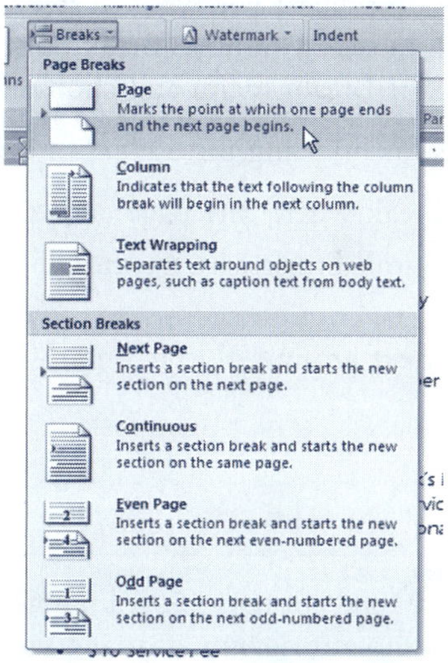

5. Select **Page** from the menu. A manual page break is inserted.

6. On the **Home** tab, in the **Paragraph** group, click the **Show/Hide ¶** button. The hidden paragraph marks, page break markers, and other formatting marks are displayed.

7. Scroll to the first page and notice the manual page break marker, shown in Figure 7-6.

Figure 7-6

Manual page break with hidden formatting marks displayed

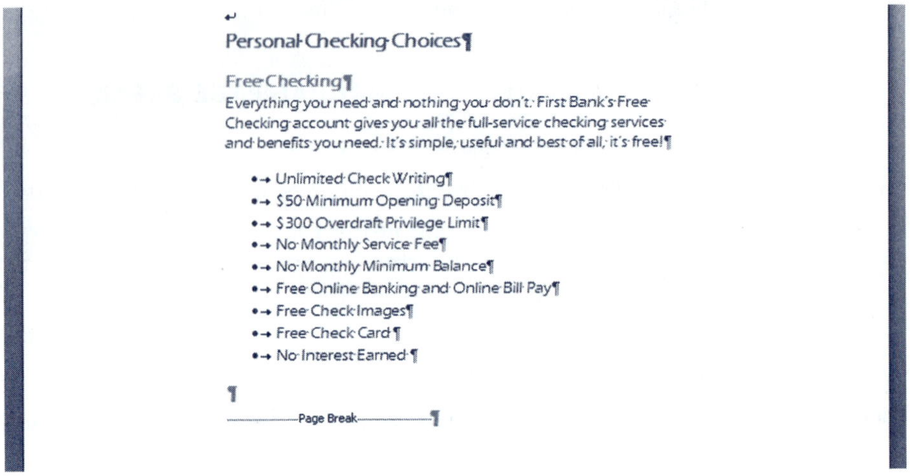

Personal Checking Choices¶

Free Checking¶

Everything you need and nothing you don't. First Bank's Free Checking account gives you all the full-service checking services and benefits you need. It's simple, useful and best of all, it's free!¶

- Unlimited Check Writing¶
- $50 Minimum Opening Deposit¶
- $300 Overdraft Privilege Limit¶
- No Monthly Service Fee¶
- No Monthly Minimum Balance¶
- Free Online Banking and Online Bill Pay¶
- Free Check Images¶
- Free Check Card¶
- No Interest Earned ¶

¶

Page Break ¶

CERTIFICATION READY?
How do you force a page break?
2.3

8. Select the **Page Break marker** and press the **Backspace** key. The page break is deleted.
9. Select the **Page Break marker** below the Value Checking information and press the **Backspace** key.
10. **SAVE** the document.

PAUSE. LEAVE the document open to use in the next exercise.

A ***page break*** is the location in a document where one page ends and a new page begins. Pages are easy to distinguish in Word. In Print Layout view, Word displays a document page by page, one after the other, on a blue background (as was shown earlier in Figure 7-4).

TAKE NOTE*

Click the **Show/Hide ¶** button to view page breaks and section breaks for editing purposes.

In this exercise, you inserted page breaks using two different methods. To insert a manual page break, position the insertion point where you want to start a new page. Then, on the Insert tab, in the Pages group, click to select the Page Break button. Or, on the Page Layout tab, in the Page Setup group, click the Breaks menu and choose Page.

The Breaks menu contains options for inserting three types of breaks:

- Page: inserts a manual page break where one page ends and a new page begins
- Column: inserts a manual column break where text will begin in the next column after the column break
- Text Wrapping: separates the text around objects on a Web page, such as caption text from body text

ANOTHER WAY

You can also insert a manual page break by pressing **Ctrl+Enter**.

Inserting Section Breaks

You can use section breaks to create a section, or separate portion, of a document. For example, you can create a section in your document that contains a page that has different margins than the rest of the document.

INSERT A SECTION BREAK

USE the document that is open from the previous exercise.

1. Position the insertion point before the *F* in the *Free Checking* heading. Press **Enter** to insert a blank line.

2. On the **Page Layout** tab, in the **Page Setup** group, click the **Breaks** menu.
3. Under Section Breaks, select **Continuous**. A section break is inserted, as shown in Figure 7-7.

Figure 7-7

Section Break

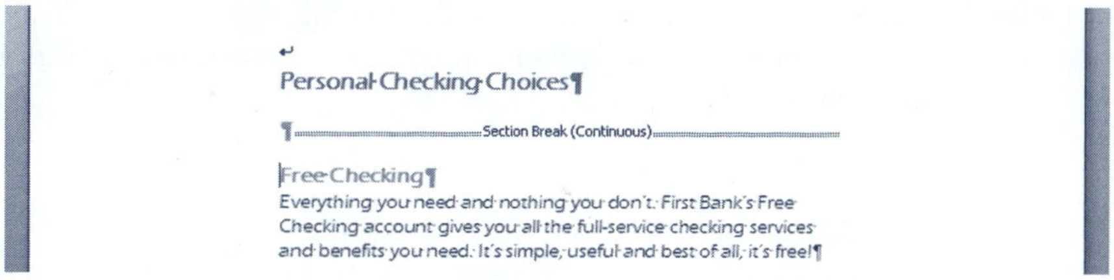

4. On the **Page Layout** tab, in the **Page Setup** group, click **Margins** and select **Narrow**. The margins of the section are changed while the margins of the other part of the document remain the same.
5. **SAVE** the document.

PAUSE. LEAVE the document open to use in the next exercise.

CERTIFICATION READY?
How do you insert a section break?
2.3, 2.5, 2.3.2

A ***section break*** is used to create layout or formatting changes in a portion of a document. In this exercise, you inserted a Continuous section break and then changed the margins of that section.

It is useful to insert a section break when you want to change the following types of formatting for a portion of your document:

- Columns
- Footnotes and endnotes
- Headers and footers
- Line numbering
- Margins
- Page borders
- Page numbering
- Paper size or orientation
- Paper source for a printer
- Vertical alignment of text on a page

To insert a section break, position the insertion point where you want the section to begin. On the Page Layout tab, in the Page Setup group, click the Breaks menu and then select one of the four available options for creating section breaks:

- Next Page: inserts a section break and starts the new section on the next page
- Continuous: inserts a section break and starts the new section on the same page
- Even Page: inserts a section break and starts the new section on the next even-numbered page
- Odd Page: inserts a section break and starts the new section on the next odd-numbered page

You can select and delete section breaks just as you can remove page breaks. Just remember that when you delete a section break, you remove the section formatting as well.

Setting Up Columns

THE BOTTOM LINE

Columns are often used in newspapers, magazines, and newsletters that contain large amounts of text. When text is formatted into columns, the lines are shorter, white space is added, and a document generally becomes more reader friendly. When setting up columns in a document, you can specify the number of columns, formatting options, and column widths.

Creating Columns

You can create columns for all the text within a document or for only a portion of the text.

CREATE COLUMNS

USE the document that is open from the previous exercise.

1. On the **Page Layout** tab, in the **Page Setup** group, click **Columns**. The Columns menu appears, as shown in Figure 7-8.

Figure 7-8

Columns menu

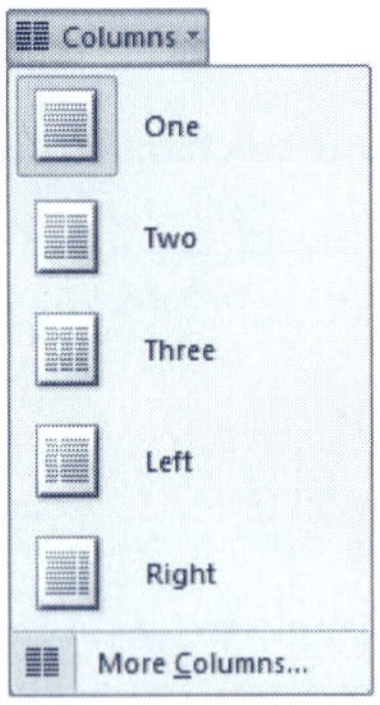

2. Select **Two**. The text in the document following the *Personal Checking Choices* heading is formatted into two columns.
3. **SAVE** the document.

PAUSE. LEAVE the document open to use in the next exercise.

Columns are vertical blocks of text in which text flows from the bottom of one to the top of the next. As you learned in this exercise, you can easily create columns in your document. On the Page Layout tab, in the Page Setup group, the Columns menu, shown in Figure 7-8, lists options for creating common column formats:

- One: formats the text into a single column
- Two: formats the text into two even columns
- Three: formats the text into three even columns
- Left: formats the text into two unequal columns—a narrow one on the left and a wide one on the right
- Right: formats the text into two uneven columns—a narrow one on the right and a wide one on the left
- More Columns: contains options for customizing columns

CERTIFICATION READY?
How do you create columns?
1.2.3

Formatting Columns

In addition to Word's common column formats, you can customize column formats to fit the text and the purpose of your document.

FORMAT COLUMNS

USE the document that is open from the previous exercise.

1. On the **Page Layout** tab, in the **Page Setup** group, click the **Columns** menu.
2. Select **More Columns**. The Columns dialog box appears, as shown in Figure 7-9.

Figure 7-9

Columns Dialog box

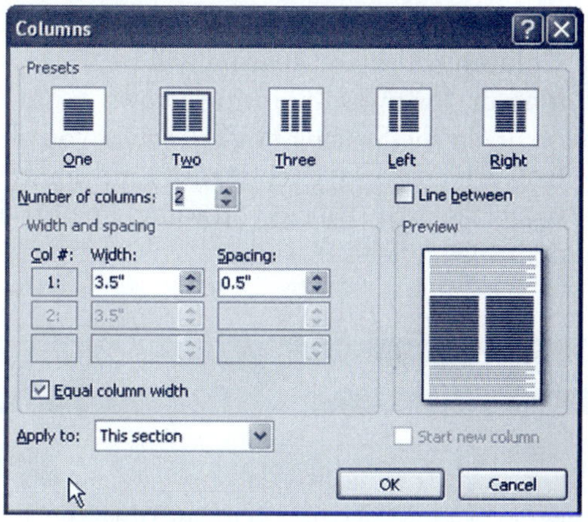

3. Select **2**, if necessary, in the Number of Columns box and key **3**.
4. Click the **Line Between** box.
5. Click **OK**.
6. Position the insertion point before the *S* in the *Senior Preferred* heading.
7. On the **Home** tab, **Paragraph** group, click the **dialog box launcher**. In the Line and Page Breaks tab, click to deselect the **Page Break Before** box and click **OK**.
8. **SAVE** the document.

PAUSE. LEAVE the document open to use in the next exercise.

CERTIFICATION READY?
How do you format columns?
1.2.3

You have many options for formatting columns. The More Columns command at the bottom of the Columns menu displays the Columns dialog box. From here, you can choose one of the preset column formats or create a format of your own containing up to 15 columns.

Click the Line Between box to insert a vertical line between columns.

Changing Column Widths

Documents that contain columns with even widths are formal and conservative. If you want to make a document more casual, or if the information you are displaying calls for columns of different widths, you can specify varying column widths easily in Word.

CHANGE COLUMN WIDTHS

USE the document that is open from the previous exercise.

1. On the **Page Layout** tab, in the **Page Setup** group, click the **Columns** menu.
2. Select **More Columns**. The Columns Dialog Box appears.
3. Key **2** in the Number of columns box.

4. Select the text in the **Width** box and key 3.25. Press the Tab key to move to the Spacing box. Notice that the spacing adjusted automatically to 1. Click **OK.**
5. On the **Page Layout** tab, in the **Page Setup** group, click the **Columns** menu and select **More Columns**.
6. Click the **Three** columns button. Select the text in the **Width** box and key **2.3.** Press the Tab key to move to the Spacing box. Notice that the spacing adjusted automatically to .3. Click **OK.**
7. **SAVE** the document.

PAUSE. LEAVE the document open to use in the next exercise.

CERTIFICATION READY?
How do you change column widths?
1.2.3

Columns can be formatted with even or uneven widths in the Columns dialog box. If you want all the columns in a document to have the same widths, make sure the Even column width box is checked. Column width and spacing will be displayed for the first column only. Click the upward-pointing or downward-pointing arrows in the Width box or key in a specific width. The measurements in the Spacing box change as you change the width. If you want to change the spacing between columns, click the upward-pointing or downward-pointing arrows in the Spacing box or key the spacing you want. The preview adjusts to show your changes. When you are finished, click OK.

Inserting a Blank Page into a Document

THE BOTTOM LINE

When creating or editing a document, you may need to insert a blank page on which to add more text, graphics, or a table. Rather than pressing the Enter key enough times to insert a blank page, Word provides a Blank Page command.

Inserting a Blank Page

You can insert a blank page at any point within a document—the beginning, middle, or end.

INSERT A BLANK PAGE

USE the document that is open from the previous exercise.

1. Position the insertion point after the *k* in *First Bank*.
2. On the **Insert** tab, in the **Pages** group, click **Blank Page**. A blank page is inserted.
3. Click the **Undo** button on the Quick Access toolbar.
4. Click the **Show/Hide ¶** button.
5. **SAVE** and **CLOSE** the document.

STOP. CLOSE Word.

CERTIFICATION READY?
How do you insert a blank page?
1.1.6

In this exercise, you inserted a blank page in the middle of the document. To insert a blank page wherever you need it, position the insertion point and click the Blank Page command in the Pages group on the Insert tab. To delete a blank page, use the Show/Hide ¶ button to display hidden characters, then select and delete the page break.

SUMMARY SKILL MATRIX

In this lesson you learned	Matrix Skill	Skill Number
To control widows and orphans	Control pagination	2.3
To keep a paragraph's lines on the same page	Control pagination	2.3
To keep two paragraphs on the same page	Control pagination	2.3
To force a paragraph to the top of a page	Control pagination	2.3
To force a page break	Control pagination	2.3
To insert section breaks	Control pagination, Insert sections, Create and modify sections	2.3, 2.5, 2.3.2
To create columns	Create and format columns	1.2.3
To format columns	Create and format columns	1.2.3
To change column widths	Create and format columns	1.2.3
To insert a blank page into a document	Insert blank pages or cover pages	1.1.6

Knowledge Assessment

Matching

Match the term in Column 1 to its description in Column 2.

Column 1	Column 2
1. widow	**a.** vertical blocks of text in which text flows from the bottom of one column to the top of the next
2. orphan	**b.** used to create layout or formatting changes in a portion of a document
3. page break	**c.** displays the Columns dialog box
4. section break	**d.** keeps two paragraphs together on the same page
5. columns	**e.** keeps all lines of a paragraph together on the same page
6. Blank Page command	**f.** the last line of a paragraph that is left alone at the top of a page
7. More Columns command	**g.** keeps at least two lines together at the bottom of the page or at the top of a new page
8. Keep with Next	**h.** the location in a document where one page ends and a new page begins
9. Keep Lines Together	**i.** the first line of a paragraph that is left alone at the bottom of a page
10. Widow/Orphan Control	**j.** inserts a blank page at the insertion point

True / False

Circle T if the statement is true or F if the statement is false.

T | F 1. Widow/Orphan Control is turned on by default.

T | F 2. Use Widow/Orphan Control to keep all the lines of a paragraph together on the same page.

T | F 3. Word considers a heading a paragraph.

T | F 4. Columns can be formatted with even or uneven widths.

T | F 5. You can see page break and section break markers in Print Layout view.

T | F 6. A Continuous section break starts the new section on the next page.

T | F 7. A page break is the location in a document where one page ends and a new page begins

T | F 8. The Even column width box should be checked only when you want all columns to have the same width.

T | F 9. You can only insert a blank page at the beginning or at the end of a document.

T | F 10. Section breaks are useful when you want to change the margin setting for a portion of the document.

Competency Assessment

Project 7-1: YMCA Newsletter

Format some data for the YMCA into a two-column newsletter.

CD

The *ynews* document is available on the companion CD-ROM.

GET READY. Launch Word if it is not already running.

1. **OPEN** *ynews* from the data files for this lesson.
2. Click the **Show/Hide ¶** button.
3. Position the insertion point before the *M* in *Mother's Day Out*. . . .
4. On the **Page Layout** tab, in the **Page Setup** group, click the **Breaks** menu and select **Continuous**.
5. On the **Page Layout** tab, in the **Page Setup** group, click the **Columns** menu and select **Two**.
6. Position the insertion point before the *F* in the *Fall Soccer*. . . heading.
7. On the **Page Layout** tab, in the **Page Setup** group, click the **Breaks** menu and select **Column**.
8. On the **Page Layout** tab, in the **Page Setup** group, click the **Columns** menu and click **More Columns**.
9. In the **Columns** dialog box, click the **up arrow** on the Width box until it reads **2.8**. The number in the Spacing box should adjust to **.9"**.
10. Click the **Line Between** box and click **OK**.
11. Click the **Show/Hide ¶** button.
12. **SAVE AS** ***ymcanewsletter*** and **CLOSE** the document.

PAUSE. LEAVE Word open for the next project.

Project 7-2: Computer Use Policy

The **computerusepolicy** document is available on the companion CD-ROM.

You are updating First Bank's computer use policy and you need to adjust the flow of text on the page.

1. **OPEN** *computerusepolicy* from the data files for this lesson.
2. Scroll to the top of page 3. Position the insertion point before the *e* in *engaging in illegal activity.*
3. On the **Home** tab, in the **Paragraph** group, click the **dialog box launcher**. On the **Line and Page Breaks** tab, click to select the **Widow/Orphan Control** box and click **OK**.
4. Position the insertion point in the last line of page 3 that begins *D. Anyone obtaining....*
5. On the **Home** tab, in the **Paragraph** group, click the **dialog box launcher**. On the Line and Page Breaks tab, click the **Keep Lines Together** box and click **OK**.
6. Position the insertion point before the *S* in the *Section Ten* heading.
7. On the **Home** tab, in the **Paragraph** group, click the **dialog box launcher**. On the Line and Page Breaks tab, click the **Page Break Before** box and click **OK**.
8. **SAVE** the document as *newcupolicy* and **CLOSE** the file.

PAUSE. LEAVE Word open for the next project.

Proficiency Assessment

Project 7-3: Coffee Shop Brochure

The **coffeemenu** document is available on the companion CD-ROM.

Your supervisor at the Grand Street Coffee Shop asks you to format the information within their coffee menu as a brochure.

1. **OPEN** *coffeemenu* from the data files for this lesson.
2. Change the page orientation to **Landscape**.
3. Position the insertion point before the *M* in the *Menu* heading and insert a **Continuous** section break.
4. Create an uneven, two-column format using the **Left** column setting.
5. Position the insertion point before the *N* in the *Nutritional* heading and insert a **Column** break.
6. Increase the amount of space between columns to **.7″**.
7. **SAVE** the document as *coffeeshopbrochure* and **CLOSE** the file.

PAUSE. LEAVE Word open for the next project.

Project 7-4: Mom's Favorite Recipes

The **recipes** document is available on the companion CD-ROM.

Your mom asks you to help her create a small cookbook filled with her favorite recipes that she can share with family and friends. She has emailed you a Word document containing a few recipes to help you get started with creating a format.

1. **OPEN** *recipes* from the data files for this lesson.
2. Click the **Show/Hide ¶** button to display hidden formatting marks.
3. Position the insertion point before the *C* in the *Chicken Pot Pie* heading and insert a **Continuous** section break.
4. Position the insertion point before the *B* in the *Breads* heading and insert a **Next Page** section break.
5. Position the insertion point before the *B* in the *Banana Nut Bread/Chocolate Chip Muffins* headings and insert a **Continuous** section break.

6. Position the insertion point anywhere within the Chicken Pot Pie recipe.
7. Format the recipes in this section into two even columns with **.7″** spacing between columns and a line between.
8. Position the insertion point anywhere within the Banana Nut Bread recipe.
9. Format the recipes in this section into two even columns with **.7″** spacing between columns and a line between.
10. Position the insertion point before the *R* in the *Ranch Chicken* heading and insert a column break.
11. Position the insertion point before the *E* in the *Easy Pumpkin Bread/Muffins* heading and insert a column break.
12. Position the insertion point before the *C* in the *Chocolate Zucchini Bread* heading and insert a column break.
13. Position the insertion point in the *Main Dishes* heading and insert the Alphabet header style. Select the *Title* placeholder and key **Mom's Favorite Recipes**.
14. Click the **Show/Hide ¶** button to hide formatting marks.
15. SAVE the document as ***favorite recipes*** and **CLOSE** the file.

PAUSE. LEAVE Word open for the next project.

Mastery Assessment

CD

The ***checkingacctchoices*** document is available on the companion CD-ROM.

Project 7-5: Three-fold Bank Brochure

Reformat the Checking Choices document to create a three-fold brochure.

1. **OPEN** ***checkingacctchoices*** from the data files for this lesson.
2. Reformat the document using a page size of 8 1/2 X 14 with landscape orientation. Create the brochure to look like the one shown in Figure 7-10.

Figure 7-10

Checking brochure

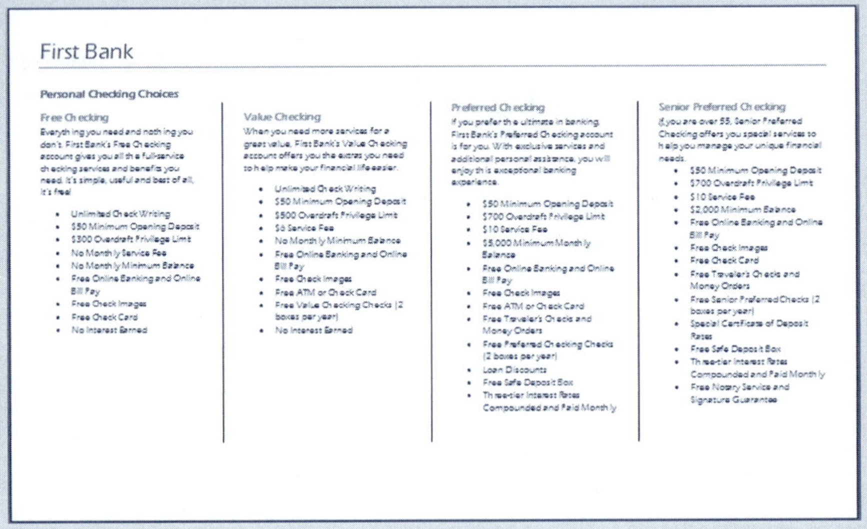
First Bank

Personal Checking Choices

Free Checking

Everything you need and nothing you don't. First Bank's Free Checking account gives you all the full-service checking services and benefits you need. It's simple, useful and best of all, it's free!

- Unlimited Check Writing
- $50 Minimum Opening Deposit
- $300 Overdraft Privilege Limit
- No Monthly Service Fee
- No Monthly Minimum Balance
- Free Online Banking and Online Bill Pay
- Free Check Images
- Free Check Card
- No Interest Earned

Value Checking

When you need more services for a great value, First Bank's Value Checking account offers you the extras you need to help make your financial life easier.

- Unlimited Check Writing
- $50 Minimum Opening Deposit
- $500 Overdraft Privilege Limit
- $6 Service Fee
- No Monthly Minimum Balance
- Free Online Banking and Online Bill Pay
- Free Check Images
- Free ATM or Check Card
- Free Value Checking Checks (2 boxes per year)
- No Interest Earned

Preferred Checking

If you prefer the ultimate in banking, First Bank's Preferred Checking account is for you. With exclusive services and additional personal assistance, you will enjoy this exceptional banking experience.

- $50 Minimum Opening Deposit
- $700 Overdraft Privilege Limit
- $10 Service Fee
- $5,000 Minimum Monthly Balance
- Free Online Banking and Online Bill Pay
- Free Check Images
- Free ATM or Check Card
- Free Traveler's Checks and Money Orders
- Free Preferred Checking Checks (2 boxes per year)
- Loan Discounts
- Free Safe Deposit Box
- Three-tier Interest Rates Compounded and Paid Monthly

Senior Preferred Checking

If you are over 55, Senior Preferred Checking offers you special services to help you manage your unique financial needs.

- $50 Minimum Opening Deposit
- $700 Overdraft Privilege Limit
- $10 Service Fee
- $2,000 Minimum Balance
- Free Online Banking and Online Bill Pay
- Free Check Images
- Free Check Card
- Free Traveler's Checks and Money Orders
- Free Senior Preferred Checks (2 boxes per year)
- Special Certificate of Deposit Rates
- Free Safe Deposit Box
- Three-tier Interest Rates Compounded and Paid Monthly
- Free Notary Service and Signature Guarantee

3. Make any adjustments necessary to format the document professionally.
4. **SAVE** the document as ***checkingbrochure*** and **CLOSE** the file.

PAUSE. LEAVE Word open for the next project.

Project 7-6: Reformat the YMCA Newsletter

As an alternative to the layout you created earlier, reformat the YMCA newsletter with two uneven columns.

CD

The ***ynewsletter*** document is available on the companion CD-ROM.

1. Open *ynewsletter* from the data files for this lesson.
2. Reformat the newsletter with two uneven columns using the **Right** column setting.
3. Make any adjustments necessary to format the document professionally on one page.
4. **SAVE** the document as *rightymcanewsletter* and **CLOSE** the file.

   CLOSE Word.

INTERNET READY

Have you considered starting your own business someday? Use the Internet to research small business checking accounts for three different banks. What are the fees? What services are offered? What are the restrictions? Create a three-column document comparing the account features of each bank side by side.

8 Editing Basics

LESSON SKILL MATRIX

Skills	Matrix Skill	Skill Number
Using Built-In Building Blocks	Insert building blocks in documents	4.1.1
Inserting a Field from Quick Parts	Insert fields from Quick Parts	4.1.4
Creating Your Own Building Blocks	Save frequently used data as building blocks	4.1.2
Using the Clipboard to Copy Text	Cut, copy, and paste text	2.2.1
Using the Clipboard to Move Text	Cut, copy, and paste text	2.2.1
Using the Mouse to Copy or Move Text	Cut, copy, and paste text	2.2.1
Finding Text in a Document	Find and replace text, Move through a document quickly by using the Find and Go To commands	2.2.2, 5.1.1
Replacing Text in a Document	Find and replace text, Move around in a document quickly by using the Find and Go To commands	2.2.2, 5.1.1
Using the Go To Command	Move through a document quickly by using the Find and Go To commands	5.1.1
Using the Document Map	Change window views	5.1.2

You are a content manager for Flatland Hosting Company, a position in which you are responsible for writing and editing all client-facing material, such as hosting guidelines and agreements. When creating and revising documents, several Word commands can help you work more efficiently. In this lesson, you will learn how to add content to a document using Quick Parts, copy and move text using the Clipboard and the mouse, find and replace text, and navigate a long document.

KEY TERMS

building blocks
copy
cut
field
paste
wildcards

Using Quick Parts to Add Content to a Document

THE BOTTOM LINE

Word has many features that can help simplify the process of creating documents. The Quick Parts feature enables you to easily insert reusable pieces of content within your document. In these activities, you will learn how to use built-in building blocks and how to create your own. You will also learn how to insert Quick Parts such as fields into a document.

Using Built-In Building Blocks

To save time when creating a document, you can use built-in building blocks already stored in galleries. Just choose the one you want and insert it.

USE BUILT-IN BUILDING BLOCKS

NEW FEATURE

CD

The ***hosting*** document is available on the companion CD-ROM.

GET READY. Before you begin these steps, be sure to launch Microsoft Word.

1. **OPEN** ***hosting*** from the data files for this lesson.
2. On the Insert tab, in the Text group, click the **Quick Parts** button to display the menu shown in Figure 8-1.

Figure 8-1

Quick Parts menu

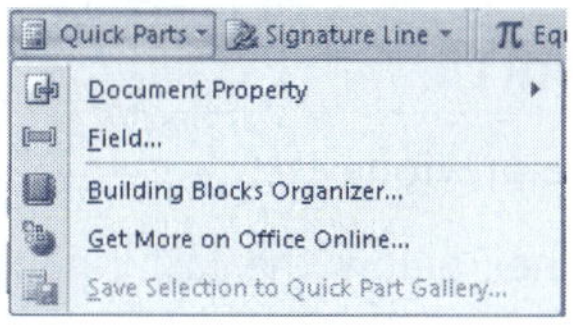

3. Click **Building Blocks Organizer** to display the dialog box shown in Figure 8-2.

Figure 8-2

Building Blocks Organizer

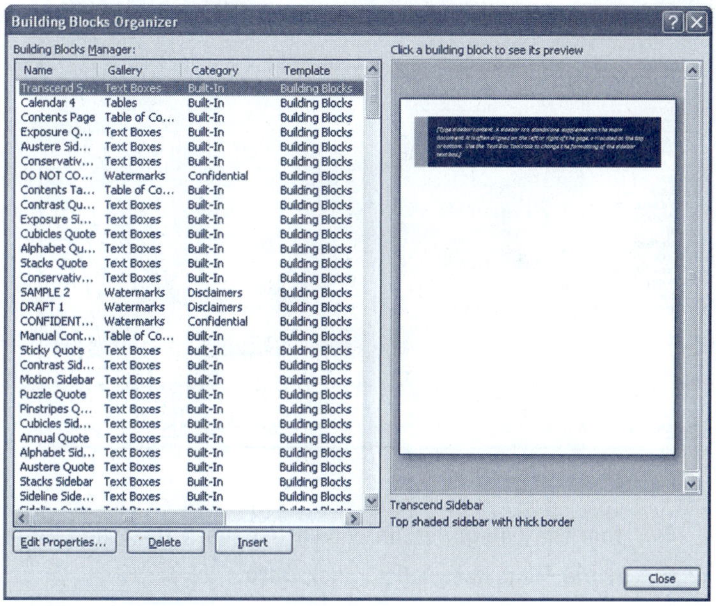

4. Click the **Name** heading to sort the building blocks by name.
5. Scroll down and select the **Confidential 1** building block.

TROUBLESHOOTING If the names are not entirely visible, you can change the width of the Name column by pointing to the right edge of the heading and dragging the resize bar to the right.

CERTIFICATION READY?
How do you insert building blocks in a document?
4.1.1

6. Click the **Insert** button. The Confidential watermark appears behind the text on each page of your document.
7. **SAVE** the document as ***hosting_terms***.

   PAUSE. LEAVE the document open to use in the next exercise.

X REF
Headers and footers are another type of building block. You already learned how to insert headers and footers from Quick Parts in Lesson 5.

Building blocks are reusable pieces of content or other document parts that are stored in galleries and can be inserted into a document whenever needed. The Building Blocks Organizer enables you to manage building blocks by editing, deleting, and/or inserting them. You can sort the building blocks by name, gallery, category, or template, and you can also preview any of the building blocks that are stored in the galleries. A description of a selected building block appears below the preview pane.

Inserting a Field from Quick Parts

When you add fields from Quick Parts into a document, Word automatically inserts specific information in place of each field when you open the document.

INSERT A FIELD FROM QUICK PARTS

USE the document that is open from the previous exercise.

1. Place the insertion point two lines below the last line in the document.
2. Key **Last Updated:** in bold.
3. On the Insert tab, in the Text group, click the **Quick Parts** button.
4. Click **Field** on the menu. The dialog box shown in Figure 8-3 will be displayed.

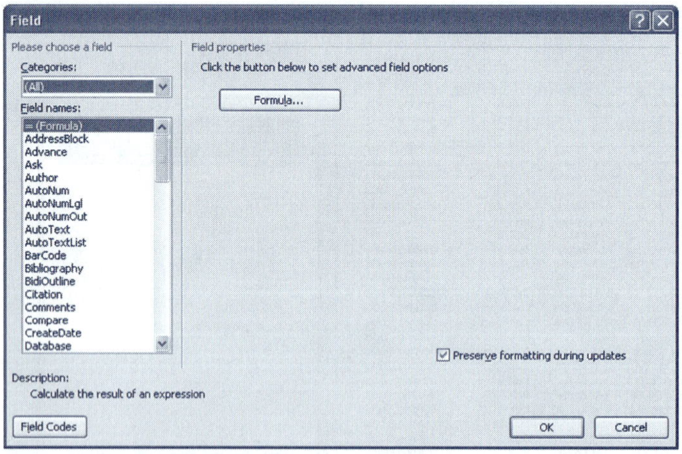

Figure 8-3
Field dialog box

5. From the Categories dropdown list, click **Date and Time**.
6. In the Field Names list, click **Date**.
7. In the Date Formats list, select the ninth option with the **d MMMM yyyy** format and click **OK**. The end of your document should look similar to Figure 8-4.

Figure 8-4

Document with Date and Time field inserted

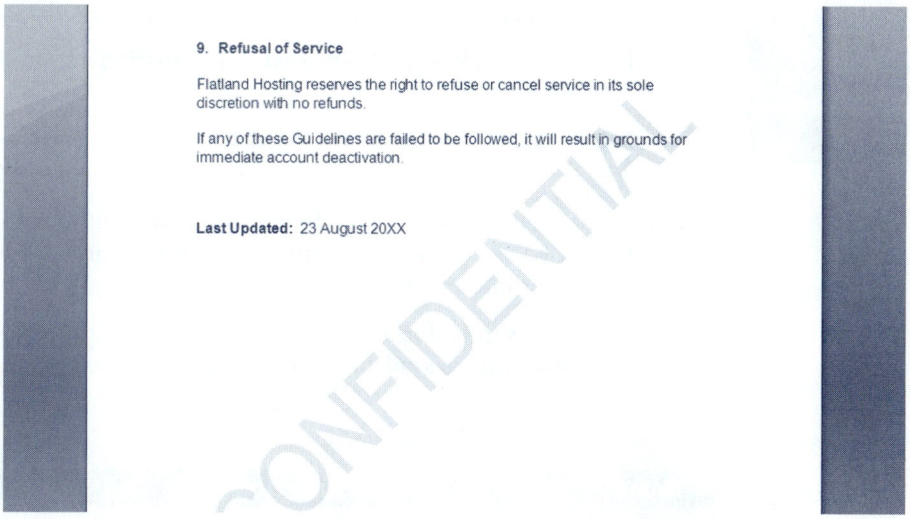
9. **Refusal of Service**

Flatland Hosting reserves the right to refuse or cancel service in its sole discretion with no refunds.

If any of these Guidelines are failed to be followed, it will result in grounds for immediate account deactivation.

Last Updated: 23 August 20XX

CONFIDENTIAL

CERTIFICATION READY?
How do you insert fields from Quick Parts?
4.1.4

8. **SAVE** the document.

   PAUSE. LEAVE the document open to use in the next exercise.

A ***field*** is a placeholder that tells Word to insert changeable data into a document. Word automatically uses fields when you use certain commands, such as inserting a page number or creating a table of contents. You can also manually insert fields into your document. Word automatically updates fields when a document is opened, so the information stays up to date.

Fields—also called field codes—appear between curly brackets ({ }) when displayed. To display field codes in your document instead of the resulting information, press **Alt+F9**. To edit a field, right-click the field and then click Edit Field.

Creating Your Own Building Blocks

If you have customized text that you frequently insert into documents, you can store it as a building block and then reuse it again whenever you need it.

CREATE YOUR OWN BUILDING BLOCKS

USE the document that is open from the previous exercise.

1. Select the four paragraphs of text under the *2. Account Information* heading.
2. On the Insert tab, in the Text group, click the **Quick Parts** button.
3. Click **Save Selection to Quick Part Gallery** on the menu. The Create New Building Block dialog box appears, as shown in Figure 8-5.

Figure 8-5

Create New Building Block dialog box

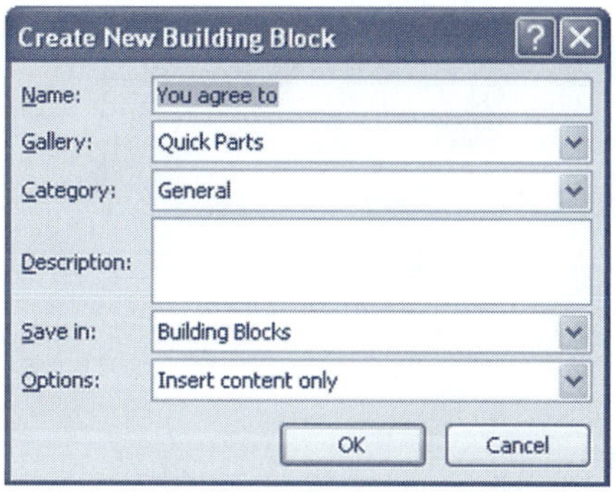

CERTIFICATION READY?
How do you save frequently used data as building blocks?
4.1.2

4. In the Name: box, key **Account Information XXX (where XXX = your initials)**.
5. In the Description: box, key **text from hosting terms document**.
6. Click **OK**.

PAUSE. LEAVE the document open to use in the next exercise.

Building blocks enable you to store frequently needed information so that it can be easily accessed and used again. In this activity, you stored the account information text so that you can easily insert it into other documents in the future.

Table 8-1 describes the information you fill out in the Create New Building Block dialog box. This same information is available if you need to modify a building block.

Table 8-1

Create New Building Block information

Name	Description
Name	Unique and descriptive name for the building block.
Gallery	Gallery where the building block will appear.
Category	Category in which the building block will be located. User may choose an existing category from the dropdown list or create a new category.
Description	General description of the building block.
Save In	Name of the template where the building block will be saved, selected from the dropdown list.
Options	The **Insert Content in Its Own Page** option ensures the building block is placed on a separate page. The **Insert Content in Its Own Paragraph** option is used for content that should not become part of another paragraph. The **Insert Content Only** option is used for all other content.

TROUBLESHOOTING

To store paragraph formatting such as indentation, alignment, line spacing, and pagination in a building block, you must include the paragraph mark (¶) in the selection. To view paragraph marks, from the Home tab, in the Paragraph group, click Show/Hide¶.

When you close Word, a message will appear asking if you want to save the changes you have made to building blocks, as shown in Figure 8-6. To keep the changes, click Yes.

Figure 8-6

"Save changes to building blocks" message

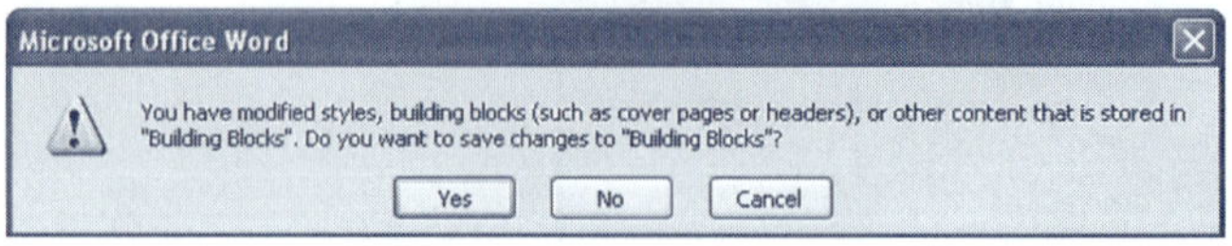

Copying and Moving Text

THE BOTTOM LINE

It is often necessary to copy or remove text from one location in a document and place it in another. In the following activities, you will learn two different ways to copy and move text—using the Clipboard and using the mouse.

Using the Clipboard to Copy and Move Text

The Clipboard enables you to cut or copy multiple items and paste them into any Office document.

USE THE CLIPBOARD TO COPY AND MOVE TEXT

USE the document that is open from the previous exercise.

1. In the first section of the document, select the entire second paragraph, which begins *Questions or comments regarding . . ..*
2. On the Home tab, in the Clipboard group, click the **Cut** button shown in Figure 8-7.

Figure 8-7

Clipboard group on the Home tab

ANOTHER WAY

To copy items to the Clipboard using the keyboard, press **Ctrl+C**. To cut an item using the keyboard, press **Ctrl+X**.

3. Place the insertion point on the line below the document title.
4. On the Home tab, click the **Clipboard dialog box launcher** to display the Clipboard task pane.
5. Move your mouse pointer to the text you just collected on the Clipboard and click the downward-pointing arrow, as shown in Figure 8-8.

Figure 8-8

Clipboard task pane

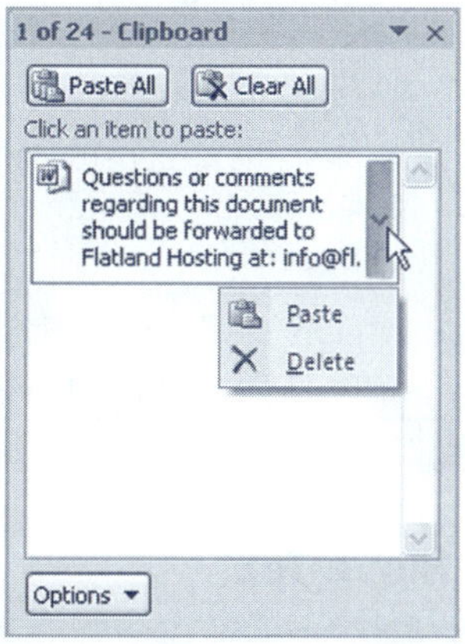

TAKE NOTE*

Your Clipboard task pane may look different depending on how many items have been collected there.

6. Click **Paste** to insert the text into the document in the new location.

> **ANOTHER WAY**
>
> To paste the item most recently collected on the Clipboard, press **Ctrl+V** on the keyboard.

> **CERTIFICATION READY?**
> How do you cut, copy and paste text?
> **2.2.1**

7. Click the **Close** button on the Clipboard task pane.
8. **SAVE** the document.

PAUSE. LEAVE the document open to use in the next exercise.

When you ***cut*** text, you remove it. When you ***copy*** text, you make a duplicate. When you ***paste*** text, you place the cut or copied text in a different location. In this activity, you moved text to a new location in a document. The process for copying an item is the same.

When you cut or copy an item, it is added to the Clipboard collection. Collected items stay on the Clipboard until you exit all Office programs or click the Clear All button. To turn off the Clipboard, click the Close button on the Clipboard task pane.

The Clipboard holds up to 24 items. If you add a 25th item, the first item is deleted from the Clipboard. The newest entry is always added to the top. Each entry includes an icon representing the source Office program and a portion of copied text or a thumbnail of a copied graphic. By default, a message appears in the lower corner of your screen when you collect an item on the Clipboard, as shown in Figure 8-9.

Figure 8-9

Clipboard icon and status message

To control how the Clipboard is displayed, click the Options button on the Clipboard task pane. Table 8-2 describes the various options available.

Table 8-2

Options for displaying the Clipboard

Option	Description
Show Office Clipboard Automatically	Automatically displays the Clipboard when copying items.
Show Office Clipboard When Ctrl+C Pressed Twice	Automatically displays the Clipboard when you press **Ctrl+C** twice.
Collect Without Showing Office Clipboard	Automatically copies items to the Clipboard without displaying the Clipboard task pane.
Show Office Clipboard Icon on Taskbar	Displays the Clipboard icon in the status area of the system Taskbar when the Clipboard is active. Turned on by default.
Show Status Near Taskbar When Copying	Displays the "collected item" message when copying items to the Clipboard. Turned on by default.

Using the Mouse to Copy or Move Text

When you want to move a selection of text, you can use your mouse to drag and drop the selection.

USE THE MOUSE TO COPY OR MOVE TEXT

USE the document that is open from the previous exercise.

1. Select the phrase *Flatland Hosting* in the second paragraph of *6. Security/Software*.
2. Press the **Ctrl** key as you click, drag, and drop the phrase in the first paragraph before the words *login ID and password*. As you can see in Figure 8-10, the pointer shows a plus sign (+) as you drag, indicating that you are copying the selected text.

Figure 8-10

Copying text using the drag-and-drop feature

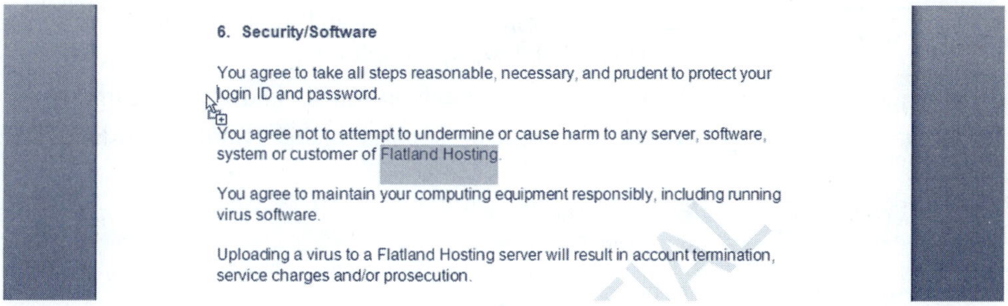
6. Security/Software

You agree to take all steps reasonable, necessary, and prudent to protect your login ID and password.

You agree not to attempt to undermine or cause harm to any server, software, system or customer of Flatland Hosting.

You agree to maintain your computing equipment responsibly, including running virus software.

Uploading a virus to a Flatland Hosting server will result in account termination, service charges and/or prosecution.

CERTIFICATION READY?
How do you cut, copy and paste text?
2.2.1

3. **SAVE** the document.

   PAUSE. LEAVE the document open to use in the next exercise.

To move or copy text by using the mouse, first select the text and then click the selection. Drag the text to a new position, or hold the Ctrl key while you drag to copy the text. As you drag, the pointer shows a box when you are moving text or a box with a plus sign (+) when you are copying it. When you copy or move text using the mouse, the item is not stored on the Clipboard.

TROUBLESHOOTING

By default, drag-and-drop editing is turned on so that you can drag the pointer to move and copy text. This option can be turned on or off by clicking the Microsoft Office Button and then clicking Word Options.

Click Advanced and, under Editing options, select or clear the Allow Text to Be Dragged and Dropped checkbox.

Finding and Replacing Text

THE BOTTOM LINE

A big advantage of online documents over hard copy is the ability to quickly search for and/or replace text. These features may be accessed from the Find and Replace dialog box.

Finding Text in a Document

You can use the Find command to search for specific text in a document, or you can use it to move quickly to a particular word or place in the document.

FIND TEXT IN A DOCUMENT

USE the document that is open from the previous exercise.

1. Place the insertion point at the beginning of the document.
2. On the Home tab, in the Editing group, click the **Find** button, shown in Figure 8-11.

Figure 8-11

Editing group on Home tab

ANOTHER WAY

To open the Find tab in the Find and Replace dialog box using the keyboard, press **Ctrl+F**.

3. The Find tab of the Find and Replace dialog box should be displayed. In the Find What box, key **Products**.
4. Click the **Find Next** button to find each occurrence.
5. When a message appears saying "Word is finished searching the document," click **OK**.
6. Click the **More >>** button, if necessary, to display more search options (see Figure 8-12).

Figure 8-12

Find tab of the Find and Replace dialog box

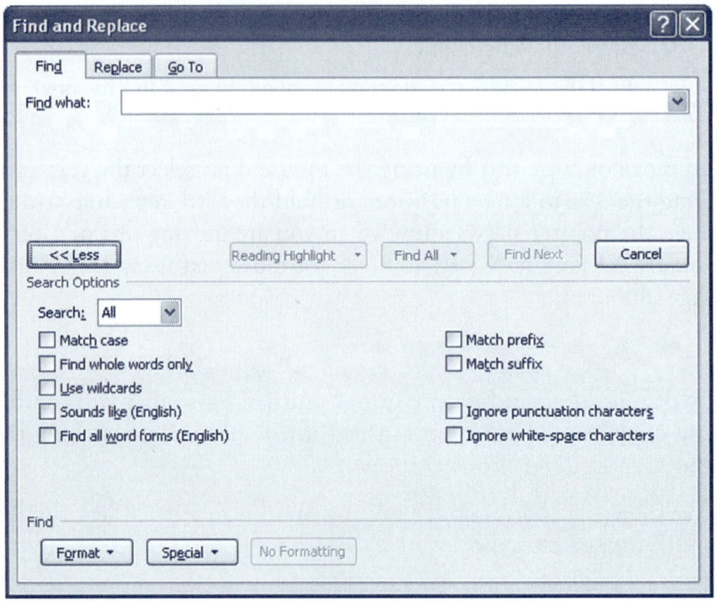

TAKE NOTE*

To cancel a search in progress, press **Esc**.

7. In the Search dropdown list, click **All** if it is not already selected.
8. Click to select the **Match Case** checkbox.
9. Click **Find Next**. Notice that this time Word only finds one occurrence because all the others are lowercase.
10. **SAVE** the document.

PAUSE. LEAVE the document open to use in the next exercise.

CERTIFICATION READY?
How do you find and replace text? How do you move around in a document quickly by using the Find and Go To commands?
2.2.2, 5.1.1

In the Find dialog box, key the text that you want to search for and click Find Next to locate the next instance of the word or phrase. To find all instances of a specific word or phrase in the document, click Find All and then click Main Document.

TAKE NOTE*

Do not select text before starting the search. Otherwise, Word will only search through the selected text, rather than the entire document.

To highlight every occurrence of a word or phrase on the screen, click Reading Highlight and then click Highlight All. The highlighting will not be visible when the document is printed. To clear the highlighting, click Reading Highlight and click Clear Highlighting. Figure 8-13 shows part of a document with reading highlight applied to the word *information*.

Figure 8-13

Text with reading highlight

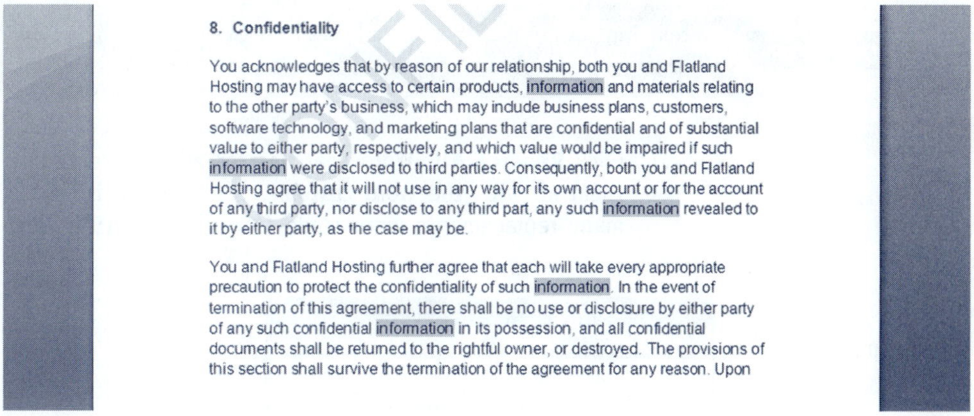

8. **Confidentiality**

You acknowledges that by reason of our relationship, both you and Flatland Hosting may have access to certain products, information and materials relating to the other party's business, which may indude business plans, customers, software technology, and marketing plans that are confidential and of substantial value to either party, respectively, and which value would be impaired if such information were disclosed to third parties. Consequently, both you and Flatland Hosting agree that it will not use in any way for its own account or for the account of any third party, nor disclose to any third part, any such information revealed to it by either party, as the case may be.

You and Flatland Hosting further agree that each will take every appropriate precaution to protect the confidentiality of such information. In the event of termination of this agreement, there shall be no use or disclosure by either party of any such confidential information in its possession, and all confidential documents shall be returned to the rightful owner, or destroyed. The provisions of this section shall survive the termination of the agreement for any reason. Upon

For more options, click the More>> button and choose additional criteria to refine the search process, such as matching the case or finding whole words only. You can use ***wildcard*** characters to find words or phrases that contain specific letters or combinations of letters. Key a question mark (?) to represent a single character—for example, keying b?t will find *bat, bet, bit,* and *but.* Key an asterisk (*) to represent a string of characters—for example, m*t will find *mat, moment,* or even *medium format.*

Click the Format button to find specific formatting such as a font, paragraph, or style. Click the Special button to find special elements in a document such as a field, footnote mark, or section break.

Replacing Text in a Document

The Replace command can be used to automatically replace a word or phrase with another. The Replace tab of the Find and Replace dialog box is similar to the Find tab, except that it enables you to replace text instead of just searching for it.

REPLACE TEXT IN A DOCUMENT

USE the document that is open from the previous exercise.

1. Place the insertion point at the beginning of the document.
2. On the Home tab, in the Editing group, click the **Replace** button.
3. Click to deselect the **Match case** checkbox. Click the **<< Less** button to hide the options. The Replace tab of the Find and Replace dialog box should now look similar Figure 8-14.

Figure 8-14

Replace tab of Find and Replace dialog box

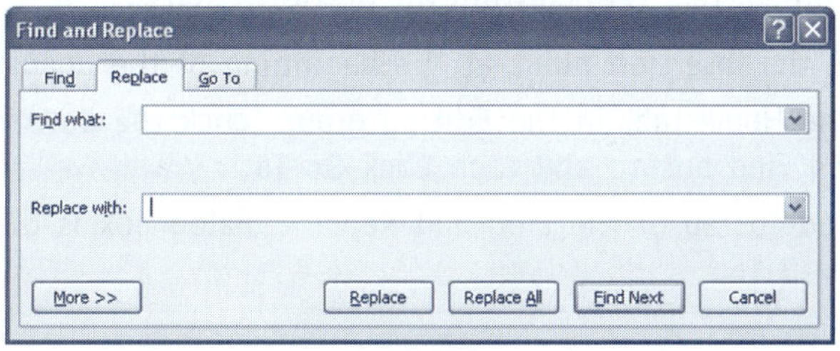

ANOTHER WAY

To open the Replace tab in the Find and Replace dialog box using the keyboard, press **Ctrl+H**.

4. In the Find What box, key **clients**.
5. In the Replace With box, key **customers**.
6. Click **Find Next**. Word searches for the first occurrence of the word *clients* and highlights it.
7. Click **Replace**.

TAKE NOTE* When replacing text, it is usually a good practice to click Replace instead of Replace All so that you can confirm each replacement to make sure it's correct.

8. Click **Replace All**. Word searches for all occurrences of the word *clients*, replaces them all with the word *customers*, and then displays a message telling you how many replacements were made (see Figure 8-15).

Figure 8-15

Find and replace message

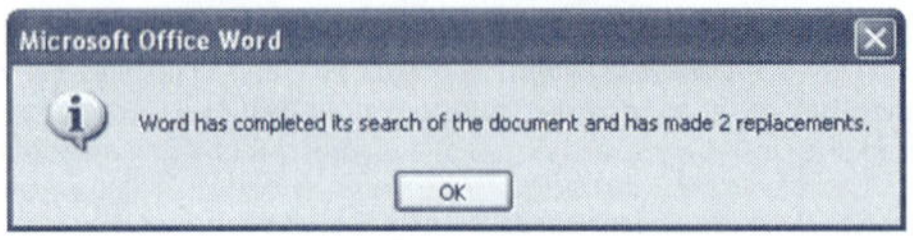

9. Click **OK**.
10. Click the **Close** button to close the Find and Replace dialog box.
11. **SAVE** the document.

PAUSE. LEAVE the document open to use in the next exercise.

CERTIFICATION READY?
How do you find and replace text? How do you move around in a document quickly by using the Find and Go To commands?
2.2.2, 5.1.1

The Replace command is versatile. Besides text, you can also search for and replace formatting. For example, you can find a specific word or phrase and change the font color, or find specific formatting such as italics and remove or change it. It is also possible to search for and replace special characters and document elements such as page breaks and tabs.

■ Navigating a Long Document

THE BOTTOM LINE In a longer document, you might want to go directly to a specific place without having to scroll or quickly locate a particular heading. The Go To and Document Map commands provide ways to navigate through longer documents easily.

Using the Go To Command

You can navigate to a specific page, line number, footnote, comment, or other object using the Go To command.

USE THE GO TO COMMAND

USE the document that is open from the previous exercise.

1. Place the insertion point at the beginning of the document.
2. On the Home tab, in the Editing group, click the **downward-pointing arrow** next to the Find button and then click **Go To**.
3. The Go To tab of the Find and Replace dialog box is displayed, as shown in Figure 8-16.

Figure 8-16

Go To tab in Find and Replace dialog box

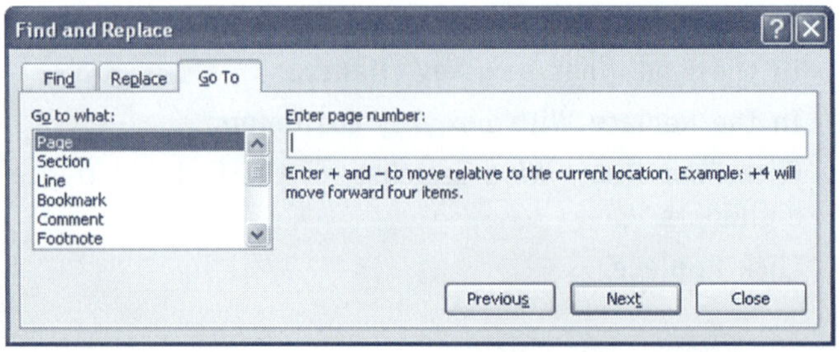

ANOTHER WAY

To open the Go To tab in the Find and Replace dialog box using the keyboard, press **Ctrl+G**.

CERTIFICATION READY?
How do you find and replace text? How do you move around in a document quickly by using the Find and Go To commands?
2.2.2, 5.1.1

4. In the Go To What box, **Page** should be selected. In the Enter Page Number box, key **6** and then click **Go To**. The insertion point moves to page 6 of the document.
5. In the Go To What box, select **Line**. In the Enter Line Number box, key **23** and then click **Go To**. The insertion point moves to line 23 in the document.
6. In the Go To What box, select **Field**. In the Enter Field Number box, **Any Field** should be selected. Click **Next**. The insertion point moves to the field you inserted into the document earlier in this lesson.
7. Click the **Close** button to close the Find and Replace dialog box.

PAUSE. LEAVE the document open to use in the next exercise.

You can use the Go To command to jump to a specific page, table, graphic, equation, or other item in your document. To go to the next or previous item of the same type, leave the Enter box empty and then click Previous or Next.

TAKE NOTE*

Word keeps track of the last three locations where you typed or edited text. To go to a previous editing location in your document, press **Shift+F5**.

Using the Document Map

Use the Document Map to quickly navigate through a document and keep track of your location within it.

USE THE DOCUMENT MAP

USE the document that is open from the previous exercise.

1. Place the insertion point at the beginning of the document.
2. On the View tab, in the Show/Hide group, click to select the **Document Map** checkbox.
3. The Document Map pane appears, as shown in Figure 8-17.

Figure 8-17
Document Map pane

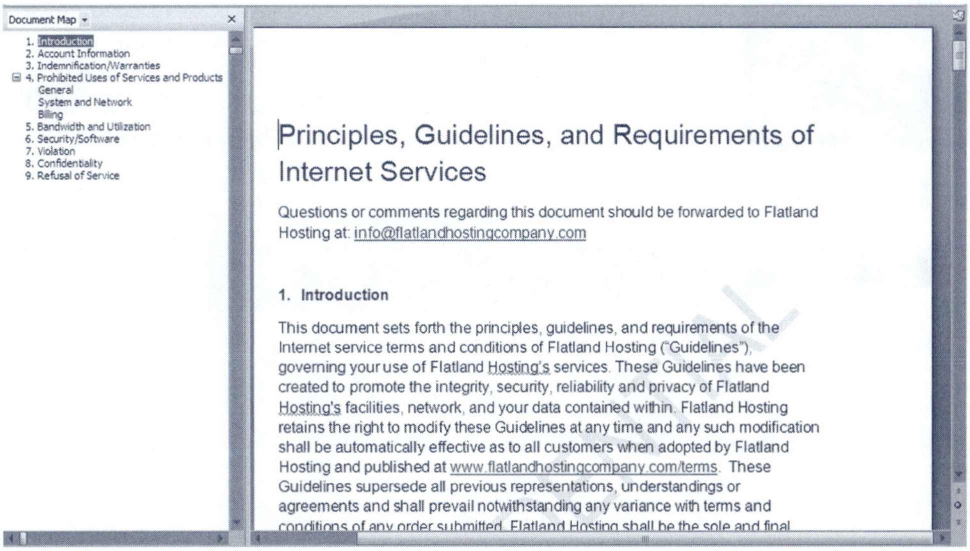

TROUBLESHOOTING

If the headings are too long, you can change the width of the Document Map by pointing to the right edge of the pane and dragging the resize bar to the right. Or you can hover the pointer over an individual heading to view it.

4. In the Document Map pane, click the *5. Bandwidth and Utilization* heading. The insertion point moves to that location in the document.
5. Click the minus sign (-) next to the *4. Prohibited Uses of Products and Services* heading to collapse the subheadings.
6. Click the downward-pointing arrow next to the Document Map dropdown list and click **Thumbnails**. The pane shows a thumbnail of each page, as shown in Figure 8-18.

Figure 8-18

Document Map thumbnails

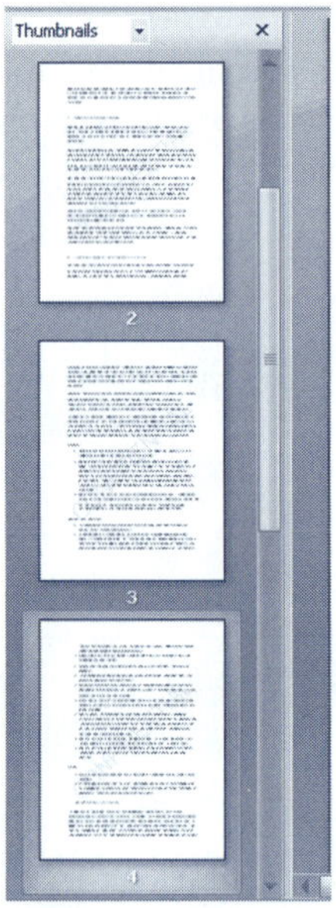

7. Click the **Close** button to close the Document Map pane.
8. **SAVE** and **CLOSE** the document.

STOP. CLOSE Word.

CERTIFICATION READY?
How do you find and replace text? How do you move through a document quickly by using the Find and Go To commands? How do you change window views?
2.2.2, 5.1.1, 5.1.2

The Document Map is a pane that displays a list of headings so that you can navigate through a structural view of the document. When you click a heading in the pane, Word jumps to the corresponding heading in the document and highlights it in the Document Map. You can display small versions of each page by clicking the downward-pointing arrow in the Document Map pane and then clicking Thumbnails.

TROUBLESHOOTING

Document headings must be formatted with built-in heading styles to display in the Document Map.

You can choose the level of detail to display in the Document Map by right-clicking a heading and clicking a number on the shortcut menu, as shown in Figure 8-19. To display the subheadings under a heading, click the plus sign (+) next to it. To collapse the subheadings under a heading, click the minus sign (-). To close the Document Map, click the Close button.

Figure 8-19

Document Map shortcut menu

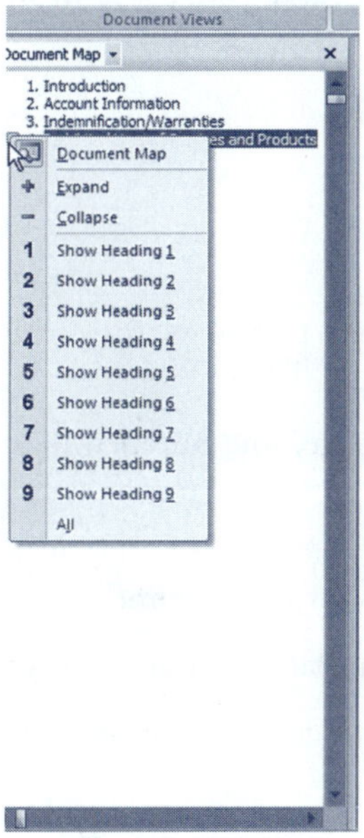

SUMMARY SKILL MATRIX

In this lesson you learned	Matrix Skill	Skill Number
To use built-in building blocks	Insert building blocks in documents	4.1.1
To insert a field from building blocks	Insert fields from Quick Parts	4.1.4
To create your own building blocks	Save frequently used data as building blocks	4.1.2
To use the Clipboard to copy text	Cut, copy, and paste text	2.2.1
To use the Clipboard to move text	Cut, copy, and paste text	2.2.1
To use the mouse to copy or move text	Cut, copy, and paste text	2.2.1
To find text in a document	Find and replace text, Move through a document quickly by using the Find and Go To commands	2.2.2, 5.1.1
To replace text in a document	Find and replace text, Move through a document quickly by using the Find and Go To commands	2.2.2, 5.1.1
To use the Go To command	Move through a document quickly by using the Find and Go To commands	5.1.1
To use the Document Map	Change window views	5.1.2

Knowledge Assessment

Fill in the Blank

Complete the following sentences by writing the correct word or words in the blanks provided.

1. The Building Blocks __________ gives you a way to manage building blocks by editing, deleting, and/or inserting them.
2. A __________ is a placeholder that tells Word to insert changeable data into a document.
3. When you copy or move text using the __________, the item is not stored on the Clipboard.
4. You can use __________ characters to find words or phrases that contain specific letters or combinations of letters.
5. You can navigate to a particular page, line number, footnote, comment, or other object using the __________ command.
6. The __________ Map is a pane that displays a list of headings so that you can navigate through a structural view of the document.
7. When you __________ text, you place it in another location.
8. If you add more items to the Clipboard than it can hold, the first item is __________.
9. When you want to move a selection of text, you can use the __________ feature with your mouse.
10. The Replace command is very similar to the __________ command, except that you can replace text instead of just searching for it.

Multiple Choice

Select the best response for the following statements.

1. You can sort the building blocks by all EXCEPT which of the following?
   a. name
   b. creator
   c. gallery
   d. category
2. The Clipboard holds up to how many items?
   a. 10
   b. 14
   c. 20
   d. 24
3. To control how the Clipboard is displayed, click which button in the Clipboard task pane?
   a. Options
   b. Display
   c. Settings
   d. View

4. To copy text using the mouse, which key do you hold while you drag?
   a. Tab
   b. Shift
   c. Alt
   d. Ctrl
5. To highlight every occurrence of a word or phrase on the screen, click
   a. Reading Highlight.
   b. Highlight All.
   c. View All.
   d. Highlight Next.
6. You can display small versions of each page by clicking the downward-pointing arrow in the Document Map pane and clicking
   a. Display Small.
   b. Thumbnails.
   c. View Page.
   d. Miniature.
7. When displayed in the document, field codes appear between what?
   a. parentheses
   b. quotations
   c. curly brackets
   d. dashes
8. If you have customized text that you frequently insert into documents, you can reuse it by storing it as
   a. a wildcard.
   b. Clipboard content.
   c. a Document Map.
   d. a building block.
9. The Replace command can be used to search for
   a. text.
   b. formatting.
   c. special characters.
   d. all of the above.
   e. none of the above.
10. Which command could NOT be used to navigate a longer document?
   a. Find
   b. Go To
   c. Clipboard
   d. Document Map

Competency Assessment

Project 8-1: Compiling Books and Beyond Handbook

In your job at Books and Beyond, you have started compiling the documents you have been working on into an employee handbook.

GET READY. Launch Word if it is not already running.

1. **OPEN** ***perdiemrates*** from the data files for this lesson.
2. Press Ctrl+A to select all the text in the ***perdiemrates*** document.
3. On the Home tab, in the Clipboard group, click the **Copy** button to copy the text to the Clipboard.
4. Click the **Microsoft Office Button** and click **Close** to close the ***perdiemrates*** document.
5. **OPEN** ***booksbeyond*** from the data files for this lesson.
6. On the Home tab, in the Editing group, click the **Find** arrow and then click **Go To**.
7. In the Go To What box, select **Page** if necessary. In the Enter Page Number box, key **6**.
8. Click the **Go To** button to go to page 6, which is blank.
9. Click the **Close** button to close the Find and Replace dialog box.
10. On the Home tab, click the **Clipboard task pane launcher**.
11. In the Clipboard task pane, click the per diem text you just copied to the Clipboard to insert it on page 6.
12. Click the **Close** button to close the Clipboard task pane.
13. **SAVE** the document as ***booksbeyond_handbook***.

PAUSE. LEAVE the document open to use in the next project.

CD

The ***perdiemrates*** document is available on the companion CD-ROM.

CD

The ***booksbeyond*** document is available on the companion CD-ROM.

Project 8-2: Editing Books and Beyond Handbook

Now that you have compiled all the individual documents into one employee handbook for Books and Beyond, you need to make some changes.

1. Place the insertion point at the beginning of the document.
2. On the Home tab, in the Editing group, click the **Find** arrow and then click **Go To**.
3. In the Go To What box, select **Line**. In the Enter Line Number box, key **1**.
4. Click the **Go To** button to go to the first line of the document.
5. Click the **Replace** tab in the Find and Replace dialog box.
6. In the Find What box, key **HR**.
7. In the Replace With box, key **Human Resources**.
8. Click the **More >>** button, if necessary, to display more options.
9. Select the **Match Case** box.
10. Click **Find Next** and then **Replace**.
11. Click **Replace All** and then **OK** to close the message box when all replacements have been made.
12. Click **Close** to close the Find and Replace dialog box.
13. On the Insert tab, in the Text group, click the **Quick Parts** button.
14. Select **Building Blocks Organizer** on the menu.
15. Sort by name and then scroll down and click the **Draft 1** building block.
16. Click the **Insert** button to insert the watermark into the document.

17. **SAVE** the document then **CLOSE** the file.

PAUSE. LEAVE Word open for the next project.

Proficiency Assessment

Project 8-3: Inserting Your Custom Building Block

You are creating a new hosting agreement document for Flatland Hosting and to save time, you want to use the building block that you saved earlier.

CD
The ***agreement*** document is available on the companion CD-ROM.

1. **OPEN** ***agreement*** from the data files for this lesson.
2. Place the insertion point at the end of the document.
3. On the Insert tab, in the Text group, click the **Quick Parts** button.
4. Select **Building Blocks Organizer** from the menu.
5. Insert the **Account Information XXX** building block that you saved earlier in the document.
6. **SAVE** the document as ***flatland_agreement*** and then **CLOSE** the file.

PAUSE. LEAVE Word open for the next project.

Project 8-4: Editing a Document

As an employee of Cornwall Village Bank and Trust, you frequently work with bank documents. The bank has just started a new service for customers called the Discretionary Overdraft Service, and you need to make some changes to the document describing it.

CD
The ***overdraft*** document is available on the companion CD-ROM.

1. **OPEN** ***overdraft*** from the data files for this lesson.
2. Select the first paragraph under the Introduction title.
3. Create a reusable building block named **Cornwall Intro XXX (where XXX = your initials)**.
4. Search for every occurrence of the & symbol in the document and replace it with the word *and*.
5. Use the Document Map to navigate to the *If You Need Help* heading.
6. Copy the phone number from the end of that paragraph.
7. Use the Go To command to go to the first page.
8. Paste the phone number on first line below the title of the document.
9. **SAVE** the document as ***overdraft_service*** and then **CLOSE** the file.

PAUSE. LEAVE Word open for the next project.

Mastery Assessment

Project 8-5: Store a Personal Quick Part

It would be helpful to be able to insert your name, class name, and the date on documents that you create in class without keying the items each time. You decide to create a personal building block for this purpose.

1. **OPEN** a new blank document.
2. Create a building block that includes your name, the class, and the current date. Use a field to insert the date.

3. Format the text however you want. You could even put the information in a header or footer.
4. Save the building block as your full name.
5. Open a document you have previously created in class and insert the building block you just created.
6. **SAVE** the document as ***personal_block*** and then **CLOSE** the file.
7. Without saving, close the document you used to create the building block.
8. **SAVE** the changes to building blocks when prompted.

PAUSE. LEAVE Word open for the next project.

Project 8-6: Building Blocks Help

You want to be able to create a report template that provides your template users with two cover letter types to choose from when they create their own report based on your template. You have heard that it is possible to do this by saving and distributing building blocks with a template, and you decide to use Word Help to find out more.

1. **OPEN** a new blank document.
2. Use Word Help to look up information on building blocks.
3. Find the information that deals specifically with saving and distributing building blocks with a template.
4. Read the Word Help information and then copy and paste the information into the blank document.
5. **SAVE** the document as ***buildingblocks_help*** and **CLOSE** the document.

CLOSE Word.

INTERNET READY

One benefit to being connected to the Internet while you are working in Word is that you have access to additional resources. As you saw in Figure 8-1 at the beginning of this lesson, the Quick Parts menu has a **Get More on Office Online** choice. Select this option to go directly to the Word building blocks page in the online Templates site. This resource improves as more people contribute. Consider submitting a building block others might find useful to the Community Templates section. Or, download an existing building block and then participate by rating or commenting on it.

Creating Tables and Lists

9

LESSON SKILL MATRIX

Skills	Matrix Skill	Skill Number
Inserting a Table by Dragging	Create tables and lists	4.2.1
Using the Insert Table Dialog Box	Create tables and lists	4.2.1
Drawing a Table	Create tables and lists	4.2.1
Inserting a Quick Table	Create tables and lists	4.2.1
Applying a Quick Style to a Table	Apply Quick Styles to tables	4.3.1
Turning Table Style Options On or Off	Modify table properties	4.3.2
Resizing a Row or Column	Modify table properties	4.3.2
Moving a Row or Column	Modify table properties	4.3.2
Setting a Table's Horizontal Alignment	Modify table properties	4.3.2
Creating a Header Row	Modify table properties	4.3.2
Sorting a Table's Contents	Sort content	4.2.2
Performing Calculations in Table Cells	Perform calculations in tables	4.3.4
Merging and Splitting Table Cells	Merge and split table cells	4.3.3
Changing the Position of Text in a Cell	Change the position and direction of cell contents	4.3.5
Changing the Direction of Text in a Cell	Change the position and direction of cell contents	4.3.5
Creating an Outline-Style List	Create tables and lists	4.2.1
Sorting a List's Contents	Sort content	4.2.2
Changing a List's Formatting	Modify list formats	4.2.3

Karen Archer is an executive recruiter. Many large companies hire her to find professional talent to fill communications and marketing executive positions within their firms. You have just been hired as her assistant. Although the business is small, you are still expected to display a high degree of professionalism, confidentiality, and integrity. Because it is a small business, you will be asked to perform many different duties. One of your main duties is to assist Ms. Archer with the constant updating of tables that contain data related to current clients, potential clients, and potential candidates for placement. Microsoft Word's table tools can help you successfully manage this information. In this lesson, you will learn to format lists as well as create, format, and manage tables.

KEY TERMS

ascending
cells
descending
formula
header row
merge cells
Quick Tables
sort
split cells
table

■ Creating Tables

THE BOTTOM LINE

Tables are ideal for organizing information in an orderly manner. Calendars, invoices, and contact lists are all examples of tables that you see and use every day. Word gives you several options for creating tables. You can create a table using the dragging method, the Insert Table dialog box, by drawing a table, or inserting a Quick Table.

Inserting a Table by Dragging

When you know exactly how many rows and columns you need for a new table, the quickest way to create a table is by dragging over the Table grid in the Tables menu to select the desired number of rows and columns.

INSERT A TABLE BY DRAGGING

OPEN a new blank Word document.

1. On the **Insert** tab, in the **Tables** group, click the **Table** button. The Insert Table menu appears.
2. Point to the cell in the **fifth column, second row**. The menu title should read *5X2 Table*, as shown in Figure 9-1. Click the mouse button to create the table.

Figure 9-1

Insert Table menu

CERTIFICATION READY?
How do you insert a table by dragging?
4.2.1

3. Click below the table and press **Enter** to insert a blank line.
4. **SAVE** the document as ***tables***.

PAUSE. LEAVE the document open to use in the next exercise.

A ***table*** is an arrangement of data made up of horizontal rows and vertical columns. ***Cells*** are the rectangles that are formed when rows and columns intersect. See Figure 9-2.

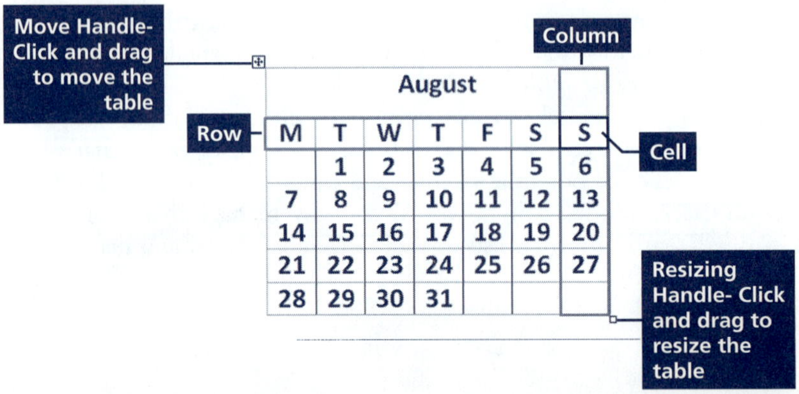

Figure 9-2

Table

As you just learned in the previous exercise, you can quickly create a table from the Table menu by dragging the mouse pointer to specify the number of rows and columns that you want. In this way, you can create a new empty table with up to 8 rows and 10 columns.

Using the Insert Table Dialog Box

The Insert Table dialog box lets you create large tables by specifying up to 63 columns and thousands of rows. You probably will not be working with tables that large very often, but the Insert Table dialog box gives you the option of creating a table with exactly the number of columns and rows you need.

USE THE INSERT TABLE DIALOG BOX

USE the document that is open from the previous exercise.

1. On the **Insert** tab, in the **Tables** group, click the **Table** button. Select **Insert Table** from the menu. The Insert Table dialog box appears.
2. In the **Number of Columns** box, click the upward-pointing arrow until **9** is displayed.
3. In the Number of rows box, click the upward-pointing arrow until **3** is displayed, as shown in Figure 9-3.

Figure 9-3

Insert Table dialog box

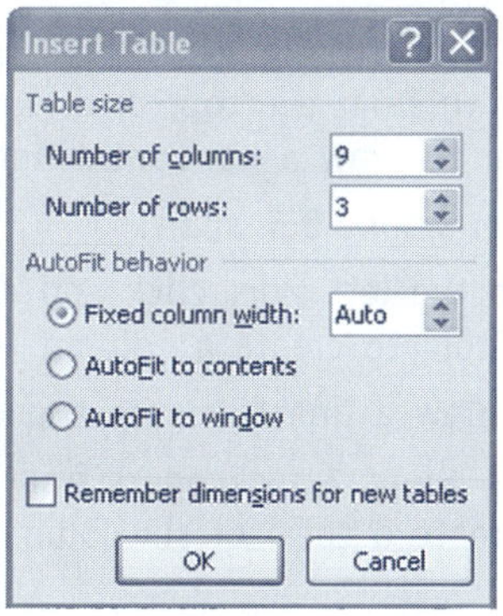

CERTIFICATION READY?
How do you create a table using the Insert Table dialog box?
4.2.1

4. Click **OK** to insert the table.
5. Click below the table and press **Enter** to insert a blank line.
6. **SAVE** the document.

PAUSE. LEAVE the document open to use in the next exercise.

You just used the Insert Table dialog box to insert a table with nine columns and three rows. From the Insert Table dialog box, you can click the upward- and downward-pointing arrows or key in the number of columns and rows you want in a table.

Drawing a Table

When you need to draw a complex table, you can use the Draw Table command, which lets you draw a table as you would with a pencil and piece of paper. The Draw Table command enables you to draw an outline of a table and then draw the rows and columns exactly where you want them.

DRAW A TABLE

USE the document that is open from the previous exercise.

1. Click the **View Ruler** button to display the rulers, if necessary.
2. On the **Insert** tab, in the **Tables** group, click the **Table** button. Select **Draw Table** from the menu. The pointer becomes a pencil tool.

3. To begin drawing the table shown in Figure 9-4, click at the blinking insertion point and drag down and to the right until you draw a rectangle that is approximately 3 inches high and 6 inches wide.

Figure 9-4

Draw a Table

4. Starting at about 0.5 inch down from the top, click and drag the pencil from the left border to the right border to draw a horizontal line.
5. Draw two more horizontal lines about 0.5 apart.
6. Starting at about 1 inch from the left side, click and drag the pencil from the first line you drew to the bottom to create a column (see Figure 9-4).
7. Move over about 1 inch and draw a line from the top of the table to the bottom.
8. Draw three more vertical lines about 1 inch apart from the first horizontal line to the bottom of the table to create a total of six columns. Your table should look similar to Figure 9-4.
9. Click below the table and press **Enter** to create a blank line.
10. **SAVE** the document.

PAUSE. LEAVE the document open to use in the next exercise.

When you choose the Draw Table command from the Table menu, the mouse pointer becomes a pencil tool you can use to draw a table.

TAKE NOTE*

You have learned four ways to insert a blank table. If you have data that is separated by commas, tabs, paragraphs, or another character, you can easily convert it to a table with the Convert Text to Table command on the Table menu.

TROUBLESHOOTING

When you are drawing tables with the pencil tool, remember that it will draw squares and rectangles as well as lines. If you are trying to draw a straight line and you move the pencil off your straight path, Word may think you are trying to draw a rectangle and insert one for you. If this happens, just click the Undo button on the Quick Access toolbar and try again. It might take a little bit of practice to learn the difference between drawing straight lines and rectangles.

CERTIFICATION READY?
How do you draw a table?
4.2.1

Inserting a Quick Table

As you have learned in previous lessons, Word provides many predefined building blocks, such as headers and footers, that can help you create professional-looking documents. In the same way, Word provides a variety of Quick Tables you can insert into your documents.

INSERT A QUICK TABLE

USE the document that is open from the previous exercise.

1. On the **Insert** tab, in the **Tables** group, click the **Table** button. Select **Quick Tables** from the menu. A gallery of built-in Quick Tables appears, as shown in Figure 9-5.

Figure 9-5

Built-in Quick Table gallery

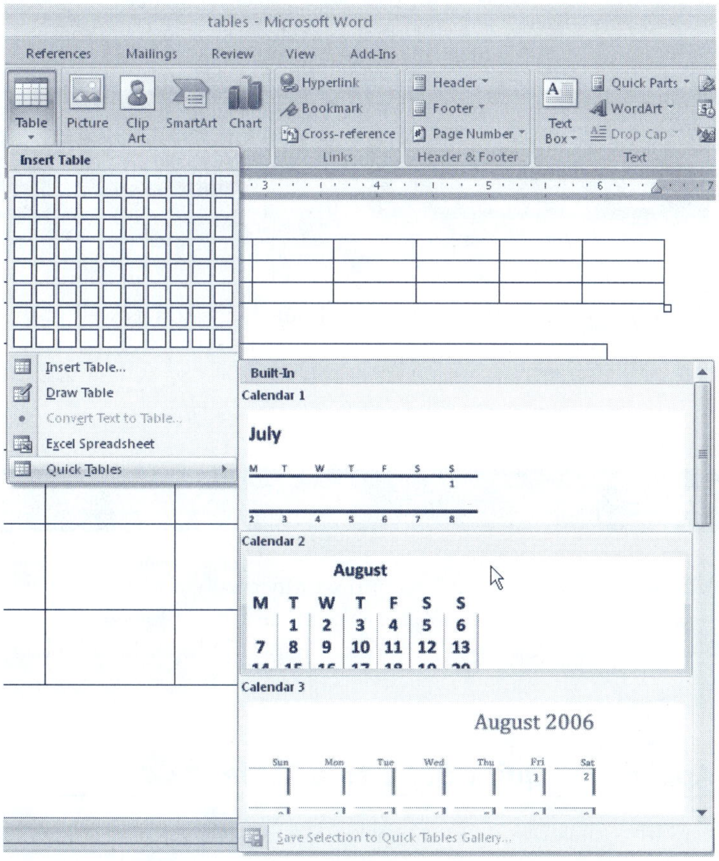

2. Select **Calendar 2**.
3. **SAVE** the document and **CLOSE** the file.

   PAUSE. LEAVE Word open to use in the next exercise.

CERTIFICATION READY?
How do you insert a Quick Table?
4.2.1

Quick Tables are built-in preformatted tables, such as calendars and tabular lists, you can insert and use in your documents.

You just inserted a Quick Table calendar into a document. You can edit a calendar, if necessary, to reflect the current month and year.

TAKE NOTE*

You can move a table to a new page or a new document by clicking the Move handle to select the table and then using the Cut and Paste commands. Use the Copy command to leave a copy of the table in the original location.

Software Orientation

Design Tab on the Table Tools Ribbon

After you insert a table, Word displays Table Tools in the ribbon as shown in Figure 9-6. You can use these tools to work with your table. Because this is a new set of tools you have not seen before, it is important to become familiar with the commands that are available.

Figure 9-6

Design Tab on the Table Tools Ribbon

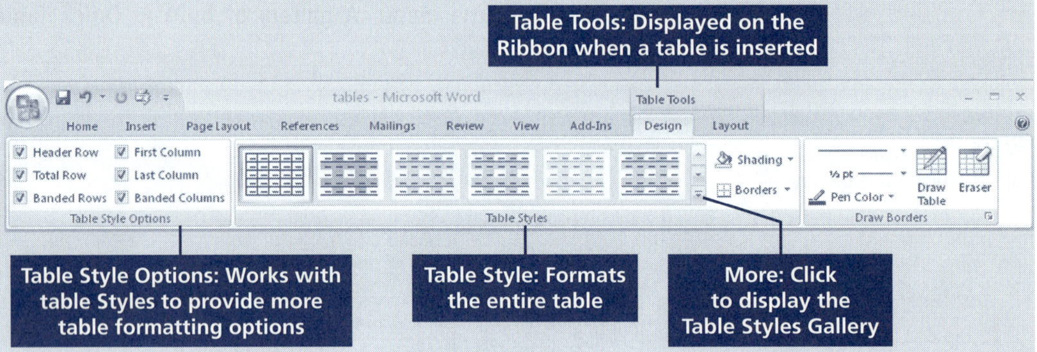

Use this figure as a reference throughout this lesson as well as the rest of this book.

Formatting a Table

THE BOTTOM LINE

You can format rows and columns individually and experiment with different combinations of formats, which would take some time. However, if you are interested in creating a professional-looking table quickly, apply a Quick Style. Then, if you need to, you can adjust the style using Table Style Options.

Applying a Quick Style to a Table

NEW FEATURE

With Quick Styles, Word makes it easy to quickly change a table's formatting. You can apply styles to tables in much the same way you learned to apply styles to text in previous lessons.

APPLY A QUICK STYLE TO A TABLE

OPEN ***clients*** from the data files for this lesson.

CD

The *clients* document is available on the companion CD-ROM.

1. Click anywhere in the table to position the insertion point.
2. On the **Design** tab, in the **Table Styles** group, click the **More** button to view a gallery of Quick Styles.
3. Scroll through the available styles. Notice that as you point to a style, Word displays a live preview, showing you what your table will look like if you choose that style.
4. Scroll down to the fourth row under the Built-in section and select the fourth style over in the row, the green **Medium Shading 1 - Accent 3** style, shown in Figure 9-7.

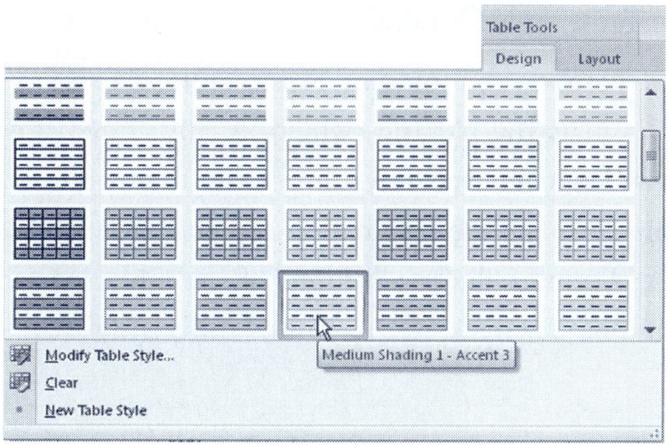

Figure 9-7

Quick Style gallery

CERTIFICATION READY?
How do you apply a Quick Style to a table?
4.3.1

5. **SAVE** the document as ***client_table***.

   PAUSE. LEAVE the document open to use in the next exercise.

In the previous exercise, you applied a Quick Style to a table. Remember to position the insertion point in the table before selecting a style from the Quick Styles gallery. If you decide later that you do not like the current style, you can always go back and use the same procedure to choose a different style.

Turning Table Style Options On or Off

Table Style Options work with Quick Styles to give you even more formatting options.

TURN TABLE STYLE OPTIONS ON OR OFF

USE the document that is open from the previous exercise.

1. Position the insertion point anywhere in the table.
2. On the **Design** tab, in the **Table Style Options** group, click the **First Column** checkbox. Notice that the format of the first column of the table changes, as do the Table Styles in the Quick Style gallery.
3. Click the **Banded Rows** checkbox to turn the option off. Color is removed from the rows.
4. Click the **Banded Rows** checkbox to turn it on again. Color is reapplied to every other row.
5. **SAVE** the document.

   PAUSE. LEAVE the document open to use in the next exercise.

CERTIFICATION READY?
How do you turn Table Style Options on or off?
4.3.2

In the previous exercise, you learned to turn Table Style Options on or off by clicking each option's checkbox. Table Style Options are used globally throughout the table. For example, if you turn on Banded Columns, all even columns in the table will be formatted differently than the odd columns. Table Style Options relate back to the Table Styles. So, if you turn on an option, such as Banded Columns, the Table Style gallery will include various designs with banded columns.

The following are Table Style Options you can turn on or off:

- Header Row: Formats the top row of the table specially
- Total Row: Formats the last row, which usually contains column totals, specially
- Banded Rows: Formats even rows differently than odd rows
- First Column: Formats the first column of the table specially
- Last Column: Formats the last column of the table specially
- Banded Columns: Formats even columns differently than odd columns

SOFTWARE ORIENTATION

Layout Tab on the Table Tools Ribbon

As you have already learned, when you are working with tables, Word displays Table Tools in the ribbon. You can switch between the Design tab and the Layout tab to edit tables. The Layout tab, as shown in figure 9-8, includes commands for changing the format of an entire table as well as commands for changing the appearance of individual table components, such as cells, columns, and rows.

Figure 9-8

Layout Tab on the Table Tools Ribbon

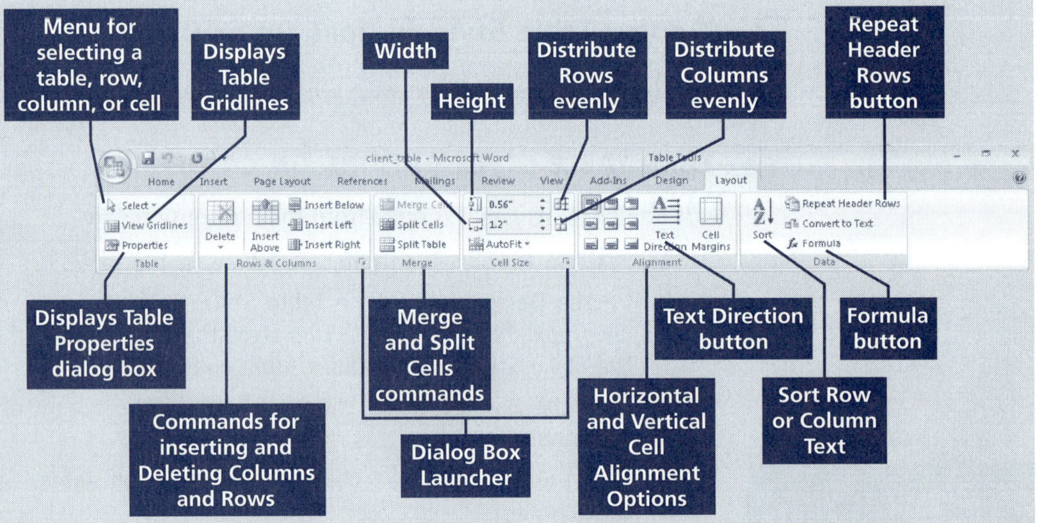

Use this figure as a reference throughout this lesson as well as the rest of this book.

Managing Tables

THE BOTTOM LINE

After you create a table, you can resize rows or columns, move rows or columns, set a table's horizontal alignment, create a header row, sort a table's contents, perform calculations, merge and split cells, change the position of text in a cell, and change the direction of text in a cell.

Resizing a Row or Column

As with any document that you edit, some adjustments are always necessary when you work with tables. You may need to resize columns or rows to better fit your data.

RESIZE A ROW OR COLUMN

USE the document that is open from the previous exercise.

1. On the **Layout** tab, in the **Table** group, click the **View Gridlines** button.
2. Position the mouse pointer over the right border of the table, in the first row. The pointer changes to a double-headed arrow, shown in Figure 9-9.

Figure 9-9

Double-headed arrow

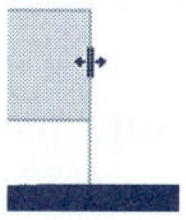

3. Click and drag the border to the right until you reach the 6.5-inch mark on the ruler.
4. On the **Layout** tab, in the **Cell Size** group, click the **AutoFit** button. On the dropdown menu, click **AutoFit Contents**, as shown in Figure 9-10. Each column width changes to fit the data in the column.

Figure 9-10

AutoFit button and menu

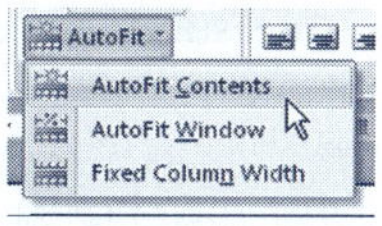

5. Position the pointer outside the table, above the column with the phone numbers. The pointer changes to a downward-pointing selection arrow. Click to select the column.
6. On the **Layout** tab, in the **Cell Size** group, click the upward-pointing arrow in the **Width** box until it reads **1.1**. The column width changes.
7. Select the first row. On the **Layout** tab, in the **Cell Size** group, click the **Dialog Box Launcher**. The Table Properties dialog box appears.
8. Click the **Row** tab. Click the **Specify Height** checkbox. In the Height box, click the upward-pointing arrow until the box reads **0.5″**, as shown in Figure 9-11.

Figure 9-11

Table Properties dialog box

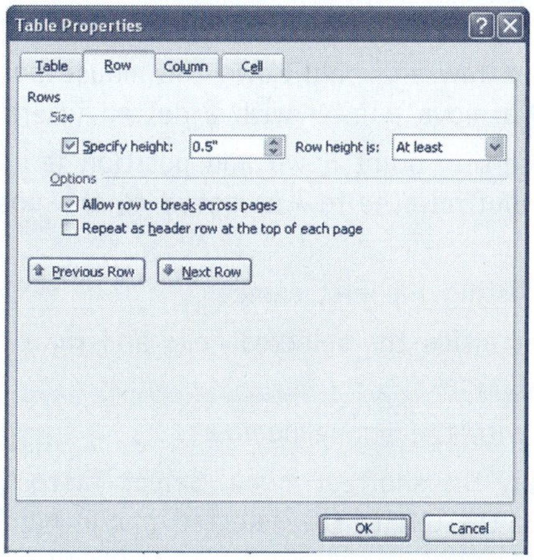

9. Click the Next Row button. Notice the selection moves down one row. Click **OK**.
10. Click in any cell to remove the selection.
11. **SAVE** the document.

PAUSE. LEAVE the document open to use in the next exercise.

As you just saw, Word makes it easy to resize a column or row instantly. When you position the pointer over a row or column boundary, it becomes a double-headed arrow pointer. Now you can click and drag the boundary to resize the row or column.

Displaying a table's gridlines can make editing easier. The View Gridlines button is located on the Layout tab in the Table group.

You can also resize a column or row using the commands in the Cell Size group on the Layout tab. Select cells or an entire row and click the arrows in the Height box to adjust the height. Select cells or a column and click the arrows or key in a measurement to adjust the width. The AutoFit command provides three options for automatically adjusting column width:

- AutoFit Contents: Adjusts column width to fit the size of its contents
- AutoFit Window: Adjusts column width to fit the size of the window
- Fixed Column Width: Forces a column to remain at a fixed width

CERTIFICATION READY?
How do you resize a row or column?
4.3.2

If you need to be more precise or change the size of several rows or columns at one time, select the rows or columns you want to resize and use the Table Properties dialog box to specify the height of a row or the width of a column. You can also specify whether you want the row height or column width to be exactly that measurement or at least that measurement.

ANOTHER WAY You can access the Table Properties dialog box from the shortcut menu by right-clicking anywhere in the table and selecting Table Properties.

Moving a Row or Column

When you are working with tables, it is important to know how to rearrange columns and rows to better display your data.

MOVE A ROW OR COLUMN

USE the document that is open from the previous exercise.

1. Select the fourth row of data, which contains the information for Proseware, Inc.
2. Click on the selected row and hold down the mouse button. Notice the mouse pointer changes to a move pointer with a dotted insertion point. 
3. Drag the dotted insertion point down and position it before the *W* in *Wingtip Toys*. Release the mouse button. The row is moved to the position above the Wingtip Toys row.
4. Select the column listing the first names.
5. Position the pointer inside the selected cells and right-click to display the shortcut menu. Select **Cut**.
6. Select the column with the phone numbers.
7. Right-click to display the shortcut menu. Select **Paste Columns**. The first name column is moved to the left of the selected phone number column.
8. **SAVE** the document.

   PAUSE. LEAVE the document open to use in the next exercise.

You can use drag-and-drop editing to move rows or columns. Select the entire column or row that you want to move and then click within the selection and hold the mouse button. The mouse pointer changes to a move pointer, which looks like a pointer with an empty rectangle underneath it. The insertion point becomes a dotted line. Drag the dotted insertion point to the location where you want to move the row or column and release the mouse button.

Another way to move rows and columns is to cut and paste. You have already learned to cut and paste text. The concept is the same for rows and columns. Select the entire row or column. Right-click to display the shortcut menu and then select the Cut command. Select the column to the right or the row below where you want the copied data to appear and select either Paste Columns or Paste Rows from the shortcut menu.

TAKE NOTE* When moving a row, you can click the Home tab and use the Cut and Paste commands in the Clipboard group. However, using the commands on the shortcut menu saves you time by keeping the Table Tools displayed in the Ribbon.

Setting a Table's Horizontal Alignment

A table can be aligned on a page at the left margin, right margin, or in the center. When you insert a table within a report, such as a sales projections table, you can adjust its horizontal alignment on the page to maintain the flow of the report.

SET A TABLE'S HORIZONTAL ALIGNMENT

USE the document that is open from the previous exercise.

1. Position the insertion point anywhere inside the table. On the **Layout** tab, in the **Table** group, click the **Select** button. Then click **Select Table** from the menu.
2. On the **Layout** tab, in the **Table** group, click **Properties**. The Table Properties dialog box appears.
3. Click the **Table** tab. In the Alignment section, click **Center**, as shown in Figure 9-12.

Figure 9-12

Table Properties dialog box

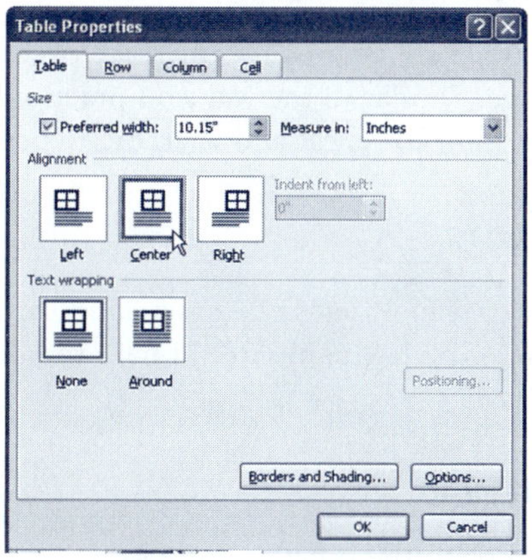

4. Click **OK**. The table is centered horizontally on the page.
5. **SAVE** the document.

PAUSE. LEAVE the document open to use in the next exercise.

To set a table's horizontal alignment, click in any table cell to position the insertion point somewhere within the table you want to align. Alternatively, you can select the table. On the Layout tab, in the Table group, click Properties to display the Table Properties dialog box. In the Alignment section, click Left, Center, or Right. If you want to indent the table from the left margin, first choose Left in the Alignment section, then use the upward- and downward-pointing arrow or key in the amount of space you want to indent from the left margin.

CERTIFICATION READY?
How do you set a table's horizontal alignment?
4.3.2

Creating a Header Row

When you specify a header row in the Table Style Options group, the row is formatted specially and provides a great place for column headings.

CREATE A HEADER ROW

USE the document that is open from the previous exercise.

1. Select the first row of the table.
2. On the **Layout** tab, in the **Rows & Columns** group, click **Insert Above**. A new blank row is inserted.
3. On the **Design** tab, in the **Table Style Options** group, click the **Header Row** checkbox. The header row is formatted differently.
4. Key headings in each cell within the first row of the table, as shown in Figure 9-13.

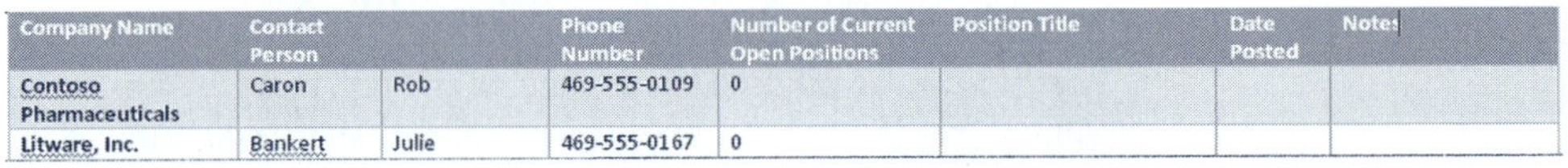

Company Name	Contact Person		Phone Number	Number of Current Open Positions	Position Title	Date Posted	Notes
Contoso Pharmaceuticals	Caron	Rob	469-555-0109	0			
Litware, Inc.	Bankert	Julie	469-555-0167	0			

Figure 9-13

Header row

5. Select the first row of the table.
6. On the **Layout** tab, in the **Data** group, click the **Repeat Header Rows** button. Scroll down and see that the headings have been repeated on the second page.
7. **SAVE** the document.

PAUSE. LEAVE the document open to use in the next exercise.

TAKE NOTE*

Repeating rows are only visible in Print Layout view or on a printed document.

A ***header row*** is the first row of the table that is formatted differently, and it usually contains headings for the entire table. When you click the Header Row checkbox in the Header Style Options group, you specify special formatting for the header row.

CERTIFICATION READY?
How do you create a header row?
4.3.2

When you have long tables that are split across two or more pages, you may need to repeat the header row or rows on each page. Similar to the way you practiced in the previous exercise, select the row or rows that you want to repeat and click the Repeat Header Rows button.

Sorting a Table's Contents

It is often helpful to display data in order. For example, an office contact list that displays employees in alphabetical order by last name would help the reader find information for a particular employee quickly.

SORT A TABLE'S CONTENTS

USE the document that is open from the previous exercise.

1. Select the **Company Name** column.
2. On the **Layout** tab, in the **Data** group, click the **Sort** button. The Sort dialog box appears, as shown in Figure 9-14.

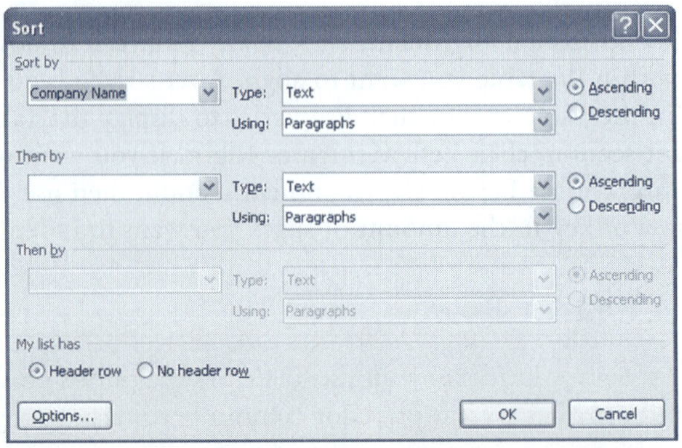

Figure 9-14

Sort dialog box

3. Click **OK.** Note that the table now appears sorted in ascending alphabetical order by company name.
4. **SAVE** the document.

PAUSE. LEAVE the document open to use in the next exercise.

To ***sort*** data means to arrange it alphabetically, numerically, or chronologically. Word can sort text, numbers, or dates in ascending or descending order. ***Ascending*** order sorts text from beginning to end, such as from A to Z, 1 to 10, and January to December. ***Descending*** order sorts text from the end to the beginning, such as from Z to A, 10 to 1, and December to January.

To sort text, numbers, or dates in a column, you first need to select the column. Then click the Sort command on the Layout tab in the Data group to display the Sort dialog box. The column you have selected will be displayed in the Sort By box. Select the type of data you are sorting, then choose ascending or descending order.

CERTIFICATION READY?
How do you sort a table's contents?
4.2.2

The Sort dialog box lets you sort up to three columns of data in a table. For example, you could sort text in one column by last name, and then sort text in another column by first name.

Performing Calculations in Table Cells

Tables provide a professional format for displaying numbers, such as sales figures. In a Word table, you can easily perform basic calculations, such as adding all of the sales figures in a column.

PERFORM CALCULATIONS IN TABLE CELLS

USE the document that is open from the previous exercise.

1. Select the *Woodgrove Bank* row.
2. On the **Layout** tab, in the **Rows & Columns** group, click the **Insert Below** button . A new blank row is inserted at the bottom of the table.
3. On the **Design** tab, in the **Table Styles Options** group, click the **Total Row** checkbox.
4. Click in the last cell of the *Number of Current Open Positions* column, which should be an empty cell.
5. On the **Layout** tab, in the **Data** group, click the **Formula** button. The Formula dialog box appears, as shown in Figure 9-15.

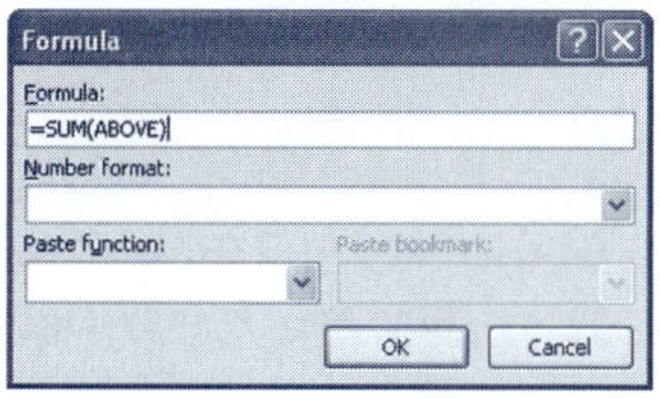

Figure 9-15
Formula dialog box

6. Click **OK** to accept the default settings. The sum is displayed in the formula cell.
7. Key **TOTAL** in the first cell of the Total row.
8. **SAVE** the document.

PAUSE. LEAVE the document open to use in the next exercise.

A ***formula*** is a set of mathematical instructions used to perform calculations in a table cell. Word provides basic formulas that can be used in tables to perform calculations like totaling sales figures in a column.

To insert a formula, click the cell that will contain the formula and click the Formula button on the Data group. The Formula dialog box appears from which you can key in a formula or insert one from the Paste Functions menu.

A formula must begin with an equal sign (=)for Word to consider any text that follows to be a formula. Next, key a function in all caps or choose one of the 18 functions available from the Paste Functions menu. Functions include SUM, AVERAGE, and COUNT. In parentheses after the function, key the addresses of the cells you want Word to consider in the calculation. You can key ABOVE to tell Word to consider all the cells above the formula cell. You can also specify cell references such as LEFT, RIGHT, or BELOW.

TAKE NOTE*

If you want to specify individual cells, combine the column letter with the row number. For example, the cell in the first column in the first row would be A1. This is known as the cell address.

CERTIFICATION READY?
How do you perform calculations in table cells?
4.3.4

Merging and Splitting Table Cells

The ability to merge and split table cells gives you flexibility to create tables that fit your data.

MERGE AND SPLIT TABLE CELLS

USE the document that is open from the previous exercise.

1. Scroll to the header row located at the top of page 1. Select the cell that contains the *Contact Person* heading and the empty cell to the right of it.
2. On the **Layout** tab, in the **Merge** group, click the **Merge Cells** button.
3. In the *Position Title* column, on the *Lucerne Publishing* row, select the cell that contains *Director Marketing VP Public Relations*.
4. On the **Layout** tab, in the **Merge** group, click the **Split Cells** button. The Split Cells dialog box appears, as shown in Figure 9-16.

Figure 9-16
Split Cells dialog box

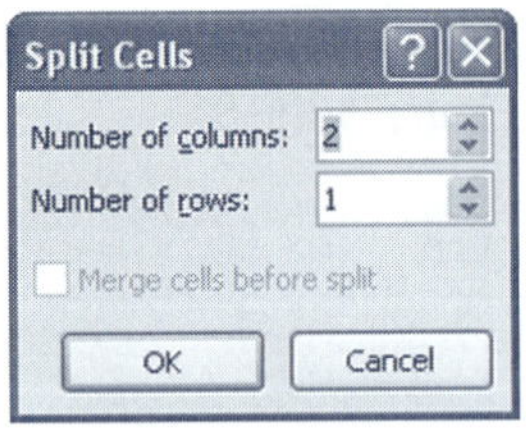

5. Click **OK** to accept the settings as they are. A new column is inserted within the cell.
6. Select *VP Public Relations* and press the **Backspace** key to delete it.
7. Position the insertion point in the new cell and key **VP Public Relations**.
8. **SAVE** the document.

PAUSE. LEAVE the document open to use in the next exercise.

ANOTHER WAY
You can access the Merge Cells command on the shortcut menu.

To ***merge cells*** means to combine two or more cells into one. Merging cells is useful when you want to create a heading that spans several columns. Merging cells is simple. Select the cells you want to merge and click the Merge Cells command, located in the Merge group of the Layout tab.

CERTIFICATION READY?
How do you merge and split table cells?
4.3.3

To ***split cells*** means to divide one cell into two or more cells. You may want to split cells when you have more than one type of data that needs to fit in one cell. To split a cell, select it and click the Split Cells command. The Split Cells dialog box enables you to split a cell vertically into columns or horizontally into rows. Use the upward- and downward-pointing arrows or key in the number you want and click OK.

Changing the Position of Text in a Cell

Word provides you with nine options for aligning text in a cell. These options enable you to control the horizontal and vertical alignment of cells, such as Top Left, Top Center, and Top Right.

CHANGE THE POSITION OF TEXT IN A CELL

USE the document that is open from the previous exercise.

1. Select the first row, with the headings.
2. On the **Layout** tab, in the **Alignment** group, click the **Align Bottom Center** button.
3. Select the *Number of Current Open Positions* column and click the **Align Center** button.
4. **SAVE** the document.

PAUSE. LEAVE the document open to use in the next exercise.

CERTIFICATION READY?
How do you change the position of text in a cell?
4.3.5

As you just practiced, you can easily align text in a cell. Select the cell or cells you want to align and click one of the nine alignment buttons in the Alignment group on the Layout tab (see Figure 9-8). These alignment buttons let you align the text horizontally and vertically within the cell.

Changing the Direction of Text in a Cell

Rotating text in a cell provides you with additional options for creating interesting and effective tables. Changing the direction of text in a heading can be especially helpful.

CHANGE THE DIRECTION OF TEXT IN A CELL

USE the document that is open from the previous exercise.

1. Select the cell that contains the *Company Name* heading.
2. On the **Layout** tab, in the **Alignment** group, click the **Text Direction** button three times to see the rotating text option.
3. **SAVE** the document and **CLOSE** the file.

PAUSE. LEAVE Word open to use in the next exercise.

CERTIFICATION READY?
How do you change the direction of text in a cell?
4.3.5

As you just saw, you can change the direction of text in a cell. Clicking the button three times will cycle you through the three available directions.

Working with Lists

THE BOTTOM LINE

From lists of supplies needed for a project to To Do lists, everyone uses lists. Bulleted lists, numbered lists, and multilevel lists are used in documents to provide small, quick, user-friendly pieces of information. Word can help you create and format lists to fit your documents.

Creating an Outline-Style List

Outline-style lists, also called multilevel lists, are often used to create outlines for long documents. Outline-style lists are also used to create documents such as meeting agendas and legal documents.

CREATE AN OUTLINE-STYLE LIST

CD

The *outline* document is available on the companion CD-ROM.

OPEN ***outline*** from the data files for this lesson.

1. Position the insertion point on the blank line after the *Discussion Outline* heading.
2. On the **Home** tab, in the **Paragraph** group, click the **Multilevel** List button. A menu of list formats appears. Notice that when you position the mouse pointer over the formats, they enlarge and expand.
3. Click the format style in the *Current List* section, as shown in Figure 9-17. The number *1.* is inserted for you.

Figure 9-17

Multilevel List menu

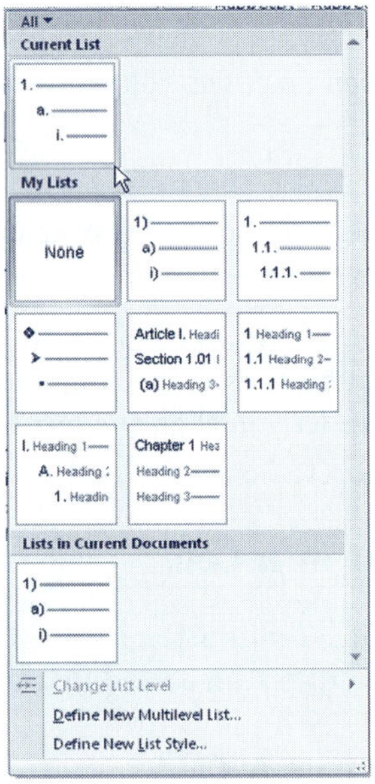

4. Key **Experience** and press the Enter key.
5. Key **Communication with Client** and press the Enter key.
6. Press the Tab key and key **Initial Meeting**. Press the Enter key.
7. Press the Tab key and key **Identify Position**. Press the Enter key.
8. Press the Tab key and key **Qualifications**. Press the Enter key.
9. Key **Compensation Package** and press the Enter key.
10. Key **Time Frame** and press the Enter key.
11. Press Shift + Tab twice to move back two levels. Key **Progress Reporting** and press the Enter key.
12. Press Shift + Tab to move back one level. Key **Methods for Finding Candidates** and press the Enter key.
13. Press the Tab key. Key **Database** and press the Enter key.
14. Key **Contacts** and press the Enter key.
15. Key **Networking**.
16. **SAVE** the document as ***discussion_outline***.

PAUSE. LEAVE the document open for use in the next exercise.

CERTIFICATION READY?
How do you create an outline-style list?
4.2.1

To create a multilevel list, position the insertion point at the location where you want the list to begin. Click the Multilevel List button in the Paragraph group of the Home tab. Select a multilevel list style from the gallery. Key the list, using the Tab key or Shift+Tab to move to different levels.

Sorting a List's Contents

You can sort a single-level list in much the same way as you sort a column in a table.

SORT A LIST'S CONTENTS

USE the document that is open from the previous exercise.

1. Select the bulleted list under the *Philosophy* section.
2. On the **Home** tab, in the **Paragraph** group, click the **Sort** button. The Sort Text dialog box appears. Click **OK.**
3. **SAVE** the document.

PAUSE. LEAVE the document open to use in the next exercise.

You just sorted a bulleted list. The Sort Text dialog box probably looked familiar because it is the same as the one you used for sorting text in a table. Like sorting column content, you can specify to sort lists with text, numbers, or dates in ascending or descending order.

CERTIFICATION READY?
How do you sort a list's contents?
4.2.2

You can sort single-level lists, such as bulleted lists or numbered lists, but if you sort a multi-level list, Word will alphabetize each line and your outline will become jumbled and out of correct order.

Changing a List's Formatting

Word provides several options for changing the look of a list. You can change a list's formatting by changing the type of bullet or numbering that is displayed. Some formats, such as round bullets, work well for most documents. Sometimes, however, you may prefer to use different shaped bullets.

CHANGE A LIST'S FORMATTING

USE the document that is open from the previous exercise.

1. Select the bulleted list.
2. On the **Home** tab, in the **Paragraph** group, click the downward-pointing arrow on the **Bullets** button. A menu appears.
3. Click the square bullet format in the Bullet Library, as shown in Figure 9-18.

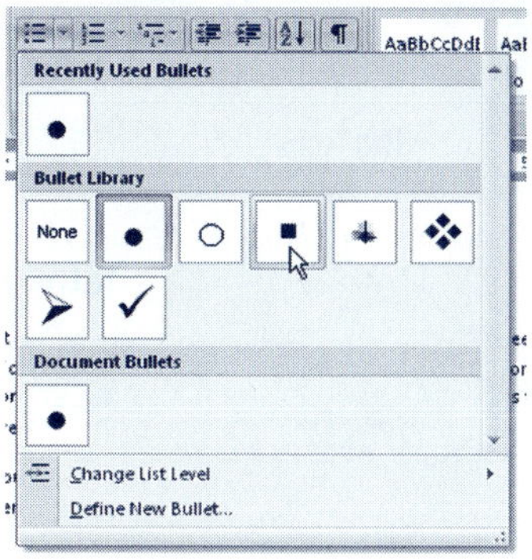

Figure 9-18
Bullets menu

4. Select the multilevel list you keyed earlier.
5. On the **Home** tab, in the **Paragraph** group, click the downward-pointing arrow on the **Multilevel List** button. A menu appears.
6. Under List Library, click the second format on the top row.
7. **SAVE** the document and **CLOSE** the file.

STOP and **CLOSE** Word.

CERTIFICATION READY?
How do you change a list's formatting?
4.2.3

As you just learned, you can change the formatting of lists easily by highlighting the list and choosing a new format from the library of formats on the Bullets, Numbering, or Multilevel List menus. You can also customize bullets, numbering, or multilevel lists with the Define New commands on the menus.

SUMMARY SKILL MATRIX

In This Lesson You Learned	Matrix Skill	Skill Number
To insert a table by dragging	Create tables and lists	4.2.1
To use the Insert Table dialog box	Create tables and lists	4.2.1
To draw a table	Create tables and lists	4.2.1
To insert a Quick Table	Create tables and lists	4.2.1
To apply a Quick Style to a table	Apply Quick Styles to tables	4.3.1
To turn Table Style options on or off	Modify table properties	4.3.2
To resize a row or column	Modify table properties	4.3.2
To move a row or column	Modify table properties	4.3.2
To set a table's horizontal alignment	Modify table properties	4.3.2
To create a header row	Modify table properties	4.3.2
To sort a table's contents	Sort content in tables and lists	4.2.2
To perform calculations in table cells	Perform calculations in tables	4.3.4
To merge and split table cells	Merge and split table cells	4.3.3
To change the position of text in a cell	Change the position and direction of cell contents	4.3.5
To change the direction of text in a cell	Change the position and direction of cell contents	4.3.5
To create an outline-style list	Create tables and lists	4.2.1
To sort a list's contents	Sort content in tables and lists	4.2.2
To change a list's formatting	Modify list formats	4.2.3

Knowledge Assessment

Matching

Match the term in Column 1 to its description in Column 2.

Column 1	Column 2
1. sort	**a.** to combine two or more cells into one
2. ascending	**b.** an arrangement of data made up of horizontal rows and vertical columns
3. descending	**c.** built-in preformatted tables you can insert and use in your documents
4. merge cells	**d.** the rectangles that are formed when rows and columns intersect
5. split cells	**e.** sorts text from the end to the beginning
6. table	**f.** a set of mathematical instructions used to perform calculations in a table cell
7. header row	**g.** sorts text from the beginning to the end
8. formulas	**h.** to arrange data alphabetically, numerically, or chronologically
9. Quick Tables	**i.** to divide one cell into two or more cells
10. cells	**j.** the first row of a table that is formatted differently from the rest of the table and usually contains headings for the entire table

True / False

Circle T if the statement is true or F if the statement is false.

T | F **1.** When you know how many rows and columns you need in a table, the quickest way to create one is by dragging over a grid in the Table menu.

T | F **2.** Turning Table Style Options on or off has no effect on the Quick Styles in the Table Styles gallery.

T | F **3.** The Total Row is the first row of the table.

T | F **4.** You can move a column or row using Cut and Paste.

T | F **5.** You can only sort one column of data at a time.

T | F **6.** A formula must begin with an equal sign (=).

T | F **7.** You can align text horizontally and vertically in a cell.

T | F **8.** Word gives you four options for changing the direction of text in a cell.

T | F **9.** You can sort single-level lists, such as bulleted lists or numbered lists, but you should not sort multilevel lists.

T | F **10.** In a multilevel list, press Shift+Alt to move the insertion point back one level.

Competency Assessment

Project 9-1: Placements Table

Ms. Archer, the executive recruiter, asks you to start working on a placements table that will list the candidates that have been placed, the companies that hired them, and the date of hire.

CD

The *placements* document is available on the companion CD-ROM.

GET READY. Launch Word if it is not already running.

1. **OPEN** *placements* from the data files for this lesson.
2. Select the last column.
3. On the **Layout** tab, in the **Cell Size** group, click the downward-pointing arrow in the **Width** box until it reads .9".
4. Select the first column.
5. On the **Layout** tab, in the **Cell Size** group, click the downward-pointing arrow in the **Width** box until it reads .9".
6. Select the *Company* column and change the width to 1.5".
7. Select the *Date of Placement* column and change the width to 1.3".
8. On the **Design** tab, in the **Table Style Options** group, click the **Header Row** checkbox and **Banded Rows** checkbox to turn them on.
9. On the **Design** tab, in the **Table Styles** group, select the **Medium Shading 1 - Accent 1** style in the fourth row.
10. Select the *Last* column.
11. On the **Layout** tab, in the **Data** group, click the **Sort** button. In the Sort dialog box, click **OK**.
12. On the **Layout** tab, in the **Table** group, click the **Select** menu and choose **Select Table**.
13. On the **Layout** tab, in the **Table** group, click the **Properties** button.
14. In the Table Properties dialog box, click **Center** alignment and click **OK**.
15. Select the first row, the header row.
16. On the **Layout** tab, in the **Alignment** group, click **Align Center**.
17. **SAVE** the document as *placements_table* and **CLOSE** the file.

PAUSE. LEAVE Word open for the next project.

Project 9-2: Quarterly Sales Data

Create a table showing the quarterly sales for Coho Vineyard.

1. Create a new blank document.
2. On the **Insert** tab, in the **Tables** group, click the **Table** button. Drag to create a table that has 5 columns and 7 rows.
3. Enter the following data in the table:

20XX Sales				
	First Quarter	Second Quarter	Third Quarter	Fourth Quarter
Mark Hanson	19,098	25,890	39,088	28,789
Terry Adams	21,890	19,567	32,811	31,562
Max Benson	39,400	35,021	19,789	21,349
Cathan Cook	34,319	27,437	28,936	19,034
Totals				

4. Select the first row. On the **Layout** tab, in the **Merge** group, click the **Merge Cells** button.
5. With the row still selected, center the title. On the **Layout** tab, in the **Alignment** group, click the **Align Center** button.
6. Position the insertion point in the second column, bottom row.
7. On the **Layout** tab, in the **Data** group, click the **Formula** button to insert a **SUM** formula in the *Totals* row. In the Formula dialog box, click **OK.**
8. Insert SUM formulas in the *Totals* row for the *Second Quarter, Third Quarter* and *Fourth Quarter* columns.
9. On the **Design** tab, in the **Table Styles Options** group, click the **Total Row** checkbox to turn it on. The Header Row, First Column, and Banded Rows options should be turned on already.
10. On the **Design** tab, in the **Table Styles** gallery, click the **More** button to display the gallery. On the eleventh row, seventh column, choose the orange **Dark List - Accent 6**.
11. **SAVE** the document as ***quarterly_sales*** and **CLOSE** the file.

PAUSE. LEAVE Word open for the next project.

Proficiency Assessment

Project 9-3: Sales Table

Ms. Archer asks you to create a sales table including data from the past two years. She can use this table to set goals and project future income.

CD

The ***sales*** document is available on the companion CD-ROM.

1. **OPEN** ***sales*** from the data files for this lesson.
2. Select the columns with the months and change the text direction for all the months so that they begin at the bottom of the column and extend to the top.
3. Increase the row height of the row with the months to 0.9 inches so that the text all fits on one line.
4. Select all the columns with the months and select **AutoFit Contents**.
5. Insert SUM formulas in the bottom row for each month.
6. Make sure the **Header Row**, **Total Row, Banded Columns**, and **First Column** Table Style Options are the only ones turned on.
7. Merge all the cells in the first row.
8. Merge all the cells in the second row.
9. Choose the **Medium Shading 2 - Accent 2** Table Style format.
10. **SAVE** the document as ***sales_table*** and **CLOSE** the file.

PAUSE. LEAVE Word open for the next project.

Project 9-4: Client Contact Table

Ms. Archer needs you to create a quick contact list.

CD

The ***client_table_2*** document is available on the companion CD-ROM.

1. **OPEN** ***client_table_2*** from the data files for this lesson.
2. Delete the last four columns: *Number of Current Open Positions, Position Title, Date Posted,* and *Notes.*
3. Change the page orientation to **Portrait**.
4. Change the width of the *Company Name* column to 1.9 inches.

5. Select the *Contoso Pharmaceuticals* row and change its height to 0.2 inches.
6. Delete the *Total* row and turn off the Total Row option in Table Styles Options.
7. Change the style to the blue **Light Grid–Accent 1** style.
8. Center the table horizontally on the page.
9. Select the header row and change its height to 0.4 inches.
10. **SAVE** the document as ***new_client_table*** and **CLOSE** the file.

    PAUSE. LEAVE Word open for the next project.

Mastery Assessment

Project 9-5: Correct the Quarterly Sales Table

The Coho Winery's Quarterly Sales Table includes some formatting mistakes. Find and correct the five problems within this document.

CD

The ***problem*** document is available on the companion CD-ROM.

1. **OPEN** ***problem*** from the data files for this lesson.
2. Find and correct five errors in the table.
3. **SAVE** the document as ***fixed_quarterly_sales*** and **CLOSE** the file.

   PAUSE. LEAVE Word open for the next project.

Project 9-6: Soccer Team Roster

As coach of your child's soccer team, you need to distribute a roster to all of your players with contact information, uniform numbers, and assigned snack responsibilities. You received a rough list from the league and you would like to convert it to table form. You haven't converted text to a table before, but you're confident you can do it.

CD

The ***soccer_team*** document is available on the companion CD-ROM.

1. Open ***soccer_team*** from the data files for this lesson.
2. Select all the text.
3. On the **Insert** tab, in the **Tables** group, click the **Table** button. Select **Convert Text to Table** from the menu.
4. In the Convert Text to Table dialog box, key **4** in the Number of Columns box. Click the **Commas** button under the Separate Text At section and click **OK**.
5. Use what you learned in this lesson to format the table. Start by removing extra spaces or words, adjusting column widths, and aligning text. Sort the table by snack date, insert a header row with headings for each column, and choose a Table Style format.
6. **SAVE** the document as ***soccer_roster*** and **CLOSE** the file.

   STOP and **CLOSE** Word.

INTERNET READY

Search the Internet for job openings that interest you. Create a table to record data about at least five positions. Include columns for the job title, salary, location, contact person, and any other information that would help you in a job search. Use what you have learned in this chapter to format the table in an attractive way that you could easily maintain.

Workplace Ready

Creating Tables and Performing Calculations in Word

Most everyone working in business is familiar with the many advantages of using Excel for creating tables and performing calculations. What some people may not realize is that Word provides many of these same capabilities. By creating a table and performing basic calculations directly within a Word document, you can turn an ordinary word processing document into a comprehensive business illustration.

Having just completed your college education, you are excited to begin your new career with Woodgrove Bank. As a Banking Associate in the Mortgage Department, one of your main responsibilities will be to produce a monthly Mortgage status memo. This memo will include monthly information on the number of new mortgage applications, the dollar amount of each, and their current status.

Presenting this information in a table format will provide for the most appealing design. However, you also need to include a brief introductory paragraph recapping the monthly information, as well as calculations for the total dollar amount of new mortgage applications. This report should be sent out in a memo format. By using Word, you can easily meet all of your objectives in just one program.

A co-worker reminds you that Word provides several memo templates, and you decide to choose one when initially creating your document. Memo templates provide replaceable text for To, From, Subject, Date and CC information. Below this, you can enter your monthly recap paragraph. Finally, you can use Word's Table options to create and format a table with the desired number of columns and rows.

Once the table has been created and the information has been entered into the appropriate cells, you can use Word's Table Layout and Design tools to enhance your table's appearance. Word provides many of the same capabilities you would find in Excel, such as merging cells, splitting cells, aligning text, auto-fitting text, sorting and much more. You can also insert formulas to perform basic calculations.

With so many possibilities, Word is a true all-in-one business tool.

INTEROFFICE MEMORANDUM

TO: WOODGROVE BANK MORTGAGE DEPARTMENT

FROM: SHAUN BEASLEY

SUBJECT: OCTOBER MORTGAGE STATUS MEMO

DATE: 2/4/20XX

CC: FILE

OCTOBER MORTGAGE STATUS MEMO

Although we saw a slight decrease in the number of new mortgage applications in October, the total dollar amount of new mortgage applications actually increased over the previous month. This is likely due to the increase in new and existing home sale prices throughout the tri-state region.

Woodgrove Bank October 20XX Mortgage Statistics		
New Mortgages	**Mortgage $ Amount**	**Current Status**
Alexander, Michelle	$149,000	Approved
Bischoff, Jim & Denise	$234,900	Pending
Harrington, Mark	$210,500	Denied
MacDonald, Scott	$180,000	Approved
Steele, Bill & Laura	$205,500	Approved
Wood, John & Karen	$199,900	Pending
TOTAL $ AMOUNT	**$1,179,800**	

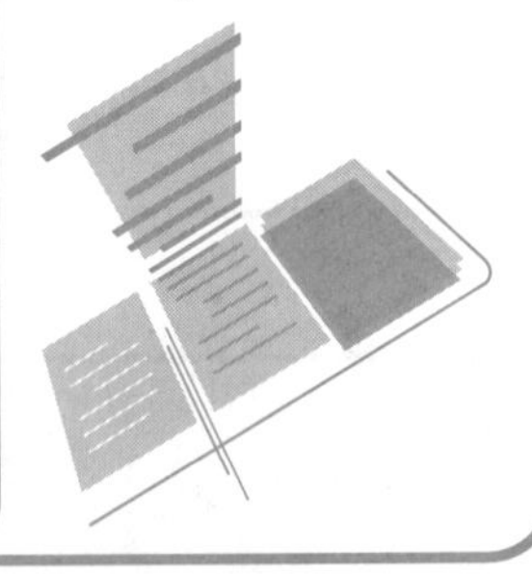

Adding Pictures and Shapes to a Document

LESSON SKILL MATRIX

Skills	Matrix Skill	Skill Number
Using SmartArt Graphics	Insert SmartArt graphics; Add text to SmartArt graphics and shapes	3.1.1, 3.2.5
Inserting and Resizing a Clip Art Picture	Insert pictures from files and clip art; Format by sizing, scaling, and rotating	3.1.2, 3.2.2
Inserting a Picture from a File	Insert pictures from files and clip art	3.1.2
Inserting Lines and Other Shapes	Insert shapes	3.1.3
Creating a Flowchart	Insert shapes	3.1.3
Adding Text to a Shape	Add text to SmartArt graphics and shapes	3.2.5
Cropping, Sizing, Scaling, and Rotating a Picture	Format by sizing, scaling, and rotating	3.2.2
Applying a Quick Style to a Picture	Apply Quick Styles	3.2.3
Adjusting a Picture's Brightness, Contrast, and Color	Set contrast, brightness, and coloration	3.2.4
Arranging Text Around a Picture	Format text wrapping	3.2.1
Compressing a Picture	Compress pictures	3.2.6

You work as a travel agent at Margie's Travel, a full-service travel agency that specializes in providing services to senior citizens. Margie's Travel offers tours, cruises, adventure activities, group travel, and vacation packages all geared toward seniors. On the job, you frequently need to enhance a document with graphics, pictures, or drawings. Word makes it easy to provide eye-catching travel information, signs, brochures, and flyers using SmartArt, clip art, and shapes. In this lesson, you will learn how to insert SmartArt graphics, clip art, pictures, and shapes containing text in a document. You will work with pictures to resize; scale; crop; rotate; apply a Quick Style; adjust color, brightness, and contrast; and compress.

KEY TERMS

clip art
compress
crop
embedded object
floating object
inline object
linked object
reset
SmartArt graphics

Software Orientation

Illustrations Group on Insert Tab

The Insert tab, shown in Figure 10-1, contains a group of features that you can use to add graphics to your document. The Illustrations group has options for several types of graphics you can use to enhance your Word documents—Shapes, SmartArt, charts, pictures, and clip art.

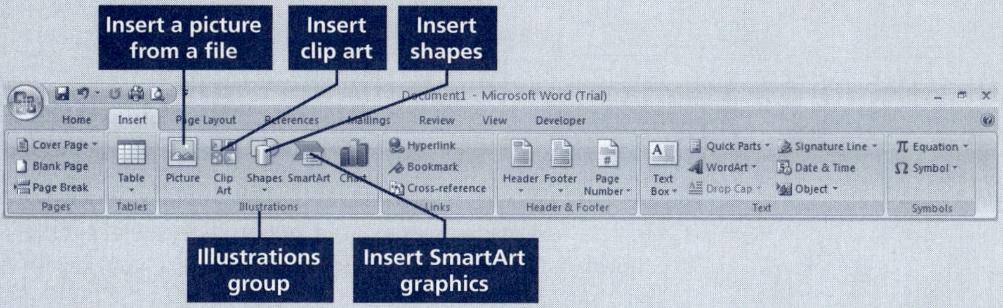

Figure 10-1

Illustrations group on the Insert tab

Use this figure as a reference throughout this lesson, as well as the rest of the book.

Inserting a Picture

THE BOTTOM LINE SmartArt, pictures, and clip art are graphics that can be inserted into a document and then formatted using a variety of options.

Using SmartArt Graphics

SmartArt graphics, designer-quality illustrations, can be quickly and easily created by choosing from among many different available layouts, depending on what information you want to convey. SmartArt graphics can be used to illustrate a process, hierarchy, cycle, or relationship.

USE SMARTART GRAPHICS

NEW FEATURE

GET READY Before you begin these steps, be sure to launch Microsoft Word and **OPEN** a new, blank document.

1. On the **Insert** tab, in the **Illustrations** group, click **SmartArt**. The Choose a SmartArt Graphic dialog box appears.

2. Click the **Relationship** category and then click **Equation** as shown in Figure 10-2.

Figure 10-2

Choose a SmartArt graphic dialog box

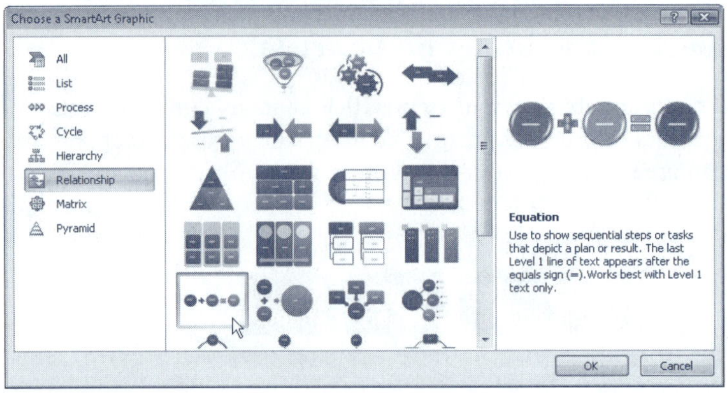

3. Click **OK** to insert the SmartArt into your document.
4. In the Text pane, replace the bulleted text placeholders with the information shown in Figure 10-3. Notice how the text you key in the placeholder also appears on the graphic.

Figure 10-3

Replace SmartArt graphic text with your own

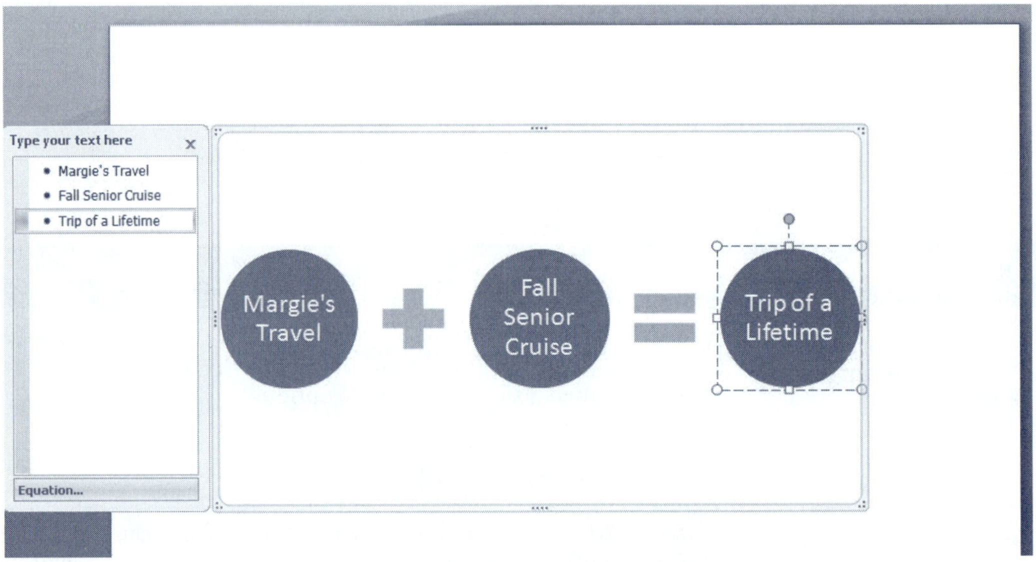

5. SmartArt Tools are available to make changes to SmartArt graphics. On the **Design** tab, in the **Layouts** group, click **Vertical Equation**.
6. Click the **Change Colors** button and then click **Colorful-Accent Colors**, shown in Figure 10-4. Your document should also look similar to the figure.

CERTIFICATION READY?
How do you insert SmartArt graphics? How do you add text to SmartArt graphics and shapes?
3.1.1, 3.2.5

Figure 10-4

SmartArt Tools and document

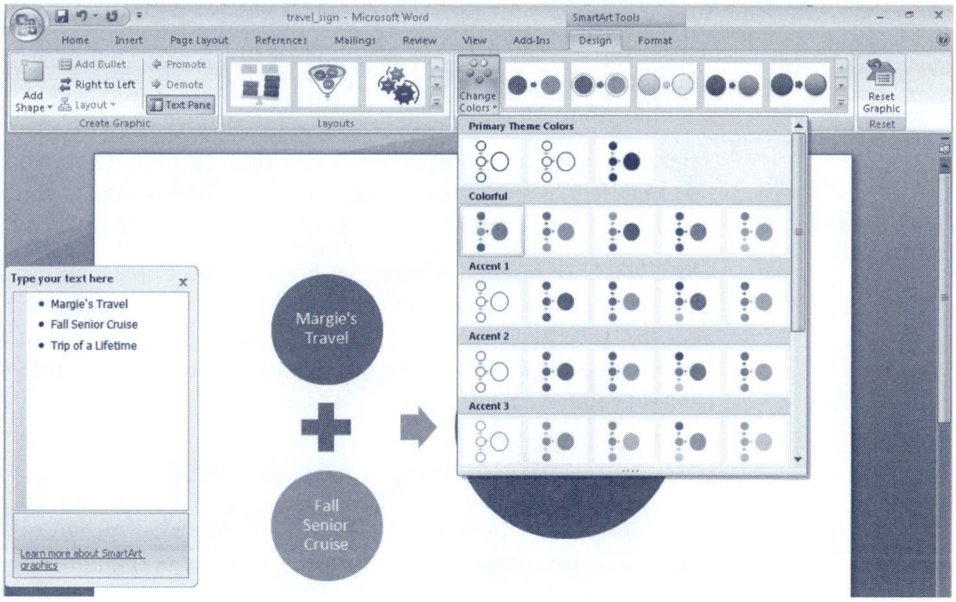

7. **SAVE** the document as ***travel_sign*** and **CLOSE** the file.

PAUSE. LEAVE Word open to use in the next exercise.

SmartArt graphics are visual representations of information that can help communicate your message or ideas more effectively. Table 10-1 gives some examples of the type of information you can display with each category of SmartArt graphics.

Table 10-1

SmartArt graphic categories

Type	Purpose
List	Show nonsequential or grouped blocks of information
Process	Show a progression of steps in a process, timeline, task, or workflow
Cycle	Show a continuing sequence of stages, tasks, or events in a circular flow
Hierarchy	Show a decision tree or create an organization chart
Relationship	Illustrate connections or interlocking ideas; show related or contrasting concepts
Matrix	Show how parts relate to a whole
Pyramid	Show proportional, foundation-based, containment, overlapping, or interconnected relationships

When a SmartArt graphic is selected, the Text pane appears to the left. As you key text to replace the placeholders, the text appears in the corresponding location on the Text pane. You can choose to show or hide the Text pane by clicking the Text Pane button in the Create Graphic group on the Design tab.

After you choose a layout, it is easy to switch to a different layout. Most of your text and other content, colors, styles, effects, and text formatting are automatically carried over to the new layout. Try different layouts until you find one that works best with your message.

Once you have inserted a SmartArt graphic, you can alter it using the SmartArt Tools. There are many options for changing the graphic. For example, you can add shapes to the graphic, alter the direction, change the layout, and change the colors. At any time if you want to revert to the original graphic, click the Reset Graphic button to discard the formatting changes you have made.

Inserting and Resizing a Clip Art Picture

To illustrate a specific concept in your document, you can insert clip art pictures—including drawings, movies, sounds, or stock photography.

INSERT AND RESIZE A CLIP ART PICTURE

OPEN a new, blank Word document.

1. Centered on the page, key **Explore the Globe** in Cambria, 48 pt. font.
2. Press **Enter**.
3. On the **Insert** tab, in the **Illustrations** group, click **Clip Art**. The Clip Art pane appears to the right of your document.
4. In the **Search For** box, key **travel**.
5. In the **Search In** box, click the downward-pointing arrow and click **Everywhere**.
6. In the **Results Should Be** box, click the downward-pointing arrow and select only the **Clip Art** checkbox.
7. Click **Go**.
8. In the Results pane, click the clip art with **baggage and Earth**, as shown in Figure 10-5.

Figure 10-5

Clip art pane

9. Hold the **Shift** key (to maintain the proportions of the clip art picture) as you click and drag the **bottom right sizing handle** of the clip art to make it larger, as shown in Figure 10-6.

Figure 10-6

Resizing clip art

XREF

Besides resizing, there are many other ways to format clip art. You will learn to use the various Picture Tools options later in this lesson.

10. **SAVE** the document as ***travel_flyer***.

PAUSE. LEAVE the document open to use in the next exercise.

Clip art refers to picture files that can be inserted into a document. In the Clip Art task pane, you can also search for photographs, movies, and sounds. To include any of those media types, select the checkbox next to each in the *Results Should Be* box.

CERTIFICATION READY?
How do you insert pictures from files and clip art?
3.1.2

In the Clip Art pane, you can click Organize Clips... to open the Microsoft Clip Organizer, shown in Figure 10-7. From here, clips can be arranged and categorized into collections for easy access. You can also add, delete, copy, and move clips, as well as change keywords and captions.

Figure 10-7

Microsoft Clip Organizer

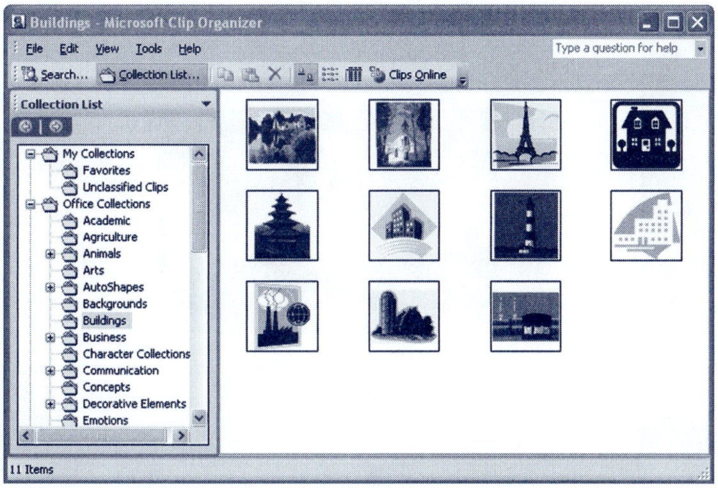

Inserting a Picture from a File

Additional sources of graphics include photographs or pictures that you might have stored on your computer. If you have your own picture that you would like to add to a document, you can insert it from a file.

INSERT A PICTURE FROM A FILE

USE the document that is open from the previous exercise.

1. On the line below the clip art, centered on the page, key **Picture Yourself Here** in Cambria, 28 pt. font.
2. Press **Enter**.
3. On the **Insert** tab, in the **Illustrations** group, click **Picture**. The Insert Picture dialog box appears, similar to Figure 10-8. (Your screen will look different, depending on the pictures that you have in the My Pictures folder on your computer.)

Figure 10-8

Insert Picture dialog box

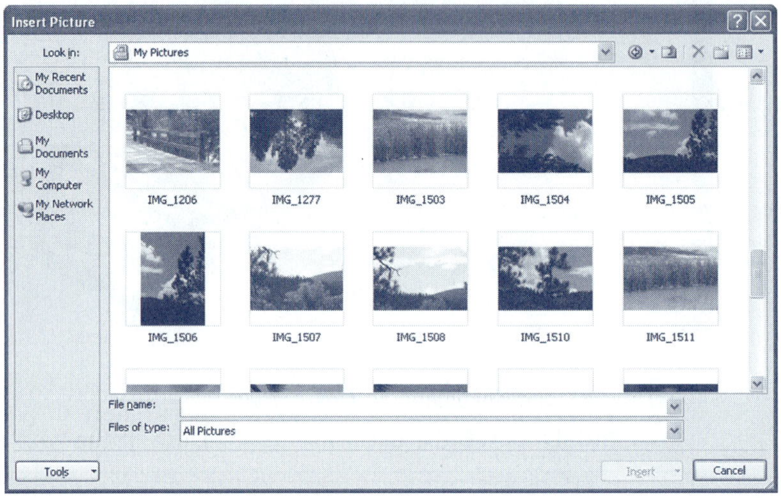

4. Navigate to where the data files for this lesson are located. Select the picture file named ***beach***.
5. Click **Insert**.
6. Hold the **Shift** key (to maintain the proportions of the picture) as you click and drag the **bottom right sizing handle** of the picture to make it smaller. Reduce the size of the picture until the entire document fits on one page. The bottom half of the document should look similar to Figure 10-9.

CD

The ***beach*** picture file is available on the companion CD-ROM.

Figure 10-9

Picture inserted into a document

X REF

You will learn more about how to format a picture using Picture Tools later in this lesson.

CERTIFICATION READY?
How do you insert pictures from files and clip art?
3.1.2

7. **SAVE** the document.

PAUSE. LEAVE the document open to use in the next exercise.

When you insert a picture into a document, Word makes it an ***embedded object*** by default, which means that it becomes part of the document. Another option is to insert the pictures as a ***linked object***, which creates a connection between the document and picture. This can reduce the file size of the document. In the Insert Picture dialog box, click the arrow next to Insert and then click Link to File.

You can copy or move a picture just as you would any other object or text. Select the picture and then choose the Copy, Cut, or Paste command.

SOFTWARE ORIENTATION

Shapes Menu and Drawing Tools Format

When you click the Shapes button in the Illustrations group, the Shapes menu is displayed, as shown in Figure 10-10. This menu contains options for a variety of ready-made shapes, including lines, arrows, stars, and banners. After inserting a shape, you can use the Drawing Tools, shown in Figure 10-11, to format a shape's style, fill, color, outline, and many other attributes.

Figure 10-10
Shapes menu

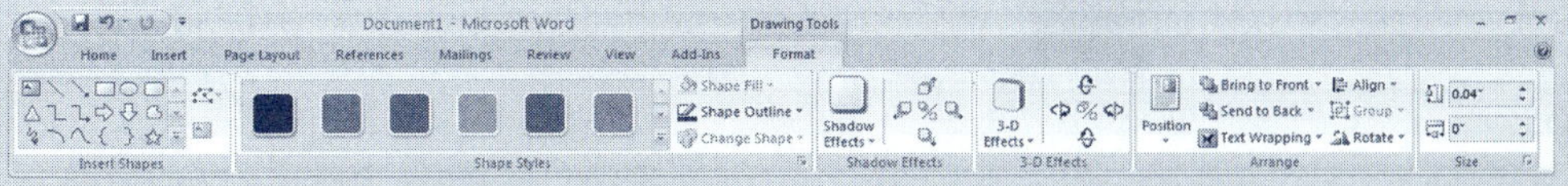

Figure 10-11
Drawing Tools

Use these figures as a reference throughout this lesson, as well as the rest of the book.

Adding Shapes

THE BOTTOM LINE

A drawing refers to a single drawing object or multiple drawing objects that are grouped together. A drawing object can include lines, arrows, callouts, stars, banners, or any other shape.

When inserting a drawing object in Word, you can place it in a drawing canvas—a frame-like boundary between the drawing and the rest of the document. Because a drawing canvas can help keep multiple drawing objects together, it is best to use one when adding more than one shape to your illustration—for example, if you are creating a flowchart.

Inserting Shapes

With a few simple clicks, you can insert a variety of different shapes into your Word document. There are many ready-made shapes to choose from—lines, basic shapes, block arrows, flowchart symbols, callouts, stars, and banners.

INSERT SHAPES

USE the document that is open from the previous exercise.

1. Select the *Picture Yourself Here* text and the picture below it.
2. On the **Home** tab, in the **Paragraph** group, click the **Align Text Right** button.
3. On the **Insert** tab, in the **Illustrations** group, click the **Shapes** button to display the Shapes menu.
4. In the **Block Arrows** section, click the **Curved Right Arrow** shape. The insertion point turns into a crosshair (+).
5. Place the crosshair in front of the word *Picture*. Click and drag downward and toward the chairs on the left of the photograph to create the arrow shown in Figure 10-12.

Figure 10-12

Block arrow shape

TROUBLESHOOTING

If the shape you are drawing does not turn out the right size the first time, you can adjust the shape by selecting it and then dragging one of the sizing handles.

6. On the **Insert** tab, in the **Illustrations** group, click the **Shapes** button to display the Shapes menu.
7. In the **Basic Shapes** section, click the **Smiley Face** shape.

8. Place the crosshair (+) inside the curve of the arrow. Click and drag to create a small smiley face that fits in the space available there.
9. **SAVE** the document and **CLOSE** the file.

PAUSE. LEAVE Word open to use in the next exercise.

CERTIFICATION READY?
How do you insert shapes?
3.1.3

The shapes on the Shapes menu are all inserted the same way. Click to select the one you want to insert. Then click in the document where you want to begin drawing and drag until the shape is the size and shape you want.

Drawing Tools provides many options for formatting shapes. Click the More button in the Shape Styles group to see the Quick Style options for changing the overall visual style of the shape, as shown in Figure 10-13.

Figure 10-13

Shape Styles gallery

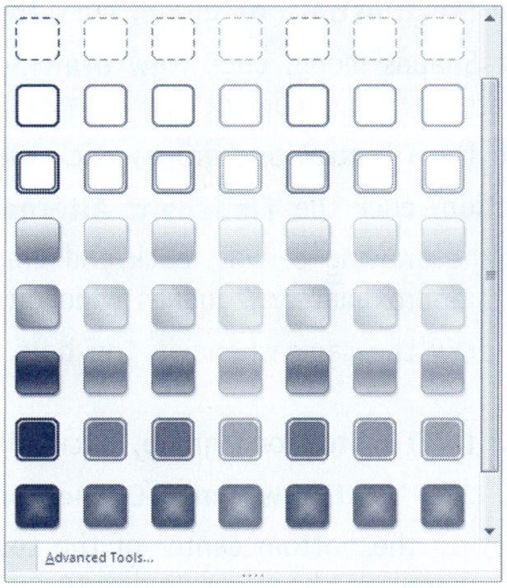

You can change the look of your shape by changing its fill or by adding effects, such as shadows, glows, reflections, soft edges, bevels, and 3-D rotations. For example, click the Shadow Effects button to see all the options for applying a shadow to your shape. Or, click the 3-D Effects button to enhance your shape with a 3-D effect, as shown in Figure 10-14. There are so many ways to format a shape that it is not possible to cover them all here—but, do not be afraid to experiment.

Figure 10-14

3-D Effects button and menu

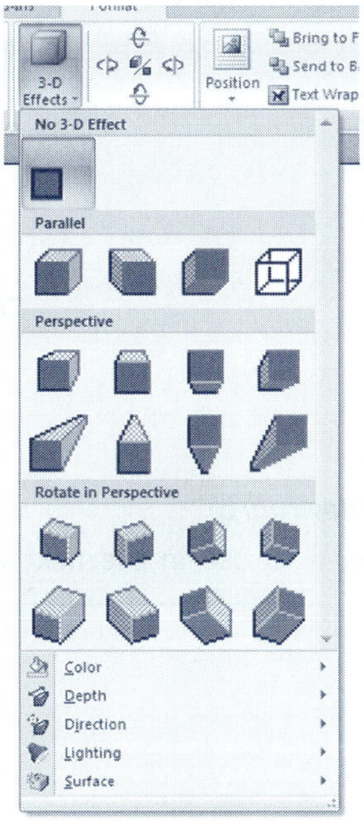

Creating a Flowchart

A flowchart can be created using the flowchart symbols available on the Shapes menu. You can then connect the symbols using a variety of line options—arrows, connectors, curves, freeform, and even scribbles.

CREATE A FLOWCHART

OPEN a new, blank Word document.

1. At the top of the document, centered on the page, key **Margie's Travel** in Cambria, 24 pt. font. Press **Enter**.
2. Centered on the page, key **Organization Chart** in Cambria, 20 pt. font. Press **Enter**.
3. On the **Insert** tab, in the **Illustrations** group, click the **Shapes** button.
4. At the bottom of the Shapes menu, click **New Drawing Canvas**. The frame of a drawing canvas appears on the document.
5. On the **Insert** tab, in the **Illustrations** group, click the **Shapes** button.
6. In the **Flowchart** section, click the **Flowchart: Alternate Process** symbol.
7. At the top center of the drawing canvas, click and drag the crosshair (+) to create a shape that is approximately 2 inches wide by 1 inch high.
8. Repeat steps 5–7 to draw the same shape in the bottom left of the drawing canvas.
9. On the **Insert** tab, in the **Illustrations** group, click the **Shapes** button.
10. In the Lines section, click the **Elbow Arrow Connector** symbol.
11. Click the crosshair (+) on the bottom center of the top shape and drag to the top center of the bottom shape, as shown in Figure 10-15.

Figure 10-15

Flowchart shapes and connector

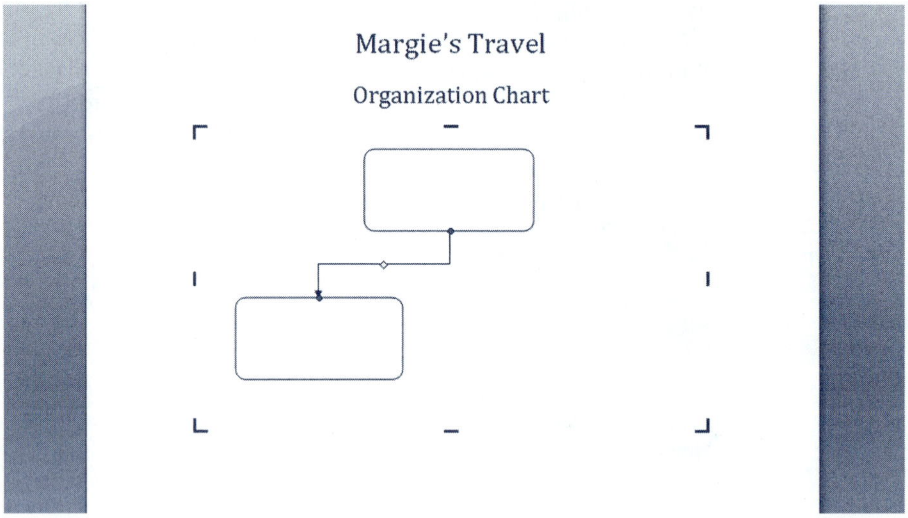

CERTIFICATION READY?
How do you insert shapes?
3.1.3

12. **SAVE** the document as ***travel_flowchart***.

PAUSE. LEAVE the document open to use in the next exercise.

Flowcharts are useful for creating process documents, decision trees, or small organization charts. Because a flowchart is comprised of multiple drawing objects, it is easier to arrange them by first clicking New Drawing Canvas on the Shapes menu to insert a document canvas.

Insert flowchart symbols and size them just as you would any other shape. To connect them, use the connector options in the Lines section of the Shapes menu.

ANOTHER WAY To create organization charts that are already formatted and arranged, choose a SmartArt graphic from the Hierarchy category.

Adding Text to a Shape

You can add text to shapes and then format or edit the text just as you would text in a document. You can also use the Text Box Tools to format the text box just as you would a shape.

ADD TEXT TO A SHAPE

USE the document that is open from the previous exercise.

1. Select the top box.
2. On the **Format** tab, in the **Insert Shapes** group, click the **Edit Text** button. An insertion point appears within the shape.
3. Key **Josh Barnhill**, press **Enter**, and key **President**.
4. Select the text and use the Mini toolbar that appears to **center** the text and change it to **14 pt**.
5. Select the bottom box.
6. On the **Format** tab, in the **Insert Shapes** group, click the **Edit Text** button. An insertion point appears within the shape.
7. Key **Jeanne Bourne**, press **Enter**, and key **Vice President**.
8. Select the text and use the Mini toolbar that appears to **center** the text and change it to **12 pt**.
9. Click outside the drawing canvas. Your document should look similar to Figure 10-16.

Figure 10-16

Shapes with text inserted

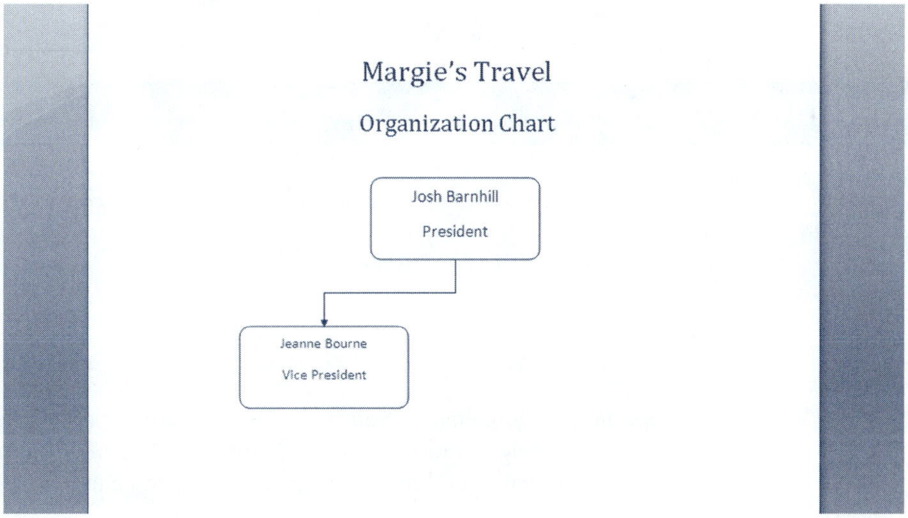

CERTIFICATION READY? How do you add text to SmartArt graphics and shapes? **3.2.5**

10. **SAVE** the document and **CLOSE** the file.

PAUSE. LEAVE Word open to use in the next exercise.

To add text to a flowchart symbol, or any shape, select the symbol or shape and then click the Edit Text button in the Insert Shapes group on the Format tab. An insertion point appears within the shape. After keying text, you can format or edit it just as you would regular text. The Text Box Tools, shown in Figure 10-17, are available at the top of the screen for formatting the text box.

Figure 10-17

Text Box Tools

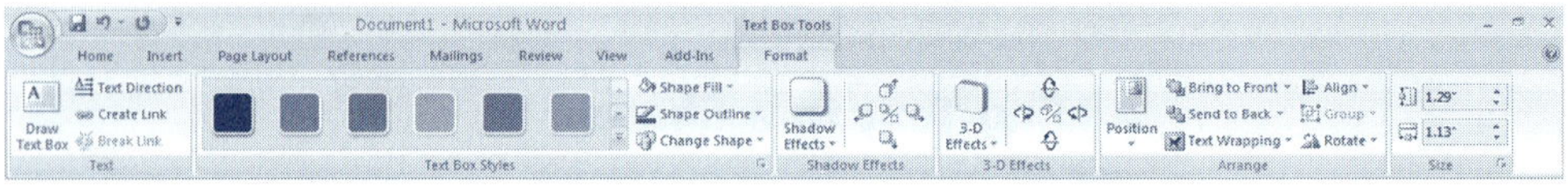

TAKE NOTE* If the shape does not allow for text, such as a line, then the Edit Text button will be unavailable.

■ SOFTWARE ORIENTATION

Picture Tools

The Picture Tools tab, shown in Figure 10-18, is a contextual command tab that appears only when a picture is selected. Many formatting options are available for you to make changes, including borders, effects, cropping, and resizing.

Figure 10-18

Picture Tools

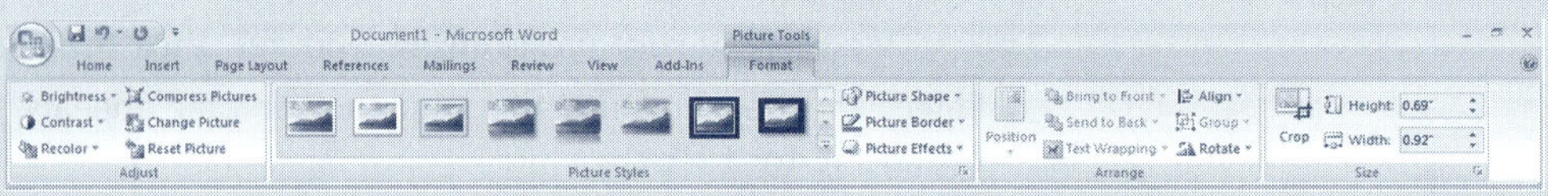

Use this figure as a reference throughout this lesson, as well as the rest of the book.

■ Formatting Pictures

THE BOTTOM LINE To format a picture, first select the picture. Then you can choose from the many Picture Tools options, such as adjusting the contrast, rotating the picture, or compressing the picture to reduce the size.

Cropping, Resizing, Scaling, and Rotating a Picture

Cropping a picture enables you to remove unwanted parts. You can resize a picture by changing the height and width measurements or scale the picture by changing the height and width percentages. You can rotate a picture to change its position.

CROP, RESIZE, SCALE, AND ROTATE A PICTURE

OPEN a new, blank Word document.

1. Key **Visit the Palm Trees of California** centered on the first line of the document.
2. On the **Home** tab, in the **Styles** group, click the **More** button.
3. Click the **Title** option in the Quick Style gallery to apply the style and then press **Enter**.
4. On the **Insert** tab, in the **Illustrations** group, click the **Picture** button.
5. Navigate to the data files for this lesson, select the ***palms*** picture, and click **Insert**. The picture should be selected and the Picture Tools displayed.
6. On the **Format** tab, in the **Size** group, click the **Crop** button. The insertion point becomes a cropping tool and cropping handles appear on the edges of the picture.
7. Position the cropping tool over the **top right cropping handle**. Then click and drag down and left until it is past the street signs in the picture, as shown in Figure 10-19.

CD

The ***palms*** picture file is available on the companion CD-ROM.

Figure 10-19

Cropping a picture

8. Release the mouse button to crop the picture. Click the **Crop** button again to remove the cropping handles.
9. On the **Format** tab, click the **Size Dialog Box Launcher** to display the Size dialog box, similar to Figure 10-20.

Figure 10-20

Size dialog box

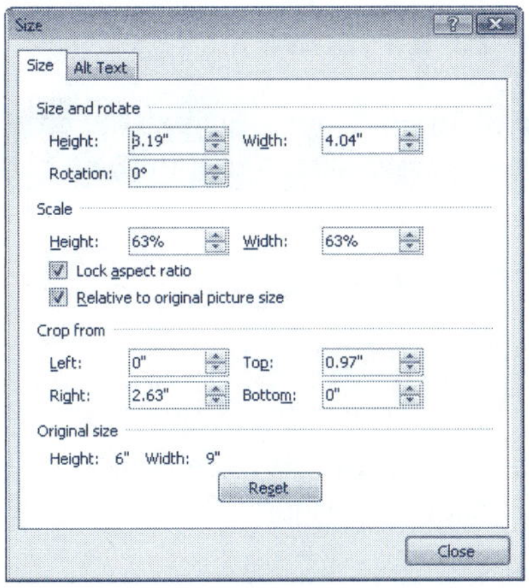

10. In the **Size and Rotate** section, click the **Height downward-pointing arrow** until **3"** appears. Click the **Rotation downward-pointing arrow** until **350°** appears.

ANOTHER WAY You can also rotate a picture by selecting it and dragging the rotation handle—the round arrow that appears at the top of a selected picture or shape—in the direction you want to rotate the picture.

11. In the **Scale** section, both checkboxes should be selected. Click the **Height upward-pointing arrow** until **65%** appears.
12. Click the **Close** button.
13. **SAVE** the document as ***travel_palms***.

PAUSE. LEAVE the document open to use in the next exercise.

CERTIFICATION READY? How do you format by sizing, scaling, and rotating? **3.2.2**

When you ***crop*** a picture, you trim the horizontal or vertical edges to get rid of unwanted areas. To crop a picture, select the picture and click the Crop button. The insertion point becomes a cropping tool and cropping handles appear on the edges of the picture. Drag the cropping handles until only the portion of the picture you want to remain is outlined. Release the mouse button and then click the Crop button again to remove the cropping handles. You can also crop by precise measurements using the Size box.

To resize, scale, rotate, or crop a picture, click the Size Dialog Box Launcher. In the Size dialog box, you can either resize the picture by changing the exact measurements of the height and width or rescale it by changing the height and width percentages. If the Lock Aspect Ratio box is selected, the width will change proportionally when you change the height or vice versa. If the Relative to Original Picture Size box is selected, the size and scale numbers are displayed with respect to the original size of the picture, which is shown at the bottom. To reset a picture to its original size, click the Reset button.

You can also rotate a picture right 90° or left 90°, flip it horizontally, or flip it vertically by clicking the Rotate button in the Arrange group, as shown in Figure 10-21.

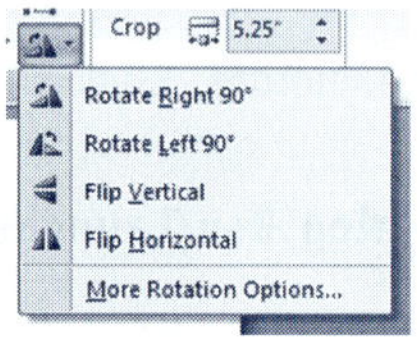

Figure 10-21
Rotate button and menu

Applying a Quick Style to a Picture

Applying a Quick Style to a picture is similar to applying a Quick Style to text. You can choose from the preformatted options available in the gallery.

APPLY A QUICK STYLE TO A PICTURE

USE the document that is open from the previous exercise.

1. To display the Picture Tools, select the picture if it is not already selected,.
2. On the **Format** tab, in the **Picture Styles** group, click the **More** button to display the Quick Style gallery, shown in Figure 10-22.

Figure 10-22

Picture Quick Style gallery

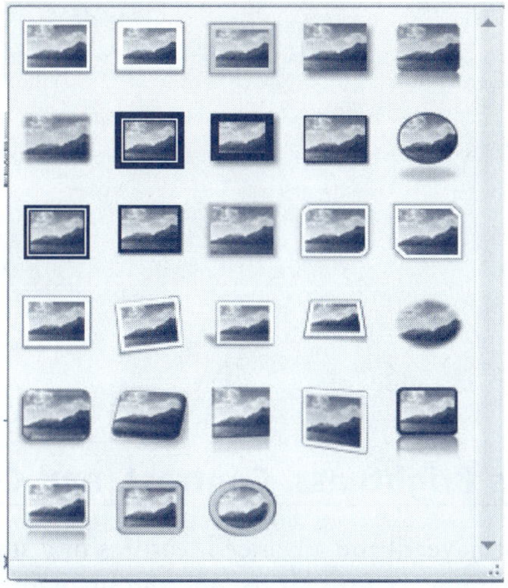

3. Click **Bevel Rectangle**. Your document should look similar to Figure 10-23.

Figure 10-23

Picture with Quick Style applied

CERTIFICATION READY?
How do you apply QuickStyles?
3.2.3

4. **SAVE** the document.

   PAUSE. LEAVE the document open to use in the next exercise.

You can use a Quick Style to add interest to your picture. Some styles are shown in the Picture Styles group. Click the More button to see the other options. In the Picture Styles group, you can also add a border using the Picture Border menu, shown in Figure 10-24, to specify the color, width, and line style for the outline of the picture. Or you can add an effect using the Picture Effects menu, shown in Figure 10-25. To see an effect without actually applying it, just hover the mouse cursor over the option for a live preview.

Figure 10-24

Picture Border menu

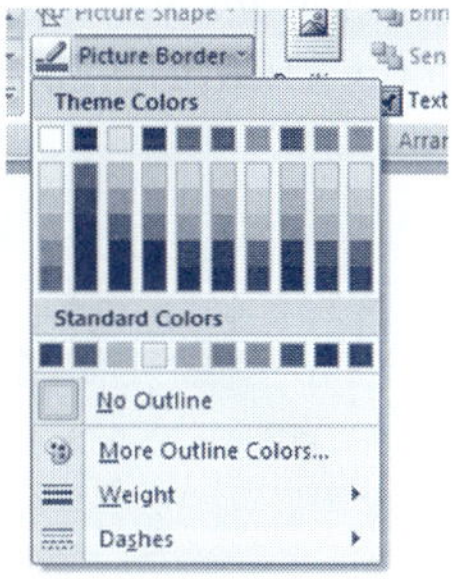

Figure 10-25

Picture Effects menu

Adjusting a Picture's Brightness, Contrast, and Color

Although Word does not have all the advanced features of a stand-alone photo editing program, it does offer many ways for you to make adjustments to a picture—including changing a picture's brightness, contrast, and color.

ADJUST A PICTURE'S BRIGHTNESS, CONTRAST, AND COLOR

USE the document that is open from the previous exercise.

1. To display the Adjust Tools, select the picture if it is not already selected.
2. On the **Format** tab, in the **Adjust** group, click the **Brightness** button to display the menu shown in Figure 10-26.

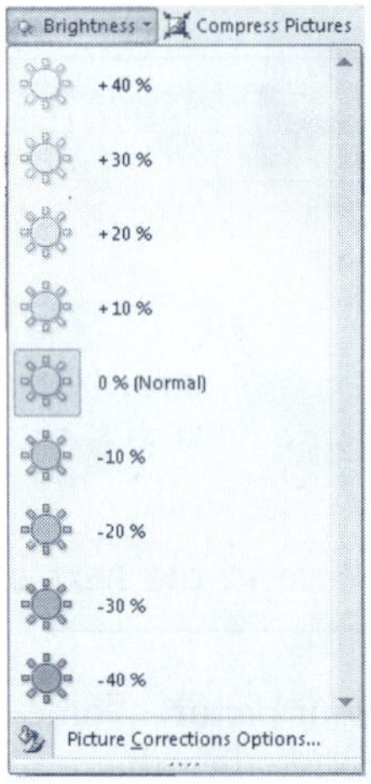

Figure 10-26

Brightness menu

3. Click **+10%** to increase the brightness of the picture.
4. On the **Format** tab, in the **Adjust** group, click the **Contrast** button to display the menu.
5. Click **–20%** to decrease the contrast of the picture.
6. On the **Format** tab, in the **Adjust** group, click the **Recolor** button to display the menu shown in Figure 10-27.

Figure 10-27

Recolor menu

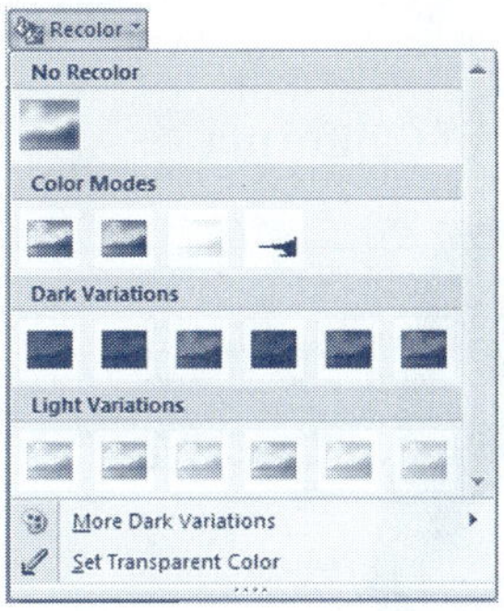

CERTIFICATION READY?
How do you set contrast, brightness, and coloration?
3.2.4

7. In the **Dark Variations** section, click the **Accent color 3 Dark** option.
8. **SAVE** the document.

   PAUSE. LEAVE the document open to use in the next exercise.

You can quickly make adjustments to a picture that has been inserted into a document by using the Brightness, Contrast, and Recolor menus. On the Brightness and Contrast menus, choose the percentage that you want the picture to vary from normal. On the Recolor menu, turn the picture into a grayscale, sepia-toned, washed-out, or black-and-white version or apply a light or dark color variation.

Arranging Text around a Picture

The Text Wrapping command changes the way text wraps around the picture or other drawing object.

ARRANGE TEXT AROUND A PICTURE

USE the document that is open from the previous exercise.

1. Place the insertion point on the line below the picture and key the following text:

   Our charming desert cities, warm sun, and hot mineral springs make California the perfect vacation destination. So come visit the palm trees and experience this magical place.
2. To display the Adjust Tools, select the picture if it is not already selected.
3. On the **Format** tab, in the **Arrange** group, click the **Text Wrapping** button to display the menu shown in Figure 10-28.

Figure 10-28

Text Wrapping options

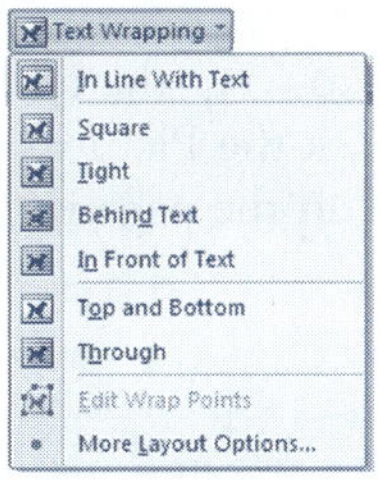

4. Click **Square**. All the text moves to the right, including the title.
5. Select the picture and drag it downward slightly until the title returns to the top and all the text is positioned on the right of the picture, as shown in Figure 10-29.

Figure 10-29

Text wrapped around a picture

6. **SAVE** the document.

   PAUSE. LEAVE the document open to use in the next exercise.

CERTIFICATION READY?
How do you format text wrapping?
3.2.1

To configure the picture as an ***inline object*** that moves along with the text around it, select the In Line with Text option. Or, you can choose a text wrapping style that changes a picture to a ***floating object*** that can be positioned precisely on the page, including behind or in front of text.

Click More Layout Options on the Text Wrapping menu to open the Advanced Layout dialog box, shown in Figure 10-30.

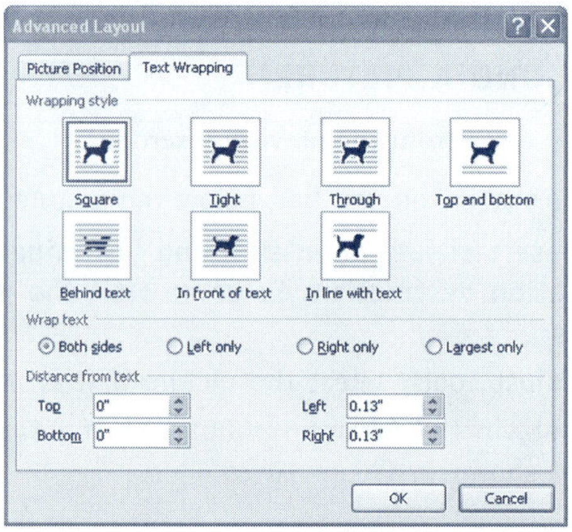

Figure 10-30

Advanced Layout dialog box

In this dialog box, you can choose precisely how to wrap the text and determine the distance between the text and the picture. You can also click the Picture Position tab to choose options for exactly how you want to position the picture on the page vertically or horizontally.

Compressing a Picture

When you compress a picture, it reduces the file size and makes documents easier to manage.

COMPRESS A PICTURE

USE the document that is open from the previous exercise.

1. To display the Adjust Tools, select the picture if it is not already selected.
2. On the **Format** tab, in the **Adjust** group, click the **Compress Pictures** button to display the Compress Pictures dialog box, shown in Figure 10-31.

Figure 10-31

Compress Pictures dialog box

3. Click the **Options** button to display the Compression Settings dialog box, shown in Figure 10-32.

Figure 10-32

Compression Settings dialog box

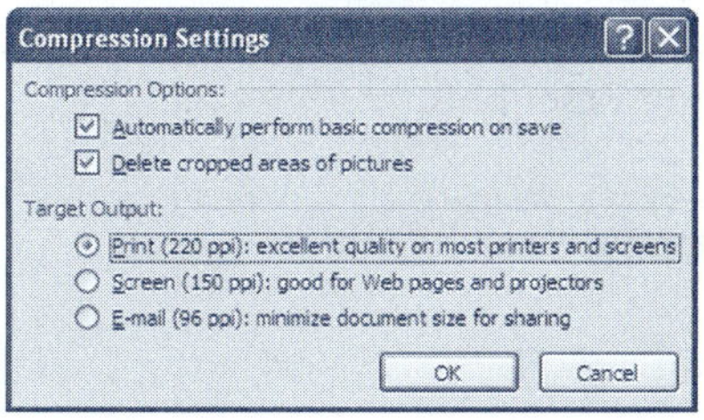

4. In the Target Output section, select **E-mail (96 ppi)**.
5. Click **OK**.
6. In the Compress Pictures dialog box, select the **Apply to Selected Pictures Only** checkbox.
7. Click **OK**.

TROUBLESHOOTING

You will not see the compression take place. To verify that the file is smaller after compressing pictures, you can compare the document's properties before and after performing the command. Keep in mind that if your picture is already smaller than the compression option chosen, no compression will occur.

CERTIFICATION READY?
How do you compress pictures?
3.2.6

8. **SAVE** the document.

   PAUSE. LEAVE the document open to use in the next exercise.

When you ***compress*** a picture, you decrease the size of the file by reducing the resolution. Inserting large picture files can make a document difficult to manage. You can work more efficiently by compressing the pictures to reduce the file size of the document. This helps save room on your hard disk, enables documents to open and save more quickly, and reduces download time for files you plan to share.

In the Compression Settings dialog box, you can choose to reduce the resolution to print, screen, or email quality, depending on what you plan to do with the pictures. You can also choose to delete cropped areas of pictures, which discards the extra information for the hidden parts of the picture that are still stored in the file after the picture is cropped.

Resetting a Picture

Resetting a picture will discard all formatting changes you made to the picture, including changes to contrast, color, brightness, and style.

RESET A PICTURE

USE the document that is open from the previous exercise.

1. To display the Picture Tools, select the picture if it is not already selected.
2. On the **Format** tab, in the **Adjust** group, click **Reset Picture**. Formatting changes you made to the picture are discarded.

3. **SAVE** the document as ***travel_reset*** and **CLOSE** the file.
   STOP and **CLOSE** Word.

Reset a picture when you want to discard all the formatting changes that you made. You can undo changes that you made to a picture's contrast, color, or brightness using the Reset Picture command. Or, you can choose to discard only certain formatting changes. In the Picture Styles group, click the dialog box launcher to open the Format Picture dialog box. To reset just the brightness and contrast, click Picture and then click the Reset Picture button. Or, to remove a style that you applied, click 3-D Format to display the options shown in Figure 10-33. Then click the Reset button.

Figure 10-33

Format Picture dialog box

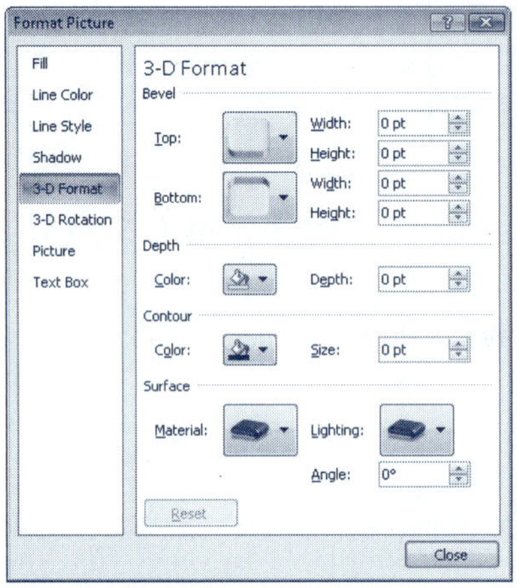

SUMMARY SKILL MATRIX

In This Lesson You Learned	Matrix Skill	Skill Number
To use SmartArt graphics	Insert SmartArt graphics; Add text to SmartArt graphics and shapes	3.1.1, 3.2.5
To insert and resize a clip art picture	Insert pictures from files and clip art; Format by sizing, scaling, and rotating	3.1.2, 3.2.2
To insert a picture from a file	Insert pictures from files and clip art	3.1.2
To insert lines and other shapes	Insert shapes	3.1.3
To create a flowchart	Insert shapes	3.1.3
To add text to a shape	Add text to SmartArt graphics and shapes	3.2.5
To crop, size, scale, and rotate a picture	Format by sizing, scaling, and rotating	3.2.2
To apply a Quick Style to a picture	Apply Quick Styles	3.2.3
To adjust a picture's brightness, contrast, and color	Set contrast, brightness, and coloration	3.2.4
To arrange text around a picture	Format text wrapping	3.2.1
To compress pictures	Compress pictures	3.2.6

Knowledge Assessment

Fill in the Blank

Complete the following sentences by writing the correct word or words in the blanks provided.

1. ______________ graphics can be used to illustrate a process, hierarchy, cycle, or relationship.
2. To illustrate a specific concept in your document, you can insert a ______________ picture—including drawings, movies, sounds, or stock photography.
3. It is easier to arrange multiple drawing objects by first creating a document __________.
4. Picture Tools is a contextual command tab that appears only when a picture is ______________.
5. You can ______________ a picture by changing the height and width measurements.
6. The ______________ command changes the way text wraps around the picture or other drawing object.
7. A ______________ object is a picture or drawing object that can be positioned precisely on the page, including behind or in front of text.
8. When you insert a picture into a document, Word makes it an ______________ by default, which means that it becomes part of the document.
9. ______________ are useful for creating process documents, decision trees, or small organization charts.
10. When you scale a picture, you change the height and width ______________.

Multiple Choice

Select the best response for the following statements.

1. In the Clip Art pane, you can click Organize Clips ... to open the
   - **a.** ClipArt Organizer.
   - **b.** Result task pane.
   - **c.** Microsoft Clip Organizer.
   - **d.** Manage Pictures dialog box.
2. What is it called when you decrease the size of a picture file by reducing the resolution?
   - **a.** compress
   - **b.** rotate
   - **c.** crop
   - **d.** resize
3. Lines, block arrows, stars, and banners are examples of what?
   - **a.** diagrams
   - **b.** shapes
   - **c.** flowcharts
   - **d.** Quick Styles
4. Which tools provide options for formatting shapes?
   - **a.** Drawing
   - **b.** Picture
   - **c.** Text
   - **d.** Effects

5. Which is *not* a type of line option?
   a. connectors
   b. callouts
   c. freeform
   d. scribbles
6. Which command enables you to remove unwanted parts from a picture?
   a. SmartArt
   b. Contrast
   c. Rotate
   d. Crop
7. Which option is *not* available on the Recolor menu?
   a. Grayscale
   b. Position
   c. Sepia
   d. Washout
8. Which type of picture is configured to move along with the text around it?
   a. inline
   b. wrap
   c. square
   d. flipped
9. Which is *not* an option in the Compression Settings dialog box?
   a. print
   b. optimal
   c. screen
   d. e-mail
10. Which command do you use to discard all the formatting changes you made to a picture?
    a. Original
    b. Undo
    c. Reset
    d. Discard

Competency Assessment

Project 10-1: House for Sale

In your position at Tech Terrace Real Estate, you are asked to add a photo to a flyer advertising a house for sale and format it attractively.

CD

The ***tech_house*** document is available on the companion CD-ROM.

GET READY Launch Word if it is not already running.

1. OPEN *tech_house* from the data files for this lesson.
2. Place the insertion point on the first line of the document.
3. On the **Insert** tab, in the **Illustrations** group, click **Picture**.
4. Navigate to the data files for this lesson and select the *housephoto* file.
5. On the **Format** tab, in the **Size** group, click the **Crop** button.
6. Click the **bottom right cropping handle** and drag up until the sidewalk is outside the selection area and release the mouse button to crop out the sidewalk.

CD

The ***housephoto*** picture file is available on the companion CD-ROM.

7. On the **Format** tab, in the **Picture Styles** group, click the **More** button.
8. Click **Reflected Bevel, Black** in the gallery.
9. On the **Format** menu, in the **Adjust** group, click the **Recolor** button.
10. In the **Color Modes** section, click **Grayscale**.
11. **SAVE** the document as ***house_flyer*** and **CLOSE** the file.

PAUSE. LEAVE Word open for the next project.

Project 10-2: Server Model

In your position at Flatland Hosting Company, you are asked to create a process diagram to present to clients. Your development process operates on a three-server model, so you want to find a SmarArt graphic that fits the information you are trying to illustrate.

1. **OPEN** a new, blank Word document.
2. On the first line, key **Flatland Hosting Company Development Process**.
3. On the **Home** tab, in the **Styles** group, click the **More** button.
4. Click the **Heading 1** option in the gallery.
5. On the **Home** tab, in the **Paragraph** group, click **Center** to center the text.
6. Press **Enter**.
7. On the **Insert** tab, in the **Illustrations** group, click the **SmartArt** button.
8. Click **Process** in the list on the left.
9. Click the **Alternating Flow** option.
10. In the Text pane, enter the text shown below:
    - **Dev Server**
        - **internal**
        - **developer access**
    - **Stage Server**
        - **intermediate**
        - **client access**
    - **Live Server**
        - **launched**
        - **public access**
11. **SAVE** the document as ***server_model*** and **CLOSE** the file.

PAUSE. LEAVE Word open for the next project.

Proficiency Assessment

Project 10-3: Adding to the Organization Chart

You need to make some additions and changes to the organization chart your created for Margie's Travel.

1. **OPEN** ***travel_flowchart*** from the location where you saved it earlier in this lesson.
2. Use the knowledge you have gained about shapes in this lesson to add to the organization chart and format it, as shown in Figure 10-34.

Figure 10-34
Formatted organization chart

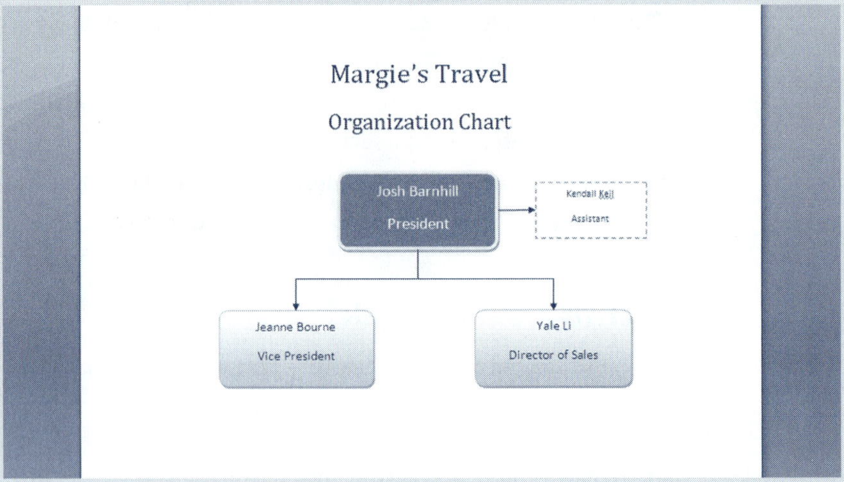

3. **SAVE** the document as ***travel_orgchart*** and **CLOSE** the file.

   PAUSE. LEAVE Word open for the next project.

Project 10-4: Creating a Room Layout

Your teacher needs your help creating a drawing of your classroom's layout, including various shapes to indicate the location of desks, computers, printers, and any other significant items.

1. **OPEN** a new, blank Word document.
2. On the **Insert** menu, in the **Illustrations** group, click the **Shapes** button and choose **New Drawing Canvas** to insert a document canvas.
3. Use the available shapes to draw a layout map of the classroom.
4. Label each shape and format the shapes attractively.
5. **SAVE** the document as ***room_layout*** and **CLOSE** the file.

   PAUSE. LEAVE Word open for the next project.

Mastery Assessment

Project 10-5: Party Invitation

You are having a party and want to create your own invitation using Word and clip art.

1. **OPEN** a new, blank Word document.
2. Use the knowledge you have gained in this lesson to create a party invitation using at least two pieces of clip art that reflect the type of party you are having.
3. Include the time, date, and location of the party. Use the Text Wrapping command to position the clip art around your text. Be creative!
4. **SAVE** the document as ***party_invitation*** and **CLOSE** the file.

   PAUSE. LEAVE Word open for the next project.

Project 10-6: Formatting a Flyer

CD

The ***rose_bushes*** document is available on the companion CD-ROM.

A coworker at Keyser Garden & Nursery tried to create a sales flyer about roses, but was not familiar with formatting tools and ran into trouble. She asks if you can open the file and try to correct the problems and help format it.

1. **OPEN** ***rose_bushes*** from the data files for this lesson.

2. Use the skills learned in this lesson to correct the problems and format the document to look like Figure 10-35.

Figure 10-35
Formatted flyer

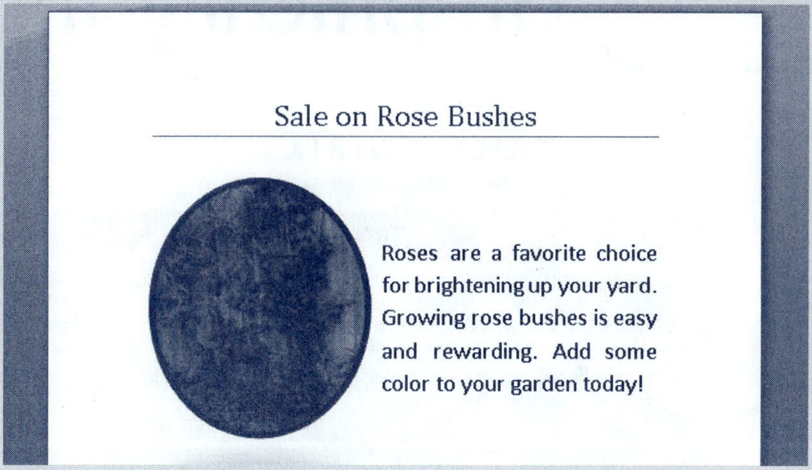

3. **SAVE** the document as ***rose_sale*** and **CLOSE** the file.
CLOSE Word.

INTERNET READY

When creating a document, you are not limited to inserting only the clip art and other media that comes installed with Word. A single click can open up a whole new world of options. At the bottom of the Clip Art pane, notice the Clip Art on Office Online link. Click the link to connect to the Clip Art and Media home page, as shown in Figure 10-36. You can browse dozens of categories, download the clip of the day, view featured collections, and get clip tips. Next time you need to enhance your document with clip art or other media, expand your options by going online.

Figure 10-36
Clip Art and Media page

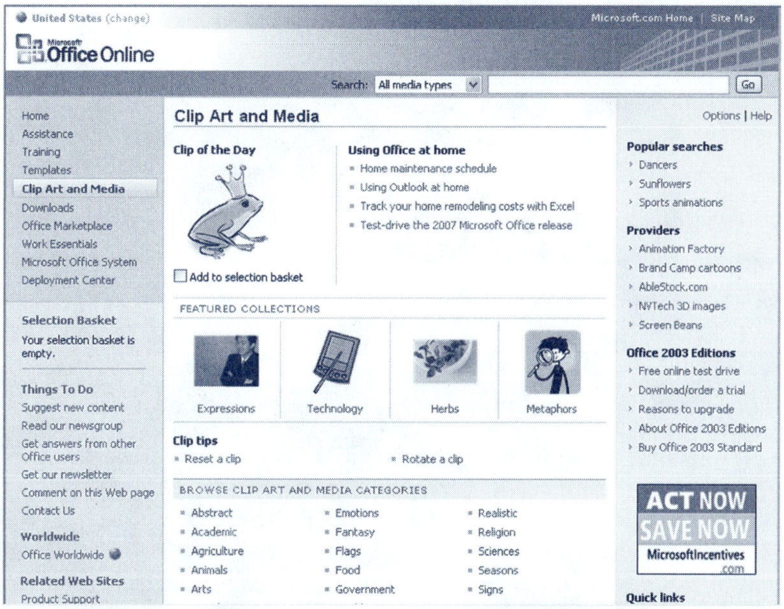

11 Making Text Graphically Interesting

LESSON SKILL MATRIX

Skills	Matrix Skill	Skill Number
Creating Drop Caps	Insert and modify drop caps	3.3.3
Formatting Text as a Pull Quote	Insert pull quotes	3.3.2
Inserting WordArt	Insert and modify WordArt	3.3.1
Editing WordArt Text	Insert and modify WordArt	3.3.1
Changing the Shape of WordArt	Insert and modify WordArt	3.3.1
Inserting a Text Box	Insert text boxes	3.4.1
Formatting a Text Box	Format text boxes	3.4.2
Linking Multiple Text Boxes Together	Link text boxes	3.4.3

The Coho Winery is a family-owned business that leads the industry in innovative winemaking techniques and natural farming practices. After three decades of winemaking success, the Coho Winery has many loyal customers who enjoy visiting the winery and attending special events. As the director of customer relations, you are responsible for furthering this relationship by fostering communication with current customers as well as potential customers. Part of your job includes the creation of a monthly newsletter that is mailed to members of Coho's wine club. This newsletter is used to communicate information concerning special events and special offers not available to the general public. Word is a perfect tool for creating this newsletter. In this lesson, you will learn to insert drop caps, format pull quotes, create WordArt, and work with text boxes.

KEY TERMS

drop cap
pull quote
WordArt
text box

Creating a Drop Cap

THE BOTTOM LINE

Drop caps are used to give interest to newsletters or magazine articles. Because they are often used at the beginning of an article or story, they also serve as a visual clue, telling the reader where to start reading. Rather than having to set tabs and adjust indents to place a drop cap, Word's Drop Cap command performs this formatting automatically, making it easy to insert drop caps wherever they are needed.

CREATE A DROP CAP

CD

The *coho* document is available on the companion CD-ROM.

GET READY. Before you begin these steps, be sure to launch Microsoft Word and **OPEN** the ***coho*** document from the data files for this lesson.

1. In the first paragraph of the article written by John Kane, select the *S* in *Since wine is my business.*
2. On the **Insert** tab, in the **Text** group, click the **Drop Cap** button. A menu appears.
3. Select **Dropped** from the menu, as shown in Figure 11-1. A drop cap is inserted.

Figure 11-1

Drop Cap menu

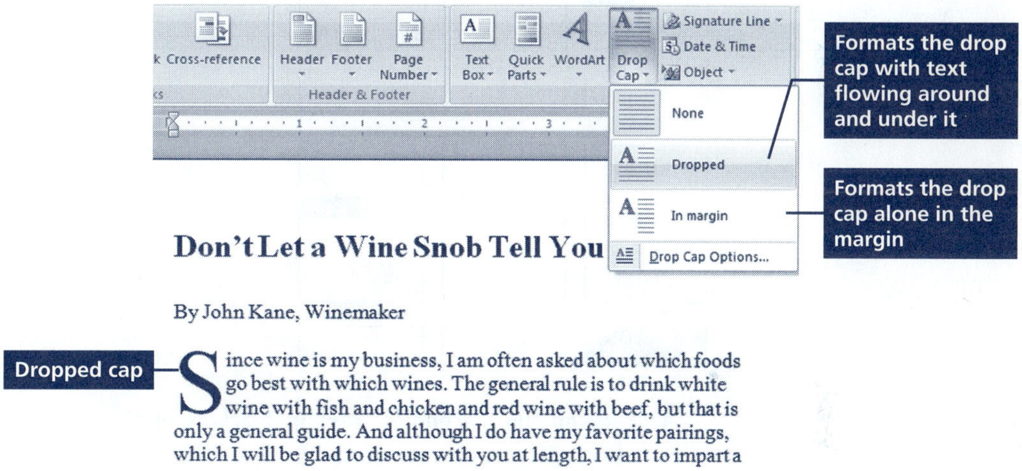

CERTIFICATION READY?
How do you insert and modify drop caps?
3.3.3

4. **SAVE** your document as ***coho_newsletter***.

PAUSE. LEAVE the document open to use in the next exercise.

A ***drop cap*** is a large initial letter that drops down two or more lines at the beginning of a paragraph. Drop caps are often used to add interest to a document, such as a newsletter.

As you saw in Figure 11-1, Word offers two types of drop caps: Dropped and In Margin. When you choose Dropped, as you did in the previous exercise, paragraph text wraps around the dropped capital letter and flows below it. The In Margin option places the dropped initial cap alone in the margin.

If you want to customize a drop cap, click the Drop Cap Options command at the bottom of the Drop Cap menu. The Drop Cap dialog box appears, from which you can adjust the font of the drop cap, the number of lines to drop (the default number is three), and the distance of the drop cap from the rest of the text.

■ Formatting Text as a "Pull Quote"

THE BOTTOM LINE

Pull quotes are often used along with drop caps in newsletters, advertisements, and magazines. Although a pull quote is made of text, pulling it out of the text and emphasizing it gives it a graphical quality that adds to the design of the page. Word's Text Box command lets you insert professionally formatted pull quotes quickly.

CREATE A "PULL QUOTE" NEW FEATURE

USE the document that is open from the previous exercise.

1. On the **Insert** tab, in the **Text** group, click the **Text Box** button. A menu of built-in quotes and sidebars appears.
2. Scroll down and select **Contrast Quote**, as shown in Figure 11-2. The pull quote box is inserted into the document in the same position as shown on the thumbnail in the menu.

Figure 11-2

Text Box button and Built-in Quotes and Sidebars menu

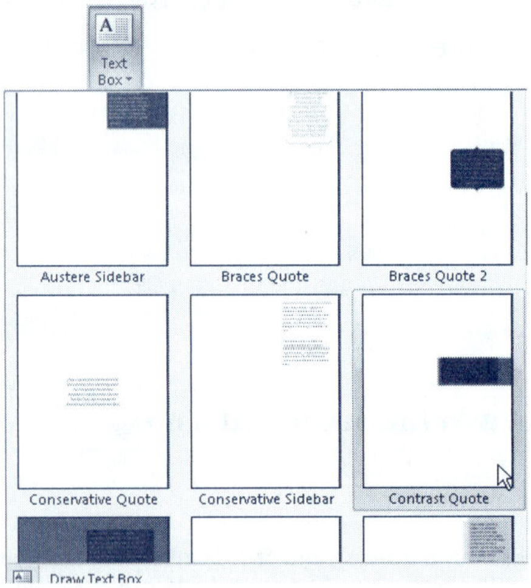

3. Click on the placeholder text in brackets of the pull quote box. Key **Life is too short. If you want a glass of wine with your frozen burrito, you should have it.**
4. Click outside the pull quote to check your work.
5. Click inside the pull quote to select it. Blue circle-shaped selection handles appear around the quote, as shown in Figure 11-3.

Figure 11-3

Pull quote

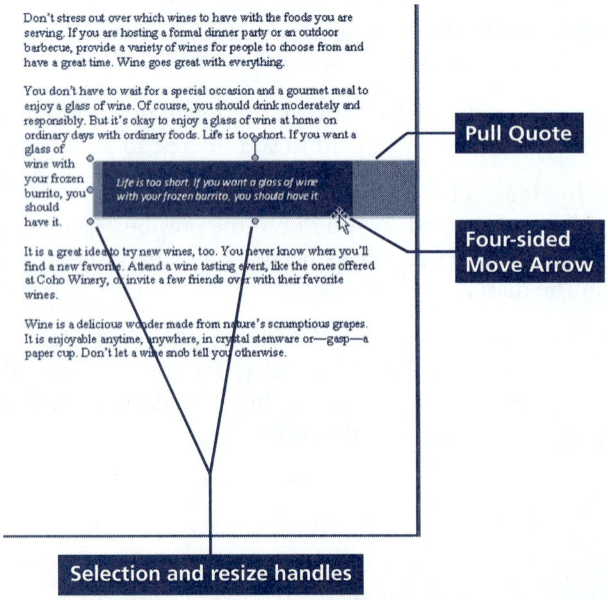

CERTIFICATION READY?
How do you insert text as a "pull quote"?
3.3.2

6. Position the insertion point on the bottom border until the pointer becomes a four-sided move arrow.
7. Click and drag the quote down the page until it is about ⅔ of the way down to the bottom of the page, as shown in Figure 11-3.
8. **SAVE** the document.

PAUSE. LEAVE the document open to use in the next exercise.

You just created a pull quote using Word's Text Box command. A ***pull quote*** is a sentence or other text that is copied from a document, then enlarged and displayed separately on the page for emphasis.

As you saw, the menu displays built-in, preformatted quote formats that you can insert into a document. Click the one you want, select the placeholder text, and key the text for your quote. You can place the pull quote anywhere on the page by clicking to select the box and then dragging to move it to a desired location.

TAKE NOTE* After you insert a pull quote, you can select the text and use the Mini toolbar to change its font, size, color, alignment, or effects.

Software Orientation

WordArt Tools in the Ribbon

Before you begin working with WordArt, it is a good idea to become familiar with the new tools that will be displayed in the Ribbon. When you insert WordArt, WordArt Tools appear in the Ribbon as shown in Figure 11-4.

Figure 11-4
WordArt Tools in the Ribbon

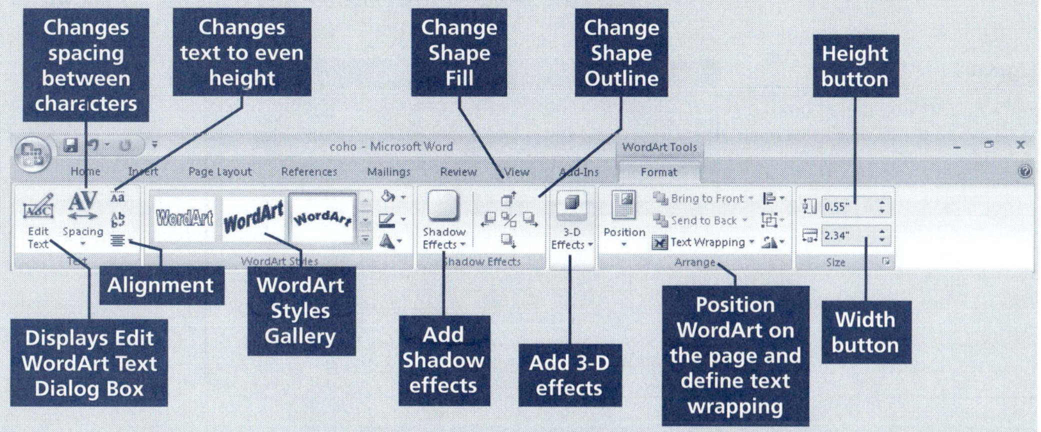

The WordArt Tools provide commands for editing text boxes. Use this figure as a reference throughout this lesson as well as the rest of this book.

Creating Artistic Text with WordArt

THE BOTTOM LINE

WordArt enables you to format text into a variety of shapes and alignments. You can insert, edit, and change the shape of text created in WordArt. You can add shadows and 3-D effects, as well as customize the outline and fill of text created in WordArt.

Inserting WordArt

Word provides many WordArt styles, including rainbow-colored text or rainbow-shaped text. Be sure to choose WordArt that is appropriate for your document. WordArt with rainbow-colored text might be appropriate for a spring company picnic flyer, but not for the annual report.

INSERT WORDART

USE the document that is open from the previous exercise.

1. In the first column of the newsletter about halfway down, select the words *Wine Facts.*
2. On the **Insert** menu, in the **Text** group, click the **WordArt** button. A gallery of WordArt styles appears.
3. Select **WordArt style 3**, as shown in Figure 11-5.

Figure 11-5
WordArt gallery of styles

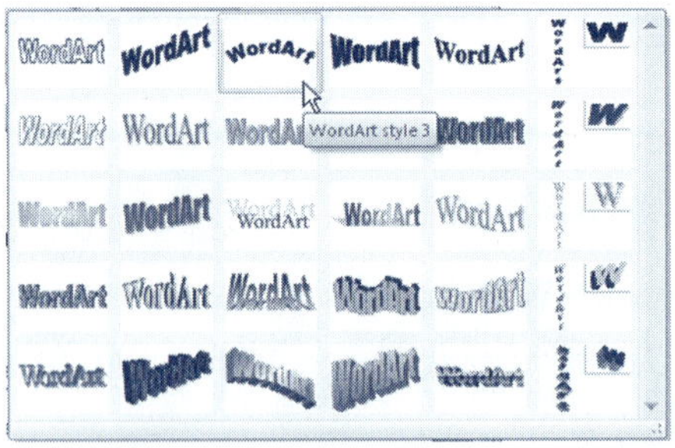

4. The **Edit WordArt Text** dialog box appears, as shown in Figure 11-6.

Figure 11-6
Edit WordArt Text dialog box

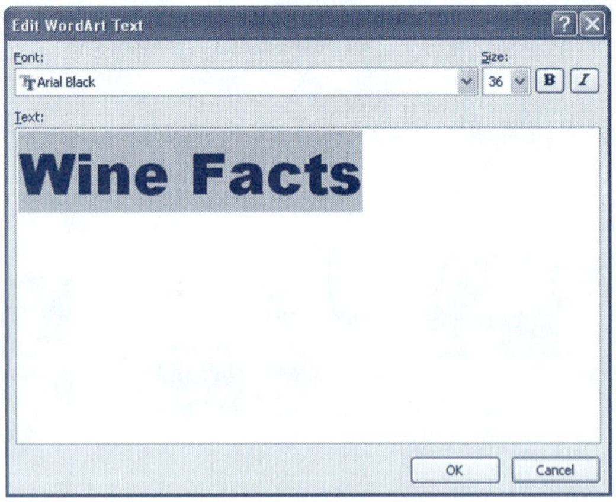

5. Click **OK**. The WordArt is inserted into the document.
6. **SAVE** the document.

PAUSE. LEAVE the document open to use in the next exercise.

WordArt is a feature that creates decorative effects with text. The WordArt gallery provides you with many options for decorative text.

CERTIFICATION READY?
How do you insert WordArt?
3.3.1

You just practiced creating WordArt by selecting existing text and choosing the WordArt command. You can also click the WordArt command and key the text for your WordArt in the Edit WordArt Text dialog box.

The Edit WordArt Text dialog box includes commands for changing the font and size, as well as the bold and italic style of WordArt.

Editing WordArt

After you insert WordArt, you can edit it using the WordArt tools that are displayed in the Ribbon. Editing WordArt allows you to customize it for your document.

EDIT WORDART

USE the document that is open from the previous exercise.

1. Click the *Wine Facts* WordArt to select it, if necessary. Notice that the WordArt tools are displayed in the Ribbon.
2. On the **Format** tab, in the **Text** group, click the **Edit Text** button. The Edit WordArt Text dialog box appears.
3. With *Wine Facts* selected in the dialog box, key **Did You Know?**
4. Click the **Size** menu and select **18**.
5. Click the **Bold** button.
6. Click **OK**.
7. On the **Format** tab, in the **Text** group, click the **Spacing** button. A menu of spacing options appears. Select **Tight**.
8. Click the **Even Height** button to change all the characters to the same height.
9. Click the **Even Height** button again to change it back.
10. Click the **WordArt Vertical Text** button to change the WordArt text to a vertical design.
11. Click the **WordArt Vertical Text** button again to change it back.
12. **SAVE** the document.

PAUSE. LEAVE the document open to use in the next exercise.

After you insert WordArt, the Ribbon displays the WordArt tools. The WordArt tools enable you to edit the text, change the WordArt style, add a shadow effect, arrange the WordArt, and adjust its size.

As you practiced in this exercise, you can edit the text of WordArt you have already created. Select the WordArt graphic and click the Edit Text button in the Text group to display the Edit WordArt Text dialog box. From here, you can key the new text. You can also change the font, size, and bold or italic styles of the text.

CERTIFICATION READY?
How do you modify WordArt?
3.3.1

You learned to use the commands in the Text group to adjust the spacing between characters in the text. You also experimented with two commands that toggle off and on. The Even Height command changes the height of all the characters—lowercase and uppercase—to the same size. The WordArt Vertical Text command changes the alignment of WordArt from horizontal to vertical.

Changing the Shape of WordArt

Once you have created a piece of WordArt, you may decide that the chosen design does not work well in your document. You learned in the previous exercise that you can easily edit WordArt text. You can just as easily edit design elements of WordArt. The WordArt Styles group of tools enables you to change the shape, shape color, and shape outline of WordArt.

CHANGE THE SHAPE OF WORDART

USE the document that is open from the previous exercise.

1. Select the *Did You Know?* WordArt, if it isn't selected already.
2. On the **Format** tab, in the **WordArt Styles** group, click the **Change WordArt Shape** button. A menu of shapes appears. Notice that as you point to each shape, Word displays a live preview of what your text would look like if you chose that shape.
3. Click the **Deflate** shape, as shown in Figure 11-7.

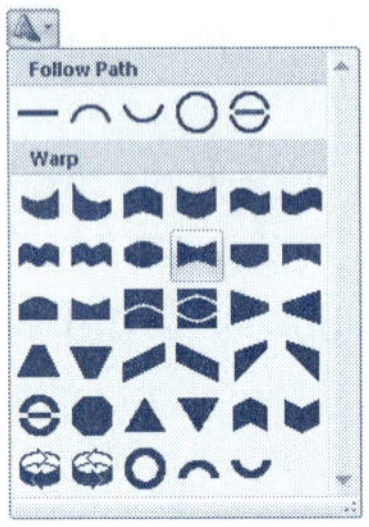

Figure 11-7
Change WordArt Shape button and menu

4. Click the **Shape Fill** button. A menu of colors and fills appears.
5. Click the **Olive Green, Accent 3, Darker 25%** color, as shown in Figure 11-8.

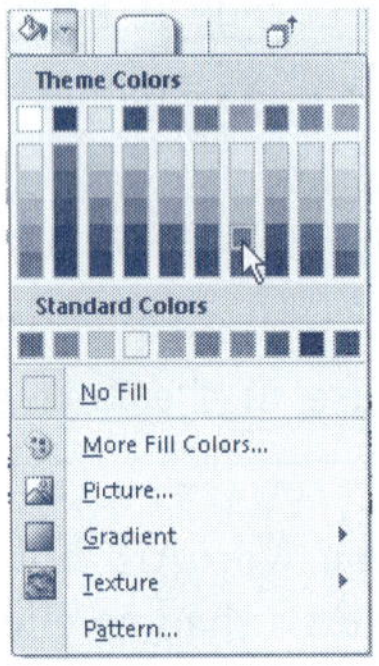

Figure 11-8
Shape Fill menu

6. Click the **Shape Outline** button. A menu of colors and lines appears.
7. Select **No Outline** from the menu, as shown in Figure 11-9.

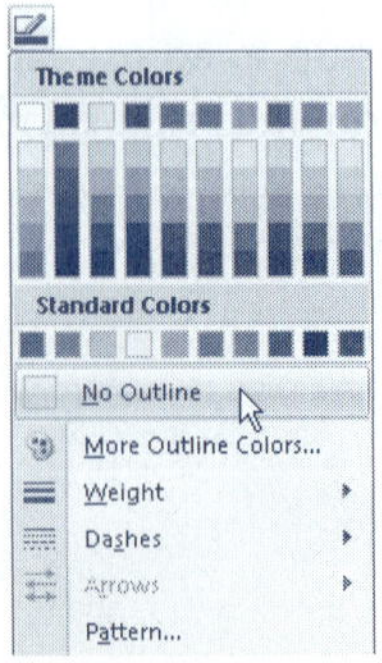

Figure 11-9
Shape Outline menu

CERTIFICATION READY?
How do you modify WordArt?
3.3.1

8. **SAVE** the document.

PAUSE. LEAVE the document open to use in the next exercise.

You can always change WordArt—even its shape—as you just did in the previous exercise.

The Change WordArt Shape button displays a menu of shapes you can use to change your WordArt graphic. It displays Follow Path shapes in which the text follows a path such as a circle. The Warp shapes twist and turn, warping the text.

The Shape Fill button displays a gallery of Theme colors and Standard colors. In addition, the menu lists options for No Fill and More Fill Colors, so you can select a custom color. The Picture command enables you to fill the shape with a picture of your choice. The Gradient, Texture, and Pattern commands provide galleries of endless choices for filling WordArt shapes.

You can also resize and reposition WordArt. Just click to select the WordArt, then drag the resize handles to increase or decrease its size. To change its position on the page, use the Position command in the Arrange group. To delete the WordArt, click to select it and then press the Delete key.

SOFTWARE ORIENTATION

Text Box Tools in the Ribbon

Before you begin working with text boxes, it is a good idea to become familiar with the new tools available in the Ribbon. When you insert a text box, the Text Box tools appear in the Ribbon, as shown in Figure 11-10.

Figure 11-10
Text Box Tools in the Ribbon

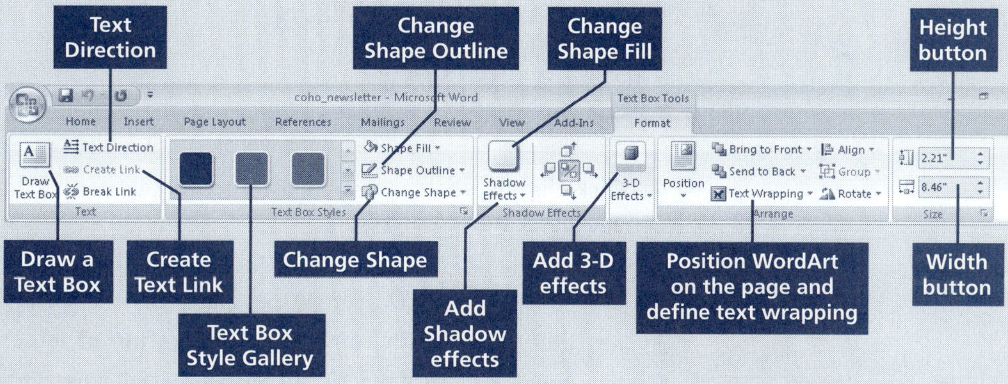

The Text Box tools provide commands for editing text boxes. Use this figure as a reference throughout this lesson as well as the rest of this book.

Creating Text Boxes

THE BOTTOM LINE

Text boxes can be used for a variety of purposes. Most often, they are used to insert text within other document text or to lay out text. After you insert a text box, you can format it as well as link it to other text boxes.

Inserting a Text Box

As you have already learned in this lesson, Word provides a gallery of built-in text boxes with pull quotes and sidebars that you can insert in a document. When you need a different kind of text box, you can draw and insert your own empty, unformatted text box.

INSERT A TEXT BOX

USE the document that is open from the previous exercise.

1. Click before the *H* in *Harvest Celebration* . . . to position the insertion point at the beginning of the document.
2. On the **Insert** tab, in the **Text** group, click the **Text Box** button. A menu of built-in quotes and sidebars appears.
3. Click **Contrast Sidebar**, as shown in Figure 11-11. The text box is inserted at the top of the document.

Figure 11-11

Text Box button and menu

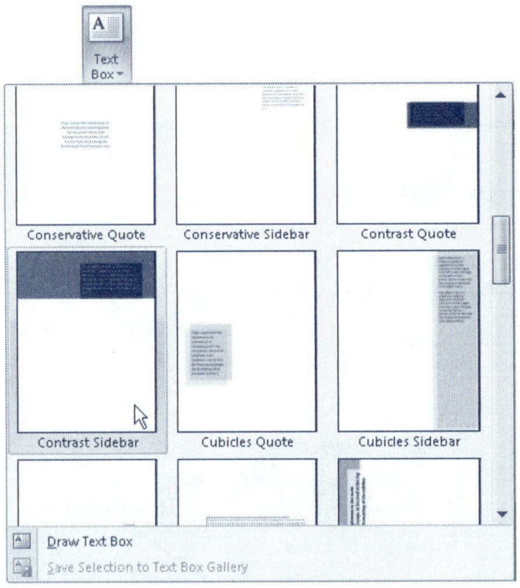

4. Click the placeholder text in brackets to select it, if necessary. Key **Coho Winery** and press the **Enter** key.
5. Press the **Enter** key again to insert a blank line.
6. Key **September 20XX Newsletter** and press the **Enter** key.
7. Key **Daily tours with complimentary tasting of wines**. Then press the **Enter** key.
8. Key **Monday–Saturday: 10 am to 5 pm** and press **Enter**.
9. Key **Sunday: Noon to 5 p.m.**
10. Select the text box.

CERTIFICATION READY?
How do you insert a text box?
3.4.1

11. On the **Format** tab, in the **Text** group, click the **Draw Text Box** button. The mouse pointer becomes a crosshair (+). Click just below the *Did You Know?* paragraph and drag down and to the right to draw a square that is approximately 2½ inches wide and 2½ inches high, as shown in Figure 11-12.

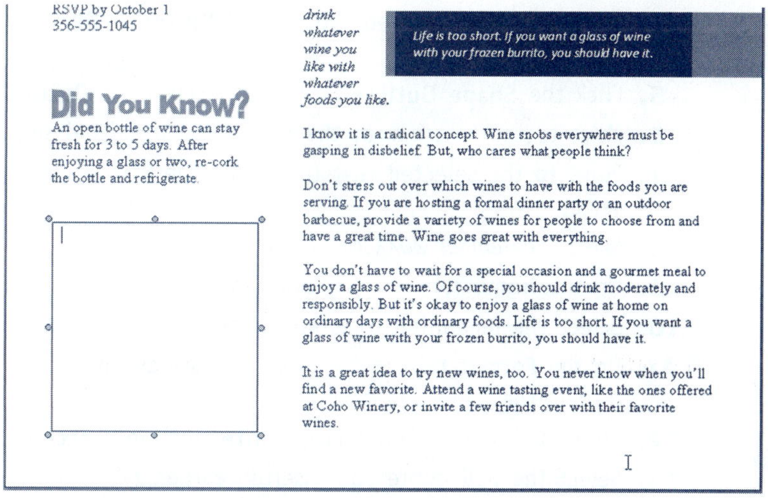

Figure 11-12

Text box inserted using the Draw Text Box command

12. **SAVE** the document.

PAUSE. LEAVE the document open to use in the next exercise.

You just inserted a text box using one of Word's preformatted built-in designs. A ***text box*** is an invisible, formatted box in which you can insert and position text and/or graphic objects.

You added text by selecting the placeholder text and keying the new text. You did not need to move this text box, but you could click and drag it to a new location just as you moved the pull quote earlier in this lesson.

You also learned to draw and insert an empty, unformatted text box using the Draw Text Box command. This is easy to do and gives you the flexibility of drawing a box with the exact size and in the exact location that you want. You can choose to format it from scratch if desired.

Formatting a Text Box

After you insert a text box, the Text Box tools are displayed in the Ribbon. You can use these tools to format a text box for your specific purpose.

FORMAT A TEXT BOX

USE the document that is open from the previous exercise.

1. Click on the new, empty text box to select it, if necessary.
2. On the **Format** tab, click the **Position** button and select **Position in Bottom Left with Square Text Wrapping**, as shown in Figure 11-13.

Figure 11-13

Position button and menu

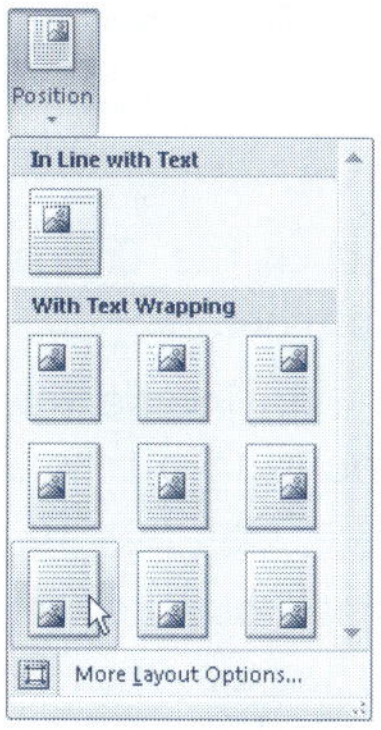

3. On the **Format** tab, in the **Text Box Styles** group, click the **More** button to display the gallery of styles.

4. Click the black **Colored Fill, White Outline - Dark** style in the Text Box Styles gallery.
5. Click the **Shape Outline** button and select **No Outline**.
6. Move to the text box at the top of the page and select *Coho Winery*.
7. Point to the selected text to display the Mini toolbar. Click the Size menu and select **36**.
8. Select *September 20XX Newsletter.*
9. On the **Home** tab, in the **Paragraph** group, click the **Align Text Right** button.
10. Select the remaining lines and click the **Center** button.
11. On the **Format** tab, in the **Text Box Styles** group, click the **More** button to display the gallery of text box styles.
12. Click the green **Colored Fill, White Outline - Accent 3** style in the first row.
13. Select the pull quote you inserted earlier. (Do not worry if it has moved to a new page. You will make adjustments in the next exercise.)
14. On the **Format** tab, in the **Text Box Styles** group, click the green **Colored Fill, White Outline - Accent 3** style in the styles gallery.
15. **SAVE** the document.

PAUSE. LEAVE the document open to use in the next exercise.

CERTIFICATION READY?
How do you format a text box?
3.4.2

As you just practiced, you can format a text box using the Text Box tools displayed in the Ribbon. Some of the tools may look familiar because they are also available for WordArt.

In this lesson, you defined a position and text wrapping style for the new text box with the Position command and chose a text box style from the gallery. You further customized the look of the text box using the Shape Outline menu.

Because a text box does not expand when text is added, you need to resize or reposition it as necessary. Click and drag the move pointer to reposition it in the document or use the resize handles to increase or decrease the size.

You can select and format text inside a text box just as you would any other text. The Mini toolbar is handy for making these changes.

If you need to delete a text box, select it and press the Backspace or Delete key.

Linking Multiple Text Boxes Together

When you want text to flow from one text box to another, you can create a link using Word's Create Link command.

LINK TEXT BOXES

USE the document that is open from the previous exercise.

1. Select the text box at the top of the page.
2. On the **Format** tab, in the **Text** group, click the **Create Link** button. The mouse pointer changes to a filled pitcher.
3. Position the mouse on the empty text box in the lower left corner of the newsletter. The pointer changes to a pouring pitcher. Click the empty text box to link the two. Text flows from the top text box to the lower one.
4. Select the top text box and click the small blue resize circle at the bottom center of the text box. Drag the dotted resize line up until it rests below *September 20XX Newsletter,* as shown in Figure 11-14, and click to release it.

CERTIFICATION READY?
How do you link multiple text boxes?
3.4.3

Figure 11-14

Resizing a text box

5. Position the insertion point before the *D* in *Daily*.
6. Press **Enter** to insert a blank line.
7. **SAVE** and **CLOSE** the document.

   CLOSE Word.

As you just learned, the process for linking text boxes is quite simple. Select the original text box and choose the Create Link button in the Text group of the Format tab. When the mouse pointer changes to a pouring pitcher, click the empty destination text box to create the link. Now text can flow from the first text box to the second text box.

SUMMARY SKILL MATRIX

In this lesson you learned	Matrix Skill	Skill Number
To create drop caps	Insert and modify drop caps	3.3.3
To format text as a pull quote	Insert pull quotes	3.3.2
To insert WordArt	Insert and modify WordArt	3.3.1
To edit WordArt text	Insert and modify WordArt	3.3.1
To change the shape of WordArt	Insert and modify WordArt	3.3.1
To insert a text box	Insert text boxes	3.4.1
To format a text box	Format text boxes	3.4.2
To link multiple text boxes together	Link text boxes	3.4.3

■ Knowledge Assessment

Matching

Match the term in Column 1 to its description in Column 2.

Column 1	Column 2
1. drop cap	**a.** a feature that creates decorative effects with text
2. pull quote	**b.** a command that changes the height of all the characters—lowercase and uppercase—to the same size

3. WordArt	**c.** a command that displays a menu of shapes you can use to change a WordArt graphic
4. text box	**d.** a command used to draw a text box
5. Even Height	**e.** a command for positioning a text box and defining its text wrap style
6. Position	**f.** a command used to link text boxes
7. Draw Text Box	**g.** a large initial letter that drops down two or more lines at the beginning of a paragraph
8. pouring pitcher	**h.** indicates that text is ready to be linked to another text box
9. Change WordArt Shape	**i.** an invisible, formatted box that enables you to insert and position text and/or graphic objects
10. Create Link	**j.** a sentence or two that is copied from the text and enlarged and displayed separately on the page for emphasis

True / False

Circle T if the statement is true or F if the statement is false.

T | F **1.** Text wraps around and flows underneath an in-margin drop cap.

T | F **2.** You can insert a pull quote with the Text Box command.

T | F **3.** Once you create WordArt, you cannot go back and change it.

T | F **4.** You can create WordArt by selecting existing text and clicking the WordArt command.

T | F **5.** An in-margin drop cap is placed alone in the margin.

T | F **6.** You can fill WordArt with a picture of your choice.

T | F **7.** When linking text boxes, you select the destination text box first.

T | F **8.** The Create Link command looks like a chain link.

T | F **9.** A text box does not expand when you add text to it.

T | F **10.** All the WordArt and Text Box tools displayed in the Ribbon are exactly the same.

Competency Assessment

Project 11-1: CD Case Insert

Your friend's birthday is coming up and you have decided to burn a CD of his favorite songs. Create an insert for the front of the CD case.

GET READY. Launch Word if it is not already running.

1. Create a new, blank document.
2. Create a custom paper size of 5″×5″ with Narrow margins.
3. On the Insert tab, in the Text group, click the **Text Box** button and select **Draw Text Box** from the menu.
4. Draw a square box 4″×4″ on the page at the margins, leaving approximately half an inch margin space on all sides.
5. On the **Format** tab, in the **Arrange** group, click the **Position** button and select **Position in Middle Center with Square Text Wrapping**.

6. Click the **Shape Fill** button and select **Picture** from the menu. Double-click the **Sample Pictures** folder, select **Blue Hills**, and click **Insert**.
7. Click outside the text box.
8. On the **Insert** tab, in the **Text** group, click the **WordArt** button and select **WordArt style 22** in the fourth row.
9. Key **Ian's Favorite Tunes** and click **OK**.
10. On the **Format** tab, in the **Arrange** group, click the **Position** button and select **Position in Middle Center with Square Text Wrapping**.
11. **SAVE** the document as *cd_insert* and then **CLOSE** the file.

PAUSE. LEAVE Word open for the next project.

Project 11-2: Coho Winery Note Cards

Create note cards for the Coho Winery.

CD

The ***notecard*** document is available on the companion CD-ROM.

1. **OPEN** *notecard* from the data files for this lesson.
2. Select the text box in the bottom half of the document.
3. On the **Format** tab, in the **Text Box Styles** group, click the **Shape Fill** button and select **Olive Green, Accent 3, Lighter 80%**.
4. On the **Format** tab, in the **Text Box Styles** group, click the **Shape Outline** button and select **Olive Green, Accent 3, Darker 25%**.
5. Click outside the text box to deselect it.
6. On the **Insert** tab, in the **Text** group, click the **Text Box** button and select **Contrast Quote**.
7. Select the placeholder text, key **Coho Winery**, and press the Enter key.
8. Key **Bringing you fine wines** and press the Enter key.
9. Key **Since 1969**.
10. Select **Coho Winery** and change the font size to **14**.
11. On the **Format** tab, in the **Text Box Styles** group, click the **More** button to display the gallery of text box styles.
12. Click the **Colored Fill, White Outline - Accent 3** style in the first row.
13. Click the **Shape Outline** button and select **No Outline**.
14. Select the pull quote and resize it using the up and down arrows in the Size group. Click the down arrow on the **Height** button until it reads **.9"** and click the up arrow on the **Width** button until it reads **3.5"**.
15. Move the pull quote into position on the note card, as shown in Figure 11-15.

Figure 11-15

Coho note card

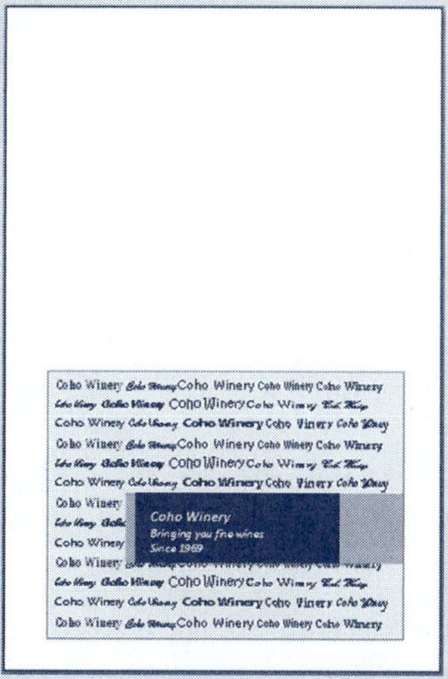

16. **SAVE** the document as ***coho_notecard*** and then **CLOSE** the file.

PAUSE. LEAVE Word open for the next project.

Proficiency Assessment

Project 11-3: Happy Birthday Card

Create a birthday card for your friend.

1. Create a new, blank document.
2. Change the orientation to Landscape with Narrow margins.
3. Insert WordArt with **WordArt Style 16** and the text **Happy Birthday!**
4. Increase the size of the text to **60** points.
5. Position the WordArt graphic **Middle Right with Square Text Wrapping**.
6. Click the **Shadow Effects** button and select **Shadow Style 3** from the Drop Shadow section of the menu.
7. **SAVE** the document as ***birthday_card*** and **CLOSE** the file.

PAUSE. LEAVE Word open for the next project.

Project 11-4: Coho One-Panel Brochure

CD

The ***brochure*** document is available on the companion CD-ROM.

Create an informational one-panel brochure about the special event services offered at the Coho winery.

1. **OPEN** ***brochure*** from the data files for this lesson.
2. Create and format the brochure as shown in Figure 11-16.

Figure 11-16

Coho one-panel brochure

3. Insert two Contrast Quote text boxes and key the text as shown for each. Do not forget to change the color to green and change the outline to none. Resize and position as shown.
4. Create a customized in-margin drop cap. Use the Drop Cap Options command to change the lines to drop to 5 and the distance from text to 0.1 inches.
5. **SAVE** the document as *coho_brochure* and then **CLOSE** the file.

PAUSE. LEAVE Word open for the next project.

Mastery Assessment

Project 11-5: Update the YMCA Newsletter

Now that you have improved your Word skills, update the YMCA newsletter created in an earlier lesson.

CD

The ***ymcanewsletter*** document is available on the companion CD-ROM.

1. **OPEN** *ymcanewsletter* from the data files for this lesson.
2. Create WordArt for the *Fall Soccer Registration* heading, using WordArt Style 10. Change the shape fill to red.
3. Create drop caps for the *Mother's Day Out* article and the *Get Movin' Challenge* article. Change the color of the drop caps to red.
4. Replace the title of the newsletter with the **Transcend Sidebar**. Key the title in the sidebar and change the text color to red.
5. Replace the membership box in the lower right corner with the **Transcend Quote** text box. Copy and paste the text and center it. Change the text color to red.
6. Make any adjustments necessary so that all the text fits on one page.
7. **SAVE** the document as *updated_ymcanewsletter* and **CLOSE** the file.

PAUSE. LEAVE Word open for the next project.

Project 11-6: Fix the Coho Newsletter

Someone has gone into the Coho newsletter file and messed it up. Go in and return it to the way it was.

CD

The ***problem_coho_newsletter*** document is available on the companion CD-ROM.

1. **OPEN** *problem_coho_newsletter* from the data files for this lesson.
2. Fix the newsletter to make it the way it was.
3. **SAVE** the document as *coho_newsletter_corrected*.

CLOSE Word.

INTERNET READY

Search the Internet for tips on how to create reader-friendly, professional-looking newsletters, brochures, and other types of desktop publishing documents. Use the information you find to create a newsletter. Include a pull quote, drop cap, text box, and WordArt in your newsletter.

Workplace Ready

Using WordArt

There was a time when doing anything other than simply typing sentences and paragraphs in a word processing document was unheard of. To enhance a document with graphics used to require the use of a separate desktop publishing program. Desktop publishing programs are not only costly to purchase, but can often be somewhat difficult to master. Word provides you with many of the same graphical capabilities you find in today's desktop publishing programs, but without the added cost or the learning curve.

As the Marketing director for Alpine Ski House, a non-profit organization that provides discounted ski equipment to underprivileged children, you are often called upon to create promotional materials. These materials are used to promote your organization's mission, as well as to solicit donations. Being a non-profit organization, your company tries to keep their operating costs as low as possible, so you work within an extremely tight budget.

You need to create several different promotional pieces for your upcoming annual donation drive. These materials include items such as brochures, flyers, and pledge cards. Outsourcing the design work to a professional desktop publisher or printer is absolutely out of the question, given your limited budget. You decide to put your knowledge of Word's many formatting options to use and design the items yourself.

You find that using WordArt to format your company's name is the perfect way to enhance each document. With just one click on a predefined style from the WordArt gallery, your company's name is completely transformed.

Circling Back

As the scheduling manager for Consolidated Messenger, a full-service conference and retreat center, you use Word to create and revise all documents and forms used in coordinating the facility's events.

Project 1: CREATING A LOGO

In recent years, the conference center has expanded and changed its focus. The owner needs your help in creating a new logo for all of the business' documents.

GET READY. Launch Word if it is not already running.

1. Use WordArt, shapes, pictures, and/or clip art to create a logo for Consolidated Messenger. Be creative.
2. Place the logo at the top of a blank Word document.
3. **SAVE** the document as ***consolidated_logo***.

   PAUSE. LEAVE the ***consolidated_logo*** document open for the next project.

Project 2: EDITING A DOCUMENT

You are working on a promotional piece for the conference center, but need to make some changes and add the logo. Open and revise the document.

USE the document that is open from the previous project.

> **CD** The ***consolidated_intro*** file is available on the companion CD-ROM.

1. Select the logo and copy it to the Clipboard.
2. OPEN ***consolidated_intro*** from the data files for this lesson.
3. Place the insertion point on the first line of the document and paste the logo.
4. On the **Home** tab, in the **Editing** group, click the **Find** button.
5. In the **Replace** tab, search for all occurrences of the word *Gallery* and replace them with the word *Theatre*.
6. Select the first two paragraphs of the document.
7. On the **Insert** tab, in the **Text** group, click the **Quick Parts** button.
8. Click Save Selection to Quick Parts Gallery with the name ***consolidatedXXX*** **(where XXX = your initials)**.
9. Place the insertion point at the beginning of the first sentence of the document.
10. On the **Insert** tab, in the **Illustrations** group, click the **Picture** button.
11. Locate ***conference_photo*** in the data files for this lesson and click **Insert**.
12. On the **Format** tab, in the **Arrange** group, click the **Text Wrapping** button.
13. Click **Square**.
14. On the **Format** tab, in the **Size** group, click the **Crop** button.
15. Crop the picture and position it in the document so that it looks similar to Figure 1.

> **CD** The ***conference_photo*** picture file is available on the companion CD-ROM.

Figure 1
Promotional document with photo

Consolidated Messenger Conference and Retreat Center is perfectly suited to serve the needs of conferences, seminars, receptions, and meetings.

This state-of-the-art facility sets new and higher standards for excellence for the conference and training events of association, business, and government groups. We offer a comfortable and stimulating environment, an eager staff, and the latest communications and multi-media technology.

The Great Hall Theatre on the grounds is a restored 1930's vintage movie house. Technologically, however, the facility is all 21st Century. Equipped with a state-of-the-art presentation system, superb lighting and sound, full-size screen and projection unit, the Theatre makes an excellent gathering point for keynote addresses, plenary sessions, and, of course, entertainment.

Upstairs, the renovated Conference Center can be configured as four break-out rooms to accommodate simultaneous sessions - or opened fully to serve up to 250 participants. This space also houses an expansive catering kitchen and technological amenities amidst

16. On the **Format** tab, in the **Picture Styles** group, click the **More** button.
17. Click the **Rotated, White** option.
18. Make any adjustments necessary to fit the entire document on one page.
19. **SAVE** the document as ***consolidated_promo*** and **CLOSE** the file.

PAUSE. LEAVE the document open to use in the next project.

Project 3: AUDIO VISUAL EQUIPMENT TABLE

Create a table that contains a list of the audio and visual equipment available for rent at the conference center.

USE the *consolidated_logo* document that is open from the previous project.

1. Place the insertion point below the logo.
2. In Cambria, 24 pt. font, key the title **Audio Visual Equipment Rental**.
3. Create a table that has three columns and eight rows.
4. Change column widths as necessary and key the information shown in Figure 2 into the table.

Figure 2
Audio visual equipment table

AUDIO VISUAL EQUIPMENT RENTAL

CODE	DESCRIPTION	DAILY RENTAL
LCD	High-resolution LCD data projector	$325
VID	Low-resolution video projector with VCR and monitor	$120
OHP	Overhead projector	$35
FSM	Color 42" flat screen monitor mounted on the front wall	$90
CAM	Mini DVD camcorder with tripod	$95
CDP	Stereo CD player with cassette deck and radio	$25
KEY	Full-size electronic keyboard with stool	$75

5. Place the insertion point anywhere in the table.
6. On the **Design** tab, in the **Table Styles** group, click the **More** button to view a gallery of Quick Styles.
7. Scroll down and click the **Medium Shading 1 - Accent 1** option.
8. On the **Layout** tab, in the **Data** group, click the **Sort** button. Sort by the *Daily Rental* column in descending order.
9. Select the first row.
10. On the **Layout** tab, in the **Alignment** group, click **Align Top Center.**
11. Select all the numbers in the *Daily Rental* column.
12. On the **Layout** tab, in the **Alignment** group, click **Align Center Right**.
13. **SAVE** the document as ***consolidated_equipment*** and **CLOSE** the file.

PAUSE. LEAVE Word open for the next project.

Project 4: FORMATTING A DOCUMENT

You began creating a document to serve as a guide for introducing guests to the conference center. Open and format the document.

CD

The ***consolidated_guests*** file is available on the companion CD-ROM.

1. **OPEN** ***consolidated_guests*** from the data files for this lesson.
2. Use what you have learned in this unit to complete the following tasks. You do not have to complete them in this order, but your goal is to make the document look similar to Figure 3.

Figure 3

Finished document

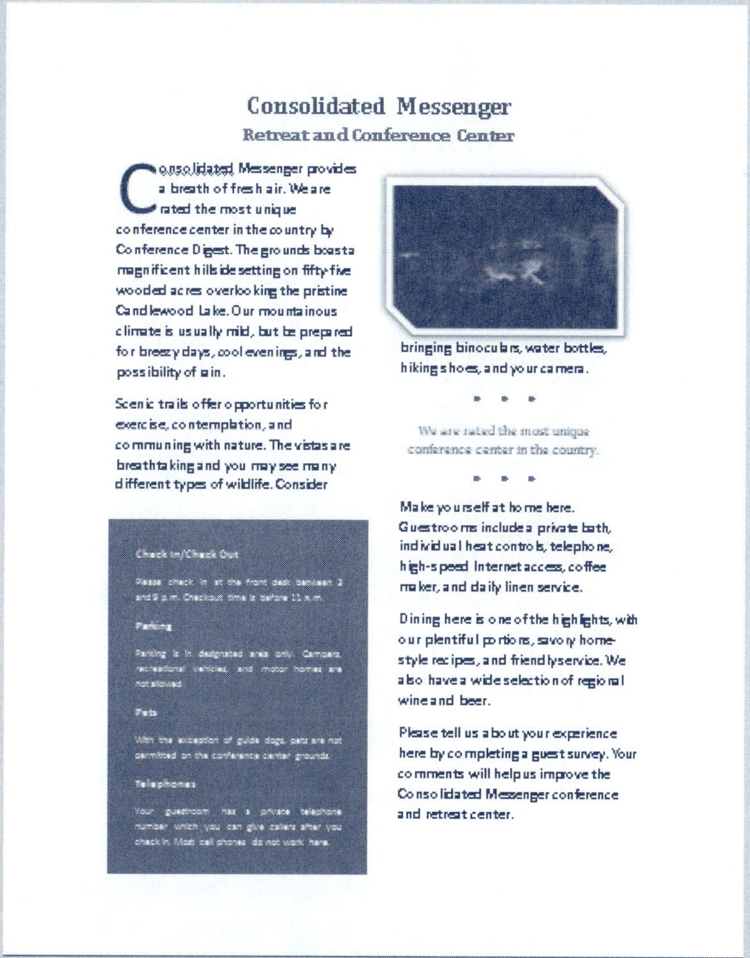
Consolidated Messenger
Retreat and Conference Center

Consolidated Messenger provides a breath of fresh air. We are rated the most unique conference center in the country by Conference Digest. The grounds boast a magnificent hillside setting on fifty-five wooded acres overlooking the pristine Candlewood Lake. Our mountainous climate is usually mild, but be prepared for breezy days, cool evenings, and the possibility of rain.

Scenic trails offer opportunities for exercise, contemplation, and communing with nature. The vistas are breathtaking and you may see many different types of wildlife. Consider bringing binoculars, water bottles, hiking shoes, and your camera.

* * *

We are rated the most unique conference center in the country.

* * *

Make yourself at home here. Guestrooms include a private bath, individual heat controls, telephone, high-speed Internet access, coffee maker, and daily linen service.

Dining here is one of the highlights, with our plentiful portions, savory home-style recipes, and friendly service. We also have a wide selection of regional wine and beer.

Please tell us about your experience here by completing a guest survey. Your comments will help us improve the Consolidated Messenger conference and retreat center.

Check In/Check Out

Please check in at the front desk between 2 and 9 p.m. Checkout time is before 11 a.m.

Parking

Parking is in designated area only. Campers, recreational vehicles, and motor homes are not allowed.

Pets

With the exception of guide dogs, pets are not permitted on the conference center grounds.

Telephones

Your guestroom has a private telephone number which you can give callers after you check in. Most cell phones do not work here.

a. Use section breaks to create a section for the text and then put the text into two columns.

b. Create a drop cap for the first sentence.

c. Apply Snip Diagonal Corner, White to the photograph.

d. Create a pull quote using the **Tiles Quote** style in the **Accent 2** theme color using this text: *We are rated the most unique conference center in the country.*

e. Arrange elements on the page and make any other necessary adjustments to make your document look like Figure 3.

3. **SAVE** the document as ***consolidated_guide*** and **CLOSE** the file.

STOP. CLOSE Word.

Adding Navigation Tools to a Document

12

LESSON SKILL MATRIX

Skills	Matrix Skill	Skill Number
Inserting a Bookmark	Insert document navigation tools	1.3.4
Editing a Bookmark	Insert document navigation tools	1.3.4
Deleting a Bookmark	Insert document navigation tools	1.3.4
Referring to a Bookmark in a Document	Insert document navigation tools	1.3.4
Using Styles to Create a Document Map	Insert document navigation tools; Change window view	1.3.4 5.1.2

You are employed as a communications intern at Lucerne Publishing, where you frequently deal with long documents such as manuscripts and contracts. Instead of scrolling through documents to find certain text, you can save time by using bookmarks. In this lesson, you will learn how to insert, edit, and delete a bookmark. You will also learn how to refer to a bookmark in a document and use styles to create a document map.

KEY TERMS

bookmark
cross-reference

Software Orientation

Bookmark Dialog Box

When you work with bookmarks in a document, you use the Bookmark dialog box, shown in Figure 12-1. This is where you add, delete, sort, and go to bookmarks.

Figure 12-1

Bookmark dialog box

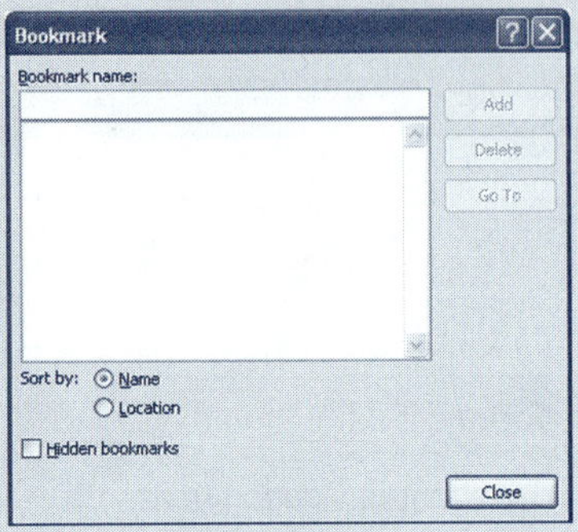

Use this figure as a reference throughout this lesson as well as the rest of this book.

Working with Bookmarks

THE BOTTOM LINE

Bookmarks can be used to identify locations within a document. This enables users to locate important information more quickly. Just as readers use bookmarks to save places within books, Word bookmarks are used to indicate locations within a document.

Inserting a Bookmark

Rather than scrolling through text trying to locate a certain place in the document, you can insert a bookmark that will provide faster and more efficient navigation.

INSERT A BOOKMARK

GET READY. Before you begin these steps, be sure to launch Microsoft Word.

CD

The ***lucerne_publishing*** file is available on the companion CD-ROM.

1. **OPEN** ***lucerne_publishing*** from the data files for this lesson.
2. In the first paragraph, select the author's name, *Kevin A. Cavallari*.
3. On the Insert tab, in the Links group, click the **Bookmark** button to display the Bookmark dialog box.
4. In the Bookmark name box, key **author**.
5. Click the **Add** button.
6. In the first sentence of section 1c, select the phrase *provisions of 17 U.S.C. 211B*.
7. On the Insert tab, in the Links group, click the **Bookmark** button to display the Bookmark dialog box.

8. In the Bookmark box, key **provisions**.
9. Click the **Add** button.
10. Select the fourth numbered heading, *4. Amendments*.
11. Insert a bookmark named **Amendments**.
12. In the second paragraph of section 5, place the insertion point before the word *signatures*.
13. Insert a bookmark named **signatures**.
14. **SAVE** the document as ***lucerne_agreement***.

PAUSE. LEAVE the document open to use in the next exercise.

CERTIFICATION READY?
How do you insert document navigation tools?
1.3.4

A ***bookmark*** is a location or a selection of text that you name and identify for future reference. Select the text or item to which you want to assign a bookmark, or click where you want to insert a bookmark. In the Bookmark dialog box, key a name in the Bookmark box and then click Add.

Bookmark names can contain numbers, but they must begin with a letter. You cannot have any spaces in a bookmark name, so use an underscore to separate words, or put the words together. For example, *Trade_Secrets* or *TradeSecrets.*

Bookmarks can be sorted by name or by location in the Bookmark dialog box. To jump to the location of a bookmark in a document, select the bookmark from the Bookmark dialog box and click the Go To button.

Editing a Bookmark

To edit a bookmark, you must first display all bookmarks in the document.

EDIT A BOOKMARK

USE the document that is open from the previous exercise.

1. Click the **Microsoft Office Button** and then click **Word Options**.
2. Click **Advanced** and then select the **Show bookmarks** checkbox in the Show document content section, as shown in Figure 12-2.

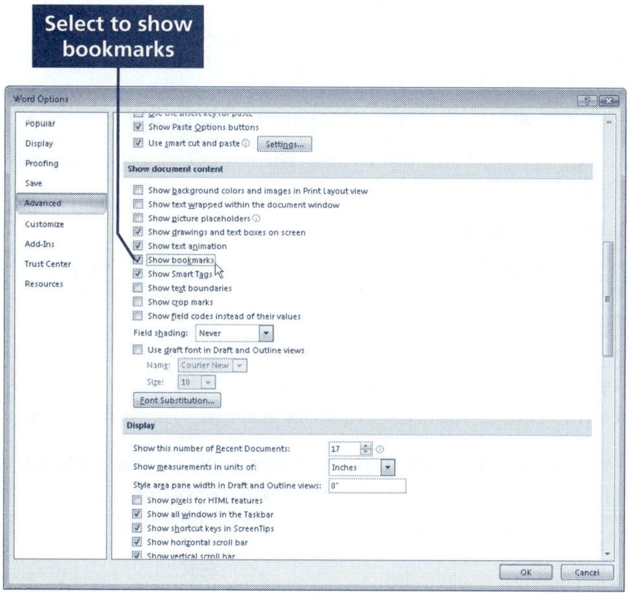

Figure 12-2

Word Options dialog box

TROUBLESHOOTING Bookmarks are not displayed by default in a document, but if other people have used your computer, they may have already selected the Show bookmarks checkbox in the Advanced section of the Word Options dialog box.

3. Click **OK**. Bookmarks in the document are indicated by either square brackets, when an entire block of text has been bookmarked, or a single I-beam (see Figure 12-3).

Figure 12-3

Bookmarks displayed in text

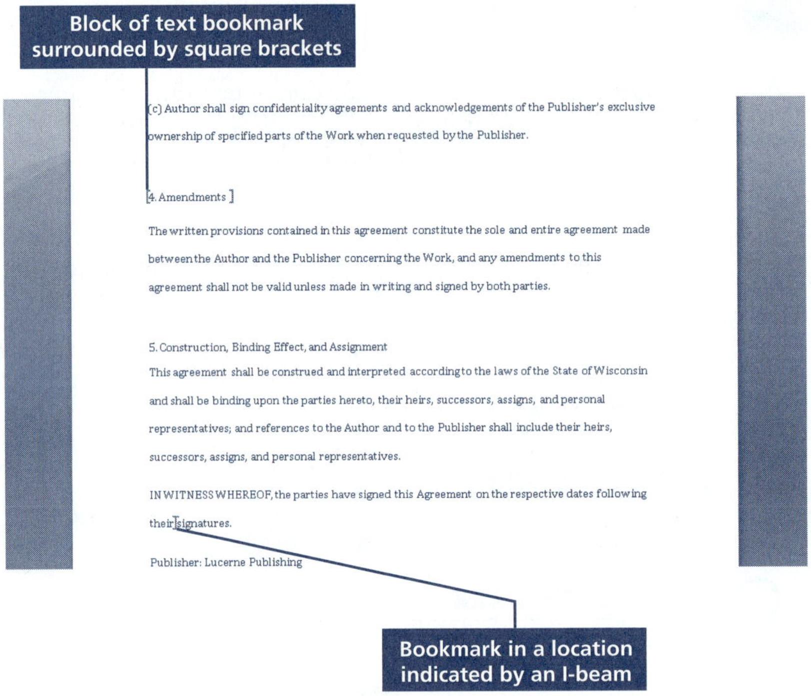

4. On the Insert tab, in the Links group, click the **Bookmark** button to display the Bookmark dialog box.
5. In the Bookmark name list, select **provisions**.
6. Click the **Go To** button.
7. Click **Close** to close the Bookmark dialog box.
8. Change *211B* to ***106A*** within the selected text. Any edits that you make within the brackets become part of the bookmark.
9. **SAVE** the document.

PAUSE. LEAVE the document open to use in the next exercise.

CERTIFICATION READY?
How do you insert document navigation tools?
1.3.4

When you assign a bookmark to a block of text, Word surrounds the text with square brackets on the screen. When you add a bookmark to a location, the bookmark appears as an I-beam. The bookmark indicators are not visible when you print the document.

You can cut, copy, and paste items that are marked with a bookmark. You can also add text to, and delete text from, marked items. When you change a bookmarked item, make sure that you change the text or graphics inside the brackets. Table 12-1 describes the changes you can make to bookmarks.

Table 12-1

Changes you can make to bookmarks

When you	This happens
Copy and paste all or part of a bookmarked item to another location in the same document	The bookmark remains with the original item; the pasted text does not have a bookmark
Copy an entire bookmarked item to another document	Both documents contain identical items and identical bookmarks
Cut an entire bookmarked item and paste it in the same document	The item and the bookmark move to the new location
Delete part of a bookmarked text	The bookmark stays with the remaining text
Click within the brackets of a bookmarked item and add text or graphics to the item	The addition is included in the bookmark
Click directly before or after the brackets that enclose a bookmarked item and add text or graphics	The addition is not included in the bookmark

Referring to Bookmarks in a Document

Cross-references can be inserted to refer to bookmarks in other locations of a document.

REFER TO BOOKMARKS IN A DOCUMENT

USE the document that is open from the previous exercise.

1. On the Insert tab, in the Links group, click the **Bookmark** button to display the Bookmark dialog box.
2. In the Bookmark name list, select **signatures**.
3. Click the **Go To** button.
4. Click **Close** to close the Bookmark dialog box.
5. Scroll down and place the insertion point on the line below the *Author* signature line.
6. On the Insert tab, in the Links group, click the **Cross-reference** button to display the Cross-reference dialog box.
7. In the Reference type box, click the downward-pointing arrow and select **Bookmark**. The list of bookmarks in your document is displayed, as shown in Figure 12-4.

Figure 12-4

Cross-reference dialog box

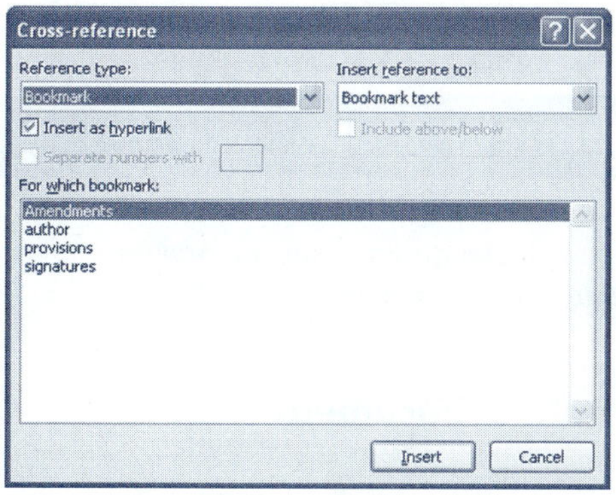

CERTIFICATION READY?
How do you insert document navigation tools?
1.3.4

8. In the Insert reference to box, **Bookmark text** should be selected.
9. In the For which bookmark list, click **author**.
10. Click the **Insert** button. The bookmarked text is inserted into the document.
11. Press Ctrl and click the author's name that you just inserted. The insertion point jumps to that bookmark in the document.
12. **SAVE** the document.

PAUSE. LEAVE the document open to use in the next exercise.

You can refer to items such as figures, tables, footnotes, or bookmarks with an inserted cross-reference. A ***cross-reference*** is a notation or direction at one place to relevant information in another. For example, after you insert a bookmark in a document, you can refer to that bookmark from other places in the text by creating cross-references to it.

Cross-references are automatically updated if the content is moved to another location. By default, cross-references are inserted as hyperlinks. Pressing Ctrl and clicking the cross-referenced text moves to the bookmark in the document. If the bookmark is deleted, the cross-reference will no longer be linked.

Deleting a Bookmark

A bookmark that is no longer needed can easily be removed using the Bookmark dialog box.

DELETE A BOOKMARK

USE the document that is open from the previous exercise.

CERTIFICATION READY?
How do you insert document navigation tools?
1.3.4

1. On the Insert tab, in the Links group, click the **Bookmark** button to display the Bookmark dialog box.
2. In the Bookmark name list, select **Amendments**.
3. Click the **Delete** button.
4. In the Bookmark name list, select **signatures**.
5. Click the **Delete** button.
6. Click the **Close** button.
7. **SAVE** the document.

PAUSE. LEAVE the document open to use in the next exercise.

To delete a bookmark, first select the name of the bookmark that you want to delete in the Bookmark dialog box and then click the Delete button. If you want to delete both the bookmark and the bookmarked item (such as a block of text), select the item and then press the Delete button on the keyboard.

Using Styles to Create a Document Map

THE BOTTOM LINE You learned how to display a Document Map in previous lessons. Now you will learn how to use styles to create a Document Map.

Using Styles to Create a Document Map

You can create, or add to, a Document Map by applying heading styles to your document.

USE STYLES TO CREATE A DOCUMENT MAP

X REF

You previously learned about the Document Map in Lesson 1 and in Lesson 8.

USE the document that is open from the previous exercise.

1. On the View tab, in the Show/Hide group, click to select the **Document Map** check box to display the Document Map pane.
2. Below the first paragraph in the document, select the line *WITNESSETH:*, including the paragraph mark.
3. On the Home tab, in the Styles group, click the **More** button.
4. Click **Heading 2**. Notice the heading is now added to the Document Map.
5. Select the first numbered heading, *1. Title and Copyright Assignment*.
6. On the Home tab, in the Styles group, click the **More** button.
7. Click **Heading 3**.
8. Repeat steps 6 and 7 for each of the remaining numbered headings in the document. Your document window and the Document Map pane should look similar to Figure 12-5.

Figure 12-5

Document Map pane and document with styles applied

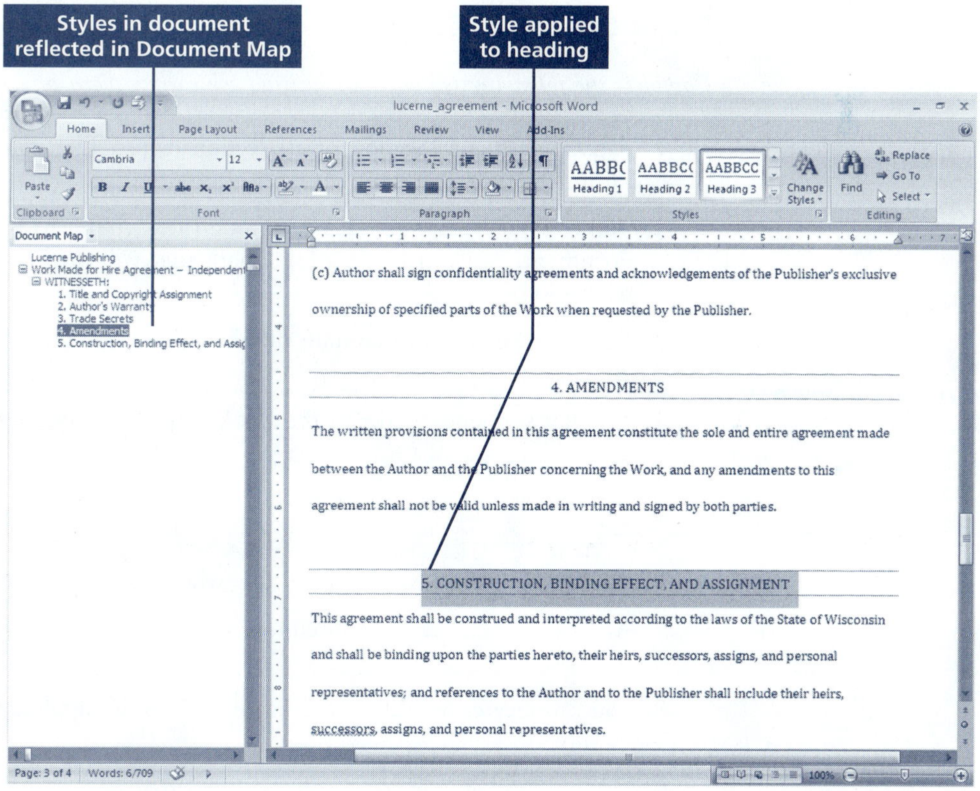

9. **SAVE** the document and **CLOSE** the file.

STOP. CLOSE Word.

CERTIFICATION READY?
How do you insert document navigation tools? How do you use the Document Map? How do you change window views?
1.3.4, 5.1.2

When you display the Document Map, headings that are formatted with built-in heading styles or look like headings are displayed. If Word is unable to locate any headings, the Document Map will be blank. As you apply styles to headings in your document, those headings are added to the Document Map.

SUMMARY SKILL MATRIX

In This Lesson You Learned	Matrix Skill	Skill Number
To insert a bookmark	Insert document navigation tools	1.3.4
To edit a bookmark	Insert document navigation tools	1.3.4
To delete a bookmark	Insert document navigation tools	1.3.4
To refer to a bookmark in a document	Insert document navigation tools	1.3.4
To use styles to create a document map	Insert document navigation tools; Change window views	1.3.4 5.1.2

Knowledge Assessment

Fill in the Blank

Complete the following sentences by writing the correct word or words in the blanks provided.

1. A bookmark is a location or a selection of text that you name and identify for future ______________.
2. Rather than ______________ through text trying to locate a certain place in the document, you can insert a bookmark that will provide faster and more efficient navigation.
3. Bookmark names can contain numbers, but they must begin with a ______________.
4. You can sort bookmarks in the Bookmark dialog box by name or by ______________.
5. Bookmarks in a document are indicated by either square brackets or an I-____________.
6. Bookmark indicators are not visible when you ______________ a document.
7. A ______________ is a notation or direction at one place to relevant information in another.
8. You can create, or add to, a Document Map by applying heading ______________ to your document.
9. If Word is unable to locate any headings that are formatted with built-in heading styles or that look like heading styles, the Document Map will be ______________.
10. Use the ______________ dialog box to show bookmarks in a document.

Multiple Choice

Select the best response for the following statements.

1. Which action is possible in the Bookmark dialog box?
   a. rename
   b. view cross-reference
   c. sort
   d. all of the above
   e. none of the above

2. Bookmark names cannot include what?
   a. an underscore
   b. a capital letter
   c. a number
   d. a space
3. To jump to the location of a bookmark in a document, click which button?
   a. Jump
   b. Go To
   c. Link
   d. Cross-reference
4. To edit bookmarks in a document, you must first do what?
   a. sort them
   b. display them
   c. rename them
   d. cross-reference them
5. By default, cross-references are inserted as
   a. Building Blocks.
   b. headings.
   c. text boxes.
   d. hyperlinks.
6. To jump from a cross-reference to its respective bookmark in a document, what button do you press while clicking the cross-referenced text?
   a. Tab
   b. Shift
   c. Ctrl
   d. Enter
7. If you want to delete both the bookmark and the bookmarked item, select the entire item and then press what?
   a. Remove
   b. Delete
   c. Esc
   d. Ctrl
8. On which tab do you find the Bookmark button?
   a. Home
   b. Insert
   c. Page Layout
   d. Review
9. Which command can you NOT perform from the Bookmark dialog box?
   a. Move
   b. Add
   c. Go To
   d. Delete
10. Which is an example of an acceptable bookmark name?
    a. 3rd_Heading
    b. Title and Copyright
    c. Author_Warranty
    d. hire agreement

Competency Assessment

Project 12-1: Inserting Bookmarks

In your position within the service department at Cornwall Bank and Trust, you frequently use a document that explains the discretionary overdraft service. Open the document and insert bookmarks to help you navigate to specific text more quickly.

CD

The ***cornwall*** document is available on the companion CD-ROM.

GET READY. Launch Word if it is not already running.

1. **OPEN** ***cornwall*** from the data files for this lesson.
2. Select the phone number below the title.
3. On the Insert tab, in the Links group, click **Bookmark**.
4. In the Bookmark name box, key **phone_number**.
5. Click **Add**.
6. On page two, select the bolded phrase *discretionary service* in the first sentence.
7. Insert a bookmark named **discretionary_service**.
8. On the last page, select the subheading *If You Need Help*.
9. Insert a bookmark named **help**.
10. **SAVE** the document as ***cornwall_overdraft*** and **CLOSE** the file.

PAUSE. LEAVE Word open for the next project.

Project 12-2: Editing a Bookmark and Creating a Cross-Reference

In your position as an account manager for Flatland Hosting, you often refer to the same information within a client document you use and have already added several bookmarks. Now you need to make a change to one of the bookmarks and create a cross-reference.

CD

The ***principles*** document is available on the companion CD-ROM.

1. **OPEN** ***principles*** from the data files for this lesson.
2. On the Insert tab, in the Links group, click **Bookmark**.
3. In the Bookmark name box, select **maximum_transfer**.
4. Click **Go To**.
5. Click **Close**.
6. Within the brackets, change the number *5* to **10**.
7. Scroll to the end of the document, place the insertion point after the word *information* and before the period in the last sentence.
8. Insert a space, key the word **at**, and then insert another space.
9. On the Insert tab, in the Links group, click the **Cross-reference** button to display the Cross-reference dialog box.
10. In the Reference type box, click the downward-pointing arrow and select **Bookmark**.
11. In the Insert reference to box, **Bookmark text** should be selected.
12. In the For which bookmark list, click **email**.
13. Click the **Insert** button. The bookmarked text is inserted into the document.
14. Click the **Close** button.
15. Press Ctrl and click the email address that you just inserted. The insertion point jumps to that bookmark in the document.
16. **SAVE** the document as ***principles_flatland*** and **CLOSE** the file.

PAUSE. LEAVE Word open for the next project.

Proficiency Assessment

Project 12-3: Editing a Document Map and Creating a Cross-Reference

You need to make additional changes to the discretionary overdraft service document that you use frequently in the service department at Cornwall Bank and Trust. Open the document to edit the Document Map and create a cross-reference.

1. **OPEN** ***cornwall_overdraft*** from the location where you saved it in Project 12-1.
2. On the View tab, in the Show/Hide group, select the **Document Map** checkbox.
3. In the Document Map pane, click **CUSTOMER OPT-OUT** to navigate to the *CUSTOMER OPT-OUT* heading.
4. On the Home tab, in the Styles group, apply the **Heading 2** style to this heading.
5. Apply the Heading 2 style to the *If You Need Help* and *Always a Discretionary Service* headings. Notice that the Document Map reflects these changes.
6. In the *If You Need Help* section, place the insertion point between the word *bank* and the period at the end of the paragraph.
7. Key a space, the word **at**, and then another space.
8. Insert a cross-reference for the **phone_number** bookmark.
9. Click the **Insert** button.
10. **SAVE** the document as ***cornwall_dos*** and **CLOSE** the file.

PAUSE. LEAVE Word open for the next project.

Project 12-4: Adding Bookmarks and Styles

The manager of the marketing department at LostArt Photos, where you are employed as a marketing assistant, has discussed adding more information to a promotional document. Because you anticipate the document will become lengthy, you decide to plan ahead by adding bookmarks and styles to the document.

CD

The ***lostart*** document is available on the companion CD-ROM.

1. **OPEN** ***lostart*** from the data files for this lesson.
2. Format each of the four subheadings with a Heading 2 style.
3. Display the Document Map to verify that the headings appear there.
4. Create a bookmark for each of the same four headings.
5. **SAVE** the document as ***lostart_prints***.

PAUSE. LEAVE the document open for the next project.

Mastery Assessment

Project 12-5: Format the Document Map

While working with the Document Map, you find it hard to read and decide to change its formatting. You have not done this before, but you are already familiar with styles and use those skills to perform this new task.

USE the document that is open from the previous project.

1. Display the Document Map.
2. On the Home tab, click the **Styles dialog box launcher**.
3. Click the downward-pointing arrow next to Document Map and then click **Modify** to open the Modify Style dialog box.

4. In the Formatting section, select **12** in the font size box and select **Dark Blue, Text 2** in the color box.
5. Click **OK** to close the dialog box.
6. Close the Styles dialog box.
7. Now the text is too big to read the entire heading in the Document Map pane. Place the insertion point over the right edge of the pane until it turns into a resizing tool with double arrows, as shown in Figure 12-6.

Figure 12-6

Resize the Document Pane window

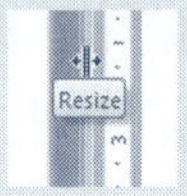

8. Drag the resizing arrows to the right until all the text is visible in the Document Map pane.
9. **SAVE** the document as ***lostart_format*** and **CLOSE** the file.

PAUSE. LEAVE Word open for the next project.

Project 12-6: Using Styles to Create a Document Map

You want to see a structural view of the Books and Beyond Employee Handbook, but when you open the Document Map, it does not display correctly. Apply styles to the headings to create the Document Map.

CD

The ***books_employee*** document is available on the companion CD-ROM.

1. **OPEN** ***books_employee*** from the data files for this lesson.
2. On the View tab, in the Show/Hide group, select the **Document Map** checkbox.
3. Apply Heading 1, Heading 2, and Normal styles to text where appropriate to make the Document Map look like Figure 12-7.

Figure 12-7

Document Map corrected

4. **SAVE** the document as ***books_handbook*** and **CLOSE** the file.

CLOSE Word.

INTERNET READY

The skills you are learning in this book are a good foundation for using Word in the workplace. There may be times when you want to perform a task that goes beyond what you have already learned. The Internet can be a great resource for finding additional information. Use the Internet to search for information about one of the following bookmark topics and then write a brief paragraph answering the topic's question or explaining how to accomplish the task. Document your sources by including the URL in your answer.

- The Bookmark dialog box has a Hidden Bookmarks checkbox. What is the purpose of this checkbox? Is it possible to hide a bookmark? If so, how?
- It is easy to delete a bookmark using the Bookmark dialog box. Suppose you want to protect bookmarks from being deleted. Is this possible? If so, how? If not, why not?
- List the steps you would follow to create a hyperlink in an HTML page to a bookmark in a Word document.
- You want to highlight the bookmarks in your document by making them bold so you can see them better. Is this possible? If so, how?

13

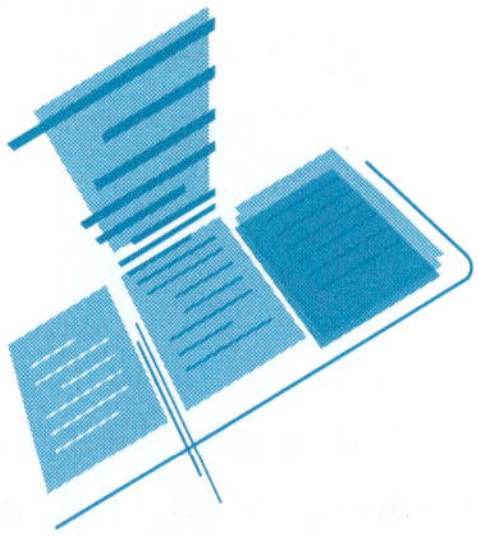

Creating a Table of Contents and Index

LESSON SKILL MATRIX

Skills	Matrix Skill	Skill Number
Creating a Table of Contents from Heading Styles	Create, modify, and update tables of contents	1.3.1
Adding Selected Text to a Table of Contents	Create, modify, and update tables of contents	1.3.1
Updating a Table of Contents	Create, modify, and update tables of contents	1.3.1
Marking an Entry for an Index	Create, modify, and update indexes	1.3.2
Creating a Subentry and a Cross-Reference	Create, modify, and update indexes	1.3.2
Creating an Index	Create, modify, and update indexes	1.3.2
Formatting an Index	Create, modify, and update indexes	1.3.2
Updating an Index	Create, modify, and update indexes	1.3.2

You have just begun a new career as a project manager at Proseware, Inc., a Web Development company. One of the responsibilities of this position includes meeting with new clients who want to develop new Web sites or redesign existing sites. To help make this process easier, you decide to create a template that you can use to plan Web site development for each client. Although the template is only about seven pages long, you know it will get longer as the sections are filled in and completed for each client. In this lesson, you will create a table of contents and an index so that all sections of the document can be referred to easily amongst client representatives and coworkers during the planning and development of Web sites.

KEY TERMS

index
main entry
subentry
tab leaders
table of contents

Creating a Table of Contents

THE BOTTOM LINE

A table of contents is usually found at the beginning of a long document, and it helps readers quickly locate topics of interest. Word includes several options that make creating a table of contents easy. These include creating a table of contents from heading styles, adding selected text to a table of contents, and updating a table of contents.

Creating a Table of Contents from Heading Styles

One advantage of using Word's Quick Styles to format headings in a document is the ability to easily create a table of contents. In an instant, Word searches your document for the properly formatted headings and compiles them into a table of contents with page numbers.

CREATE A TABLE OF CONTENTS

GET READY. Before you begin these steps, be sure to launch Microsoft Word and **OPEN** the ***website*** document from the data files for this lesson.

CD

The ***website*** document is available on the companion CD-ROM.

1. On the first page, fourth line, select *Planning the site*.
2. On the Home tab, in the Styles group, click **Heading 1**.
3. On the next line, select *Research*. On the Home tab, in the Styles group, click the **More** button, if necessary, to display the Styles gallery. Click the **Heading 2** style.
4. On the next line, select *Research and scheduling*. On the Home tab, in the Styles group, click the **Heading 3** style.
5. Scroll through the document to verify that all the other headings have the correct styles applied to them.
6. Click on a blank line above the *Web Site Creation Strategy* title.
7. On the References tab, in the Table of Contents group, click the **Table of Contents** button. A gallery of Built-in styles and a menu appears, as shown in Figure 13-1.

Figure 13-1

Table of Contents button and menu

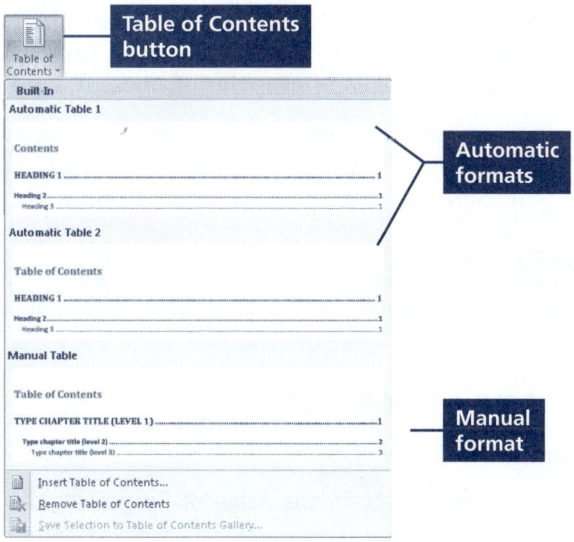

8. Click the **Automatic Table 2** style. The table of contents is inserted in the document (see Figure 13-2).

Figure 13-2

Table of Contents

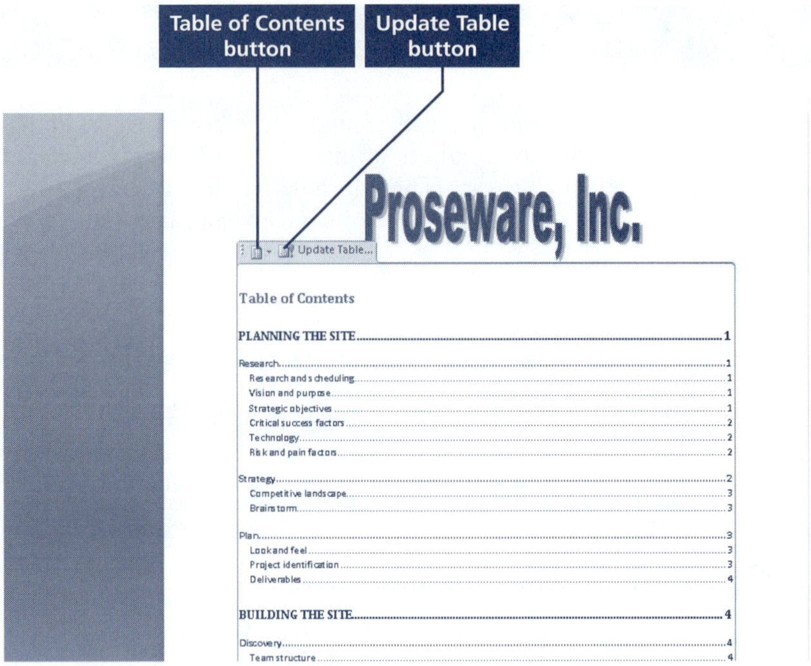

CERTIFICATION READY?
How do you create a table of contents from headings?
1.3.1

9. **SAVE** your document as ***website_template***.

   PAUSE. LEAVE the document open to use in the next exercise.

A ***table of contents*** is an ordered list of the topics in a document, along with the page numbers on which they are found. Word makes inserting a table of contents easy using the built-in gallery of styles on the Table of Contents menu. The menu includes two automatic formats and one manual format.

When you choose one of the automatic formats, as you did in the previous exercise, Word automatically builds your table of contents using the Heading 1, Heading 2, and Heading 3 styles. If you want Word to create a table of contents for you, make sure the headings in your document have been formatted using these styles.

You can also choose to create a table of contents manually, independent from the contents of the document, by choosing the Manual Table from the gallery. Word inserts a common format that you can use to create your own table of contents.

Word inserts a built-in table of contents as a block of text with a light blue background. For easy access, Word also inserts a Table of Contents button and the Update Table button at the top of the table of contents.

ANOTHER WAY

To delete a table of contents, select the Remove Table of Contents command from the Table of Contents menu.

FORMAT A TABLE OF CONTENTS

USE the document that is open from the previous exercise.

1. On the References tab, in the Table of Contents group, click the **Table of Contents** button.
2. Select **Insert Table of Contents from the menu**. The Table of Contents dialog box appears, as shown in Figure 13-3. The Print Preview box lists all styles that were used to create the table of contents.

Figure 13-3

Table of Contents dialog box

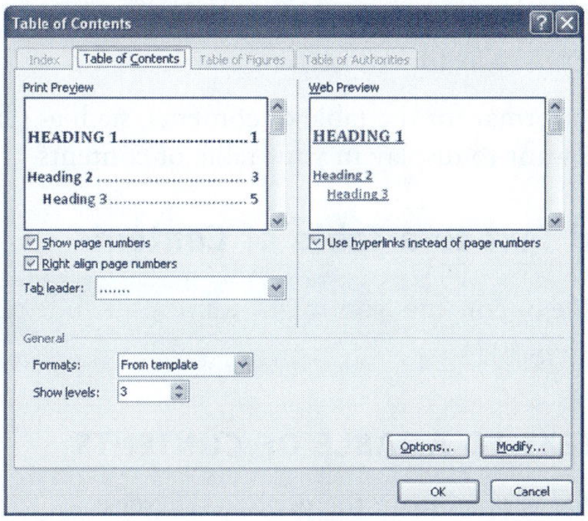

3. Click the **Options** button. The Table of Contents Options dialog box appears, as shown in Figure 13-4.

Figure 13-4

Table of Contents Options dialog box

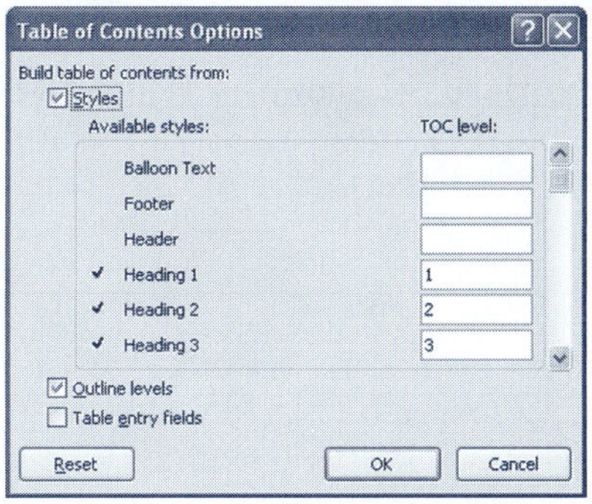

4. In the Build table of contents from section, scroll through the TOC level list. Notice the styles and their levels marked for inclusion in the table of contents.
5. Click **Cancel**. The Table of Contents dialog box appears.
6. Click the downward-pointing arrow on the Formats menu and select **Formal**.
7. Click the downward-pointing arrow on the Tab leader menu and select **...... (dots)**, if necessary.
8. Click **OK**. Word displays a prompt asking you if you want to replace the selected table of contents. Click **Yes**.
9. Notice the new format of the table of contents.
10. **SAVE** the document.

PAUSE. LEAVE the document open to use in the next exercise.

Even after you have created a table of contents, you can create the format you want using the Table of Contents Options dialog box.

You can use styles other than Heading 1, Heading 2, and Heading 3 to create a table of contents. The Table of Contents Options dialog box provides options for choosing which styles you want to include and at what level you want them to appear in the table of contents.

The Table of Contents dialog box has other options you can specify, including whether to show page numbers and whether to right align those page numbers. You can also specify ***tab leaders***, which are the symbols that appear between the table of contents topic and the tab set for the corresponding page number. You can choose for these to appear as periods, dashes, lines, or none.

You can also choose a format for the table of contents, such as Classic or Modern, as well as how many levels you want to display in your table of contents.

Adding Selected Text to a Table of Contents

Sometimes in a table of contents you might want to include text that has not been formatted with a heading style.

ADD SELECTED TEXT TO A TABLE OF CONTENTS

USE the document that is open from the previous exercise.

1. Scroll to page 2 of the document and position the insertion point before the *W* in *Web Site Creation Strategy*.
2. On the Insert tab, in the Pages group, click the **Page Break** button.
3. Select the *Web Site Creation Strategy* text.
4. On the References tab, in the Table of Contents group, click the **Add Text** button to display the menu. 

5. Select **Level 1** from the menu, as shown in Figure 13-5.

Figure 13-5

Add Text button and menu

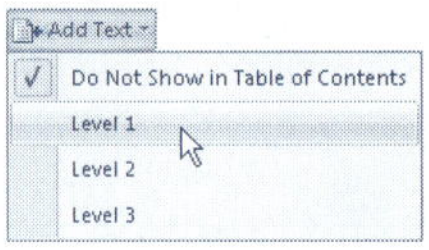

CERTIFICATION READY?
How do you add selected text to a table of contents?
1.3.1

6. **SAVE** the document.

PAUSE. LEAVE the document open to use in the next exercise.

You just added selected text to a table of contents. After you selected the text and clicked the Add Text button, a menu of levels appeared. This menu enables you to choose the level at which the new text will appear. The levels available in the previous exercise were Do Not Show in Table of Contents, Level 1, Level 2, and Level 3. When working with tables of contents in other documents that have more levels, additional options may be available on the menu.

ANOTHER WAY

You can create an entire table of contents using the Add Text method.

Updating a Table of Contents

After you add new text or make other changes to a table of contents, you will need to update the table of contents.

UPDATE A TABLE OF CONTENTS

USE the document that is open from the previous exercise.

1. On the References tab, in the Table of Contents group, click the **Update Table** button. 

2. The **Update Table of Contents** dialog box appears. Click the **Update entire table** button, as shown in Figure 13-6, and click **OK**.

Figure 13-6

Update Table of Contents dialog box

CERTIFICATION READY?
How do you update a table of contents?
1.3.1

3. Scroll to the table of contents pages and notice the addition and the page number updates.
4. **SAVE** the document.

PAUSE. LEAVE the document open to use in the next exercise.

When you make changes to a document that affect the table of contents, such as adding a page or adding text, you need to update the table of contents as you did in the previous exercise. When you click the Update Table button, the Update Table of Contents dialog box appears, providing a choice between updating page numbers only or updating the entire table.

ANOTHER WAY

You can also update a table of contents by clicking the Update Table button at the top of the table of contents in the document.

Creating an Index

THE BOTTOM LINE

An index helps readers find the location of specific topics, words, or phrases in a document. When you mark entries for an index, Microsoft Word can compile those entries and insert a formatted index. You can also add subentries, format the index, and update the index.

Marking an Entry for an Index

The first step in creating an index is marking the words you want to include. When making these decisions, be sure to consider how the reader will use the index and what words will be helpful to include.

MARK AN ENTRY FOR AN INDEX

USE the document that is open from the previous exercise.

1. Scroll to page 4. In the Technology section, select the first instance of *Server*.
2. On the References tab, in the Index group, click the **Mark Entry** button. The Mark Index Entry dialog box appears, as shown in Figure 13-7.

Figure 13-7

Mark Index Entry dialog box

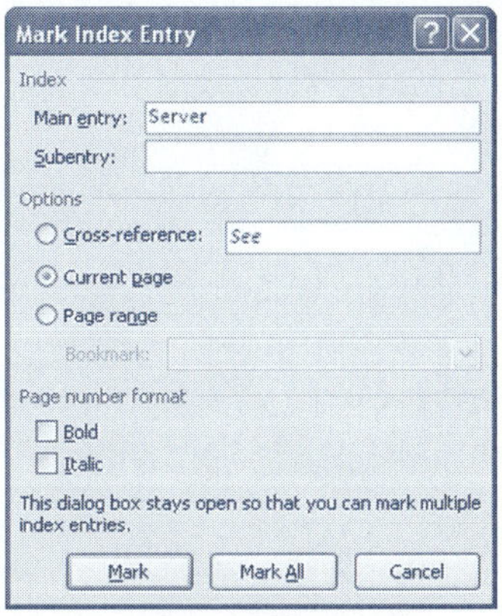

ANOTHER WAY You can also mark an entry by selecting it and pressing **Alt+Shift+X** to display the Mark Index Entry dialog box.

3. Click **Mark**. The word is marked as an index entry with an XE field, as shown in Figure 13-8. The Mark Index Entry dialog box remains on the screen so that you can mark more entries.

Figure 13-8

Index entry

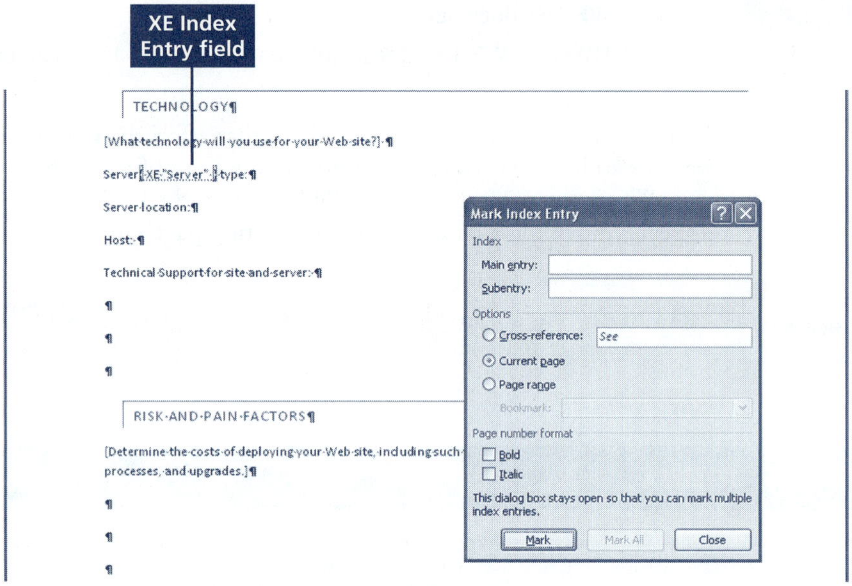

4. Two lines down, select *Host*.
5. Click anywhere in the **Mark Index Entry** dialog box. The word *Host* appears in the Main entry box. Click **Mark**.
6. Scroll to page 7. In the *Technology Architecture* section, select the word *databases*. Click anywhere in the Mark Index Entry dialog box and click **Mark**.
7. Two rows down, select *Shopping cart*. Click anywhere in the Mark Index Entry dialog box and click **Mark**.
8. **SAVE** the document.

PAUSE. LEAVE the document open to use in the next exercise.

An ***index,*** usually located at the end of a document, is an alphabetical list of topics that includes the page numbers on which they are found (see Figure 13-9).

Figure 13-9

Index

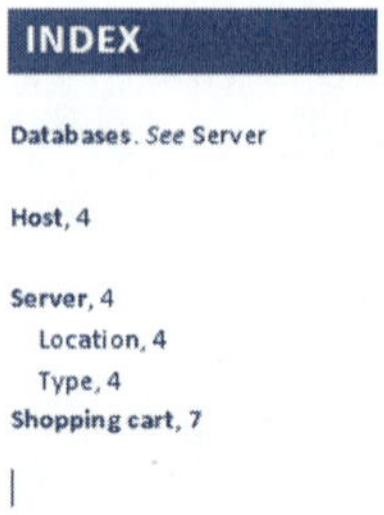

TAKE NOTE*

When you mark an entry and the *XE* field is inserted, Word automatically turns on the Show/Hide ¶ command so you can view the fields in the document. Remember that you can access this command on the Home tab, in the Paragraph group, whenever you need to view these hidden fields.

You just marked an entry for an index by selecting it and choosing the Mark Entry button. When the Mark Index Entry dialog box appears, the entry is displayed in the Main entry box.

ANOTHER WAY

You can also mark an index entry by clicking the insertion point where you want the entry to appear, clicking the Mark Entry button, and then keying text for the entry into the dialog box.

A ***main entry,*** like the ones you marked in the previous exercise, is the top-level entry in an index.

XREF

Cross-references were also discussed in Lesson 12.

In the Options section of the Main Index Entry dialog box, you can insert a cross-reference or mark the entry as being on the current page or on a range of pages. In the Page Number section, you can indicate if you would like the page numbers to appear in bold or italic text.

When you want to mark an entry on the current page, click the Mark button. By clicking the Mark All button, every occurrence of a particular word in the document will be marked.

When you mark an index entry, Word inserts a special *XE* field that includes the marked main entry and any subentry or cross-reference information that you choose to include.

CERTIFICATION READY?
How do you mark an entry for an index?
1.3.2

After you mark an entry, the Mark Index Entry dialog box remains on the screen so you can continue marking entries without having to open and close the dialog box each time. When you are finished marking entries, click the Close button to remove the dialog box from the screen.

Creating a Subentry and a Cross-Reference

When you need subcategories under a main entry, you can list them in the index by creating a subentry. For example, Microsoft Office would be a main entry, while Word, Excel, and PowerPoint would each be subentries. You can also create a cross-reference to point the reader to a related word in the index.

CREATE A SUBENTRY AND A CROSS-REFERENCE

USE the document that is open from the previous exercise.

1. On page 4, in the *Technology* section, select the first occurrence of *Server*.
2. Click the **Mark Index Entry** dialog box. *Server* appears in the Main entry box.
3. Key **type** in the Subentry box and click **Mark**.
4. On the next line, select *Server*. Click the **Mark Index Entry** dialog box.
5. Key **location** in the Subentry box and click **Mark**.
6. Scroll to page 7. In the *Technology Architecture* section, select *databases*. Click the **Mark Index Entry** dialog box.
7. Click the **Cross-reference** button and key **Server** following *See*.
8. Click **Mark**.
9. Click **Close**.
10. **SAVE** the document.

PAUSE. LEAVE the document open to use in the next exercise.

A ***subentry*** is a subcategory of a main entry. It is used to specify more about the main entry. As you saw in the previous exercise, it is easy to insert a subentry, even after you've marked the main entry. Just select the entry again, click the Mark Index Entry dialog box, and key the subentry.

CERTIFICATION READY?
How do you create a subentry?
1.3.2

In a similar way, you can specify a cross-reference, which is a reference to a related part of the document. In the Mark Index Entry dialog box, just click the Cross-reference button under Options and key the related word following the word *See* in the text box.

Creating an Index

After you mark the entries, subentries, and cross-references that you want to include in your index, it is time to create the index.

CREATE AN INDEX

USE the document that is open from the previous exercise.

1. Scroll to the end of the document and insert a page break.
2. Key **Index** and press the **Enter** key.
3. Apply the **Heading 1** style to the Index title.
4. Click on the paragraph mark below the heading.
5. On the References tab, in the Index group, click the **Insert Index** button. The Index dialog box appears, as shown in Figure 13-10. 

Figure 13-10

Index dialog box

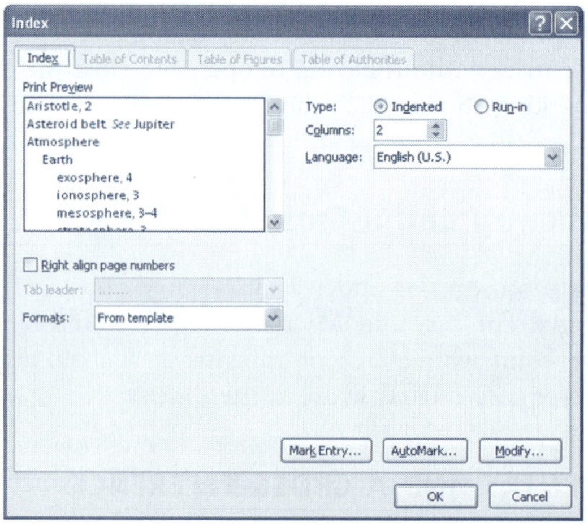

6. Click the downward-pointing arrow on the **Columns** box to change the value to 1.
7. Click the **Formats** menu and select **Bulleted**.
8. Click **OK**. The index is inserted in the document.
9. **SAVE** the document.

PAUSE. LEAVE the document open to use in the next exercise.

CERTIFICATION READY?
How do you create an index?
1.3.2

You created an index in the previous exercise using the Index dialog box, which contains options for choosing an index's layout. The Type section lets you choose between indented or run-in entries, and the Columns box lets you indicate how many columns to use. You can choose to right align page numbers or keep them next to the entry. The Formats menu has a list of seven index formats you can choose from. The Print Preview window shows you what your choices will look like in the index.

Once you have made your choices in the Index dialog box and you have selected the OK button, Word compiles the entries, alphabetizes them, and inserts the index.

Formatting an Index

You can format index entries by going back to the *XE* field for each entry you would like to change and making changes there. You can also reformat the entire index.

FORMAT AN INDEX

USE the document that is open from the previous exercise.

1. Click on any part of the index to select it.
2. On the References tab, in the Index group, click the **Insert Index** button. The Index dialog box appears.
3. Click the **Formats** menu, and select **Simple**.
4. Click **OK**.
5. Word will display a prompt asking if you want to replace the existing index. Click **OK**. The new index is inserted.
6. Scroll to page 4 of the document and locate the entries you marked for the index.
7. In the first *XE* field, double-click *Server* (inside the quotation marks) to select it, as shown in Figure 13-11.

CERTIFICATION READY?
How do you format an index?
1.3.2

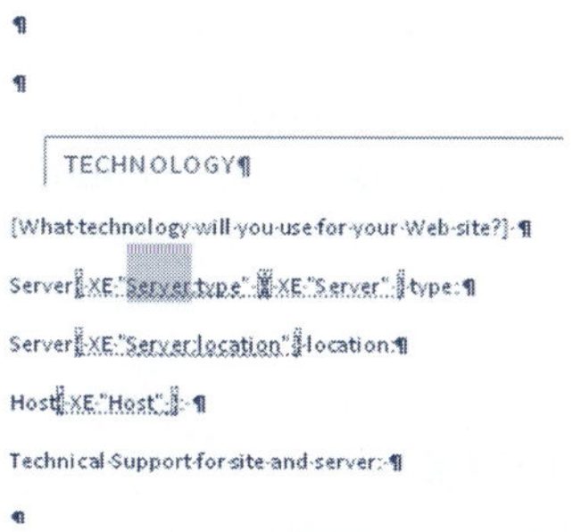
TECHNOLOGY¶
[What·technology·will·you·use·for·your·Web·site?]·¶
Server{·XE·"Server·type"·}{·XE·"Server"·}·type:¶
Server{·XE·"Server·location"·}·location:¶
Host{·XE·"Host"·}·¶
Technical·Support·for·site·and·server:·¶

Figure 13-11
XE field

8. On the Home tab, in the Font group, click the **Bold** button.
9. Within the *XE* field, select the *t* in the word *type* and key an uppercase **T**.
10. On the next line, double-click *Server* (inside the quotation marks) to select it.
11. On the Home tab, in the Font group, click the **Bold** button.
12. Delete the lowercase *l* in *location* and key an uppercase **L**.
13. In the same way, select the *Host* entry and apply bold formatting.
14. Scroll to page 7. Within the *XE* field for the word *database*, select the *d* and key an uppercase **D**. Select the word *Databases* and apply bold formatting.
15. Select the *Shopping Cart* entry and apply bold formatting.
16. **SAVE** the document.

PAUSE. LEAVE the document open to use in the next exercise.

After creating an index, you can reformat it as well as the entries you have marked for it.

As you just practiced, you can select an entire index just by clicking any part of it. Click the Insert Index button to display the Index dialog box, where you can choose a new format or make adjustments to the current format. After you finish making decisions about the format, you will replace the current index with the new one.

To change the format of index entries, you must select the text in quotation marks within the *XE* field in your document. You can use the ribbon or the Mini toolbar to apply formatting changes to the text. The formatting changes will appear in your index after you update it.

TAKE NOTE*

If you want to delete an index entry, select the entire *XE* field, including the braces ({}), and press the **Delete** key.

Updating an Index

You can make changes to index entries even after you have created the index. However, in order for the changes to take effect, you need to update the index.

UPDATE AN INDEX

CERTIFICATION READY?
How do you update an index?
1.3.4

USE the document that is open from the previous exercise.

1. Scroll to the end of the document.
2. Click on any part of the index to select it.
3. On the References tab, in the Index group, click the **Update Index** button. The index is updated.
4. On the Home tab, in the Paragraph group, click the **Show/Hide ¶** button to turn it off.
5. **SAVE** the document and **CLOSE** the file.

   STOP. CLOSE Word.

ANOTHER WAY

You can also press the **F9** key to update an index

After you make changes to an index entry, you need to update the index so that the changes will be applied to your document's index. First, select the index. Then, as you just practiced, click the Update Index button.

SUMMARY SKILL MATRIX

In This Lesson You Learned	Matrix Skill	Skill Number
To create a table of contents from heading styles	Create, modify, and update tables of contents	1.3.1
To add selected text to a table of contents	Create, modify, and update tables of contents	1.3.1
To update a table of contents	Create, modify, and update tables of contents	1.3.1
To mark an entry for an index	Create, modify, and update indexes	1.3.2
To create a subentry and a cross-reference	Create, modify, and update indexes	1.3.2
To create an index	Create, modify, and update indexes	1.3.2
To format an index	Create, modify, and update indexes	1.3.2
To update an index	Create, modify, and update indexes	1.3.2

Knowledge Assessment

Matching

Match the term in Column 1 to its description in Column 2.

Column 1	Column 2
1. table of contents	**a.** enables you to add selected text to a table of contents
2. tab leaders	**b.** a reference to a related part of the document
3. Add Text	**c.** indicates that a word or phrase has been marked for inclusion in the index
4. Update Table	**d.** a subcategory of a main entry
5. index	**e.** symbols that appear between the table of contents topic and the tab set for its page number
6. *XE* field	**f.** a top-level entry in an index
7. subentry	**g.** a command that updates the index so that changes will be applied to the index
8. cross-reference	**h.** updates a table of contents by applying changes that have been made in the document
9. Update Index	**i.** usually located at the beginning of a document, an ordered list of the topics in a document, along with the page numbers on which they are found
10. main entry	**j.** usually located at the end of a document, an alphabetical list of topics in a document, along with the page numbers on which they are found

True / False

Circle T if the statement is true or F if the statement is false.

T | F **1.** A table of contents is usually found at the end of a document.

T | F **2.** The Manual Table of Contents option allows you to create a table of contents on your own.

T | F **3.** You can use a line as a tab leader.

T | F **4.** Only text formatted with a heading style can be included in a table of contents.

T | F **5.** You can choose to update only the page numbers in a table of contents.

T | F **6.** An index is usually located at the beginning of a document.

T | F **7.** Click the Mark All button to have Word mark every occurrence of a selected word in the document.

T | F **8.** To change the format of a marked index entry, you must make changes to the text within the *XE* field.

T | F **9.** An *XE* field is only visible when it is inserted.

T | F **10.** You can select an entire index by clicking any part of it.

Competency Assessment

Project 13-1: Mom's Favorite Recipes

You know that your mom will be sending you more recipes for her cookbook. You decide to create a table of contents using headings in the cookbook, making it easy to update as recipes are added.

CD: The ***momsfavorites1*** document is available on the companion CD-ROM.

GET READY. Launch Word if it is not already running.

1. **OPEN** ***momsfavorites1*** from the data files for this lesson.
2. Scroll to page 3. Select the *Breads* heading and apply the **Heading 1** style to it.
3. Select the *Banana Nut Bread/Chocolate Chip Muffins* heading and apply the **Heading 2** style.
4. Apply the **Heading 2** style to the remaining recipe headings.
5. On page 1, position the insertion point before the *M* in *Main Dishes*.
6. On the References tab, in the Table of Contents group, click the **Table of Contents** button. Select **Automatic Table 1** from the menu.
7. Center *Contents* and apply the **Title** style.
8. Select the table and click the **Update Table** button. Update the page numbers only.
9. **SAVE** the document as ***moms_recipes_toc*** and **CLOSE** the file.

   PAUSE. LEAVE Word open for the next project.

Project 13-2: Index Mom's Favorite Recipes

Add an index to your mom's cookbook.

CD: The ***momsfavorites2*** document is available on the companion CD-ROM.

1. **OPEN** ***momsfavorites2*** from the data files for this lesson.
2. On page 2 in the fourth line of the recipe, select *chicken*.
3. On the References tab, in the Index group, click **Mark Entry**. Click **Mark All**.
4. On page 4, in the last line of the recipe, select *chocolate*. Click the Mark Index Entry dialog box. In the Subentry box, key **mini chips**. Click **Mark**.
5. On page 5, in the second line, select *pumpkin*. Click the Mark Index Entry dialog box. In the Subentry box, key **canned**. Click **Mark**.
6. On page 6, in the last line of the recipe, select *chocolate*. Click the Mark Index Entry dialog box. In the Subentry box, key **mini chips**. Click **Mark**.
7. On page 8, on the ninth line, select *blueberries*. Click the Mark Index Entry dialog box. Click **Mark**.
8. On page 8, in the first line of the last paragraph, select *muffins*. Click the Mark Index Entry dialog box and select the word *muffins* in the Main entry box. Right-click and select Font from the menu. In the Font Style box, click **Regular** and click **OK**. In the Subentry box, key **blueberry**. Click **Mark**.
9. On page 4, in the *Banana Nut Bread/Chocolate Chip Muffins* heading, click to position the insertion point before the *M* in *Muffins*. Click the Mark Index Entry dialog box. Key **muffins** in the Main entry box. In the Subentry box, key **chocolate chip**. Click **Mark**. Click the **Close** button.
10. Move to the end of the document and insert a page break.
11. Key **Index** and format it with the Heading 1 style. Press the **Enter** key.
12. On the References tab, in the Index group, click **Insert Index**. Choose the **Classic** format with **2** columns. Click **OK**.

13. Move to the table of contents at the beginning of the document. Select the entire table of contents and click the **Update Table** button. Choose to update the entire table to include the index you just inserted.
14. **SAVE** the document as ***moms_recipes_index*** and **CLOSE** the file.

PAUSE. LEAVE Word open for the next project.

Proficiency Assessment

Project 13-3: Computer Use Policy

CD

The ***computeruse1*** document is available on the companion CD-ROM.

The First Bank Computer Use Policy document is almost ready for distribution to employees. You decide to create an index for the document.

1. **OPEN** ***computeruse1*** from the data files for this lesson.
2. Find and mark the following words for inclusion in the index.

Location	Word	Action
Section One	e-mail	Mark All
Section Four	Internet	Mark All
Section Five	viruses	Mark All
Section Six	hacking	Mark All
Section Seven	passwords	Mark All
Section Nine	termination	Mark All

3. Insert a page break at the end of the document.
4. Key **Index** and press the Enter key. Apply the **Heading 1** style.
5. Insert the index on the last page using the Simple format with 1 column.
6. **SAVE** the document as ***computer_use_index*** and **CLOSE** the file.

PAUSE. LEAVE Word open for the next project.

Project 13-4: Computer Use Policy Contents

CD

The ***computeruse2*** document is available on the companion CD-ROM.

Add a table of contents to the Computer Use Policy document.

1. **OPEN** ***computeruse2*** from the data files for this lesson.
2. Select the title, *Computer Use Policy*, and apply the **Title** style.
3. Select *Section One* and apply the **Heading 1** style.
4. Select *Purpose* and apply the **Heading 2** style.
5. In the same manner, continue applying the **Heading 1** and **Heading 2** styles to the headings for the remainder of the document.
6. On page 1, position the insertion point before the *C* in *Computer Use Policy* and insert a built-in table of contents using the **Automatic Table 1** style.
7. Update the entire table of contents.
8. **SAVE** the document as ***computer_use_toc*** and **CLOSE** the file.

PAUSE. LEAVE Word open for the next project.

Mastery Assessment

Project 13-5: Web Site Creation Strategy

You need to mark more entries for the Web Site Creation Strategy template, update the index, and update the table of contents to include the index.

CD
The ***websitecreation*** document is available on the companion CD-ROM.

1. **OPEN** ***websitecreation*** from the data files for this lesson.
2. Scroll to the index, located at the end of the document.
3. Find the *XE* fields of the main entries *budget* and *testing*. Capitalize the first letter of the entries and apply bold formatting.
4. On page 8, delete the *Templates* heading and the explanation that follows. You can leave the three blank lines in the document.
5. Update the entire table of contents.
6. Change the index format to Simple with 3 columns.
7. Update the entire index.
8. **SAVE** the document as ***website_creation_completed*** and **CLOSE** the file.

PAUSE. LEAVE Word open for the next project.

Project 13-6: USA Proposal

You need to add a table of contents to the USA Proposal document. However, the document was created without using heading styles and you cannot change the format of the document. Use the Add Text command to create a table of contents.

CD
The ***USAproposal*** document is available on the companion CD-ROM.

1. **OPEN** ***USAproposal*** from the data files for this lesson.
2. Use the Add Text command to create a table of contents with three levels. Level 1 will be the Proposal Description, Level 2 will be the three Options, and Level 3 will be the cities listed under each option.
3. Create a Manual table of contents with dot leaders at the beginning of the document.
4. Update the table of contents as needed.
5. **SAVE** the document as ***USA_proposal_toc*** and **CLOSE** the file.

CLOSE Word.

INTERNET READY

Search the Internet for information about project managers in the computer technology industry. What do they do? What kind of companies do they work for? What are their duties and responsibilities? What kind of work experience or education is needed to become a project manager? What is the salary range for a project manager? Write out the answers to these questions.

Workplace Ready

Creating an Index in Word

As you are working your way through the lessons of this text, you may have need to quickly refer to a specific topic or other useful information found elsewhere within the book. At times such as this, you will likely realize the value of having an index to reference. Although it may appear that this item would be quite time consuming to create, actually the opposite is true. An index for a Word document can be generated with just a few clicks of your mouse.

As a freelance indexer, you contract with companies to compile indexes for various publications. Your work ranges from small projects, including intercompany business documents and directories, to larger projects such as textbooks and other publications. No matter how small or large the job, you find that using Word's index options enables you to quickly and easily compile the most thorough index.

You have contracted to compile an index for a new cookbook. Since the publisher has provided you with a copy of the cookbook as a Word document, you are able to create the index using the options found in Word's Index group. Before you can create the index, you must first mark each word to be included as an entry. Your publisher has asked that only the recipe names be included as main entries within the index. However, Word also provides the ability to include sub-entries and cross-reference information within an index. You can choose to mark just a single instance of a word, or all instances within a document.

Now that you will be using Word to create your indexes, just think of all the extra projects you'll be able to take on in your spare time!

INDEX

Apple Pie, 10
Banana Bread, 1
Banana Cream Pie, 11
Blueberry Quick Bread, 2
Breads, 1
Butter Cake, 5
Cakes, 5
Caramel Pie, 12
Cheesecake, 6
Chocolate Cream Pie, 13
Chocolate Pudding Cake, 7
German Chocolate Cake, 8
Italian Wedding Cake, 9
Lemon Pie, 14
Pecan Pie, 15
Pies, 10
Pumpkin Bread, 3
Pumpkin Pie, 17
Raisin Nut Bread, 4

14

Working with Captions

LESSON SKILL MATRIX

Skills	Matrix Skill	Skill Number
Adding a Caption to a Figure	Insert citations and captions	4.4.2
Adding a Caption to an Equation	Insert citations and captions	4.4.2
Adding a Caption to a Table	Insert citations and captions	4.4.2
Editing and Deleting Captions	Insert citations and captions	4.4.2
Inserting a Table of Figures	Create, modify, and update tables of figures and tables of authorities	4.4.5
Updating a Table of Figures	Create, modify, and update tables of figures and tables of authorities	4.4.5
Deleting a Table of Figures	Create, modify, and update tables of figures and tables of authorities	4.4.5

You are employed at Fabrikam, Inc., a Web development company that creates websites for small businesses. As an information architect, you help design the layout, organization, and flow of each site for optimal end-user experience. One step in this process is to create wireframes—skeletal drawings that provide a visual presentation of the structure of Web pages. You often insert figures and graphics into Word documents when producing client presentations. Therefore, having the ability to label figures and graphics in Word is helpful. In this lesson, you will learn how to add captions to figures or other items, as well as how to delete and edit captions. You will also learn how to insert, update, and delete a table of figures.

KEY TERMS

caption
table of figures

Software Orientation

Caption Dialog Box

When working with captions in a document, you will use the Caption dialog box, shown in Figure 14-1. From here you can select various caption options, including labels and numbering.

Figure 14-1
Caption dialog box

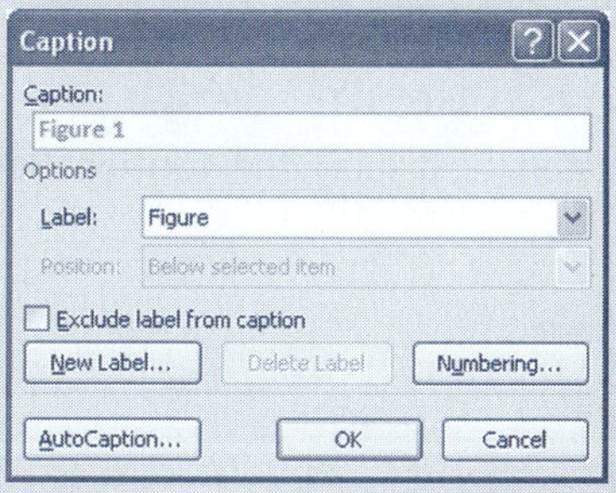

Use this figure as a reference throughout this lesson as well as the rest of this book.

Adding Captions to a Document

THE BOTTOM LINE You can add a numbered label, such as "Figure 1," to a figure, equation, table, or other item by adding a caption. Captions can be added, edited, deleted, or moved.

Adding Captions to a Figure

You can choose to have Word automatically add captions when you insert tables, figures, or other objects into your document or you can manually add captions to items that are already inserted.

ADD CAPTIONS TO A FIGURE

CD The ***Homepage*** figure file is available on the companion CD-ROM.

GET READY. Before you begin these steps, be sure to launch Microsoft Word.

1. **OPEN** a new, blank Word document.
2. On the Insert tab, in the Illustrations group, click the **Picture** button.
3. In the Insert Picture dialog box, navigate to the data files for this lesson, select ***Homepage***, and click **Insert**.

ANOTHER WAY To insert a picture into the document, double-click the name of the file in the Insert Picture box.

CD The ***Portraits*** figure file is available on the companion CD-ROM.

4. Insert a blank line after the picture.
5. On the Insert tab, in the Illustrations group, click the **Picture** button.
6. In the Insert Picture dialog box, navigate to the data files for this lesson, select ***Portraits***, and click **Insert**.

7. Click to select the first picture.
8. On the References tab, in the Captions group, click the **Insert Caption** button to display the Caption dialog box.

ANOTHER WAY Right-click the selected picture and choose Insert Caption from the shortcut menu to display the Caption dialog box.

9. In the Options section, select **Figure** in the Label box and **Above selected item** in the Position box.
10. Click the **Numbering** button to display the Caption Numbering dialog box, as shown in Figure 14-2.

Figure 14-2

Caption Numbering dialog box

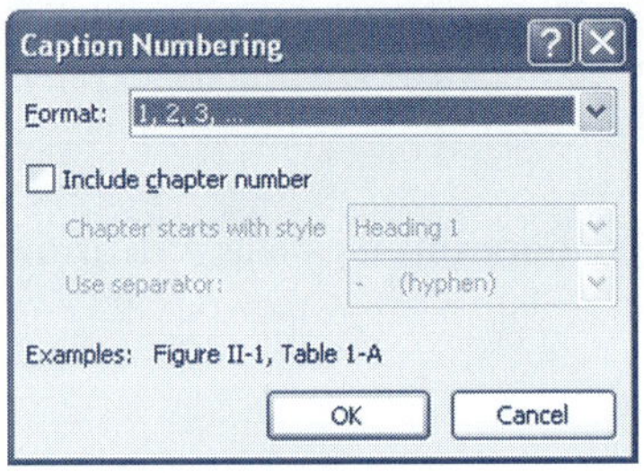

11. In the Format box, select **A, B, C, ...**
12. Click **OK** to close the Caption Numbering dialog box.
13. Click **OK** to close the Caption dialog box and insert the caption, as shown in Figure 14-3.

Figure 14-3

Caption inserted above figure

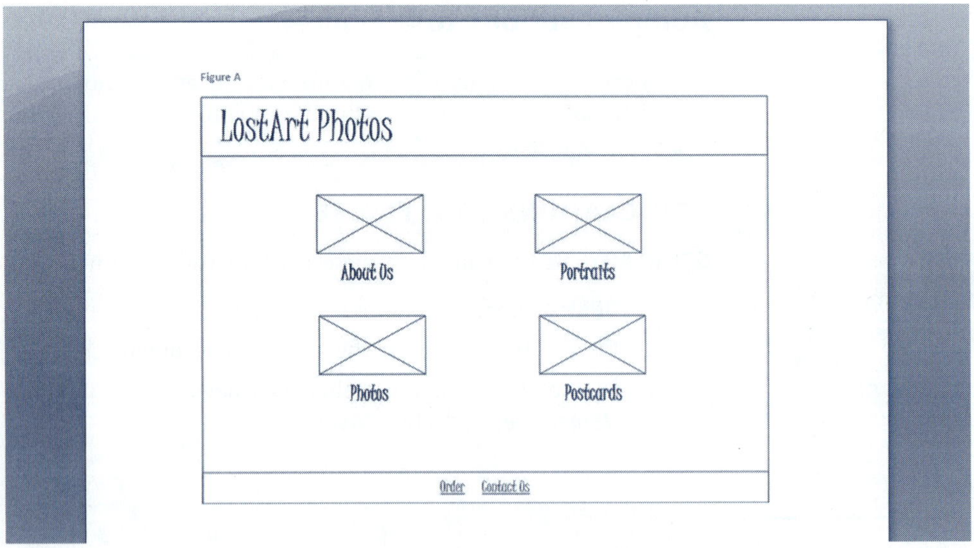

CERTIFICATION READY?
How do you insert citations and captions?
4.4.2

14. Click to select the second picture.
15. On the References tab, in the Captions group, click the **Insert Caption** button to display the Caption dialog box. Notice Word has automatically updated the caption to *Figure B*.
16. Click **OK**.
17. Adjust the document margins as necessary to fit everything on a single page.
18. **SAVE** the document as ***wireframes*** and **CLOSE** the file.

PAUSE. LEAVE Word open to use in the next exercise.

Use the Insert Caption command to add a caption to a figure or other item. A ***caption*** is a line of text that describes an object. For example, "Figure 1: Islands." A caption may appear above or below the object it describes.

In this exercise, you learned how to insert a caption manually. You can also add captions automatically when you insert a figure, table, equation, or other item into a document. In the Caption dialog box, click the AutoCaption . . . button to display the AutoCaption dialog box, shown in Figure 14-4.

Figure 14-4
AutoCaption dialog box

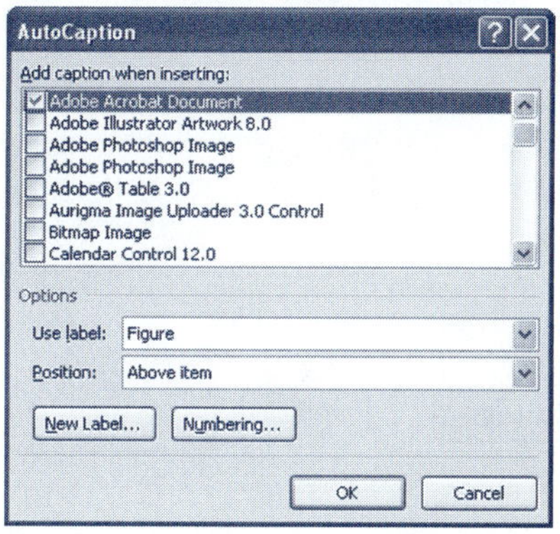

Select the objects for which you want Word to insert captions. Then select the options you want, similar to what you do in the Caption dialog box. Word automatically adds the appropriate caption and a sequential number to each inserted object that you selected. If you want to add more text to a caption, click after a caption and type the additional text.

TROUBLESHOOTING

Word inserts captions as text, but the sequential caption number is inserted as a field. If your caption looks similar to {SEQ Figure * ALPHABETIC}, Word is displaying field codes instead of field results. To see the field results, press **Alt+F9**.

Adding Captions to an Equation

The process for adding a caption to an equation, table, or other item is the same as adding it to a figure. Simply select a different item in the Label list—or create a new label.

ADD CAPTIONS TO AN EQUATION

OPEN a new, blank Word document.

1. On the Insert menu, in the Symbols group, click the downward-pointing arrow next to the **Equation** button to display the menu shown in Figure 14-5.

Figure 14-5

Equation menu

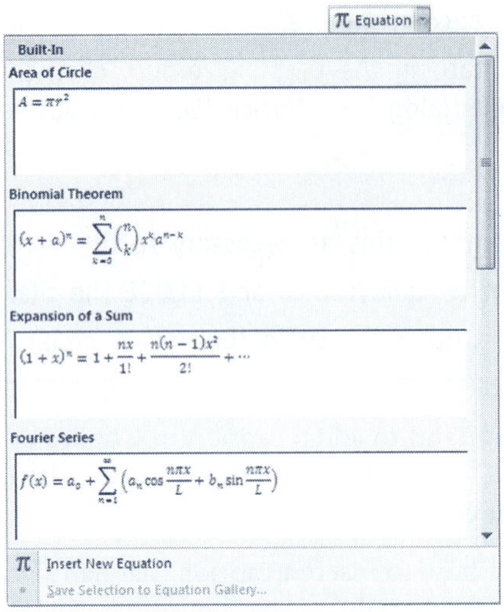

2. Click **Area of a Circle** to insert the equation into the document.
3. Click the downward-pointing arrow on the equation, click **Justification**, and click **Left** on the shortcut menu, as shown in Figure 14-6.

Figure 14-6

Equation shortcut menu

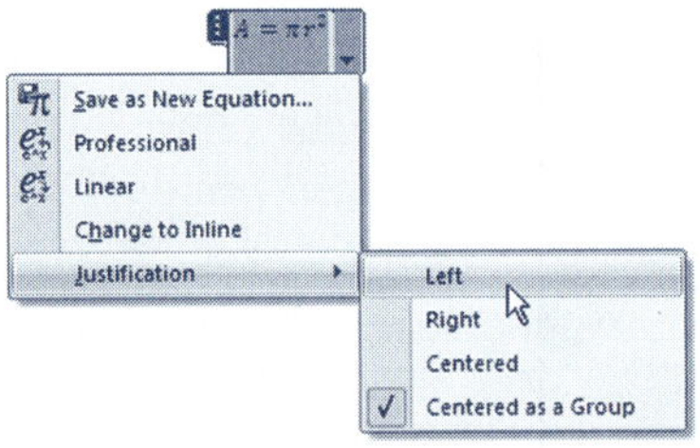

4. Click to select the tab to the left of the equation.
5. On the References tab, in the Captions group, click the **Insert Caption** button to display the Caption dialog box.
6. In the Label box, select **Equation** and in the Position box, select **Below selected item**.
7. Click **OK**.
8. Press **Enter** twice.
9. On the Insert menu, in the Symbols group, click the downward-pointing arrow next to the **Equation** button.
10. Click **Pythagorean Theorem**.
11. Click the tab to the left of the equation to select it.
12. On the References tab, in the Captions group, click the **Insert Caption** button.
13. In the Caption dialog box, click **OK**.
14. **SAVE** the document as ***equations***.

PAUSE. LEAVE the document open to use in the next exercise.

CERTIFICATION READY?
How do you insert citations and captions?
4.4.2

In the Label list of the Caption dialog box, select the label that best describes the object, such as a picture or equation—or create a new label for an item that is not listed. You can have different caption labels and number formats for different types of items—for example, "Table IV" or "Equation 3-A." Select the Exclude label from caption check box if you do not want the label to appear with the caption—for example, only "A" will appear instead of "Figure A."

When you open the Caption dialog box, the previously selected label and numbering format will be displayed along with the next sequential number. For example, if you inserted the caption "Equation 1," the next time you open the Caption dialog box in that document, "Equation 2" will be displayed.

Adding Captions to a Table

Use the same process to add captions to a table as you would for any other object.

ADD CAPTIONS TO A TABLE

USE the document that is open from the previous exercise.

1. Place the insertion point two lines below the second equation.
2. On the Insert menu, in the Tables group, click the **Table** button.
3. On the menu, click Quick Tables and then click **Calendar 1**.
4. On the References tab, in the Captions group, click the **Insert Caption** button to display the Caption dialog box.
5. Click the **New Label** button to display the New Label dialog box, shown in Figure 14-7.

Figure 14-7

New Label dialog box

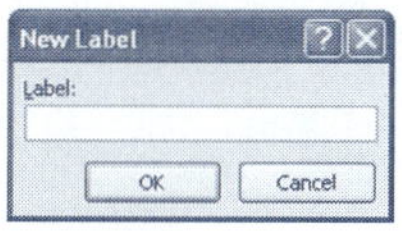

6. In the Label box, key **Calendar**.
7. Click **OK**.
8. In the Position box, select **Above selected item**.
9. Click **OK**.
10. **SAVE** the document as ***equations_calendar*** and **CLOSE** the file.

PAUSE. LEAVE Word open to use in the next exercise.

CERTIFICATION READY?
How do you insert citations and captions?
4.4.2

The process for adding captions to a table is the same as for any other object. If you want to use a label that is not listed, click the New Label button in the Caption dialog box. Key a new label in the New Label box and click OK. This label is now available on the Label list for adding a caption to any object you insert.

To delete a label from the Label list, select the label and click the Delete Label button. If you delete a label from the list, it is no longer available. However, any captions that you inserted using that label will remain.

Editing and Deleting Captions

When a new caption is inserted, Word automatically updates all caption numbers. However, when a caption is moved or deleted, all captions will need to be manually updated.

EDIT AND DELETE CAPTIONS

OPEN the ***wireframes*** document you saved earlier in this lesson.

1. Place your insertion point on the line after the first figure.
2. On the Insert tab, in the Illustrations group, click the **Picture** button.

CD

The ***About_us*** figure file is available on the companion CD-ROM.

3. In the Insert Picture dialog box, navigate to the data files for this lesson, select ***About_us***, and click **Insert**.
4. With the figure selected, on the References tab, in the Captions group, click the **Insert Caption** button to display the Caption dialog box.
5. In the Label box, select **Figure** and in the Position box, select **Above selected item**.
6. Click **OK** to insert the caption. Notice how Word automatically updated the caption numbering so the newly inserted figure is now "Figure B."
7. Select the Figure A caption and the accompanying figure.
8. Press **Delete**. Notice that the remaining figures are not automatically renumbered.
9. Press **Ctrl**+**A** to select the entire document.
10. Right-click the first caption and select **Update Field** from the shortcut menu, shown in Figure 14-8, to renumber the figures.

Figure 14-8

Update Field command

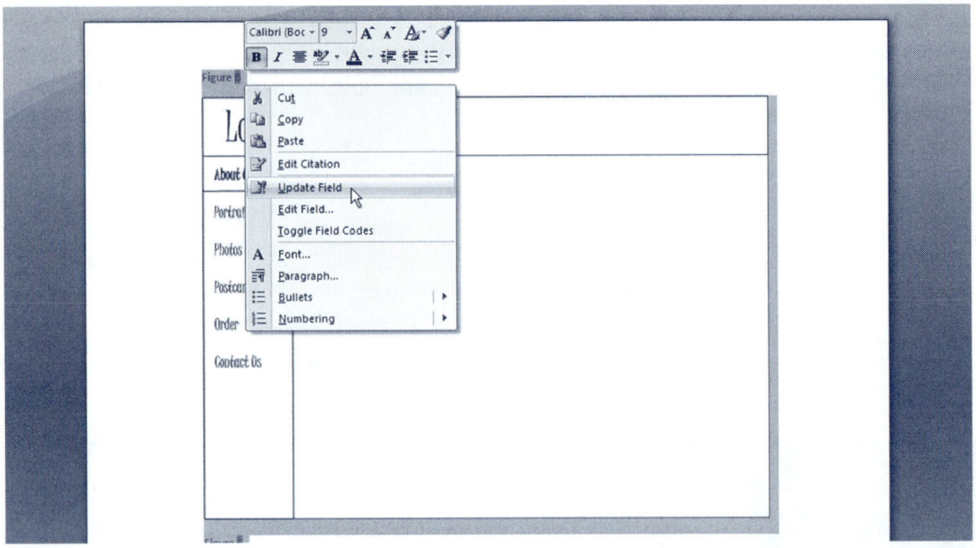

11. Select the Figure B caption and open the Caption dialog box.
12. Click the **Numbering** button.
13. In the Format box, select **I, II, III...** and click **OK**.
14. **SAVE** the document as ***wireframes_update***.

PAUSE. LEAVE the document open to use in the next exercise.

CERTIFICATION READY?
How do you insert citations and captions?
4.4.2

To make changes to a caption—for example, changing "Figure 5" to "Table 5"— open the Caption dialog box and select a different label from the list.

When you add a caption to a document, Word automatically renumbers the others to be sequential. If you delete or move a caption, you can easily update all caption numbers at once. To update all captions after making changes, press Ctrl+A to select the entire document, right-click on a caption, and then click Update Field on the shortcut menu.

Software Orientation

Table of Figures Dialog Box

When you work with a table of figures in a document, you will use the Table of Figures dialog box, shown in Figure 14-9. From here you can preview the table and select formatting and style options.

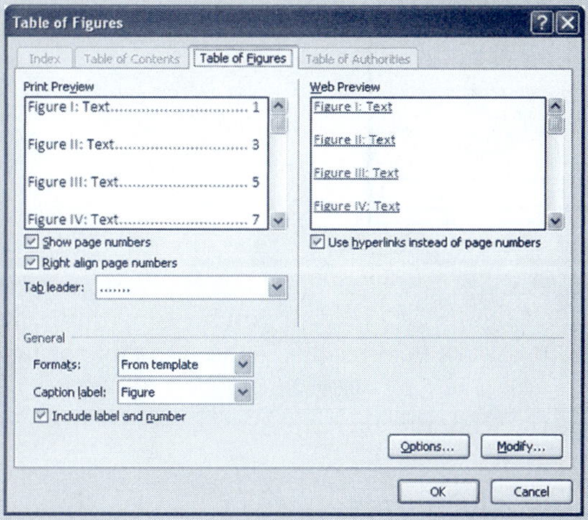

Figure 14-9
Table of Figures dialog box

Use this figure as a reference throughout this lesson as well as the rest of this book.

Creating a Table of Figures

THE BOTTOM LINE When you insert a table of figures, Word searches the document for captions, sorts them by number, and displays them along with the page number each caption appears on.

Inserting a Table of Figures

The Insert Table of Figures command inserts a table of figures at the location of the insertion point in the document.

INSERT A TABLE OF FIGURES

USE the document that is open from the previous exercise.

1. Place the insertion point on a new page at the end of the document.
2. On the References tab, in the Captions group, click the **Insert Table of Figures** button to display the Table of Figures dialog box.
3. In the General section, in the Formats box, select **Simple**.
4. In the Tab Leader box, select the dashed line (---------).
5. Click **OK**. The table of figures is inserted in the document.
6. **SAVE** the document as ***table_of_figures***.

PAUSE. LEAVE the document open to use in the next exercise.

CERTIFICATION READY?
How do you create, modify, and update tables of figures and tables of authorities?
4.4.5

A ***table of figures*** is a list of the captions for all figures, tables, or equations in a document. To insert a table of figures, place the insertion point where you want the table to appear and then choose the Insert Table of Figures command. Choose the type of caption labels to be compiled in the table of figures and select the other options you want.

If you already applied custom styles to your figure captions, you can specify the style settings for Word to use when the table of figures is built. Click the Options button in the Table of Figures dialog box to display the Table of Figures Options dialog box, shown in Figure 14-10.

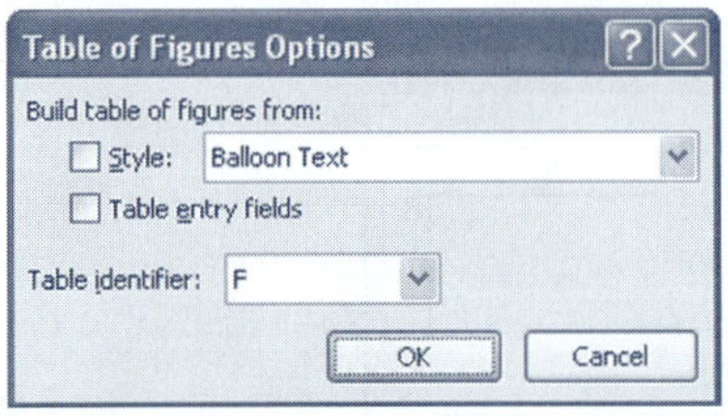

Figure 14-10
Table of Figures Options dialog box

TROUBLESHOOTING

Word inserts a table of figures as a field. If you see something like {TOC}, the field codes are being displayed instead of field results. To see the table of figures, select the entire field and press **Shift+F9**.

Updating a Table of Figures

If you add, delete, move, or edit captions or other text in a document, you should update the table of figures.

UPDATE A TABLE OF FIGURES

USE the document that is open from the previous exercise.

1. Place the insertion point before the Figure II caption.
2. Press Ctrl + Enter to insert a page break.
3. Place the insertion point before the table of figures.
4. Press Ctrl + Enter to insert a page break.
5. Place the insertion point after the Figure I caption and key **: About Us**.
6. Place the insertion point after the Figure II caption and key **: Portraits**.
7. Select the table of figures.
8. On the References tab, in the Captions group, click the **Update Table** button to display the Update Table of Figures dialog box, shown in Figure 14-11.

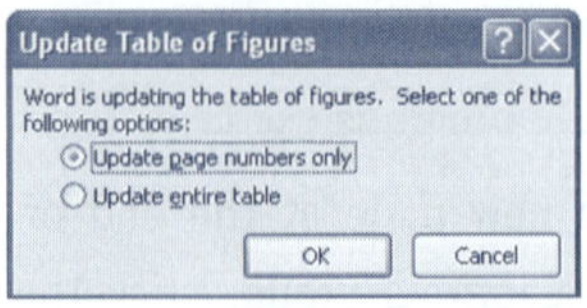

Figure 14-11
Update Table of Figures dialog box

ANOTHER WAY

Right-click the table of figures and choose Update Field from the shortcut menu.

9. Select the **Update entire table** option.
10. Click **OK**. The captions and the page numbers are updated in the table of figures.
11. Place the insertion point in the table of figures and click the **Insert Table of Figures** button.
12. Click the **Modify** button to display the Style dialog box, shown in Figure 14-12.

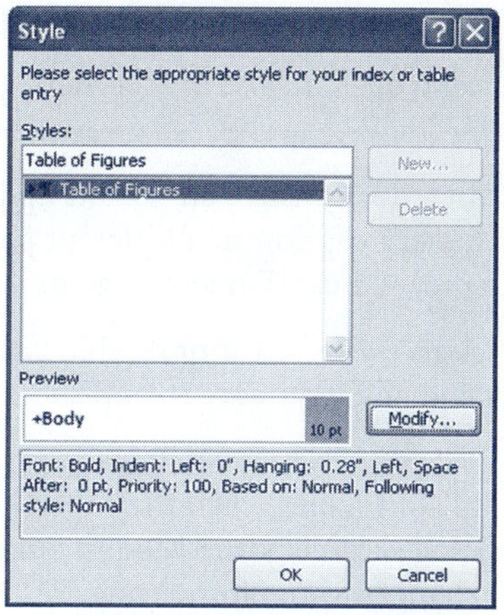

Figure 14-12

Style dialog box

13. Click the **Modify** button to display the Modify Style dialog box, shown in Figure 14-13.

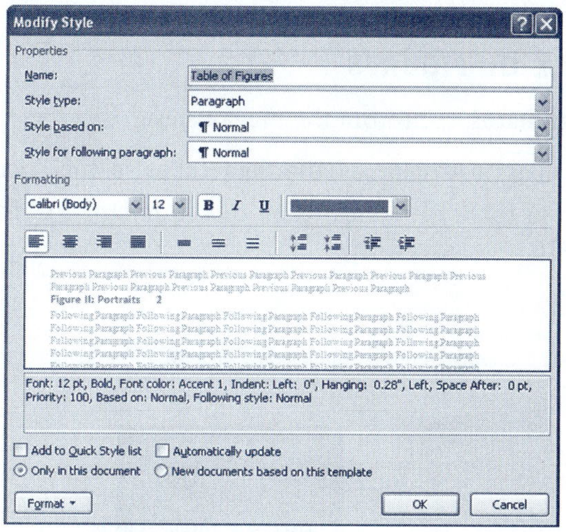

Figure 14-13

Modify Style dialog box

14. In the Formatting section, select font size **12**.
15. In the Font Color box, choose **Blue, Accent 1**.
16. Click **OK** to close the Modify Style dialog box.
17. Click **OK** to close the Style dialog box.
18. Click **OK** to close the Table of Figures dialog box.
19. When a message appears, as shown in Figure 14-14, click **OK**.

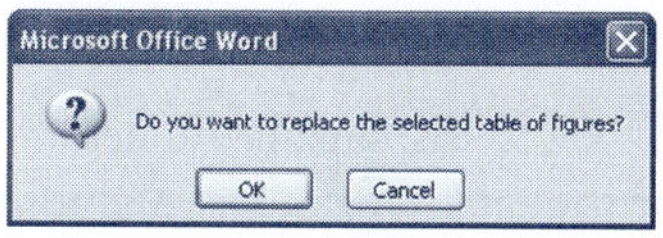

Figure 14-14

Replace table of figures message

20. The format of the table of figures is modified and should now look similar to Figure 14-15.

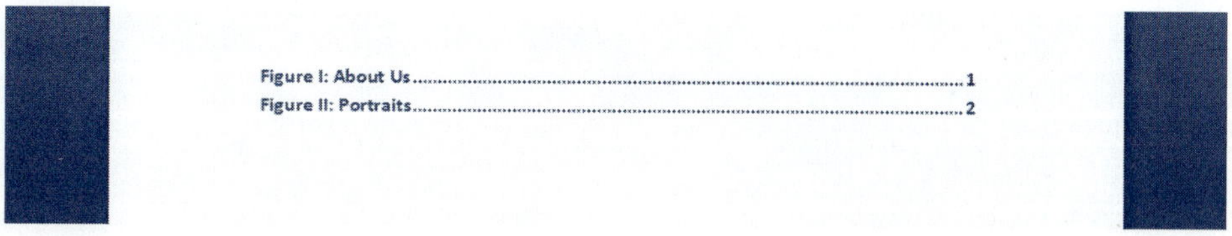

Figure 14-15

Updated table of figures

CERTIFICATION READY?
How do you create, modify, and update tables of figures and tables of authorities?
4.4.5

21. **SAVE** the document as ***updated_figures***.

PAUSE. LEAVE the document open to use in the next exercise.

After making any changes to text in a document, you should update the table of figures. For example, if you edit a caption or move a caption to a different page, you should make sure that the table of figures reflects the revised caption and page number.

To update the table of figures, click to the left of it or double-click to select it. Then press F9. In the Update Table of Figures dialog box, you have the option of updating just page numbers or updating the entire table.

To change the appearance of a Table of Figures, click the Modify button in the Table of Figures dialog box. In the Style dialog box, click the Modify button to open the Modify Style dialog box and make any desired changes to the formatting.

Deleting a Table of Figures

To delete a table of figures, select the table and press Delete.

DELETE A TABLE OF FIGURES

USE the document that is open from the previous exercise.

1. Press Alt + F9 to display all the field codes in the document.
2. To select the table of figures, click to the left of the field code, which is shown in Figure 14-16.

Figure 14-16
Field code for table of figures

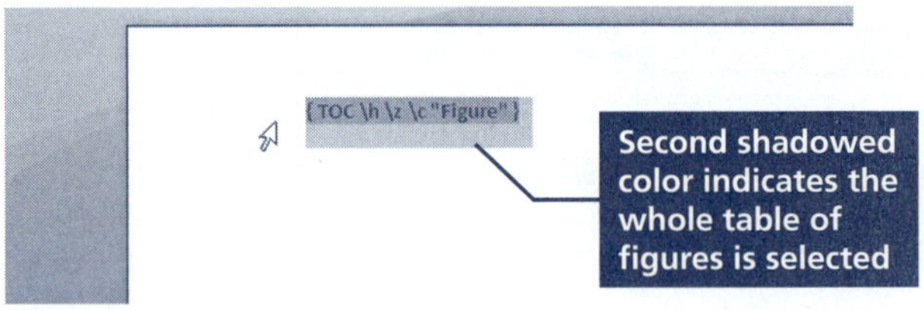

3. Press Delete to delete the table of figures.
4. Press Backspace until the page break is deleted and page 3 is removed.
5. Press Alt + F9 to display all the field results in the document again.
6. **SAVE** the document as ***no_table*** and **CLOSE** the file.

STOP. CLOSE Word.

CERTIFICATION READY?
How do you create, modify, and update tables of figures and tables of authorities?
4.4.5

To delete a table of figures, press Alt+F9 to display all the field codes in the document. Click to the left to select the field code for the table of figures, including the brackets, and then press Delete. Another method is to click and drag to select all of the information in the table of figures and then press Delete.

SUMMARY SKILL MATRIX

In this lesson you learned	Matrix Skill	Skill Number
To add a caption to a figure	Insert citations and captions	4.4.2
To add a caption to an equation	Insert citations and captions	4.4.2
To add a caption to a table	Insert citations and captions	4.4.2
To edit and delete captions	Insert citations and captions	4.4.2
To insert a table of figures	Create, modify, and update tables of figures and tables of authorities	4.4.5
To update a table of figures	Create, modify, and update tables of figures and tables of authorities	4.4.5
To delete a table of figures	Create, modify, and update tables of figures and tables of authorities	4.4.5

Knowledge Assessment

Fill in the Blank

Complete the following sentences by writing the correct word or words in the blanks provided.

1. When working with captions in a document, you use the ______________ dialog box.
2. You can choose to have Word automatically add captions when you ______________ objects into your document.
3. A ______________ is a line of text that appears above or below an object to describe it.
4. Word inserts captions as text, but inserts the sequential caption number as a ______________.
5. To delete a label from the Label list, select the label and click the ______________ button.
6. When a new caption is inserted, Word automatically updates the caption ______________.
7. A ______________ is a list of captions for all figures, tables, or equations in a document.
8. If you edit a caption or move it to a different page, you should ______________ the table of figures.
9. In the Update Table of Figures dialog box, you have the option to update just the ______________ or to update the entire table.
10. To delete a table of figures, click to the left to select the field code, including the brackets, and then press ______________.

Multiple Choice

Select the best response for the following statements.

1. Which of the following is *not* a default option on the Label list?
   a. Figure
   b. Equation
   c. Footnote
   d. Label
2. You can add captions automatically using which dialog box?
   a. AutoLabel
   b. AutoCaption
   c. AutoInsert
   d. AutoAdd
3. Which is an example of excluding a label from a caption?
   a. Figure B
   b. B
   c. Figure B-3
   d. none of the above
4. Which dialog box would you open to use a label that is not listed?
   a. New Caption
   b. Add Caption
   c. Add Label
   d. New Label
5. Where is the table of figures inserted?
   a. at the beginning of the document
   b. at the end of the document
   c. where the insertion point is located
   d. immediately preceding the first figure
6. To update the table of figures, click to the left of the table and press
   a. F9.
   b. Ctrl+Enter.
   c. Ctrl+Tab.
   d. F1.
7. The Captions group appears on which tab?
   a. Home
   b. References
   c. Insert
   d. View
8. If you want to add a caption to an item that does not appear in the Label list, you can
   a. use a text box to create a caption.
   b. insert the caption into a table of figures.
   c. create a new label.
   d. all of the above.

9. When you open the Caption dialog box, the previously selected label and numbering format will be displayed along with
   a. the next sequential number.
   b. a table of figures.
   c. a thumbnail of the object.
   d. an editing toolbar.
10. If a caption is moved or deleted, the remaining captions will need to be
   a. deleted.
   b. manually updated.
   c. inserted into a table of figures.
   d. highlighted.

Competency Assessment

Project 14-1: Historic Homes

You are a volunteer for the local Society for the Preservation of Historic Homes and have compiled a document with thumbnail photos of some of the historic homes. Now you want to label them.

GET READY. Launch Word if it is not already running.

CD
The ***historic*** document is available on the companion CD-ROM.

1. **OPEN** *historic* from the data files for this lesson.
2. Select the first photograph.
3. On the References tab, in the Captions group, click the **Insert Caption** button.
4. Click the **New Label** button.
5. Key **Historic Home**.
6. Click **OK**.
7. In the Position box, choose **Above selected item**.
8. Click **OK**.
9. Select the second photograph.
10. On the References tab, in the Captions group, click the **Insert Caption** button.
11. Click **OK**.
12. Label the rest of the photographs by selecting each one and repeating steps 10 and 11.
13. **SAVE** the document as *historic_homes* and **CLOSE** the file.

PAUSE. LEAVE Word open for the next project.

Project 14-2: House for Sale Clip Art

As the office manager at Tech Terrace real estate, you frequently use clip art to create newsletters, brochures, and flyers of houses for sale. You have compiled some of the clip art into a single document for easy access and now want to add captions.

GET READY. Launch Word if it is not already running.

CD
The ***sale*** document is available on the companion CD-ROM.

1. **OPEN** *sale* from the data files for this lesson.
2. Select the first piece of clip art.
3. On the References tab, in the Captions group, click the **Insert Caption** button.

4. In the Label list, choose **Figure**.
5. In the Position list, choose **Below selected item**.
6. Click the **Numbering** button.
7. In the Format list, choose **1,2,3 ...** .
8. Click **OK**. Click **OK** again.
9. Select the second piece of clip art.
10. On the References tab, in the Captions group, click the **Insert Caption** button.
11. Click **OK**.
12. Label the rest of the clip art by selecting each one and repeating steps 10 and 11.
13. **SAVE** the document as ***sale_clipart***.

PAUSE. LEAVE the document open for the next project.

Proficiency Assessment

Project 14-3: Clip Art Table of Figures

You plan to continue adding clip art to your documents of houses for sale and decide it would be helpful to have a table of figures as a reference.

USE the document that is open from the previous project.

1. Place the insertion point at the beginning of the document.
2. On the References tab, in the Captions group, click the **Insert Table of Figures** button.
3. Select **Figure** as the caption label and the **dots** as the tab leaders.
4. Click the **Modify** button.
5. Click the **Modify** button again.
6. Select **12** as the font size and **Dark Blue, Text 2** as the font color.
7. Click **OK** three times to close the dialog boxes and insert the table of figures.
8. **SAVE** the document as ***clipart_table*** and **CLOSE** the file.

PAUSE. LEAVE Word open for the next project.

Project 14-4: Updating Historic Homes

You want to add a table of figures and update the historic homes document.

1. **OPEN** the ***historic_homes*** document you created in Project 14-1.
2. Place your insertion point at the end of the document.
3. On the References tab, in the Captions group, click the **Insert Table of Figures** button.
4. Select the **dashed line** as the tab leaders.
5. Click **OK**.
6. Place the insertion point between the first and second photograph.
7. On the Insert menu, in the Illustrations group, click **Picture**.
8. Navigate to the data files for this lesson and select ***english_home***.
9. Click **OK**.
10. On the References tab, in the Captions group, click the **Insert Caption** button.
11. Click **OK**.

CD

The ***english_home*** photo file is available on the companion CD-ROM.

12. Select the table of figures.
13. On the Reference tab, in the Captions group, click the **Update Table** button.
14. Select **Update the entire table**.
15. Click **OK**.
16. **SAVE** the document as ***historic_update*** and **CLOSE** the file.

PAUSE. LEAVE Word open for the next project.

Mastery Assessment

Project 14-5: List of Equations

As a mathematics professor, you decide to give your students a list of common mathematical equations for reference. Use Word to create this list with labels.

1. **OPEN** a new, blank Word document.
2. Use the Equation and Insert Caption commands to create the document shown in Figure 14-17.

Figure 14-17

List of equations with labels

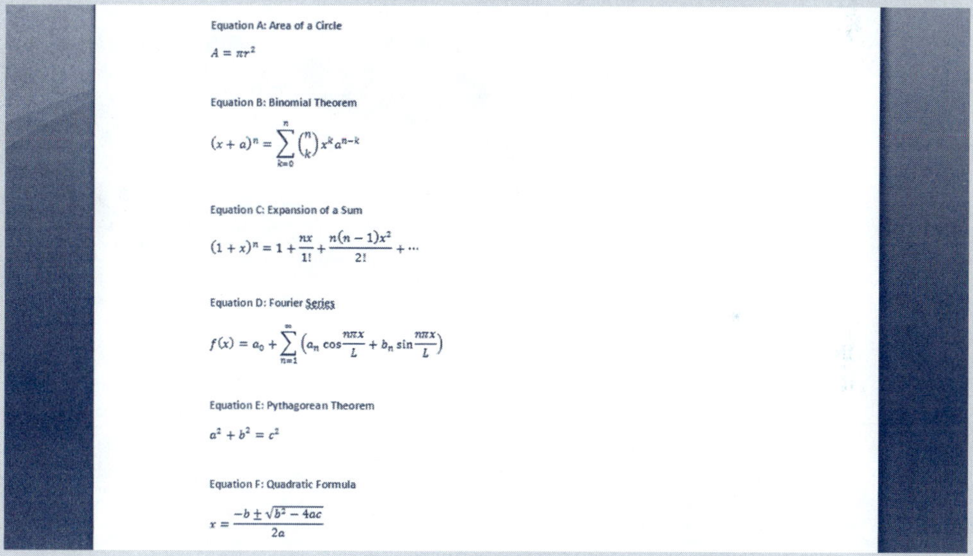

Equation A: Area of a Circle

$$A = \pi r^2$$

Equation B: Binomial Theorem

$$(x+a)^n = \sum_{k=0}^{n} \binom{n}{k} x^k a^{n-k}$$

Equation C: Expansion of a Sum

$$(1+x)^n = 1 + \frac{nx}{1!} + \frac{n(n-1)x^2}{2!} + \cdots$$

Equation D: Fourier Series

$$f(x) = a_0 + \sum_{n=1}^{\infty} \left(a_n \cos\frac{n\pi x}{L} + b_n \sin\frac{n\pi x}{L}\right)$$

Equation E: Pythagorean Theorem

$$a^2 + b^2 = c^2$$

Equation F: Quadratic Formula

$$x = \frac{-b \pm \sqrt{b^2 - 4ac}}{2a}$$

3. **SAVE** the document as ***labeled_equations*** and **CLOSE** the file.

PAUSE. LEAVE Word open for the next project.

Project 14-6: Nature Photos

Your cousin recently went on a nature expedition, where he took several photographs. He tried to place the photographs in a Word document, label them, and add a table of figures, but wasn't familiar with the commands. He asks for your help with editing the document.

CD

The ***nature*** document is available on the companion CD-ROM.

1. **OPEN** ***nature*** from the data files for this lesson.
2. Edit the document with the following specifications:
   - Each photo has a caption with the label "Photo" and the numbering "A,B,C . . ."
   - The caption appears at the top of each photo.
   - The photos all fit on two pages.
   - A table of figures appears on page 3 with an underline as a tab leader.

3. **SAVE** the document as ***nature_photos*** and **CLOSE** the file.

STOP and **CLOSE** Word.

INTERNET READY

Microsoft has numerous online resources available to provide solutions, services, and support for whatever business needs you may have. If you are in small business, a helpful site is the Microsoft Small Business Center. Here, you can find advice, products, tools, and information tailored to small businesses. Search the Microsoft site for the Small Business Center, shown in Figure 14-18.

Explore the resources offered on the site. In the Articles & Research section, choose a topic about which you would like to know more. Read an article that interests you and write a brief summary of what you learned.

Figure 14-18

Microsoft Small Business Center

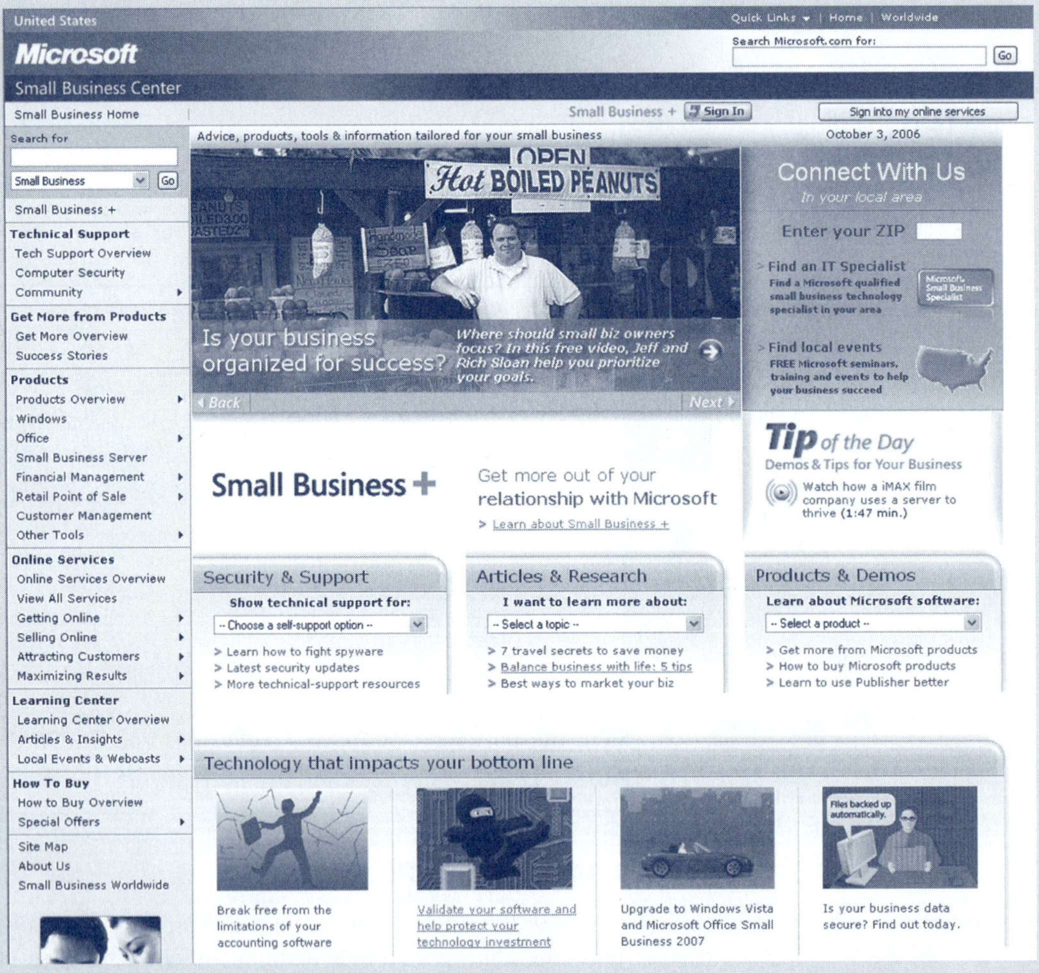

Workplace Ready

Organizing Figures in Word

By now, you realize that you can insert a variety of images into a Word document. From photographs to clipart, Word provides the tools you need to organize and identify these figures.

You have been hired as a photographer by Contoso, Ltd., a wholesale landscape supplier, to provide pictures for their Fall perennial sales brochure. Contoso, Ltd. is the Midwest's largest supplier of perennial plants. They are producing a sales brochure that will be sent to all current clients, as well as to potential clients, as a means of soliciting pre-season orders for shipment next spring.

As you begin photographing the different varieties of perennials that Contoso, Ltd. offers, you realize that many of the plants look quite similar. You decide that you need to keep a good record of each perennial's name for future reference. After inserting your photographs into a Word document, you find that adding a caption to each figure is a great way to identify the perennials. Word automatically includes a figure number with each caption, but you could easily remove this if needed. You decide to keep the figure numbers as part of each caption.

Once you have compiled all of your photographs and added the appropriate captions, you use Word's Table of Figures option to create a list of all figure captions. The list of captions, which is sorted by number, also includes the page number for each figure. This will be a handy reference tool when it comes time to add the photographs into the sales brochure.

Whether you're creating a sales brochure, a training manual or a family photo album, Word can not only help you identify your figures, but also keep them organized.

Figure 1 White Phlox

Figure 2 Purple Snowcone

Figure 3 Shasta Daisy

Figure 4 Pink Daylily

15 Adding Citations, Sources, and a Bibliography

LESSON SKILL MATRIX

Skills	Matrix Skill	Skill Number
Inserting a Citation	Insert citations and captions	4.4.2
Creating a Source	Create and modify sources	4.4.1
Applying a Style to a Citation	Select reference styles	4.4.4
Changing a Citation	Insert citations and captions	4.4.2
Modify a Source	Create and modify sources	4.4.1
Removing a Citation	Insert citations and captions	4.4.2
Inserting a Bibliography	Insert and modify bibliographies	4.4.3
Updating a Bibliography	Insert and modify bibliographies	4.4.3
Deleting a Bibliography	Insert and modify bibliographies	4.4.3

You are working a full-time job at Northwind Traders and taking night courses at the local college to finish your degree. Your history professor has assigned a research paper that is due next week. In this lesson, you will use Word's references commands to create a paper with citations, sources, and a bibliography that follows the specific reference style you need.

KEY TERMS
bibliography
citation
source

Adding Citations and Sources to a Document

THE BOTTOM LINE

When writing research papers, articles, or reports that analyze or describe research you have completed on a topic, you need to include sources in your documents, citing where the information originated. When you cite a source, you do so at the relevant place within the text. Word enables you to insert a citation and create a source at the same time. You can also easily modify citations and sources, or delete them, when necessary.

Inserting a Citation and Creating a Source

When you insert a citation, Word enables you to add the source information at the same time.

INSERT A CITATION AND CREATE A SOURCE

CD

The ***firstladies*** document is available on the companion CD-ROM.

GET READY. Before you begin these steps, be sure to launch Microsoft Word and **OPEN** the *firstladies* document from the data files for this lesson.

1. In the second paragraph, position the insertion point after *Meringolo*.
2. On the References tab, in the Citations & Bibliography group, click the **Insert Citation** button. A menu appears, as shown in Figure 15-1.

Figure 15-1

Insert Citation button and menu

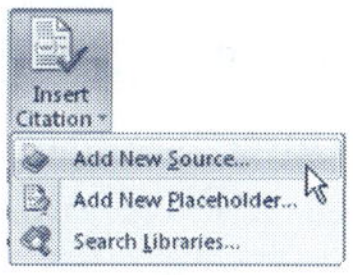

3. Select **Add New Source**. The Create Source dialog box appears.
4. If necessary, select **Book** from the Type of Source menu.
5. In the lower left corner, click the **Show All Bibliography Fields** box.
6. Key the source information that is shown in Figure 15-2.

Figure 15-2

Create Source dialog box

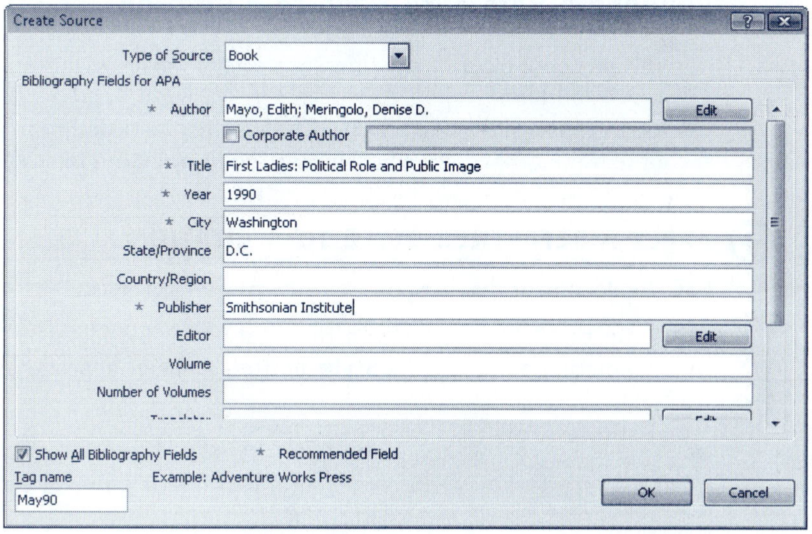

CERTIFICATION READY?
How do you insert a citation?
4.4.2

CERTIFICATION READY?
How do you create a source?
4.4.1

7. Click **OK**. The citation is added to the text and the source information is saved.
8. **SAVE** your document as *role_of_first_ladies*.

PAUSE. LEAVE the document open to use in the next exercise.

A ***citation*** is a note mentioning the source of information, as shown in Figure 15-3.

Figure 15-3

Citation

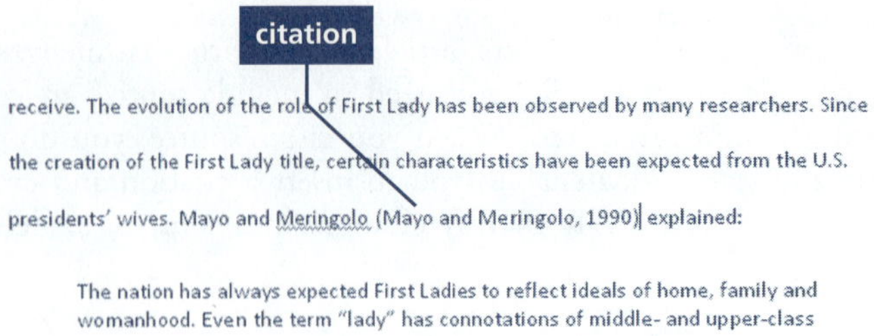

A ***source*** is the work, such as a book, report, or website, that supplied the information you used in the creation of your document.

When you add a new citation to a document, you also create a new source that will appear in the bibliography. A ***bibliography*** is a list of sources, usually placed at the end of a document, that you consulted while creating your document.

The Create Source dialog box contains fields for each part of a source, including the author, title, year of copyright, city where publisher is located, and publisher. When you have more information to include about a source, such as specifying the state/province field as you did in the previous exercise, click the Show All Bibliography Fields box to display additional fields.

Each time you create a new source in any document, the information is saved on your computer in a master list, so that you can find and use any source previously used. Word also creates a current list, which contains all sources within your current document.

When you do not have all the information for a source, you can insert a placeholder that can be filled in later. To add a placeholder, click Add New Placeholder on the Insert Citation menu.

Another useful command on the Insert Citation menu is the Search Libraries command. This option can be used to find additional sources, or additional information about sources that you are citing. For example, you can search a library database for every match of a particular topic in that library's collection. Then, you can insert the citation in the document, or you can add the source information to the current list of sources for later use.

Applying a Reference Style to a Citation

You can choose from many different reference styles when formatting your citations, sources, and bibliography. American Physcological Association (APA) and Modern Language Association (MLA) are perhaps the most common. Word enables you to choose from a list of styles and inserts the information in the correct format for you.

APPLY A REFERENCE STYLE TO A CITATION

USE the document that is open from the previous exercise.

1. On the References tab, in the Citations & Bibliography group, click the downward-pointing arrow on the **Style** button. A menu appears, as shown in Figure 15-4.

Figure 15-4

Style menu

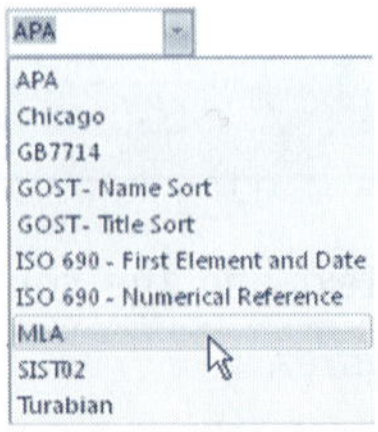

CERTIFICATION READY?
How do you apply a style to a citation?
4.4.4

2. Select **MLA**. The citation style is changed.
3. In the fourth paragraph, click to position the insertion point at the end of the second sentence following the word *speech*.
4. On the References tab, in the Citations & Bibliography group, click the **Insert Citation** button and select **Add New Source**.
5. In the Type of Source menu, select **Book**.
6. Key the source information for MLA style in the dialog box, as shown in Figure 15-5. Please note that the last word of the title, *House*, is cut off in the figure. Be sure to key the entire word.

Figure 15-5
MLA style source Information

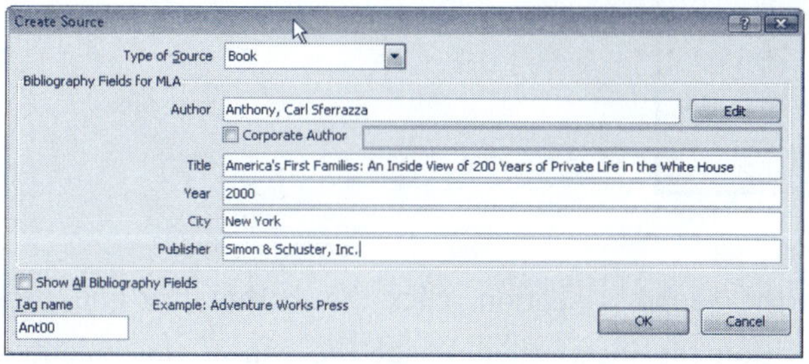

7. Click **OK**. The citation is inserted.
8. **SAVE** the document.

PAUSE. LEAVE the document open to use in the next exercise.

When you changed the reference style in the previous exercise, the new style was applied to the citations already in your document. And, the new style was used in the citations you created afterwards.

Modifying a Citation and a Source

Sometimes you need to edit previously created citations and sources. Word makes this easy by providing menus on the citation placeholders, allowing you easy access to dialog boxes used to modify citations and sources.

MODIFY A CITATION AND A SOURCE

USE the document that is open from the previous exercise.

1. At the end of the second paragraph, click on the first citation you inserted. The citation is selected and the blue placeholder around the citation appears.
2. Click the downward-pointing arrow to display a menu, as shown in Figure 15-6.

Figure 15-6
Citation placeholder and menu

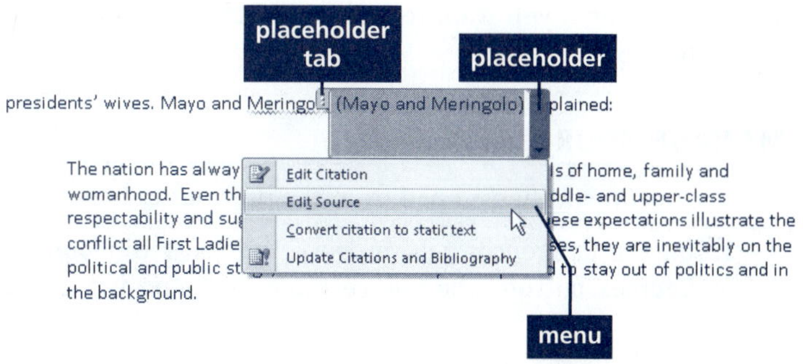

3. Select **Edit Source** from the menu. The Edit Source dialog box appears.
4. In the Year field, delete the last *0* in 1990 and key a **4** to change the year of publication to 1994.
5. Click **OK**. Word displays a prompt asking if you want to apply the changes to your master list and the current document. Click **Yes**.
6. Click the downward-pointing arrow on the placeholder again and select **Edit Citation**. The Edit Citation dialog box appears, as shown in Figure 15-7.

Figure 15-7

Edit Citation dialog box

7. In the Suppress section, click the **Author** box and click **OK**.
8. Position the insertion point at the end of the indented third paragraph, after the word *background*.
9. On the References tab, in the Citations & Bibliography group, click **Insert Citation**. The menu lists two sources that you have cited in the current document. This is your current list. Select the Mayo, Edith citation. The citation is inserted.
10. Click the citation. Click the downward-pointing arrow to display the citation options and select **Edit Citation**.
11. In the Add section, key **p. 8** and in the Suppress section, click **Author** and **Title**. Click **OK**.
12. **SAVE** the document.

PAUSE. LEAVE the document open to use in the next exercise.

CERTIFICATION READY?
How do you modify a citation?
4.4.2

CERTIFICATION READY?
How do you modify a source?
4.4.1

When you insert a citation, Word inserts it into your document inside a placeholder. You can easily modify the text within the placeholder or the source or citation data that goes along with it.

You can select the entire placeholder by clicking the small tab in the top left corner of the placeholder. Each citation placeholder also has a downward-pointing arrow at the bottom that, when clicked, displays a menu of editing choices for sources and citations.

The Edit Citation dialog box enables you to add page numbers specifying the source's page or pages to which you are referring. You can also make decisions about what to display within the citation text. You can suppress—or choose not to display—the title, year, or author.

The Edit Source dialog box appears, filled with the information you keyed earlier about the source. You can change any information in the dialog box and click OK. Word will display a prompt asking if you want to make these changes in the current document as well as the master list.

MANAGE SOURCES

USE the document that is open from the previous exercise.

1. On the References tab, in the Citations & Bibliography group, click the **Manage Sources** button. The Source Manager dialog box appears, as shown in Figure 15-8.

Figure 15-8

Source Manager

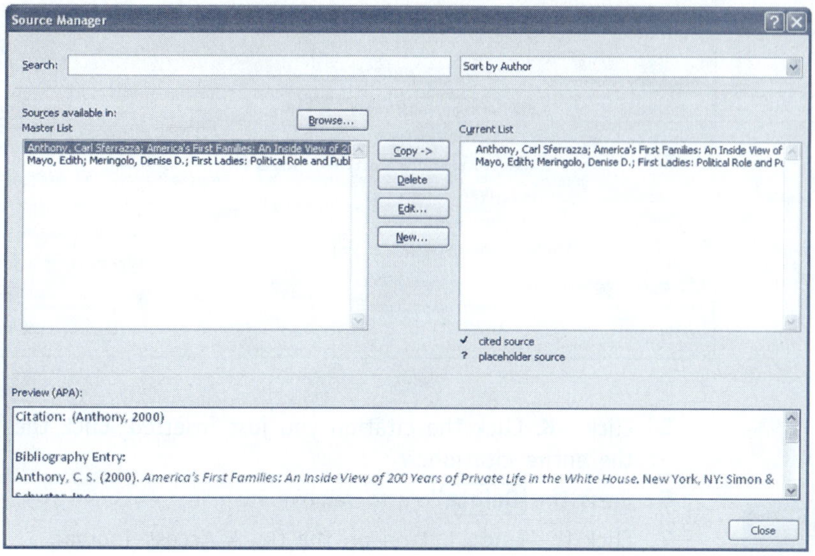

2. In the Master List section, select the Mayo and Meringolo source.
3. Click the **Edit** button. The Edit Source dialog box appears.
4. Click the **Show All Bibliography Fields** box. The Edit Source dialog box expands to include additional fields.
5. Key **NY** in the State/Province field and click **OK**.
6. Word displays a prompt asking if you want to apply the changes to your master list and the current document. Click **Yes**.
7. Click the **Close** button.
8. **SAVE** the document.

PAUSE. LEAVE the document open to use in the next exercise.

The Source Manager displays all the sources you have created and provides options for their management. The Source Manager displays two lists: the master list, which contains all the sources for all the documents you have created using Word, and the current list, which includes all sources you have created in the current document. The Source Manager enables you to manage these sources by sorting, moving, copying, deleting, or creating sources.

In the previous exercise, you edited a source by selecting it and clicking the Edit button. Word displayed the Edit Source dialog box, where you made changes.

Removing a Citation

You can remove a citation from your document without removing the source data. The source data remains saved in the current document list and in the master list. So, if you decide you need to cite that source in another location, you can choose it from the Insert Citation menu.

REMOVE A CITATION

USE the document that is open from the previous exercise.

1. In the fourth paragraph, third sentence, position the insertion point after *Anthony*.
2. On the References tab, in the Citations & Bibliography group, click the **Insert Citation** button. Select **Add New Source**.
3. On the Type of Source menu, select **Book**.
4. Key the source information that is shown in Figure 15-9.

Figure 15-9

Create Source dialog box

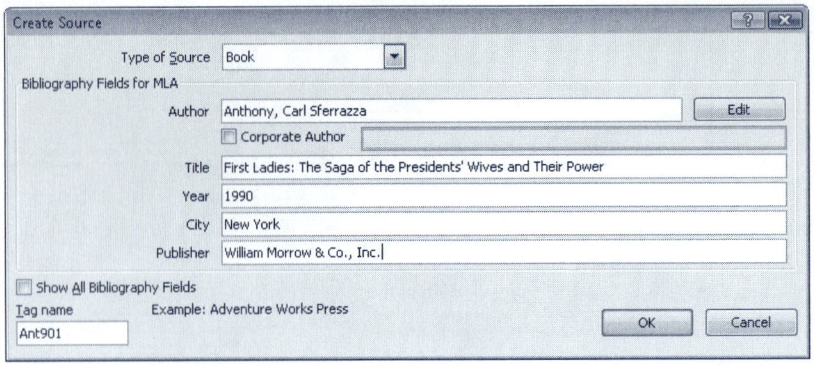

5. Click **OK**. Click the citation you just inserted. Click the placeholder tab to select the entire citation.
6. Press the **Delete** key to remove it.
7. Click the **Undo** button on the Quick Access Toolbar.
8. **SAVE** the document.

PAUSE. LEAVE the document open to use in the next exercise.

CERTIFICATION READY?
How do you remove a citation?
4.4.2

You just deleted a citation from the document. By clicking the placeholder tab, you can select the entire citation and then press the Delete key to remove it. If you change your mind, remember, you can always click the Undo button to bring it back.

ANOTHER WAY

You can remove a source from the master or current list, and from the bibliography, by selecting the source in Source Manager and clicking the Delete button.

■ Creating a Bibliography

NEW FEATURE

THE BOTTOM LINE

Word provides a gallery of bibliographies from which to choose. You can choose to insert a bibliography at the end of the document or create a new page for the bibliography. After you insert the bibliography, you can update it as you add or delete sources. You can also easily remove a bibliography.

Creating a Bibliography

Word enables you to create a bibliography using the sources you inserted with the document's citations. You can create a bibliography after at least one source has been entered.

CREATE A BIBLIOGRAPHY

USE the document that is open from the previous exercise.

1. Scroll to the end of the document and position the insertion point after the last sentence of the document. Press the **Enter** key.
2. On the References tab, in the Citations & Bibliography group, click the **Bibliography** button. A menu of built-in bibliography styles appears, as shown in Figure 15-10.

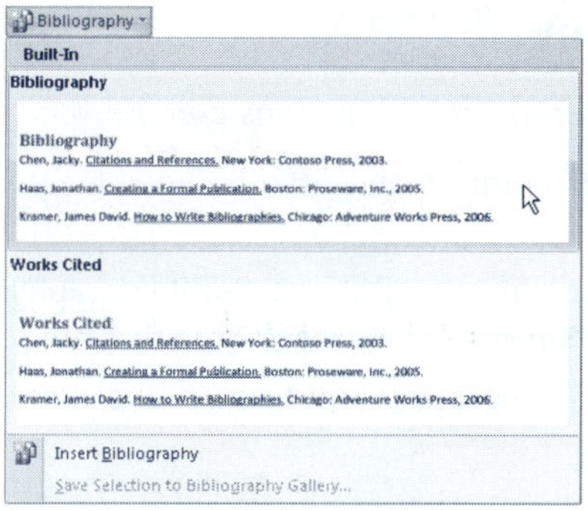

Figure 15-10

Bibliography button and menu

3. Select the **Bibliography** style. The bibliography is inserted on a new page, as shown in Figure 15-11.

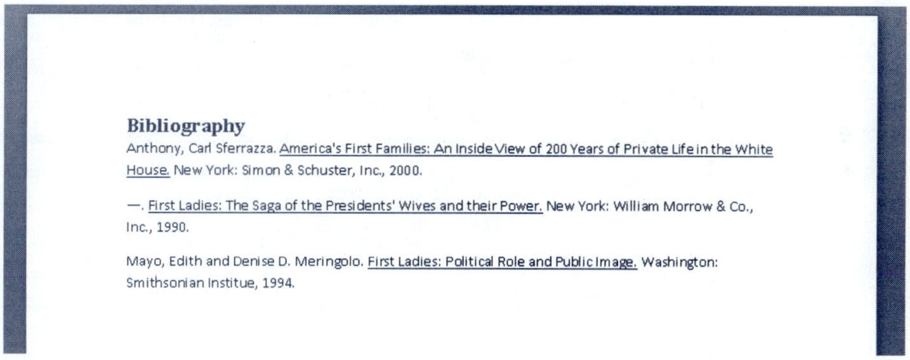

Figure 15-11

Bibliography

4. **SAVE** the document.

   PAUSE. LEAVE the document open to use in the next exercise.

Word enables you to automatically generate a bibliography based on source information you provided for a document.

The Bibliography button displays a menu of built-in bibliography formats. You can choose to insert an automatic bibliography at the end of the document or on a new page. You can also choose a works cited format at the end of the last page or on a new page.

The Insert Bibliography command inserts a bibliography without a title.

If you create a custom bibliography style that you would like to keep available for future use, you can select the entire bibliography and add it to the bibliography gallery by clicking the Bibliography menu and selecting the Save Selection to Bibliography Gallery command.

The Save Selection to Bibliography Gallery command enables you to save a bibliography as a new Building Block.

CERTIFICATION READY?
How do you insert a bibliography?
4.4.3

Updating a Bibliography

After adding new sources or modifying sources, you need to update the bibliography to reflect the changes or additions you have made.

UPDATE A BIBLIOGRAPHY

USE the document that is open from the previous exercise.

1. Position the insertion point in the fifth paragraph, at the beginning of the fifth sentence, after the word *Gutin*.
2. On the References tab, in the Citations & Bibliography group, click **Insert Citation** and select **Add New Source**. The Create Source dialog box appears.
3. Click the **Show All Bibliography Fields** box. The dialog box expands to include more fields.
4. Key the source information that is shown in Figure 15-12.

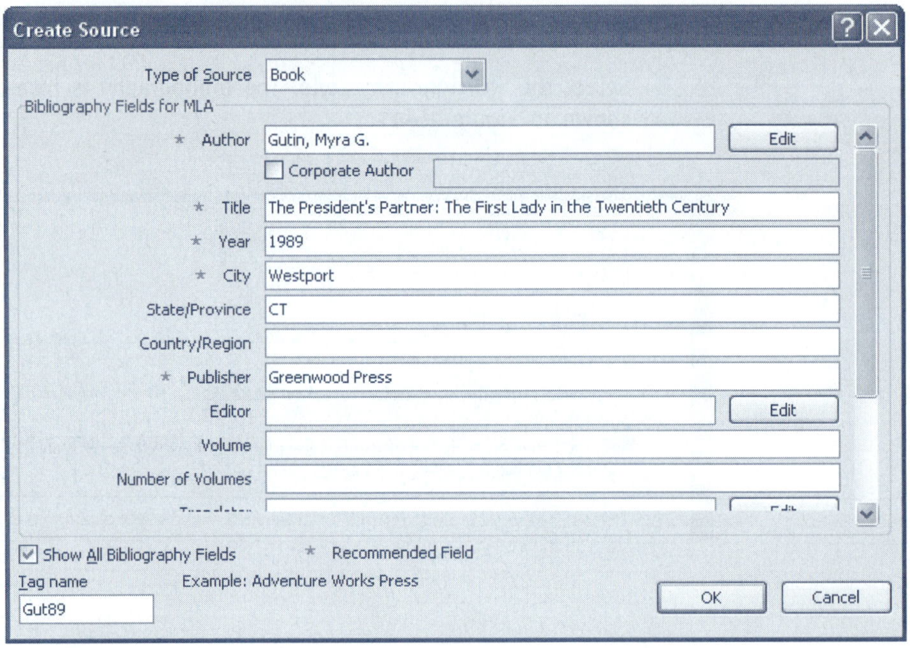

Figure 15-12

Gutin Source - Create Source dialog box

5. Click **OK**. The citation is inserted.
6. Scroll to the bibliography. Click anywhere in the bibliography to select it.
7. Click the right mouse button. A shortcut menu appears.
8. Select **Update Field** from the menu, as shown in Figure 15-13. The bibliography is updated.

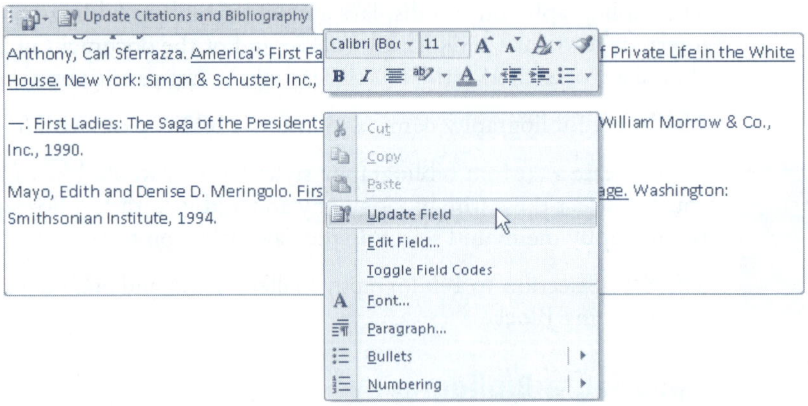

Figure 15-13

Update Field command on the shortcut menu

9. **SAVE** the document.

PAUSE. LEAVE the document open to use in the next exercise.

CERTIFICATION READY?
How do you modify a bibliography?
4.4.3

Word inserts a bibliography within a placeholder, similar to the way it inserts citations. Thus, you can select the bibliography using the placeholder tab.

In the previous exercise, you updated the bibliography by updating the field. Word uses hidden fields in the placeholders to compile your source data into a bibliography. To update the bibliography, you need to update the field. Just select the placeholder and right-click to display the shortcut menu, then select Update Field.

When you delete or make a change in the Source Manager, the bibliography is automatically updated when you close the Source Manager dialog box.

You can change the formatting of a bibliography by selecting the text you want to format and then choosing formatting commands on the Home tab or on the Mini toolbar.

ANOTHER WAY You can also update a bibliography by clicking the Update Citations and Bibliography button on the placeholder.

Deleting a Bibliography

You can easily delete a bibliography. However, remember that the source information is still saved with the current document, as well as within Word's master list.

DELETE A BIBLIOGRAPHY

CERTIFICATION READY? How do you delete a bibliography? 4.4.3

USE the document that is open from the previous exercise.

1. Click the placeholder tab beside the word *Bibliography* to select the entire bibliography. Click it again to select the inner placeholder for the source list.
2. Press the **Delete** key. The bibliography is deleted.
3. Click the **Undo** button on the Quick Access Toolbar.
4. **SAVE** the document and **CLOSE** the file.

STOP. **CLOSE** Word.

When Word inserts a bibliography, a placeholder is inserted within another placeholder. The outer placeholder includes the title of the bibliography, and the inner placeholder holds the source list. You can delete either the inner placeholder or both of the placeholders. When you want to delete only the source data, click its placeholder tab and press the Delete key. When you want to delete the entire bibliography, click the placeholder tab next to the title and press the Delete key.

SUMMARY SKILL MATRIX

In This Lesson You Learned	Matrix Skill	Skill Number
To insert a citation	Insert citations and captions	4.4.2
To create a source	Create and modify sources	4.4.1
To apply a style to a citation	Select reference styles	4.4.4
To change a citation	Insert citations and captions	4.4.2
To modify a source	Create and modify sources	4.4.1
To remove a citation	Insert citations and captions	4.4.2
To insert a bibliography	Insert and modify bibliographies	4.4.3
To update a bibliography	Insert and modify bibliographies	4.4.3
To delete a bibliography	Insert and modify bibliographies	4.4.3

Knowledge Assessment

Matching

Match the term in Column 1 to its description in Column 2.

Column 1	Column 2
1. citation	**a.** used to select an entire placeholder
2. source	**b.** where source information is stored
3. bibliography	**c.** displays all the sources you have created and gives you options for managing them
4. placeholder tab	**d.** command used to update a bibliography
5. reference style	**e.** style for formatting citations, sources, and a bibliography, such as MLA or APA
6. master list	**f.** a list of sources, usually placed at the end of a document, that you consulted while creating a document
7. type of source	**g.** a list of the sources you have entered for the current document
8. Source Manager	**h.** the work, such as a book, report, or web site, which supplied you with information for creating your document
9. current list	**i.** the type of work you are referencing, including books, websites, reports, and journals
10. Update field	**j.** a note mentioning the source of information

True / False

Circle T if the statement is true or F if the statement is false.

T | F **1.** MLA is an example of a source.

T | F **2.** You can delete a citation by selecting its placeholder and pressing the Delete key.

T | F **3.** Citations appear in the bibliography.

T | F **4.** When you change the reference style, you need to update all the citations in the document.

T | F **5.** You can add page numbers to a citation.

T | F **6.** Each citation placeholder has a downward-pointing arrow that when clicked, displays a menu of choices for editing sources and citations.

T | F **7.** Bibliographies always start on a new page.

T | F **8.** Sources are saved in a master list on your computer.

T | F **9.** When you delete a bibliography, you also delete the sources in it.

T | F **10.** When Word inserts a bibliography, it inserts a placeholder within a placeholder.

Competency Assessment

Project 15-1: Health Benefits Paper

You are director of customer relations for Coho Winery & Vineyard, but you are also a graduate student at a local university studying oenology, the study of wine. As part of your course work, you are required to conduct and write research on various related topics. You are writing one now and are at the point where you need to edit and insert citations and sources for the document.

CD

The ***healthbenefits*** document is available on the companion CD-ROM.

GET READY. Launch Word if it is not already running.

1. **OPEN** ***healthbenefits*** from the data files for this lesson.
2. Select the citation at the end of the first paragraph. Click the downward-pointing arrow to display the citations options nd select **Edit Source**.
3. In the Name of Web Page field, key **Red Wine and Your Heart** and click **OK**.
4. Select the citation at the end of the second paragraph. Click the downward-pointing arrow to display the menu and select **Edit Source**.
5. In the Name of Web Site field, key **Wikipedia: The Free Encyclopedia** and click **OK**.
6. Select the Stuttaford citation at the end of the fourth paragraph. Click the downward-pointing arrow to display the menu and select **Edit Source**.
7. Delete the text in the Name of Web Page field and key **Is Red Wine Good for You?**
8. In the Name of Web Site field, key **Healthspan**.
9. In the Year field, key **2005**.
10. In the Month field, key **May**. Then click **OK**.
11. In the second to last paragraph, position the insertion point after the quotation mark following the word *meal*.
12. On the References tab, in the Citations & Bibliography group, click **Insert Citation** and select **Add New Source**. The Create Source dialog box appears.
13. Key the source data that is shown in Figure 15-14.

Figure 15-14

Add new source data

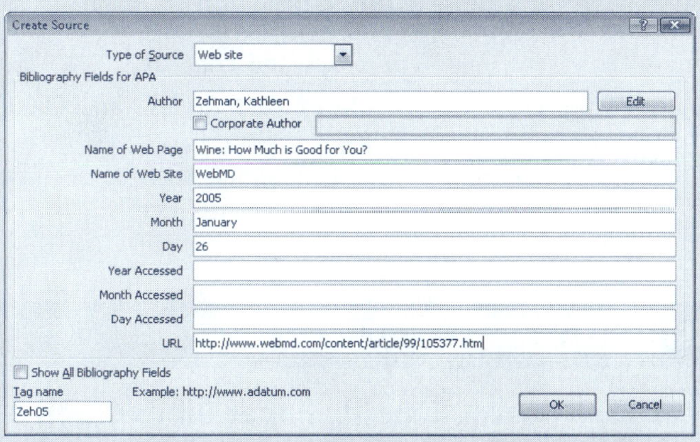

14. Click **OK**.
15. **SAVE** the document as ***health_benefits_of_wine*** and **CLOSE** the file.

PAUSE. LEAVE Word open for the next project.

Project 15-2: Research Paper Citations and Sources

You need to edit and insert more citations and sources for your research paper.

1. **OPEN** ***firstladies2*** from the data files for this lesson.
2. Scroll to the first sentence of the sixth paragraph, after the word *activism*.

CD The *firstladies2* document is available on the companion CD-ROM.

3. Click on the *Mayo and Meringolo* citation. Click the downward-pointing arrow and select **Edit Citation** from the menu.
4. Key **pp. 8-9** in the Pages box. In the Suppress section, click the **Author**, **Year**, and **Title** boxes. Click **OK**.
5. Position the insertion point at the end of the sixth paragraph after the word *added*.
6. On the References tab, in the Citations & Bibliography group, click the **Insert Citation** button and select the **Mayo, Edith** citation from the menu.
7. Click the citation. Click the downward-pointing arrow and select **Edit Citation** from the menu.
8. Key **p. 43** in the Pages box. In the Suppress section, click the **Author**, **Year**, and **Title** boxes and click **OK**.
9. Position the insertion point at the end of the indented eighth paragraph, after the word *power*.
10. On the References tab, in the Citations & Bibliography group, click the **Insert Citation** button and select the **Mayo**, **Edith** citation from the citations options menu.
11. Edit the citation. Key **p. 75** in the Pages box. In the Suppress section, click the **Author**, **Year**, and **Title** boxes and click **OK**.
12. Position the insertion point in the second sentence of the ninth paragraph, after the word *Gutin*.
13. On the References tab, in the Citations & Bibliography group, click the **Insert Citation** button and select the **Gutin**, **Myra G.** source from the menu.
14. Edit the citation. In the Suppress section, click the **Author** box and click **OK**.
15. In the fourth sentence of the same paragraph, after the word *added*, insert the **Gutin**, **Myra G.** source.
16. Edit the citation. Key **p. 176** in the Pages box. In the Suppress section, click the **Author**, **Year**, and **Title** boxes and click **OK**.
17. Position the insertion point at the end of the document, after the quotation mark following the word *life*. Insert the **Mayo, Edith** source.
18. Edit the citation. Key **p. 75** in the Pages box. In the Suppress section, click the **Author**, **Year**, and **Title** boxes and click **OK**.
19. **SAVE** the document as ***role_of_first_ladies2*** and **CLOSE** the file.

PAUSE. LEAVE Word open for the next project.

Proficiency Assessment

Project 15-3: Health Benefits Paper Bibliography

Now, you decide that you are ready to create a bibliography for your article.

CD The *healthbenefits2* document is available on the companion CD-ROM.

1. **OPEN** ***healthbenefits2*** from the data files for this lesson.
2. On the References tab, in the Citations & Bibliography group, click the **Style** button and select **Chicago** from the menu.
3. Position the insertion point on a blank line below the last paragraph and press the **Enter** key.
4. On the References tab, in the Citations & Bibliography group, click the **Bibliography** button and select **Works Cited**.

5. Select the Wikipedia citation at the end of the second paragraph. Press the **Delete** key.
6. On the References tab, in the Citations & Bibliography group, click the **Manage Sources** button.
7. In the current list, select the **Wikipedia** source and press the **Delete** key.
8. Click the **Close** button.
9. Scroll to the bibliography to make sure it was automatically updated.
10. **SAVE** the document as ***health_benefits_of_wine2*** and **CLOSE** the file.

PAUSE. LEAVE Word open for the next project.

Project 15-4: Research Paper Bibliography

CD

The *firstladies3* document is available on the companion CD-ROM.

You need to insert a new source and create a new bibliography for your research paper.

1. **OPEN** ***firstladies3*** from the data files for this lesson.
2. Position the insertion point in the first sentence of paragraph nine, after the word *Greer*.
3. Insert a new source. Key the data that is shown in Figure 15-15.

Figure 15-15

Add new source data

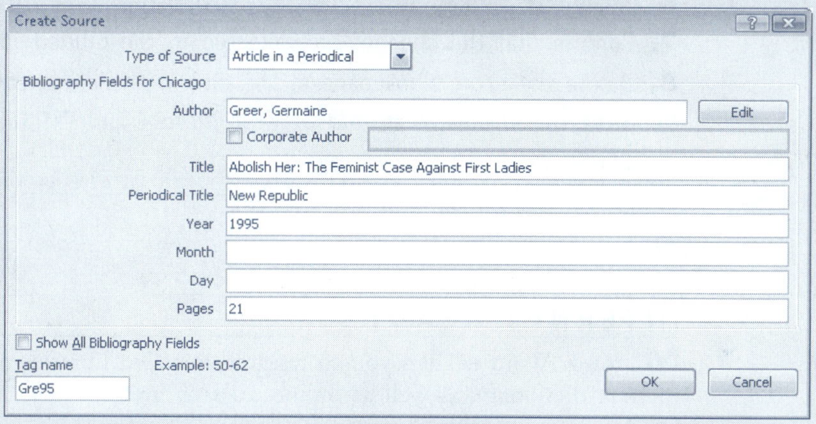

4. Edit the citation to suppress the author.
5. Scroll to the bibliography and select the entire bibliography.
6. Click the **Bibliographies** button at the top of the placeholder and select the **Works Cited** style.
7. Make sure the new source is included in the bibliography.
8. **SAVE** the document as ***role_of_first_ladies3*** and **CLOSE** the file.

PAUSE. LEAVE Word open for the next project.

Mastery Assessment

Project 15-5: Manage Sources for the Health Benefits Paper

CD

The *healthbenefits3* document is available on the companion CD-ROM.

You need to edit and delete sources in your article.

1. **OPEN** ***healthbenefits3*** from the data files for this lesson.
2. Click on the citation at the end of the fifth paragraph. Edit the source. Capitalize some of the words in the Web page title so that it reads New White Wine 'Good for Heart'.
3. Delete the Stuttaford citation at the end of the fourth paragraph.
4. Open the Source Manager. Select the Stuttaford source in the current list. Click the **Copy** button to move it to the master list.

5. Delete the Stuttaford source from the current list and close the Source Manager.
6. Confirm that the bibliography has been updated.
7. If necessary, delete the extra blank page at the end of the document.
8. **SAVE** the document as ***health_benefits_of_wine3*** and **CLOSE** the file.

PAUSE. LEAVE Word open for the next project.

Project 15-6: Manage Sources for the Research Paper

You're almost finished with the research paper. You just need to make a few final edits to the sources.

CD

The ***firstladies4*** document is available on the companion CD-ROM.

1. **OPEN** ***firstladies4*** from the data files for this lesson.
2. On the second page, following the quotation mark after the word *shakers*, insert a citation for the Anthony 1990 source that displays only the page number, **p. 8**.
3. Access the Source Manager.
4. Edit the Greer source. Key the word **The** in the periodical title to change it to *The New Republic*.
5. Show all the bibliography fields and key **212** as the volume number.
6. Apply the changes to the master list and the current list.
7. Confirm that the changes are reflected in the bibliography.
8. Delete the extra blank page at the end of the document.
9. **SAVE** the document as ***role_of_first_ladies4*** and **CLOSE** the file.

CLOSE Word.

INTERNET READY

Microsoft Word enables you to research installed libraries of research books, such as the Encarta dictionary, as well as online research and financial sites like MSN Money Stock Quotes. Practice using these services.

1. Select Search Libraries from the Insert Citations menu. The Research pane opens on your screen. Key first lady in the Search for box.
2. Click the downward-pointing arrow beside All Reference Books to display a menu. Select All Research Sites to search for occurrences of *first lady* in online research libraries.
3. Scroll down to view the various articles and websites that were found. Find *First Ladies: More Than Just Supportive Spouses* and click Encarta Feature. The online quiz opens in your web browser. Take the quiz just for fun.

Experiment more with the other research options available. Look up the current stock quote for MSFT under the All Business and Financial Sites, MSN Money Stock Quotes.

Circling Back

As a fourth grade writing teacher at a private elementary school, you have been asked to present a research paper at a national conference. You use Word to write and edit the research paper.

Project 1: BOOKMARKS AND DOCUMENT MAP

While working on the research paper, you often refer to the same places in the document. Insert bookmarks to help you jump to certain text more quickly. Apply styles to the headings to create the Document Map.

CD

The ***research*** file is available on the companion CD-ROM.

GET READY. Launch Word if it is not already running.

1. Open ***research*** from the data files for this lesson.
2. On page 2, select the *Introduction* heading.
3. On the Home tab, in the Styles group, click the More button to display the Quick Styles gallery.
4. Click the **Heading 1** option.
5. Apply the Heading 1 style to the remaining headings in the document: *Community in the Classroom, Technology within Literature Circles, Computer-Mediated Discussion Groups,* and *Conclusion*.
6. On the View tab, in the Show/Hide group, click the **Document Map** check box to display the Document Map.
7. Close the Document Map.
8. On page 2, select the *Introduction* heading.
9. On the Insert tab, in the Links group, click the **Bookmark** button.
10. In the Bookmark dialog box, key **Introduction** in the Bookmark name box.
11. Click the **Add** button.
12. Create a bookmark for each of the remaining headings in the document. Use the following abbreviated headings as bookmark names: *Community, Technology, Discussion,* and *Conclusion*.
13. **SAVE** the document as ***research_navigate***.

    PAUSE. LEAVE the document open for the next project.

Project 2: TABLE OF CONTENTS AND INDEX

A table of contents helps readers quickly locate topics of interest, and an index helps readers find the location of specific topics, words, and phrases. Because your research paper is a long document, both of these would be helpful. Insert a table of contents and an index so that all sections of the document can be referred to easily.

USE the document that is open from the previous project.

1. Place the insertion point on page 1 on a line after the author's name.
2. Press **Ctrl**+**Enter** to insert a page break.
3. On the References tab, in the Table of Contents group, click the **Table of Contents** button to display the gallery of built-in styles.
4. Click the **Automatic Table 2** style to insert a table of contents on its own page. (If necessary, place the insertion point after the table and press **Ctrl**+**Enter** to insert another page break.)
5. On the Home tab, in the Editing group, click the **Find** button.

6. In the Find what box, key **literature circles**.
7. Click the **Find Next** button. An occurrence of *literature circles* is selected in the document.
8. On the References tab, in the Index group, click the **Mark Entry** button.
9. In the Mark Index Entry dialog box, click **Mark All**.
10. Use the same process to mark all the occurrences of the following words/phrases: *community, network, journaling, technology, blogs, discussion groups*.
11. Cancel the Find and Replace dialog box and close the Mark Index Entry dialog box.
12. Scroll to the end of the document and insert a page break.
13. Key **Index** and press the Enter key.
14. Apply the **Heading 1** style to the Index title.
15. Click on the paragraph mark below the heading.
16. On the References tab, in the Index group, click the **Insert Index** button.
17. In the Index dialog box, click the downward-pointing arrow on the **Columns** box to change the value to 1.
18. Click the **Formats** menu and select **Bulleted**.
19. Click **OK**. The index is inserted in the document.
20. **SAVE** the document as ***research_contents***.

PAUSE. LEAVE the document open for the next project.

Project 3: Captions and Table of Figures

You want to include several screen captures in the paper as an appendix. Insert the figures and then insert a table of figures as a reference.

CD

The ***website1, website2,*** and ***website3*** figure files are available on the companion CD-ROM.

1. Place the insertion point at the end of the document and press Ctrl+Enter to insert a page break.
2. On the Insert tab, in the Illustrations group, click the **Picture** button.
3. In the Insert Picture dialog box, navigate to the data files for this lesson, select ***website1***, and click **Insert**.
4. From the data files, insert the ***website2*** and ***website3*** figures below the first.
5. On the References tab, in the Captions group, click the **Insert Caption** button to display the Caption dialog box.
6. In the Options section, select **Figure** in the Label box and **Above selected item** in the Position box.
7. Click **OK**.
8. Insert captions for the other two figures.
9. On page 2, place the insertion point on a line below the table of contents.
10. Key **Table of Figures** and copy the format from the Table of Contents heading.
11. Place the insertion point below the heading you just created.
12. On the References tab, in the Captions group, click the **Insert Table of Figures** button to display the Table of Figures dialog box.
13. In the General section, in the Formats box, select **Simple**.
14. In the Tab Leader box, select the dotted line (---------).
15. Click **OK**.
16. **SAVE** the document as ***research_figures***.

PAUSE. LEAVE the document open for the next project.

Project 4: Citations and Bibliography

You have already added many citations to the master source list for the document. Add another citation and then create a works cited page at the end of the research paper.

1. Place the insertion point in the *Introduction* section, third paragraph, at the end of the second sentence after the words *overcome underlying differences*.
2. On the References tab, in the Citations & Bibliography group, click the **Insert Citation** button.
3. Select **Add New Source**. The Create Source dialog box appears.
4. Select **Electronic Source** from the Type of Source menu.
5. Key the following fields:

Title:	**Rethinking networks and communities in a wired society.**
City:	**Los Angeles**
State/Province:	**CA**
Country/Region:	**USA**
Year:	**1999**
Month:	**December**
Day:	**10**

6. Scroll to the end of the document and place the insertion point below the last figure.
7. On the References tab, in the Citations & Bibliography group, click the **Bibliography** button. A menu of built-in bibliography styles appears.
8. Select the **Works Cited** style. The bibliography is inserted on a new page.
9. **SAVE** the document as ***research_references*** and **CLOSE** the file.

CLOSE Word.

16

Performing Mail Merges

LESSON SKILL MATRIX

Skills	Matrix Skill	Skill Number
Setting up a Main Document	Create merged documents; Merge data into form letters	4.5.1, 4.5.2
Selecting Recipients for the Mailing	Create merged documents; Merge data into form letters	4.5.1, 4.5.2
Preparing Merge Fields	Create merged documents; Merge data into form letters	4.5.1, 4.5.2
Previewing the Merged Letters	Create merged documents; Merge data into form letters	4.5.1, 4.5.2
Completing the Mail Merge	Create merged documents; Merge data into form letters	4.5.1, 4.5.2
Creating Envelopes for a Group Mailing	Create envelopes and labels	4.5.3
Creating Labels for a Group Mailing	Create envelopes and labels	4.5.3

You are employed at Graphic Design Institute as an admissions officer in the Office of Enrollment Services. Because you frequently send out letters containing the same content to different recipients, it is essential that you know how to perform mail merges. In this lesson, you will learn how to create merged documents and merge data into form letters. You will also learn how to create envelopes and labels for a group mailing.

KEY TERMS

data source
mail merge fields
main document

Software Orientation

Mailings Tab

Commands on the Mailings tab are used to perform mail merges, as well as to create envelopes and labels for a group mailing.

Figure 16-1

Mailings tab

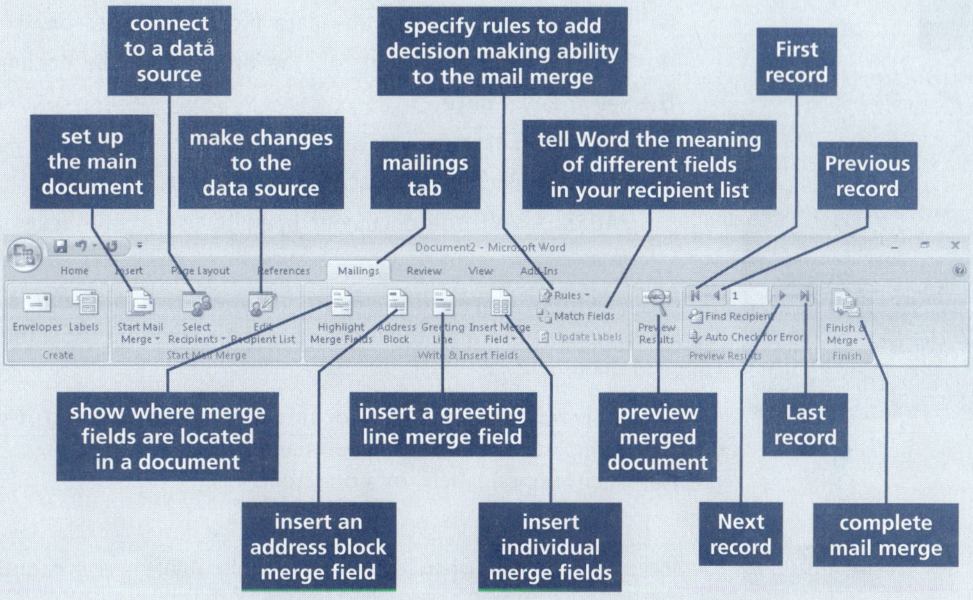

Use Figure 16-1 as a reference throughout this lesson as well as the rest of this book.

Creating a Mail Merge Document

THE BOTTOM LINE

Mail merges are useful for creating multiple documents that have the same basic content, yet are personalized with unique information from a data source—for example, a form letter that is sent to multiple customers using different recipient names and addresses.

Setting up a Main Document

Start a mail merge by first setting up the main document that you intend to print or email multiple times. You can open an existing document or create a new one.

SET UP A MAIN DOCUMENT

GET READY. Before you begin these steps, be sure to launch Microsoft Word.

1. On the Mailings tab, in the Start Mail Merge group, click the **Start Mail Merge** button to display the menu, shown in Figure 16-2.

Figure 16-2

Start Mail Merge menu

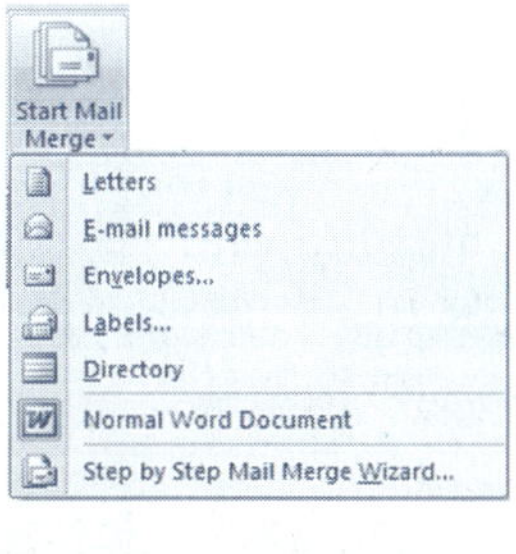

2. Click **Letters**.

ANOTHER WAY

You can also perform a mail merge by using the Mail Merge task pane, which leads you step by step through the process. To use the task pane, on the Start Mail Merge menu, click Step by Step Mail Merge Wizard.

CD

The ***scholarship*** file is available on the companion CD-ROM.

3. OPEN ***scholarship*** from the data files for this lesson.
4. Place the insertion point on the first line of the document.
5. Key **today's date**.
6. Press the **Enter** key twice.
7. **SAVE** the document as ***scholarship_letter***.

PAUSE. LEAVE the document open to use in the next exercise.

CERTIFICATION READY?
How do you create merged documents? How do you merge data into form letters?
4.5.1, 4.5.2

In this activity, you opened the main document that you will use for the mail merge. The ***main document*** contains the text and graphics that are the same for each version of the merged document.

You can also create a new main document by choosing the type of document you want to create on the Start Mail Merge menu and then keying your text. You can create letters, email messages, envelopes, labels, or a directory.

TROUBLESHOOTING

A document must be opened in Word for the mail merge commands to be available.

Or you can choose the Step by Step Mail Merge Wizard, which opens the Mail Merge task pane, shown in Figure 16-3, to walk you through the process of performing a mail merge.

Figure 16-3

Step by Step Mail Merge wizard task pane

Selecting Recipients for the Mailing

Choose the list of people to whom you intend to send the letter. You can key your own list, use your Outlook contacts, or connect to a database.

SELECT RECIPIENTS FOR THE MAILING

USE the document that is open from the previous exercise.

1. On the Mailings tab, in the Start Mail Merge group, click the **Select Recipients** button to display the menu shown in Figure 16-4.

Figure 16-4

Select Recipients menu

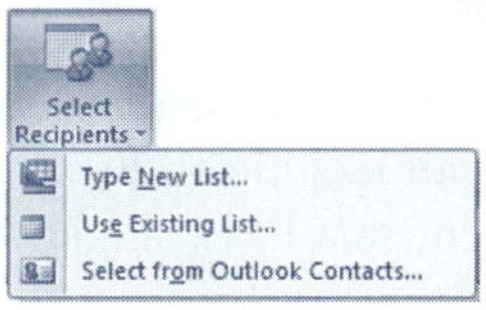

2. Click **Use Existing List** to open the Select Data Source dialog box, shown in Figure 16-5.

Figure 16-5

Select Data Source dialog box

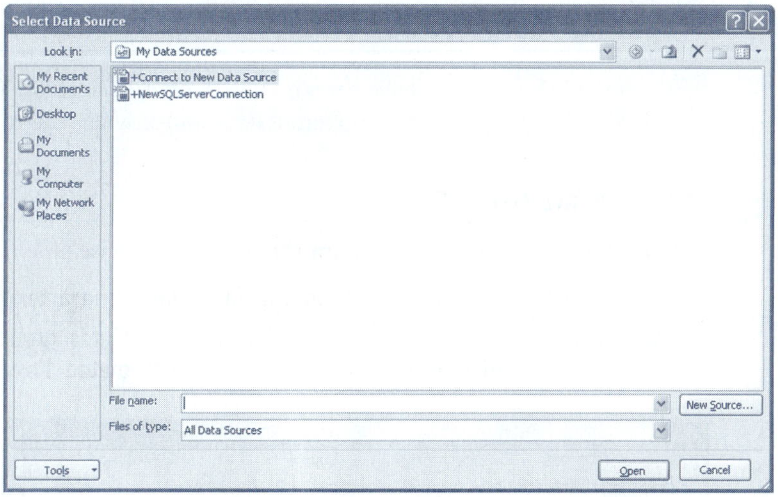

CD

The ***student_list*** file is available on the companion CD-ROM.

3. Navigate to the data files for this lesson and select the ***student_list*** file.
4. Click **Open**.
5. On the Mailings tab, in the Start Mail Merge group, click the **Edit Recipient List** button to display the Mail Merge Recipients dialog box, shown in Figure 16-6.

Figure 16-6

Mail Merge Recipients dialog box

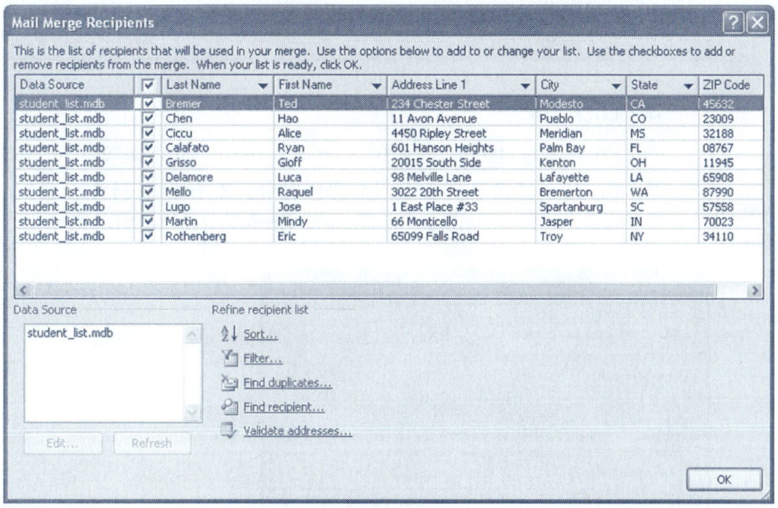

6. Click to clear the check boxes for *Alice Ciccu* and *Jose Lugo*.
7. Click the **Last Name** header to sort the list alphabetically by last name.

CERTIFICATION READY?
How do you create merged documents? How do you merge data into form letters?
4.5.1, 4.5.2

8. Click **OK**.

   PAUSE. LEAVE the document open to use in the next exercise.

To merge information into a main document, you must connect the document to a data source or a data file. A ***data source*** is a file that contains the information to be merged into a document, for example, names and addresses.

To connect to a data source, you can type a new list, use an existing list, or select recipients from your Outlook contacts. Existing lists can include an Excel spreadsheet, an Access database, an HTML file or a Word document that has a single table, an electronic address book, or any text file that has data fields.

To make changes to a list of recipients and decide who should receive your letter, click the Edit Recipient List button. In the Mail Merge Recipients dialog box that opens, you can also sort, filter, find and remove duplicates, and validate addresses from the list.

Preparing Merge Fields

When mail merge fields have been inserted into a document, Word will automatically replace them with information from a data source when the mail merge is performed.

PREPARE MERGE FIELDS

USE the document that is open from the previous exercise.

1. Place the insertion point on the first blank line after the date.
2. On the Mailings tab, in the Write & Insert Fields group, click the **Address Block** button to display the Insert Address Block dialog box, shown in Figure 16-7.

Figure 16-7
Insert Address Block dialog box

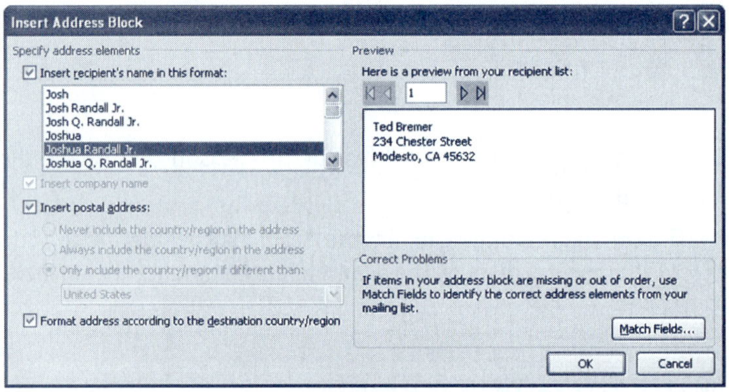

3. Click **OK**.
4. Press the **Enter** key to place a blank line after the Address Block field.
5. On the Mailings tab, in the Write & Insert Fields group, click the **Greeting Line** button to display the Insert Greeting Line dialog box, shown in Figure 16-8.

Figure 16-8
Insert Greeting Line dialog box

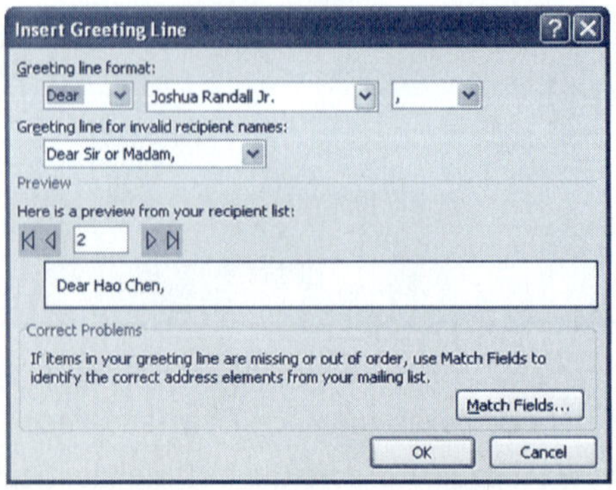

CERTIFICATION READY?
How do you create merged documents? How do you merge data into form letters?
4.5.1, 4.5.2

6. In the Greeting line format section, click the arrow on the second dropdown list and click **Joshua**.
7. Click **OK**.
8. On the Mailings tab, in the Write & Insert Fields group, click the **Highlight Merge Fields** button. This shows where the merge fields are located in your document.
9. Click the **Highlight Merge Fields** button again to remove the highlight.
10. **SAVE** the document as ***scholarship_fields***.

PAUSE. LEAVE the document open to use in the next exercise.

After connecting a main document to a data file, the next step is to add mail merge fields to the document. ***Mail merge fields*** are placeholders—such as Name and Address—that are filled with information from the data source file when the mail merge is performed.

TAKE NOTE*

When you insert a mail merge field into a main document, the field name is surrounded by chevrons (« »). These chevrons will not show up in the merged documents. They are just included to help you distinguish the fields in the main document from the regular text.

By putting a field in a main document, you indicate that you want a certain category of information to appear in that location. Fields correspond to the column headings in the data file that you select. Rows in a data file represent records of information. Word generates a copy of the main document for each record when you perform a mail merge.

You can combine fields and separate them by punctuation marks. For example, to create a partial address, you can set up the fields in your main document like this: «City», «State» «Postal code»

On the Mailings tab, in the Write & Insert Fields group, click the Address Block or Greeting Line buttons to insert an address or greeting. To add an individual field, such as first name or telephone number, click the Insert Merge Field button.

TROUBLESHOOTING

To make sure that Word can find a column in your data file that corresponds to every name or address, you may need to map the mail merge fields in Word to the columns in your data file. On the Mailings tab, in the Write & Insert Fields group, click Match Fields.

Database and spreadsheet programs store information that you key in cells as raw data. Formatting that you apply, such as fonts and colors, is not stored with the raw data. When you merge information from a data file into a Word document, you are merging the raw data without the applied formatting.

To format the data in the document, select the mail merge field and format it, just as you would format any text. Make sure that the selection includes the chevrons (« ») that surround the field.

Previewing the Merged Letters

Before completing the merge, you can preview the merged documents and make any necessary changes.

PREVIEW THE MERGED LETTERS

USE the document that is open from the previous exercise.

1. On the Mailings tab, in the Preview Results group, click the **Preview Results** button.

2. Select the three lines in the address block.
3. On the Page Layout tab, in the Paragraph group, click the downward-pointing arrow in the Spacing Before box until it reaches **0 pt**.
4. Select the date.
5. On the Page Layout tab, in the Paragraph group, click the **upward-pointing arrow** in the Spacing After box until it reaches **12 pt**.
6. On the Mailing tab, in the Preview Results group, click the **Next Record** button.
7. Continue clicking the **Next Record** button until you have previewed all the records.
8. On the Mailing tab, in the Preview Results group, click the **Find Recipient** button to display the Find Entry dialog box, shown in Figure 16-9.

Figure 16-9

Find Entry dialog box

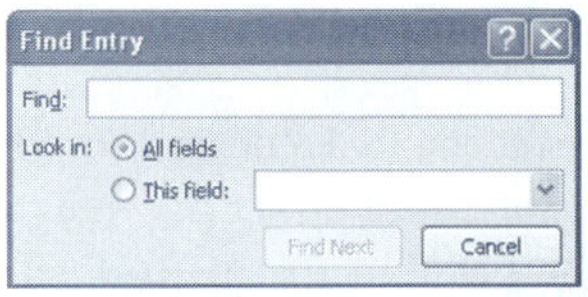

9. In the Find box, key **Ted**. The preview results moves to the record for Ted Bremer.
10. Click **Cancel** to close the Find Entry dialog box.
11. On the Mailing tab, in the Preview Results group, click the **Auto Check for Errors** button to display the Checking and Reporting Errors dialog box, shown in Figure 16-10.

Figure 16-10

Checking and Reporting Errors dialog box

CERTIFICATION READY?
How do you create merged documents? How do you merge data into form letters?
4.5.1, 4.5.2

12. Click the button for **Simulate the merge and report errors in a new document**.
13. Click **OK**.
14. A message appears that no mail merge errors were found. Click **OK**.
15. **SAVE** the document as ***scholarship_preview***.

PAUSE. LEAVE the document open to use in the next exercise.

After you add fields to a main document, you are ready to preview the merge results. On the Mailings tab, in the Preview Results group, click the Preview Results button or page through each merged document by using the Next Record and Previous Record buttons.

Word replaces the merge fields in your document with actual data from the recipient list so you can preview what the document looks like. When you are satisfied with the preview, you can complete the merge.

Preview a specific record in the recipient list by clicking the Find Recipient button. Click the Auto Check for Errors button to check for mail merge errors.

Completing the Mail Merge

When you complete the mail merge, Word replaces the merge fields in your document with actual data from the recipient list.

COMPLETE THE MAIL MERGE

USE the document that is open from the previous exercise.

1. On the Mailings tab, in the Finish group, click the **Finish & Merge** button to display the menu shown in Figure 16-11.

Figure 16-11

Finish & Merge menu

2. Click **Edit Individual Documents** to open the Merge to New Document dialog box, shown in Figure 16-12.

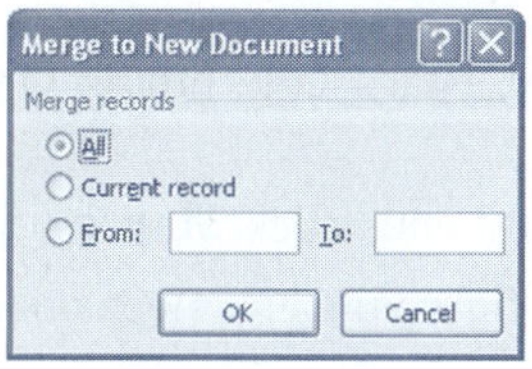

Figure 16-12

Merge to New Document dialog box

3. The **All** button should be selected. Click **OK**.
4. The mail merge is performed and a new file is created. Scroll through to see that each individual merged letter appears on a separate page. The document should contain a total of eight letters.
5. **SAVE** the new document as ***scholarship_merged*** and **CLOSE** the file.
6. **CLOSE** the ***scholarship_preview*** document, saving any changes if necessary.

PAUSE. LEAVE Word open to use in the next exercise.

CERTIFICATION READY?
How do you create merged documents? How do you merge data into form letters?
4.5.1, 4.5.2

When you perform a merge, information from the first row in the data file replaces the fields in the main document to create the first merged document. Information from the second row in the data file replaces the fields to create the second merged document, and so on.

The Finish & Merge button contains three options: merge to a new document, merge to a printer, or merge to email. You can modify the documents individually. You can print or change all or just a subset of the documents.

The merged documents are separate from the main document. It is a good idea to save the merged document and also save the main document itself if you plan to use it for another mail merge.

When you save a main document, you also save its connection to the data file. As shown in Figure 16-13, the next time that you open the main document, a message prompts you to choose whether you want the information from the data file to be merged again into the main document.

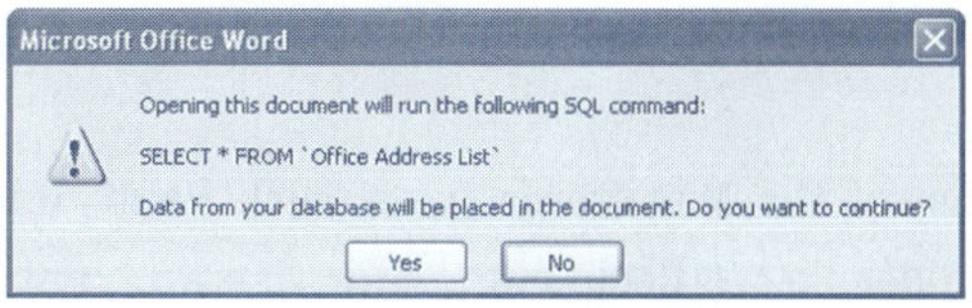

Figure 16-13

Connection to data file message

Creating Envelopes and Labels for a Mail Merge

THE BOTTOM LINE

The mail merge process for envelopes and labels entails the same overall steps as for creating a mail merge document.

XREF

You learned the basics about creating envelopes and labels in Lesson 2.

Creating Envelopes for a Group Mailing

Use mail merge to create a batch of envelopes for sending a mass mailing to your address list.

CREATE ENVELOPES FOR A GROUP MAILING

OPEN a new, blank Word document.

1. On the Mailings tab, in the Start Mail Merge group, click the **Start Mail Merge** button.
2. On the Start Mail Merge options menu, click **Step by Step Mail Merge Wizard.**
3. In the Mail Merge pane on the right, under Select document type, select **Envelopes**.
4. At the bottom of the Mail Merge pane, click **Next: Starting document** to move to the next wizard step.
5. In Step 2, under Select starting document, select **Change document layout.**
6. Under Change document layout, click **Envelope options** to display the Envelope Options dialog box, shown in Figure 16-14.

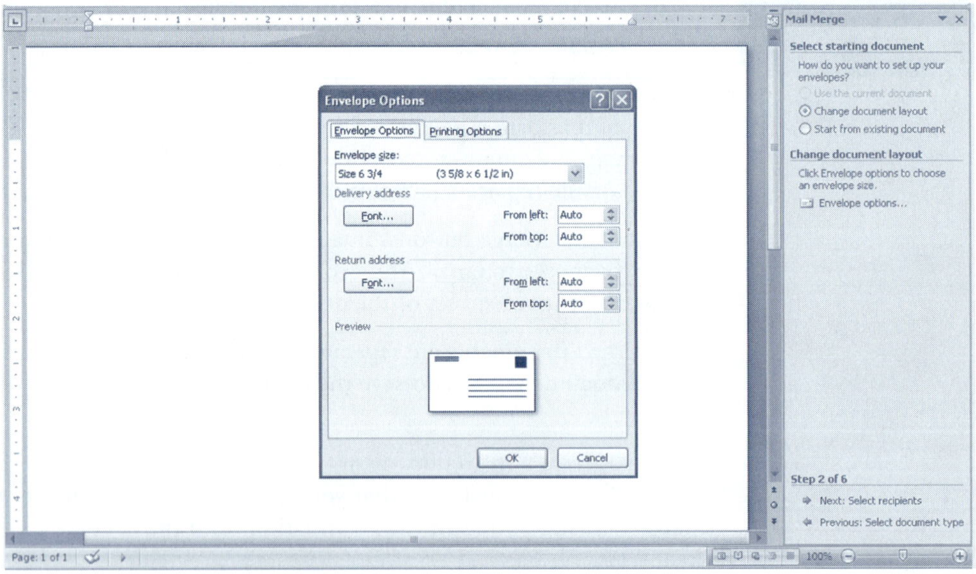

Figure 16-14

Mail Merge Wizard, Step 2: and Envelope Options dialog box

7. In the Envelope size list, choose **Size $6^3/_4$ ($3^5/_8$ x $6^1/_2$)**.
8. Click **OK**.
9. At the bottom of the Mail Merge pane, click **Next: Select recipients.**
10. In Step 3, under Select Recipients, click **Use an existing list.**
11. Under Use an existing list, click **Browse**.

CD

The ***student_list*** file is available on the companion CD-ROM.

TROUBLESHOOTING

If you later want to make any changes to the recipient list, click the Edit Recipient List option in the Mail Merge Wizard.

12. In the Select Data Source dialog box, navigate to the data files for this lesson and select ***student_list***.
13. Click **Open**.
14. Click to clear the checkboxes for *Alice Ciccu* and *Jose Lugo*.
15. Click the **Last Name** header to sort the list alphabetically by last name.
16. Click **OK**.
17. At the bottom of the Mail Merge pane click **Next: Arrange your envelope**.
18. In Step 4, click to place the insertion point on the lower center of the envelope, approximately where a recipient address would appear.
19. Under Arrange your envelope, click **Address Block**.
20. In the Insert Address Block dialog box, click **OK**. An address block merge field is inserted on the envelope, similar to Figure 16-15.

Figure 16-15

Mail Merge Wizard, Step 4: Arrange Your Envelope

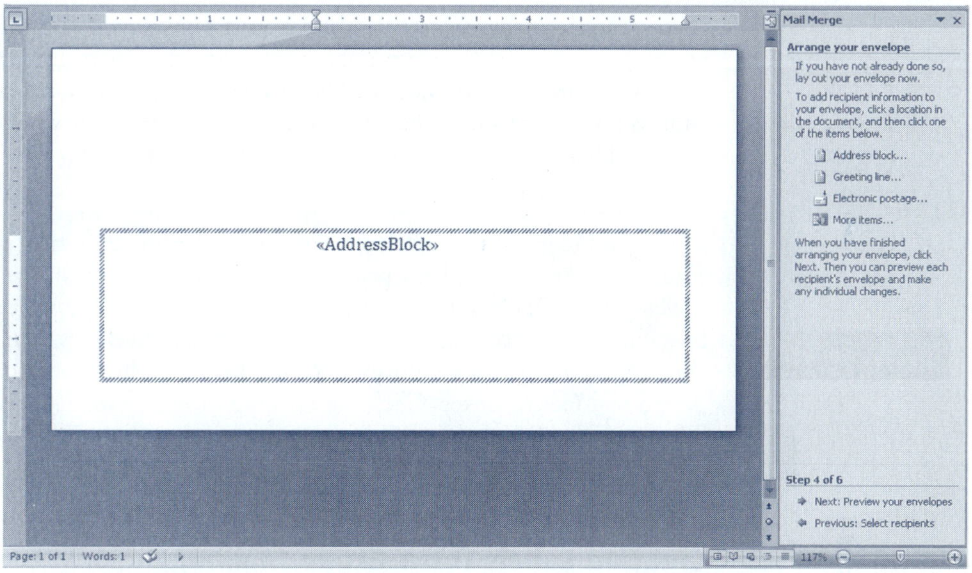

21. At the bottom of the Mail Merge pane, click **Next: Preview your envelopes**.
22. In Step 5, under Preview your envelopes, click the **arrows** to scroll through and preview each envelope, as shown in Figure 16-16.

Figure 16-16

Mail Merge Wizard, Step 5: Preview Your Envelopes

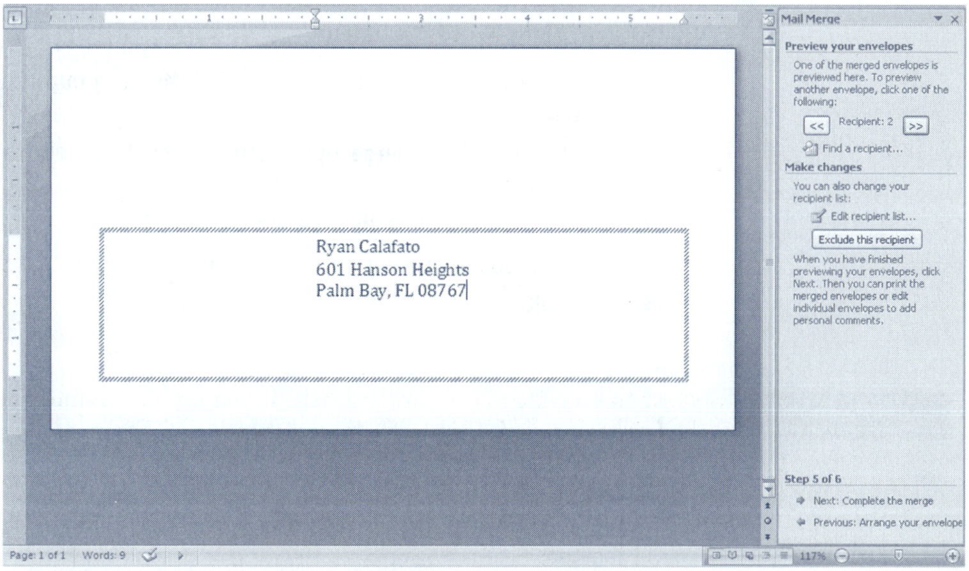

23. At the bottom of the Mail Merge pane, click **Next: Complete the merge**.
24. In Step 6, under Merge, click **Edit individual envelopes . . . .**
25. In the Merge to New Document dialog box, click **All** and then click **OK**.
26. The mail merge is performed and a new file is created. Scroll through to see that each individual merged envelope appears on a separate page. The document should contain a total of eight envelopes.
27. **SAVE** the new merged document as ***scholarship_envelopes*** and **CLOSE** the file.
28. **SAVE** the main document as ***envelopes_main*** and **CLOSE** the file.

PAUSE. LEAVE Word open to use in the next exercise.

CERTIFICATION READY?
How do you create envelopes and labels?
4.5.3

The mail merge process for envelopes follows the same overall steps as for creating a mail merge document. In this activity, you used the Mail Merge Wizard to create envelopes for a mass mailing. The wizard walks you through each step needed to complete a mail merge.

If you want to include a return address on the envelopes, you can set this up before you start working on an envelope main document. Click the Microsoft Office Button and then click Word Options. Click Advanced. Under General, type your return address in the Mailing address box. Word stores the address so that you can use it whenever you want to insert your return address in a document.

TROUBLESHOOTING

It is a good idea to print a few test envelopes first, to verify that your printing options are configured correctly for your printer. On the Mailings tab, in the Create group, click Envelopes. Click Options and then click the Envelope Options tab. In the Envelope size box, click the choice that matches the size of your envelopes. If none of the choices matches your envelope size, click Custom size and then type the dimensions of your envelope in the Width and Height boxes. Click the Printing Options tab. The printer driver sends the information to Word about which way the envelope should be loaded into the printer. This information is displayed on the Printing Options tab of the Envelope Options dialog box.

Creating Labels for a Group Mailing

To create address labels for sending a mass mailing, use mail merge to create a sheet of address labels. Each label will contain an address from the address list.

CREATE LABELS FOR A GROUP MAILING

OPEN a new, blank Word document.

1. On the Mailings tab, in the Start Mail Merge group, click the **Start Mail Merge** button.
2. On the Start Mail Merge options menu, click **Labels** to display the Label Options dialog box.
3. In the Label vendors list, select **Avery US Letter**.
4. In the Product number box, select **5160**.
5. Click **OK**.

TROUBLESHOOTING

Word uses a table to lay out the labels. If you do not see lines separating the labels, click the Layout tab under Table Tools, and then in the Table group, click View Gridlines.

6. On the Mailings tab, in the Start Mail Merge group, click the **Select Recipients** button.
7. On the menu, click **Type New List** to display the New Address List dialog box.

8. Click the **Customize Columns** button to display the Customize Address List dialog box, shown in Figure 16-17.

Figure 16-17

Customize Address List dialog box

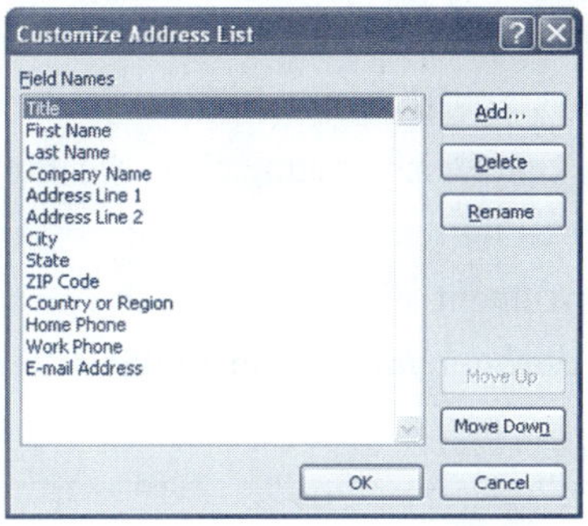

9. In the Field Names box, select **Title**.
10. Click **Delete**. When a confirmation message appears, click **Yes**.
11. Repeat step 10 for the following field names: Company Name, Address 2, Country or Region, Home Phone, Work Phone, and E-mail Address.
12. Click **OK** to close the Customize Address List dialog box.
13. Key the recipient information shown in Figure 16-18 into the table in the New Address List dialog box.

Figure 16-18

New Address List dialog box

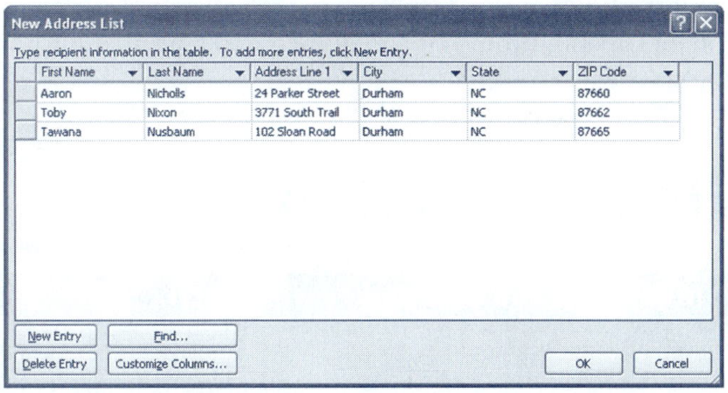

14. Click **OK**.
15. In the Save Address List dialog box, **SAVE** the document as ***durham_addresses***.
16. The labels main document appears with the insertion point in the first label. On the Mailings tab, in the Write & Insert Fields group, click the **Address Block** button. Click **OK**.
17. On the Mailings tab, in the Write & Insert Fields group, click the **Update Labels** button. Your document should look similar to Figure 16-19.

Figure 16-19

Labels main document

18. On the Mailings tab, in the Preview Results group, click the **Preview Results** button.
19. Click the **Preview Results** button again to return to the merge fields.

20. On the Mailings tab, in the Preview Results group, click the **Auto Check for Errors** button.
21. In the Checking and Reporting Errors dialog box, click **Simulate the merge and report errors in a new document** and then click **OK**.
22. Click **OK** to close the message that no mail merge errors have been found.
23. On the Mailings tab, in the Finish group, click the **Finish & Merge** button.
24. Click **Edit Individual Documents**.
25. In the Merge to New Document dialog box, click **All** and then click **OK**.
26. **SAVE** the document as ***durham_labels*** and **CLOSE** the file.

STOP. CLOSE Word.

CERTIFICATION READY?
How do you create envelopes and labels?
4.5.3

Like envelopes, the mail merge process for labels follows the same overall steps as for creating a mail merge document.

To set up a label main document, choose the information in the Label Options dialog box that corresponds with the labels that you will be using. If you do not already have a data source, you can create one during the mail merge process by using the New Address List dialog box. In the Customize Columns dialog box, you can specify which field names will be used.

You can add, delete, or rename fields in the first label of a label main document. You can also key text that you want repeated on each label or add a graphic, such as a company logo. Then update all the labels in the document to use information from the recipient list by clicking the Update Labels button. For a mail merge to a printed document or email, this command is not necessary.

SUMMARY SKILL MATRIX

In This Lesson You Learned	Matrix Skill	Skill Number
To set up a main document	Create merged documents; Merge data into form letters	4.5.1, 4.5.2
To select recipients for the mailing	Create merged documents; Merge data into form letters	4.5.1, 4.5.2
To prepare merge fields	Create merged documents; Merge data into form letters	4.5.1, 4.5.2
To preview merged letters	Create merged documents; Merge data into form letters	4.5.1, 4.5.2
To complete a mail merge	Create merged documents; Merge data into form letters	4.5.1, 4.5.2
To create envelopes for a group mailing	Create envelopes and labels	4.5.3
To create labels for a group mailing	Create envelopes and labels	4.5.3

Knowledge Assessment

Fill in the Blank

Complete the following sentences by writing the correct word or words in the blanks provided.

1. The ________________ contains the text and graphics that are the same for each version of the merged document.
2. A ________________ is a file that contains the information to be merged into a document, for example, names and addresses.
3. Mail merge fields are ________________ that are filled with information from the data source file when the mail merge is performed.
4. To set up the label main document, choose the information in the ________________ dialog box that corresponds with the labels that you will be using.
5. In the Customize Columns dialog box, you can specify which ________________ will be used.
6. The ________________ command is not necessary for a mail merge to a printed document or email.
7. To make changes to the list of recipients and decide which of them should receive your letter, click the ________________ button.
8. ________________ correspond to the column headings in the data file that you select.
9. Word generates a ________________ of the main document for each record when you perform a mail merge.
10. Before completing the merge, you can ________________ the merged documents and make any necessary changes.

Multiple Choice

Select the best response for the following statements.

1. Which tab contains the commands used to perform mail merges?
   - **a.** Merge
   - **b.** Mailings
   - **c.** Mail Merge
   - **d.** Insert
2. What is the first step in performing a mail merge?
   - **a.** Set up the main document
   - **b.** Insert merge fields
   - **c.** Preview the results
   - **d.** Select the recipients
3. Which command walks you through the process of creating a mail merge?
   - **a.** AutoMerge
   - **b.** Create Mail Merge
   - **c.** MergeWizard
   - **d.** Step by Step Mail Merge Wizard

4. Which is NOT an option for selecting a list of recipients for the mail merge?
   - **a.** download from an online directory
   - **b.** type a new list
   - **c.** use an existing list
   - **d.** use your Outlook contacts
5. To merge information into your main document, you must first connect the document to a(n)
   - **a.** address validator.
   - **b.** form letter.
   - **c.** data source.
   - **d.** Website.
6. When mail merge fields have been inserted into a document, Word will automatically replace them with information from a data source when
   - **a.** the main document is saved.
   - **b.** the recipients are selected.
   - **c.** the merge fields are inserted.
   - **d.** the mail merge is performed.
7. Mail merge fields are enclosed by
   - **a.** quotation marks (" ").
   - **b.** chevrons (<< >>).
   - **c.** apostrophes (' ').
   - **d.** brackets ([ ]).
8. When previewing the mail merge document, Word replaces the merge fields with
   - **a.** sample data.
   - **b.** blank spaces.
   - **c.** actual data.
   - **d.** highlighted headings.
9. Which is NOT an option on the Finish & Merge menu?
   - **a.** Edit Individual Documents
   - **b.** Create New Merge Document
   - **c.** Print Documents
   - **d.** Send E-mail Messages
10. When you save the main document, you also save
    - **a.** all the data in an Excel spreadsheet.
    - **b.** any other open file.
    - **c.** the default return address for Word.
    - **d.** its connection to the data file.

Competency Assessment

Project 16-1: Business Students Contest Judge

As the director of business and marketing education at the School of Fine Art, you have recruited professional members of the local business community to serve as volunteers for judging a state contest for high school business students. You are sending a mail merge letter that contains necessary information for the judges and want to set up the main document.

CD

The *judges* document is available on the companion CD-ROM.

CD

The *judges_list* document is available on the companion CD-ROM.

GET READY Launch Word if it is not already running.

1. **OPEN** ***judges*** from the data files for this lesson.
2. Place the insertion point on the first line of the document.
3. On the Mailings tab, in the Start Mail Merge group, click the **Select Recipients** button.
4. Click **Use Existing List.**
5. Navigate to the data files for this lesson, select ***judges_list***, and click the **Open** button.
6. On the Mailings tab, in the Start Mail Merge group, click the **Edit Recipient List** button.
7. Click the **ZIP Code** header to sort the recipients by ZIP code.
8. Click **OK.**
9. On the Mailings tab, in the Write & Insert Fields group, click the **Address Block** button.
10. Preview the addresses in the Insert Address Block dialog box and click **OK.**
11. Press **Enter**.
12. On the Mailings tab, in the Write & Insert Fields group, click the **Greeting Line** button.
13. Preview the greeting lines in the Insert Greeting Line dialog box and click **OK.**
14. **SAVE** the main document as ***judges_letter***.

PAUSE. LEAVE the document open to use in the next project.

Project 16-2: Business Students Contest Judge

You are ready to complete the mail merge to the list of professional members of the local business community volunteering to judge a state contest for high school business students.

USE the document that is open from the previous exercise.

1. On the Mailings tab, in the Preview Results group, click the **Preview Results** button.
2. Select the four lines in the address block.
3. On the Page Layout tab, in the Paragraph group, click the downward-pointing arrow in the Spacing After box until it reaches **0 pt.**
4. Select the greeting line.
5. On the Page Layout tab, in the Paragraph group, click the upward-pointing arrow in the Spacing Before box until it reaches **12 pt.**
6. On the Mailings tab, in the Preview Results group, click **Next Record** and continue until you have previewed each letter.
7. Click the **Preview Results** button again.
8. On the Mailings tab, in the Finish group, click the **Finish & Merge** button.
9. Click **Edit Individual Documents.**
10. In the Merge to New Document dialog box, select **All** and click **OK.**
11. On page 1 of the new document, edit the address to change *Routh* to **Roth.**
12. **SAVE** the merged document as ***judges_merged*** and **CLOSE** the file.
13. **SAVE** the main document as ***contest_judges*** and **CLOSE** the file.

PAUSE. LEAVE Word open for the next project.

Proficiency Assessment

Project 16-3: PTA Officers

As president of the PTA at the local elementary school, you need to address envelopes to send information to the PTA officers about the upcoming school year. Create a new recipient list and perform an envelope mail merge.

OPEN a new Word document.

1. Start a new envelope mail merge document. Use **Size 10 (4$^{1}/_{8}$ x 9$^{1}/_{2}$)** as the envelope size.
2. Type a new address list using the information shown in Figure 16-20.

Figure 16-20

New Address List data

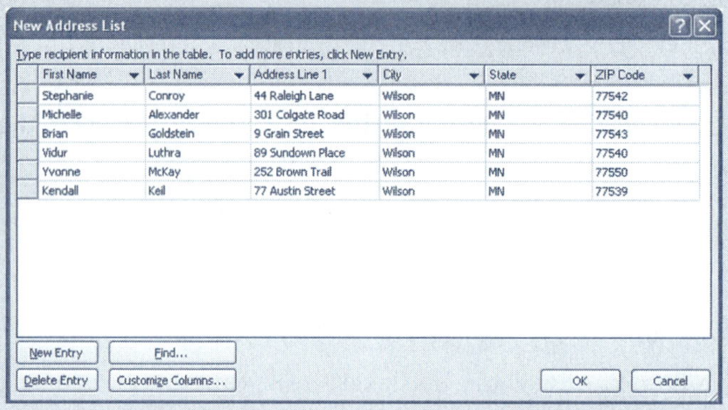

3. **SAVE** the new data source as ***pta_addresses***.
4. Add an address block to the envelope main document.
5. Preview the envelopes and auto check the document for errors.
6. Complete the mail merge.
7. **SAVE** the merged document as ***pta_envelopes*** and **CLOSE** the file.
8. **SAVE** the main document as ***pta_main*** and **CLOSE** the file.

PAUSE. LEAVE Word open for the next project.

Project 16-4: Student Labels

As an admissions officer at the Graphic Design Institute, you frequently send promotional material to prospective students. You need to address a catalog and are using the mail merge feature in Word to create labels.

CD

The ***student_list*** document is available on the companion CD-ROM.

1. **OPEN** a new Word document.
2. Set up a new main document for labels.
3. Set the labels using **Avery US Letter** as the label product and **5160** as the product number.
4. Use the ***student_list*** database found in the data files for this lesson as the data source.
5. Change the font size on the labels to **12 pt**.
6. Complete the mail merge.
7. **SAVE** the merged label document as ***student_labels*** and **CLOSE** the file.
8. **SAVE** the label main document as ***student_main*** and **CLOSE** the file.

PAUSE. LEAVE Word open for the next project.

Mastery Assessment

Project 16-5: Personal Address Labels

You are sending a personal invitation and want to create mailing labels to use for addressing the envelopes to your friends and family.

OPEN a new, blank Word document.

1. Set up a label mail merge using the **5160** label size.
2. Use the New List option on the Select Recipients menu to create a data source that includes the addresses of at least ten friends and family members. Customize the columns as needed.
3. **SAVE** the data source as ***friends_family***.
4. Create a label mail merge that connects to the data source that you just created.
5. Perform the mail merge.
6. **SAVE** the merged document as ***invitation_labels*** and **CLOSE** the file.
7. **SAVE** the main document as ***invitation_main*** and **CLOSE** the file.

   PAUSE. LEAVE Word open for the next project.

Project 16-6: Email Message Mail Merge

You are the office manager at Coho Winery & Vineyard where a select group of customers are invited to join the Cellar Select Friends, who receive special promotions and offers. Create an email message main document that will be used to send out the welcome message.

CD

The *cellar_select* document is available on the companion CD-ROM.

OPEN a new, blank Word document.

1. Set up the mail document for email messages.
2. Use ***cellar_select*** as the recipient list.
3. Key the message and insert merge fields as shown in Figure 16-21.

Figure 16-21

Email message main document

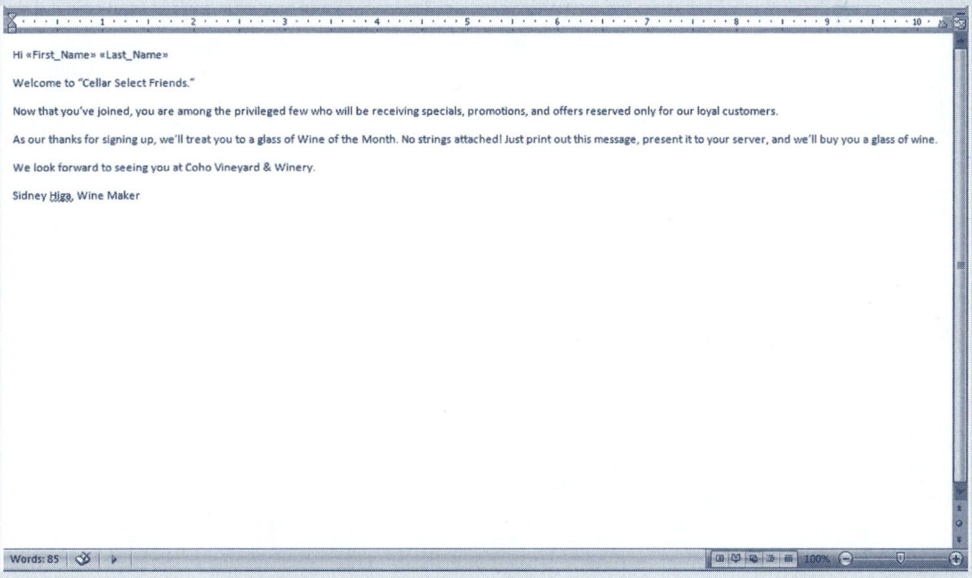

4. Preview the results and auto check for errors.
5. **SAVE** the main document as ***cellar_email*** and **CLOSE** the file. (You must have a compatible email program to complete the merge, so only finish and merge if your instructor asks you to do so.)

   STOP. CLOSE Word.

INTERNET READY

Blogs can be a fun way to pass time, but they can also be a great source of business information. If you enjoy blogs, check out some of the business-related blogs available, such as The Microsoft Connections Blog, shown in Figure 16-22. The URL for this blog is *http://blogs.msdn.com/conblog/default.aspx.* Search for information on mail merges or another topic of interest to you and see what you can find.

Figure 16-22

The Microsoft Connection Blog

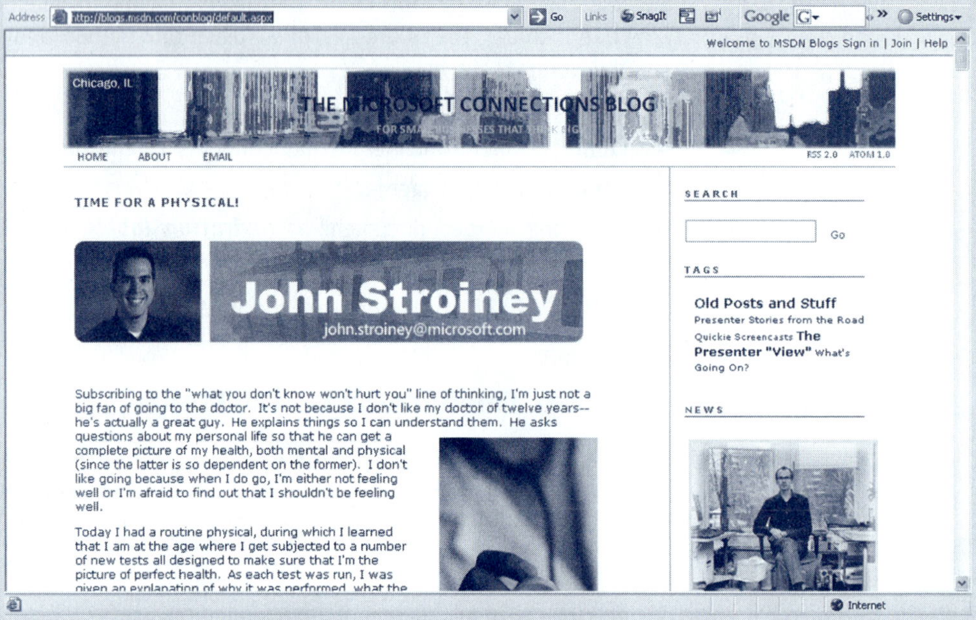

Workplace Ready

Using Word's Mail Merge

Creating correspondence is likely the most popular business use for Word. Often, companies create standard business letters that they can personalize with individual contact names, addresses, company names, and more. As the Director of Charities for Children's Hospital, you need to send out thank you letters to the nearly 200 corporate donors for this year's toy drive. To create each personalized letter, you have two choices; manually inserting the personalized information into individual letters for all of the donors, or using Word's Mail Merge.

The first option would require manually searching through each letter, finding the appropriate spot where each piece of personalized information should be inserted, then typing in the information. If several copies of this letter need to be sent to different individuals or companies, this process would need to be completed for each letter; a very cumbersome task.

You decide that a much better choice is using the Mail Merge option found in Word. This option provides the ability to insert text holders for personalized information into a letter. An existing word document can be selected during the mail merge process, or you can choose to create a new letter. You already have an Access database containing the necessary information for all donors, such as company name, contact name, and address, so you choose to import this information from the database. At the end of the process, you preview how the letters will appear and click to complete the task.

By using Word's Mail Merge, you saved yourself a great deal of time and aggravation. Now, if only all your business decisions could be so obvious!

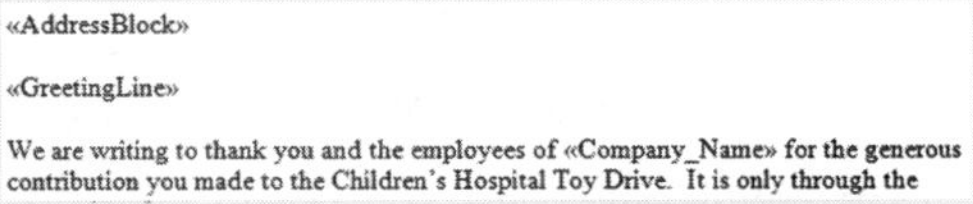
«AddressBlock»

«GreetingLine»

We are writing to thank you and the employees of «Company_Name» for the generous contribution you made to the Children's Hospital Toy Drive. It is only through the

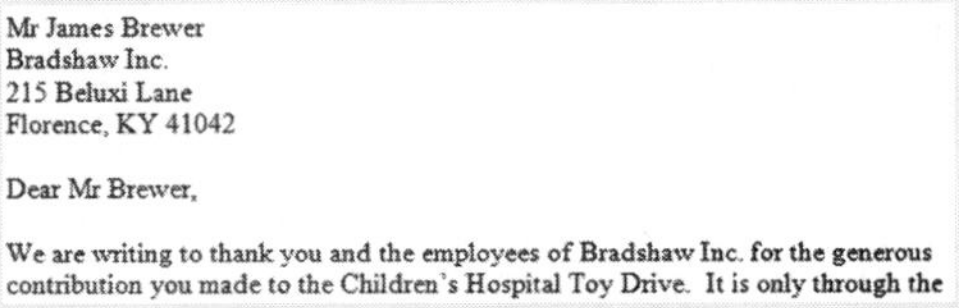
Mr James Brewer
Bradshaw Inc.
215 Beluxi Lane
Florence, KY 41042

Dear Mr Brewer,

We are writing to thank you and the employees of Bradshaw Inc. for the generous contribution you made to the Children's Hospital Toy Drive. It is only through the

17

Securing and Sharing Documents

LESSON SKILL MATRIX

Skills	Matrix Skill	Skill Number
Setting Permissions for a Document	Restrict permissions to documents	6.2.1
Marking a Document as Final	Mark documents as final	6.2.2
Setting an Access Password for a Document	Set passwords	6.2.3
Protecting a Document	Protect documents	6.2.4
Using a Signature to Authenticate a Document	Authenticate documents by using digital signatures	6.3.1
Inserting a Digital Signature in a Document	Insert a line for a digital signature	6.3.2
Using the Compatibility Checker	Identify document features that are not supported by previous versions	6.1.2
Using the Document Inspector	Remove inappropriate or private information by using Document Inspector	6.1.3
Inserting Comments	Insert, modify, and delete comments	5.4
Viewing Comments	Insert, modify, and delete comments	5.4
Editing Comments	Insert, modify, and delete comments	5.4
Deleting Comments	Insert, modify, and delete comments	5.4
Viewing Comments Inline	Insert, modify, and delete comments	5.4
Viewing Comments as Balloons	Insert, modify, and delete comments	5.4
Using the Reviewing Pane	Insert, modify, and delete comments	5.4
Revealing Document Markup	Display markup	5.3.1
Turning Change-Tracking On and Off	Enable, disable, accept, and reject tracked changes	5.3.2
Inserting Tracked Changes	Manage track changes	5.3
Deleting Your Changes	Manage track changes	5.3
Accepting Changes from Another User	Enable, disable, accept, and reject tracked changes	5.3.2
Rejecting Changes from Another User	Enable, disable, accept, and reject tracked changes	5.3.2
Setting Track Change Options	Change tracking options	5.3.3
Comparing Two Versions of a Document	Compare document versions	5.2.1
Merging Different Versions of a Document	Merge document versions	5.2.2
Combining Changes Made by Different Authors	Combine revisions from multiple authors	5.2.3

Blue Yonder Airlines is a large company with hundreds of employees. In your job as a human resources specialist, you are involved in hiring, employee benefit programs, and employee communications. Because many of the documents you work with relate to employee issues, you have to be very careful about keeping documents confidential and available only to those who are authorized to have access. In this lesson, you will learn different ways to guard the security of documents. You will prepare an employee evaluation for sharing with a supervisor and work together with a colleague to create an offer letter.

KEY TERMS
certificate
certificate authority
digital signature
legal blackline
markup

SOFTWARE ORIENTATION

Prepare Commands on the Microsoft Office Button

When you click the Microsoft Office Button and point to the arrow beside the Prepare command, a menu of options appears. These options help you prepare a document for distribution.

Figure 17-1
Prepare the document for distribution menu

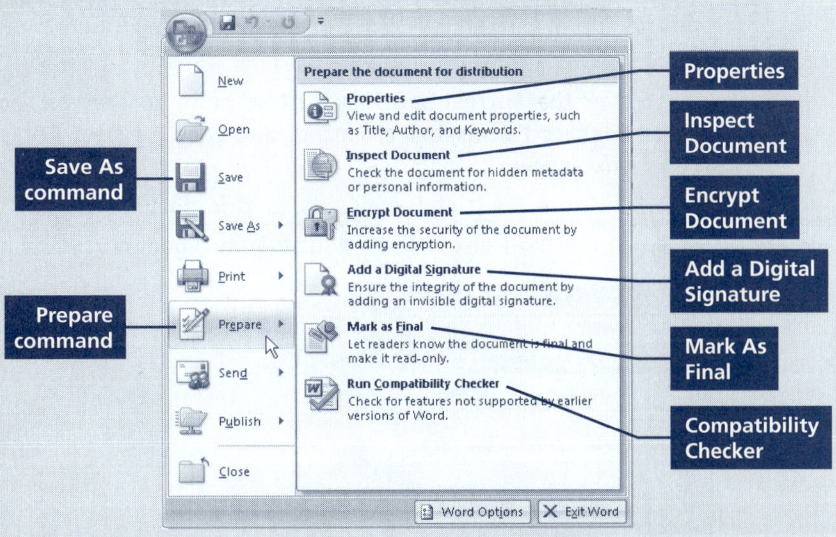

The Prepare the document for distribution menu enables you to set security options for documents. Use Figure 17-1 as a reference throughout this lesson as well as the rest of this book.

Restricting Access to a Document

THE BOTTOM LINE

When you are working in a business setting, there will be times when you are asked to create or review sensitive documents, such as budgets, employee evaluations, or hiring correspondence, that others may be unauthorized to access. To help you manage these tasks and maintain security, Word has commands you can use to restrict access to a document. You can set the permissions for a document, mark a document as final, set an access password for a document, or protect a document.

Setting Permissions for a Document

The Restrict Permissions command enables you to specify the users who have permission to read, change, copy, or print a document. This helps prevent sensitive information from being printed, forwarded, or copied by unauthorized people.

TAKE NOTE*

The Advanced Information Rights Management and Policy Capabilities are only available in Microsoft Office Ultimate 2007, Microsoft Office Professional Plus, or Microsoft Office Enterprise 2007. You must have Word from one of these packages in order to work with this feature.

CD

The ***peerreview*** document is available on the companion CD-ROM.

SET PERMISSIONS FOR A DOCUMENT

GET READY. Before you begin these steps, be sure to launch Microsoft Word and **OPEN** the ***peerreview*** document from the data files for this lesson.

TROUBLESHOOTING

To use the Restrict Permission command, you need to download and install the Windows Rights Management software. Information Rights Management (IRM) is the use of a server to authenticate the credentials of people who create or receive documents with restricted permission. Some organizations use their own rights management servers. For Microsoft Office users without access to one of these servers, Microsoft provides a free trial IRM service. If you do not already have the software, you will be prompted to download it when you access the Do Not Distribute or Restrict Permission As commands. Downloading and using the software requires a .NET Passport account. (If you have a Hotmail or MSN email account, you already have a .NET Passport.) Check with your instructor about whether you should download the software and install it on the computer you are using. If you choose to download it, a wizard will appear providing step-by-step instructions for installation.

1. Click the **Microsoft Office Button**, point to **Prepare**, point to the arrow on the **Restrict Permission** command, and click **Restrict Access**. The Permission dialog box appears.
2. Click the **Restrict Permission to this document** box.
3. In the Read box, key **GregGuzik@blueyonderairlines.com:**, as shown in Figure 17-2.

Figure 17-2

Permission dialog box

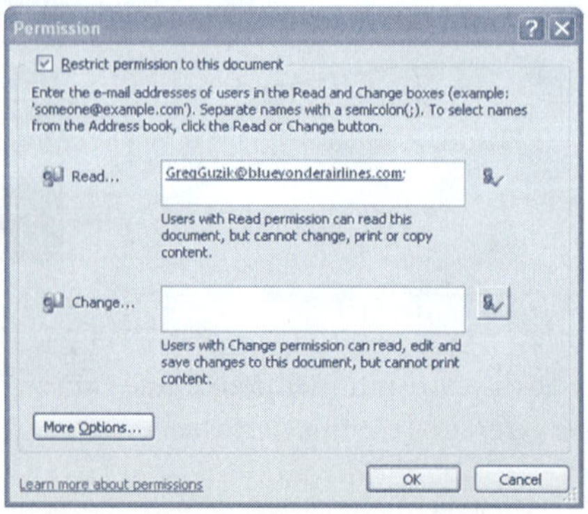

4. You do not want to give any permission to make changes to the document, so leave the Change box empty.
5. Click **OK**. In Figure 17-3, notice that below the Ribbon, a message bar is inserted stating that permissions are restricted.

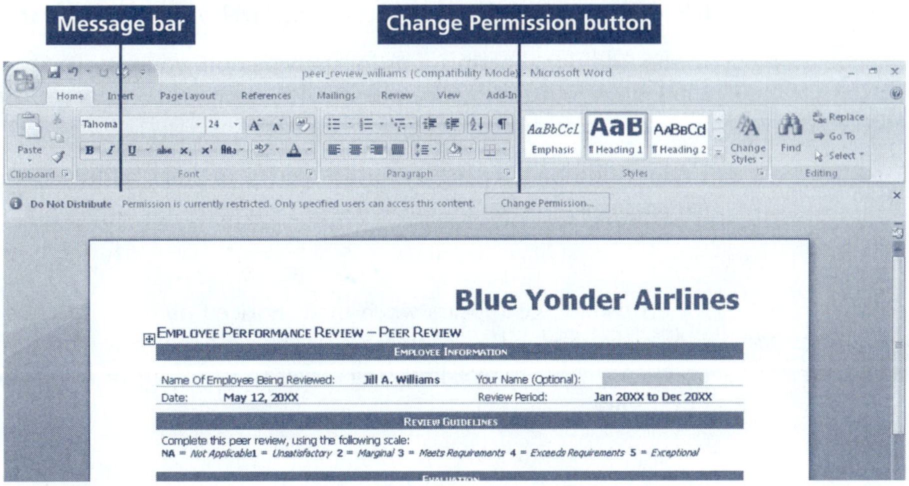

Figure 17-3

Restricted Permissions message bar

CERTIFICATION READY?
How do you set permissions for a document?
6.2.1

6. Click the **Change Permission** button on the message bar. The Permission dialog box appears.
7. Click the **Restrict Permissions to this document** box to remove the checkmark and remove restrictions. The message bar is removed. Click **OK**.
8. **SAVE** your document as ***peer_review_williams***. **CLOSE** the file.

PAUSE. LEAVE Word open to use in the next exercise.

The Restrict Permissions command makes it possible to limit another user's ability to read or make changes to a document.

As you just practiced, you specify users by entering their email addresses. In the Permission dialog box, you can click the Read or Change button to select an email address from your address book.

Click the Options button to display the Permission dialog box, shown in Figure 17-4, where the users with permissions to the document are listed. You can change the permissions level here or add users.

Figure 17-4

Permission dialog box—More Options

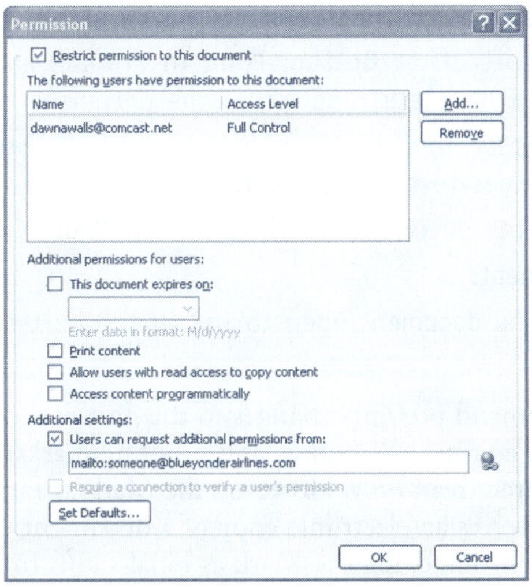

Users with Read permission can read the document but cannot copy, print, or change the document. Users with Change permission can read, edit, and save the document, but they cannot print. Typically, the author of the document has Full Control permission, which means he or she can do anything to a document. The author can grant Full Control permission to other users by selecting the user's email address and clicking the Access Level title, which becomes a permissions level menu. The author can then choose either Read, Change, or Full Control to specify the level of permission for that user.

In the Additional permissions for users section, you can specify a document expiration date, allow users to print the document, allow users with read permission to copy content, or allow users to access content programmatically.

Under Additional settings, you can specify an email address users can send a message to requesting additional permissions.

TROUBLESHOOTING

An error message appears when unauthorized users try to open the document. The first time an authorized user attempts to open a document with restricted permission, the user must connect to a licensing server to verify his or her credentials and download a use license.

Marking a Document as Final

When you want to share a document but prevent recipients from making changes to it, you can use the Mark As Final command to let the readers know that the document is read-only.

MARK A DOCUMENT AS FINAL

GET READY. OPEN the *reviewform* document from the data files for this lesson.

1. Click the **Microsoft Office Button**. Point to **Prepare** and select **Mark as Final**. A dialog box appears, as shown in Figure 17-5.

Figure 17-5

Microsoft Office Word dialog box

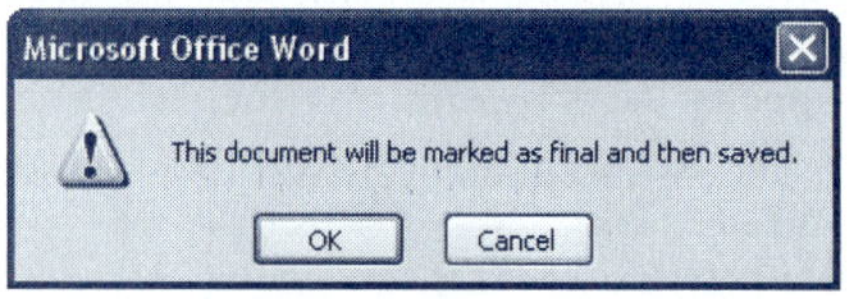

2. Click **OK**. The document is now read-only. (If another dialog box appears confirming that the document has been marked as final, click **OK** to close the dialog box.)
3. Select the title and try to delete it or make a change. Notice that you cannot make changes to the document.
4. Click the **Microsoft Office Button**. Point to **Prepare** and select **Mark as Final** to remove Mark as Final status and return the document to its original status.
5. Select the *B* in *Blue Yonder Airlines* and press the **Delete** key. Notice that you can again make changes to the document.
6. Click the **Undo** button on the Quick Access Toolbar.
7. **SAVE** the document.

   PAUSE. LEAVE the document open to use in the next exercise.

CERTIFICATION READY?
How do you mark a document as final?
6.2.2

The Mark as Final command prevents changes to the document. When a document is marked as final, typing, editing commands, and proofing marks are disabled or turned off, and the document becomes read-only. However, the Mark as Final command is not a security feature. Anyone who receives an electronic copy of a document that has been marked as final can edit that document by removing the Mark as Final status from the document.

TAKE NOTE* Documents that have been marked as final in a 2007 Microsoft Office system program will not be read-only if they are opened in earlier versions of Microsoft Office programs.

Setting an Access Password for a Document

You can protect a document with a password so that only people with access to the password can open or modify the document.

SET AN ACCESS PASSWORD FOR A DOCUMENT

USE the document that is open from the previous exercise.

1. Click the **Microsoft Office Button** and then click the **Save As** button. The Save As dialog box appears.
2. Click the **Tools** button. Select **General Options** from the menu, as shown in Figure 17-6. The General Options dialog box appears.

Figure 17-6

Save As dialog box and Tools menu

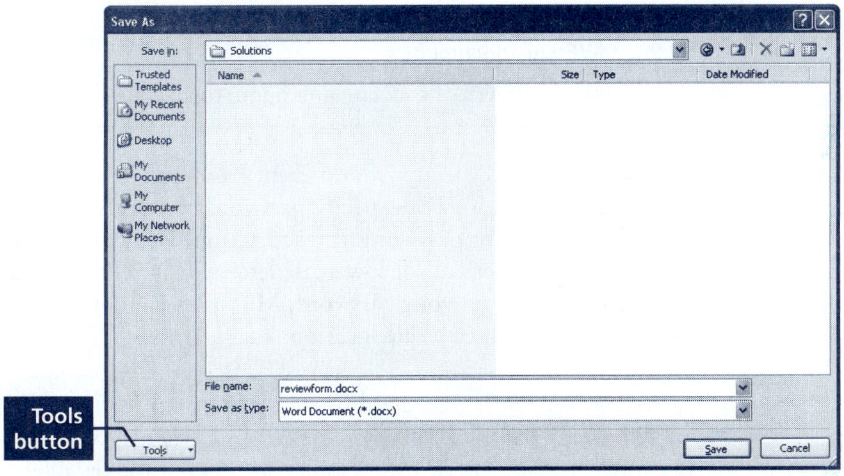

3. Key **HRform_peer** in the Password to open box, as shown in Figure 17-7.

Figure 17-7

General Options dialog box

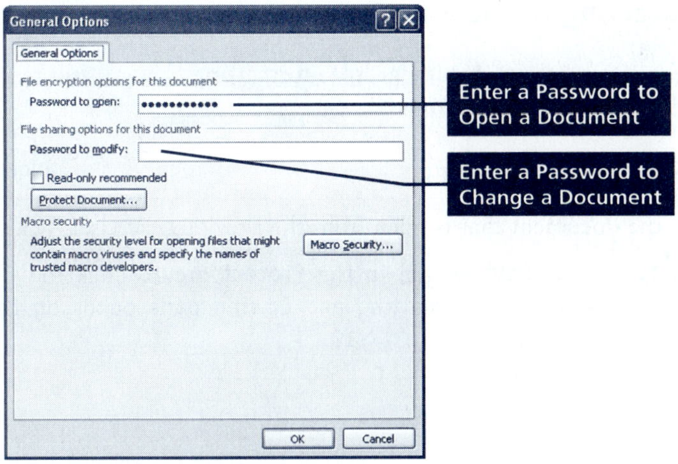

4. Click **OK**. The Confirm Password dialog box appears, as shown in Figure 17-8.

Figure 17-8

Confirm Password dialog box

CERTIFICATION READY?
How do you set an access password for a document?
6.2.3

5. Key **HRform_peer** in the Reenter password to open box and click **OK**.
6. Click **Save** in the Save As dialog box.
7. Close the document.
8. Open the document. A dialog box appears, as shown in Figure 17-9.

Figure 17-9
Password dialog box

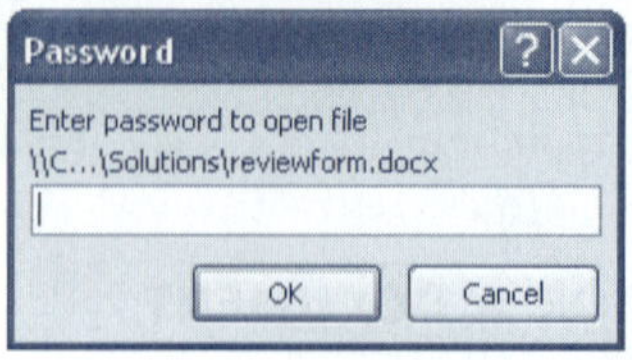

9. Key **HRform_peer** in the box and click **OK**. The document opens.
10. Remove the password protection by clicking the **Microsoft Office Button**, then **Save As**. In the Save As dialog box, click **Tools** and then select **General Options** from the menu.
11. If necessary, select the dots in the Password to open box, press the **Delete** key, and click **OK**.
12. **SAVE** the document.

PAUSE. LEAVE the document open to use in the next exercise.

Word enables you to specify two different passwords—one to open a document and one to modify a document. You can specify passwords for both actions if you want. Just make sure you specify a different password for each action. Passwords are case-sensitive, which means you can specify upper and/or lowercase letters. It is very important for you to remember your password. If you forget your password, Microsoft cannot retrieve it for you. Write down the password and store it in a safe location.

TAKE NOTE*

Use strong passwords that combine uppercase and lowercase letters, numbers, and symbols. Weak passwords do not mix these elements. Strong password: W5!dk8. Weak password: CAR381. Passwords should be 8 or more characters in length. A pass phrase that uses 14 or more characters is better.

Protecting a Document

You can protect a document from formatting changes and restrict editing by using the Protect Document command.

PROTECT A DOCUMENT

USE the document that is open from the previous exercise.

1. On the **Review** tab, in the **Protect** group, click the **Protect Document** button. The Restrict Formatting and Editing pane opens on the right side of your screen, as shown in Figure 17-10.

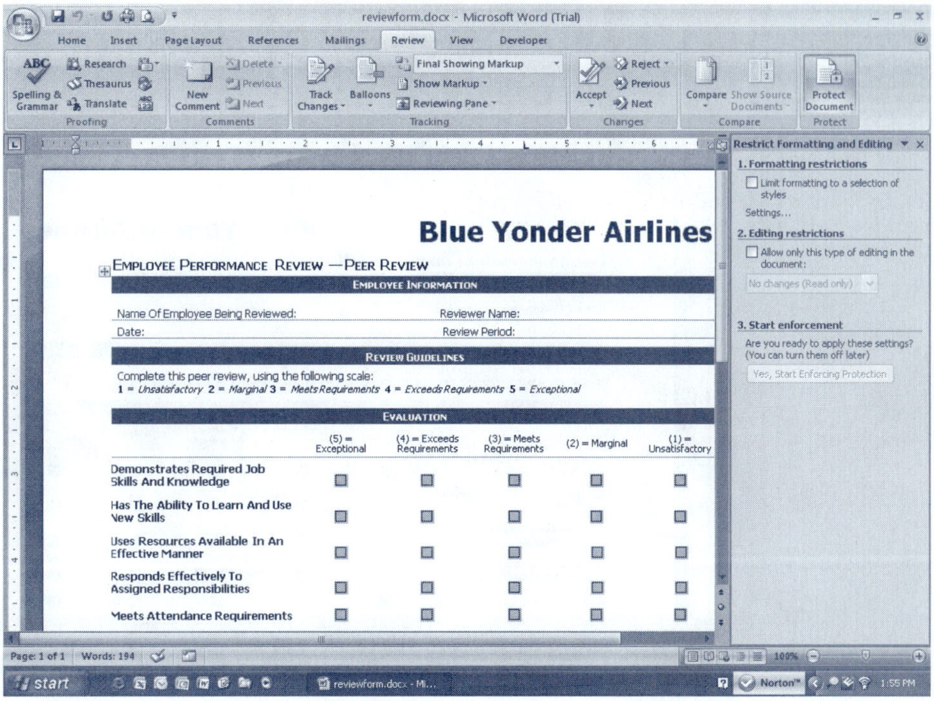

Figure 17-10

Restrict Formatting and Editing pane

2. In the Editing restrictions section, click the **Allow only this type of editing in the document** box.
3. Click the **downward-pointing arrow** of the text box and select Filling in forms from the dropdown menu.
4. In the Start Enforcement section, click the **Yes, Start Enforcing Protection** button. The Start Enforcing Protection dialog box appears, as shown in Figure 17-11.

Figure 17-11

Start Enforcing Protection dialog box

5. Key **BYA_HRDept** in the Enter new password box and in the Reenter password to confirm box and click OK.
6. The Restrict Formatting and Editing pane displays your permissions, as shown in Figure 17-12 and indicates that you may only fill in forms.

Figure 17-12

Your permissions pane

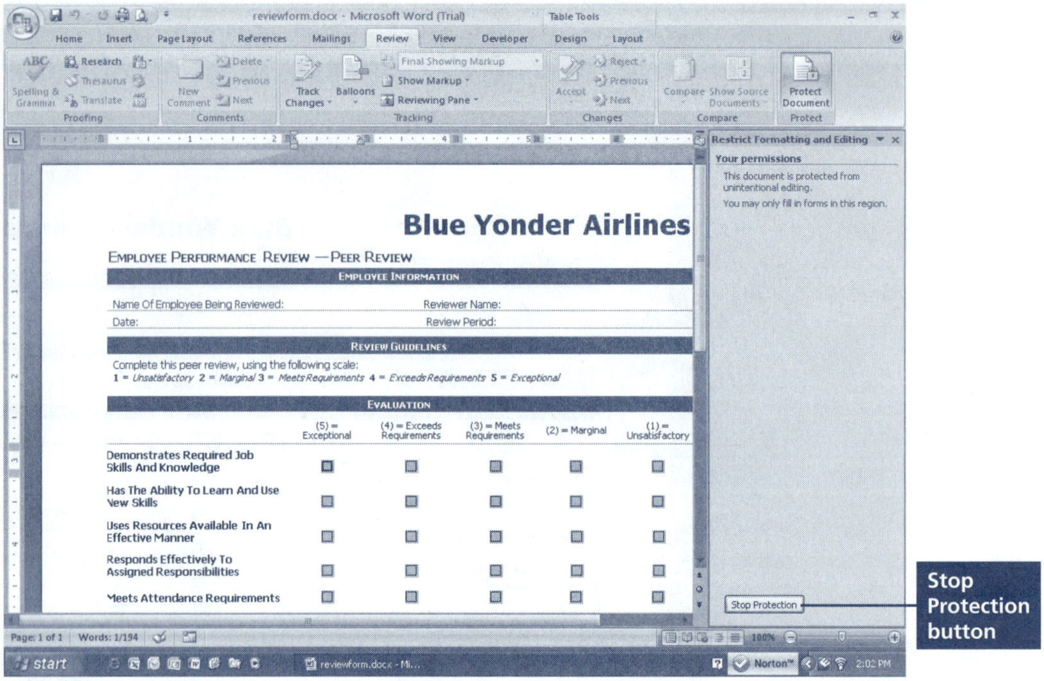

7. Click the **Stop Protection** button. The Unprotect Document dialog box is displayed. Enter the password **BYA_HRDept** and click **OK**.
8. Click the **Allow only this type of editing in the document** box to remove the checkmark.
9. Click the **Protect Document** button on the Ribbon to remove the Restrict Formatting and Editing pane.
10. **SAVE** the document.

PAUSE. LEAVE the document open to use in the next exercise.

CERTIFICATION READY?
How do you protect a document?
6.2.4

The Protect Document pane enables you to set formatting restrictions and editing restrictions, and to start enforcement of protection.

From the Formatting restrictions section of the Protect Document pane, click the Limit formatting to a selection of styles box and then click the Settings link. From the Formatting Restrictions dialog box that appears, you can choose the styles you will allow to be used in the document. By limiting the formatting, you prevent others from modifying styles and applying formatting directly to the document.

You can also restrict editing, as you did in the previous exercise. Click the Allow only this type of editing in the document box and choose an option from the menu: Tracked changes, Comments, Filling in forms, or No changes (Read only). The Exceptions section enables you to select parts of the document to exclude from the restrictions and specify which users or groups are allowed to edit them.

In the Start enforcement section, click the Yes, Start Enforcing Protection button to turn on the limits you have set.

Using Digital Signatures

NEW FEATURE

THE BOTTOM LINE

Important documents often require signatures, and now Word enables you to sign a document electronically using a digital ID that ensures the signature is authentic. You can add a visible signature line to sign a document, or you can add an invisible digital signature, which has no visible signature line displayed, to a document.

Using a Signature to Authenticate a Document

You can digitally sign a document to give it authenticity, just as you would sign a letter or other printed document with a pen and ink. A digital signature is saved along with the code of the file and is not visible unless you insert a digital signature line, which you will practice in a later exercise.

USE A SIGNATURE TO AUTHENTICATE A DOCUMENT

USE the document that is open from the previous exercise.

1. Click the **Microsoft Office Button** and point to **Prepare**. Select **Add a Digital Signature**. A Microsoft Office Word dialog box about digital signatures appears, as shown in Figure 17-13.

Figure 17-13

Microsoft Office Word dialog box

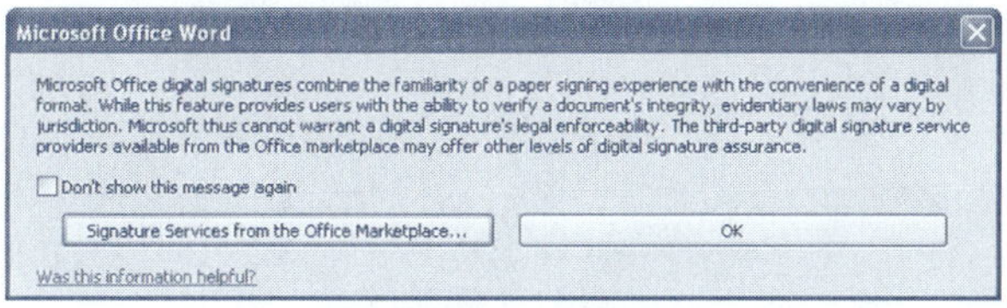

2. Click **OK**. The Get a Digital ID dialog box appears, as shown in Figure 17-14.

Figure 17-14

Get a Digital ID dialog box

3. Click the **Create your own digital ID** button and click **OK**. The Create a Digital ID dialog box appears.
4. Enter information into the dialog box as shown in Figure 17-15.

Figure 17-15

Create a Digital ID dialog box

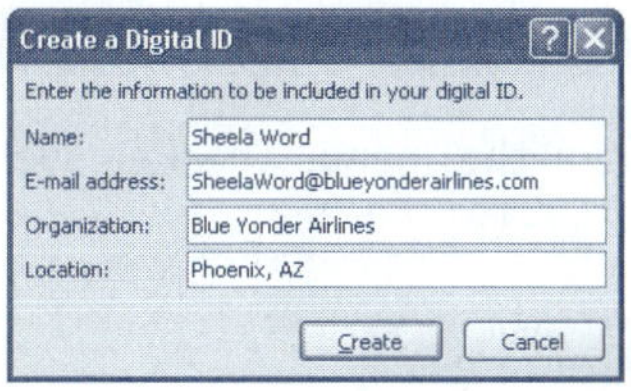

5. Click **Create**. The Sign dialog box appears, as shown in Figure 17-16.

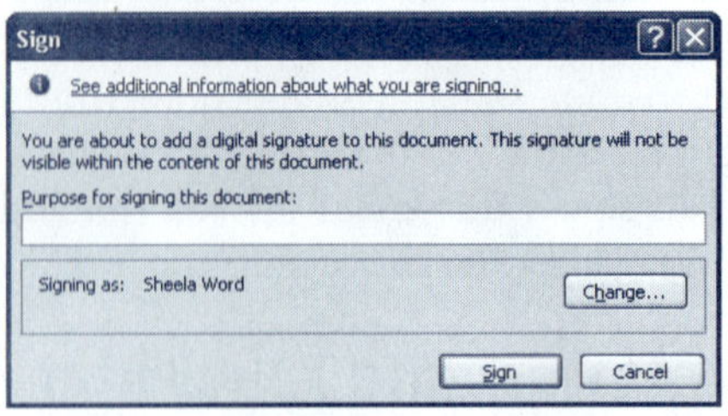

Figure 17-16

Sign dialog box

6. Key **Validation** in the Purpose for signing this document box and click **Sign**. The Signature Confirmation dialog box appears, as shown in Figure 17-17.

Figure 17-17

Signature Confirmation dialog box

7. Click **OK**. A Signatures pane appears on the right side of your screen.
8. In the Signatures pane, shown in Figure 17-18, point to Sheela Word to display the downward-pointing arrow. Click the downward-pointing arrow to display a menu.

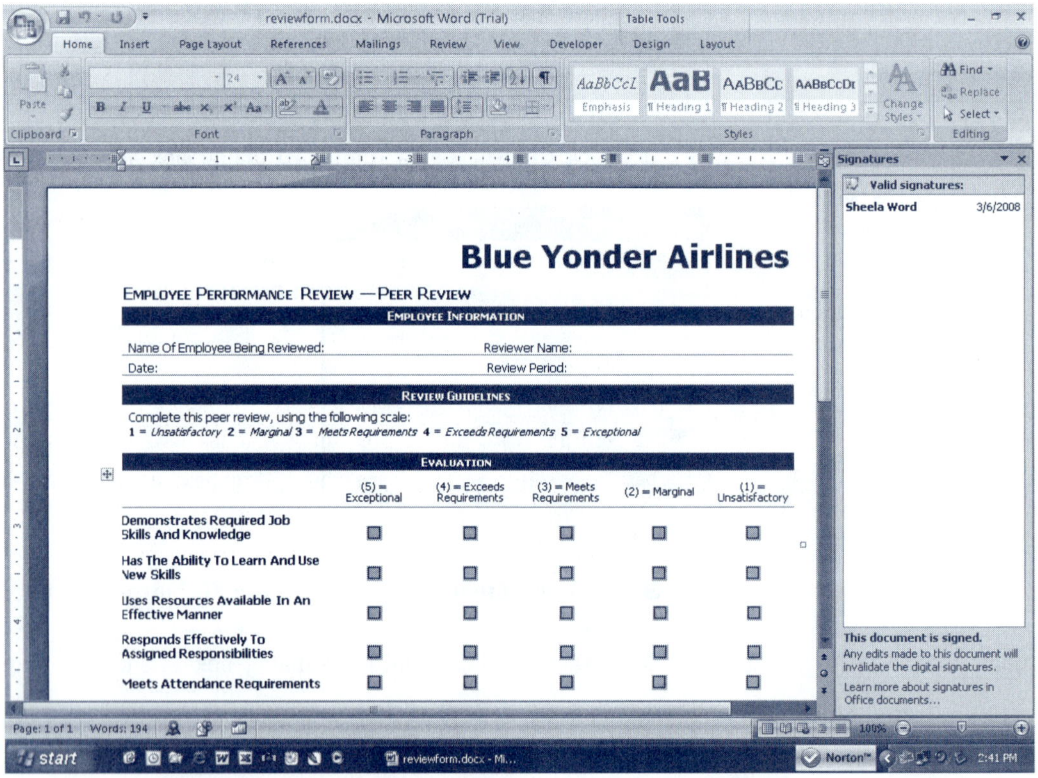

Figure 17-18

Signatures pane

9. Select **Remove Signature** from the menu. The Remove Signature dialog box appears, as shown in Figure 17-19.

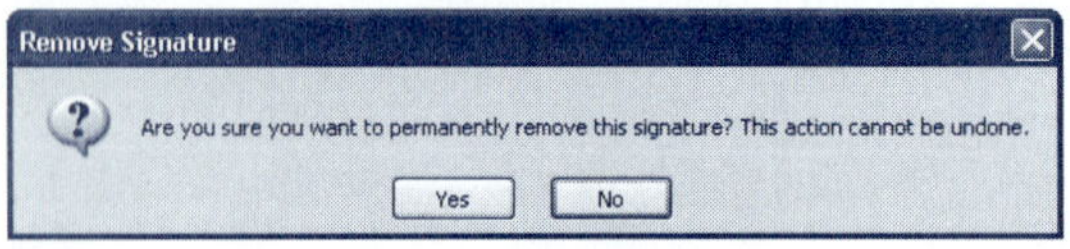

Figure 17-19

Remove Signature dialog box

10. Click **Yes**. A dialog box appears.
11. Click **OK**.
12. Click the **Close** box on the Signatures pane to remove it.
13. **SAVE** the document.

PAUSE. LEAVE the document open to use in the next exercise.

A ***digital signature*** is an electronic signature that verifies that the signer of a document is the person he or she claims to be and the content has not been changed since it was signed. It also helps prove the origin of the signed content.

To digitally sign a document, you need a certificate, also called a Digital ID. A ***certificate*** is a digital means of proving identity and authenticity. You need to either purchase a certificate or create one yourself.

To provide authenticity, the certificate must be issued from a trusted ***certificate authority***, which is a company that issues digital certificates, keeps track of assigned certificates, verifies a certificate's validity, and tracks revoked or expired certificates.

CERTIFICATION READY?
How do you use a signature to authenticate a document?
6.3.1

As you just practiced, you can sign a document by clicking the Microsoft Office Button, pointing to Prepare, and selecting Add a Digital Signature. The Microsoft Office dialog box appears with information about purchasing a digital signature from the Microsoft Office Marketplace. Or, click OK to display the Get a Digital ID dialog box. Here you can click to Get a digital ID from a Microsoft partner or Create your own digital ID. Note that if you choose to create your own Digital ID, no one else can verify the authenticity of your signature.

Inserting a Digital Signature in a Document

Using a visible signature line in a document makes it possible for organizations to get signatures for important documents such as contracts more quickly. Signature lines eliminate the need to print and mail or fax hard copies of documents back and forth.

INSERT A LINE FOR A DIGITAL SIGNATURE

USE the document that is open from the previous exercise.

1. Position the insertion point at the bottom of the document, on a blank line below *Additional Comments*.

2. On the Insert tab, in the Text group, click the **Signature Line** button. The Microsoft Office Word dialog box appears. Click **OK**. The Signature Setup dialog box appears.
3. Enter information into the dialog box, as shown in Figure 17-20.

Figure 17-20
Signature Setup dialog box

4. Click **OK**. The signature line is inserted.
5. Click the Signature line to select it. Right-click to display the shortcut menu. Select **Sign** from the menu.
6. Click **OK** in the Microsoft Office Word dialog box. The Sign dialog box appears.
7. Key **Sheela Word** next to the X, as shown in Figure 17-21.

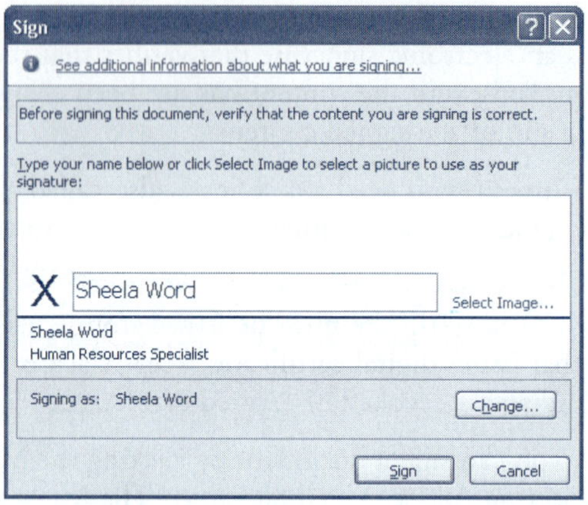

Figure 17-21
Sign dialog box

8. Click **Sign**. The Signature Confirmation dialog box appears. Click **OK**. The signature is inserted and saved with the document, as shown in Figure 17-22.

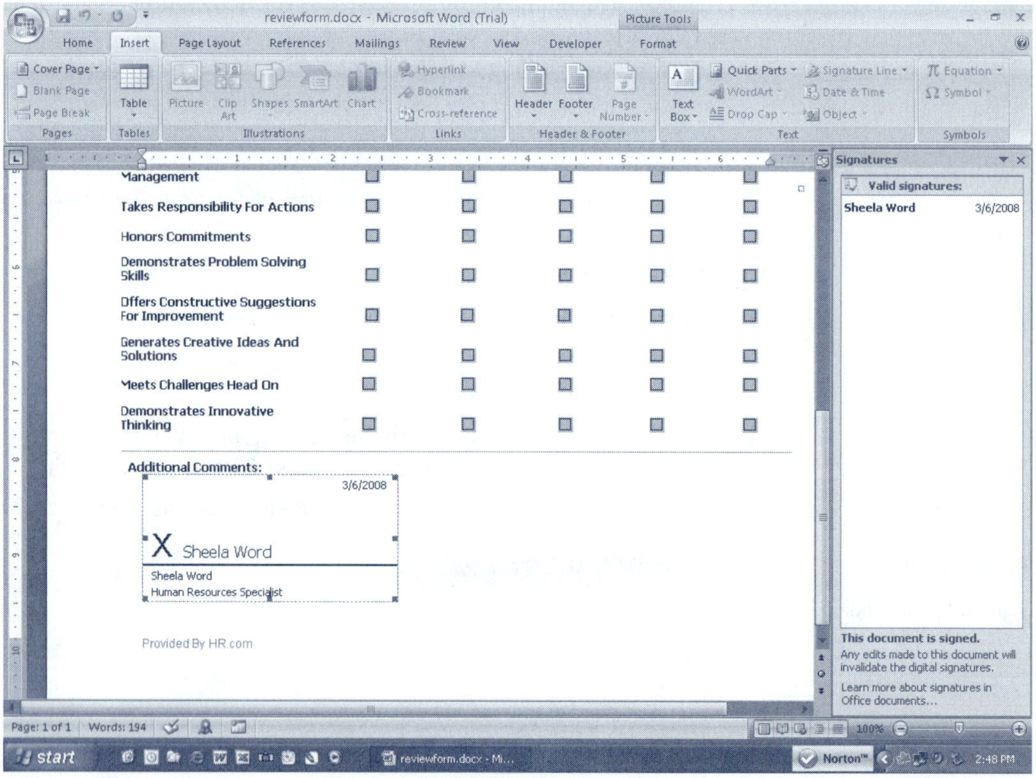

Figure 17-22
Signature

9. Click the **Close** button on the Signatures pane.
10. **SAVE** the document as ***reviewform_signed*** and **CLOSE** the file.

PAUSE. LEAVE Word open to use in the next exercise.

You just inserted a visible line for a digital signature. A signature line looks like a typical signature placeholder that might appear in a print document, but it works differently. When a signature line is inserted into an Office document, the document author can specify information about the intended signer, as well as instructions for the signer. When the document is sent electronically to the intended signer, this person sees the signature line and a notification that his or her signature is requested.

The signer can then click the signature line to digitally sign and either type a signature, select a digital image of his or her signature, or write a signature by using a Tablet PC.

When the signer adds a visible representation of his or her signature to the document, a digital signature is added at the same time to authenticate the identity of the signer. After a document is digitally signed, it will become read-only to prevent anyone from making changes to its content.

CERTIFICATION READY? How do you insert a digital signature in a document? 6.3.2

To remove a signature, you can select it, right-click to display the shortcut menu, and select Remove Signature.

Making Sure a Document is Safe to Share

THE BOTTOM LINE

Before you share documents, you probably check the spelling, formatting, and grammar to make sure everything is correct and appears professional. For these same reasons, it is a good idea to use Word's Compatibility Checker to ensure that a document's features are compatible with other versions of Word. You should also use Word's Document Inspector to remove any hidden or unwanted data.

Using the Compatibility Checker

When you share documents with users who have earlier versions of Word software, you will need to save the document in the Word 97-2003 format for them to be able to open the file. Thus, it is a good idea to use the Compatibility Checker to ensure the features you have included in your document will not be removed or changed when you save it in the Word 97-2003 format.

USE THE COMPATIBILITY CHECKER

CD: The *empoffer* document is available on the companion CD-ROM.

1. **OPEN** the ***empoffer*** document from the data files for this lesson.
2. Save the document as ***employment_offer***.
3. Click the **Microsoft Office Button**, point to **Prepare**, and select **Run Compatibility Checker**. The Microsoft Office Word Compatibility Checker dialog box appears, as shown in Figure 17-23.

Figure 17-23

Microsoft Office Word Compatibility Checker dialog box

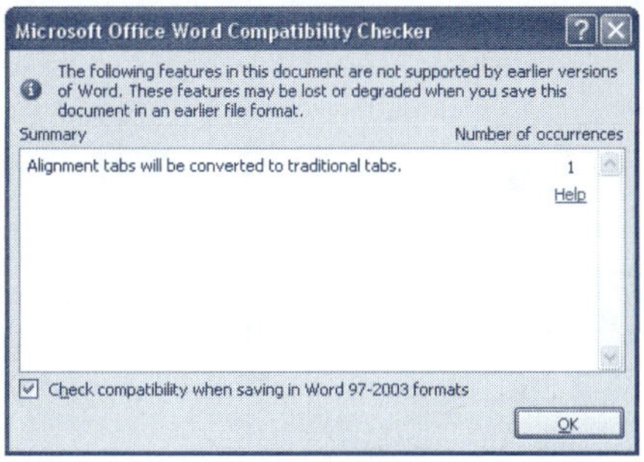

4. Click **OK**.
5. Click the **Microsoft Office Button** and select **Save As**.
6. Key **employment_offer2003** in the File name box.
7. Click the arrow on the Save as type menu and select **Word 97-2003 Document**. Click **Save**. The Microsoft Office Word Compatibility Checker dialog box appears, as shown in Figure 17-24.

Figure 17-24

Microsoft Office Word Compatibility Checker dialog box

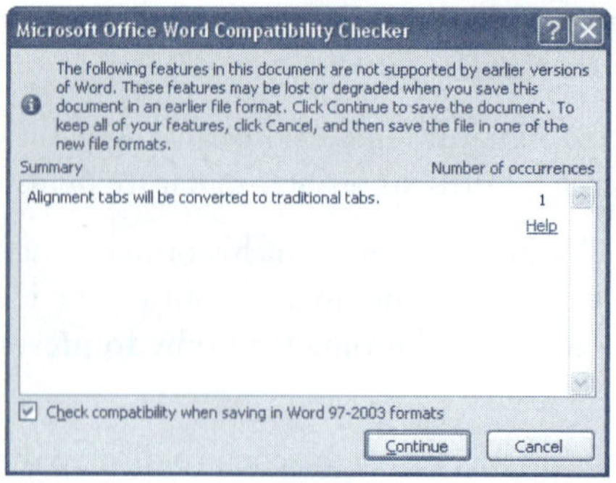

CERTIFICATION READY?
How do you use the Compatibility Checker?
6.1.2

8. Click **Continue** to save the document.

   PAUSE. LEAVE the document open to use in the next exercise.

The Compatibility Checker searches a document for features that are not supported by earlier versions of Word and lists a summary of these features. You can then decide if you need to make changes to the document or if it is okay to save the document in the Word 97-2003 format as it is. Features not supported in the previous versions will be permanently changed when you save a document as a Word 97-2003 format, and those features cannot be converted back to the Office Word 2007 format. This is why it is a good idea to first make a copy of the document and then run the Compatibility Checker on the copy.

Using the Document Inspector

NEW FEATURE

When you share documents, it is a good idea to use Word's Document Inspector to remove any personal data, tracked changes, or other unwanted information.

USE THE DOCUMENT INSPECTOR

USE the document that is open from the previous exercise.

1. Click the **Microsoft Office Button**, point to **Prepare**, and click **Inspect Document**. The Document Inspector dialog box appears, as shown in Figure 17-25.

Figure 17-25

Document Inspector dialog box

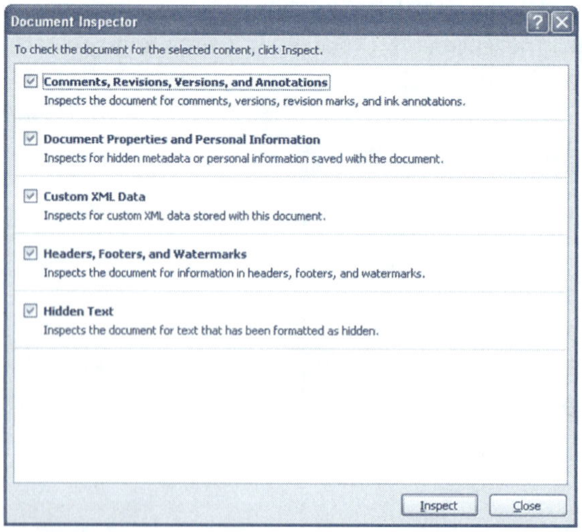

2. Click **Inspect**. The Document Inspector appears, as shown in Figure 17-26.

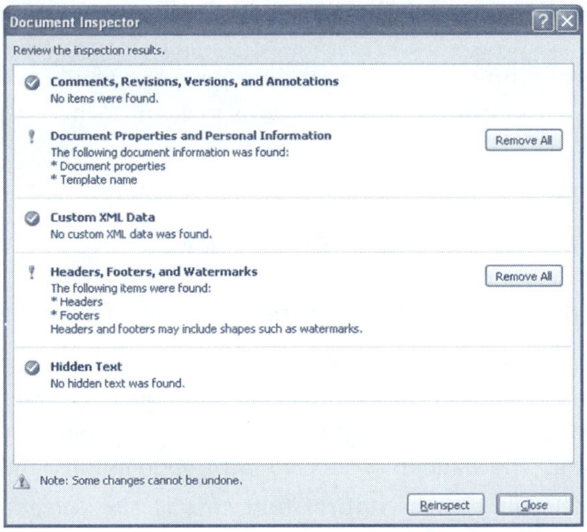

Figure 17-26

Document Inspector dialog box—Reinspect

3. In the Document Properties and Personal Information section, click **Remove All**. The items are removed and the dialog box is updated.
4. You decide to leave the Headers, Footers, and Watermarks as is. Click **Close**.
5. **SAVE** the document and **CLOSE** the file.

PAUSE. LEAVE Word open to use in the next exercise.

CERTIFICATION READY?
How do you use the Document Inspector?
6.1.3

The Document Inspector can remove comments, tracked changes, personal data, and other unwanted information from your documents.

You can use the Document Inspector to find and remove hidden data and personal information in Word 2007 documents as well as earlier versions. It is a good idea to use the Document Inspector before you share an electronic copy of your Office document, such as in an email attachment.

Software Orientation

Review Tab

The Review tab in the Ribbon contains commands for editing documents.

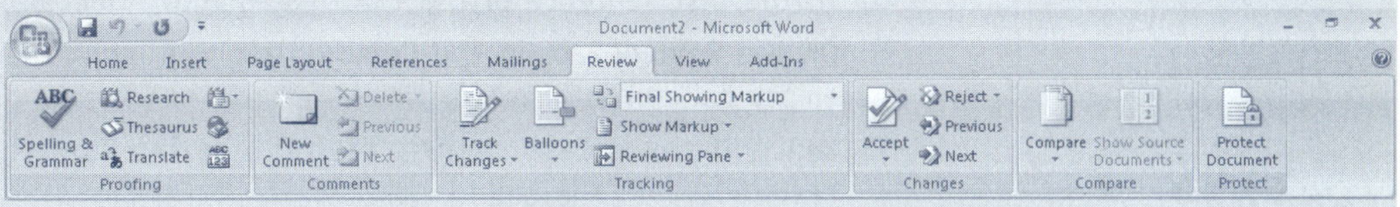

Figure 17-27

Review tab

Use Figure 17-27 as a reference throughout this lesson as well as the rest of this book.

Working with Comments

THE BOTTOM LINE

Word's comment feature enables document reviewers to easily express comments, concerns, or questions in a format that does not get in the way of the text.

Inserting, Editing, and Deleting a Comment

When you are editing or reviewing a document and you have questions or comments about the text, you can key those concerns in a comment. You can also edit and delete comments.

INSERT, EDIT AND DELETE A COMMENT

CD

The ***empoffer*** document is available on the companion CD-ROM.

1. **OPEN** the ***empoffer*** document from the data files for this lesson.
2. In the first sentence of the second paragraph, select *$55,000*.
3. On the Review tab, in the Comments group, click the **New Comment** button. A balloon appears in the right margin of the document where you can key your comment. The balloon is labeled with your initials and the comment number.
4. Key **Will you please confirm that this is the correct salary?** in the balloon, as shown in Figure 17-28.

Figure 17-28

Comment

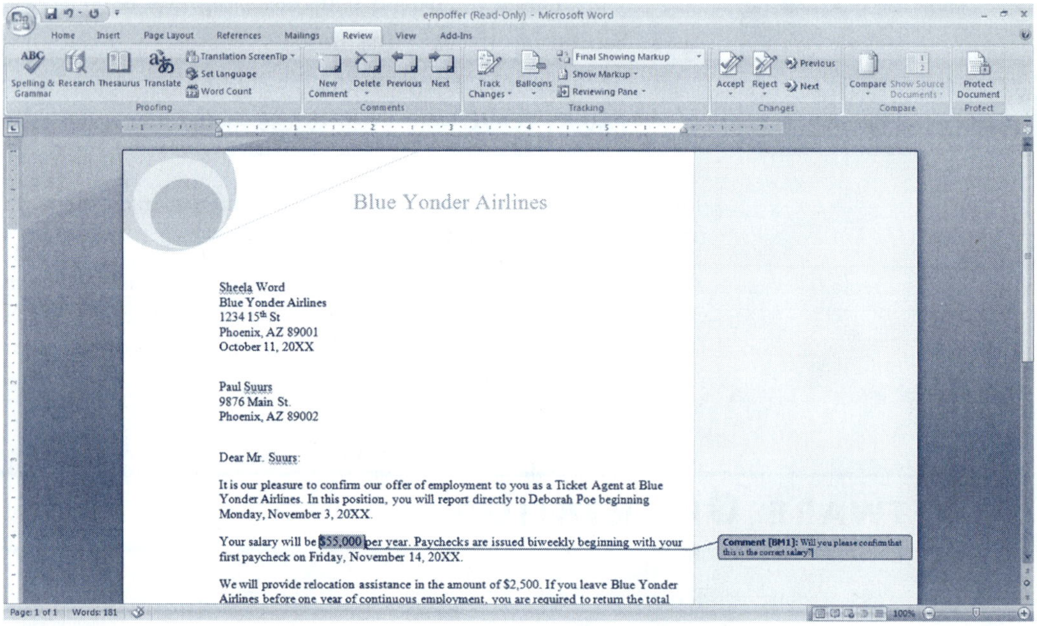

5. In the first sentence of the third paragraph, select *$2,500*.
6. On the **Review** tab, in the **Comments** group, click the **New Comment** button. An empty balloon is inserted.
7. Key **Will you please confirm that this is the correct amount of relocation assistance?** in the balloon.
8. In the second comment balloon, select *is the correct amount of relocation assistance?* and key **person is not eligible for relocation assistance since he lives here in Phoenix?**
9. Right-click the second comment to display the shortcut menu. Select **Delete Comment**. The comment is removed.
10. **SAVE** the document as ***employment_offer_edit***.

PAUSE. LEAVE the document open to use in the next exercise.

CERTIFICATION READY?
How do you insert a comment?
5.4

CERTIFICATION READY?
How do you edit a comment?
5.4

CERTIFICATION READY?
How do you delete a comment?
5.4

As you just learned, inserting a comment in a Word document is easy. Select the text about which you have a question or comment and click the New Comment button. Word inserts a comment balloon on the right side of your screen. The text you selected is highlighted with the same color as the balloon. Word labels each balloon with your initials and the sequential comment number. You can view a comment on the page by hovering the mouse pointer over the highlighted text where the comment is located.

If you need to edit the text in a comment balloon, just click in the balloon and edit the text.

If you want to delete a comment, right-click the comment text or the balloon and select Delete Comment from the shortcut menu.

ANOTHER WAY

You can also delete a comment using the Delete button and menu in the Comments group. Select the comment and click the Delete button. The Delete menu also lets you choose to delete All Comments Shown or All Comments in Document.

Viewing Comments

If you would rather not display the comments as balloons in the margins of your documents, you can choose to view them inline. It is easy to switch back and forth using the Balloons menu.

VIEW COMMENTS INLINE AND AS BALLOONS

USE the document that is open from the previous exercise.

1. On the Review tab, in the Tracking group, click the arrow on the **Balloons** button and select **Show all revisions inline**, as shown in Figure 17-29.

Figure 17-29

Balloons button and menu

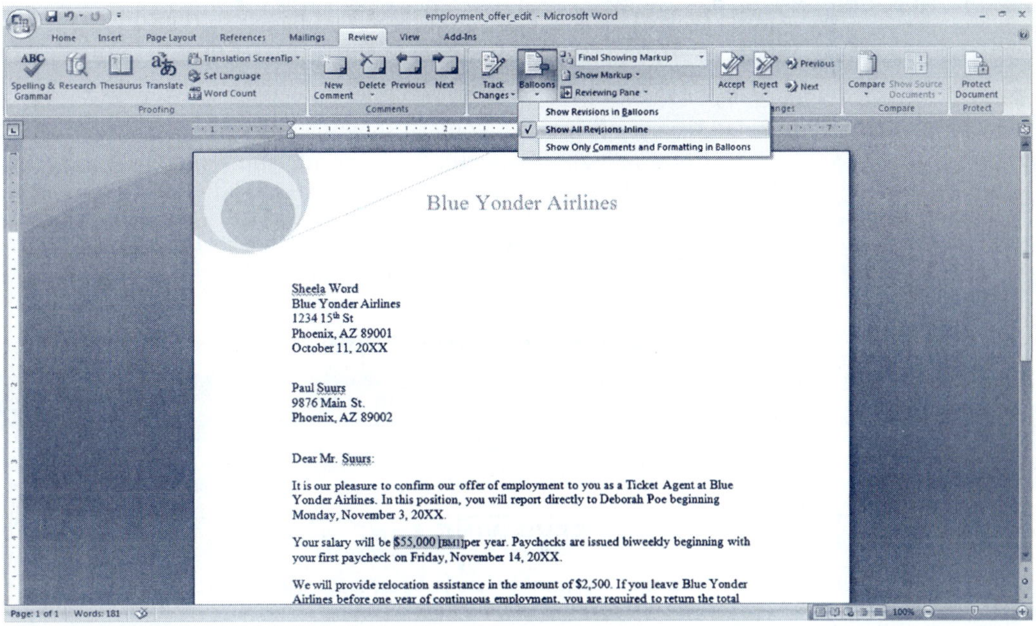

2. Position the mouse pointer over your initials. The comment appears in a ScreenTip, as shown in Figure 17-30.

Figure 17-30

Inline comment shown in a ScreenTip

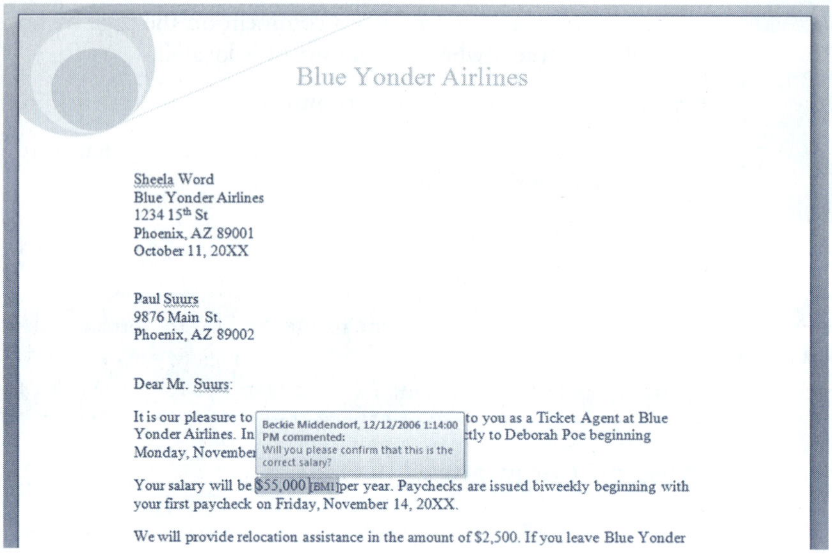

CERTIFICATION READY?
How do you view comments inline?
5.4

CERTIFICATION READY?
How do you view comments as balloons?
5.4

3. On the Review tab, in the Tracking group, click the arrow on the **Balloons** button and select **Show revisions in balloons**. The comment is shown in a balloon again.
4. **SAVE** the document.

PAUSE. LEAVE the document open to use in the next exercise.

The Balloons button contains commands for viewing comments and revisions in balloons or inline. You can also choose to show only comments and formatting in balloons. When you view comments inline, the comments are hidden, but the reviewer's initials are inserted in brackets beside the selected text that relates to the comment. Both the selected text and the reviewer's comments are highlighted. Hover over the initials with the mouse pointer, and the comment appears in a ScreenTip.

As you just learned, you can show comments inline by selecting Show all revisions inline from the Balloons menu. If you decide you want to see the comments in balloons again, select Show revisions in balloons or Show only comments and formatting in balloons.

You can use the Next and Previous buttons in the Comments group to move from comment to comment throughout a document.

Using the Reviewing Pane

The Reviewing Pane contains a summary of the changes that have been made to a document. You can use the Reviewing Pane to make sure you have addressed all the changes in a document

USE THE REVIEWING PANE

USE the document that is open from the previous exercise.

1. On the Review tab, in the Tracking group, click the **Reviewing Pane** button. The Reviewing Pane appears in a window on the left side of the document, as shown in Figure 17-31.

Figure 17-31

Reviewing Pane

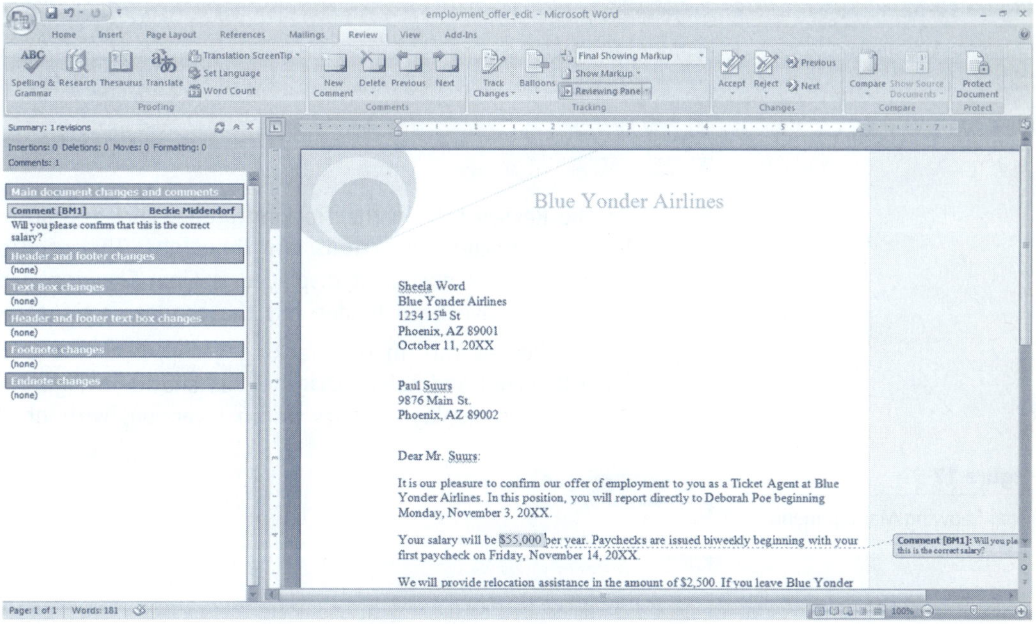

2. On the Review tab, in the Tracking group, click the arrow on the **Reviewing Pane** button and select **Reviewing Pane Horizontal**.
3. On the Review tab, in the Tracking group, click the arrow on the **Reviewing Pane** button and select **Reviewing Pane Vertical**.
4. **SAVE** the document and **CLOSE** the file.

PAUSE. LEAVE Word open to use in the next exercise.

CERTIFICATION READY?
How do you use the reviewing pane?
5.4

In the previous exercise, you displayed the Reviewing Pane. The Reviewing Pane displays all of the changes that currently appear in a document, the total number of changes, and the number of changes of each type.

As you go through a document, you can update the Reviewing Pane by clicking the Update Revision Count button.

The Reviewing Pane menu enables you to choose to display the Reviewing Pane vertically or horizontally.

Revealing Document Markup

If you would like to view only the comments in a document, you can hide the other markups using the Show Markup command.

REVEAL DOCUMENT MARKUP

CD

The *byaemploymentoffer* document is available on the companion CD-ROM.

1. **OPEN** the ***byaemploymentoffer*** document from the data files for this lesson.
2. On the Review tab, in the Tracking group, click the arrow on the **Show Markup** button and select **Comments**, as shown in Figure 17-32. All comments in the document are hidden.

Figure 17-32

Show Markup menu

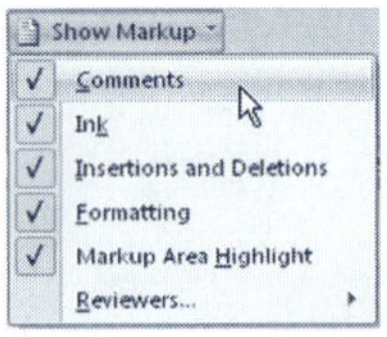

3. On the Review tab, in the Tracking group, click the arrow on the **Show Markup** button and select **Insertions and Deletions**. The insertions and deletions are hidden. Notice that the document displayed is Final Showing Markup, which means the revision marks have been hidden but the changes are incorporated into the document.
4. On the Review tab, in the Tracking group, click the arrow on the **Final Showing Markup** menu and select **Original**, as shown in Figure 17-33. Notice that the document is displayed in its Original version, without changes displayed.

Figure 17-33

Final Showing Markup menu

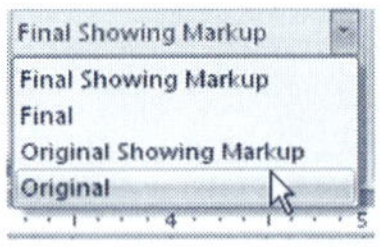

5. On the Review tab, in the Tracking group, click the arrow on the **Original** menu and select **Final Showing Markup**.
6. On the Review tab, in the Tracking group, click the **Show Markup** menu and select **Comments**. All comments are displayed in the document.
7. On the Review tab, in the Tracking group, click the **Show Markup** menu and select **Insertions and Deletions** to display them.
8. **SAVE** the document as ***bya_employment_offer***.

PAUSE. LEAVE the document open to use in the next exercise.

TAKE NOTE*

If you use a TabletPC, you can record and insert Voice comments inside balloons.

Markup includes comments and tracked changes such as insertions, deletions, and formatting changes in a document.

The Show Markup button displays or hides markup. In the Show Markup menu, you can choose to display Comments, Ink (used for inserting comments with a TabletPC), Insertions and Deletions, Formatting, Markup Area Highlight, and the changes from All Reviewers or specific individuals.

Turning Track Changes On and Off

You can begin tracking changes made to a document, including insertions, deletions, and formatting changes, by turning on the Track Changes option.

TURN TRACK CHANGES ON AND OFF

USE the document that is open from the previous exercise.

1. Notice that on the Review tab, in the Tracking group, the **Track Changes** button is orange, indicating it is turned on. Click the **Track Changes** button and select **Track Changes** from the menu, as shown in Figure 17-34. Track Changes is now turned off.

Figure 17-34

Track Changes button and menu

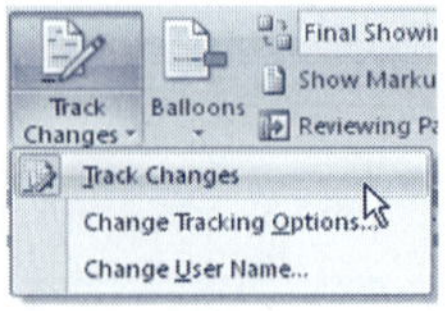

2. Change the date below Sheela Word's address to read **October 12, 20XX**. Notice you can make changes without any revision marks being inserted.

CERTIFICATION READY?
How do you enable and disable tracked changes?
5.3.2

3. On the Review tab, in the Tracking group, click the **Track Changes** button and select **Track Changes** from the menu. Track Changes is now turned on again.
4. **SAVE** the document.

PAUSE. LEAVE the document open to use in the next exercise.

To turn on Track Changes, click the arrow on the Track Changes button and select Track Changes from the menu. When Track Changes is turned on, the button color changes to orange.

To turn off Track Changes, click the Track Changes button and select Track Changes again to remove the icon.

Inserting and Deleting Tracked Changes

When you need to make a change that others need to know about, you can easily turn on Track Changes and insert, delete, or modify text. If you make a mistake while you are inserting changes, you can simply delete your insertions or use the Undo command.

INSERT AND DELETE TRACKED CHANGES

USE the document that is open from the previous exercise.

1. On the Review tab, in the Tracking group, click the **Balloons** button and select **Show only comments and formatting in balloons**.
2. Change the date back to read **October 11, 20XX**. Notice that a revision mark is inserted.
3. At the end of the last sentence of the letter after the fax number, key **or mail to the address above**.
4. Position the insertion point at the top of the document after *Sheela Word* and press the **Enter** key.
5. Key **Human Resources Specialist**.
6. At the end of the last sentence of the letter, delete the words you inserted earlier. Select *or mail to the address above* and press the **Delete** key.
7. **SAVE** the document.

PAUSE. LEAVE the document open to use in the next exercise.

CERTIFICATION READY?
How do you insert and delete tracked changes?
5.3

Inserting and deleting tracked changes is as easy as keying or deleting text. With Track Changes turned on, you simply key new text where you want it or use the Backspace or Delete key to delete words or characters. The Track Changes feature does the rest for you, inserting the revision marks for your insertions, deletions, moves, and comments, as shown in Figure 17-35.

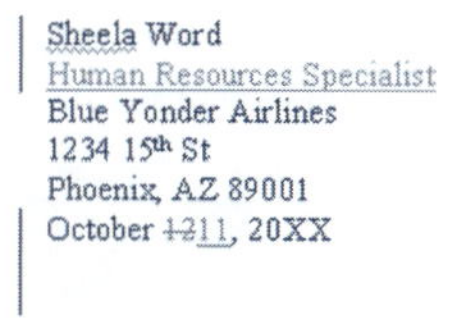
Sheela Word
Human Resources Specialist
Blue Yonder Airlines
1234 15th St
Phoenix, AZ 89001
October ~~12~~11, 20XX

Figure 17-35
Tracked changes

Accepting and Rejecting Changes from Another User

As you review the insertions, deletions, moves, and comments in a document, you can choose to accept or reject each change or accept or reject all changes.

ACCEPT AND REJECT CHANGES FROM ANOTHER USER

CERTIFICATION READY?
How do you accept changes from another user?
5.3.2

CERTIFICATION READY?
How do you reject changes from another user?
5.3.2

USE the document that is open from the previous exercise.

1. Move the insertion point to the beginning of the document.
2. On the Review tab, in the Changes group, click the **Next** button. Human Resources Specialist is selected.
3. On the Review tab, in the Changes group, click the arrow on the **Accept** button and select **Accept and Move to Next** from the menu. The *12* in the October date is selected.
4. Click the arrow on the **Reject** button and select **Reject and Move to Next**. The 11 in the October date is selected.
5. Click the **Reject** button.
6. Click the arrow on the **Accept** button and select **Accept All Changes in Document**.
7. Right-click the comment balloon and select **Delete Comment** from the shortcut menu.
8. **SAVE** the document.

   PAUSE. LEAVE the document open to use in the next exercise.

The Changes group contains commands for moving to Next and Previous changes and for Accepting and Rejecting changes. The Accept and Reject buttons have menus of options for accepting and rejecting changes. As you just practiced, you can Accept and Move to Next change to easily accept and view individual revisions in sequential order. Choose Accept All Changes in Document to accept all changes at one time. In a similar fashion, you can choose to Reject and Move to Next change or Reject All Changes in Document.

Setting Track Change Options

If you do not like seeing red insertion and deletion marks in a document, you can change the color by using the Change Tracking Options command on the Track Changes menu. You can also change the way moves are tracked and the way deletions are marked. The customizations you choose are saved with the document you are working on and will also affect new documents thereafter.

SET TRACK CHANGE OPTIONS

USE the document that is open from the previous exercise.

1. On the Review tab, in the Tracking group, click the arrow on the **Track Changes** button and select **Change Tracking Options**. The Track Changes Options dialog box appears, as shown in Figure 17-36.

Figure 17-36

Track Changes Options dialog box

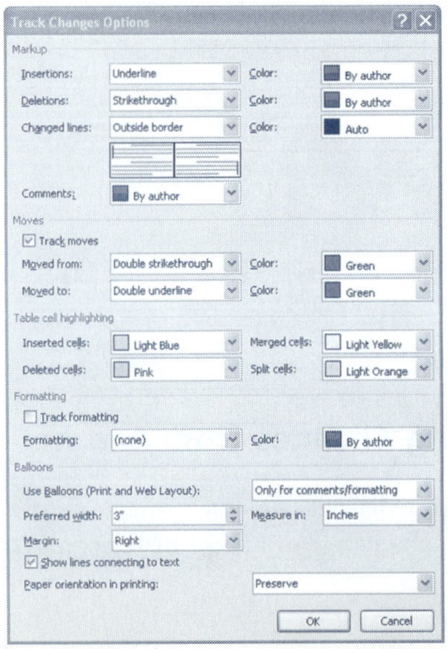

2. In the Markup section, click the menu beside Insertions and select **Color only**.
3. Click the menu beside Deletions and select **Double Strikethrough**.
4. In the Moves section, click the menu beside the Moved from color and select **Yellow**.
5. Click **OK**.
6. Select the three lines of the Paul Suurs address and use a drag-and-drop operation to move it to the top of the page above the Sheela Word address. Notice the Move from color is yellow.
7. Click the **Undo** button on the Quick Access Toolbar.
8. **SAVE** the document and **CLOSE** the file.

PAUSE. LEAVE Word open to use in the next exercise.

CERTIFICATION READY?
How do you set track change options?
5.3.3

The Track Changes Options dialog box enables you to set options for tracking changes. The dialog box contains the following categories of options you can change for tracking purposes.

- Markup: Modify the way insertions, deletions, changed lines, and comments are displayed, as well as the colors used to identify them.
- Moves: This section changes the color and the way moved items are identified.
- Table Cell Highlighting: Enables you to set colors for modifications made to cells in tables.
- Formatting: This section enables you to track formatting and change the way the changes are displayed.
- Balloons: This section lets you set options for when and how to use balloons to display comments or formatting changes.

Comparing and Combining Documents

NEW FEATURE

THE BOTTOM LINE

When you have multiple document versions or authors, Word can help you compare and combine documents so that all the revisions are incorporated.

Comparing and Merging Two Versions of a Document

You can compare two versions of a document by using the Compare command. You also have the option of merging the two versions into a new third document or into one of the existing documents.

COMPARE AND MERGE TWO VERSIONS OF A DOCUMENT

GET READY. Launch Word if it is not already running.

1. On the Review tab, in the Compare group, click the **Compare** button to display the Compare options. Select **Compare** from the list. The **Compare** Documents dialog box appears.
2. In the Original document menu, select ***empoffer***, as shown in Figure 17-37. If you need to browse to find the document, click the folder icon or choose Browse from the dropdown menu and navigate to the data files for this lesson.

Figure 17-37

Compare Documents dialog box

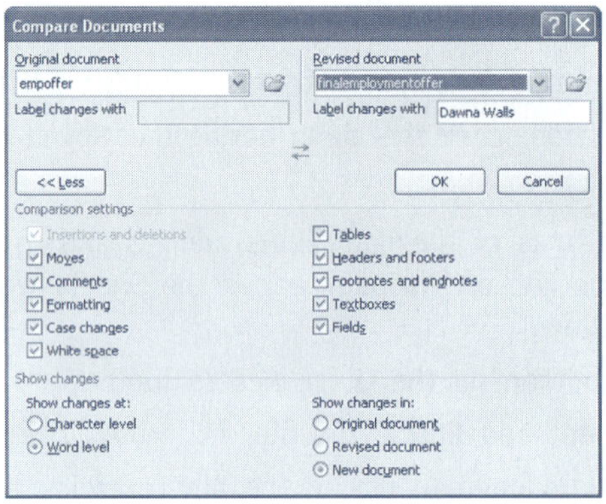

3. In the Revised document menu, select ***finalemploymentoffer*** from the data files for this lesson.
4. If necessary, click the **More** button to view all the options available. Make sure the **New Document** button is selected in the Show Changes section.
5. Click **OK**. A new document appears with all the differences displayed.
6. On the Review tab, in the Compare group, click the **Show Source Documents** button and if necessary, select **Show Both** from the menu. Your screen should look similar to Figure 17-38.

Figure 17-38

Compared Document and Source Documents

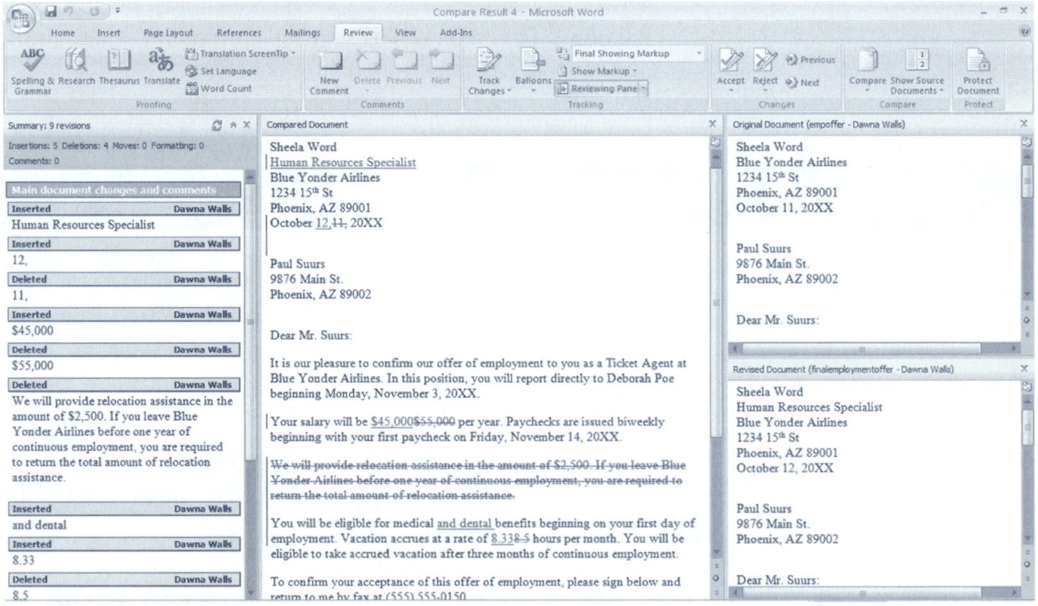

7. On the Review tab, in the Compare group, click the **Show Source Documents** button and select **Hide Source Documents** from the menu.
8. **SAVE** the document as ***employment_offer_merge*** and **CLOSE** the file.

PAUSE. LEAVE Word open to use in the next exercise.

CERTIFICATION READY?
How do you compare two versions of a document?
5.2.1

When you need to compare two versions of a document, you can do so by selecting the Compare command. The Compare command compares two documents and displays only what changed between them. The documents that are being compared are not changed. The comparison is displayed by default in a new third document, referred to as a ***legal blackline*** document.

ANOTHER WAY If you like to view two documents or two versions of a document side-by-side, you can choose the View tab, in the Window group, and click the View Side by Side button.

CERTIFICATION READY? How do you merge different versions of a document? 5.2.2

Combining Changes Made by Different Authors

Combining the changes made by multiple authors is a great way to make sure you have incorporated everyone's suggestions.

COMBINE CHANGES MADE BY DIFFERENT AUTHORS

GET READY. Launch Word if it is not already running.

1. On the Review tab, in the Compare group, click the **Compare** button and select **Combine** from the menu. The Combine Documents dialog box appears.
2. In the Original document menu, select ***flightattendant***, as shown in Figure 17-39. If you need to browse to find the document, click the folder icon or choose Browse from the dropdown menu and navigate to the data files for this lesson.

Figure 17-39

Combine Documents dialog box

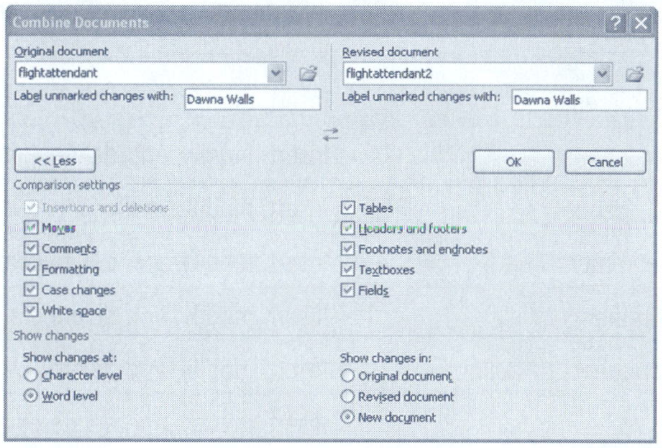

3. On the Revised document menu, select ***flightattendant2*** from the data files for this lesson.
4. Click **OK**. A new document appears.
5. On the Review tab, in the Compare group, click the **Show Source Documents** button and select **Show Both** from the menu.
6. On the Review tab, in the Compare group, click the **Show Source Documents** button and select **Hide Source Documents** from the menu.
7. **SAVE** the document as ***flight_attendant_combined*** and **CLOSE** the file.

CLOSE Word.

CERTIFICATION READY? How do you combine changes made by different authors? 5.2.3

You just combined two documents from two different authors. You could combine more than two documents; you just have to combine them two at a time until all the documents are merged into one.

The Show Source Documents button is useful when you want to show or hide just one or both of the source documents.

SUMMARY SKILL MATRIX

In This Lesson You Learned	Matrix Skill	Skill Number
To set permissions for a document	Restrict permissions to documents	6.2.1
To mark a document as final	Mark documents as final	6.2.2
To set an access password for a document	Set passwords	6.2.3
To protect a document	Protect documents	6.2.4
To use a signature to authenticate a document	Authenticate documents by using digital signatures	6.3.1
To insert a digital signature in a document	Insert a line for a digital signature	6.3.2
To use the Compatibility Checker	Identify document features that are not supported by previous versions	6.1.2
To use the Document Inspector	Remove inappropriate or private information by using Document Inspector	6.1.3
To insert comments	Insert, modify, and delete comments	5.4
To view comments	Insert, modify, and delete comments	5.4
To edit comments	Insert, modify, and delete comments	5.4
To delete comments	Insert, modify, and delete comments	5.4
To view comments inline	Insert, modify, and delete comments	5.4
To view comments as balloons	Insert, modify, and delete comments	5.4
To use the reviewing pane	Insert, modify, and delete comments	5.4
To reveal document markup	Display markup	5.3.1
To turn change-tracking on and off	Enable, disable, accept, and reject tracked changes	5.3.2
To insert tracked changes	Manage track changes	5.3
To delete your changes	Manage track changes	5.3
To accept changes from another user	Enable, disable, accept, and reject tracked changes	5.3.2
To reject changes from another user	Enable, disable, accept, and reject tracked changes	5.3.2
To set track change options	Change tracking options	5.3.3
To compare two versions of a document	Compare document versions	5.2.1
To merge different versions of a document	Merge document versions	5.2.2
To combine changes made by different authors	Combine revisions from multiple authors	5.2.3

Knowledge Assessment

Matching

Match the term in Column 1 to its description in Column 2.

Column 1	Column 2
1. digital signature	**a.** searches a document for features that are not supported in earlier versions of Word and lists a summary of them
2. certificate	**b.** enables you to set options for tracking such as moves, insertions, deletions, formatting, table cells, and balloons
3. certificate authority	**c.** enables you to show or hide source documents when comparing or combining documents
4. markup	**d.** displays all of the changes that currently appear in a document, the total number of changes, and the number of changes of each type
5. Compatibility Checker	**e.** changes a document to read-only and prevents changes to a document
6. Document Inspector	**f.** an electronic signature that verifies the signer of a document is the person he or she claims to be and the content has not been changed since it was signed
7. Reviewing Pane	**g.** the tracked changes and comments such as insertions, deletions, and formatting changes in a document
8. Mark as Final	**h.** also called a digital ID, it is a digital means of proving identity and authenticity
9. Track Changes Options	**i.** removes comments, tracked changes, metadata, or other unwanted information from your documents
10. Show Source Documents	**j.** a company that issues digital certificates, keeps track of assigned certificates, verifies a certificate's validity, and tracks revoked or expired certificates

True / False

Circle T if the statement is true or F if the statement is false.

T | F **1.** The Restrict Permissions command uses a password to limit another user's ability to read or make changes to a document.

T | F **2.** You can specify two different passwords—one to open a document and one to modify it.

T | F **3.** You can create your own digital ID.

T | F **4.** You should run the Compatibility Checker on original files.

T | F **5.** You can insert visible or invisible digital signatures.

T | F 6. Anyone who receives an electronic copy of a document that has been marked as final can edit that document by removing the Mark as Final status from the document.

T | F 7. You cannot delete a visible digital signature.

T | F 8. Features not supported in previous versions of Word will be permanently changed when you save a document in a Word 97-2003 format.

T | F 9. You can accept all changes to a document at once.

T | F 10. When you compare two versions of a document, you must merge them into a third document.

Competency Assessment

Project 17-1: Prepare the Coho Winery Document for Review

You are ready to send an article entitled "How to Reap the Health Benefits of Wine" to a classmate for review. Inspect the document and mark it as final.

CD The ***benefitsofwine*** document is available on the companion CD-ROM.

GET READY. Launch Word if it is not already running.

1. **OPEN** ***benefitsofwine*** from the data files for this lesson.
2. Click the **Microsoft Office Button**, point to **Prepare**, and click **Inspect Document**. The Document Inspector appears.
3. Click **Inspect**.
4. In the Document Properties and Personal Information section, click **Remove All**.
5. Leave the Custom XML Data as is.
6. Click **Close**.
7. Click the **Microsoft Office Button**, point to **Prepare**, and click **Mark as Final**.
8. Click **OK**.
9. Click the **Microsoft Office Button**, point to **Finish**, and click **Mark as Final** to unmark the option.
10. **SAVE** the document as ***benefits_of_wine*** and **CLOSE** the file.

PAUSE. LEAVE Word open for the next project.

Project 17-2: Review Comments in the Coho Winery Document

Your classmate has returned your article with comments and revisions. Review the comments.

CD The ***benefitsofwineedits*** document is available on the companion CD-ROM.

1. **OPEN** ***benefitsofwineedits*** from the data files for this lesson.
2. On the Review tab, in the Changes group, click the arrow on the **Accept** button and select **Accept and Move to Next**. The capital *T* is selected.
3. Click the **Accept** button. The lowercase *t* is selected.
4. Click the **Accept** button. The deleted comma is selected.
5. Click the **Reject** button. The *(USDA)* insertion is selected.
6. Click the **Accept** button. The word *the* is selected.
7. Click the **Accept** button. The deleted words *the key* are selected.
8. Click the **Accept** button. The words *very important* are selected.
9. Click the **Accept** button. A Microsoft Office Word dialog box appears.
10. Click **OK**.
11. On the Review tab, in the **Tracking** group, click the **Reviewing Pane** button to make sure you addressed all the revisions in the document.

12. On the Review tab, in the Tracking group, click the **Reviewing Pane** button again to remove it.
13. **SAVE** the document as ***benefits_of_wine_edits*** and **CLOSE** the file.

PAUSE. LEAVE Word open for the next project.

Proficiency Assessment

Project 17-3: Blue Yonder Airlines Stockholder Agreement

You need to make changes to the stock agreement for participating employees at Blue Yonder Airlines.

CD
The ***stockagreement*** document is available on the companion CD-ROM.

1. **OPEN** ***stockagreement*** from the data files for this lesson.
2. Modify Change Tracking Options for insertions so that they are displayed with an underline and change the color to blue.
3. Display the Reviewing Pane.
4. Use the Accept and Move to Next command to accept each revision in sequence.
5. Close the Reviewing Pane.
6. **SAVE** the document as ***stock_agreement*** and **CLOSE** the file.

PAUSE. LEAVE Word open for the next project.

CD
The ***stockagreement2*** document is available on the companion CD-ROM.

Project 17-4: Prepare the Stock Agreement for Distribution

Make sure the stock agreement is ready to be distributed to eligible employees.

1. **OPEN** ***stockagreement2*** from the data files for this lesson.
2. Inspect the document. Remove all Document Properties and Personal Information as well as Headers, Footers, and Watermarks.
3. Reinspect the document. Remove all Comments, Versions, Revisions, and Annotations as well as Headers, Footers, and Watermarks.
4. Click **Close**.
5. Select the second paragraph that begins with *Agreement made . . . .* and click the **Protect Document** button.
6. Click the **Allow only this type of editing in the document** box and click the **Everyone** box under Exceptions.
7. Click **Yes, Start Enforcing Protection** and enter the password BYA_agree in the dialog box. Close the Restrict Formatting and Editing pane.
8. **SAVE** the document as ***stock_agreement_2*** and **CLOSE** the file.

LEAVE Word open for the next project.

Mastery Assessment

Project 17-5: Employment Offer Letter with Signature Line

CD
The ***byasignature*** document is available on the companion CD-ROM.

You decide to insert a line for a digital signature at the bottom of the Blue Yonder Airlines employment offer letter.

1. **OPEN** ***byasignature*** from the data files for this lesson.
2. Turn off Track Changes.

3. Select and delete the signature line and date at the bottom of the letter.
4. Insert a Microsoft Office Signature Line for Paul Suurs to sign. You do not have his title or email address information.
5. **SAVE** the document as ***bya_signature*** and **CLOSE** the file.

PAUSE. LEAVE Word open for the next project.

Project 17-6: Create a Document with a Password

Create a document that only you can access.

1. **OPEN** a new, blank document.
2. Key your name, address, and telephone number.
3. Protect it with a strong password that you can remember easily or that you can write down and store in a safe place.
4. SAVE the document as ***my_info*** and **CLOSE** the file.

CLOSE Word.

INTERNET READY

Research digital signatures and the Microsoft Partners that provide certificate services. Start by accessing the Add a Digital Signature command from the Microsoft Office Button, on the Prepare menu. Click Signature Services from the Office Marketplace to access the Internet and a list of companies that provide these services. Follow some of the links to find out more information about digital signature services.

Workplace Ready

Word's Security Options

In today's electronic world, sending a document to a coworker as an email attachment is quickly replacing the use of interoffice mail. Along with the many advantages of sending a file in electronic format, rather than as a hard copy, there remains the concern over who may be able to access the file once it leaves your computer.

Securing sensitive business information has always been a top priority for even the smallest of companies. Word provides many security options than can help with achieving this goal. You work as a research analyst for A Datum Corporation, an investment consulting firm. You regularly prepare confidential research reports on investment opportunities for various clients. Each report is prepared exclusively for a specific client and you need to ensure that the information contained in each report cannot be accessed by unauthorized individuals.

You find that assigning a password to each file is the perfect way to ensure that a report is viewed only by the intended client. You choose to set a password for opening each file, then provide your clients with the password information for their documents. Only users with access to a file's password will be able to open that particular file. If needed, you could also set a separate password for modifying a document. Once set, a document can only be modified if the user has provided the appropriate password.

With the security options offered in Word, you can feel confident knowing you will retain control over your documents long after they leave your desk.

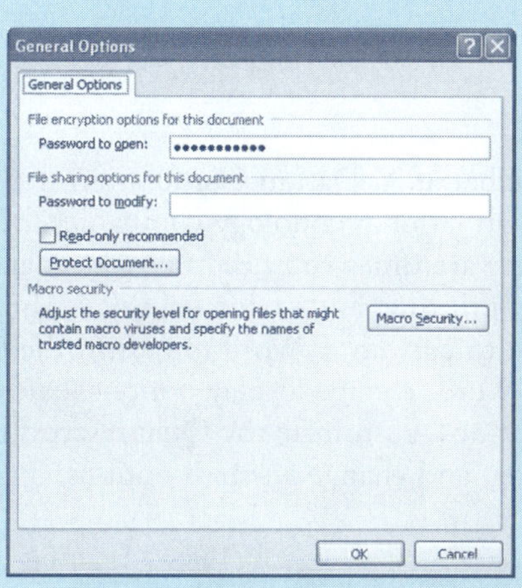

18

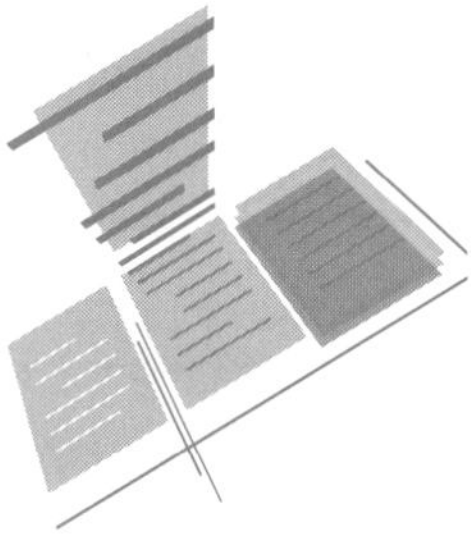

Customizing Word

LESSON SKILL MATRIX

Skills	Matrix Skill	Skill Number
Personalizing Word	Customize Word options	1.4.1
Changing Display Options	Customize Word options	1.4.1
Configure Proofing Options	Customize Word options	1.4.1
Setting Save Options	Customize Word options	1.4.1
Using Advanced Options	Customize Word options	1.4.1
Customizing the Quick Access Toolbar	Customize Word options	1.4.1
Viewing and Managing Add-Ins	Customize Word options	1.4.1
Protecting Your Computer	Customize Word options	1.4.1
Changing Research Options	Change research options	1.4.2

You are employed as a researcher at A. Datum Corporation, a company that provides custom consulting services to information technology companies. Many of the default options for Word are suitable, but there are times you need to make changes to settings for features such as compatibility, editing, printing, and saving. In this lesson, you will learn how to access options that enable you to customize Word to best fit the tasks that you perform. You will learn how to personalize Word, change display options, configure proofing options, set save options, use advanced options, customize the Quick Access toolbar, view and manage add-ins, protect your computer, and change research options.

KEY TERMS

add-in

Software Orientation

Word Options

The Word Options dialog box provides a wide variety of methods to customize how Word is used. Nine different option groups are provided. To access these options, click the Microsoft Office Button and then click the Word Options button on the menu, as shown in Figure 18-1.

Figure 18-1

Word Options button

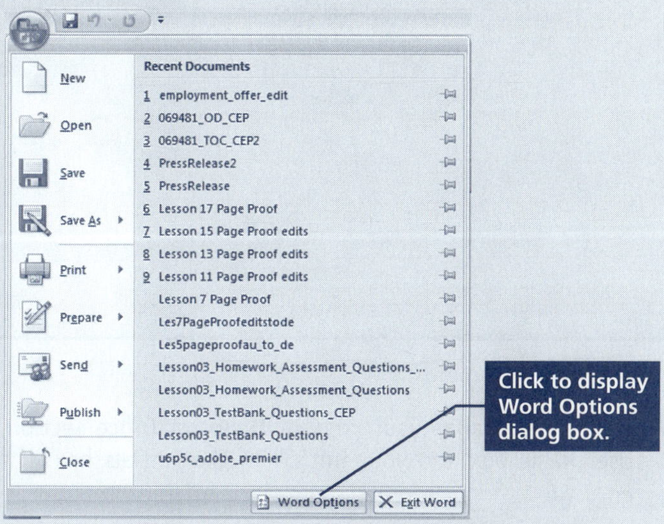

Use this figure as a reference throughout this lesson as well as the rest of this book.

Customizing Word

THE BOTTOM LINE Word can be customized through the different options available in the Word Options dialog box.

Personalizing Word

The Popular screen of the Word Options dialog box contains some of the most popular options that can be customized in Word, including changing your name and initials.

PERSONALIZE WORD

GET READY. Before you begin these steps, be sure to launch Microsoft Word.

1. **OPEN** ***a_datum*** from the data files for this lesson.
2. Click the **Microsoft Office Button** and then click the **Word Options** button to display the Word Options dialog box.
3. Click **Popular** on the left to display the personalize options, shown in Figure 18-2.

CD: The *a_datum* file is available on the companion CD-ROM.

Figure 18-2

Popular options screen

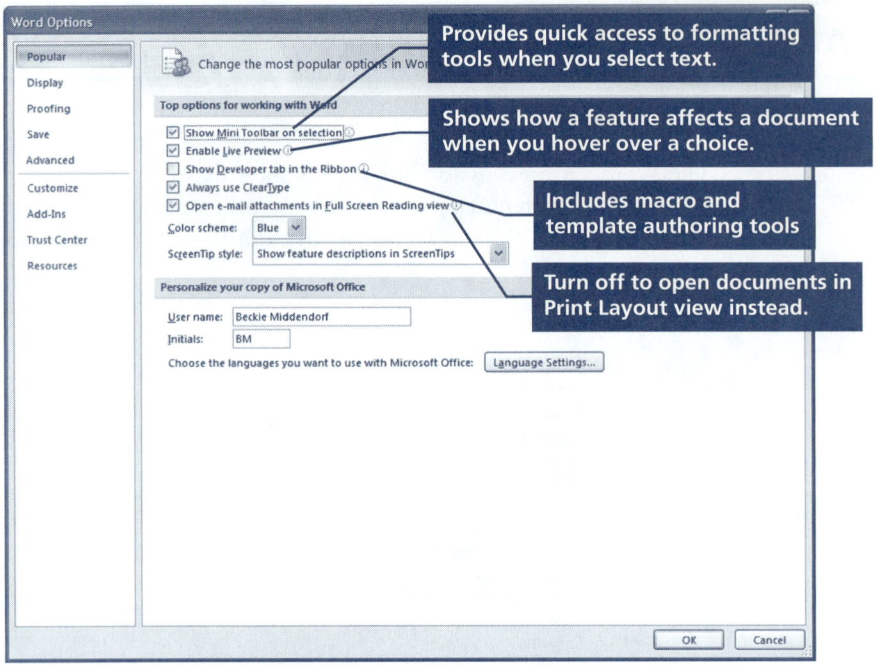

4. In the Personalize your copy of Microsoft Office section, key your name in the User Name box and your initials in the Initials box, if they are not there already.
5. Click **OK**.
6. Click the **Microsoft Office Button**, click **Prepare**, and then click **Properties**. Notice the Author box in the Document Information Panel has your name.
7. Click the **Close** button to close the Document Information Panel.

PAUSE. LEAVE the document open to use in the next exercise.

CERTIFICATION READY?
How do you customize Word options?
1.4.1

The popular options are some of the most frequently used when customizing Word. When creating a new document, Word sets the Author property based on the user name setting. The user name and initials specified here are also displayed in comments and tracked changes.

Take time to explore the contents of each screen of the Word Options dialog box, because there are too many choices to cover in this lesson, The more familiar you become with the options available, the better able you will be to customize Word to suit your needs.

Changing Display Options

The Display screen of the Word Options dialog box contains options for changing how document content is displayed both on the screen and when printed.

CHANGE DISPLAY OPTIONS

USE the document that is open from the previous exercise.

1. Click the **Microsoft Office Button** and then click the **Word Options** button to display the Word Options dialog box.
2. Click **Display** on the left to view the display options, shown in Figure 18-3.

Figure 18-3

Display options screen

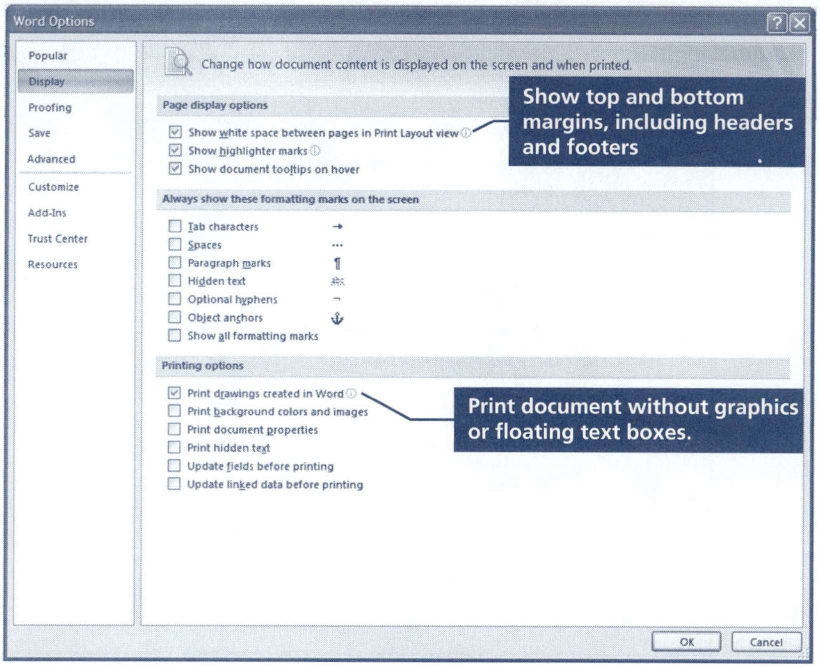

3. In the Always show these formatting marks on the screen section, select the **Paragraph Marks** checkbox.
4. Click **OK**. Notice the paragraph marks are displayed in the document.
5. Open the Word Options dialog box and deselect the **Paragraph Marks** checkbox on the Display screen.
6. Click **OK**.
7. **CLOSE** the document without saving the changes.

PAUSE. LEAVE Word open to use in the next exercise.

CERTIFICATION READY?
How do you customize Word options?
1.4.1

Changing options on the Display screen of the Word Options dialog box affects how content is displayed both on your computer screen and when printed for all documents, not just the document that is currently open. Select or deselect the checkbox for any option you want to turn on or off.

Configuring Proofing Options

The Proofing screen of the Word Options dialog box contains options for changing how Word corrects and formats your text.

CONFIGURE PROOFING OPTIONS

OPEN a new, blank Word document.

1. Click the **Microsoft Office Button** and then click the **Word Options** button to display the Word Options dialog box.
2. Click **Proofing** on the left to display the Proofing options screen, shown in Figure 18-4.

Figure 18-4

Proofing options screen

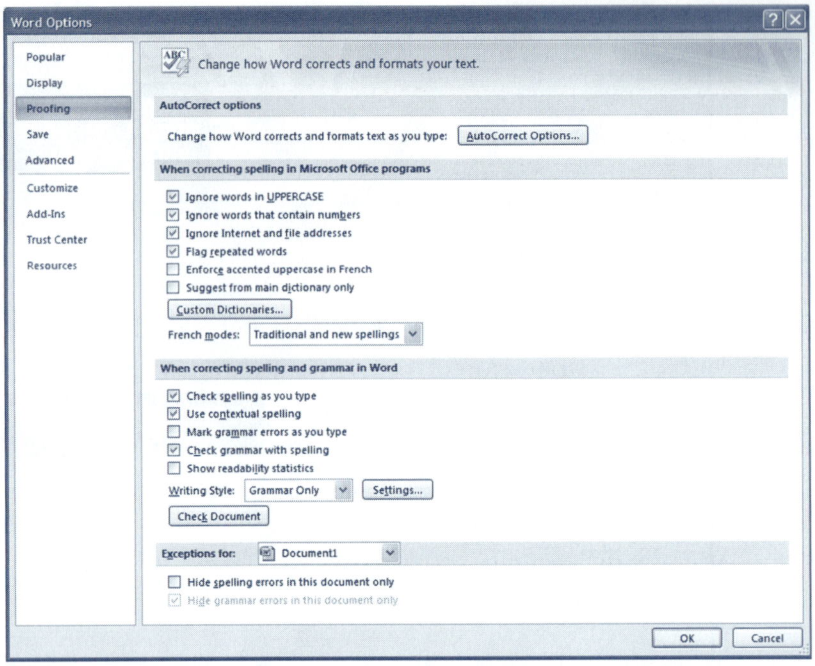

3. Click the **AutoCorrect Options** button to display the AutoCorrect: English (U.S.) dialog box, shown in Figure 18-5.

Figure 18-5

AutoCorrect: English (U.S.) dialog box

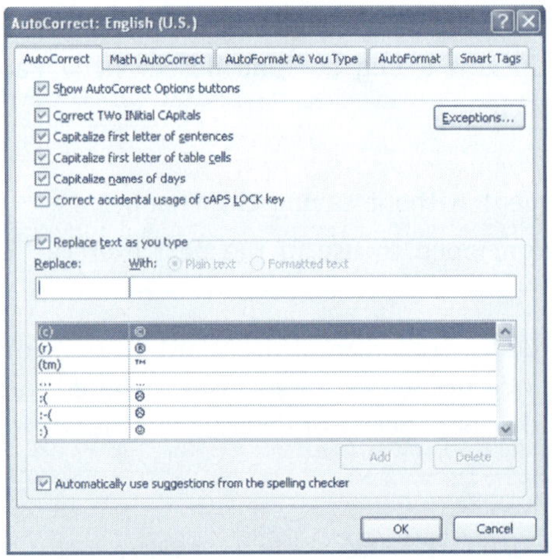

4. Click each of the tabs at the top to view the various options in the AutoCorrect dialog box.
5. Click **OK**.
6. In the When correcting spelling and grammar in Word section, click the **Settings** button to open the Grammar Settings dialog box, shown in Figure 18-6.

Figure 18-6

Grammar Settings dialog box

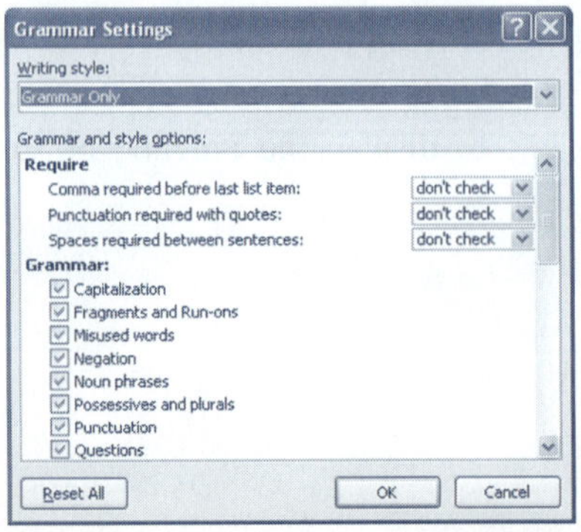

> **CERTIFICATION READY?**
> How do you customize Word options?
> **1.4.1**

7. Scroll down to see all the grammar and style options.
8. Click **OK**.
9. Leave the Word Options dialog box open for the next exercise.

PAUSE. LEAVE Word open to use in the next exercise.

Use the proofing options to specify how Word corrects spelling and grammar. The default options usually work well for most people, but you can customize options to suit your needs.

Click the AutoCorrect Options button to open the AutoCorrect dialog box and make choices about how Word corrects and formats text as you type—for example, having Word automatically correct capitalization errors or replace certain text as you type. Click the Settings button to open the Grammar Settings dialog box and choose which grammar and style options you want Word to check.

Setting Save Options

> The Save screen of the Word Options dialog box contains options for customizing how documents are saved.

SET SAVE OPTIONS

1. From the Word Options dialog box, click **SAVE** on the left to display the save options, shown in Figure 18-7.

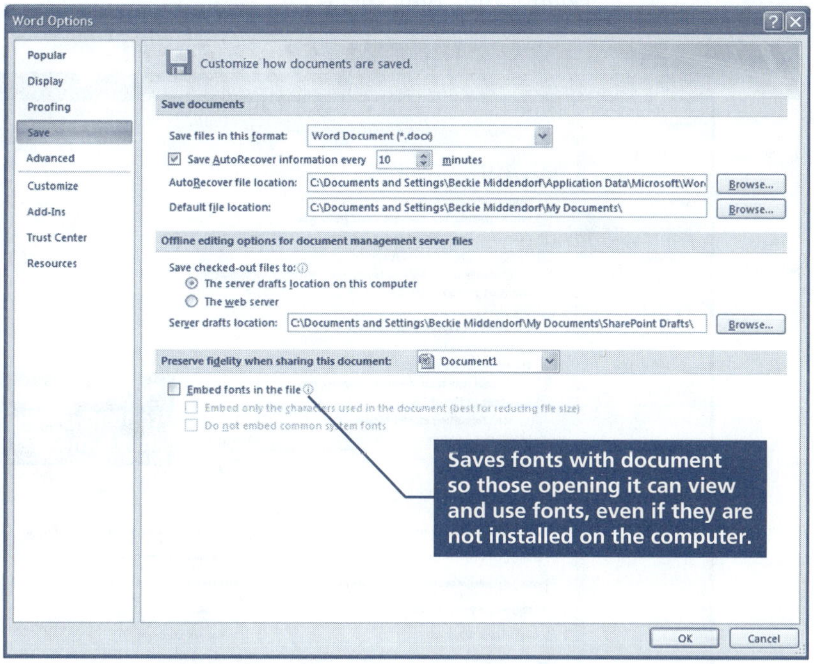

Figure 18-7

Save options screen

2. In the Save documents section, click the **downward-pointing arrow** in the Save files in this format box. The menu displays the options available for changing the default file format used when saving backup files.
3. In the Save AutoRecover information every box, click the **downward-pointing** arrow to change the number of minutes to **9**.
4. Leave the Word Options dialog box open for the next exercise.

PAUSE. LEAVE Word open to use in the next exercise.

> **CERTIFICATION READY?**
> How do you customize Word options?
> **1.4.1**

Use the save options to determine how documents are saved, including backup files for preserving information for your documents, sharing files using a document management server, and embedding fonts in a file.

For example, you can change the default format used to save documents or you can change how often your documents are backed up by using the AutoRecover feature. The My Documents folder, located on drive C, is the default working folder for all the documents created in Microsoft Office programs. On the Save screen, you can choose a different default working folder.

TAKE NOTE*

Any change made to the default working folder applies only to the program that you are currently using. For example, if a different default working folder is selected for Word, the default working folder for Excel will remain My Documents.

Using Advanced Options

The Advanced screen of the Word Options dialog box contains advanced options for working with Word.

USE ADVANCED OPTIONS

1. From the Word Options dialog box, click **Advanced** on the left to display the advanced options. There are several advanced options, many of which are shown in Figures 18-8 thru 18-11.

Figure 18-8

Advanced options screen; Editing and Cut, copy, and paste options

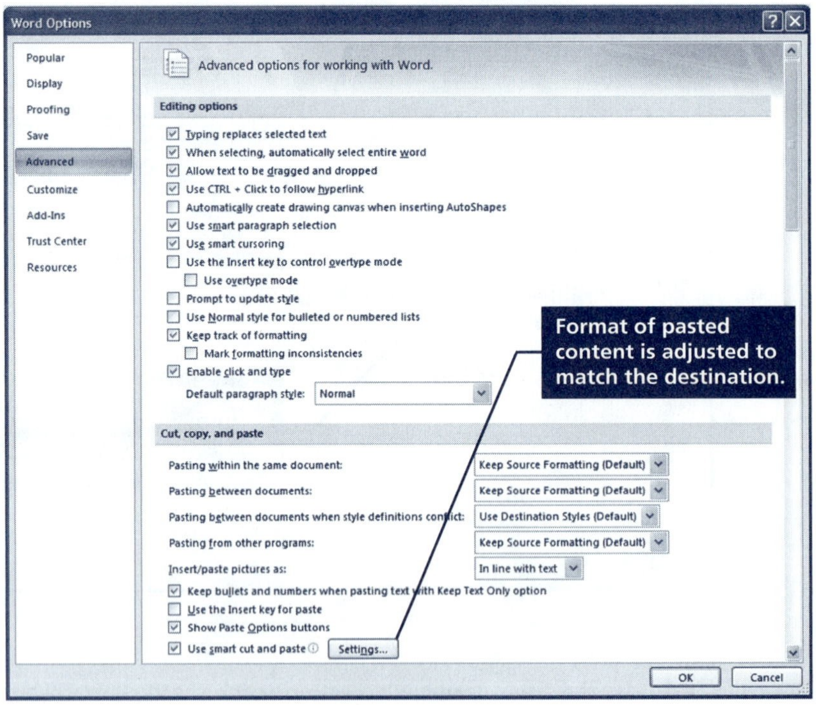

2. Scroll down and in the Display section (shown in Figure 18-9), click the upward-pointing arrow in the Number of documents in the Recent Document list box to change it to **10**.

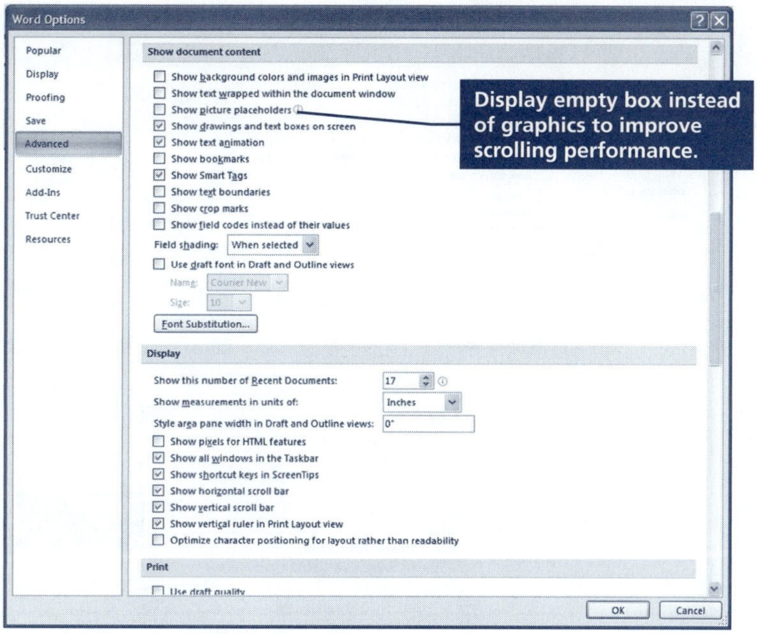

Figure 18-9

Advanced options screen; Show document content and Display options

3. Click **OK**.
4. Click the **Microsoft Office Button** and notice that the Recent Document list now displays ten documents, but only the first nine are numbered.
5. Click the **Word Options** button to display the Word Options dialog box.
6. On the Advanced screen, scroll down to the Save section (shown in Figure 18-10) and click to select the **Prompt before saving Normal template** checkbox. Now if you change the default template, Word will ask if you want to save the changes.

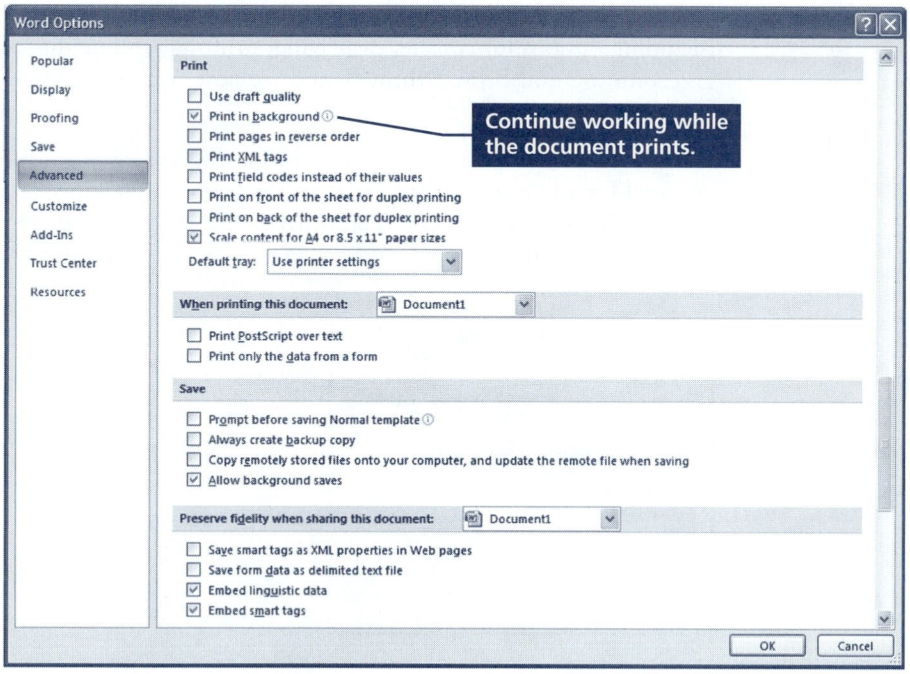

Figure 18-10

Advanced options screen; Print and Save options

7. In the General section (shown in Figure 18-11), key your name and address in the Mailing address box.

Figure 18-11

Advanced options screen; General and Compatibility options

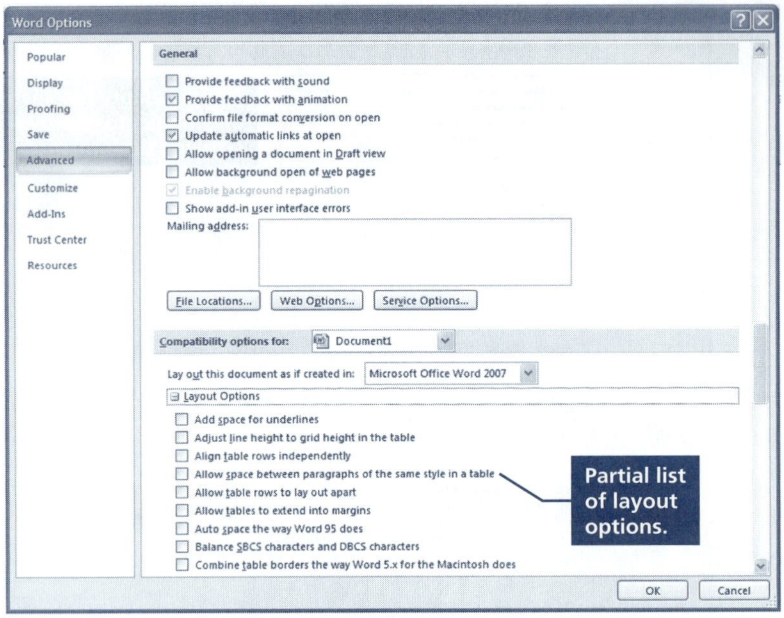

8. Click **OK**.
9. **OPEN** a new, blank Word document if necessary.
10. On the Mailings tab, in the Create group, click the **Labels** button.
11. In the Envelopes and Labels dialog box, click to select the **Use return address** checkbox. Notice that your name and address is displayed in the Address box.
12. Click **Cancel**.

PAUSE. LEAVE Word open to use in the next exercise.

The Advanced screen contains many advanced choices for working with Word documents, including options for editing, displaying, printing, and saving. Some are selected by default and some are not. Browse through and see how you might use some of the options to work more efficiently in Word.

In addition to the multitude of options found on this screen, several dialog boxes can be accessed for additional customization. For example, clicking the Settings button will open the Settings dialog box, shown in Figure 18-12. From here, you can set formatting options to be used when cutting, copying, and pasting.

Figure 18-12

Settings dialog box

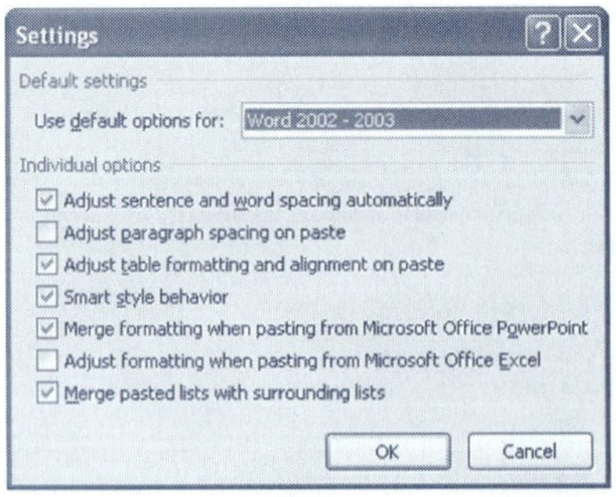

Customizing the Quick Access Toolbar

The Customize screen of the Word Options dialog box enables you to customize the Quick Access Toolbar and keyboard shortcuts.

CUSTOMIZE THE QUICK ACCESS TOOLBAR

1. From the Word Options dialog box, click **Customize** on the left to display the customization options, shown in Figure 18-13.

Figure 18-13

Customize options screen

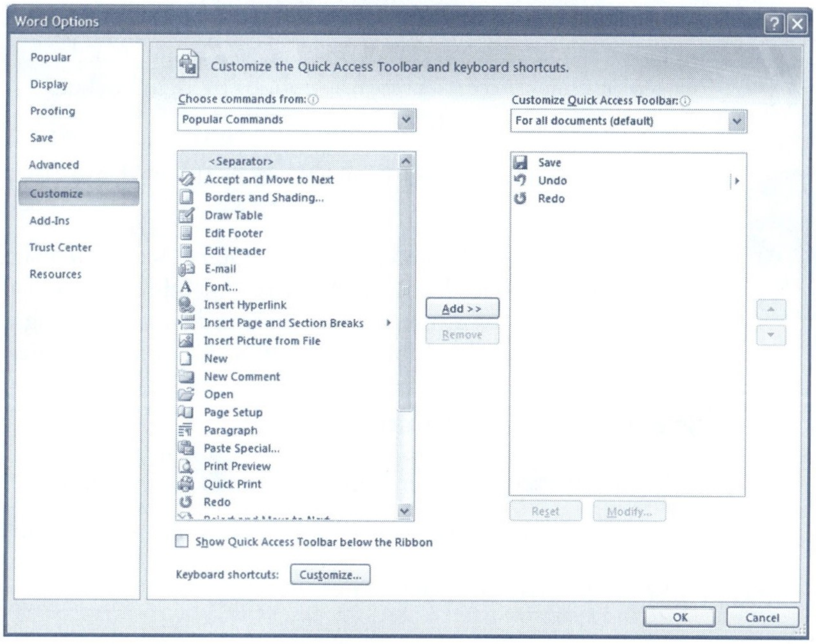

X REF You first learned about the Quick Access Toolbar in Lesson 1.

2. In the Choose commands from list, choose **Office Menu**.
3. In the list of commands, click **New**.
4. Click **Add**.
5. Click **OK**. Notice the New command button is now on the Quick Access Toolbar.
6. Open the Word Options dialog box, click **Customize** on the left, and from the customization screen, click the **Customize** button. The Customize Keyboard dialog box appears, as shown in Figure 18-14.

Figure 18-14

Customize Keyboard dialog box

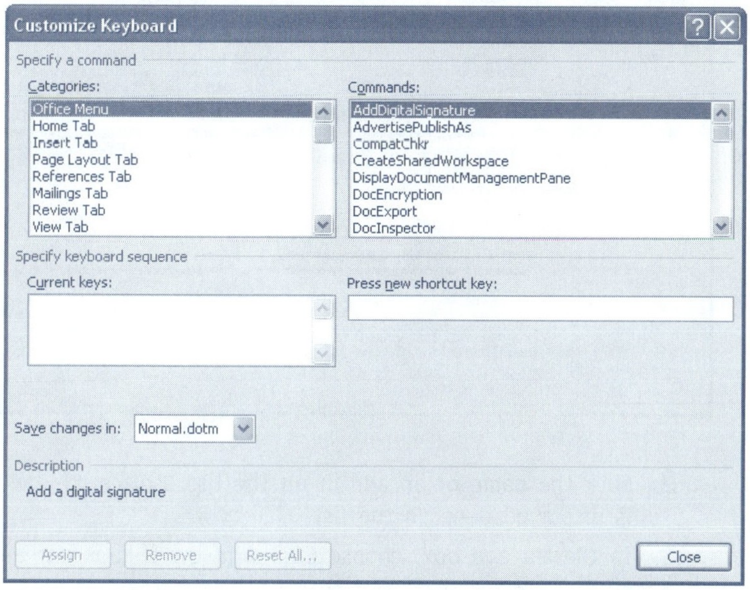

7. In the Categories box, click **Home Tab**.
8. In the Commands box, click **Bold**.
9. In the Current keys box, select **Ctrl**+**Shift**+**B**.

10. Click the **Remove** button.
11. Click **Close**.
12. Leave the Word Options dialog box open for the next exercise.

ANOTHER WAY You can also add an item to the Quick Access Toolbar in the Ribbon by clicking the Customize Quick Access Toolbar button, or by right-clicking anywhere on the bar.

PAUSE. LEAVE Word open to use in the next exercise.

Adding frequently used commands to the Quick Access Toolbar ensures that those commands are always just a single click away. Only commands can be added to the Quick Access Toolbar. The contents of most lists, such as indent and spacing values and individual styles, which also appear on the Ribbon, cannot be added to the Quick Access Toolbar.

Viewing and Managing Add-Ins

The Add-Ins screen of the Word Options dialog box provides a way to view and manage Office add-ins.

VIEW AND MANAGE ADD-INS

1. From the Word Options dialog box, click **Add-Ins** on the left to display the add-ins options, shown in Figure 18-15.

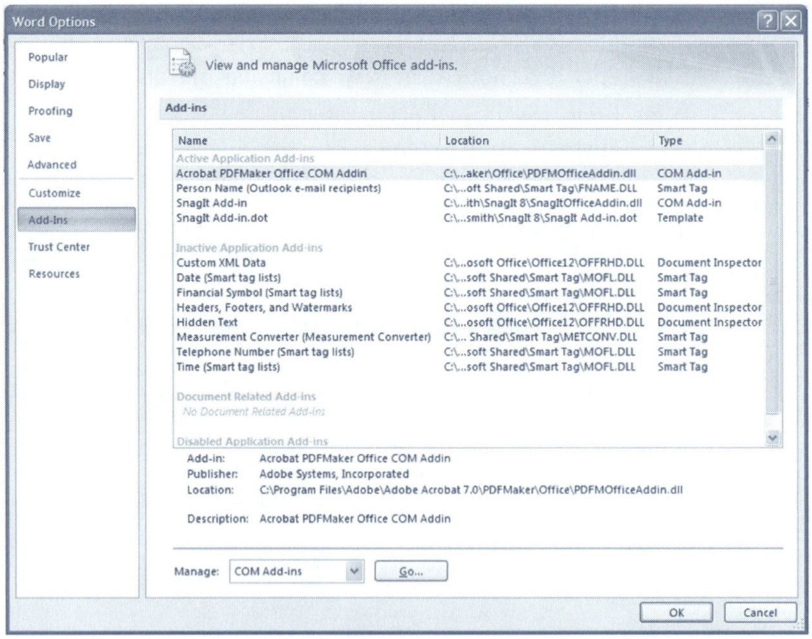

Figure 18-15
Add-Ins options screen

2. Click the name of an add-in on the list. Notice the description of the program is displayed beneath the list.
3. In the Manage box, choose **COM Add-ins** if it is not already selected.
4. Click the **Go** button. The COM Add-ins dialog box is displayed, as shown in Figure 18-16. Use this dialog box to add or remove add-ins.

Figure 18-16

COM Add-ins dialog box

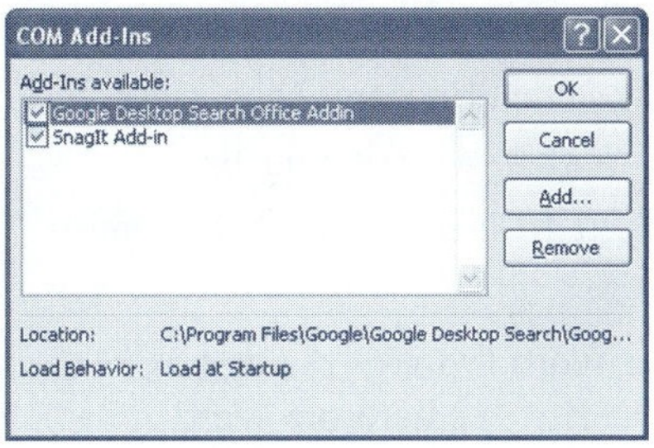

5. Click **Cancel**.

PAUSE. LEAVE Word open to use in the next exercise.

An ***add-in*** is a supplemental program that can be installed to extend the capabilities of Word by adding custom commands and specialized features. An example of an add-in program would be the Google Desktop Search Office Add-in.

TAKE NOTE*

Once you've added an add-in program, it can be accessed from the Add-Ins tab on the Ribbon.

For an add-in to be available whenever Word is started, the add-in must be stored in the Startup folder. To conserve memory and increase the speed of Word, it is a good idea to unload add-in programs that are not often used. When an add-in that is located in your Startup folder is unloaded, it is made unavailable for the current Word session but is automatically reloaded the next time Word is started. To delete an add-in from Word, remove it from the COM Add-ins dialog box.

Protecting Your Computer

The Trust Center screen of the Word Options dialog box provides ways to keep your documents safe, your computer secure, and your privacy protected.

PROTECT YOUR COMPUTER

1. Click the **Microsoft Office Button** and then click the **Word Options** button to display the Word Options dialog box.
2. Click **Trust Center** on the left to display the Trust Center options, shown in Figure 18-17.

Figure 18-17

Trust Center options screen

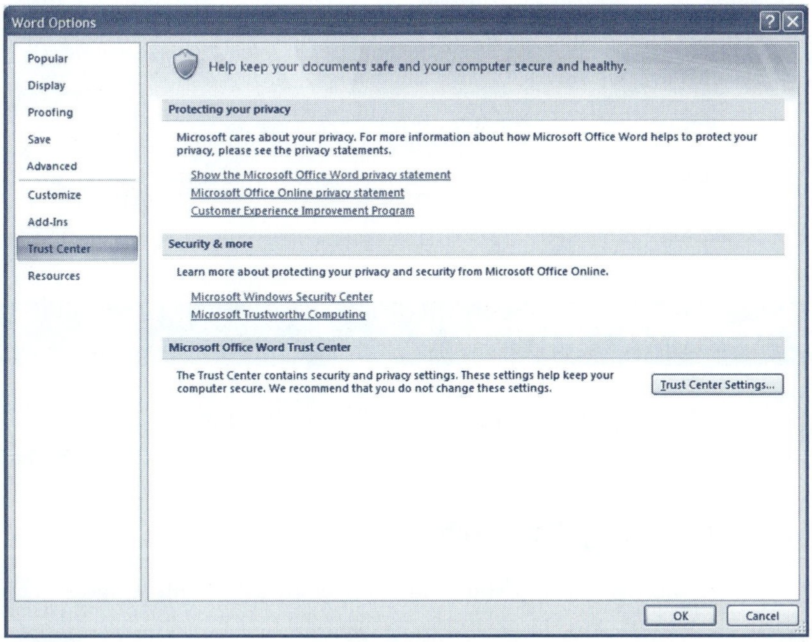

3. In the Security & more section, click the **Microsoft Trustworthy Computing** link.
4. Read about trustworthy computing and then close the browser window.
5. Click **OK** to close the Word Options dialog box.

PAUSE. LEAVE Word open to use in the next exercise.

The Trust Center screen of the Word Options dialog box contains links to information about protecting your privacy and security in Microsoft Word.

Clicking the Trust Center Settings button opens the Trust Center dialog box, which contains security and privacy settings to help keep your computer secure. It is recommended that these settings *not* be changed.

SOFTWARE ORIENTATION

Research Task Pane

The Research Task Pane, shown in Figure 18-18, enables you to search various research and reference services for information related to keyed-in text.

Figure 18-18

Research Task Pane

Use this figure as a reference throughout this lesson as well as the rest of this book.

Changing Research Options

THE BOTTOM LINE The Research command is used to search through available reference materials. The Research Options dialog box enables you to activate a service for searching.

Changing Research Options

Manage the available research options by adding, removing, and updating services, or setting parental controls.

CHANGE RESEARCH OPTIONS

1. On the Review tab, in the Proofing group, click the **Research** button. The Research Task Pane is displayed.

ANOTHER WAY

Another way to open the Research Task Pane is by clicking the Alt key, then clicking on a word in your Word document. Note that the word you click on will automatically be entered into the Search for box of the task pane.

2. Click **Research Options** to display the Research Options dialog box, shown in Figure 18-19.

Figure 18-19

Research Options dialog box

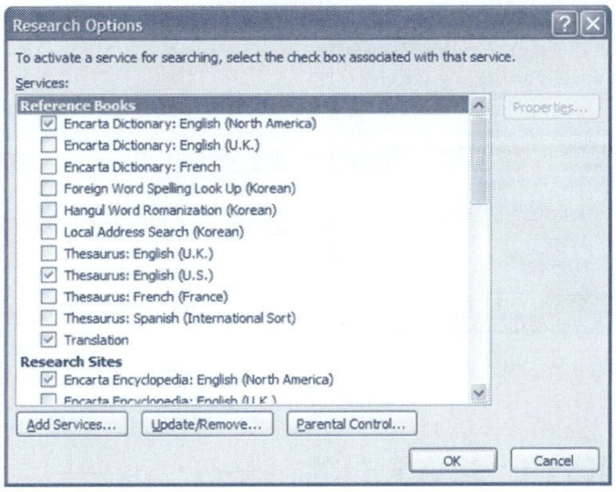

3. Scroll down to the Research Sites section, select **Factiva iWorks™**, and click **Properties** to display the Service Properties dialog box, shown in Figure 18-20.

Figure 18-20

Service Properties dialog box

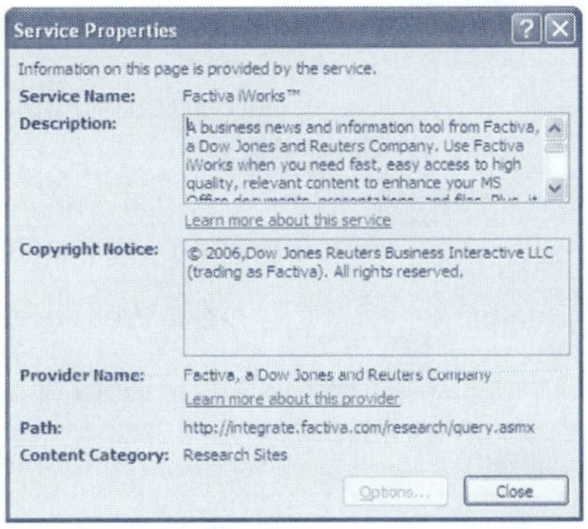

4. Click **Close**.
5. Click **Cancel**.
6. In the Search for box in the Research Task Pane, key **immigration**.
7. Click the **Start searching** green arrow beside the box.
8. Scroll down to see the search results.
9. Just below the Search for box, click the **downward-pointing** arrow and select **All Research Sites**.
10. Scroll down to see the search results.
11. Just below the Search for box, click the **downward-pointing** arrow and select **All Business and Financial Sites**.
12. Click the **plus sign (+)** next to Thomson Gale Company Profiles to display the available information.

13. Click the **Close** button to close the Research Task Pane.

STOP. CLOSE Word.

Open the Research Task Pane to search reference materials such as dictionaries, encyclopedias, and translation services. Click the Research Options link to open the Research Options dialog box, where you can manage the available search services. To see details about a service, select it and click the Properties button.

Clicking the Parental Controls button opens the Parental Controls dialog box, shown in Figure 18-21, where you can choose to filter content to ensure that services block offensive material. You can also ensure that only search services that have the ability to block offensive material are used. By specifying a password on this dialog box, you prevent unauthorized users from changing the Parental Control settings.

Figure 18-21

Parental Controls dialog box

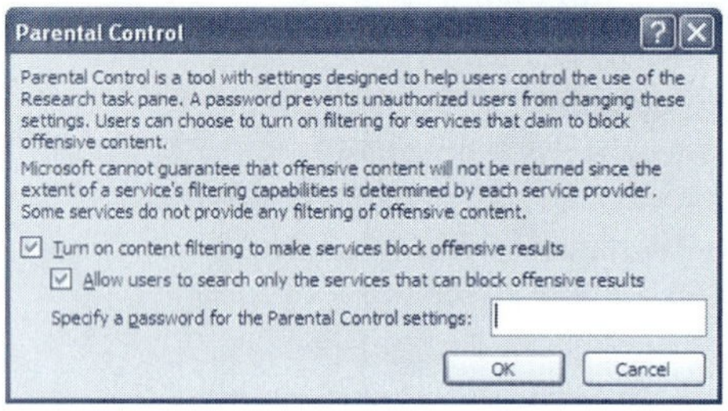

SUMMARY SKILL MATRIX

In This Lesson You Learned	Matrix Skill	Skill Number
To personalize Word	Customize Word options	1.4.1
To change display options	Customize Word options	1.4.1
To configure proofing options	Customize Word options	1.4.1
To set save options	Customize Word options	1.4.1
To use advanced options	Customize Word options	1.4.1
To customize the Quick Access Toolbar	Customize Word options	1.4.1
To view and manage add-ins	Customize Word options	1.4.1
To protect your computer	Customize Word options	1.4.1
To change research options	Change research options	1.4.2

Knowledge Assessment

Fill in the Blank

Complete the following sentences by writing the correct word or words in the blanks provided.

1. You can change your name and initials on the ______________ screen of the Word Options dialog box.
2. The Display screen of the Word Options dialog box contains options to change how document content is displayed on the ______________ and when ______________.

3. The _______________ screen contains options to change how Word corrects and formats your text.
4. The option for choosing a different default file format is found on the _______________ screen.
5. The _______________ folder is the default working folder for all the documents created in Microsoft Office programs.
6. The _______________ screen contains the largest number of options available in the Word Options dialog box.
7. The Customization screen of the Word Options dialog box enables you to customize the Quick Access Toolbar and _______________.
8. An _______________ is a supplemental program that can be installed to extend the capabilities of Word by adding custom commands and specialized features.
9. The _______________ screen of the Word Options dialog box provides ways to keep your documents safe, your computer secure, and your privacy protected.
10. The _______________ command is used to search through available reference materials and services.

Multiple Choice

Select the best response for the following statements.

1. How many option groups are listed in the Word Options dialog box?
   - **a.** three
   - **b.** five
   - **c.** seven
   - **d.** nine
2. What button do you click to display the menu with the Word Options button?
   - **a.** Insert
   - **b.** Advanced
   - **c.** Microsoft Office Button
   - **d.** Display
3. Which Word Office dialog box screen contains the most popular options?
   - **a.** Popular
   - **b.** Save
   - **c.** Resources
   - **d.** Tools
4. Changes made to options on the Display screen will affect
   - **a.** all Word documents.
   - **b.** the document currently in use.
   - **c.** all Office documents.
   - **d.** any document in the My Documents folder.
5. Correct TWo INitial CAps is a proofing option found in which dialog box?
   - **a.** CorrectCaps
   - **b.** AutoCorrect
   - **c.** Grammar Settings
   - **d.** Exceptions

6. The Quick Access Toolbar is for
   a. frequently used commands.
   b. commands from the File menu.
   c. contents of lists on the Ribbon.
   d. recently used documents.
7. Which dialog box is used to add or remove add-ins?
   a. Add/Remove Add-Ins
   b. Manage Add-ins
   c. Add-in Wizard
   d. COM Add-ins
8. It is recommended that the settings in the Trust Center
   a. be updated regularly.
   b. not be changed.
   c. be accessed using keyboard shortcuts.
   d. all of the above.
9. Which reference materials or services are available using the Research Task Pane?
   a. dictionaries
   b. encyclopedias
   c. translation services
   d. all of the above
10. You can choose to filter content to block offensive material in which dialog box?
    a. Filter Content
    b. Parental Control
    c. Block Material
    d. User Controls

Competency Assessment

Project 18-1: Lost Art Photos Return Address

In your position as a marketing assistant at Lost Art Photos, you frequently mail promotional letters. You prepare envelopes for these mailings in Word, and making the company's return address your default option would save time. Change your Word options to set this up.

GET READY. Launch Word if it is not already running.

1. **OPEN** a new, blank Word document.
2. Click the **Microsoft Office Button** and then click the **Word Options** button to display the Word Options dialog box.
3. Click **Advanced** on the left to display the advanced options.
4. Scroll down to the General section and in the Mailing address box, key:
   LostArtPhotos
   5500 Bissell Street
   Grand Junction, CO 98445
5. Click **OK**.
6. On the Mailings tab, in the Create group, click **Envelopes**.

7. In the Envelopes and Labels dialog box, key your name and address in the Delivery address box. Notice that the company's return address is already in the Return address box.
8. Click the Add to Document button.
9. **SAVE** the document as ***lostart_envelope*** and **CLOSE** the file.

PAUSE. LEAVE Word open for the next project.

Project 18-2: Set Research Options

A. Datum Corporation has an overseas branch in the United Kingdom. In your position as a researcher, you sometimes need to take this into account when using Word to look up information. Set the research options accordingly.

1. On the Review tab, in the Proofing group, click the **Research** button to display the Research Task Pane.
2. Click **Research Options** to display the Research Options dialog box.
3. In the Reference Books section, click the checkboxes to select **Encarta Dictionary: English (U.K.)** and **Thesaurus: English (U.K.)**.
4. In the Research Sites section, click the checkboxes to select **Encarta Encyclopedia: English (U.K.)** and **MSN Search U.K.**
5. In the Business and Financial Sites section, click the checkbox to select **MSN Money Stock Quotes U.K.**
6. Click **OK**. Your research options are now set to include those specific to the United Kingdom.

PAUSE. LEAVE Word open for the next project.

Proficiency Assessment

Project 18-3: Customizing the Quick Access Toolbar

As a paralegal in a busy legal practice, you are always looking for ways to streamline your work. As you learn more about Word, you want to use the available options to help customize the program for your daily tasks.

1. **OPEN** the Word Options dialog box.
2. Display the Customization screen.
3. Choose five commands that you use frequently, but that are not currently located on the Quick Access Toolbar. Add the commands to the Quick Access Toolbar.
4. **CLOSE** the Word Options dialog box.

PAUSE. LEAVE Word open for the next project.

Project 18-4: Finding Readability Statistics

You are a fourth grade teacher, and a research paper that you are presenting at a national conference will be distributed to members of a discussion panel. You are interested in finding out the readability statistics of your paper, an option that you know is available in Word.

CD

The ***research_readability*** document is available on the companion CD-ROM.

1. **OPEN** ***research_readability*** from the data files for this lesson.
2. Open the Word Options dialog box and display the Proofing screen.
3. In the When correcting spelling and grammar in Word section, select the **Show readability statistics** checkbox if is not already selected.
4. Click **OK**.

5. On the Review tab, in the Proofing group, click the **Spelling & Grammar** button.
6. Click **Ignore All** each time Word displays a possible spelling mistake.
7. When a message appears that the spelling and grammar check is complete, click **OK**. The Readability Statistics dialog box is displayed.
8. On a piece of paper, jot down the numbers displayed for the Flesch Reading Ease and the Flesch-Kincaid Grade Level tests.
9. Click **OK** to close the dialog box.

PAUSE. LEAVE the document open for the next project.

Mastery Assessment

Project 18-5: Understanding Readability Statistics

Now that you have found the readability statistics for your research paper, you need to understand what they mean. Use Word help to locate this information.

1. **OPEN** Word help and search for **readability**.
2. Read the information about testing a document's readability.
3. In a new Word document, briefly explain the Flesch Reading Ease test and the Flesch-Kincaid Grade Level test.
4. List the readability scores that you wrote down for the ***research_readability*** document and explain whether they are considered good scores.
5. **SAVE** the document as ***test_scores*** and **CLOSE** the file.
6. **CLOSE** the ***research_readability*** document without saving.

PAUSE. LEAVE Word open for the next project.

Project 18-6: Word Options

You are a volunteer in the business office of the ANHH (Association of National Historic Homes) and have been assigned a variety of tasks that require an advanced knowledge of Word options.

1. **OPEN** a new, blank Word document.
2. Using what you have learned in this lesson, explore the Word Options dialog box as needed to find the answers to the following questions:
   a. You want to use XML-related features. How would you display the necessary commands in the Ribbon?
   b. You want blank boxes to be printed in place of graphics. What option would you disable?
   c. You do not want Word to replace fractions (1/2) with fraction characters (½). What option in what dialog box would you access to change this?
   d. You want Word to always check and require a comma before the last item in a list. What setting would you change?
   e. You want to use draft quality to print the rough draft of a long document. Where would you access this option?
   f. You want to diagnose and repair a problem with your Office applications. How would you do this from the Word Options dialog box?
3. Key your answers into the Word document.
4. **SAVE** the document as ***word_options*** and **CLOSE** the file.

CLOSE Word.

INTERNET READY

From the Resources screen of the Word Options dialog box, shown in Figure 18-22, you can contact Microsoft, find online resources, and maintain the health and reliability of your Office applications.

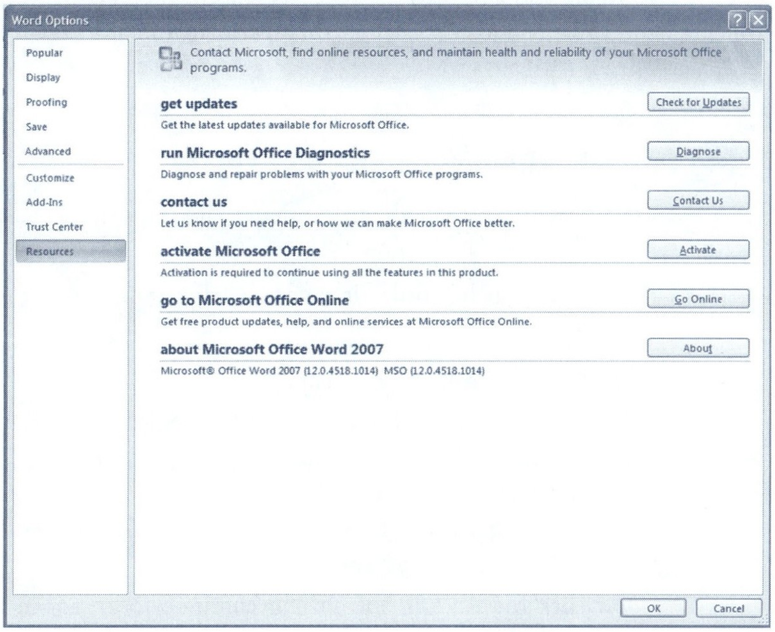

Figure 18-22

Resources screen of Word Options dialog box

To ensure that your computer is up-to-date, click the Check for Updates button to open the Microsoft update site, shown in Figure 18-23. From here, you can check to see if you need updates for your programs, hardware, or devices.

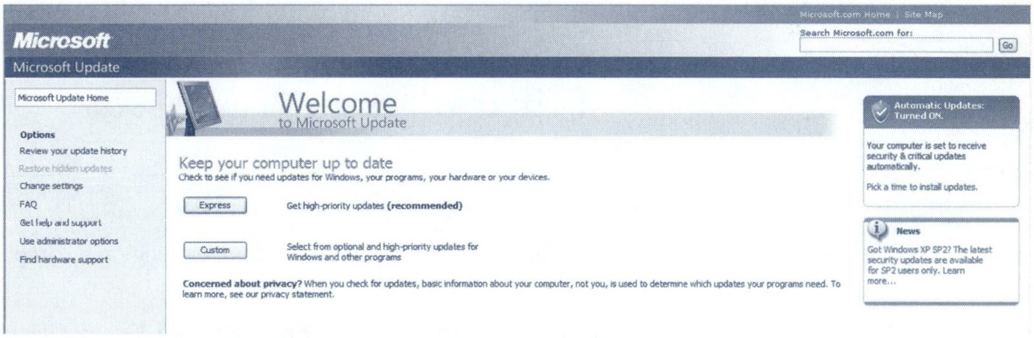

Figure 18-23

Microsoft update site

Circling Back

The annual professional development conference for the NAPC (National Association of Professional Consultants) is over and was a huge success. As membership manager for the association, you helped plan the conference and secure speakers. Now it is time to write and mail thank you letters to the speakers who made presentations at the conference. You use Word to write and edit a letter, then perform a mail merge to create individual letters and labels for each speaker.

Project 1: Reviewed Speaker Letter

You have written a draft thank you letter and sent it to a colleague for review. Accept or reject each change he suggested.

CD

The ***speakerthankyou*** file is available on the companion CD-ROM.

GET READY. Launch Word if it is not already running.

1. **OPEN** ***speakerthankyou*** from the data files for this lesson.
2. Display the Reviewing Pane.
3. If necessary, position the insertion point at the beginning of the document.
4. On the Review tab, in the Changes group, click the **Next** button. The first change is selected.
5. On the Review tab, in the Changes group, click the arrow on the **Accept** button and select **Accept and Move to Next**.
6. Click the **Accept** button and continue to accept all the changes suggested by the reviewer until you get to the inserted sentence, *I enjoyed meeting with you.* Reject that change before moving to the next one.
7. Accept all the remaining changes.
8. Click on the first comment to select it. On the Review tab, in the Comments group, click the **Delete Comment** button.
9. Turn off Track Changes.
10. Close the Reviewing Pane.
11. **SAVE** the document as ***speaker_thank_you*** and **CLOSE** the file.

PAUSE. LEAVE Word open for the next project.

Project 2: Inspected Speaker Letter

Now that you have incorporated the changes suggested, prepare the document for distribution.

CD

The ***speakerthankyou2*** file is available on the companion CD-ROM.

1. **OPEN** ***speakerthankyou2*** from the data files for this lesson.
2. Click the **Microsoft Office Button**, click **Prepare**, and select **Inspect Document** from the menu.
3. Run the Document Inspector and choose **Remove All Document Properties and Personal Information**. Leave Headers, Footers, and Watermarks as is and close the window.
4. Save the document as ***thank_you_inspected***.
5. Click the **Microsoft Office Button**, click **Prepare**, and click the **Compatibility Checker**. No compatibility issues were found.
6. Click **OK** and **CLOSE** the file.

PAUSE. LEAVE Word open for the next project.

Project 3: Main Document

Insert merge fields to create a main document.

CD
The *speakerthankyou3* file is available on the companion CD-ROM.

CD
The *speakerlist* file is available on the companion CD-ROM.

1. **OPEN** *speakerthankyou3* from the data files for this lesson.
2. Leave one blank line after the date and position the insertion point on the following line.
3. On the Mailings tab, in the Start Mail Merge group, click the **Select Recipients** button. Then select **Use Existing List** from the menu.
4. Navigate to the data files for this lesson and select *speakerlist*.
5. Click the **Address Block** button and click **OK** to accept the format.
6. Press the Enter key.
7. Leave one blank line after the Address Block and position the insertion point on the following line. Click the **Greeting Line** button and click **OK** to accept the *Dear Mr. Slade* format.
8. Position the insertion point at the end of the first sentence, after the blank space following the word *on*.
9. Click the arrow on the **Insert Merge Field** button and select **Date** from the menu.
10. Position the insertion point in the second sentence, after the space following the word *presentation*. Key **on** and press the **Spacebar**.
11. Click the arrow on the **Insert Merge Field** button and select **Topic** from the menu. Press the **Spacebar** to insert a blank space after the Topic field.
12. **SAVE** the main document as *speaker_thank_you_main*.

PAUSE. LEAVE the document open for the next project.

Project 4: Merged Thank You Letters

Merge the speaker thank you letters and preview the results.
USE the document that is open from the previous project.

1. On the Mailings tab, in the Preview Results group, click the **Preview Results** button.
2. On the Mailings tab, in the Preview Results group, click **Next Record** and continue until you have previewed each letter.
3. Click the **Preview Results** button again.
4. On the Mailings tab, in the Finish group, click the **Finish & Merge** button.
5. Click **Edit Individual Documents**.
6. In the Merge to New Document dialog box, select **All** and click **OK**.
7. Save the *merged* document as *thank_you_merge* and **CLOSE** the file.
8. **CLOSE** the *speaker_thank_you_main* file without saving.

PAUSE. LEAVE Word open for the next project.

Project 5: Speaker Labels

Create labels for the envelopes that you will use to mail the letters.

1. **OPEN** a new, blank Word document.
2. On the Mailings tab, in the Start Mail Merge group, click the **Start Mail Merge** button and select **Labels** from the menu.
3. Set the labels using **Avery US Letter** as the label product and **5160** as the product number and click **OK**.

CD

The *speakerlist* document is available on the companion CD-ROM.

4. In the Mailings tab, in the Start Mail Merge group, click the **Select Recipients** button.
5. As the data source, use the ***speakerlist*** database found in the data files for this lesson.
6. Click the **Address Block** button and click **OK.**
7. Click the **Update Labels** button.
8. Click the **Preview Results** button.
9. Click the **Preview Results** button again.
10. On the Mailings tab, in the Finish group, click the **Finish & Merge** button.
11. Click **Edit Individual Documents.**
12. In the Merge to New Document dialog box, select **All** and click **OK.**
13. **SAVE** the *merged label* document as ***speaker_labels*** and **CLOSE** the file.
14. **SAVE** the *label main* document as ***labels_main*** and **CLOSE** the file.

CLOSE Word.

MATRIX SKILL	SKILL NUMBER	LESSON NUMBER
Work with templates	1.1.1	6
Apply Quick Styles to documents	1.1.2	2
Format documents by using themes	1.1.3	2
Customize themes	1.1.4	2
Format document backgrounds	1.1.5	5
Insert blank pages or cover pages	1.1.6	6, 7
Format pages	1.2.1	5
Create and modify headers and footers	1.2.2	5
Create and format columns	1.2.3	7
Create, modify, and update tables of contents	1.3.1	13
Create, modify, and update indexes	1.3.2	13
Modify keywords to document properties	1.3.3	2
Insert document navigation tools	1.3.4	12
Customize Office Word 2007 options	1.4.1	18
Change research options	1.4.2	18
Apply styles	2.1.1	3
Create and modify styles	2.1.2	3
Format characters	2.1.3	3
Format paragraphs	2.1.4	4
Set and clear tabs	2.1.5	4
Cut, copy, and paste text	2.2.1	8
Find and replace text	2.2.2	8
Control pagination	2.3	7
Create and modify sections	2.3.2	7
Insert sections	2.5	7
Insert SmartArt graphics	3.1.1	10
Insert pictures from files and clip art	3.1.2	10
Insert shapes	3.1.3	10
Format text wrapping	3.2.1	10
Format by sizing, scaling, and rotating	3.2.2	10
Apply Quick Styles	3.2.3	10
Set contrast, brightness, and coloration	3.2.4	10
Add text to SmartArt graphics and shapes	3.2.5	10
Compress pictures	3.2.6	10
Insert and modify WordArt	3.3.1	11
Insert pull quotes	3.3.2	11
Insert and modify drop caps	3.3.3	11

continued

MATRIX SKILL	SKILL NUMBER	LESSON NUMBER
Insert text boxes	3.4.1	11
Format text boxes	3.4.2	11
Link text boxes	3.4.3	11
Insert building blocks in documents	4.1.1	8
Save frequently used data as building blocks	4.1.2	8
Insert formatted headers and footers from Quick Parts	4.1.3	5
Insert fields from Quick Parts	4.1.4	8
Create tables and lists	4.2.1	4, 9
Sort content	4.2.2	9
Modify list formats	4.2.3	9
Apply Quick Styles to tables	4.3.1	9
Modify table properties	4.3.2	9
Merge and split table cells	4.3.3	9
Perform calculations in tables	4.3.4	9
Change the position and direction of cell contents	4.3.5	9
Create and modify sources	4.4.1	15
Insert citations and captions	4.4.2	14, 15
Insert and modify bibliographies	4.4.3	15
Select reference styles	4.4.4	15
Create, modify, and update tables of figures and tables of authorities	4.4.5	14
Create merged documents	4.5.1	16
Merge data into form letters	4.5.2	16
Create envelopes and labels	4.5.3	2, 16
Move through a document quickly by using the Find and Go To commands	5.1.1	8
Change window views	5.1.2	1, 8, 12
Compare document versions	5.2.1	17
Merge document versions	5.2.2	17
Combine revisions from multiple authors	5.2.3	17
Manage track changes	5.3	17
Display markup	5.3.1	17
Enable, disable, accept and reject tracked changes	5.3.2	17
Change tracking options	5.3.3	17
Insert, modify, and delete comments	5.4	17
Save to appropriate formats	6.1.1	1, 2
Identify document features that are not supported by previous versions	6.1.2	17
Remove inappropriate or private information by using Document Inspector	6.1.3	17
Restrict permissions to documents	6.2.1	17
Mark documents as final	6.2.2	17
Set passwords	6.2.3	17
Protect documents	6.2.4	17
Authenticate documents by using digital signatures	6.3.1	17
Insert a line for a digital signature	6.3.2	17

COMPONENT	REQUIREMENT
Computer and processor	500 megahertz (MHz) processor or higher[1]
Memory	256 megabyte (MB) RAM or higher[1, 2]
Hard disk	2 gigabyte (GB); a portion of this disk space will be freed after installation if the original download package is removed from the hard drive.
Drive	CD-ROM or DVD drive
Display	1024x768 or higher resolution monitor
Operating system	Microsoft Windows(R) XP with Service Pack (SP) 2, Windows Server(R) 2003 with SP1, or later operating system[3]
Other	Certain inking features require running Microsoft Windows XP Tablet PC Edition or later. Speech recognition functionality requires a close-talk microphone and audio output device. Information Rights Management features require access to a Windows 2003 Server with SP1 or later running Windows Rights Management Services.
	Connectivity to Microsoft Exchange Server 2000 or later is required for certain advanced functionality in Outlook 2007. Instant Search requires Microsoft Windows Desktop Search 3.0. Dynamic Calendars require server connectivity.
	Connectivity to Microsoft Windows Server 2003 with SP1 or later running Microsoft Windows SharePoint Services is required for certain advanced collaboration functionality. Microsoft Office SharePoint Server 2007 is required for certain advanced functionality. PowerPoint Slide Library requires Office SharePoint Server 2007. To share data among multiple computers, the host computer must be running Windows Server(R) 2003 with SP1, Windows(R) XP Professional with SP2, or later.
	Internet Explorer 6.0 or later, 32 bit browser only. Internet functionality requires Internet access (fees may apply).
Additional	Actual requirements and product functionality may vary based on your system configuration and operating system.

[1]1 gigahertz (GHz) processor or higher and 512 MB RAM or higher recommended for **Business Contact Manager**. Business Contact Manager not available in all languages.

[2]512 MB RAM or higher recommended for **Outlook Instant Search**. Grammar and contextual spelling in Word is not turned on unless the machine has 1 GB memory.

[3]Office Clean-up wizard not available on 64 bit OS

A

add-in supplemental program that can be installed to extend the capabilities of Word by adding custom commands and specialized features

ascending sorting text from beginning to end, such as from A to Z, 1 to 10, and January to December

B

badges small square labels that contain key tips

bibliography a list of sources, usually placed at the end of a document, that you consulted while creating a document

bookmark a location or a selection of text that you name and identify for future reference

Building Blocks reusable pieces of content or other document parts that are stored in galleries and can be inserted into a document whenever needed

C

caption a line of text that appears above or below an object to describe it

cells rectangles that are formed when rows and columns intersect

certificate a digital means of proving identity and authenticity

certificate of authority digital certificate issued by a company to keep track of assigned certificates, verify a certificate's validity, and track revoked or expired certificates

character any single letter, number, symbol, or punctuation mark

character styles styles that are applied to individual characters or words that you have selected within a paragraph rather than affecting the entire paragraph

citation a note mentioning the source of information

clip art picture files that can be inserted in a document

columns vertical blocks of text in which text flows from the bottom of one column to the top of the next

command a button you click or a box where you enter information that tells Word what you want it to do

Content controls tiny programs that include a label for instructing you on the type of text to include and a placeholder that reserves a place for your new text

Connection Status menu a menu that lets you choose between searching help topics online and help topics offline

compress decrease the size of a picture file by reducing the resolution

copy duplicate a selection so it can be pasted in another location

cover sheet the first page of a document; typically includes an author, title, and date

crop trim the vertical or horizontal edges of an object

cross-reference a notation or direction at one place to relevant information in another

cut remove a selection from its location

D

data source a file that contains the information to be merged into a document

descending sorting text from the end to the beginning, such as from Z to A, 10 to 1, and December to January

desktop the main screen that appears once the computer is started

dialog box a box that displays options or information you can specify to execute a command

dialog box launcher a small arrow in the lower right corner of a group that you click to launch a dialog box

digital signature an electronic signature that verifies the signer of a document is the person he or she claims to be and that the content has not been changed since it was signed

document map shows you the structure of a document in a left window pane

document properties details about a file that describe or identify it

document theme a set of predefined formatting options that include sets of theme colors, fonts, and effects

drop cap a large initial letter that drops down two or more lines at the beginning of a paragraph

E

embedded object an inserted picture that becomes part of the document

F

field a placeholder that tells Word where to insert changeable data into a document

first-line indent in a paragraph, the first line indents more than the following lines

floating object a picture or drawing object that can be positioned precisely on the page, including behind or in front of text

font a set of characters that have the same design

footer text that is printed at the bottom of a page

formula a set of mathematical instructions used to perform calculations in a table cell

G

gridlines a grid of vertical and horizontal lines that helps you align graphics and other objects in your documents

groups related commands within the tabs on the Ribbon

H

hanging indent in a paragraph, the first full line of text is not indented, but the following lines are

header text that is printed at the top of a page

header row in a table, the first row; it is formatted differently and usually contains headings for the entire table

horizontal alignment how text is positioned between the left and right margins, including left-aligned, centered, right-aligned, and justified

I

I-beam shape of the mouse pointer when it is moved over the text area of a document

indent the space between a paragraph and the document's left and/or right margin

index an alphabetical list of information in a document, along with the page numbers on which they are found, usually found at the end of a document

inline object a picture or drawing object that moves along with the text around it

insertion point a blinking vertical line that signals you can begin keying text

K

key tips small letters and numbers that appear on the Ribbon when you press Alt; used for executing commands with the keyboard

keywords words or sets of words that describe a document

L

landscape orientation page setup in which a page is wider than it is tall

leaders dotted, dashed, or solid lines that fill the space before a tab

legal blackline a document that displays the comparison of two documents, showing what changed between them

line spacing the amount of space between lines of text in a paragraph

linked object an inserted object that includes a connection to the object's source

M

mail merge fields placeholders that are filled with information from the data source file when the mail merge is performed

main document contains the text and graphics that are the same for each version of the merged document

main entry the top level entry in an index

margins the blank areas at the top, bottom, and sides of a document

markup the tracked changes and comments such as insertions, deletions, and formatting changes in a document

menu a list of additional options from which you can choose

merge cells combine two or more cells into one

Microsoft Office Button displays a menu of basic commands for opening, saving, and printing files as well as more advanced options

Mini toolbar a small toolbar with popular commands that appears when you point to selected text

multi selection a feature that enables you to select multiple pieces of text that are not next to each other

N

negative indent a paragraph that extends into the left margin

nonprinting characters symbols that Word inserts into a document when you use certain formatting commands, such as paragraph and indents

O

orphan a line of text that is left alone at the bottom of a page

P

page break the location in a document where one page ends and a new page begins

paragraph spacing the amount of space above or below a paragraph

paragraph styles formats that are applied to all the text in the paragraph where your insertion point is located, whether or not you have it all selected

paste place a cut or copied selection in the chosen location

point size refers to the height of characters, with one point equaling approximately 1/72 of an inch

portrait orientation page setup in which the page is taller than it is wide

Print Preview command that enables you to view your document as it will look when it is printed, and also provides the ability to make changes

pull quote a sentence or other text that is copied from a document and enlarged and displayed separately on the page for emphasis

Q

Quick Access Toolbar a toolbar at the top left of the screen that contains the commands that you use most often, such as Save, Undo, and Redo

Quick Styles predefined formats that you can apply to your document to instantly change its look and feel

Quick Tables built-in preformatted tables, such as calendars and tabular lists, you can insert and use in your documents

R

redo repeat your last action

reset discard all the formatting changes that you made to a picture

Ribbon located across the top of the screen, it contains tabs and groups of commands

ruler a measuring tool that helps you align text and displays indents, tabs, and margins

S

Save store a document for future use

Save As save a document with a new name or in a different location

Scrollbars appear on the right and/or bottom of the document window; contain buttons and boxes you can use to move through the document

Scroll box a box you can click and drag to move more quickly horizontally or vertically through the document

Scroll buttons buttons you can click to move up or down through the document one line at a time

section break used to enable layout or formatting changes in a portion of a document

Shortcut menu a menu of useful commands that appears when you click the right mouse button

SmartArt graphics a visual representation of your information; can help communicate your message and ideas

sort to arrange data alphabetically, numerically, or chronologically

source the work, such as a book, report, or website, that supplied you with information for creating your document

split cells to divide one cell into two or more cells

subentry a subcategory of a main entry

T

tab leaders the symbols that appear between the table of contents topic and the tab set for its page number

table an arrangement of data made up of horizontal rows and vertical columns

table of contents an ordered list of the topics in a document, along with the page numbers on which they are found, usually placed at the beginning of a document

table of figures a list of the captions for all figures, tables, or equations in a document

tabs areas of activity in the Ribbon

template master document that has predefined page layout, fonts, margins, and styles and is used to create new documents that will share the same basic formatting

text box an invisible, formatted box that enables you to insert and position text and/or graphic objects

thumbnail a small picture of a page

U

undo cancel or undo your last command

V

vertical alignment how text is positioned between the top and bottom margins of the page

W

watermark text or graphic that is printed lightly behind text on a page

widow a line of text that is left alone at the top of a page

wildcard symbol that represents a character or multiple characters in a search string

WordArt a feature that creates decorative effects with text

Photo Credits

Lesson 1
Digital Vision

Lesson 2
Corbis Digital Stock

Lesson 3
Purestock/Superstock

Lesson 4
Corbis Digital Stock

Lesson 5
PhotoDisc, Inc.

Lesson 6
Nick Clements/PhotoDisc, Inc.

Lesson 7
Corbis Digital Stock

Lesson 8
Purestock/Superstock

Lesson 9
PhotoDisc, Inc.

Lesson 10
Digital Vision

Lesson 11
PhotoDisc, Inc.

Lesson 12
Digital Vision

Lesson 13
Corbis Digital Stock

Lesson 14
PhotoDisc, Inc.

Lesson 15
PhotoDisc, Inc.

Lesson 16
PhotoDisc, Inc./ Getty Images

Lesson 17
PhotoDisc, Inc./ Getty Images

Lesson 18
Corbis Digital Stock